Medieval History

This series includes pioneering editions of medieval historical accounts by eye-witnesses and contemporaries, collections of source materials such as charters and letters, and works that applied new historiographical methods to the interpretation of the European middle ages. The nineteenth century saw an upsurge of interest in medieval manuscripts, texts and artefacts, and the enthusiastic efforts of scholars and antiquaries made a large body of material available in print for the first time. Although many of the analyses have been superseded, they provide fascinating evidence of the academic practices of their time, while a considerable number of texts have still not been re-edited and are still widely consulted.

The Chartulary of St John of Pontefract

The prosperous Cluniac priory of St John the Evangelist, Pontefract, was founded around 1090 by Robert de Lacy, remaining subject to its mother-house of La Charité-sur-Loire until the fourteenth century. The charters in this two-volume work have been arranged by type: seigniorial charters; episcopal and papal charters; royal charters; and those relating to priory property, arranged geographically according to proximity to Pontefract. The cartulary is particularly valuable for topographical studies and local and family history – in many cases the names of all witnesses have been transcribed. The manuscript was originally compiled in the first half of the thirteenth century, with additions made on blank leaves over the following centuries (not included by the editor). Volume 2, published in 1902, contains charters 234–556, on local property holdings and leases, and an index to the whole work. Each Latin charter is preceded by a brief English summary.

Cambridge University Press has long been a pioneer in the reissuing of out-of-print titles from its own backlist, producing digital reprints of books that are still sought after by scholars and students but could not be reprinted economically using traditional technology. The Cambridge Library Collection extends this activity to a wider range of books which are still of importance to researchers and professionals, either for the source material they contain, or as landmarks in the history of their academic discipline.

Drawing from the world-renowned collections in the Cambridge University Library and other partner libraries, and guided by the advice of experts in each subject area, Cambridge University Press is using state-of-the-art scanning machines in its own Printing House to capture the content of each book selected for inclusion. The files are processed to give a consistently clear, crisp image, and the books finished to the high quality standard for which the Press is recognised around the world. The latest print-on-demand technology ensures that the books will remain available indefinitely, and that orders for single or multiple copies can quickly be supplied.

The Cambridge Library Collection brings back to life books of enduring scholarly value (including out-of-copyright works originally issued by other publishers) across a wide range of disciplines in the humanities and social sciences and in science and technology.

The Chartulary of
St John of Pontefract

*From the Original Document in the Possession
of Godfrey Wentworth, Esq., of Woolley Park*

VOLUME 2

EDITED BY RICHARD HOLMES

CAMBRIDGE
UNIVERSITY PRESS

CAMBRIDGE UNIVERSITY PRESS

Cambridge, New York, Melbourne, Madrid, Cape Town,
Singapore, São Paolo, Delhi, Mexico City

Published in the United States of America by Cambridge University Press, New York

www.cambridge.org
Information on this title: www.cambridge.org/9781108058681

© in this compilation Cambridge University Press 2013

This edition first published 1902
This digitally printed version 2013

ISBN 978-1-108-05868-1 Paperback

THE PONTEFRACT CHARTULARY.

VOLUME II.

The Yorkshire Archæological Society.

FOUNDED 1863.   INCORPORATED 1893.

RECORD SERIES.

VOL. XXX.

FOR THE YEAR 1901.

THE CHARTULARY

OF

St. JOHN OF PONTEFRACT.

VOL. II.

EDITED BY

THE LATE RICHARD HOLMES.

PRINTED FOR THE SOCIETY,

1902

INTRODUCTION.

VOLUME II.

OF the two portions into which for convenience sake I have considered it better to divide the Chartulary, the second is of not much less importance than the first. For, although dealing with the smaller and more trivial affairs of the monastery, rather than with the seigniorial, regal and ecclesiastical charters and its more general privileges, it affords much useful information and illustration even to the general student.

The **Seventh Fasciculus,** which is the first of this volume, opens with a charter (No. 234) concerning land at Wick (now Keswick, near Leeds).

Wike (now Keswick) is in the neighbourhood of Alwoodley and to the north of Leeds. It is more easily accessible from Kirkstall than from Pontefract, and the monks of the latter place did not retain their holding there permanently. No. 235 is from Thomas son of Warin, who had possessions in Harewood, near Leeds. He is described as the son of Gerold, and in the *Dodsworth MS.* G. (vol. 127) 19, 20, his daughter Margaret[1] de Ripariis, described as his heir, is stated, in the full power of her widowhood, to have granted the mill of Harewood to the monks of Bolton. This identifies the family connection as being that of Warin fitz Gerold. Warin and his brother Henry fitz Gerold were successively royal chamberlains to kings Stephen and Henry II., there being only a small interval in 2 Henry II. (1156), when a Stephen Camerarius occurs.[2]

---

(1) The husband of Margaret de Ripariis was Baldwin, heir apparent to the earldom of Devonshire, who died before his father on September 1, 1216.

(2) It may however be noted that this last-named Camerarius was of a lower office than that of royal chamberlain, and that he is then so called only in connection with a payment on the Yorkshire portion of the *Pipe Roll*, which was made "in the chamber of the king" to "Stephen

It is interesting to note also that the Final Concord, 2 Henry III. (No. 243) rehearses the names of two justices itinerant (John de Vipont and Richard Duket), not known to Foss.

Featherstone, with which charters No. 244 and No. 247 are concerned, had connection, and intimate connection, with two monastic communities, the Augustinian canons of Nostell, and the Cluniac monks of Pontefract. These met in friendly rivalry within its borders, each having possessions there, leading to dealings with regard to its church, under the following circumstances.

At the time of the Domesday Survey, the associated manors of Featherstone, Purston, West Hardwick and Nostell had two churches, the ownership of which was very shortly afterwards divided—no evidence remains how; the church of Featherstone (that is to say, its advowson and the possibility of a revenue from it) was, however, given to the monks of Pontefract between 1086 and 1122, it is not clear by whom, while, and naturally enough, that at Nostell (Wragby) came into the possession of the canons there.

But in the early days subsequent to the Survey, a second place of worship had been built in Pontefract for the convenience of the inhabitants of Pontefract proper, and at first this was called the church of St. Mary of Pontefract, though afterwards (see No. 3) the church of St. Mary de Foro. This newly-established foundation was held in medieties by the canons of Nostell and the monks of Pontefract, an arrangement which pointed to the fact that there had been a joint endowment by these two founders; but there is now no evidence to show the particulars, for all deeds respecting it, except those below, appear to have been destroyed when superseded.

Camerarius" by William de Clarfait. But mention of him occurs ten years afterwards on the Yorkshire portion of *Liber Niger* as H. Stephen filius Herberti Camerarii (where Hearne, probably correctly, thinks the first H to be superfluous), as holding a knight's fee of the king himself. With but one knight's fee, however, he is ranked between Roger de Mowbray with 88, and Henry de Lascy with 60 fees; so that, if not wealthy, he had a considerable position. If Stephen fitz Herbert had no body of tenants under him, he was at least entitled to take rank among the chief of the county. The same document, *Dodsworth*, vol. 127, ff. 19, 20, makes Alice de Courcy to be the wife of Warin and mother of Thomas, who thus appears to have died *s.p.*; and as in 18 John (1216) there was a second Warin fitz Gerold, in possession of Stoke Courcy evidently by right of this marriage, confusion between the two Warins, each a fitz Gerold, has resulted. In the charter before us, however, we may be certain of the generation at least, and of the date within a few years; for Peter de Tolleston who married the de Dai heiress, and Alan his brother, belonged to the latter half of the twelfth century. See No. 96 and No. 238.

What is certain is that the church of St. Mary did not exist at the time of the Domesday Survey in 1086, and that when, shortly afterwards, in 1090, the monks secured their early charter, that document contained no hint of their possession of such an endowment, or any part of it. But probably in 1106 or 1107, while the estates were in the king's hands, the church had been built, endowed, and, with regard to the property, divided between Nostell and Pontefract. This joint possession had probably so undesirable a result that at the first opportunity Hugh de Laval terminated the arrangement, and gave both medieties to the Pontefract monks in exchange for more valuable rights in Featherstone Church, which were allotted to Nostell. This exchange, as one affecting property, needed ratification and confirmation from the king, which it obtained shortly afterwards by the following royal charter, not enrolled in the Pontefract Chartulary, but to be found in that of Nostell:—

Carta H. Regis Anglie[1] de Ecclesia de Fetherstana.[2] Cir. 1123.

[Henry, king of England, to Thurstan, archbishop of York, and to the justiciaries, and to all his barons and faithful of Yorkshire, greeting. Know that I have permitted the exchange which has been made by Thurstan the archbishop of York and Hugh de Val between the monks of St. John of Pontefract and the canons of St. Oswald; that is to say, to the said canons the church of Featherstone, with the lands and all things to that church belonging, which the aforesaid monks give to them in exchange for the half of the church of St. Mary of Pontefract and for the half of the district belonging to that church. And besides, I confirm to the aforesaid monks 45 shillings rent yearly, which Hugh de Val gives to them for the aforesaid exchange; that is to say the church of Ledsham with its rents, and with other rents to complete those 45 shillings; and they may hold the exchange as if- certainly theirs, both well and in peace and quietly. Witness, &c.]

H[enricus] rex Anglie T[urstino] Eboracensi archiepiscopo et vicariis et omnibus baronibus et fidelibus suis de Eboraciscira[3] salutem. Sciatis me concessisse escambium quod factum est per Turstinum archiepiscopum Eboracensem et Hugonem de Valle[3] inter monachos sancti Johannis de Pontefracto[4] et canonicos sancti Oswaldi, videlicet ipsis canonicis ecclesiam de Federstana, cum terris et omnibus rebus ipsi ecclesie pertinentibus, quam predicti monachi eis dant in excambium pro medietate ecclesie sancte Marie de Pontefracto, et pro medietate parochie pertinentis eidem ecclesie. Et preterea concedo prefatis monachis xlv

---

(1) *Sic.* This seems to dispose of the statement sometimes made, that this king was always called "Rex Anglorum," not "Rex Anglie." (2) *Cott. MSS.* Vesp. E. xix. fo. 101.—Fetherstan, No. 2.

(3) *Sic,* in each case.

(4) This is, I believe, the very earliest instance of Pontefract being so called.

solidos redditus per annum quos Hugo de Valle eis dat pro predicto excambio; videlicet ecclesiam de Ledeshama cum redditibus suis, et cum aliis redditibus usque ad perficere illos xlv solidos; et bene et in pace et quiete teneant amodo utique suum excambium. Teste,[1] &c.

Carta Turstini Eboracensis Archiepiscopi.   Cir. 1112.

[Thurstan, by the grace of God, archbishop of York, to all the clergy and people of the church of St. Peter at York, and also to all the sons of the Catholic Church, greeting and blessing. We notify to you a certain agreement made in our presence between the church of Featherstone and the church of St. Oswald. For the monks of Charitè and the priest of Featherstone, who were alleging it to be attached to the parish of Featherstone [and the canons], have claimed it, free and quit from all custom and service, so that the canons may regularly serve God there, and may have a cemetery for their use and for that of their tenants in every respect, near those of them dwelling in the land which is called Nostel. And in this agreement the clerks of St. Oswald have quit-claimed to the church of Featherstone all ecclesiastical customs which they used to have from Hardwick. I, Thomas the second, archbishop, and Robert de Lascy, and Anfrid and Bernwin the priest, and Ralph the clerk, being present and confirming. And this was done on the first day during the dedication of the church of St. Oswald. Witness, &c.]

Turstinus[2] dei gratia Eboracensis Archiepiscopus, toti clero et populo Eborascensis ecclesie sancti Petri, immo omnibus universalis ecclesie filiis, salutem et benedictionem. Notificamus vobis quandam conventionem factam in presentia nostra inter ecclesiam de Federstan et ecclesiam Sancti Oswaldi. Monachi namque de Caritate et sacerdos de Federstan qui calumpniabantur eam adjacere parochie de Fetherstana[3] clamaverunt eam solutam et quietam ab omni consuetudine et servicio, ita quod canonici regulariter deo ibi serviant et habeant cemiterium ad opus suum et serviencium suorum omnique juxta eos habitancium in terra que dicitur Nostlet. Et in hac conventione clamaverunt clerici sancti Oswaldi quietas omnes ecclesiasticas consuetudines quas habebant de Hardewic[4] ecclesie de Fetherstan, me Thoma archiepiscopo ijᵒ et Rodberto de Laceio, et Anfrido, et Bernewino presbitero, et Radulfo clerico presentibus et confirmantibus. Et hoc factum est prima feria in dedicatione ecclesie sancti Oswaldi. Teste,[5] &c.

Thus the building which for above six hundred years, from 1180 to 1790, was called the "chapel" of St. Giles, is in these two charters called the "church" of St. Mary (de Pontefracto or de Foro). This fact, and the statement with regard to the church of St. Oswald, confirm the theory I have ventured to form that the constitution of parish churches with their subordinate chapels was not known, at least in this part of the country, till the time of archbishop Roger,

---

(1) *Sic*; singular number.

(2) *Sic*, at full; though it was possibly only an extension of T. (for Thomas) made by the fourteenth century clerk.   (3) " Et canonici" interlined with poor ink, in a feeble hand.

(4) " W." interlined in the same manner, indicating West Hardwick, which is on the southern border of Featherstone,   (5) *Sic*.

but that till then every separate ecclesiastical building was called a "church;" and that the name of chapel (which was ultimately given to those few "churches" to which the status of parish was not assigned because they had no sufficient grant of land to constitute what was considered a suitable independent maintenance for a parson or parish priest) was afterwards extended to those places of worship also which were erected within the parish of the earlier church to which the privileges of tithes and revenues had already been awarded.[1]

Having thus obtained the entire property in the church of St. Mary, the monks seem to have enlarged it by building the church of St. Giles, retaining however the older building as the chancel of their new church.[2]

The Whitwood group of ten charters, No. 249 to No. 258, points to the probability, almost amounting to certainty, that Hameric was a son of the Robert de Stapleton who married Claricia de Reineville,[3] that he was a younger brother of the William (II.) who on his father's death became the head of the family, who was at this time fluctuating between his paternal home at Stapleton and his mother's manor at Cudworth and who ultimately, before 1200, with his mother Claricia, obtained permission from John Tyrel, then parson of Royston, to have a private chapel within their manor house at Cudworth. In return for this permission, they gave six acres of land in Cudworth to be an addition to the endowment of the church of Royston. And as one of the conditions of the transaction was that the anniversary of Robert de Stapleton, the husband of Claricia, should be celebrated there, it is probable that Robert's death and

---

(1) Chirch or Church in the parish of Whalley was another singular illustration. The place was called Chirch because in its earlier times it had a church; and yet under the ecclesiastical system of the middle ages the building ranked as a "chapel" only—as the chapel of Chirch in the parish of Whalley. This alone shows that the building which was formerly considered a "church," and had thus even given its name to the manor in which it was planted, had under the new ecclesiastical arrangements ceased to be more than a "chapel;" just as St. Giles's, similarly, about half a century afterwards, lost its status as "church," and became "chapel" only.

(2) Although the circumstances seem to indicate that the monks and the canons were the joint founders of St. Mary de Foro, there is nothing to show how Featherstone Church had come to belong to the monks of Pontefract. But the rights over it which the canons obtained by this exchange were much more extensive than those over the other churches (except Wragby) in their patronage. So much so that when, in 1247, archbishop Gray made a fresh arrangement of the ecclesiastical patronage belonging to them, neither the Church of Featherstone nor that at Wragby was mentioned in the decree, and they continued to possess the advowsons of both on the ancient terms. These were modified in the case of Featherstone, only in the fourteenth century, while Wragby continued to be a simple donative—independent of the archbishop so far as patronage was concerned—even as it has done until the present day.

(3) See pedigree, Introduction, xlvi.

the succession of his son William had occasioned these family re-arrangements.

For just before this time another son of Stapleton "hived out," also abandoning his patronymic. This was Hugh son of Robert, and therefore brother of William II. and of Hamericus, who, as appears from the following extract, received about 1190 a grant from Robert de Lascy. He was thenceforward known as Hugh de Horton.

HORTON (LITTLE), MORLEY Hundred, WEST RIDING
(*Harl MSS.*, 797, fo. 33).[1]

Robert de Lacy, lord of the Honor of Pontefract, who lived in the time of H. 2, and dyed 4 R. I. [1193], gave and granted to Hugh, son of Robert de Stapleton, 4 carucates of land in fee and inheritance. To hold of him by the 3rd part of one Knight's fee, to wit—In great Horton 20 oxgangs of land, in Little Horton 14 oxgangs of land, and in Clayton 6 oxgangs of land, with the appurtenances. Witnesses, . . . Pinnell and . . . Rainevill.

This grant (whether by purchase or by gift) was thus the foundation of the medieval family of de Horton ; which continued in the wapentake of Morley for several generations.

At the Mere it is evident that, besides the group which owned Hameric as their progenitor, there were two clearly distinct families, some of each of which called themselves de Mara ; those who centre round Robert son of Robert, and those connected with Master Raimond, the clerk or parson of Methley. And that these may be thus grouped :—

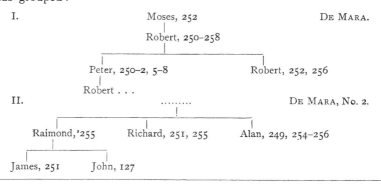

I.   Moses, 252   DE MARA.
                             Robert, 250–258

                Peter, 250–2, 5–8   Robert, 252, 256
                Robert . . .
II.   . . . .   DE MARA, No. 2.

       Raimond,'255   Richard, 251, 255   Alan, 249, 254–256

   James, 251   John, 127

---

(1) The above, which is repeated under Great Horton, is a translated extract from *Dodsworth* vol. 118, fo. 122b, which Dodsworth describes as one among a series extracted from the Collections of John Hanson of Woodhouse ; but he gives Hanson's authority only.

Some of this second group have already appeared above our horizon with sufficient circumstance to indicate the extreme likelihood that Raimond was the Master Raimond who became clerk, that is parson or rector, of the adjoining parish of Methley, and was probably a younger brother of the lord there. For it cannot be too constantly remembered by those attempting to understand the ecclesiastical history of the twelfth century that it was the century of much of the endowment of the church in this district; that that endowment emanated, not from the state, but from the squire; and that practically the endowment for a parson was also in many cases the provision for a younger son.

This Raimond, clerk of Methley, was a considerable property owner in Pontefract[1]; and he witnessed Roger de Lascy's charter in 1194,[2] while his son James,[3] apparently as a childless man, made by No. 127 very large donations to the monks.

But in No. 255 another clerk of Methley appears, one Henry, apparently the Henry son of Susanna of No. 251, and perhaps the last signatory of No. 173. So that while Richard brother of Raimond, with his brother Alan,[4] each appeals to his relationship to Raimond, the place of that once powerful cleric—whose name as a young but distinguished scholar, "Master Raimond," still remains attached to the Pontefract town charter—knoweth him no more.

No. 259 affords a striking illustration of the fact that the use of seals, on which were engraved some insignium of the user, was in the first half of this thirteenth century becoming more and more general, till it was at the time of this charter so universal that the absence of one had to be accounted for. In this case the grantor, a lady with no seal of her own, seems to have felt that the use of one was necessary to the validity of the document; and not merely that it should be affixed in evidence that she, whose private mark it bore, so to say, had consented to the transaction. Of this use of borrowed plumes, I have met with another even more curious example, because it shows that the seal of one brother was not

---

(1) See No. 119, No. 135, and No. 141.   (2) See page xl.   (3) No. 150.
(4) No. 255—called in No. 254 Alan de Mara, and in No. 255 Alan de Lamar.

necessarily that of another; that, in fact, at this time a seal belonged to a person, not to a family. It is in the Additional Charters, No. 7423, a confirmation charter to Byland Abbey granted by Symon son of Henry de Denebi (a younger brother of Adam fitz Swain). It adds, "and because I have not a seal, I have sealed this charter with the seal of Jordan my brother." The original charter from Henry de Denby is in the same collection (7416), as is an earlier Denby charter (7427) from William son of Osbert de Denby, which is witnessed by Robert Butivelein, dean of York, who also witnessed R 86, similarly confirmed by a borrowed seal.

The Hugh (de Swillington) who tests No. 262 as bailiff of the West Riding, and had tested No. 263 and No. 264 in immediate succession to his father Walter, the then holder of that office, was Hugh IV., son of Walter of the younger branch of the family of that Hugh who was the progenitor of the de Swillingtons. The Hugh of the document next before us is never styled de Swillington, so far as I have ascertained, though he appears on several occasions as if he were himself king's bailiff, thus as it were inheriting the office of his father, Walter. (See also No. 248, in which Walter signs as king's bailiff in 1189.) It is probable that he was the Hugh who married Roais, sister to Humphrey de Villeio,[1] and ultimately branched off in some as yet unascertained direction, taking a name of adoption from the place at which he settled. Of nine members of the Swillington family whose names I have on my notes four were named Hugh, three of whom were lords during five generations, this Hugh being the fourth. Thus it is easy to confuse the four Hughs de Swillington.

No. 267 is remarkable as containing one of the earliest mentions of a Savile in this neighbourhood—the Henry de Savile who has already passed before us as testing No. 227. Dodsworth copied the charter into his volume 151 (one of his later volumes); where it appears among a group of documents witnessed by members of this Savile family, or in which the name of Savile occurs. For he seems to have had at one time a scheme for correcting and adding to the

---

(1) *Dodsworth*, vol. 127, fo. 116.

earlier portion of their pedigree, which by means of these Pontefract documents he considered that he had traced to its origin in the Staincross wapentake. There is, however, no evidence that he carried out the idea. Perhaps he discovered that he could not gather sufficient reliable materials; or it might have been that, although the full development of the branch enquiry would have to some extent supplied further illustration, he found that the compilation and publication of the *Monasticon* made such demands upon his time and energies as to prevent him from devoting further attention to a subject which lay somewhat beyond what had then become his main scheme.

Bilham, to which the group of charters No. 272 to No. 277 relates, was a small manor to the south of Hooton Pagnell. In Domesday there were three distinct interests in it. The most important in the time of the Confessor had with Hooton belonged to earl Edwin, as a manor of ten carucates; but Richard de Surdeval was after the Conquest enfeoffed there under the earl of Mortain; and three generations afterwards a descendant in the female line gave his name to it, which it still retains, as Hooton Pagnell. To this portion belonged the mill and the demesne land, which last employed three of the nine ploughs of the whole manor. The remaining two-thirds were farmed by twelve villanes, with six ploughs. It is to land in this part of the Paganel fee at Bilham that these six Pontefract charters refer. It belonged to the ecclesiastical parish of Hooton. The second interest was a possession of six carucates which with Barnborough had belonged to Osul or Osulf, but which fell to Roger de Busli, and ultimately became and continued part of the ecclesiastical parish of Barnborough. These two portions of Bilham afterwards constituted the Bilham township of 536 acres, of which the 369 of the Paganel fee belonged to Hooton parish, and 167 of the Busli fee to that of Barnborough. As I have said, they had been reckoned at Domesday with Hooton and Barnborough respectively. The third was a smaller interest of a sokeman and a bordar with half a plough. This fell to William de Warene, and was afterwards altogether included in the Conisborough fee and parish.

Thus the interests of three fees, and subsequently the jurisdiction of three ecclesiastical parishes, bordered each other within the bounds of this small Domesday manor. The Sir Andrew Luterel who tested No. 275 in 1238 was the chief lord of Hooton, whose son Geoffrey ultimately inherited all the Paganel rights in that manor, and in 37 Henry III. had a charter for a market there, which has however been long discontinued, if it ever was held. The following had been the descent of the manor of Hooton. At the Conquest it was granted to Robert earl of Mortain, who enfeoffed Richard (de Surdeval). Richard (sometimes erroneously called Surdus, the deaf) left an heiress Matilda, married to Ralph eldest son of William Paganel, the Domesday grantee of that name. Ralph re-founded Holy Trinity, York, and with his wife's consent (showing that he held the property by her right) gave to that hospital the church of Hooton. He died about 1130, and Jordan their second son had Hooton, his mother's manor, by heirship. On the death of Jordan (though it is sometimes said there was an interval during which it was possessed by his stepson, Stephen de Meynill) the manor went to his youngest brother Alexander. Alexander had two sons, William and Jordan. The latter inherited a moiety of the Fossard property through his mother, the co-heiress of Robert Fossard, and was the father of the elder Henry de Vernoil (see No. 231); but William inherited the paternal property at Hooton. He was wealthy, and reported the possession of 14 knights' fees in 1166; but having no male heirs, he gave much of his wealth to religious purposes and was a large benefactor to Kirkstall, Nostell, Roche Abbey, and other religious houses. His co-heiresses were Frethesanta, who married (1) Geoffrey de Luterel, the elder brother of Sir Andrew, and (2) Henry de Newmarch, the father of Adam; and Isabel, who married William the Bastard. All the Hooton property ultimately went to the Luterels; and this Sir Andrew, having been sheriff of Lincoln-shire for a half-year in 1250, gave the king three marks of gold for future exemption from the offices of justiciary, sheriff, and bailiff, and that he should not be put on assizes, juries, or recognizances. That year he answered for 15 knights' fees, the number that belonged to the barony of Hooton Pagnell, and for twelve and a half belonging to the honour of Maurice de Gaunt, of Leeds, which also he had inherited.

Among the instances in which the Pontefract Chartulary furnishes a missing link to a twelfth century pedigree, No. 271 is not the least important, for that charter makes a very useful addition to the uncertain pedigree of the Malebise family of Acaster Malbis, and shows that there were about 1180 four brothers, Richard the eldest (the Malabestia of the Jews' massacre at York in 1190), Geoffrey (of whom no more seems to be known), William and Hugh. These last two appear twice in the Whitby Chartulary, No. 112 and No. 141, with Richard their elder brother, named brother to Hugh, as a testing witness in each case. William and Hugh are generally coupled as brothers but unrelated to Richard, although Roger de Houeden states that Richard and *his brother* Hugh had been excommunicated in 1191 by the Pope as accessories with earl John in his machinations against the kingdom of his brother. But this present mention in the Pontefract Chartulary is unequivocal.

Moreover, from G 643, G 644 and G 645, c. 1220-1234, we learn that Hugh, and therefore Richard, had a sister named Amicia married to Stephen de Blaby, to whose descendants much of Hugh's lands ultimately came. Collating the charters here named, and from other sources, the following pedigree is now obtainable :—

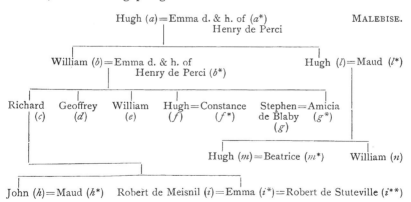

(a) 1138. Gave the vale of Bagby, &c., to Byland (*Dodsworth's Monasticon*, 778).
　c. 1145. Tests Roger de Mowbray's gifts of Welburn, &c., to Rievaux.
　c. 1145. Confirmed all Stainton, &c., to Rievaux, R 73, R 74, R 75. After the shrievalty of Ranulph (*temp.* King Stephen), R 67.
　1147. Dapifer to Roger Mowbray (*Dodsworth's Monasticon*, 1030).

(a*) (b*) Foss says that Emma was the mother of Richard and the wife of Hugh. But he does not give his authority for the statement which he has thus mangled.

(b) . . . . Confirmed his father's gift of Bagby, &c., to Byland . . . .

    c. 1160. Dapifer to Roger Mowbray, W 256.

    1166. Named in *Pipe Rolls* 12 Henry II., as holding land, which in *Pipe Rolls* 13 Henry II., is said to be at Acaster (Malbis).

    1166. Had land in Ryedale, *Pipe Rolls* 12 Henry II.

(c) 1190. Took part in the slaughter of the Jews at York. Richard and his brother Hugh are mentioned by Roger de Houeden as excommunicated for adherence to the cause of earl John against the new king (Richard I.).

    c. 1190. Richard endowed Newbo, in Lincolnshire, with lands at Entwistle, his charter being confirmed by Robert de Lascy II., who died 1193-4.

    1199. Gave to the new king (John) £100, two Norway hawks, two leash of greyhounds, and four palfreys, for having seisin of the manors of Scawton, Dale and Albi (Hawnby), also lands at Marton, Tolesby, Newenham and Bagby, and rent at Moreton and Steinton (*Oblatis* 41).

    1200. There was a suit, Richard Malebise *v.* abbot and monks of Rievaux, concerning the boundaries between Hawnby and Laskill (*Feet of Fines*, 2 John, No. 16).

    1200. He had a charter (*Oblatis*, 68) of free warren in Acaster, Copmanthorpe, Scawton, and Hawnby.

    1200. He grants to Rievaux lands in the territory between Scawton and Byland, R 300, for the good of Hugh his uncle and Hugh his son, R 304.

    1200. Had a licence to fortify a castle at Qweldric (Wheldrake), but the citizens of York obtained a withdrawal of the permission (Roger de Houeden).

    1202. The advowson of Handale or Grendale was given by Richard de Percy to Richard Malebise (*Dodsworth's Monasticon*, 427-8), the gift being witnessed by William de Stoteville, sheriff, who filled that office in 1201-3.

    1203. There was a suit, Richard Malebise *v.* William de Tameton, concerning the manor of Raisdale in Bilsdale (*Feet of Fines*, 5 John No. 236).

    1207. Richard Malebise *v.* Hugh de Bolton (who was living in 1208, *Feet of Fines* 9 John, No. 315 and 10 John, No. 417) concerning Hugh's failure to do homage for his lands at Coldrick (Wheldrake—*Burton*, 280; the misspelling is, however, in the original)—(*Finibus*, 379).

    . . . . King John gave leave to Richard M. to stub 80 acres and the pasture and forest between Ouse and Derwent at Queldrick (Wheldrake) (*Burton*, 192).

    . . . . Richard Malebise gave the assart to Fountains, and rights in Thickhet in Wheldrake to Thickhet; and these the prioress of Thickhet (c. 1214) transferred to Fountains (Burton, 280).

    . . . . Richard Malebise gave an acre in Acaster, and the service there of Richard Malebise, his nepos, to Fountains.

    1209. Richard Malebise died 11 John (*Foss*).

(*d*) Nothing has occurred to me of Geoffrey, except his mention in P 271 (cir. 1180). He probably died early, and *s.p.*

(*e*) 1206. Deforciant in a suit for dower moved by Constance, widow of his brother Hugh (*Feet of Fines*, 8 John, No. 281).

    . . . . Gave all his land at Bracanhoo in Marton to Whitby (W 112). Witnesses, Richard M. and Hugh his brother. The lands are defined (W 141) as those which Hugh his father and Hugh his (that is William's) brother had before given.

(*f*) 1200. Named in 300 R and 304 R.

    1205. Gave 200 marks and two palfreys that he might have the good will of the king and seisin of his lands, and that he might be restored to all he held before the king was incensed with him (*Finibus*, 334).

(*f**) 1206. There was a suit between Constance his widow and Robert de Lutterington her second husband *v.* Richard Malebise for dower from lands in Hawnby and Scawton (*Feet of Fines*, 8 John, No. 281). Also, the same *v.* William Malebise for dower from lands in Marton, Bagby, Tolesby and Newenham (*Feet of Fines*, 8 John, No. 282).

(*g*) and (*g**) Stephen de Blaby and Amicia his wife gave lands in Marton to Guisborough, G 643, G 644, G 645.

(*h*) and (*h**) 1231. Maud widow of John sold her dowry in Golstaindale for six marks to Guisborough, G 692.

(*i*), (*i**) and (*i***) 1207. Emma Malebise, whose first husband was Robert de Meisnil, married Robert de Stutevill (G 695). Richard her father with the intending husband made a fine of 300 marks on account of the marriage (*Finibus*, 384).

(*l*) c. 1200. Named in R 304 as uncle of Richard.

    . . . . Named in Byland Register, 176, according to Burton, 332, 334, 337, 338.

(*m*)) 1200. Named in R 304 as son of Hugh.

    . . . . Hugh and Beatrice gave to Fountains common pasture for their sheep at Greneburg, in the territory of Ellerton (*Burton*, 164, 167).

    1203. Granted dower (by *Feet of Fines*, 5 John, No. 227A) in Wensley and Ellerton (both in the North Riding) to Helewisa widow of Wimar, son of Warner.

    1205. Held half the church of Wensley (*Finibus*, 309).

    1208. (*Feet of Fines* 10 John, No. 394.) Hugh and Beatrice recover half a knight's fee in Bolton and Theakston (each in North Riding) from Robert son of William de Preston.

(*n*) 1166. Named in *Pipe Rolls* 1 R. I., under Nottingham and Derbyshire.

That the monks had had a carucate of land in the manor of Swillington, however short was the time of their ownership, we learn from the catalogue of possessions contained in the second charter of king Henry II. (No. 73), granted at Northampton in January

1155, in the very opening of the reign of that monarch; but as the grant was not included among those confirmed by Henry de Lascy at the consecration in 1159 (No. 10), or by the papal legate, archbishop Theobald (No. 57), the probability is that the gift was very soon alienated. From No. 238, it would appear that Richard son of Swain fitz Ailric held the manor when that charter was granted, about 1180, for he speaks of his "demesne" meadow there; but there is nothing to show how the carucate thus given to the monks by Thomas Campion had reverted to the donor or what, if anything, was given to the monks in exchange.

No. 297 is of a distinctly later date than No. 238, for it names Robert de Lascy, who was lord between 1187 and 1194; and it is remarkable that John, who had been dean of Kellington (see No. 208), here signs himself as dean of Pontefract. There can be no doubt of the man; for his identity is proved by the co-signatures of his brother and of two of his sons; and as there is a small but excessively interesting piece of ecclesiastical history revealed by this document, or rather the full outline of which is completed by it, I may well devote a few lines to the subject.

From an inventory of the lands of the Knights Templar in England, taken in 1185, we learn that John de Kellington held the church there at that date, Henry de Lascy having the patronage. This was in the very infancy of the parochial system in the diocese of York, when parishes had been but recently constituted, as they remained for some centuries; and there is nothing to show whence this first known incumbent of Kellington sprang, or how his rights came to be hereditary and overborne only after the death of his grandson.

Henry de Lascy subsequently transferred the advowson of Kellington Church to the Knights Templar of (Temple) Hirst; but whatever might be the force of this grant, the church remained in the possession of John's very clerical family for at least three generations. It would, indeed, appear as if it had been looked upon in the light of a family living, or rather a family estate; for John's next brother Henry seems to have been in orders, and at one time rector expectant. But John lived so long as to see both his son Thomas and his son Adam attain the canonical age; whereupon he obtained for himself the promotion to Pontefract, of which No. 297 shows him to have been then in possession.

In that charter the name of dean evidently signifies no more than the rector or parson of a parish containing several manors, the three names of dean, rector and parson being used indifferently, and it being at the time uncertain which was to be permanently selected to indicate the position. Pontefract, Kellington, Swillington, Ledsham, the Ainsty were all "deaneries" in the last quarter of the twelfth century, though we do not find Kippax, Smeaton, Womersley, Darrington, Castleford, or Methley ever so designated.

The Knights Templar had the legal right of presentation to Kellington; but in those disturbed times, with archbishop Geoffrey only a nominal ruler, it would appear that possession was nine points of the law. In any case, on the departure of John for the deanery of Pontefract, whenever that happened, he left the rectory in the possession of his son Thomas; and in No. 925 of the Selby Chartulary there is what seems an expression of bewilderment on the part of those patrons as to how Thomas had obtained possession. The document is dated 12 November, 1202, and was the result of a commission issued by Pope Innocent III. to the abbot of Meaux and the priors of Guisborough and Newborough to partition the tithes of Whitley, near Pontefract, between the churches of Kellington and Snaith. All parties were summoned, and appeared in the Chapter House at York, where Thomas even alleged his independence of the Knights-Templar. The point seems to have been settled by his continued possession, and he remained rector or parson at least till the reign of Henry III., as appears by No. 895 (Selby). No. 381 of the same chartulary shows that he had a son named Alexander, who, as we shall learn from No. 550, succeeded his father in the living, or at least some share of it. The Knights Templar obtained full possession only after Alexander's death, as may be seen by a comparison of No. 377 and No. 427 on archbishop Gray's roll, dated 1239 and 1244 respectively, and they had ultimately to make a second presentation, which reserved the rights of Alexander as vicar.

NOTE to the SECOND VOLUME.

We regret to record that the death of Mr. Holmes occurred when only four sheets of the present volume had been printed. His notes, however, were left in such order and completeness that he who took up his work had merely to see them through the press. They have, however, not had the great advantage of Mr. Holmes's final revision.

The thanks recorded in the former volume the present editor here gratefully repeats. The same ready assistance in reading of proofs, &c., has been accorded to him, a perfect stranger, as had been accorded to Mr. Holmes.

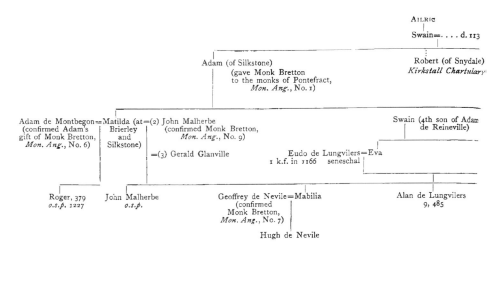

A.

The following is the pedigree as given in folio 85 of the Pontefract Chartulary. Its transcript in the Monasticon is somewhat obscured by an incorrect punctuation:—

Suayn filius Alrick feofavit domum de Pontefracto et monachos ibidem deo servientes de ecclesia de Silkeston cum sex bovatis terre in eadem villa.

Et de dicto Suayn venit Adam filius ejus, et confirmavit feofamentum patris sui. scilicet de ecclesia de Silkeston cum sex bovatis terre.

Et de dicto Ada venit Matilda et Anabilla, et de Matilda venit Rog. de Munbegum, Mabilia et Clementia de Lungvilers, de Clementia venit Johannes de Lungvilers.

Et de dicto Johanne de Lungvilers venit alius Johannes de Lungvilers, et de illo Johanne venit Mabilia et Margareta uxor Galfridi de Neovile.

Et de Mabilia venit Willielmus Lamare, et de Willielmo Delamare venit alia Mabilia, et de illa Mabilia venit Hugo de Neovile.

Et de Anabella filia Adæ venit Sarra, et de Sarra venit Thomas de Burgo, et de Thoma de Burgo alius Thomas de Burgo et Johannes, et dictus Thomas expiravit sine hærede, et de Johanne venit Thomas de Burgo qui nunc est.

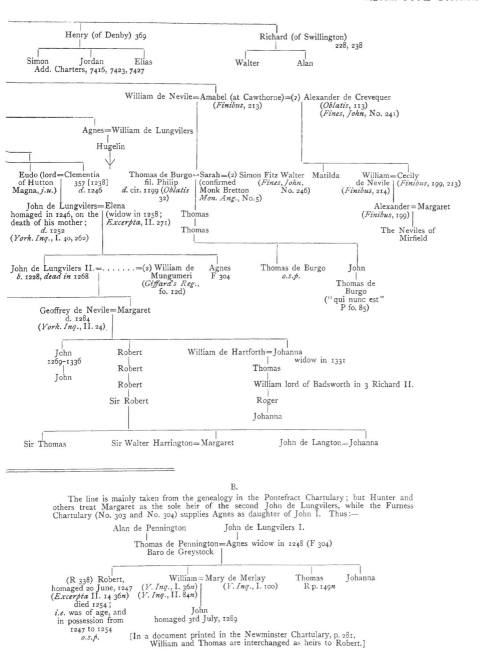

B.

The line is mainly taken from the genealogy in the Pontefract Chartulary; but Hunter and others treat Margaret as the sole heir of the second John de Lungvilers, while the Furness Chartulary (No. 303 and No. 304) supplies Agnes as daughter of John I. Thus:—

RAMOSVILLE or REINEVILLE.

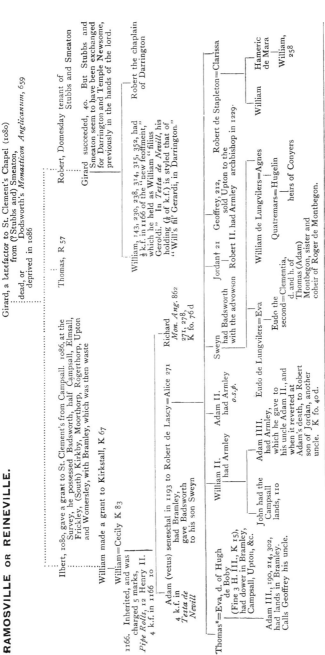

Girard, a benefactor to St. Clement's Chapel (1080) from (?Stubbs and) Smeaton, dead, or Dodsworth's *Monasticon Anglicanum*, 659 deprived in 1086.

Ilbert, 1080, gave a grant to St. Clement's from Campsall. 1086, at the Survey, he possessed Badsworth, half Campsall, Elmsall, Frickley, (South) Kirkby, Moorthorp, Rogerthorp, Upton and Womersley, with Bramley, which was then waste

William made a grant to Kirkstall, K 67

William=Cecily K 83

1166. Inherited, and was charged 5 marks, *Pipe Rolls*, 12 Henry II. 4 k.f. in 1166 10

Adam (vetus) seneschal in 1193 to Robert de Lascy=Alice 271
4 k.f. in *Testa de Nevill*

Thomas, R 57

Robert, Domesday tenant of Stubbs and Smeaton

Girard succeeded, 40. But Stubbs and Smeaton seem to have been exchanged for Darrington and Temple Newsome, previously in the hands of the lord.

Robert the chaplain of Darrington

William, 143, 230, 238, 314, 315, 352, had ⅔ k.f. in 1166 of the "new feoffment," which he held as William "filius Geroldi." In *Testa de Nevill*, his holding (⅔ of k.f.) is styled that of "Will's fil' Gerardi, in Darrington."

Richard
Mon. Ang. 862
271, 278,
K fo. 76 d

Sweyn
had Badsworth
with the advowson

Robert II. had Armley

Jordan† 21
sold Upton to the
archbishop in 1229.

Geoffrey, 212,

Robert de Stapleton=Clarissa

William de Lungvilers=Agnes
heirs of Conyers

William

Hameric de Mara

William, 258

Eudo the second=Clementia, d. and h. of Thomas (Adam) Montbegon, sister and coheir of Roger de Montbegon.

Quatremars=Hugelin
Thomas (Adam)

Thomas*=Eva, d. of Hugh de Boby (Fine 3 H. III., K 15), had dower in Bramley, Campsall, Upton, &c.

Adam III., 190, 214, 302, had lands in Bramley. Calls Geoffrey his uncle.

William II. had Armley

Adam II. had Armley *o.s.p.*

Eudo de Lungvilers
had Bramley, gave Badsworth to his son Sweyn

John had the Campsall lands, 110

Adam IIII. had Armley, which he gave to his uncle Adam II., and when it reverted at Adam's death, to Robert son of Jordan, another uncle. K fo. 40 d.

Eudo begat of Eva the heirs of Lungvilers. William begat of Agnes a daughter named Hugelin, from whom came the heirs of Conyers.

Eudo and William de Lungvilers came to Adam de Reyneville (IIII.) and said that he had unjustly given Armley to Robert son of Jordan his uncle, after the death of Adam his uncle, because he himself was lord and heir; but that Armley fell to them, Eudo and William, because they had [in marriage] the heirs of Sweyn de Reyneville, to whom belonged the heirship after Adam IIII. son of William, the firstborn of Adam de Reyneville.

† Jordan, son of a deceased Reineville, is mentioned in a Fine of 1208, concerning 36 acres of land in Ramesholme, in Kellington, Jordan Foliot being petitioner as against Henry de Vernoil (son of Jordan Paganel) and Matilda his wife, with Jordan de Reneville her son. (*Feet of Fines, John*, No. 371.) I have not traced this earlier Jordan, whose father was dead in 1208. See also *ante*, p. 266.

* The Kirkstall genealogy (K fo. 40 d) names only *four* of the six sons of Adam Vetus, ignoring Thomas and Geoffrey. Thus:—

Adam Vetus had four sons—(1) William, whom the Kirkstall Chartulary calls his firstborn; (2) Adam, (3) Sweyn, and (4) Jordan.
William his firstborn begat a son, Adam (IIII.) by name, who had the town of Bramley, entire, by bereditary right.
Adam (IIII.) gave Armley, a member of Bramley, to Adam (II.) his uncle, who died without heir.
Adam (IIII.) retook Armley into his hands, and gave it to Robert de Reineville, son of Jordan his uncle.
Moreover, the old Adam gave to Sweyn his son Badsworth, with the advowson of the church.

Sweyn had two daughters, Eva and Agnes.
Eudo de Lungvilers married Eva.
William de Lungvilers married Agnes.

Fasciculus VII.

THE SEVENTH FASCICULUS of the Pontefract Chartulary commences
with folio 46. It is of the normal size of ten folios, but contains
as many as seventy-seven charters, from No. 234 to No. 310.

Catton-on-Swale, mentioned in No. 235, was a manor in the
neighbourhood of Thirsk, between Topcliffe and Skipton; and it is
new to find that the Pontefract Priory ever had a property in
that North Riding hamlet, though, as was the case with so many of
their outlying possessions (for instance the two bovates at Smeaton
given, in No. 269, by Alan son of Robert, and the "land" at Chivet
in No. 267), the monks did not retain it in their own hands, but
freed themselves from it as soon as they conveniently could do so.

The importance of No. 238 must have been considerable, for it
was attested by representatives of most of the principal tenants in
the neighbourhood. Otto de Tilli (afterwards the seneschal at
Conisborough of Hamelin, Earl Warren); Robert the lord of
Stapleton; Reyner the Fleming (the first witness to No. 207,
another Swillington charter); Herbert de Arches, of the family that
left their name at Thorp Arch; Robert the progenitor of the
Swillingtons, and Walter the king's bailiff, the two younger sons of
Hugh the former lord of Stapleton, and the uncles of the present
lord; Humphrey de Veilly, the lord of Newton (Wallis); and Peter
de Toulston, were all typical men, each of paramount importance
in his own district in this third quarter of the twelfth century.
And these great men were backed and supported by smaller but
still important potentates; by Alan of Smeaton, Ralph son of
Nicholas of Cridling (whose son Adam of Cridling in the next
generation sold Cridling and Cridling Stubbs to Roger de Lascy),
William of Darrington, Alan de Toulston, and so "many others"
that the countryside must have been collected to give dignity to
the transaction. For it is difficult to say who, of those holding any
considerable position in the locality for many miles in the Pontefract
direction and beyond, was not present to sanction this charter of
sale made by Richard youngest son of Swain fitz Ailric to William
son of Hervey of Ledstone.

The family of the Domesday tenant, Ralph, who called himself Ralph de Featherstone, seems to have continued to flourish there, and there can be little doubt that most of the large number of owners and witnesses, who in these charters so called themselves, were his lineal descendants, with whom his prenomen was in considerable favour, even at the distance of a century and a half from his time. The *inq. p. m.* of this thirteenth century Ralph is 28 Henry III. [1244], No. 16. It reports that he had lived with a certain woman, Emma by name, for ten years before marriage, and had had by her a son Richard; that he then married, and had by her a daughter named Olive, aged 16½ years at the time of the inquisition; which Olive was declared to be the heir of the deceased, superseding the illegitimate Richard. His possessions had been—

	s.	d.
30 acres at Featherstone, worth 4d. per year	10	0
One messuage	2	0
5 acres of meadow at 6d.	2	6
Some pasture	14	0
2¾ bovates of land in villanage, at 4s. per bovate	11	0
Rent of free men in Featherstone	49	3½
Rent of Assize in Chevet	13	4
Rent of Assize in Stubbs [Walding]	0	3
Total	102	4½

He had also in Featherstone a yearly rent of a pound of pepper and two pounds of cumin, so that he was on the whole a wealthy man, especially as his interests did not extend very much beyond the lordship in which he and his forefathers had so long dwelt. Now, however, as we learn from this inquisition, the legitimate male line had failed in 1244, and the property would have to find a new line by marriage. I have not, however, traced it in any subsequent escheat.

I may notice that, although Ralph de Featherstone is called "dominus" when he attests No. 246, the honorary title is not given to him in his *inq. p. m.* The probability, therefore, is that it was one of courtesy only, which had at the time a wider scope than that ultimately given to it.

No. 248 had a datal clause of the circumlocutory character usual to the twelfth century, one so characteristic of a people who had not a long past behind them. The date referred to may, however, be ascertained without much investigation, for as the king "took the Cross" in January, 1187-8, this charter was made in the Lent of 1189, only a few weeks before his sudden demise the following summer.

Contemporary with this large owner was a second Ralph, who might have been uncle or cousin. He calls himself both " de Fetherstana " and "de eadem villa : " and follows William in No. 252. There was also a second Richard, who cannot have been the Richard son of the above Ralph ; for he would have been an older man, as he had a son, possibly a third Ralph, to follow him in the attestation clause of No. 246. But the concurrence in each case of a Ralph and of a Richard tends to lead to the inference that all were of the same family, with a common respect for their founder, the original Ralph de Featherstone of 1086.

No. 247 concludes the Featherstone series, and the Chartulary takes up next that of Whitwood and the Mere.

Whitwood had belonged to Ligulf in the time of Edward the Confessor, but when Ilbert de Lascy received his large fee he subinfeudated that manor to Roger Pictavus, who obtained Altofts also. When the Chapel of St. Clement's was being founded Roger made a contribution from Altofts ; but as he gave nothing from Whitwood, the inference would be that he had already lost his proprietorship there, though if so, Whitwood does not appear among Ilbert's possessions enumerated in the foundation charter of St. Clement's in the Castle. However, when Robert, son of Ilbert, succeeded to the fee, and founded the Priory of St. John's, Whitwood and the Mere were both in his hands, and by him conferred upon the monks by the original endowment charter (No. 1). To this grant Roger Pictavus gave his assent by testing the document, and thenceforward those two manors appear to have been held by the monks, who granted them out to various sub-tenants, if not in fee, certainly with a tenure nearly as good.

The charter No. 248 evidences that the monks had been asserting claims as if they felt that their rights were being infringed, and asserting them so successfully that the holder—a Pictavus—was glad to give them in settlement of all dispute, "from his demesne " (wherever that was), the churchman's portion of two bovates, roughly about sixteen acres.

There were two independent gifts to the monastery from this lordship ; that referred to here, which had dated from the time of Paganus de Land, "of two-thirds of Peckfield," and another from Hugh de Stiveton of the remaining third. Neither is referred to in any way in the Consecration Charter, possibly because the house held them as tenants, subject to rent, but in the charters of King Henry II., No. 71 and No. 73, made at Northampton in the opening of his reign (five years before the second dedication of the monastery), the latter witnessed by Henry de Lascy himself, both are duly enumerated as "all the land of Peckfield, that is to say two parts in perpetual alms and the third part at fee for sixteen pence each year." They are also catalogued in the pontifical charter of archbishop Theobald (No. 57), which is a few years later, but with the difference that the monks are therein said to hold all Peckfield at a yearly rent of four shillings. In the original charters (No. 311 and No. 317), as here, they are said to possess, attached to this larger share of the property, a common right in Micklefield; but this common right is not named in either of the royal charters or in that of the archbishop, while the rent named in each of those charters is here commuted for a payment in kind.

This Robert, son of Jordan de Land, was the great grandson of the donor, Paganus de Laland. See No. 317.

Walter de Byram, now developing into an influential local man, was a youngest son in the fourth generation (the latest generation with which the original part of the Chartulary has to deal) of that important magnate, Ailric of Ledstone. Ailric had four sons, named with himself in No. 206. These were Jordan and his company of three brothers, Reginald (of Aberford), Roger (of Ledstone), and Walter (of Micklefield and Wheldrake). Jordan, the eldest, had Hervey, whose second wife was Agnes widow of Henry Wallis. Hervey's son William, by his first wife, called "my lord" in No. 263 and No. 264, had two brothers, the elder of whom was the Robert here referred to, the younger being the Adam de Byram named in this charter as the father of Walter, at this time in possession. Adam's brotherhood is not here mentioned, but as, in No. 264, he calls William his "lord and brother," the fraternal relationship of the three is established.

Walter, the grantor of No. 262, thus belonged to the fifth generation, reckoning from the foundation of the monastery; and this charter seems to have been granted by him when, as a young man, in the lifetime of his father, he received his portion and went forth to establish an independent name and home, and to outlive the transaction by at least thirty years.

There were two Smeatons, separated by the river Went, and soon afterwards allotted to different parishes, but at this time in the same hand. Each had been an important place, and the larger, Kirk Smeaton, had had a pre-Domesday church which must have been built 1070–86, and therefore by the then lord Ramosville or Reineville. Being surrounded on every side by manors with churches (hemmed in by Campsall, South Kirkby, Badsworth, Ackworth, Darrington, and Womersley, each either bordering it or being close upon its borders), when the parochial arrangements were made, a century after Domesday, only one manor, that of Kirk Smeaton, was retained under the jurisdiction of the church there— Little Smeaton, on the other side of the river, the Smeaton without a church, being allotted to Womersley.

The Reinevilles first appear as donors to the foundation of St. Clement's Chapel, Ilbert having a manor in Campsall and Girard in Smeaton and perhaps Stubbs, from which each made a contribution. At the time of Domesday Ilbert had obtained Badsworth also, with Upton, Rogerthorp, Womersley, South Elmsall, South Kirkby, Moorthorp, Frickley, and Bramley, a group which continued in his descendants for some generations; while Stubbs and Smeaton had fallen to Robert, apparently by inheritance from his father Gerald. Whether Robert's branch of the Reinevilles was dispossessed or died out, or adopted a new name, I have seen nothing to show, but they never made such progress as that made by the branch which looked up to Ilbert for its head; and certain it is that even in 1166 only one de Reineville was reported as holding knights' fees, a William who held four, and who must have been two or three generations from the original Ilbert. There was, however, "of the new feoffment," *i.e.* enfeoffed under the new order of things which commenced with King Stephen, a William son of Gerold who held a third of a knight's fee, and it is evident from Testa de Nevill that it was he who was still possessed of Darrington, where his holding is represented as having diminished to a sixth part of a knight's fee. In No. 315 we shall find him described more fully as Willelmus filius Geroldi "de Dardingtona." But both Smeaton and Stubbs were at least as early as the return of 1166 in the possession of the descendants of Siward at Smeaton, and of Walden at Stubbs, though neither of the tenants was returned as holding by military service.

In Dodsworth's *Monasticon*, page 862, is a charter of "Robert de Lascy," which might easily be rejected as being probably spurious and certainly corrupt. By it Robert de Lascy is represented as giving to Kirkstall (1) the vaccarium near Roundhay, (2) common at Winmoor, (3) the wood at Roundhay, (4) an acre in Wenet, which Warin Lorimer held on the west side of the bridge. The charter professes to be tested by fifteen witnesses, but when examined these prove to belong to two different generations. They are (1) Osbert the archdeacon [who ceased to hold that office soon after 1166], (2) Ralph son of Nicholas [who tested the Kirkstall confirmation charter of 1153], (3) Robert de Stapleton. [His father William held 4 knights' fees in 1166, and his own many gifts to Nostell were confirmed by Pope Urban in 1186; while he lived well into the last decade of the century.] (4) William de Busli. [With (6) Adam de Reineville, and (11) to (15), he tests many Pontefract charters belonging to *cir.* 1193.] (5) Hugh de Tilli [as the father of Otto, Ralph and Roger, he, on the other hand, belongs to the earlier generation]. (6) Adam de Reineville. [He could hardly have come of age before 1170 or 1180.] (7) Richard his brother. [He is thus definitely mentioned in this charter only.] (8) Eudo de Lungvilers. [He had 1 knight's fee in 1166.] (9) William, his brother. [These two married the two co-heiresses of Sweyn, son of Adam Vetus.] (10) Burnell. [He witnesses P 8, P 12, and P 231, all belonging to late in the century. In P 12 he is described as dapifer to the earl of Warren (1164-1201).] The last five witnesses, (11) Elias the chamberlain, (12) Richard de Lewis, (13) Gilbert de Lascy, (14) Ralph Cocus and (15) Adam Pincerna, all appear with William de Bulli on P 5; (11) and (13) both test P 8, while (12) and (13) appear on P 240; but I trace Ralph Cocus and Adam Pincerna nowhere else, except that Ralph Cocus was in 1202, the deforciant of a bovate of land in Ribston. *Fines, John* No. 267. Thus this charter contains two groups of witnesses; of which (1) (2) (5) (8) and (9) belong to the middle of the twelfth century, and the remaining ten to its last decade.

In reading No. 278 it must be remembered that Reiner the father of the grantor is Reginald, one of the brothers of the great Jordan of Ledstone, and that Shippen is a hamlet in the fee of Hillam (see No. 210). This charter is somewhat out of position; it should have been between No. 175 and No. 173, Elinor having settled down as the wife of Elias of Aberford. To the earliest in date of these three charters, (No. 175), was appended a memorandum that Hugh son of Walter de Swillington, the final witness, was from the wapentake of Skyrack, Aberford, to which so many of the parties belonged, being in that wapentake, while the land itself was in Barkston Ash.

The eighteen acres in the Fields of Ferry (now Ferrybridge), afterwards the "territory" of that manor, appear to have been in three separate Fields, and probably in different parts of the manor. For the Fields or "territory"—it is called each in these charters indifferently —was the land bordering on neighbouring townships which had not been brought into cultivation so early as the Domesday carucates. Each carucate was a nucleus round which population clustered, while the Fields or "territory" were the outlying portions which belonged to the manor, but which had not been subjugated so early, and the boundaries of which had not indeed been fixed in many cases.

The six charters entered under the common title of No. 283, seem to be a number altogether disproportionate to so small a quantity of land; but their number was thus large, in a great measure because they belonged to a transaction which was being completed contemporaneously with the compilation of the Chartulary, and when the relative importance or insignificance of each could not be hastily determined. When, however, they are examined, they are practically reducible to three, 283*b* being triplicated, and 283*d* duplicated. Of the copy in triplicate, 283*b* seems to have been the original, No. 282 and No. 283*a* being later and having had additional witnesses, H. parson of Rothwell and Robert de Stapleton, of Cudworth in that parish, the head of the family at Stapleton in Darrington. Similarly 283*d* and 283*e* are duplicates, the second having not only the addition of "in perpetuum." but the statement that Roger de Blackburn was "parson" at that place, and the description of the witnesses as being not only "multis" but "aliis"; while the first adds the information that the full name of the parson of Rothwell was "Henry de Nottingham." This, however, is an addition sufficient to identify him as a canon of Southwell, whom we have already had testing No. 23 and No. 230 as Henry, parson of Rothwell, and who in 1234 tested the ordination of St. John's Hospital, Nottingham, as recorded in archbishop Gray's Register, page 168*n.* It may be noted that the names of these early parsons of Rothwell and Blackburn are not on record elsewhere.

To account for the presence of the name of Sir John Fiton on the deeds 283*d* and 283*e*, it may be observed that he was connected with the manor of Great Harwood, in Lancashire. His brother Richard had had a grant thereof from Henry de Lascy, which was confirmed by Robert II., his son, by a deed which is fully abstracted in the *Chartulary of Whalley*, p. 845. Richard's son Hugh, and his grandson Edmund, successively inherited, and the latter transferred the manor to Richard his second cousin half removed, the son of this witness. This last Richard had no male heirs.

The following is the line :—

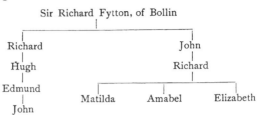

Sir Richard Fytton, of Bollin

Richard   John

Hugh   Richard

Edmund   Matilda   Amabel   Elizabeth

John

From whom the Fittons of Bolling and Gawsworth descended.

Of the co-heirs of the younger branch, Matilda married William de Hesketh, Amabel married Edmund de Leye, and Elizabeth married Roger Noel of Read.

During the two generations which had elapsed between No. 288 and No. 289, it happened that the lords of Frystone had twice failed in male heirs, and that by marriage they had changed their name as many times.

Their descent was from Gerbodo who, in the time of Domesday, held Crofton and the united manor of Wheldale and Frystone, and appears to have subsequently obtained Warmfield, for he gave the church there to Nostell. Gerbodo had two sons named in the Nostell Chartulary, William and Robert, to the latter of whom Frystone fell. Robert was the father of the William here named and of another Robert who inherited Wheldale, while William had Frystone from his father and obtained Ferry[bridge] also. The last-named manor was in the time of the Survey owned by one Hamelin, of whom I have traced nothing further than that he erected a water-mill on the Frystone Beck, where Frystone and Ferrybridge meet, which was called by his name (see No. 73 and No. 167); and that, perhaps at his death, Ferry with Hamelin's mill passed into the possession of the Frystone lord, who transferred this latter to the monks by a charter which has perished. The grant to the monks was confirmed by his son William (see No. 167) without mentioning his father's name, and only by a mere accidental annotation in the ecclesiastical confirmation of No. 57 we discover that it was Robert. Bertram, the son and heir mentioned in No. 89, dying, his sister Alice married Geoffrey Haget, whose father Bertram had founded the convent of Augustinian canons at Healaugh Park. Geoffrey was thus by inheritance the lord of Healaugh, the patron of its ecclesiastical establishments, and by marriage the lord of Frystone. But he had no male heir, and at his death his substance was divided among his daughters. Lucy, the eldest, had Wighill and the neighbouring Esdike; the second, unmarried, whose name does not occur in these documents, had Brayton; the third, Alice, had Healaugh and Frystone; but the fourth, Gundreda, had lands only. Alice married Jordan de St. Mary, but again the male line ceased, and Elizabeth, to whom Frystone came, married Henry Wallis II., whose son Richard inherited in his father's lifetime.

The Healaugh Chartulary in one place gives this rather differently, and introduces a John de Frystone as marrying Alice Haget and being father of a second Alice Haget, who inherited Healaugh, but it gives no confirmation of this bare statement, while it may generally be observed that the monks of the thirteenth century were poor genealogists, and that while their charter-evidence will generally bear investigation, their genealogical narratives fall to pieces at the slightest touch.

The following is the *inq. p. m.* of Dame Alice Haget, 31 Henry III. [1246-7], No. 33, as recently published in the *Record Series* (vol. 1, page 8) :—

Inquisition made by Henry del Greve, Ralph de Federstan, William del Greve, Simon Marshall, William Russell, Peter le Passur, Adam Chamberlain, Richard son of Robert, Adam son of Ralph, Simon Terrici, Adam de Buckden, and Robert de Sculthorpe, who say by their oath that

Alice Haget had in demesne at FRISTONE and FERI (Ferrybridge) :—

	s.	d.
10 score acres of land, at 6*d.* per acre	100	0
In demesne; meadow, 26½ acres at 3*s.*	79	6
In bondage [let to tenants]; 15 bovates of land at 2*s.*	30	0
The tenants render in work	43	9
Six cottars who pay no rent but do works worth .,.	8	3
Four other tenants ... ... pay	2	10
Fifteen free tenants... ... ... pay	54	0
A windmill there yields	26	0
Rent from MARTON	6	0
At FRICKLEY; in demesne, 64½ acres at 4*d.*	21	6
In demesne; meadow, 2 acres	2	0
In bondage [let to tenants]; 11 bovates at 5*s.* ...	55	0
The tenants render in work		22
In cottages, five acres	5	0
Four free tenants...	12	7½
Three women		23

Sum of the whole £22 10 2½

The aforesaid Alice had two heirs: Richard Wallis, son of her first daughter; and Nicholas, her other daughter.

Alice Haget thus had properties in Frystone, Ferrybridge, Marton and Frickley, and it is curious to notice their varying values. At Frystone the demesne land was worth 6*d.* per acre, at Frickley 4*d.*, and there is a corresponding value in the meadow, which was worth three times as much at Frystone as at Frickley. On the other hand, the bondage bovates were worth only 2*s.* at Frystone, while they were worth 5*s.* at Frickley. Nothing is said as to the possession of the lands at Healaugh by this " lady of Frystone," as she had probably been called while her widowhood lasted.

Dame Alice Haget, who thus retained her paternal name notwithstanding her marriage to Jordan de St. Mary, seems to have made an attempt to secure an absolute presentation to the church of Frystone without any intervention of the archbishop. She had presented William de Feugers, clerk, who had been duly instituted on 13 January, 1238-9 ; but on 6 October, 1248, Robert de Walleys, clerk, grandson of Dame Alice, and a younger brother of Richard Wallis her heir, was instituted on her presentation, although she had been dead many months and the writ for her *inq. p. m.* had issued on 3 February, 1246-7. This can be accounted for only on the supposition that on his grandmother's presentation Robert Wallis had taken possession, perhaps even years before, and that the archbishop had instituted him when he discovered the informality of his possession of the church. For by this middle of the thirteenth century, the right of the archbishop to institute to each living in his diocese had been firmly established.

This is a very interesting illustration of the manner in which Archbishop Gray maintained his rights. Nearly half a century before, in 1202, in the time of his predecessor, Archbishop Geoffrey, there was a somewhat similar state of things at Kellington, where (S 925) Thomas the son of the former rector, appeared in possession, and seems to have maintained his position independently of either presentation or institution. In the case of the Fryston church, the archbishop had evidently become strong enough to insist that the appointment, however belated, should pass through his hands. So slowly though steadily, was the constitution of our English church built up.

WICK.

CCXXXIIII. Carta Ade filii Willelmi de Alwaldleia. Cir. 1210.

[To all who shall see or hear this writing, Adam son of William of Alwoodley, greeting. I make known to all of you that I have surrendered . . . . to my lords the prior and convent of Pontefract, all right and claim . . . . in those two bovates of land which I have held from them in the town of Wick. In testimony . . . . . . Witnesses.]

Omnibus hoc scriptum visuris vel audituris Adam filius Willelmi de Alwoldeleia, salutem. Universitati vestre notum facio me sursum reddidisse, et omnino de me et heredibus meis inperpetuum quietum clamasse dominis meis Priori et conventui de Pontefracto omne jus et clamium quod habui vel habere potui in illis duabus bovatis terre quas de eis tenui in villa de Wic. In cujus rei testimonium hoc scriptum pro me et heredibus meis sigillo meo roboravi. Hiis testibus, *Ricardo de Mora, tunc ballivo,*[1] *Adam de Widentona, Henrico de Alwaldeleia*[2] *de Lofthus, Henrico de Stubbes,*[3] *Henrico de Goutorp,*[4] et multis aliis.

(1) Of Wick.   (2) "William" probably omitted. See No. 266.
    (3) Stubhouse, near Harewood.   (4) Goldthorp, near Hickleton.

CCXXXV.[1]   Carta Thome filii Warini.   Cir. 1190

[To the Archbishop of York, to all the Chapter of St. Peter of York, and to all the sons of Holy Mother Church, Thomas son of Warin greeting. Know that I have granted . . . . . . a toft in Catton . . . . . . and three roods of land ; to wit, one and a half at Garbrarth, and another and a half at Graystone; which with a toft I have [hereby] sold to my lady Adeliza, wife of Hugh son of Fulk, and she has given those roods of land, together with the toft, to the aforesaid monks . . . . These being witnesses, &c.]

Eboracensi archiepiscopo, totique capitulo sancti Petri Eboraci et omnibus sancte matris ecclesie filiis Thomas filius Warini, salutem. Sciatis me concessisse et hac mea carta confirmasse deo et monachis sancti Johannis de Pontefracto, unum toftum in Catthuna[2] qui[3] est inter domum meam et domum Hamundi, et tres perticatas terre ; unam scilicet et dimidiam ad Gairbrarth et alteram et dimidiam ad Graistana, sic quas cum tofto vendidi domine mee Adelize uxori Hugonis filii Fulconis,[4] et illas easdem perticatas terre simul cum tofto dedi prefatis monachis pro salute anime sue in puram et perpetuam elemosinam, liberas, solutas et quietas ab omni terreno servicio et

(1) Neither of these two charters appears to have been hitherto copied or even abstracted.
    (2) Catton.   (3) *Sic.*   (4) Probably Lisours of Adwick.

2 B

exactione seculari.   Hiis testibus, *Hugone filio Fulconis, Turstino monacho de Beghlanda,*[5] *Petro et Alano de Tulestuna,*[6] *Hamundo presbitero,*[7] *Thebbardo et Willelmo clerico*[8] *de Daltuna,*[9] *Helya filio Hugonis, Roberto Bond, et Ernisio de Cattuna.*

---

(5) Byland.   (6) See pedigrees under No. 143 and No. 455.

(7) Probably the parson of Catton, and the bordering owner named in the charter.

(8) *Sic* ; but query "clericis."   (9) Dalton and Catton are each in the parish of Topcliffe.

STUBBES [WALDING].

CCXXXVI.[1]   Carta Henrici filii Willelmi de Stubbes.   Cir. 1210.

[Know that I, Henry son of William of Stubbs, have granted and given . . . . to Otto my brother, an assart named Rolescroft, and a small messuage on the other side of the road, within sight of the messuage of William Burnell, to be given in religion where he will . . . . . . for the souls of our fathers and mothers, and of our ancestors.   Warranty.   Witnesses.]

Sciant presentes et futuri, quod ego Henricus filius Willelmi de Stubbes,[2] concessi et dedi et hac presenti carta mea confirmavi Otthoni fratri meo unum essartum, quod nominatur Rolescroft,[3] et unum parvum mesuagium ex altera parte vie coram mesuagio Villi[3] Burnel danda in religione ubi voluerit, in puram et perpetuam elemosinam, pro animabus patrum[3] et matrum[3] nostrorum[3] et antecessorum nostrorum.   Et ego predictus Henricus et heredes mei, warantizabimus predictam elemosinam ubi fuerit assignata inperpetuum contra omnes homines.   Hiis testibus, *Roberto Walensi, Ada de Reinevilla, et Thoma filio ejus, Thoma de Thornetona,*[4] *Thoma de*

---

(1) There is an abstract of No. 236 in the *Dodsworth* MS., vol. 136.   Stubbs and the two Smeatons were at the time of the Domesday survey in possession of Robert de Ramosville.   This Robert had two sons, the younger of whom, Girard, is recorded to have made a grant to St. Clement's Chapel of half his tithe at Smeaton, which implies that he held the manor, that the church was not then built, and that its tithes were not then dedicated.   But by what particular act of transference or exchange he was parted from those manors is uncertain, whether by his own deed or by the act of his lord.   The only certainty is that whenever Girard afterwards appears, it is as Gerald, lord of Darrington ; and as the sixth of a knight's fee, the holding was continuously reported, even as late as Testa de Nevill, as being that of "William fil' Gerardi."   But the position which Girard had held at Stubbs and Smeaton was occupied at Stubbs by Walding and his son William, and at Smeaton by Siward and his son Ralph, each of whom was a previously unknown man ; and it is evident that if this William son of Girard was the same as the William who tested No. 220, he must, like Adam Vetus, have lived to a full, ripe age.   The later holders of Stubbs (or Stubbs Walding, as it was called from the first of the family) were descended from one who is known only as Walding.   See pedigree under No. 101.   As is almost universally the case with the men of his generation, absolutely nothing but his name seems to be known of this Walding : and it is only in a succeeding generation and in connection with his son William that we meet even with that.   William is, however, constantly described as William son of Walding, but in No. 147 he is called William the soldier.   His two elder sons are called respectively Henry son of William son of Walding in No. 236, and Otto son of William son of Walding in No. 328.   But William had at least two other sons, Robert and Ralph, and two daughters, Joy and Amabel ; while, as we shall see in No. 241, Ralph became a Cluniac monk at Pontefract—an interesting evidence that French nationality was not an essential qualification for election among the monks of St. John's.   The new tenants of Stubbs gravitated towards Pontefract (see No. 101), while Ranulph and his son Alan aimed at a county position and the bailiffship of the united wapentake of Staincross and Osgoldcross.   See No. 110.   (2) See Walding pedigree, under No. 101.

(3) *Sic*, in each case.   (4) Husband of Isoulda de Preston, heir of William de Preston.

Bosevilla, Hugone filio Walteri, et Roberto fratre ejus,[5] Thoma de Lisurs, Galfrido Scorcebot, Alano filio Ranulfi, Willelmo de Sikelinghala, Johanne Albo, Willelmo de Cameshale, et aliis.

(5) The two sons of Walter, the king's bailiff. See pedigree, page xlvi.

DE TORPH.

CCXXXVII.   **Carta Acharie filie Helie de Stainforda.**   **Cir. 1190.**

[To all the sons of Holy Mother Church, Acharias daughter of Helias of Stainforth, greeting in the Lord. Know all of you that . . . . I have given, granted, and . . . . confirmed to God and St. John the Apostle and evangelist, of Pontefract, and the monks there serving God. . . . . . . a bovate of land in Thorp near Burnsall, which I bought of Arnald, the clerk, with all the easements belonging to that bovate. Warranty. Witnesses.]

Omnibus sancte matris ecclesie filiis Acharias[1] filia Helie de Stainforda, salutem in domino. Noverit universitas vestra me pro salute anime mee et omnium antecessorum et heredum meorum dedisse, concessisse et presenti carta confirmasse deo et sancto Johanni Apostolo et evangeliste de Pontefracto, et monachis ibidem deo servientibus, in puram et perpetuam elemosinam, unam bovatam terre in Torph juxta Brunsella,[2] quam emi de Arnaldo clerico, cum omnibus aisiamentis ad eamdem bovatam pertinentibus. Et ego Acharias et heredes mei prefatam bovatam terre predictis monachis warentizabimus contra omnes homines, sicut puram et perpetuam elemosinam. Hiis testibus, *Serlone de Pouele, Willelmo filio ejus, Alano de Brehae,[3] Henrico de Bramehop, Henrico de Witona, Hugone capellano, Radulfo capellano de Ottelaya, Gilleberto diacono, de eadem villa, Symone Cuinterel, Adam Forestario, Gilleberto Deirtona,[4]* et multis aliis.[5]

(1) *Sic.*

(2) **Near** Grassington. Till the end of the nineteenth century there was common land here, common to both Thorp and Burnsall, and still undivided, the condition which very generally obtained in the twelfth century throughout the West Riding.

(3) Brearey. See No. 266.   (4) Dearton is in the manor of Halifax.

(5) As No. 236, the charter of a Stubbs man, was tested mainly by his immediate neighbours, such as Alan and White of Smeaton, so No. 237 had for its principal witnesses people at Poole and Otley, belonging to that part of the wapentake of Skyrack. Nothing else occurs of Elias of Stainforth, or of Acharias his daughter.

SWINLINGTON.[1]

CCXXXVIII.   **Carta Ricardi filii Swani.[2]**   **Cir. 1180.**

[Know present and to come, that I, Richard son of Swain, ... have confirmed to William son of Hervey, the meadow of Wixstalker, in the town of Swillington. . . . . . . And if . . . . . I, Richard son of Swain, cannot warrant the

(1) The original annotator of No. 228 ascribed this charter to Byram.

(2) See No. 228 and No. 378. This early charter is from the youngest son of Swain son of Ailric, the pre-Norman magnate of Staincross and Osgoldcross. Swain had three sons, perhaps

said meadow of Wixstalker to the aforesaid William son of Hervey, before the aforesaid William son of Hervey shall be thence disseised I will give him an exchange in value from my demesne meadow in that town of Swillington. And for the gift of this meadow, the aforesaid William son of Hervey has given to me twenty shillings for acknowledgment. Witnesses.]

Sciant presentes et futuri quod ego, Ricardus filius Swani, dedi et concessi, et presentis carte testimonio confirmavi Willelmo filio Hervei,[3] pratum de Wixstalker in villa de Swinlingtona, sibi et heredibus suis tenendum de me et heredibus meis in feudo et hereditate. Reddendo inde mihi annuatim sex denarios, scilicet ad festum sancti Martini. Et si forte accidit[4] quod ego Ricardus filius Swani predictum pratum de Wixstalker predicto Willelmo filio Hervei warentizare non potero antequam predictus Willelmus filius Hervei inde dissaisiatur, excambium ad valenciam dabo illi de meo prato dominco[4] in eadem villa de Swinglingtona. Et pro hujus prati donatione predictus Willelmus filius Hervei dedit mihi xx*ti* solidos pro recognitione. Testibus istis, *Ottone de Tilli, Roberto de Stapiltona, Reinerio Flemeng, Hereberto de Archis, Roberto filio Hugonis, Petro [de] Toulestona,[7] Henrico Picot, Reinerio clerico de Derfeld, Ada filio Ormi, Willelmo de Prestona, Umfrido de Villi, Henrico filio Dolfini, Alano de Smithetona, Radulfo filio Nicholai,[5] Waltero filio Hugonis, Morando de Kirkeby, Willelmo filio Geroldi,[6] Willelmo de Hottona, Henrico filio Thome, Alano de Toulistona,[7]* et multis aliis.

---

four; Adam his principal heir, who founded Monk Bretton; Henry, who succeeded at Denby (some of whose charters with the original seal are still in the Cottonian Library); perhaps Ralph at Sharlston (see Kirkstall Chartulary; and pedigree, page 306), and this Richard, who had these demesne lands at Swillington. It may be noticed that all but the eldest son had distinctly Norman names.

(3) William son of Hervey appears as a buyer in No. 233 also. His youngest brother and ultimate heir was Adam de Byram.   (4) *Sic*, in each case.

(5) Of Cridling. He tested the Kirkstall confirmation charter, K 67, and No. 2 *Monasticon.*

(6) Of Darrington.   (7) See pedigree *ante*, page 188.

SUNDETON.
CCXXXIX.[1]   Carta Roberti Venatoris.[2]   Cir. 1180.

[Know present and to come, that I, Robert Hunter, have . . . . . . confirmed by this my charter, my curtilage in Sundeton which was Roger's, and three acres of land as they lie in three plots. And as I have held without any measurement, that they may have and hold, &c. . . . . . . Witnesses.]

Sciant presentes et futuri quod ego, Robertus Venator, donavi et concessi deo et ecclesie sancti Johannis de Pontefracto, et monachis

---

(1) No. 239, like No. 238, belongs to the third quarter of the twelfth century. The three brothers of Jordan of Ledstone test with him, and the name of each is given, so that all were then living.

(2) Robert Venator, the grantor, held of Henry de Lascy half a knight's fee in 1166, according to the valuable return to be found in *Liber Niger.*

ejusdem loci, et confirmavi hac mea carta, curtillagium meum in Sundetona quod fuit Rogeri, et tres acras terre sicut jacent in tribus agris, et sicut ego tenui sine aliqua mensuratione, ut habeant et teneant libere et quiete, in bosco et plano, in aquis et pasturis, sicut decet puram elemosinam inperpetuum, pro anima mea et animabus antecessorum et parentum meorum. Testibus, *Magistro Rainerio, Ranulfo de Sundetona, Jordano, Rainaldo, Rogero et Waltero de Ledestuna,*[3] *Symone filio Serlonis, et Benedicto fratre ejus, Raimondo filio Siwardi, et Hugone nepote ejus, Radulfo filio Hugonis, Radulfo filio Aurifabri, Gilleberto Parmenter, Johanne filio Sygeride, Michaele filio Thome,*[4] et aliis.

(3) The four Ledstone brothers. See No. 147.

(4) Michael, the last named in the charter, is Michael de Monte, afterwards Mons Monachorum —Monkhill. Thomas his father is Thomas Dapifer, one of the younger brothers of Peter fitz Asolf

---

HAREWODE: DE DUABUS BOVATIS TERRE IN COM' LANC'.

CCXL.[1]   **Carta Thome presbiteri de Harewode.**   **1192.**

[Know present and to come, that I Thomas the priest . . . . to Gilbert de Lascy and his heirs, two bovates of land in Harwood, to be held . . . . freely and quietly, in fee, and heirship, and these bovates I hold of Henry de Elland, freely and quietly, in fee and heirship, and to that extent I have his charter . . . . free and quit from all service except forensic service, for three shillings and for spurs of threepence, which Gilbert shall pay to the aforesaid Thomas yearly at the feast of St. Giles. . . . . . . A mark in acknowledgment in full wapentake at Clitheroe. Witnesses.]

Sciant presentes et futuri quod ego, Thomas presbiter, dedi et concessi Gilleberto de Lasci[2] et heredibus suis duas bovatas terre in Harewod tenendas de me et heredibus meis, libere et quiete, in feudo et hereditate, et has bovatas teneo de Henrico de Elandia, libere et quiete, in feudo et hereditate, et inde cartam ejus habeo. Concessi autem predictas bovatas predicto Gilleberto pro humagio suo et servitio eadem libertate qua illas teneo de predicto Henrico, in bosco et plano, in pratis et paschuis, in terris, in viis et semitis, in stagnis et aquis et vivariis, cum omnibus pertinentiis suis, liberas et quietas ab omni servicio preter foraneum servicium, propter tres solidos et propter calcaria

---

(1) This was copied into *Dodsworth*, vol. 151, with a memorandum that the Harwood was Harwood Magna, ten miles from Rochdale. The intention was to prevent confusion with Harewood, near Leeds. See also No. 408.

(2) The Gilbert de Lascy of this charter, whom the cartographer when classifying No. 5 mistook for one of the lords, was very clearly of an altogether different family. But see the remarks on No. 5, pages 11, 12. By a Fine 4 John (Surtees xciv., page 17), a Gilbert de Lascy and his wife Agnes held four bovates in Hippe-holme of Alice, widow of Henry de Eland.

trium denariorum quos Gillebertus reddet annuatim predicto Thome ad festum sancti Egidii et propter hoc dedit predictus Gillebertus predicto Thome unam marcam de recognitione in plenario wapentaco apud Clidh'. Hii sunt testes, *Eudo de Lungwils,*[3] *tunc senescallus, Ricardus de Tanga, Robertus filius Bernardi, Alanus vicecomes,*[4] *Ricardus de Lewes, Huffredus*[5] *de Chirche, Hospatitus*[6] *de Salesburi, Rogerus filius ejus, Gillebertus de Derwent, Hugo de Mittun, Hugo de Eleuetho, Jordanus de Cleytun, Thomas filius Roberti, Willelmus filius Roberti, Nicholaus clericus, et wapentacus.*

(3) The elder Eudo or Ivo. See also No. 9, No. 127, and the pedigree facing this Fasciculus.

(4) Alan of Kippax in No. 408. He is not named in the Official List of Sheriffs extracted from the Pipe Rolls and given in the 31st Annual Report of the Deputy Keeper of the Public Records. See note (6) to No. 27 and note (6) to No. 97.   (5) Called "Utred" in the Selby Chartulary, page 210.

(6) Gospatric. See also 283d, note (4).

SUTTON: DE CONFIRMATIONE TRIUM ACRARUM IN CAMPIS.

CCXLI.[1]   **Carte Ade filii Warneri de Suttona.**   [2]**Post 1180.**

[To all the faithful of Holy Church, Adam son of Warner, greeting. Be it known to all of you that I, Adam . . . . . confirm . . . . . the gift which William son of Roger[3] has made to them from my fee, to wit three acres in the Field of Sutton, which are called Priest dales, and a half acre on the boundary of Burg,[4] and the other half acre towards the moor, and a half toft, to wit two roods and a half rood in Sutton . . . . . to keep the anniversary of Ralph the monk, of Stubbs. Witnesses.]

Omnibus fidelibus sancte ecclesie, Adam filius Warneri salutem. Notum sit vestre universitati, quod ego, Adam, concedo et hac mea carta confirmo deo et sancto Johanni, et monachis de Pontefracto, donationem quam fecit eiis[5] Willelmus filius Rogeri de feudo meo, videlicet, tres acras in campo de Suttona que vocantur Prestedales[6] et dimidiam acram super divisum de Burg, et alteram dimidiam acram versus moram, et dimidium toftum scilicet duas rodas et dimidiam rodam in Suttona, in liberam et puram et perpetuam elemosinam, cum

(1) Since provision was now being made for celebrating the anniversary (that is, the day of his death) of Ralph the monk, it is probable that both he and Richard his son were already dead.

(2) See No. 101.   (3) Pictavensis.   (4) Burgwallis.   (5) *Sic.*

(6) In the next charter these are called "partes sacerdotis." This "Preste-dales" is thus a remarkable equivalent, and altogether No. 241 and No. 242 are singularly complementary, a remark in one completing the idea which the other has left incomplete. The extent to which they do this is noteworthy. As usual, the second is the earliest in point of date, No. 242 being the original deed of donation, No. 241 the confirmation by the lord of the fee. In the earlier charter the locality of the first plot given is said to be Middle Field, as if it were not certain to what manor it belonged; in the later, the name given to it is "the Field of Sutton;" Priest's (*sacerdotis*) portions become Priest-dales (it may be "doles"); the object of the donation—to make an anniversary for Ralph the monk, one of the grandsons of Walding of Stubbs—is defined; while his younger brother Robert, who was not named in the original charter, appears among the witnesses to the second. See also a note on the word "doles" in Rievaux Chartulary, page 294.

omnibus pertinentiis et aisiamentis ad predictam terram pertinentibus, pro anima mea et pro animabus omnium antecessorum meorum, ad faciendum anniversarium Radulfi monachi de Stubbis. Hujus rei testes sunt, *Magister Ailbinus,*[7] *Adam filius Petri,*[8] *Thomas frater suus, Robertus de Stapiltona, Petrus de Toulistona, Willelmus filius Walding, Henricus et Otto et Robertus, filii sui, Willelmus de Michlefeld,*[9] *Geraldus de Luttona,*[10] *Thomas dapifer, Willelmus frater suus,*[11] *Herebertus filius Willelmi, Henricus filius Petri, Nigellus de Witewod,* et aliis.

(7) Tests No. 324 as "Magister Ailbinus de Hanepol" (Hampole).   (8) Of Birkin.
    (9) Micklefield.   (10) Lotherton.   (11) The monks' baker.

BURG : DE TRIBUS ACRIS IN CAMPO.

CCXLII.   Carta Willelmi filii Rogeri de Burg.   Cir. 1170.

[Know present and to come, that I, William, son of Roger, have given and granted . . . . three acres in the Middle Field, which are called Priest's portions, and a half acre, adjoining the boundary of Burg, and another half acre towards the moor, and a half toft, to wit two roods and a half in Sutton. . . . . . Witnesses.]

Sciant presentes et futuri quod ego Willelmus filius Rogeri[1] dedi et concessi et hac presenti karta mea confirmavi deo et sancto Johanni et monachis de Pontefracto iij acras in medio campo que vocantur partes sacerdotis, et dimidiam acram super divisum de Burg, et alteram dimidiam acram adversus moram, et dimidium toftum scilicet duas rodas et dimidiam in Suttona, in puram et perpetuam elemosinam, cum omnibus pertinentiis et aisiamentis ad predictam terram pertinentibus, pro anima mea et pro animabus omnium antecessorum meorum. Testibus, *Adam de Rainevilla, Adam de Prestuna, Willelmo de Prestuna,*[2] *Petro de Toulistuna, Gilleberto fratre suo,*[3] *Willelmo de Stubbes, Henrico et Ottone,*[4] *filiis ejus.*

(1) Pictavensis.

(2) This is, I think, the only charter in which Adam de Preston and William de Preston concur. They were in all probability brothers, but their relationship is not named. See pedigree under No. 173. William witnessed No. 231 also.   (3) See pedigree under No. 454.

(4) See pedigree under No. 101. Consistently with the purpose of the donation, William of Stubbs and two of his sons witness each document.

SUTTON.

CCXLIII.   De Petro[1] Priore et Hugone filio Radulfi.[1]   1226.

[This is the final concord made in the court of the Lord King at York, in the octaves of All Saints, in the eleventh year . . . . . . of King Henry son of King

(1) *Sic* in each instance.

John, before Robert de Vipont, John, Robert's son, Martin de Pateshill, Brian de Insula, Richard Duket, justices itinerant . . . . . . between Hugh prior of Pontefract, plaintiff, and Ralph son of Hugh, tenant, concerning a half messuage with appurtenances in Sutton; and between the same prior, plaintiff, and the same Ralph, whom John de Roucester and Agnes his wife called to warrant . . . . . concerning four acres of land with the appurtenances in that town ; whereupon an assize was summoned &c. . . . . . . Right of the said prior . . . . . . paying thence yearly four shillings at two terms of the year ; to wit, at Whitsuntide two shillings, at the Feast of St. Martin two shillings, for all service and exaction.]

Hec est finalis concordia[2] facta in curia domini Regis apud Eboracum in octavis omnium sanctorum Anno Regni Regis Henrici filii Regis Johannis undecimo,[3] coram Roberto de Veteriponte, Johanne filio Roberti,[4] Martino de Patshill, Briano de Insula, Ricardo Dukit, Justiciariis itinerantibus et aliis domini Regis fidelibus tunc ibi presentibus, inter Hugonem Priorem de Pontefracto petentem, et Radulfum filium Hugonis tenentem, de dimidio mesuagio cum pertinentiis in Suttona ; et inter eundem priorem petentem, et eundem Radulfum quem Johannes de Boucestre[5] et Agnes uxor ejus vocaverunt ad warant[izare], et qui eis warantizavit de quatuor acris terre cum pertinentiis in eadem villa ; unde assisa summonita fuit inter eos in eadem curia ad recognoscendum utrum predictum mesuagium dimidium et terra cum pertinentiis esset libera elemosina pertinens ad ecclesiam ipsius prioris de Pontefracto, vel laicum feodum ipsorum Radulfi, Johannis, et Agnetis. Scilicet quod predictus Radulfus recognovit predictum dimidium mesuagium, et predictam terram cum pertinentiis esse jus ipsius Prioris. Et pro hac recognitione, fine[6] et concordia, idem prior concessit predicto Radulfo predictum dimidium mesuagium et predictam terram cum pertinentiis habenda et tenenda eidem Radulfo et heredibus suis de predicto priore et successoribus suis et ecclesia sancti Johannis de Pontefracto inperpetuum. Reddendo inde per annum quatuor solidos ad duos terminos anni. Scilicet ad Pentecosten duos solidos, ad festum sancti Martini duos solidos, pro omni servicio et exactione.[7]

---

(2) Final Concord was a legal phrase for a very common transaction in the King's Court, by which the ratification of an agreement to compromise legal proceedings was effected and put on record. It is sometimes by abbreviation called a "Fine," but nothing of the modern sense of the word "fine" attaches to the use of the word.   (3) 1226.

(4) Not named in Foss as a justice, but stated to have been a minor at his father's death, in 1228.

(5) Sic for Roucestre in Staffordshire, where there was a convent of Augustinian canons, founded by Richard Bacon, nephew of Ralph, earl of Chester. See note (7) to No. 171.

(6) Sic ; an early use of this form.

(7) Not one of the documents from No. 237 to No. 243 appears to have been transcribed or even abstracted, except that No. 240 and No. 243 were copied into Dodsworth's vol. 151, though with two or three very remarkable blunders, and that there is a meagre abstract of No. 242 in vol. 135.

FETHERSTANA.
CCXLIIII. Carta Willelmi de Fethurstan. Cir. 1244.

[Be it known to all who shall see or hear this writing, that I, William of Featherstone, have granted . . . . . . all the land which Hugh, the park-keeper, son of Ralph of Methley, has held of me in the Field of Featherstone, to wit, two acres and a rood upon Birk-flat. . . . . . . Warranty. Witnesses.]

Notum sit omnibus hoc scriptum visuris vel audituris quod ego, Willelmus de Fetherstana, concessi et hac presenti carta mea confirmavi deo et sancto Johanni Apostolo et evangeliste de Ponte-fracto, et monachis ibidem deo servientibus in puram et perpetuam elemosinam, totam terram quam Hugo filius Radulfi de Medeley, parcarius, de me tenuit in campo de Fetherstana, videlicet duas acras et unam perticatam super Birkflat,[1] que jacent inter terram Nicholai de Fethirstana, ex una parte, et terram meam ex altera, abuttantes versus orientem et occidentem. Tenendam et habendam dictis monachis, libere, quiete, et pacifice, et integre, in puram et perpetuam elemosinam. Et ne ego vel heredes mei contra tenorem hujus carte venire possimus, eam sigilli mei appositione roboravi. Et ad predicte terre warantizationem me et heredes meos obligavi. Hiis testibus, *Waltero de Ludham, tunc*[2] *senescallo Pontisfracti, Jordano de Insula, de Prestona,*[3] *Willelmo de Refectorio, Willelmo de Assartis, Nicholao de Fetherstana,* et aliis.

(1) It may be noticed that the bounding flat is called Birkflat and Brekflat in No. 244 and and No. 245 respectively. There was a similar metathesis in the case of Birkett or Breker in No. 127 and No. 128. (2) 1240-6.

(3) There seem to have been two of this name at this time, "Jordan de Insula de Prestona" and "Jordan de Insula de Hooton." See No. 273 and No. 443. In No. 440 this latter is called "de Brodsworth."

CCXLV. Carta Hugonis Parcarii de Pontefracto et Alicie uxoris sue. Cir. 1244.

[Know present and to come that I, Hugh, the park-keeper of Pontefract, and Alice my wife . . . . . . especially for the soul of Walter de Castley, have granted . . . . all the lands which we formerly held and possessed in the town of Featherstone, from William of Featherstone, then bailiff, Alan of Thornhill, Henry Fresel, [and] Alice and Tibba daughters of the late John Durward ; to wit a toft in the town of Featherstone lying between the toft of the late John their father and the toft of Nicholas of Featherstone, containing in breadth three rods of land, and in length eleven rods of land. And two acres and a rood upon Brekflat, which lie between the land of Nicholas of Featherstone on the one side, and the land of the aforesaid William on the other, lying towards the east and west. And two acres lying between the land of William son of Oda and the land of the aforesaid Alan, extending from the road from Featherstone towards the Park of Pontefract, and half an acre of land in the Featherstone Moor, lying between the land of William son of Roger, of Featherstone, and the land of Alexander Brun of Pontefract. And an acre of land lying between the land of Nicholas of Featherstone, and the land of Huer [? Hervey], of the same town, abutting on the house which belonged to the aforesaid sisters Alice and Tibba, stretching towards the east and west. And a rood of land and a half lying on the hill, between the land of Ralph de Featherstone and the land of William of the same town; that is to say, between the Park and Featherstone. And a half of the Woodroyd nearer the town of Featherstone, with all its appurtenances, &c. Sealed. Witnesses.]

Sciant presentes et futuri, quod ego, Hugo Parcarius de Pontefracto et Alicia uxor mea, pro salute animarum nostrarum et omnium antecessorum et successorum nostorum, et precipue pro anima Walteri de Castelleia, dedimus, concessimus, et hac presenti carta nostra confirmavimus cum corporibus nostris deo et sancto Johanni de Pontefracto et monachis ibidem deo servientibus, in puram et perpetuam [elemosinam] omnes terras quas quondam habuimus et tenuimus in villa de Fethirstana, de Willelmo de Fethirstana, tunc ballivo,[1] Alano de Tornehila, Henrico Fresel, Alicia et Tibba filiarum quondam Johannis Durwarda, videlicet unum toftum in villa de Fethirstana, jacens inter toftum Johannis quondam patris earum et toftum Nicholay de Fethirstana continens in latitudine tres perticatas[2] terre et in longitudine undecim perticatas[2] terre. Et duas acras et unam perticatam super Brekflat[3] que jacent inter terram Nicholay de Fethirstana ex una parte et terram predicti Willelmi ex altera, abuttantes versus orientem et occidentem. Et duas acras jacentes inter terram Willelmi filii Ode[4] et terram supradicti Alani extendentes a via de Fethirstana versus parcum de Pontefracto[5] et dimidiam acram terre in Mora de Fethirstana jacentem inter terram Willelmi filii Rogeri de Fethirstana et terram Alexandri Brun de Pontefracto. Et unam acram terre jacentem inter terram Nicholai de Fethirstana, et terram H'uer[6] de eadem villa, abuttantem super domum que fuit predictarum sororum Alicie et Tibbe, tendentem versus orientem et occidentem. Et unam perticatam terre et dimidiam jacentem super Hil, inter terram Radulfi de Fethirstana et terram Willelmi de eadem villa, scilicet inter parcum et Fethirstanam. Et medietatem del Wodrode propinquiorem ville de Fethirstana, cum omnibus pertinentiis suis, in pratis, in pasturis, in moris, in turbariis, in viis, in semitis et omnibus aliis libertatibus et aisiamentis ad dictas terras infra villam de Fethirstana et extra pertinentibus, tenendas et habendas libere,

---

(1) Bailiff to the earl.   (2) See note (5) to No. 168.   (3) See note (1) to No. 244.
(4) "Hoda" in No. 292, and "Odo" in No. 551.
(5) In the thirteenth century and till 1780 Pontefract Park included all that is now called the Pontefract Park District.   (6) *Sic*, ? Hervey.

quiete, et pacifice, sicut puram et perpetuam elemosinam. Et ne ego
Hugh vel Alicia uxor mea sive aliquis heredum meorum in posterum
contra tenorem hujus carte venire possimus, huic scripto sigilla nostra
apposuimus in testimonium. Hiis testibus, *Waltero de Ludhama*,[7] *tunc
senescallo, Thoma filio Jordani, Hugone capellano, Henrico*[8] *clerico de
Suth Kirkeby, Willelmo de Fethirstana, tunc ballivo, Radulfo Riche,
Willelmo de Refectorio, Jordano de Insula, Willelmo de Prestuna*, et aliis.

---

(7) 1240-6.

(8) Sir Henry the clerk (Sir Henry de Oxen), who tests No. 245, was vicar of South Kirkby
from 1230 to 1253, and the ordinations of his vicarage at each of those dates appear in archbishop
Gray's Register as No. 171 and No. 536 respectively. The Registers of archbishop Gray show
three ecclesiastics of the family name of Oxen, Oxon, or Oxonia, in possession of portions of the
church preferment in this neighbourhood. This Henry "the chaplain" was instituted on 1st June,
1230, to the perpetual vicarage of South Kirkby, with the consent of R. de Oxon, the parson and
the convent of Nostell, the patrons. On 16 Kal., February, 1252, under the name of Henry de
Kirkeby, he was preferred to the church of Normanton, though under 15 Kal., June, 1271, he is
styled Henry de Oxonia. On 8 Ides April, 1253, Peter de Oxon was similarly instituted to the
vicarage of South Kirkby at the presentation of Sir Robert de Oxon, the rector, again with the
consent of the prior and convent of Nostell, and during the following summer he was licensed to
go abroad to pursue his studies. It can hardly be doubted that Robert, Henry and Peter were of
the same family, introduced under the same patronage of Nostell to the rich pastures of South
Kirkby.

CCXLVI. **Carta Henrici Fresel.** **Ante 1244.**

[. . . . . Henry Fresel, of Featherstone, ... to Hugh, son of Ralph
of Methley, and his assigns, a half acre of land in Featherstone Moor, lying between
the land of William son of Roger of Featherstone, and the land of Alexander Brun,
of Pontefract. . . . . Paying thence . . . . yearly a silver penny.
Warranty. Seal. Witnesses.]

Sciant presentes et futuri quod ego Henricus Fresel, de Fethirstana,
vendidi, concessi, et hac presenti carta mea confirmavi, Hugoni filio
Radulfi de Medelay,[1] et assignatis suis, unam dimidiam acram terre in
Mora de Fethirstana, jacentem inter terram Willelmi filii Rogeri de
Fethirstana, et terram Alexandri Brun, de Pontefracto. Tenendam et
habendam de me et heredibus meis sibi et assignatis suis, libere,
quiete, et pacifice. Reddendo inde annuatim mihi et heredibus meis
unum denarium argenti ad Pentecosten pro omni servicio et demanda.
Pro hac autem vendicione et concessione, dedit mihi predictus Hugo
septem solidos sterlingorum pre manibus. Et ego vero Henricus
Fresel et heredes mei predicto Hugoni et assignatis suis predictam
dimidiam acram terre in omnibus pro predicto servicio et contra
omnes homines warantizabimus inperpetuum et defendemus. In
hujus rei testimonium, hanc cartam appositione sigilli mei roboravi.

---

(1) Called in the previous charter "Hugo parcarius."

Hiis testibus, *domino*[2] *Radulfo de Fethirstana, Willelmo de eadem villa, Radulfo filio Ricardi de eadem ; Thoma filio Alexandri, Ricardo filio Semani, tunc prepositis*[3] *de Pontefracto ; Roberto Marescallo, Rogero clerico,* et aliis. ⸻

(2) Probably only a courtesy title. He was not so called in his *inq. p. m.*

(3) It is noteworthy that two provosts of Pontefract test No. 246, the father of each having had a holding of land on the moor at the date of the "little charter" of 1194. See also No. 280.

⸻

CCXLVII.   **Carta Willelmi de Fetherstana.**   **Ante 1244.**

[. . . . . William of Featherstone, ... to Hugh, son of Ralph of Methley . . . . two acres of land and one rood in the Field of Featherstone, above Breke-flat. . . . . . . Paying thence yearly to me and my heirs four silver pence, at two terms . . . . Two silver marks for a fine. Warranty. Witnesses.]

Sciant presentes et futuri quod ego Willelmus de Fethirstana dedi et concessi et hac presenti carta mea confirmavi Hugoni filio Radulphi de Medeley, pro homagio et servicio suo, duas acras terre et unam perticatam in campo de Fethirstana super Brekeflat, que jacent inter terram Nicholai de Fethirstana ex una parte et terram ipsius Willelmi ex altera, abuttantes versus orientem et occidentem. Tenendas et habendas dicto Hugoni et heredibus suis et assignatis de me et heredibus meis, libere, quiete, pacifice et integre. Reddendo inde annuatim mihi et heredibus meis quatuor denarios argenti ad duos anni terminos, scilicet duos denarios ad Pentecosten et duos denarios ad festum sancti Martini in yeme pro omni servicio seculari et exactione   Pro hac autem donacione, concessione et presentis carte mee confirmacione, dedit mihi predictus Hugo duas marcas argenti in gersumma. Ego vero Willelmus et heredes mei predictam terram cum pertinentiis dicto Hugoni et heredibus suis, pro predicto servicio, contra omnes homines omnes[1] warantizabimus et defendemus in perpetuum. Hiis testibus, *Waltero de Prestuna clerico, Willelmo de Sars, Radulfo de Fethirstana, Henrico Fresel, Willelmo filio Rogeri,*[2] *Nicholao de Fethirstana, Henrico fratre suo, Johanne clerico de Castleford,* et aliis.[3]

⸻

(1) *Sic.*

(2) Two Williams, each the son of a Roger, have to do with this last charter No. 247. The grantor is a William son of Roger (see No. 246), and one of the signatories also is so described. He was probably William son of Roger Pictavus of Burg, the subsequent Burgwallis.

(3) Neither of the charters No. 244 to No. 247 was copied into the *Dodsworth* MSS. so far as I have been able to ascertain. The four form a substantial contribution to the topography of Featherstone, and by their means anyone especially interested in that manor may, probably with ease, identify the holdings dealt with.

WITEWODE.

CCXLVIII.[1]   Carta Rogeri filii Walteri de Witewode.   1189.[2]

[. . . . . Roger son of Walter, of Whitwood, ... two bovates of land with all their appurtenances from my demesne in Whitwood, next towards the east . . . . on account of the settlement of all the disputes which had arisen between me and the aforesaid church. Warranty. This charter was made in the second Lent next after King Henry II. took the Cross [1189]. Witnesses.]

Sciant presentes et futuri quod ego, Rogerus filius Walteri de Withewode, dedi et concessi, et hac mea carta confirmavi, deo et ecclesie sancti Johannis evangeliste de Pontefracto duas bovatas terre cum omnibus pertinentiis suis de dominio meo in Withewode propinquiores versus est, in puram et perpetuam elemosinam, et propter concordiam omnium querelarum que mote erant inter me et predictam ecclesiam. Et ego Rogerus et heredes mei warantizabimus predictas duas bovatas predicte ecclesie contra omnes homines. Facta est hec carta proxima secunda quadragesima postquam dominus Henricus secundus rex accepit crucem.[3] Hiis testibus, *Waltero filio Hugonis*[4] *tunc ballivo Regis de Westriding, Henrico clerico de Kellingtona,*[5] *Adam de Rainevilla, Juone*[6] *de Lungvilers, Willelmo fratre suo, Petro de Toulestona, Ricardo fratre suo,*[7] *Willelmo filio Morker, Thoma de Horbirri, Jordano fratre suo, Willelmo de Horbiri, et Thoma fratre suo, Adam filio Coleman, Jordano, Johanne et Thoma filiis Assolfi,* et multis aliis.[8]

(1) A copy of No. 248 was made for *Lansdowne* 207, but it is very imperfect. See *Yorkshire Archæological Journal* xiii., 481.

(2) There is but one document in the Chartulary dated earlier than this, No. 311, dated 30 Henry II. (1184), which is a Final Concord.

(3) Roger de Hoveden tells us that Henry II. "accepit crucem" on St. Agnes's Day (January 21), 1188.

(4) Formerly " de Stapleton," afterwards " de Swillington."   (5) See pedigree under No. 297.

(6) Eudo. See No. 27.   (7) See pedigree under No. 143 and No. 455.

(8) The concluding part of this attestation clause is very useful, as helping to connect some of the tenants. At Horbury the lord's family was branching into second cousins, Jordan and Thomas ; while three are named of the numerous family of Asolf—who do not often appear together. The youngest of these three, Thomas, "dapifer" as he is called in No. 147, the "dapifer monachorum" of No. 206, became a resident in Pontefract, and is repeatedly referred to as the father of Michael of Monkhill, who, with John his son, has been a very frequent witness to these charters.

DE MARA.

CCXLIX.[1]   Carta Willelmi filii Hamerici de Witewda.   Ante 1216.

[. . . . . William son of Hameric, of Whitwood, ... [. . . . two bovates of land which Alan, brother of Master Raimond, has held of me on lease only, in the territory of the Mere. . . . . And also all the land without withholding, with all dwelling on that land, and all other appurtenances which I have had and held in the territory of the Mere. To be held and possessed, &c. Quitclaim. Seal. Witnesses.]

(1) There is a short abstract of No. 249 in *Lansdowne* 207A.

Sciant presentes et futuri, quod ego Willelmus filius Hamerici[2] de Withewd, pro salute anime mee et omnium antecessorum et heredum meorum dedi, concessi, et presenti carta mea confirmavi deo et sancto Johanni de Pontefracto, et monachis ibidem deo servientibus, in puram et perpetuam elemosinam, nominatim illas duas bovatas terre quas Alanus frater Magistri Raimundi[3] tenuit de me tantum modo ad terminum in territorio de Mara, et de quibus bovatis terminus finitus est, et insuper totam terram sine retenemento, cum omnibus in eadem terra manentibus et omnibus aliis pertinentiis, que habui et tenui in territorio de Mara.   Tenendas et habendas prefatis monachis inperpetuum sine reclamatione mei vel heredum meorum, et totum jus et clamium quod habui vel habere potui in prefata terra aut ejus pertinentiis, prefatis monachis sursum reddidi et de me et de heredibus meis inperpetuum quietum clamavi.   Et ut hec mea donacio et quieta clamatio firma sit et stabilis, huic carte pro me et heredibus meis sigillum meum apposui.   Hiis testibus, *Henrico Walensi*,[4] *Willelmo filio Everardi*,[5] *Rogero persona de Kyppes*,[6] *Eudone*[7] *et Willelmo capellanis de Pontefracto, Ranulfo de Castelforda, Ricardo de Martona, Gaufrido de Norhamtona*,[8] et aliis.

(2) Youngest brother of William de Stapleton and Hugh de Horton.
(3) See No. 251 and No. 253.   (4) Not yet seneschal.
(5) See note (8) to No. 204.   He takes high position here without naming his former office of royal bailiff.   (6) Dead in 1233. See No. 52.
(7) Note Eudo the chaplain was dead in 1226. See No. 100.   (8) Afterwards bailiff to earl John.

CCL [1]   De conventione facta inter Priorem et
                    Petrum filium Rogeri.[2]   1223.

[. . . . . . Agreement made between the prior and convent of Pontefract on the one part, and Peter son of Robert de Mara on the other. . . . . Peter . . . . . to the aforesaid prior and convent for the term of sixty years, three bovates of land in the territory of the Mere with all their appurtenances. . . . . Paying thence yearly to the aforesaid William and his heirs three shillings . . . . . . Five marks of silver in hand. Sealed. Witnesses.]

Anno ab incarnatione domini m°cc°xx°iii° ad festum sancti Michaelis.   Hec est conventio facta inter Priorem et conventum de Pontefracto ex una parte et Petrum filium Roberti de Mara ex alia. Scilicet quod prefatus Petrus dimisit et concessit predictis Priori et conventui usque ad terminum sexaginta annorum tres bovatas terre

(1) There is a good abstract of No. 250 in *Lansdowne* 207A, and a copy in *Dodsworth* 151.
(2) *Sic.*

in territorio de Mara cum omnibus pertinentiis suis et aisiamentis ad illas pertinentibus, infra villam de Mara et extra. Illas scilicet quas idem Petrus tenuit de Willelmo filio Hamerici de Stapiltona. Reddendo inde annuatim prefato Willelmo et heredibus suis tres solidos pro omni servicio et seculari exactione, medietatem ad Pentecosten et medietatem ad festum sancti Martini. Pro hac autem concessione dederunt prefati monachi predicto Petro quinque marcas argenti pre manibus. Et ut hec conventio firma sit et stabilis, huic carte sigillorum suorum munimen apposuerunt. Hiis testibus, *Roberto de Cantia tunc senescallo de Pontefracto, Johanne de Byrkin, Henrico Walensi, Willelmo filio Evererardi,*[3] *Waltero receptore, Henrico Byset, Alano Noel, Ricardo de Martona,* et aliis.

(3) *Sic.*

CCLI.   Conventio facta inter Petrum de Mara et
Rogerum de Castelforda.   1222.

[. . . . . . Agreement between Peter de Mara and Roger of Castleford . . . . . The said Peter has demised to the said Roger and his heirs . . . . for the term of twenty years, a bovate of land in the aforesaid town of Mere with all its appurtenances . . . . . . and a half acre of land in Blackflat, and in Sandbed. To be held and possessed . . . . with all the appurtenances belonging to a bovate of land in the aforesaid town of Mere . . . . . . two shillings yearly . . . . . . doing at the assizes of the lord the king, for all service and custom and exaction, as much forinsec service as belongs to a bovate of land. Warranty . . . . twenty shillings in hand. Witnesses.]

Anno secundo post translacionem sancti Thome Martiris[1] facta est hec convencio inter Petrum de Mara[2] et Rogerum de Castelforda. Scilicet quod predictus Petrus dimisit predicto Rogero et heredibus suis a festo sancti Michaelis predicti secundi anni usque ad finem viginti annorum unam bovatam terre in predicta villa de Mara cum omnibus pertinentiis suis, illam scilicet bovatam terre que jacet ex parte solis de duabus bovatis quas predictus Petrus habet et unam dimidiam acram terre in Blakeflat et in Sandbed, tenendam et habendam predicto Rogero et heredibus suis, de predicto Petro et heredibus suis libere et quiete, et honorifice, cum omnibus pertinentiis ad unam bovatam terre in predicta villa de Mara pertinentibus. Et predictus Rogerus et heredes sui reddent inde predicto Petro et

(1) The "translation of Thomas the Martyr," from the occurrence of which this charter was dated, took place 7th July, 1221.   (2) Whitwood Mere.

heredibus suis duos solidos annuatim, scilicet duodecim denarios ad
Pentecosten, et duodecim denarios ad festum sancti Martini,
pro omni servitio, et consuetudine, et exactione, faciendo forinsecum servitium quantum pertinet ad unam bovatam terre apud
assisas domini Regis.   Et predictus Petrus et heredes sui warantizabunt predicto Rogero et heredibus suis usque ad finem
predicti termini, totam predictam terram in omnibus et contra omnes
homines.   Post finem vero predictorum viginti annorum tota predicta
terra remanebit quieta predicto Petro et heredibus suis.   Et pro hac
concessione dedit predictus Rogerus predicto Petro viginti solidos
pre manibus.   Hiis testibus, *Willelmo filio Everardi, Ricardo de
Lond[iniis],*[3] *Ivone de Medeleia, Thoma Camerario, Henrico filio
Susanne, Jacobo filio Raimundi,*[4] *Roberto filio Reginaldi, Ricardo de
Mara, Roberto de Mara, Rogero de Fetherstana, Alano de Mara,*[5]
Michaele de Snythal, et multis aliis.

(3) See No. 260.   (4) See No. 127, No. 128 and No. 150.
                    (5) Brother of Raimond. See No. 249.

CCLII.   Carta Roberti filii Roberti[1] Mose.   1216.

[. . . . . Robert son of Robert, son of Moses, of the Mere, ...
to the monks of St. John's three bovates . . . . . . in the Mere . . . . . . which
Peter my brother had before given, and by his charter confirmed, to the aforesaid
monks . . . . . . Three silver marks. Seal. Witnesses.]

Universis hoc scriptum visuris vel audituris Robertus, filius
Roberti, filii Mose, de Mara, salutem in domino.   Noverit universitas
vestra quod ego concessi et presenti carta mea confirmavi, et sine
retenemento imperpetuum de me et heredibus meis quietas clamavi,
deo et sancto Johanni de Pontefracto, et monachis ibidem deo
servientibus, tres bovatas terre in territorio de Mara, cum omnibus
ad eas infra villam et extra pertinentibus, et totum jus et clamium
quod habui vel habere potui prefatis monachis sursum reddidi.   Illas
scilicet tres bovatas quas Petrus frater meus antea dederat prefatis
monachis et carta sua confirmaverat.   Pro hac autem concessione et
quieta clamatione dederunt mihi prenominati monachi tres marcas
argenti.   Et ne ego predictus Robertus vel heredes mei in posterum
contra meam quietam clamationem venire, vel aliquid jus aut clamium
in prefatis bovatis terre vel earum pertinentiis vendicare possimus,
huic carte sigillum meum apposui.   Hiis testibus, *Henrico Walensi,*

1) *Sic.*

tunc² senescallo Pontisfracti, Johanne de Birkina, Willelmo filio Everardi, Ricardo Londiniis,³ Willelmo de Fethirstana, Radulfo de eadem villa, Rannulfo de Castelforda, Gilberto de Mara, Ricardo de Martona, et aliis.

(2) 1216-18.   (3) See No. 260.

CCLIII.   **Carta Willelmi filii Hamerici de Mara.**   **Cir. 1220.**

[. . . . . I, William son of Hameric, of the Mere . . . . have confirmed to . . . . the monks of St. John's . . . . all the land . . . . which I have held and possessed in the territory of the Mere. Seal. Witnesses.]

Sciant presentes et futuri quod ego Willelmus filius Hamerici de Mara, pro salute anime mee, et omnium antecessorum et heredum meorum, dedi, concessi, et presenti carta mea confirmavi, deo et sancto Johanni de Pontefracto, in puram et perpetuam elemosinam, et monachis ibidem deo servientibus, totam terram sine retenemento, cum omnibus pertinentiis suis, et in servitiis liberorum hominum, et in omnibus aliis rebus quam habui et tenui in territorio de Mara. Tenendam et habendam prefatis monachis inperpetuum, sine reclamatione mei vel heredum meorum, et totum jus et clamium¹ vel habere potui in prefata terra aut ejus pertinentiis prefatis monachis de me et heredibus meis sursum reddidi et inperpetuum quietam² clamavi. Et ne ego vel heredes mei in posterum contra hanc meam quietam clamationem venire vel aliquid² gravamen prefatis monachis super predicta terra facere possimus, huic carte sigillum meum apposui. Hiis testibus, *Henrico Walensi, Rogero persona de Keppeis, Willelmo filio Everardi, Ricardo Londiniis, Eudone et Willelmo capellanis de Pontefracto, Ranulfo de Castelforda, Alano de Mara,³ Ricardo de Martona, Galfrido de Northamtona,⁴* et multis aliis.

(1) "Quod unquam habui" omitted in the Chartulary.   (2) *Sic*, in each case.
(3) See No. 249.   (4) Afterwards bailiff to earl John.

CCLIIII.¹   **Carta Willelmi filii Hamerici.**   **Cir. 1220.**

[. . . . . William son of Hameric . . . . . Know that if any man shall proffer any charter of lands which I have held or possessed in the territory of the Mere, sealed in my name, I bear witness that it is forged, the prior of Pontefract and the monks of that place being excepted, to whom I have given and quitclaimed that land from me and my heirs. Warranty. Witnesses.]

(1) This charter and No. 253 seem to be contemporaneous, and the witnesses are almost identical.

2 C

Universis has litteras visuris vel audituris Willelmus filius Hamerici salutem.   Sciatis omnes quod si aliquis homo portaverit aliquam cartam de terris quas habui vel tenui in territorio de Mara, nomine meo sigillatam, testificor ipsam esse falsam, exceptis priore de Pontefracto et monachis ejusdem loci, quibus ipsam terram dedi et quietam clamavi de me et heredibus meis.   Et ego Willelmus et heredes mei prefatam terram cum omnibus pertinentiis monachis warantizabimus antedictis.   Hiis testibus, *Henrico Walensi, Rogero persona de Kippeis, Willelmo filio Everardi, Guidone*[2] *et Willelmo capellanis de Pontefracto, Alano de Mara, Ranulfo de Castleforda, Rogero Fantome, Ricardo de Martona,* et multis aliis.

----

(2) *Sic,* for Eudo.

CCLV.   **Carta Willelmi filii Hamerici de Witewod.**   **Post 1220.**

[. . . . . . I, William son of Hameric, of Whitwood . . . . . . have confirmed, to Peter son of Robert de Lamar . . . . . . for half a mark of silver given in hand, all the land without withholding, of which Robert his father was invested and seised the day he died, that is to say, three bovates of land in the Mere . . . . To be held, &c.   Paying yearly to me and my heirs six shillings . . . . . Warranty. Witnesses, &c.]

Sciant presentes et futuri quod ego Willelmus filius Hamerici de Witewod concessi et hac presenti carta mea confirmavi Petro filio Roberti de Lamar, pro homagio et servitio suo et pro dimidia marca argenti data pre manibus, totam terram sine retenemento quam Robertus pater ejus vestitus fuit et saisiatus die qua obiit, videlicet tres bovatas terre in Lamar cum pertinentiis, quas dedi Roberto patri suo pro homagio suo et servitio.   Tenendas et habendas de me et heredibus meis illi et heredibus suis in feodo et hereditate, libere et quiete, cum omnibus libertatibus, communiis et aisiamentis, infra villam et extra, eidem terre pertinentibus.   Solvendo annuatim mihi et heredibus meis sex solidos, scilicet tres solidos ad festum sancti Martini et tres solidos ad Pentecosten, pro omni servitio, et exactione, et demanda, mihi vel heredibus meis pertinentibus.   Et ego Willelmus et heredes mei prenominato Petro et heredibus suis predictam terram cum omnibus pertinentiis ubique et contra[1] homines inperpetuum warantizabimus.   Hiis testibus, *Willelmo filio Everardi, Willelmo de Featherstana, Petro de Aiktona, Roberto Morker, Ivone de Medeleia,*

----

(1) Omnes omitted.

Thoma Camerario, Henrico clerico de Medeleia, Ranulfo de Castelforda, Ricardo fratre Raimundi, Alano fratre suo,[2] *Roberto filio Reginaldi de Castleforda, Michaele de Snithale,* et aliis.

(2) As if Raimund were now dead. Compare No. 249, No. 251 and No. 256.

CCLVI.   Carta Roberti de Lamar.   Cir. 1246.

[. . . . . . I, Robert de Lamar . . . . . . have confirmed to Peter my son three bovates of land with the appurtenances in the town of Lamar, those to wit which William of Whitwood has given to me for my homage and free service ; that is to say, those bovates which lie at the east, with the messuage which is near the house of Ralph. Paying yearly . . . . 6 shillings. Warranty from William de Whitwood. Witnesses.]

Sciant presentes et futuri quod ego Robertus de Lamar, dedi et concessi, et hac presenti carta mea confirmavi Petro filio meo tres bovatas terre cum pertinentiis in villa de Lamar, illas scilicet quas Willelmus de Withewod dedit mihi pro homagio et libero servicio meo, videlicet illas bovatas que jacent apud orientem cum mesuagio quod est juxta domum Radulfi. Solvendo annuatim Willelmo de Withewod vel suis heredibus vj solidos propter predictas bovatas, scilicet medietatem ad Pentecosten, et medietatem ad festum sancti Martini, pro omnibus servitiis. Et Willelmus de Withewod et heredes sui warantizabunt predictas bovatas cum pertinentiis predicto Petro et suis heredibus inperpetuum. Hiis testibus, *Hugone de Toulistona,*[1] *Rogero Pictavensi, Roberto Morker, Thoma Camerario, Henrico clerico, Ranulfo de Castelforda, Adam filio Willelmi de Withewod,*[2] *Alano de Lamar, Ricardo fratre suo,*[3] et aliis.

(1) He was the son of Eva de Dai, and married Cecilia de Lede. See pedigree under No. 143.
(2) William son of Hameric of Stapleton. See next charter.   (3) See preceding charter.

CCLVII.   Carta Petri filii Roberti de Mara.   Cir. 1224.

[. . . . . . I, Peter son of Robert de Mara . . . . . . have confirmed . . . . . . to the monks of St. John three bovates of land in the territory of the Mere . . . . . . which I have held from William, son of Hameric de Stapleton . . . . Paying thence yearly . . . . three shillings. Seal. Witnesses.]

Sciant presentes et futuri quod ego Petrus filius Roberti de Mara pro salute anime mee et omnium antecessorum et heredum meorum dedi, concessi, et presenti carta mea confirmavi deo et sancto Johann de Pontefracto et monachis ibidem deo servientibus tres bovatas terre in territorio de Mara. Illas scilicet quas ego tenui de Willelmo filio Hamerici de Stapletona. Tenendas et habendas prefatis monachis in perpetuam elemosinam, libere et quiete, cum omnibus pertinenciis et aisiamentis ad prefatas bovatas terre infra villam de Mara et extra pertinentibus. Reddendo inde annuatim Willelmo filio Haimerici tres solidos pro omni servicio et seculari exactione, medietatem ad Pentecosten et medietatem ad festum sancti Martini. Et ut hec mea donacio firma sit et stabilis prefatis monachis per severet,[1] huic carte pro me et heredibus meis sigillum meum apposui. Hiis testibus, *Roberto de Cantia tunc senescallo de Pontefracto,*[2] *Johanne de Birkin, Henrico Walensi, Willelmo filio Everardi, Waltero receptore, Henrico Biseth, Alano Noel,* et aliis. ———

(1) *Sic*, for "perseveret." (2) 1218 to 1224.

CCLVIII.   Carta Petri filii Roberti.   Cir. 1220.

[. . . . . . I, Peter son of Robert de Mara . . . . have surrendered by my present charter . . . . . . three bovates of land in the territory of the Mere. Those, that is to say, which I have held from William, son of Hameric of Stapleton. To be held and possessed by the aforesaid monks for ever, &c., three shillings yearly . . . . in hand five silver marks. Seal. Witnesses.]

Sciant presentes et futuri quod ego Petrus filius Roberti de Mara fors juravi,[1] sursum reddidi et presenti carta mea de me et heredibus meis[2] tres bovatas terre in territorio de Mara. Illas scilicet quas ego tenui de Willelmo filio Hamerici de Stapiltona.[3] Tenendas et habendas prefatis[4] monachis inperpetuum sine reclamatione mei vel heredum meorum cum omnibus pertinentiis et aisiamentis ad prefatas bovatas terre infra villam de Mara et extra pertinentibus. Reddendo inde annuatim Willelmo filio Haymerici de Stapiltona et heredibus suis tres solidos pro omni servitio et seculari exactione, medietatem ad Pentecosten et medietatem ad festum sancti Martini. Pro hac autem quieta clamatione dederunt mihi predicti monachi quinque marcas argenti pre manibus. Et in testimonium hujus quiete mee clamationis, huic carte pro me et heredibus meis sigillum meum apposui. Hiis testibus, *Roberto de Cantia, tunc senescallo de Pontefracto, Johanne de*

(1) Two words in the original. (2) "Confirmavi" omitted. (3) See pedigree, p. xlvi.
(4) *Sic ;* but there were no "prefatis" monks.

Birkina, Henrico Walensi, Willelmo filio Everardi, Waltero receptore, Henrico Biseth, Alano Noel, et aliis.[5]

(5) Each of these ten charters was copied into *Lansdowne* 207A ; and although the accuracy of the copyist must not be insisted upon, the copies have been useful as embodying the main points of the history. They cannot, however, be used critically. This last, No. 258, was copied into vol. 151 also. The large group must be considered together, and their order in regard to time seems to have been in four small batches, 256, 252, 255 ; 251 [1221], 250 [1223] ; 257, 258 ; 249, 253, 254 : the last referring to another three bovates, and containing a general warranty from the mesne lord, which embraces a very peculiar guarantee against some apprehended forgery. By collation, it may be ascertained that the lord of the fee was William son of Hameric, called indifferently "of Stapleton," "of Whitwood," and "of the Mere." The entire absence of punctuation in the original makes the application of this local name somewhat uncertain, but I think that Hameric himself never abandoned the use of "Stapleton ;" that throughout the groups his name of Stapleton is descriptive only ; and that it was William his son who was firstly "of the Mere," afterwards "of Whitwood." I have punctuated in that sense.

BRETTON [BURTON SALMON].

CCLIX.[1]　　**Carta Alicie quondam uxoris Willelmi filii Petri.**[2]　　Cir. 1214.

[. . . . . . . I, Alice, widow of William, son of Peter de Bretton, have released . . . . . . to my lords the Prior and Convent of Pontefract, all the right and claim which I did demand in the name of dowry in the third part of that bovate of land which Matilda, my late daughter, has held of the house of Pontefract in the town of Bretton . . . . . . seal of John de Louvain . . . . . . because I had no seal of my own. Witnesses.]

Sciant presentes et futuri quod ego Alicia que fui quondam uxor Willelmi filii Petri[2] de Brettona remisi dominis meis Priori et conventui de Pontefracto ac omnino sine aliquo retenemento quietum clamavi omne jus et clamium quod petebam nomine dotis in tertiam partem[3] illius bovate terre quam Matildis quondam filia mea tenuit de domo de Pontefracto, in villa de Brettona.　Et ne ego contra hanc quietam clamationem in posterum venire possim, huic scripto sigillum Johannis de Luvayn[4] apposui quia signum proprium non habui.　Hiis testibus, *Gaufridus de Muscham, Hugone de Brodecroft, Salomone de Brettona, Petro Janitore, Ricardo Janitore,* et aliis.

(1) I have found no copy of this charter either in the British Museum or at the Bodleian. R 86, a dated charter of 1160, is similarly sealed with a borrowed seal.

(2) Peter de Bretton was a third Peter in lineal succession. His father was Peter de Bretton, and his grandfather Peter of Flockton, father of Adam fitz Peter, of Birkin.　　　(3) *Sic.*

(4) See No. 166, note (1).

PECKFIELD.[1]

CCLX.　　　**Carta Roberti filii Jordani de Landa.**[2]　　　Cir. 1214.

[. . . . . . I, Robert de Land . . . . . have confirmed . . . . . two parts of Peckfield which Paganus de Land gave to them, and my father afterwards

(1) Peckfield was a lofty moorland, afterwards divided between the manors of Kippax, Garforth, Ledstone, and Micklefield. A large area in Ledstone township is still known as Peckfield Common, while Peckfield House, Peckfield Farm, and Peckfield Lodge, each in a different township, serve to indicate the former homogeneity of the whole. No. 260 was copied into *Lansdowne* 207A ; but if it is in either of the *Dodsworth* volumes I have overlooked it.

(2) This Robert son of Jordan de Land was the great-grandson of the donor, Paganus de Laland. See No. 317.

confirmed . . . . . . to the aforesaid monks, and to all their men of Ledston and of Ledsham, full, free and entire common of all the pasture of all my land of Micklefield except meadow and corn-stalk. . . . . . . From Ledston, two skeps of wheat, for the free commonage of the aforesaid pasture, and from Ledsham two old measures of wheat at the same term . . . . . . Warranty. Witnesses.]

Omnibus sancte matris ecclesie filiis Robertus de Landa filius Jordani, salutem. Noverit universitas vestra quod ego Robertus de Landa, pro salute anime mee et antecessorum et heredum meorum concessi, et hac presenti carta mea confirmavi deo et sancti Johanni et monachis de Pontefracto, in puram et perpetuam elemosinam, duas partes de Pechfeld quas Paganus de Landa eis dedit et pater meus postea confirmavit. Insuper concessi et hac presenti carta mea confirmavi predicte ecclesie sancti Johannis et prefatis monachis ejusdem loci et omnibus hominibus suis de Ledestona et de Ledeshama plenam, liberam, et integram communam totius pasture universe terre mee de Michelfeld extra pratum et bladum. Predicti vero monachi reddent mihi et heredibus meis annuatim de Ledestona duas sceppas frumenti infra festum sancti Martini et Nathale domini pro libera communa predicte pasture, et de Ledeshama duas veteres melas frumenti ad eundem terminum, prout continetur in cartis predictorum Pagani de Landa et Jordani patris mei. Ego autem Robertus de Landa et heredes mei predictam elemosinam de Peechefeld et communam pasture de Michelfeld warentizabimus prefatis monachis contra omnes homines. Hiis testibus, *domino Henrico Walensi, Roberto de Barkestona, Ricardo de Hudlestona, Ricardo de Londoniis,*[3] *Roberto Bereforda, Waltero de Birum, Thoma de Suttona, Jordano Pateman, Rogero Pateman, Ricardo de Martona, Willelmo de Balcolm,* et aliis. ———

(3) *Sic;* at full in this instance.

BRETTON [BURTON SALMON].[1]
CCLXI.   **Carta Agnetis de Polingtona.**   1232-40.

[. . . . . . I, Agnes de Pollington, widow of Pigot de Bretton . . . . have surrendered, and . . . . . . quit-claimed to my lords the Prior and monks of Pontefract, all the right and claim which I have had, or ever could have had, in that bovate of land with its appurtenances which I have possessed and held in the name of dowry in the town of Bretton, of the fee of Pigot, formerly my husband.

(1) No particular reason appears why these isolated charters should be placed just here, apart from any other with which they might naturally be connected. They correspond with each other neither in date nor matter, while they were evidently not inserted merely to fill up space, for they are in the midst of the usual groups. No. 204 gave to the monks all the patrimonial lands which had belonged to Geoffrey Pigot in what was afterwards called Burton Salmon; and No. 261 is complementary, being from the widow, who brings her dower into the common treasury, in order that, while she is helping the monks to consolidate their acquisition, she may henceforth have no

And for this quit-claim and surrender, the said monks have received me as a sister, granting me a share in all the benefits of their house, as well temporal as spiritual. In witness of which I have placed my seal to this document, these being witnesses and present. Seal.]

Sciant presentes et futuri quod ego Agnes de Poulingtona quondam uxor Pigot[2] de Brettona in viduitate mea et ligia potestate sursum reddidi et omnino de me et omnibus meis, sine aliquo retenemento mei vel heredum meorum, inperpetuum quietum clamavi dominis meis Priori et monachis de Pontefracto omne jus et clamium quod habui vel unquam habere potui in illa bovata terre cum pertinentiis suis quam habui et tenui nomine dotis in villa de Brettona de feodo Pigot quondam viri mei. Pro hac vero quieta clamatione et sursum redditione receperunt me dicti monachi in sororem, concedentes me participationem omnium domus sue bonorum tam temporalium quam spiritualium. In cujus rei testimonium, huic scripto sigillum meum apposui. Hiis testibus et presentibus, *Gregorio monacho, camerario de Pontefracto, Jordano capellano de Snay', Gaufrido clerico, tunc ballivo domini Comitis Lincolnie,[3] Gilberto clerico de Parlingtona, Willelmo de Bladesworth, Hugone de Doddeworth, Johanne de Brettona,* et aliis.

care for herself but that of a preparation for the close of life. We shall see in No. 300 that their daughter Agnes had been already provided for. (2) Geoffrey Pigot.
(3) "Geoffrey of Northampton" in No. 249 and No. 253.

BIRUM.
CCLXII.[1]   **Carta Walteri filii Ade de Birum.**   Cir. 1212.

[. . . . I, Walter, son of Adam de Byram, ... have confirmed to . . . . . . the monks . . . . . 20 acres and one rood of land in my clearings of Byram. Of which 12 lie towards the east, near the assart of those same monks, which Roger son of Aubrey has held, and 4 acres and a half lie by themselves near the town of Pool, which Thomas son of Kaskin of Bretton has held, and 3 acres and 3 roods lie towards the south, near the clearing of the aforesaid monks, which Ralph the provost of Sutton has held. To be held and possessed, &c., and to burn from my wood, in reason, by the oversight of my forester; and to build on the said land . . . . . In exchange for a rent of 12 shillings, which the aforesaid prior and monks have quitclaimed to me and my heirs. Warranty. Witnesses.]

Sciant presentes et futuri, quod ego, Walterus, filius Ade de Birum, dedi, concessi, et presenti carta mea confirmavi deo et sancto Johanni de Pontefracto et monachis ibidem deo servientibus, in puram et perpetuam elemosinam, xx*ti* acras et unam perticatam terre in essartis meis de Birum. Ex quibus acris xii acre jacent versus est juxta

(1) There is an imperfect abstract of No. 262 in *Dodsworth.* vol. 136.

essartum eorundem monachorum, quas Rogerus filius Aubrai tenuit, et iiij*or* acre et dimidia jacent per se juxta villam de Polis, quas Thomas filius Kaskini de Brettona tenuit, et iij acre et iij perticate jacent versus Suth juxta essartum predictorum monachorum, quas Radulfus prepositus de Suttona tenuit.[2] Tenendas et habendas de me et heredibus meis, libere et quiete, cum libero introitu et exitu, et pastura, et omnibus aisiamentis ejusdem ville de Birum, et de bosco meo rationabiliter per visum forestarii mei ad ardendum, et edificandam predictam terram. Has vero xx acras et perticatam terre cum pertinentiis dedi prefatis monachis in excambium redditus xii solidorum quos predicti prior et monachi mihi et heredibus meis quietos clamaverunt, illos scilicet quos antecessores[3] mei Willelmus filius Hervei et Robertus frater suus eis dederunt et Adam pater meus eis confirmavit in puram et perpetuam elemosinam in villa de Saxeby[4] in Lindissai. Et ego, Walterus, et heredes mei warentizabimus predictas xx*ti* acras et [5]perticatas terre prenominatis monachis contra omnes homines. Hiis testibus, *Hugone de Swinlingtona et Gilleberto de Ricey, tunc balliv*[6] *de Westriding, Johanne de Birkin, Roberto Walensi, Henrico filio suo,*[7] *Jordano de Landa, Ricardo de Hudlistona, Ricardo filio suo, Ricardo de Prestuna, Ricardo de Suttona.*[8]

(2) See No. 243.   (3) *i.e.* Predecessors.

(4) Nothing else occurs in the Chartulary with regard to this rent at Saxby.

(5) *Sic.* The addition of the quantities, given in this charter, shows that the sometimes ambiguous word "perticata" is here again clearly a rood, or fourth part of an acre; for half an acre and three perticatas, being added, come out in the total as an acre and a rood. In this transitional time, when the signification of these terms was not definitely fixed, the word "terre" was frequently introduced to emphasise as it were the fact that the land division referred to was one of area.   (6) Probably plural.

(7) *i.e.* Grandson of the Henry who was the first husband of Agnes, second wife of the grantor's father.

(8) The following sketch will illustrate the position, so far at least as these charters are concerned :—

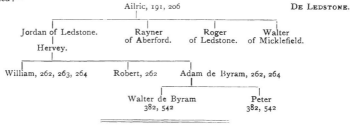

CCLXIII.[1]   Carta Willelmi de Hottona.   1189.

[To all seeing and hearing &c., I make known . . . . . . that I have granted, given, and by my present charter confirmed to God and the church of St. John of

(1) I have met with no copy of No. 263. No. 101 R shows the ownership of Flockton to have been in moieties between Peter fitz Asolf and Matthew son of Saxe; so that the Asolf moiety had been long in the Asolf family. Jordan, a brother of Peter, Peter's son, and Adam fitz Peter, in

Pontefract, and the monks there serving God, those two bovates of land in Flockton, with all their appurtenances, which my lord William, son of Hervey, has given to me, that the aforesaid monks may hold and possess in peace the aforesaid bovates of land, without any withholding, as pure and perpetual alms. Witnesses.]

Omnibus hanc cartam videntibus et audientibus, Willelmus de Hottona, salutem. Universitati vestre notum facio me pro amore dei et pro salute anime mee et domini mei Willelmi filii Hervei et omnium antecessorum et heredum suorum, et meorum, concessisse, dedisse, et presenti carta mea confirmasse, deo et ecclesie sancti Johannis de Pontefracto, et monachis ibidem deo servientibus, illas duas bovatas terre in Floctona cum omnibus pertinentiis suis quas dominus meus Willelmus filius Hervei mihi dedit, ut prefatas bovatas terre prefati monachi habeant, et in pace possideant, sine omni retenemento, sicut puram et perpetuam elemosinam. Hiis testibus, *Waltero filio Hugonis, tunc ballivo domini regis,*[2] *Hugone filio ejus, Thoma de Horbiri, Jordano et Willelmo fratribus suis, Ada filio Philippi,*[3] *Alano de Brettona, Willelmo de De Neby,*[4] *Johanne filio Harding, Willelmo filio Johannis filii Assolf,*[5] et multis aliis.

---

turn possessed it, or called themselves from it. But the ultimate right seems, after Peter's death in 1165, to have belonged to Adam the lord of Birkin, who gave a charter, No. 99 R. to the monks of Rievaux, conferring on that house rights of commonage in both Flockton and Shitlington. This was indeed cancelled in the Rievaux Chartulary, in the same way as No. 266 was cancelled in that of Pontefract, by diagonal lines from each corner meeting in the centre; but the genealogical and other literary matter is quite as useful as though the document retained the validity in regard to property which it possessed when signed. The Hotton from which William de Hotton took his name was probably the Hutton near Welburn, a few miles south-west of Malton, which belonged to Rievaux as the gift of Ralph Beler, confirmed by Roger de Mowbray and Roger de Stuteville. How William son of Hervey was "his lord," except by courtesy, is not clear. By a misreading of the word "Hotton," No. 263 was described in the original index to the Pontefract Chartulary as from "William de Flockton."

(2) Walter son of Hugh, originally of Stapleton, afterwards of Swillington, royal bailiff in the closing years of Henry II.

(3) Adam filius Philippi witnesses also R 344, a charter of Jordan son of Matthew, son of Saxe, of Horbury, and Jordan his heir, granting a culture in this same Flockton to the monks of Rievaux. See also No. 248. The following is the connection of these descendants of Saxe:—

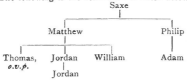

Saxe
Matthew   Philip
Thomas,   Jordan   William   Adam
o.v.p.
Jordan

(4) *Sic.*

(5) John fitz Asolf does not appear on the 1166 Pipe Roll, on which so many of his brethren were charged with succession duty after the death of their father in 1165, unless, which is probable, he is the John de Huurum who is charged a mark: but his name occurs on the Roll of 1169 (15 H. II.) as assessed at another mark, which he paid, and also as suffering a fine of forty shillings for an unjust disseisin. Half of this latter amount he paid at once and half in the following year. He had property at Wentworth and at Stansfield; for he granted a tenement in the former place to the monks of Monk Bretton, and gave five bovates of land in Stansfield in dowry at the marriage of Amabel his daughter to Roger son of Warren. Each of these deeds was witnessed by Jordan fitz Asolf and Thomas his brother, and the second names also Eustace "my son." John fitz Asolf appears at least twice subsequently on the Pipe Rolls. In 29 Henry II. he made a fine of 13s. 8d., and claimed land in Baildon against Hugh de Lelay, and two years afterwards he paid a mark for permission to compound a quarrel with Richard de Wath. Finally, his name appears in the testing clause to three charters in the Pontefract Chartulary, No. 248 and the above two.

In the first, a dated charter, he is coupled with those two of his brothers who test the Bretton deed, "Jordan, John, and Thomas, sons of Asolf." No. 263 and No. 264 are a generation later, and refer to two bovates at Flockton. They are witnessed by William son of John, son of Asolf, thus giving a brother to the Eustace named on the Stansfield deed, and adding a link to the pedigree. I should mention that Mr. Hunter thought the Flemings of Wath to have been descended from this John.

CCLXIIII.[1]   **Carta Ade de Birum.**   Cir. 1189.

[To all . . . . . Adam de Byram, greeting. I make known to all of you that . . . . for the health of my soul, and of my lord and brother William, son of Hervey . . . . I have granted, and by the present charter have confirmed to . . . . the monks, those two bovates of land in Flockton, with all their appurtenances, which my lord and brother William, son of Hervey, has given to William de Hotton, that the aforesaid monks shall have and possess them in peace, as pure and perpetual alms, which alms also I and my heirs will warrant and acquit to the aforesaid monks against all men. Witnesses.]

Omnibus sancte matris ecclesie filiis tam presentibus quam futuris, Adam de Birum, salutem. Universitati vestre notum facio me pro amore dei et pro salute anime mee et domini et fratris mei Willelmi filii Hervei et omnium antecessorum et heredum meorum concessisse et presenti carta confirmasse deo et ecclesie sancti Johannis de Pontefracto, et monachis ibidem deo servientibus, illas duas bovatas terre in Floctona[2] cum omnibus earum pertinentiis quas dominus et frater meus Willelmus filius Hervei dedit Willelmo de Hottona, ut predicti monachi eas habeant et in pace possideant sicut puram et

(1) There is an abstract of No. 264 in *Dodsworth*, vol. 136.

(2) This "Churchman's portion" of two bovates in Flockton was evidently a grant made under some very peculiar circumstances. It was an early grant, made even while the sons of those tenants who obtained such large fees at the settlement in King Stephen's time were still in possession, though dividing among themselves the improved property which their fathers had received bare and waste. But, important as the grant was at the time, the monks did not ultimately retain the holding given to them with such care and precaution. Perhaps its distance from home and its contiguity to some important possessions of Rievaux induced the Pontefract monks to relax their hold and to relinquish the property to the other monks, who could make more advantageous use of it. By careful collation the date of these documents may be ascertained to be somewhat later than 1189, the assigned date of No. 248, and they must have been granted contemporaneously, for the witnesses are the same in each. But comparing them with those who tested No. 248, I note

No. 248.	No. 263 and No. 264.
Walter son of Hugh,	The same Walter, bailiff, and
the king's bailiff.	Hugh his son.
Thomas of Horbury and	Thomas of Horbury, with
Jordan his brother.	Jordan and William, his brothers.
Jordan, John, and Thomas,	William son of John,
sons of Asolf.	son of Asolf.

There is thus a steady difference in the status of the signatories; for younger men of the same generation, or men of a newer generation, were in No. 263 and No. 264 pressing forward to take their share in such administrative acts as testing these charters. The concurrence of William son of John son of Asolf in these two deeds leads me to point out (as indeed I have done in full in a paper I contributed to the 1898 Miscellanies of the Thoresby Society) that Asolf or Essulf, the grandfather, had been in his time a very powerful man, as a tenant whose holdings extended through large portions of Osgoldcross and the neighbouring wapentakes of Barkston Ash, Agbrigg, and Morley. He lived just in the generation of which our records are most scanty, so that but little indeed is known of him, except that his shadow dominates very much in an indefinite way; and, when once attention has been called to his existence, in a way that is most tantalising. If he ever assisted to build up the monastic possessions, the succeeding generations renewed the different charters as of their own original gifts, and the primary record has in each case perished. He was a man with a large family, and each of his sons seems to have received an early portion from him. It is probable that he married when but a young man, in almost the opening portion of the reign

perpetuam elemosinam, quam etiam elemosinam ego et heredes mei prefatis monachis warentizabimus et adquietabimus contra omnes homines. Hiis testibus, *Waltero filio Hugonis, tunc ballivo domini regis,*[3] *Hugone filio ejus, Thoma de Horrebiri, Jordano et Willelmo fratribus suis, Adam filio Philippi,*[3] *Alano de Brettona, Willelmo de Deneby, Johanne filio Harding, Willelmo filio Johannis filii Assolfi,*[3] et multis aliis.

_____

of Henry I.; and, whether finding a family of many sons growing up around him, he was unwilling that they should hanker for his estates before he was ripe to leave them, or being swayed by a more statesmanlike policy, he thought it best that the eggs should not, in homely phrase, be all in one basket, he liberally divided his substance among his children. He had at least seven sons who came of age, probably eight; and by carefully collating the documents in which his and their names occur, I arrive at this order of seniority:—1, Peter fitz Asolf; 2, Jordan fitz Essulf, de Flockton, named in No. 248; 3, John, named in No. 248, No 263, and No. 264; 4, Thomas the steward, called also Thomas de Monte, named in No. 248; 5, William the baker, the almoner, the dispensator, de Whitwood and de Mara; 6, Elias, 7, Hugh; and perhaps 8, Richard of Tong. The death duties with reference to the succession to his estate are recorded in the Pipe Roll of 12 Henry II. (1166).

(3) See note (5) to previous charter.

―――――――――

CCLXV.[1]   Carta Gaufridi filii Pigot.   Cir. 1230.

[I, Geoffrey, son of Pigot de Bretton . . . . have confirmed, to Robert, son of D[avid] of Pol' (Pollington) . . . . an acre of land in the Fields of Bretton. That is to say, &c. To be held and possessed, &c. . . . . . . Paying thence, &c. For three shillings in acknowledgment . . . . . . Warrranty. Witnesses.]

Sciant presentes et futuri quod ego Gaufridus filius Pigot de Brettona dedi et concessi et hac presenti carta mea confirmavi Roberto filio Dd'[2] de Pol'[3] pro homagio et servitio suo unam acram terre in campis de Brettona. Scilicet duas perticatas et dimidiam in extremo inthac juxta venelam versus suth, et dimidiam perticatam que jacet inter terram domini et terram Prioris de Pontefracto, in rodis, et dimidiam perticatam in campis versus west, et dimidiam perticatam in crofto Reginaldi. Tenendas et habendas sibi et heredibus suis de me et de heredibus meis in feodo et heredidate, libere, quiete, et honorifice. Reddendo inde annuatim mihi et heredibus meis tres obolos, scilicet ad festum sancti Martini 1 denarium et ad Pentecosten 1 obolum. Pro hac vero donatione et concessione dedit mihi predictus R. tres solidos de recognicione. Et ego prenominatus Gaufridus et heredes mei prefatam terram predicto R. et heredibus suis vel cuicumque assignare voluerit contra omnes homines inperpetuum warantizabimus. Hiis testibus, *Osberto de*

(1) Of these four charters only No. 264 was copied into either the *Dodsworth* or the *Lansdowne* MSS. (2) If David, perhaps David the son of Harvey Kaskin. See No. 109 and No. 144.
(3) "Poles" in No. 429; ? Pollingtona.

Brettona, Waltero de Birum, Ricardo de Suttona, Ada de Brettona,[4] *Serlone de Brettuna,*[5] *Salamone de Brettona, Willelmo de Brettona, Thoma fratre ejus,* et multis aliis.[6]

---

(4) It is not clear why Adam should precede his brothers and cousins, if they were so. See also No. 212.   (5) *Sic.*

(6) From the names of the witnesses, it is clear that this acre was in Burton [Salmon], and was a part of what was called the Pigot fee (see No. 204).

CCLXVI.[1]   Carta Willelmi de Monte alto.   **Cir. 1210.**

[. . . . . . I. William de Monte alto . . . . . have confirmed to William son of Fulk, of Alwoodley, ... two bovates of land in Wick, which Robert the sergeant has held of the monks of Pontefract. To be held and possessed, &c. For twenty shillings, which the aforesaid William has given to me as acknowledgment, he and his heirs paying thence yearly to me and my heirs two shillings. . . . . . . Warranty. Witnesses.]

Notum sit omnibus presentibus et futuris quod ego Willelmus de Monte alto dedi et concessi et hac presenti carta mea confirmavi Willelmo filio Fulconis, de Alwaldeleye, pro homagio suo et servitio, duas bovatas terre in Wich quas Robertus serviens tenuit de monachis de Pontefracto. Tenendas et habendas sibi et heredibus suis, de me et heredibus meis, in feudo et hereditate, libere et quiete, et honorifice, in bosco et plano, in pratis et pasturis, et cum omnibus pertinentiis, aisiamentis et libertatibus ad predictam terram pertinentibus, infra villam et extra, pro viginti solidis quos predictus Willelmus mihi dedit ad recognitionem. Reddendo inde annuatim mihi et heredibus meis ipse et heredes sui duos solidos. Scilicet duodecim denarios ad Pentecosten, et duodecim denarios ad festum sancti Martini pro omni servitio et demanda que ad terram pertinent vel pertinere poterint. Et ego et heredes mei warantizabimus illi et heredibus suis et defendemus has predictas duas bovatas terre cum omnibus pertinentiis suis ubique et contra omnes homines. Hiis testibus, *Gaufrido de *rdington,*[2] *Hugone de Cressekelde, Alano de Bre*age,*[3] *Willelmo de Lofthus, Henrico de Alwaldleye, Henrico de*

---

(1) This charter was cancelled in the original, though, as it was included by the subsequent numerator, it would appear either that the cancellation had preceded the numeration, or that the numerator considered that the importance of the charter overruled the cancellation. A copy occurs in *Dodsworth,* vol. 151, and there is an abstract in *Lansdowne* 207. No. 266 is the corollary of No. 228 *bis,* and it is remarkable that in two charters so closely corresponding with each other as No. 228 *bis* and No. 266 there should be so many differences as occur in these In No. 228 *bis* the donor is described as William son of Symon de Mohaut, here he is "de Monte alto;" Robert de Sicklinghall of No. 228 *bis* is here Robert "Serviens," doubtless because Robert de Sicklinghall was the name of that town officer who was called a sergeant; and there are similar variations in the names of the witnesses, showing that the one charter was not a copy of the other, but that the two—while referring to the same people—were entirely independent.   (2) Arthington.

(3) Brearey. See No 237. The lines of cancellation pass over and obliterate the letters marked with a *.

Stubbes, Henrico de Mora, Hugone de Alwaldleye, Adam de Wiverdeleye, et aliis. Memorandum, quod has duas bovatas terre dedimus monialibus de Arthingtona, et Johannes de Vescy pro eisdem bovatis dedit nobis unum mesuagium in bondegate, de quo recipimus per annum ii solidos et viij denarios.

CCLXVII.[1]   Carta Alexandri de Chivet.   Cir. 1210.

[. . . . . . I, Alexander de Chivet, have . . . . . . confirmed, for the good of my soul, &c., certain "land" in the town of Chivet, having 44 feet in length and 24 in breadth. To wit, &c., which Thomas son of Rainer has held of me. To be held and possessed, &c., with free exit and entrance by the centre court of the aforesaid Thomas, without hindrance from me and my heirs. Sealed. Witnesses.]

Sciant presentes et futuri, quod ego Alexander de Chivet dedi, concessi, et hac presenti carta mea confirmavi pro salute anime mee et omnium antecessorum et heredum meorum deo et ecclesie sancti Johannis de Pontefracto et monachis ibidem deo servientibus quandam terram in villa de Chivet[2] habentem xliiij pedes in longitudine et xxiiij in latitudine. Illam scilicet que jacet inter ortum meum et ortum Willelmi de Riblesdale, quam Thomas filius Raineri tenuit de me. Tenendam et habendam prefatis monachis de me et heredibus meis in puram et perpetuam elemosinam cum libero exitu et introitu per mediam curiam predicte Thome sine impedimento mei et heredum meorum. Et ad perpetuam hujus rei memoriam huic scripto pro me et heredibus meis sigillum meum apposui in testimonium. Hiis testibus, *Willelmo de Chivet, Rogero de Nottona, Willelmo de Brettona, Adam de Holand, Henrico de Sewilla, Ricardo de Martona, Johanne filio Michaelis de Pontefracto,[3] Johanne nepote suo, Rogero Pistore,* et aliis.

(1) There is a copy of No. 266 and one of No. 267 in the *Dodsworth* MSS., vol. 151, and an abstract of each in *Lansdowne*, vol. 207.

(2) I find nothing else concerning this plot of land at Chivet. Like that at Catton (see No. 235) the monks probably parted with it at some time to suit their convenience, or capitalised it when their narrow means pressed them with more than usual severity.   (3) Of Monkhill.

CCLXVIII.[1]   Carta Helene filie Hugonis.   1241.

[. . . . . . . I, Helen, daughter of Hugh the "Waite" of Healaugh, have granted . . . . . . all the right and claim which I have ever had or in any way could have in that bovate of land in the territory of Friston, with its appurtenances,

(1) There is a copy of No. 268 in *Dodsworth*, vol. 151.

which William Marshall has given to the said monks, with his body. So that neither I, nor my heirs, nor any other on my part, can hereafter urge any right or claim. And I have promised to the said monks to keep this faithfully, and I have sworn it by touching the Holy Gospels, Simon, chaplain of Pontefract, being present, who is the witness and pledge of this deed. And for the love of God and for this my quit-claim, the said monks have given to me in hand in my great necessity eighteen shillings in silver. Seal. Witnesses. Dated 1241, on St. George's day [April 23].

Sciant presentes et futuri quod ego Helena filia Hugonis le Waite de Helaye concessi et omnino de me et heredibus meis vel meis assignatis quietum clamavi inperpetuum deo et ecclesie sancti Johannis apostoli de Pontefracto, et monachis ibidem deo servientibus, totum jus et clamium quod unquam habui vel aliquo modo habere potui in illa bovata terre in territorio de Fristona cum pertinentiis suis, quam Willelmus Marescallus dictis monachis dedit cum corpore suo. Ita quod nec ego, nec heredes mei, nec aliquis ex parte mea, in posterum aliquid juris vel clamii vendicare poterimus. Et ad hoc fideliter tenendum dictis monachis affidavi et juravi, tactis sacrosanctis evangeliis, presente Symone capellano de Pontefracto, qui hujus rei testis est et plegius. Et pro amore dei et pro hac quieta clamatione mea dederunt mihi dicti monachi in mea magna necessitate decem et octo solidos argenti pre manibus. Et ut hec mea quieta clamatio perpetue firmitatis robur optineatur,[2] huic scripto tam pro me quam omnibus heredibus meis vel assignatis si quos habere potero sigillum meum apposui. Hiis testibus, *domino Willelmo tunc persona de Helay, Gregorio de Cameria,*[2] *Thoma de Knaresburg, Nicholao et Willelmo de eadem, Roberto filio Ernis,* et aliis.[3] Facta est autem hec carta anno gracie millesimo ducentesimo xl*mo* primo in die sancti Georgii. ———

(2) *Sic* in each case.

(3) No. 268 and No. 298 are complementary, the latter being the original gift from William Marshall, which the charter before us confirms and ratifies. William, parson (or rector) of Healaugh, was a witness to each of these documents. The last-named witness, Robert son of Ernis, was a man of Pontefract extraction, and of a somewhat substantial family. His father, Ernis, appears on the Pontefract "little charter" as holding nineteen acres of the common land, while Elias, his elder brother, holds eleven, the joint possession being nearly a sixth of the whole—an illustration of the way in which such holdings naturally gravitated to each other, and by degrees fell into a few hands. This was in 1194, and I have no further mention of Ernis himself. But in No. 119 Elias son of Ernis and Robert his brother both test; and in a third generation William son of Elias (generally aspirated Helias, in the twelfth century charters) tests No. 122, No. 135, No. 153, and No. 169; after which the Pontefract Chartulary ceases to throw light upon this branch of the family. The younger brother Robert appears in company with his elder brother only once, though he tests several documents, and as his son Thomas calls himself in No. 152 Thomas son of Robert son of Ernis, the following small genealogy is well established —

```
                                    Ernis                                ERNIS.
          ┌───────────────────────────┴───────────────────────┐
          |                                                    |
      Elias, 119                          114, 119, 121, Robert 126, 126 bis, 152, 268
          |                                                    |
  William, 122, 135, 153, 169                            Thomas, 152
```

CCLXIX.[1]   Carta Alani filii Roberti filii Oliveri.   Cir. **1220.**

[. . . . . . I, Alan, son of Robert, son of Oliver, of Smeaton . . . . . . have confirmed, two acres of land in the Fields of Smeaton, with their appurtenances. Of which acres, &c. To be held and possessed, &c. Warranty. Witnesses.]

Sciant presentes et futuri quod ego Alanus[2] filius Roberti filii Oliveri de Smithetona, pro salute anime mee et omnium antecessorum et heredum meorum, dedi, concessi, et presenti carta mea confirmavi, deo et sancto Johanni de Pontefracto et monachis ibidem deo servientibus, in puram et perpetuam elemosinam, duas acras terre[3] in campis de Smithetona cum suis pertinentiis. Ex quibus acris una acra et dimidia jacent super Drakehov et extendunt se ex una parte versus Went et ex alia parte versus magnam viam que tendit versus Nortona, et dimidia acra jacet inter terram Siwardi de Norton et terram Josiane matris mee, et ex una parte percircit[4] super terram Alani filii Ranulfi, et ex alia parte inter magnam viam que tendit versus Northon. Tenendas et habendas prefatis monachis inperpetuum cum communis libertatibus et asiamentis predicte ville de Smithetona quantum ad tantum tenementum pertinet. Et ego prenominatus Alanus et heredes mei warentizabimus prefatas duas acras prefatis monachis ubique et contra omnes homines. Hiis testibus, *Alano filio Ranulfi tunc ballivo de Staincross et Osgotcros, Thebaudo de Stubbis, Petro de Stubbis, Ricardo Noel, Ricardo de Stubbis, Radulfo de Kamesal, Willelmo de Kamesal, Roberto filio Waldeni de Kamesal, Roberto filio Gilleberti, Alano filio Alani, Roberto Camberlano, Radulfo de Bateleia, Symone Pincerna,[5] Ricardo de Martona, Philippo Parcario,* et aliis.

(1) I have not met with either copy or abstract of No. 269.

(2) Alan son of Robert seems to have been more generally known by his mother's name. As he was one of the jurors who made the inquisition as to the value of the manor of Elmsall in 1264 (*Yorkshire Inquisitions* i. 99), he must at the time of the execution of No. 269 have been but a young man.

(3) The two acres granted by this charter, like the property in Catton (see No. 235) and that in Chivet (see No. 268), did not continue in the occupation of the monks, but were leased out by them immediately (see No. 502), in accordance with the plan they found most convenient and profitable.   (4) *Sic.*   (5) Dead in 1224.

CCLXX.[1]   Carta Willelmi filii Pagani.   Cir. **1206.**

[. . . . . . I, William, son of Paganus . . . . . have confirmed . . . . . two bovates of land in Hillam, with their appurtenances, which Adam de Reineville has given and confirmed to those monks in perpetual alms. Warranty. Witnesses.]

(1) There is an abstract of No. 270 in *Lansdowne* 207.

Sciant presentes et futuri quod ego Willelmus filius Pagani concessi et presenti carta mea confirmavi deo et sancto Johanni apostolo et evangeliste et monachis de Pontefracto in puram et perpetuam elemosinam, pro salute anime mee et omnium antecessorum et heredum meorum, duas bovatas terre in Hillum cum pertinentiis suis quas Adam de Reinevilla eisdem monachis donavit et confirmavit in perpetuam elemosinam. Et ego Willelmus et heredes mei predictam terram cum pertinentiis prefatis monachis warentizabimus et defendemus contra omnes homines. Hiis testibus, *Paulino capellano, Willelmo Gramatico, Adam de Reinevilla,*[2] *Thoma filio ejus,*[3] *Willelmo de Stapiltona, Raimundo clerico,* et aliis.[4]

---

(2) Adam Vetus.

(3) Thomas, Adam's eldest son, who died in 1218. See pedigree facing this Fasciculus.

(4) Of the six witnesses to this confirming charter, three are Adam the original grantee (see No. 271), Thomas his eldest son, and William de Stapleton, the husband of his daughter Clarissa.

CCLXXI[1]   **Carta Ade de Rainevilla.**[2]   **Cir. 1180.**

[. . . . . . I, Adam de Reineville . . . . . . for the good of my soul and of my wife •Alice . . . . . . two bovates of land in Hillam . . . . . . or a rent of nine shillings . . . . . . And all the land in Pontefract, which Jordan Fullo has held of me. Also . . . . . . forty pence which William son of Nun, shall pay from his rent . . . . . . And if the aforesaid William shall not faithfully pay . . . . . . distraint upon the aforesaid William, through his cattle. Witnesses.]

Omnibus sancte matris ecclesie filiis Adam de Rainevilla salutem. Notum sit universitati vestre me concessisse et dedisse et hac presenti carta mea confirmasse deo et sancto Johanni et monachis de Pontefracto, ibidem deo servientibus, pro salute anime mee et uxoris mee Aliz, et omnium antecessorum et heredum meorum, illas duas bovatas terre in Hillum cum omnibus pertinentiis suis quas Robertus filius Ulwetti tenuit de me. Has vero bovatas si ego Adam vel heredes mei warentizare non poterimus, dabimus prefatis monachis in excambio[3] redditum novem solidorum. Preter hec dedi predictis monachis totam terram in Pontefracto quam Jordanus Fullo tenuit de me. Insuper dedi eis, de redditu[3] quadraginta denariorum quos persolvet Willelmus filius Nunne de firma sua, xx denarios in festo sancti Martini, et xx denarios in Pentecosti. Si vero predictus Willelmus fideliter ad terminos prenominatos non redderit,[3] concessi ut predicti monachi prefatum Willelmum per averias suas distringant

---

(1) There is a much abridged abstract of No. 271 in *Dodsworth* 136, and a fuller, but less accurate, copy in *Lansdowne* 207   (2) Adam Vetus.   (3) *Sic*, in each case.

ad reddendum. Has vero terras et hunc redditum dedi predictis monachis in puram et perpetuam elemosinam. Hiis testibus, *Thoma de Rainevilla filio meo, Ricardo de Reinevilla,*[4] *Ricardo Malebise, Gaufrido, Willelmo, Hugone, fratribus suis,*[5] *Adam de Prestuna, Radulfo de Best', Willelmo de Novo Mercato,*[6] *Johanne clerico de Kelligtona,*[7] *Henrico, Symone, Alexandro, Moyse, fratribus suis,*[8] *Willelmo filio Everardi, Ricardo de Stagno, Jordano de Ledestuna,*[9] *Hugone de Bateleya,* et aliis.

(4) Adam's brother Richard (*Dodsworth's Monasticon* 862). See No. 278.

(5) See Introduction.

(6) Younger brother of Adam, the early benefactor of Nostell, and after 1160 having custody of his nephew the heir, till he came of age.

(7) John became dean of Pontefract about 1190. See No. 297.

(8) For pedigree see under No. 297.   (9) The eldest brother.

DE BILAMA.

CCLXXII.[1]   Carta Ricardi filii Johannis de Bilama.   1216.

[. . . . . . I, Richard, son of John of Bilham . . . . . . a rent of five shillings in the town of Bilham. Fifty shillings of silver in my great necessity. Warranty. Witnesses.]

Sciant presentes et futuri quod ego Ricardus filius Johannis de Bilama, pro salute anime mee et omnium antecessorum et heredum meorum, dedi, concessi, et hac presenti carta mea confirmavi, deo et ecclesie sancti Johannis apostoli et evangeliste de Pontefracto, et monachis ibidem deo servientibus, in puram et perpetuam elemosinam, redditum quinque solidorum in villa de Bilama, annuatim percipiendorum, videlicet de Thoma filio Thome de Bilama, decem et septem denarios pro una acra terre et dimidia et pro illo tofto quod de me tenuit; de Alexandro filio Radulfi triginta unum denarios pro uno tofto et crofto et duabus acris terre quas de me tenuit; et de Agnete filia Thome Fox duodecim denarios pro uno crofto et dimidia acra terre, quam de me tenuit. Dicti vero Thomas et heredes sui, et Alexander et heredes sui, et dicta Agnes et heredes sui reddent dictum redditum quinque solidorum dictis monachis ad duos anni terminos sicut prescriptum est. Videlicet medietatem ad Pentecosten, et alteram medietatem ad festum sancti Martini in hyeme; cum omnibus consuetudinibus, releviis et auxiliis que mihi et antecessoribus meis reddere consueverunt. Pro hac autem donatione, concessione, et confirmatione dederunt mihi dicti monachi quinquaginta solidos argenti pre manibus, in mea magna necessitate. Et ego dictus Ricardus et heredes mei dictum redditum quinque solidorum cum

(1) I have not met with either copy or abstract of this No. 272. It may be noticed that this property was acquired at ten years' purchase. For a sketch of the history of the Bilhams of the eleventh century, see Introduction.

2 D

homagiis omnium prenominatorum et cum omnibus servitiis et consuetudinibus mihi debitis vel debendis dictis monachis contra omnes homines inperpetuum warantizabimus, protegemus ac defendemus. In cujus rei testimonium tam pro me quam pro omnibus heredibus meis in perpetuum huic scripto sigillum meum apposui. Hiis testibus, *domino Willelmo de Bilama, Willelmo de Barewilla, Henrico de Camera, Willelmo filio Walteri, Waltero filio Ricardi de Broddesworda*, et aliis.

CCLXXIII.[1]   **Carta Ricardi filii Johannis de Bilam.**   **Cir. 1238.**

[. . . . . . I, Richard son of John of Bilham . . . . . . to Thomas my uncle five acres of land, in the territory of Bilham, which John son of Matthew of Bilham formerly held from me. . . . . To be had and held, &c. Fourteen pence yearly rent. Warranty. Seal. Witnesses.]

Sciant presentes et futuri quod ego Ricardus filius Johannis de Bilama, dedi et concessi et hac presenti carta mea confirmavi Thome awunculo meo quinque acras terre cum omnibus pertinentiis suis in territorio de Bilehama, quas Johannes filius Mathei de Bilama quondam tenuit de me. Tenendas et habendas de me et heredibus meis vel assignatis meis sibi et heredibus suis vel assignatis suis cum omnibus pertinentiis suis, libere et quiete. Reddendo inde annuatim mihi et heredibus meis xiiij denarios pro omni servitio seculari vel demanda, videlicet vii denarios ad Nathale domini, et vii denarios ad Pascha. Ego vero Ricardus et heredes mei vel assignati mei predictas quinque acras terre cum pertinentiis suis predicto Thome et heredibus suis vel assignatis suis warentizabimus contra omnes homines inperpetuum ac defendemus. In cujus rei testimonium huic scripto sigillum meum apposui. Hiis testibus, *Jordano de Insula de Hautun*,[2] *Henrico de Tancreslay, Willelmo de Bilama, Willelmo de Barevil, Henrico de Camera, Adam Painel*, et aliis.

(1) There is an abstract of No. 273 in *Dodsworth* 136.   (2) Hooton. See note (2) to No. 244.

CCLXXIIII.[1]   **Carta Thome filii Thome de Bilam.**   **Ante 1238.**

[. . . . . . I, Thomas, son of Thomas of Bilham . . . . . assent to . . . . . the gift which Richard son of John of Bilham has made to the monks of Pontefract, in five acres of land which I formerly held of him in the territory of Bilham. Seal. Witnesses.]

(1) I have met with no copy or abstract of No. 274.

Omnibus hoc scriptum visuris vel audituris, Thomas filius Thome de Bilham, salutem. Noverit universitas vestra me gratam et ratam habere donationem quam Ricardus filius Johannis de Bilam fecit monachis de Pontefracto, in quinque acris terre quas de eo prius tenueram in territorio de Bilam. Et ne ego dictus Thomas vel heredes mei in supradictis quinque acris terre aliquid juris vel clamii de cetero vendicare possimus huic scripto pro me et heredibus meis sigillum meum apposui. Hiis testibus, *domino Ada de Neirford tunc senescallo de Pontefracto,*[2] *Roberto de Stapiltona, Alano de Smithetona, Roberto filio Gilleberti de eadem, Willelmo de Barevilla, Henrico Camberlano,*[3] *Henrico filio Ranl' de Pontefracto, Johanne Vinitore de eadem,*[4] *Adam filio Rogeri de Balcholm,* et aliis.

---

(2) Seneschal 1232-8.   (3) De Camera in No. 272 and No. 273.
                  (4) Son of Hugh de Batley

CCLXXV.[1]   Carta Willelmi de Barevilla.   1238.

[. . . . . I, William de Bareville . . . . . a bovate of land in the territory of Bilham . . . . . called the Painel bovate. Also an acre and a-half of land . . . . . and two slips, which are called headlands, and lie towards the Cross which is between Hickleton and Bilham. To be held and possessed, &c. Warranty. Seal. Date. Witnesses.]

Sciant presentes et futuri quod ego Willelmus de Barevilla dedi, concessi, et hac presenti carta mea confirmavi deo et ecclesie sancti Johannis evangeliste de Pontefracto et monachis ibidem deo servientibus, pro salute anime mee et patris et matris mee et omnium antecessorum et heredum meorum, unam bovatam terre in territorio de Bilam, illam scilicet que vocatur bovata Painel. Et insuper unam acram terre et dimidiam que jacent inter terram Walteri Bercarii versus west et terram persone de Hoton versus est, et buttat super viam que tendit versus Broddeswd, et duas seliones que vocantur fordolis,[2] et jacent versus crucem que est inter Hykeltona et Bilama. Tenendas et habendas dictis monachis cum omnibus pertinentiis suis et aisiamentis infra villam et extra in liberam, puram et perpetuam elemosinam de me et heredibus meis sine aliquo retenemento vel contradictione mei vel heredum meorum. Ego vero Willelmus et heredes mei predictam bovatam terre et prenominatam acram et dimidiam et duas predictas seliones cum omnibus pertinentiis suis dictis monachis inperpetuum warantizabimus contra omnes homines

---

(1) There is an abstract of No. 275 in *Dodsworth* 136.   (2) *Sic.*

ac defendemus. In cujus rēi testimonium huic scripto sigillum meum apposui. Datum apud Pontefractum, anno domini m° ducentesimo tricesimo octavo. Hiis testibus, *domino. Andrea Luterel, Willelmo de Bilam, Henrico de Camera, Thoma filio Thome de Bilam, Waltero Bercario, Hugone de Claytona, Henrico filio Ranulfi de Pontefracto, Johanne Vinitore de eadem,* et aliis.

———————

CCLXXVI.[1]   Carta Ricardi filii Johannis de Bilam.   Ante 1238.

[. . . . . . I, Richard, son of John, of Bilham . . . . . . five acres of land . . . . . . in the territory of Bilham. To wit, those which Thomas son of Thomas, of Bilham, formerly held of me, and which the said Thomas has surrendered to me before the parishioners of Hooton, in the church of that town. To be held and possessed, &c. Warranty. Seal. Witnesses.]

Sciant presentes et futuri quod ego Ricardus filius Johannis de Bilam dedi, concessi, et hac presenti carta mea confirmavi deo et ecclesie sancti Johannis apostoli et evangeliste de Pontefracto et monachis ibidem deo servientibus, in puram et perpetuam elemosinam, pro salute anime mee et omnium antecessorum et heredum meorum, quinque acras terre cum omnibus pertinentiis suis in territorio de Bilam. Illas scilicet quas Thomas filius Thomas de Bilam quondam tenuit de me et quas idem Thomas mihi sursum reddidit coram parochianis de Hotona,[2] in ecclesia ejusdem ville. Tenendas et habendas dictis monachis de me et heredibus meis in liberam, puram, et perpetuam elemosinam. Ego vero Ricardus et heredes mei predictas quinque acras terre cum omnibus pertinentiis suis predictis monachis sicut puram et perpetuam elemosinam contra omnes homines warantizabimus ac defendemus inperpetuum. In cujus rei testimonium huic scripto pro me et heredibus meis sigillum meum apposui. Hiis testibus, *domino Ada de Neirford tunc*[3] *senescallo de Pontefracto, Roberto de Stapiltona, Alano de Smythetona, Roberto filio Gilleberti de eadem, Willelmo de Barevilla, Henrico Camberlano, Thoma filio Thome de Bilam,* et aliis.

———————

(1) There is an abstract of No. 276 also in *Dodsworth* 136.

(2) This surrender, "before the parishioners in the church of Hooton," it may be supposed, was at what would now be called a vestry meeting; but the absurd inference has been drawn from what appears to be this exceptional transaction that the twelfth and thirteenth century parish churches were places in which the parishioners usually held meetings for public secular purposes.

(3) 1232–8.

CCLXXVII.[1]   Carta Willelmi de Barevilla.   Ante 1238.

[. . . . . . I, William de Bareville . . . . . . a bovate of land in the territory of Bilham, to wit, that which is called the Painel bovate.   And also an acre . . . . . .   To be had and held, &c.   Warranty.   Witnesses.]

Sciant presentes et futuri, quod ego, Willelmus de Barevilla, dedi, concessi, et hac presenti carta mea confirmavi deo et ecclesie sancti Johannis de Pontefracto et monachis ibidem deo servientibus, pro salute anime mee, et patris et matris mee et omnium antecessorum et heredum meorum, unam bovatam terre in territorio de Bilam.   Illam scilicet que vocatur bovata Painel.   Et insuper unam acram terre que jacet inter terram Walteri Bercarii versus west, et terram dicti Willelmi versus est, et buttat super viam que tendit versus Broddeswrda. Habendas et tenendas dictis monachis cum omnibus pertinentiis suis et aisiamentis infra villam et extra, in liberam, puram, et perpetuam elemosinam de me et heredibus meis sine aliquo retenemento mei vel heredum meorum.   Hanc vero bovatam terre et acram prenominatam cum omnibus pertinentiis suis ego prefatus Willelmus et heredes mei predictis monachis contra omnes homines inperpetuum warentizabimus ac defendemus.   Hiis testibus, *Willelmo de Bilam, Henrico de Camera, Thoma filio Thome de Bilam, Waltero Bercario, Hugone de Claytona, Henrico filio Ranulfi de Pontefracto,*[2] *Johanne filio Michaelis de eadem, Rogero Pistore,* et aliis.

(1) This, which did not include the two "headlands," was superseded by No. 275.
(2) This "Henry son of Ralph, of Pontefract," preceding John son of Michael, might be either Henry son of Ralph of Batley (106, 139, 141) or Henry son of Ralph (and Matilda) of Smeaton.

CCLXXVIII.[1]   Carta Katherine filie Reineri.   Cir. 1210.

[. . . . . . I, Katherine, daughter of Reyner of Aberford, have given and granted, and by this my present charter have confirmed, to Elinor, daughter of Matilda my daughter, of Shippen, and her heirs, all my land of Ledstone, which I have held from Hervey son of Richard of Ledstone . . . . . . eight acres of land in the territory of Ledstone, and a meadow belonging to a bovate of land in Bondholm, towards the west, as the charter of the aforesaid Hervey witnesseth. . . . . . .   To be held, &c., freely, and quietly, and entirely.   Paying . . . . . . eightpence for all service and exaction . . . . . .   Witnesses.]

Sciant omnes tam presentes quam futuri quod ego Katerina filia Reineri de Abreforda[2] dedi et concessi et hac presenti carta mea confirmavi Alienore filie Matilde filie mee de Schipena, et heredibus

(1) This charter should have accompanied No. 173 and No. 175.
(2) See pedigree of Ailric, *ante,* page 218.

suis, totam terram meam de Ledestuna quam tenui de Herveio filio Ricardi de Ledestona. Scilicet octo acras terre in territorio de Ledestuna et pratum pertinens ad unam bovatam terre in Bondeholm versus occidentem sicut carta predicti Hervei testatur.[3] Scilicet duas acras ad Wlvegreves, et unam acram et dimidiam in Alditherodes, et unam acram et dimidiam in Stainrode, et unam acram et dimidiam in Espis, et tres rodas in Befurlonges, et tres rodas in Harethirn. Tenendam de prefato Hereveio, libere, et quiete, et integre. Reddendo inde annuatim predicto Hereveio et heredibus suis octo denarios pro omni servitio et exactione. Scilicet iiij*or* denarios ad Pentecosten, et iiij*or* denarios ad festum sancti Martini. Hiis testibus, *Willelmo Gramatico, Ricardo fratre suo,*[4] *Ada de Reinevilla, Jordano de Insula, Waltero de Abreforda,*[5] *Reginaldo de Barnebu, Ricardo de Reinevilla,*[6] *Magistro Reimundo,*[7] et multis aliis.

(3) See No. 175.

(4) See note (5) to No. 175. This was the "frater," the later of the two Richards.

(5) Formerly of Ledsham. See No. 310, and pedigree facing the Fifth Fasciculus.

(6) Younger brother of Adam de Reineville Vetus. He also witnesses No. 271, and grants K. fo. 76d.

(7) Master Raimond, the last witness of No. 278, was the head of the clerical family of Methley. He witnessed the Pontefract lord's "little charter" to his tenants of land on the moor, and, with William Grammaticus and Richard his brother, fixes the date of this last charter as about 1200. See note (5) to No. 175.

CCLXXIX.   Carta Galfridi de Ledeshama.   Cir. 1220.

[. . . . . . I, Geoffrey of Ledsham, and Cecily my wife have . . . . . quitclaimed . . . . . . to the prior of Pontefract and the monks there our dowry, in two bovates . . . . . . in the territory of Ledsham. . . . . . . A half mark of silver. Seals. Witnesses.]

Sciant presentes et futuri quod ego Galfridus de Ledeshama et Cecilia uxor mea[1] forisjuravimus et fide interposita sine retenemento de nobis inperpetuum quietum clamavimus Priori de Pontefracto et monachis ibidem deo servientibus totum jus et clamium quod per breve domini regis nomine dotarii clamavimus in duabus bovatis terre in terra dictorum monachorum in territorio de Ledeshama. Ex quibus duabus bovatis Alexander filius Rogeri filii Swani tenet unam et Ranulfus de Neuporta tenet capitale mesuagium et dimidiam bovatam et Johannes filius Radulfi aliam dimidiam bovatam. Pro

---

(1) See pedigree facing the Fifth Fasciculus. Geoffrey was the youngest son of the youngest brother Walter. Cecilia was his second wife, and he was apparently a substantial man through property acquired by marriage. He has been hitherto mainly known as a Ledsham witness to No. 102, No. 178, No. 184, No. 186, and No. 187, but he appears as of Wheldrake in No. 200 and No. 201, of Micklefield in No. 310, and as the husband of Agnes in 285. No. 279 shows him as making, through Cecilia his second wife, a claim upon two bovates in Ledsham, issuing a writ in the King's Court to enforce it, and then renouncing his claim by deed. But I have not ascertained either who was the first husband of Cecilia, through whom it is presumed he made his claim, or from which family she was descended.

hac autem quieta clamatione dederunt nobis predicti prior et monachi dimidiam marcam argenti. Et ne nos inperpetuum contra hanc nostram quietam clamationem venire possimus huic carte sigilla nostra apposuimus in testimonium. Hiis testibus, *Roberto de Kent, tunc senescallo Pontisfracti,*[2] *Johanne de Byrkina, Roberto Vavasore, Willelmo filio Everardi, Ricardo Londoniis,*[3] *Henrico Byset, Ricardo de Stagno, Thoma fratre suo, Ricardo de Martona.*

(2) 1218–1224. (3) See No. 260.

CCLXXX. Carta Alicie et Tibbe filiarum Johannis Durward. Cir. 1240.

[. . . . . I, Alice and Tibba my sister, daughters of John son of Durward, of Featherstone . . . . . have sold . . . . . to Hugh son of Ralph de Methley . . . . . a rood of land and a half . . . . . between the Park and Featherstone, and half of Woodroyd . . . . . To be held and possessed, &c. Paying . . . . . a penny at the Nativity of the Lord . . . . . A half mark of silver in hand. Warranty. Seals. Witnesses.]

Sciant presentes et futuri quod ego, Alicia, et Tibba soror mea, filie Johannis filii Durward de Fetherstana, in virginitate nostra vendidimus, concessimus, et presenti carta nostra confirmavimus Hugoni[1] filio Radulfi de Medelay, et assignatis suis, et eorum heredibus, unam percatam terre et dimidiam jacentes super hil inter terram Radulfi de Fetherstana, et inter terram Willelmi de eadem, inter parcum et Fetherstanam; et medietatem del Woderode propinquiorem ville de Fetherstana; cum omnibus pertinentibus, in pasturis, in pratis, in turbariis, et cum omnibus libertatibus, et aisiamentis, ad dictas terras infra villam de Fetherstana et extra pertinentibus. Tenendam et habendam de nobis et heredibus nostris sibi et assignatis et eorum heredibus, libere, quiete, pacifice, et integre. Reddendo inde annuatim nobis et heredibus nostris unum denarium ad nathale domini, pro omnibus servitiis secularibus et demandis. Pro hac autem venditione et concessione dedit nobis dictus Hugo dimidiam marcam argenti premanibus de recognitione. Ego vero Alicia et Tibba soror mea et heredes nostri predicto Hugoni et assignatis suis et eorum heredibus predictas terras cum omnibus pertinentiis pro predicto servicio in omnibus et contra omnes gentes warantizabimus et defendemus inperpetuum. In cujus rei testimonium

(1) This Hugh, the grantee, is called in No 245 Hugh the park-keeper, presumably of Pontefract Park. The slip which he thus purchased for a mark and a half appears to have been to the west of the park, and immediately adjoining its entrance from Featherstone. It is possible that the parent of the two vendors was either a deer-ward or a door-ward. But in the MS. the name is clearly "Durward."

hanc cartam appositione sigillorum nostrorum corroboravimus.[2] Hiis testibus, *domino Radulfo de Fetherstan, Willelmo de Fetherstan, Gregorio de Camera, Henrico de Medelay, clerico,[3] Willelmo de Knaresburga; Ricardo Lewyn, Thoma Fox, tunc prepositis de Pontefracto[4]; Willelmo filio Rogeri, Johanne de Stanlaw, clerico,* et aliis.

(2) See also No. 293, No. 308, and No. 309.

(3) He appears to have succeeded Raimond. See 278.

(4) It may be observed that here again, as in No. 122, No 130, No. 131, and perhaps No. 127, thus early in the thirteenth century, and only a generation after the granting of the Town Charter, the bailiffs of Pontefract acted in couples, each bearing the official title of "prepositus" which appears in the "Little Charter" (see page xl.). The lord's charter, it may be noticed, gave them that of "bailiff;" but the lord's officer had appropriated that particular title. See No. 162, No. 261, No. 488, etc.

DE MERKESDENA.[1]

CCLXXXI.   Carta Roberti Mey.   Cir. 1216.

[. . . . . I, Robert Mey . . . . have surrendered a bovate of land in Marsden, with all its appurtenances, and, ... touching the Holy Gospels, have sworn that I will never in future move question concerning it. . . . . . Seal.]

Sciant presentes et futuri quod ego Robertus Mey sursum reddidi et penitus abiuravi dominis meis Priori et conventui de Pontefracto et quietum clamavi de me et de heredibus meis in perpetuum omne jus et clamium, si quod habui vel habere potui aliquo modo in illa bovata terre in Merkesden cum omnibus pertinentiis quam de eis tenui, et tactis sacrosanctis evangeliis juravi quod numquam de cetero dictis monachis super dicta bovata terre cum pertinentiis movebo questionem. Ut autem ista sursum redditio seu quieta clamatio firma sit est stabilis, et ne ego vel aliquis heredum meorum aut aliquis occasione nostri contra eam in posterum venire presumat, presenti scripto sigillum meum apposui in testimonium. Hiis testibus, *Hugone Pincerna tunc senescallo de Pontefracto,[2] Symone clerico tunc ballivo,[3] Johanne clerico filio Willelmi de Kamesala, Petro de Mekesdene,[4] Roberto de Penebi,[4] Ricardo de Martona, Hugone filio Thome de Bilam, Ricardo de Keswica,* et aliis.

(1) Great Marsden in Colne, in the ancient parish of Whalley.   (2) 1211–1216.

(3) See No. 114. He tests No. 282 also, and might have been, perhaps was, the Simon de Notton of No. 114 and the Simon de Silkstone of No 347.

(4) Merkesdene and Penbirie respectively in No. 230; Penbyri in No. 282.

CCLXXXII.   Carta Roberti Mey.   1216.

[. . . . . I, Robert Mey . . . . . all the right and claim, if I ever had or could have had any, in any way, in that bovate of land in Marsden . . . . Seal. Witnesses.]

Sciant presentes et futuri quod ego Robertus Mey sursum reddidi et de me et heredibus meis inperpetuum quietum clamavi deo et ecclesie sancti Johannis de Pontefracto et monachis ibidem deo servientibus, totum jus et clamium si quod habui vel habere potui aliquo modo in illa bovata terre in Merkesdena cum omnibus pertinentiis suis quam de eis tenui. Ut autem sursum ista redditio et quieta clamatio firma sit et stabilis, et ne ego vel aliquis heredum meorum aut aliquis occasione nostri contra eam in posterum venire presumat presenti scripto sigillum meum apposui in testimonium. Hiis testibus, *domino J. de Lasci constabulario Cestrie, dominis Hugone Butel*[1] *et Gaufrido de Dutton senescallis ipsius domini J., H*[enrico] *persona de Rowelle,*[2] *domino Colino Quatremanis,*[3] *Roberto de Stapiltona, Symone clerico, tunc ballivo, Waltero receptore, Johanne clerico filio Willelmi de Kamessala, Petro de Merkesdene, Roberto de Penbyri, Ricardo de Martona,* et aliis. ———

(1) Buticularius in No. 23, Pincerne in No. 280.   (2) Henry de Nottingham in No. 283 d.
(3) Colin de Amville in No. 22.

DE MERKESDENA.
CCLXXXIII.   Carta Willelmi filii Roberti Mei.   1216.

[. . . . . . . I, William son of Robert Mey, of Marsden, have sold . . . . . . for two marks of silver and three shillings . . . . . in hand, that bovate of land, with all its appurtenances, within the town of Marsden and without, which my father and I have held of William de Vescy; and all the right and claim, &c. Seal. Witnesses.]

Sciant presentes et futuri quod ego Willelmus filius Roberti Mey de Merkesdena vendidi dominis meis Priori et conventui de Pontefracto pro duabus marcis argenti et tribus solidis quas in premanibus persolverunt illam bovatam terre cum omnibus pertinentiis suis infra villam de Merkesdena et extra, quam pater meus et ego tenuimus de Willelmo de Vescy[1]; et totum jus et clamium quod in predicta terra habui vel habere potui prefatis monachis quietum clamavi de me et de omnibus heredibus meis inperpetuum. Et in hujus rei testimonium hoc scriptum sigillo meo roboravi. Hiis testibus, *Alano clerico, tunc senescallo,*[2] *Petro receptore,*[3] *Johanne de Thelewelle, Matheo de Brereclive, Roberto filio Petri de Merkesdene, Matheo de Bredeleya, Ricardo de Catthelowe, Johanne fratre suo, Roberto Bate, Syward homine monachorum,* et multis aliis.

(1) See No. 230.
(2) Alan the clerk could not have held office long, some portion only of 1216.
(3) Peter the receiver was the predecessor in office of the oft-named Walter, who held the appointment till 1240. Walter was succeeded by another Peter, surnamed de Alpibus, and described as "physician to the Queen." He was a protégé of Queen Eleanor, who then held the presentation by grant from the king, the lord being under age. See No. 100, note (6). and No. 230, note (11).

CCLXXXIII a.[1]   **Carta Roberti Mey.**   1216.

[. . . . . . I, Robert Mey, have abjured and entirely quit-claimed . . . . all right and claim . . . . . in that bovate of land in Marsden . . . . . Seal.   Witnesses.]

Sciant presentes et futuri quod ego Robertus Mey abjuravi et de me et heredibus meis in perpetuum penitus quietum clamavi deo et ecclesie sancti Johannis de Pontefracto et monachis ibidem deo servientibus omne jus et clamium quod habui vel habere potui aliquo modo in illa bovata terre in Merkesdena cum omnibus pertinentiis suis quam tenui de Willelmo de Vescy.   Ut autem ista abjuratio et quieta clamatio firma sit et stabilis, et ne ego, vel aliquis heredum meorum, aut alius occasione nostri contra eas in posterum venire presumat, presenti scripto sigillum meum apposui in testimonium.   Hiis testibus, *J. de Lascy, constabulario Cestrie, dominis Hugone Butel', et Gaufrido de Duttona, tunc senescallis ipsius domini J., Henrico persona de Rowella,*[2] *domino Colino Quatremanis, Roberto de Stapiltona,*[2] *Symone clerico tunc ballivo, Waltero receptore, Johanne clerico filio Willelmi de Kamesala, Petro de Merkesdena, Roberto de Penbiri, Ricardo de Martona,* et aliis.

---

(1) No. 283a and No. 283b are practically triplicates with No. 252.

(2) These two witnesses are additional to those who test No 283b, Robert de Stapleton holding Cudworth, a member of Rothwell.

CCLXXXIII b.   **Carta Roberti Mey.**   1216.

[. . . . . . I, Robert Mey, have abjured and altogether quit-claimed . . . . . . all right and claim . . . . . . in that bovate in Marsden . . . . . Seal.   Witnesses.]

Sciant presentes et futuri quod ego Robertus Mey,[1] abjuravi et penitus quietum clamavi de me et de heredibus meis inperpetuum totum jus et clamium si quod habui vel aliquo modo habere potui in illa bovata terre in Merkesdena, cum omnibus pertinentiis, quam tenui de Willelmo de Vescy, deo et beato Johanni evangeliste de Pontefracto et monachis ibidem deo servientibus.   Ut autem ista abjuratio et quieta clamatio firma sit et stabilis et ne ego vel aliquis heredum meorum, aut alius occasione nostri contra eas in posterum venire presumat presenti scripto sigillum meum apposui in testimonium.   Hiis testibus, *domino J. de Lascy, constabulario Cestrie, dominis Hugone Duttone,*[2] *G. de Duttone, tunc senescallis ipsius domini J., domino Colino Quatremanis, Symone clerico,*[3] *tunc ballivo, Waltero receptore, Johanne clerico filio Willelmi de Kamesalla, Petro de Merkesdena, Roberto de Penbiri, Ricardo de Martona,* et multis aliis.

---

(1) His heirs are not included in this charter, as they were in the superseding 283 a.

(2) *Sic* for " Pincerna," or Butel'.   (3) Simon de Notton.   See note (3) to No. 306.

CCLXXXIII c.[1] **Carta Matildis uxoris quondam Roberti Mey.** 1216.

[. . . . . . I, Matilda, widow of Robert Mey . . . . . . have abjured . . . . . . all right and claim . . . . . . in all the third part . . . . which the said Robert my husband held . . . . . Half a mark of silver . . . . . Oath. Seal. Witnesses.]

Sciant presentes et futuri quod ego Matildis, uxor quondam Roberti Mey, in plena potestate viduitatis mee abjuravi et quietum clamavi Priori et monachis de Pontefracto de me et de meis totum jus et clamium si quod habui vel habere potui in tota tercia parte omnium terrarum et possessionum cum pertinentiis earum in villa de Merkesdena et extra quas dictus Robertus vir meus tenuit. Pro hac vero abjuratione et quieta clamatione intuitu pietatis dederunt michi dicti monachi in magna necessitate mea dimidiam marcam argenti pre manibus. Et ne ego vel aliquis meorum contra hanc abjurationem et quietam clamationem venire possimus, fide media et juramento interposito firmavi, et huic scripto sigillum meum apposui in testimonium. Hiis testibus, *Alano clerico, tunc senescallo*,[2] *Ricardo de Catthelawe, Johanne fratre suo, Roberto filio Petri*,[3] *Matheo de Brereclive, Matheo de Bradeley*,[4] et multis aliis.

---

(1) This is the only charter since No. 276 which was abstracted or copied. An abstract of No. 283 c will be found in *Dodsworth*, vol. 135, fo. 129.

(2) Alan succeeded Hugh Pincerna. It may be that Geoffrey Dutton had acted for Hugh Pincerna during some partial disability which preceded his dissolution. All these changes seem to have taken place in 1216.　　　　　　(3) Perhaps Robert Bate of No. 283.

(4) Such is still the local pronunciation of the name.

CCLXXXIII d.　　　　**Carta Willelmi de Vescy.**　　　　1216.

[. . . . . I, William de Vescy . . . . . to William son of Robert Mey, a bovate of land with its appurtenances in Marsden . . . . . To be held and possessed, &c. Three shillings yearly at Pontefract Fair, on the feast of St. Giles . . . . Absolute power of re-entry. Warranty. A mark of silver as fore-gift. Seal. Witnesses.]

Sciant presentes et futuri quod ego Willelmus de Vescy dedi, cóncessi, et presenti carta mea confirmavi Willelmo filio Roberti Mey unam bovatam terre cum pertinentiis in Merkesdena, illam scilicet quam pater suus aliquando de me tenuit in eadem villa. Habendam et tenendam eidem Willelmo et heredibus suis de me et heredibus meis in feudo et heredidate, libere, quiete, bene et in pace, finabiliter. Reddendo inde annuatim mihi et heredibus meis vel assignatis, pro omni servitio et exactione et rebus cunctis, tres solidos in nundinis Pontisfracti, ad festum sancti Egidii[1] sine omni impedimento. Ita quod si ipse vel heredes sui in solutione dictorum trium

---

(1) See No. 230, note (2).

solidorum termino statuto defecerint, licebit mihi et heredibus meis vel assignatis meis terram illam in manum nostram capere, et illam habere sine aliqua reclamatione dicti Willelmi vel heredum suorum. Hanc autem predictam terram cum pertinentiis ego Willelmus et heredes mei vel assignati dicto Willelmo filio Roberti et heredibus suis contra omnes homines inperpetuum warantizabimus. Pro hac autem donatione, concessione, warantizatione, et presentis carte mee confirmatione, dedit mihi dictus Willelmus unam marcam argenti in gersumma. Quod ut firmum sit et stabile presentem cartam sigilli mei appositione roboravi. Hiis testibus, *domino Henrico Walensi, tunc senescallo domini constabularii Cestrie, domino Henrico de Nottinghama,*[2] *persona de Rowella, domino Roberto de Stapiltona, domino Johanne Fituna,*[3] *Ada de Blakeburna, Rogero de Blakeburna, Huctredo de Walleya, Galfrido decano de Walleya,*[4] *Ricardo de Ekeleshill, Symone de Heric,*[5] et aliis. ——————

(2) The full name here is useful.   (3) *Ante*, page 318.

(4) This was the second successive dean of Whalley, father and son of this name, though the published Chartulary, page 1074, seems to distinguish between "Galfrid" the father and Geoffrey the son. This is, however, an error, as may be ascertained by reference to W p. 141, W p. 746, etc. The father married the daughter of Roger de Lascy, and the son married the daughter of Gospatric of Samlesbury (Hospitatus *supra* in No. 240). The deans or parsons of Whalley, it is well known, had a clearly hereditary parsonage, which had existed for ten generations (the pedigree on Whalley, page 1074, gives only nine, but, in that case, a dean is omitted between Robert and William), and we have seen such a hereditary parsonage existing for three generations at Kellington, with attempts to establish one at Darrington. The tenth and last dean of Whalley effected its conversion into an ordinary parsonage by remaining unmarried, and, as a sonless dean, ceding the preferment to Sir John de Lascy, constable of Chester.

(5) De Heriz in W p. 870, and de Herice in W p. 1057.

CCLXXXIII e.   Carta Willelmi de Vescy.   1216.

[. . . . I, William de Vescy, have . . . . . . confirmed to William, son of Robert Mey, a bovate of land with appurtenances in Marsden, that is to say, &c. To be held and possessed, &c. Paying thence yearly, &c. Power to re-enter. Warranty. A mark of silver as fore-gift. Seal. Witnesses.]

Sciant presentes et futuri quod ego, Willelmus de Vesci, dedi, concessi, et presenti carta mea confirmavi, Willelmo filio Roberti Mey, unam bovatam terre cum pertinentiis in Merkesden, illam scilicet quam pater meus[1] aliquando de me tenuit in eadem villa. Habendam et tenendam eidem Willelmo et heredibus suis de me et heredibus meis in feodo et hereditate, libere, quiete, bene et in pace, finabiliter. Reddendo inde annuatim mihi et heredibus meis vel assignatis pro omni servitio et exactione et rebus cunctis tres solidos in nundinis Pontisfracti ad festum sancti Egidii, sine

——————

(1) *Sic*, for "suus."

omni impedimento. Ita quod si ipse vel heredes sui in solutione dictorum trium solidorum termino statuto defecerint, licebit mihi et heredibus meis vel assignatis terram illam in manum nostram capere et illam habere sine aliqua reclamatione dicti Willelmi vel heredum suorum. Hanc autem predictam terram cum pertinentiis ego Willelmus et heredes mei vel assignati dicto Willelmo filio Roberti et heredibus suis contra omnes gentes warantizabimus. Pro hac autem donatione, concessione, warantisatione, et presentis carte mee confirmatione, dedit michi dictus Willelmus unam marcam argenti in gersumam. Quod ut firmum sit et stabile, presentem cartam sigilli mei appositione roboravi. Hiis testibus, *domino Henrico Walensi, tunc senescallo domini constabularii Cestrie, domino Henrico persona de Rowella, domino Roberto de Stapiltona, domino Johanne Fituna, Ada de Blakeburna, Rogero persona de Blakeburna, Huctredo de Walleya,[2] Galfrido decano de Walleya, Ricardo de Ekelishill, Symone de Heric',* et multis aliis.[3]

(2) Uchtred afterwards clerk (W 953) was fourth son of Gospatric or Hospitatus, lord of Samlesbury. In these and similar documents his name generally precedes that of the dean of Whalley.

(3) The monks seem to have obtained three bovates in Great Marsden which, though they might have adjoined, were really separate properties. These were two bovates which had been held by Richard and one which was held by Gamel his son. By No. 8 Robert de Lascy, the younger (who died in 1194), gave to the monks two bovates in Great Marsden which Uhtred formerly held, though this might have been only a confirmation as chief lord of a gift made by William de Vesci. No. 8 is witnessed by William son of Eustace, who as we know was Robert's uncle, that is his mother's brother, and who is frequently said to have been rector of Barwick, as indeed he might have been. But by No. 27 the same Robert de Lascy confirms to William son of Eustace, to whom he there refers as his uncle, at a rent of four pence or its equivalent, a (clearly third) bovate which had belonged to Gamel son of Uhtred. The occasion of these two deeds was probably the death of the former owner or lessee Uhtred; but there is another, No. 29, two generations later, in which Edmund de Lascy (under date 1258) gives Barnside to the monks and confirms to them the two bovates in Marsden, which they had of the gift of William de Vesci. And by No. 230, a second William de Vesci granted to the monks the bovate which Robert Mey had held from him, at the former chief rent of two spurs or four pence. This being witnessed by John de Heck, the date is fixed as not later than 1215. The series No. 283 follows, and welds all into one. All the eight charters (No. 281 to No. 283e) seem to have belonged to the year 1216, which was a year of great changes. It opened with king John on the throne, the aged Hugh Butler seneschal of Pontefract, and Peter the receiver for the convent; while it closed with Henry III. as king, with Sir Henry Wallis as seneschal, and with Walter as receiver; Sir Geoffrey Dutton and Alan the clerk having been seneschals in a temporary capacity in the course of the year. So many official changes probably necessitated, in some way, this numerous collection of charters with regard to this property, for all the documents seem to belong to the year. No. 283 belonged to its early portion, for it bears the name of the old Receiver, Peter; and as they were both tested by Alan the clerk, then seneschal, No. 283c must be coupled with it. On the other hand, Sir Henry Wallis, seneschal, tests No. 283d and No. 283e, on which account those two charters must be ascribed to the close of the year; while No. 283b, No. 283a, and No. 282 with Sir Hugh Butler and Geoffrey Dutton would belong contemporarily to the middle part of the year, having the same witnesses in the same order; Henry parson of Rothwell and Robert de Stapleton of Cudworth, his parishioner, being added to No. 283a and No. 282 to give them increased weight and importance.

DE FERIA.

CCLXXXIIII.   Carta Agnetis filie Rogeri de Ledestona.   Cir. 1216.

[. . . . . . . I, Agnes daughter of Roger de Ledstone, in the full power of my widowhood have demised . . . . . to Emma my sister and her heirs all right and claim in eighteen acres of land and their appurtenances lying in the territory of Ferry, which are of the fee of the Lady Alice Haget: . . . . in name of Final Concord made between us. Seal. Witnesses present.]

Notum sit omnibus hoc scriptum visuris vel audituris, quod ego
Agnes filia Rogeri de Ledestona in viduitatis mee[1] plena potestate
remisi inperpetuum et de me et heredibus meis sine aliquo
retenemento omnino quietum clamavi Emme sorori mee et heredibus
suis omne jus et clamium quod dicebam me habere in decem et
octo acris terre et earum pertinentiis jacentibus in territorio de
Feria, que sunt de feodo domine Alicie Haget; quarum sex acre
jacent juxta Welleclif et x acre jacent in Puthale et due abuttant
super limpit.[2] Has vero predictas xviii acras terre cum earum
pertinentiis remisi prefate E. sorori mee et heredibus suis quietas de
me et heredibus meis et solutas nomine nomine[3] finalis concordie
inter nos confecte, ne ipsa de cetero vel heredes sui aliquid juris
vel clamii de residuo hereditatis mee in posterum possit vendicare.
In cujus rei testimonium hoc scriptum, fide interposita, sigilli mei
munimine roboravi, presentibus hiis testibus, *Waltero receptore,*
Magistro Johanne tunc rectore hospitalis sancti Nicholai,[4] *Johanne de*
Lovain, Johanne Vinitore, Roberto Camberlano, Roberto Walensi,
Henrico filio Ranulfi, Willelmo de Aula, Rogero filio Amabilie,
Johanne filio Michaelis, Thoma de Bateleia, et aliis.

(1) Between her two marriages with (1) William of Parlington and (2) Geoffrey of Ledsham.
See pedigree facing the Fifth Fasciculus.

(2) It is worth while noticing that lime-burning was evidently a well-established industry at
Knottingley and Ferrybridge so early as the date of this charter, the first quarter of the thirteenth
century; and that lime quarries occur several times in the boundary line between Ferrybridge and
Knottingley, as if they had been the position by which the bounds between the two manors had been
originally determined. In each case the quarry belongs to Ferrybridge, the ungot lime being awarded
to Knottingley.   (3) *Sic.*   (4) In No. 285 Master John precedes Walter the receiver.

DE FERIA.

CCLXXXV.[1]   **Carta Agnetis filie Rogeri de Ledestona.**   **Cir. 1216.**

[. . . . . I hold good and valid the sale which Emma my sister, and William
her son and heir, have made to John Vintner of Pontefract, of eighteen acres of
land with their appurtenances lying in the territory of Ferry, which are of the fee
of the Lady Alice Haget. Which the same John afterwards gave to God and the
monks of Pontefract in perpetual alms. . . . . . . Quitclaim. Ten marks of silver.
. . . . . Strengthened by oath. Seals. Witnesses.]

Omnibus hoc scriptum visuris vel audituris salutem.[2] Universitati
vestre notum facio me gratam et ratam habere venditionem quam
Emma soror mea et Willelmus filius suus et heres[3] fecerunt Johanni

(1) No 285 is abstracted in *Dodsworth*, vol. 135.

(2) The name of the grantor is not mentioned in the body of the charter.

(3) William, son of William de Colne. See No. 286.

Vinitori[4] de Pontefracto in decem et octo acris terre cum pertinentiis suis jacentibus in territorio de Feria que sunt de feodo domine Alicie Haget. Quas idem Johannes postea dedit deo et monachis de Pontefracto in perpetuam elemosinam. Insuper ad instanciam et voluntatem Galfridi viri mei,[5] remisi prefatis monachis et omnino de me et heredibus meis, sine aliquo retenemento, inperpetuum quietum clamavi quicquid juris habui vel unquam habere potui in prefatis xviii acras terre et earum pertinentiis. Pro hac vero confirmacione, remissione, et quieta clamatione, dederunt nobis dicti monachi decem marcas argenti pre manibus. Et ne ego prenominata A. vel heredes mei contra hanc confirmationem, remissionem et quietam clamationem in posterum venire possimus, sacramento a nobis corporaliter prestito hoc scriptum sigillorum nostrorum munimine duximus roborandum. Hiis testibus, *domino H. Pincerna tunc senescallo, domino R. de Stapiltona, domino H. Walensi, Willelmo persona de Helage,*[6] *Magistro J. rectore Hospitalis sancti Nicholai,*[7] *Waltero receptore, Johanne de Luvayn, Johanne Vinitor, Henrico filio Ranulfi, Johanne filio Michaelis*, et aliis.

---

(4) John de Batley. See No. 286. This is an interesting example of a change of name such as was quite common in this and the two previous generations; so common, indeed, that it has to be very clearly borne in mind in all attempts to follow up the devolution of property. In this instance, John Vintner, a well-known man by that name, as also by the names of John son of Hugh, and John son of Matilda, suddenly appears in No. 286 and the following charter as John of Batley, whether because Batley was his point of origin, or because he had acquired property there, or for what reason, there is nothing yet to show.

(5) The second husband of the grantor.

(6) That William parson of Healaugh attested several of these charters may be accounted for by the fact that the church of Healaugh was in the Haget patronage.　　(7) See No. 286.

CCLXXXVI.　　Carta Willelmi filii Willelmi de Calna.　　Ante 1215.

[I, William, son of William de. Colne, with the assent of Emma my mother, have given and granted to John de Batley and his heirs, or to whom he may will to assign them, 18 acres of land in the Fields of Ferry. . . . . To be held and possessed, &c. Paying thence yearly to me or my heirs 26 pence, ... and three boon days in autumn, with one man, to the lord of Frystone. Five shillings for acknowledgment. Warranty. Witnesses.]

Willelmus filius Willelmi de Calne, de asensu[1] Emme matris mee, dedi et concessi et hac presenti carta mea confirmavi pro homagio et servitio suo, Johanni de Bateley et heredibus suis vel cui assignare voluerit xviii acras terre in campis de Feria. Quarum sex jacent in una cultura juxta Welleclif, scilicet in cultura Serlonis, et x acre in Puthale in cultura Serlonis abuttantes super montem de

---

(1) *Sic.*

Knottinglay, et ij acre abuttant super Limpith. Tenendas et habendas sibi et heredibus suis vel cui assignare voluerit, libere et quiete, pacifice et integre. Reddendo inde annuatim michi vel heredibus meis xxvi denarios, medietatem ad Pentecosten, et medietatem ad festum Sancti Martini, et tria precaria in autumpno,[1] cum homine uno, domino de Friston. Pro hac autem donatione et concessione dedit mihi dictus Johannes v solidos de recognitione. Et ego Willelmus et heredes mei dicto Johanni et heredibus suis vel cui assignare voluerit dictam terram contra omnes homines warantizabimus. Hiis testibus, *Hugone Pincerna, tunc senescallo, Waltero clerico,*[2] *Henrico filio Ranulfi, Magistro Johanne de Baghil,*[3] *Thoma de Knaresburga, Gregorio de Camera, Alano Noel, Willelmo de Aula,* et aliis.

———

(1) *Sic.*   (2) Not yet receiver.

(3) See No. 285. Comparing No. 285 and No. 286, it would appear that the full title of this Master John was "rector of the hospital of St. Nicholas," suggesting that he was "Master," not by grace of the University degree then coming into fashion, but through the earlier qualification of office.

———

DE FERIA.

CCLXXXVII.   Carta Johannis de Bateley.   **Cir. 1215.**

[. . . . . I, John de Batley, have given . . . . . eighteen acres of land with the appurtenances in Ferry Fields. . . . . To be held and possessed, &c. Paying thence yearly . . . . . twenty-six pence . . . . . and three boon days in autumn with one man to the lord of Frystone. A hundred shillings in silver. Warranty. Witnesses.]

Sciant presentes et futuri quod ego Johannes de Bateleya dedi, concessi, et hac presenti carta mea confirmavi deo et ecclesie sancti Johannis de Pontefracto, et monachis ibidem deo servientibus decem et octo acras terre cum pertinentiis in campis de Feria. Quarum sex jacent in una cultura juxta Welleclif, scilicet in cultura Serlonis, et decem acre in Puthale in cultura Serlonis, abuttantes super montem de Knottinglay, et due acre abuttantes super Limpith. Tenendas et habendas de me et heredibus meis libere, quiete, pacifice, et integre. Reddendo inde annuatim mihi et heredibus meis, vel domino de Fristona, viginti sex denarios, medietatem ad Pentecosten et medietatem ad festum sancti Martini, et tria precaria in autumpno cum uno homine, domino de Fristona.[1] Et pro hac donatione et concessione dederunt mihi predicti monachi pre manibus centum solidos argenti. Ego vero Johannes de Bateley et heredes mei

———

(1) No. 286 and No. 287 are duplicate, except that No. 287 has this additional clause, and another set of witnesses. On the other hand, No. 287 and No. 288 are duplicates, inasmuch as each has the additional clause and these same witnesses ; but No. 288 has a new clause constituting the monks the assigns of the grantor.

warantizabimus predictam terram prefatis monachis contra omnes homines.   Hiis testibus, *Hugone Pincerna tunc senescallo de Pontefracto, Willelmo capellano de Pontefracto, Johanne de Lowayn, Henrico filio Matildis, Roberto Camberlano, Johanne filio Michaelis,*[2] *Ricardo de Martona,* et aliis.   ———

(2) It thus appears that in this group John son of Michael (*i.e.* Michael de Monte) is known also as "Master John of Baghill" and "Master John, rector of St. Nicholas' Hospital."

———

CCLXXXVIII.[1]   Carta Johannis de Bateleya.   Cir. 1215.

[. . . . . . I, John of Batley, have given . . . . . . eighteen acres of land in the Fields of Ferry with their appurtenances, concerning which I have made the aforesaid monks my assigns . . . . . . To be held and possessed, &c.   Paying yearly . . . . 26 pence ; and three boon days in autumn with one man to the lord of Frystone.   The monks have given me a hundred shillings.   Warranty.   Witnesses.]

Sciant presentes et futuri quod ego Johannes de Bateleya dedi, concessi, et hac presenti carta mea confirmavi deo et ecclesie sancti Johannis de Pontefracto et monachis ibidem deo servientibus decem et octo acras terre in campis de Feria cum pertinentiis suis de quibus predictos monachos meos feci assignatos.   Quarum acrarum sex jacent in una cultura juxta Wellesclif, scilicet in cultura Serlonis, et decem acre in Puthala in cultura Serlonis, abuttantes super montem de Knottinglay, et due acre abuttantes super Limpit. Tenendas et habendas de me et heredibus meis libere, quiete, pacifice, et integre.   Reddendo inde annuatim michi et heredibus meis vel domino de Fristona xxvi denarios, medietatem ad Pente- costen et medietatem ad festum sancti Martini, et tria precaria in autumpno cum uno homine, domino de Fristona.   Et pro hac donatione et concessione dederunt mihi predicti monachi pre manibus centum solidos.   Ego vero Johannes de Bateleya et heredes mei warantizabimus predictam terram prefatis monachis contra omnes homines.   Hiis testibus, *Hugone Pincerna tunc senescallo de Pontefracto, Willelmo capellano de Pontefracto,*[2] *Johanne de Lovain, Henrico filio Matildis, Roberto Camberlano, Johanne filio Michaelis, Ricardo de Martona,* et aliis.   ———

(1) Neither No. 286, No. 287, nor No. 288 is represented either in the *Dodsworth* MSS. or in *Lansdowne* 207 A.   (2) Not yet Receiver.

2 E

CCLXXXIX.[1]   Carta Ricardi Walensis.   1248.

[Know, &c., that I, Richard Wallis, for the good of my soul and that of the Lady Alice Haget, my grandmother . . . . . . have granted, and by this my present charter confirmed, &c., those two bovates of land in the territory of Fryston with all their appurtenances, which they have of the gift of William de Fryston, and the mill and the site of the mill which is called Hamelin mill, which they have of the gift of the father of the said William, and all that culture of land which lies next the said mill, which they have similarly of the gift of the said William, with all the pool of that mill, and all the meadow which they have in the territory of Ferry, of the gift of the lord Jordan de St. Mary and the Lady Alice Haget his wife, that is to say the meadow, &c. Also . . . . . . three cultures of land in the Fields of Ferry. . . . . . . All these . . . . . . the said monks shall possess and hold, &c. Warranty. Seal. Date. Witness.]

Sciant presentes et futuri quod ego Ricardus Walensis, pro salute anime mee et domine Alicie Haget[2] avie mee, et omnium

---

(1) No. 289 is transcribed into *Dodsworth*, vol. 151, with a few errors of transcription, and there is an imperfect copy in *Lansdowne* 207 A. No. 289 and the next two are the confirmations of the new lord of Fryston, made on his assumption of his maternal inheritance, and witnessed by his younger brothers. They relate to the properties, new and old, which the monks had acquired in the fee. No. 289 and 290 were given in the lifetime of his father Henry Wallis II, but independently of him, though he was a witness assenting and consenting. In the third the name of the father disappears, that of the younger brother Robert comes forward, and John Vintner appears as John of Batley.

(2) The *inq. p. mort.* of Alice Haget, which is printed in full on page 319, was taken in 31 Henry III (1246–7), and from it we learn that she was the manorial "lord" of Fryston and that she had there six cottars who rendered no rent, but did for her, as lord, work worth 8*s*. 3*d*. Such was the character of the labour done under charter No. 289, three days' work ("precaria" or "boon-days" was the technical name) "for the lord in the time of harvest." The following is the line of descent as proved mainly from the Pontefract Chartulary:—

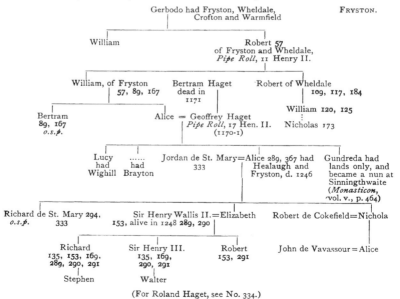

(For Roland Haget, see No. 334.)

antecessorum meorum et heredum meorum, concessi et hac presenti carta mea confirmavi deo et ecclesie sancti Johannis apostoli et evangeliste de Pontefracto et monachis ibidem deo servientibus, in liberam, puram, et perpetuam elemosinam, illas duas bovatas terre in territorio de Fristona cum omnibus pertinentiis suis quas habent ex dono Willelmi de Fristona et molendinum et situm molendini quod vocatur Hamelinemilne, quod habent ex dono patris dicti Willelmi, et totam illam culturam terre que jacet juxta dictum molendinum, quam habent similiter ex dono dicti Willelmi, cum toto stagno ipsius molendini, et totum pratum quod habent in territorio de Feria ex dono domini Jordani de sancta Maria et domine Alicie Haget[3] uxoris sue. Illud scilicet pratum quod jacet inter pratum quod fuit territi[4] de Feria versus suth et pratum Ade Russel versus north, cujus unum capud percutit super Lengelathe et tendit usque ad magnam aquam de Ayr, et illud pratum versus Helliwelle ultra rivulum qui venit de Pontefracto, quod jacet inter pratum abbatis et monachorum de Fontibus - versus north et pratum dicti territi[4] de Feria versus suth, cujus unum capud percutit super pratum hospitalis de Fulsnap et tendit usque ad magnam aquam de Ayr et fordales ejusdem prati qui percutiunt ex una parte super pratum dicti hospitalis, ex alia parte super dictam aquam de Ayr, et ex tertia parte super pratum quod fuit Roberti de Hikeltona[5] et fordales prati de Fristona qui percutiunt ex una parte super rivulum de Fristona,[6] ex alia parte super pratum Agnetis de Merstona. Item ex dono dicte domine Aliz Haget[7] tres culturas terre in campis de Feria, quarum una buttat super viam occidentalem que tendit versus Mundgoie et super Wluedale versus est, et alia buttat super predictam viam et super Howes versus est, et tertia buttat super Torndic versus north, et super Herthesti versus suth. Has omnes supranominatas terras et predictum molendinum et situm ejus et stagnum et omnia prenominata prata cum omnibus pertinentiis suis in bosco, in plano, in pratis et pascuis et pasturis, in aquis et molendinis et piscariis, in introitibus et exitibus, et in omnibus aliis libertatibus et aisiamentis ad prenominatas terras, molendinum, et prata, infra villam et extra et ubicumque pertinentibus, tenebunt et habebunt[8] dicti monachi in liberam, puram et perpetuam elemosinam, in bene[9] et

---

(3) See No. 333.

(4) *Sic* in each case ; the word which ultimately developed into "territorium," signifying the converted "Field" which had as yet no resident population.

(5) Richard of Hickleton and Robert his father are named in *De Prestitis*, p. 190.

(6) "Qui percutiunt ex una parte super rivulum de Fristona" omitted in *Dodsworth*, vol. 151.

(7) See No. 307. (8) "Herebunt" in *Dodsworth*, vol. 151. (9) *Sic.*

pace, libere, quiete, pacifice, et honorifice, sine contradictione, gravamine, vel impedimento mei vel heredum meorum. Ego vero Ricardus et heredes mei omnia supranominata cum omnibus pertinentiis suis sicut predictum est dictis monachis contra omnes homines warantizabimus, et ab omnibus servitiis secularibus et demandis adquietabimus· et defendemus inperpetuum. Et ut hec mea concessio et confirmatio perpetue firmitatis robur optineat, presenti scripto tam pro me quam pro heredibus meis sigillum meum apposui in testimonium. Actum anno ab incarnatione millessimo ducentesimo quadragesimo octavo, mensi Aprili.[10] Hiis testibus, *domino Henrico Walensi patre meo, domino Adam de Everingham, domino Roberto de Stapiltona, domino Henrico fratre meo, Johanne de Smithetona, Gregorio de Camera, Roberto et Nicholao de Knaresburga, Willelmo de Fetherstana,* et aliis. _____

(10) In Domesday, Wheldale and Fryston were reckoned together as one carucate, which was probably in Wheldale, where there was a church. But in this group of charters we have Fryston gravitating towards Ferry (bridge) and both the subject of the same instrument. No. 57, *i.e.*, the legatine confirmation of the conventual possessions at its date, names only those in Fryston, as given in No. 289, but adds two details to the catalogue, (1) that Hamelin mill was the gift of William's father "Robert," and (2) that the "culture" next the mill contained three acres. The remaining acquisitions as named in No. 289 are therefore all of a later date, the meadow in the Fields of Ferry given by Jordan de St. Mary and Alice his wife, the three cultures in the same Fields, Alice's gift as a widow, and also the eighteen acres in those Fields which John of Batley sold to them (see No. 90), and the bovate in the territory of Fryston given by Nicholas son of Ralph (see No. 294) to William Marshall, by whom (see No. 295) it was conveyed to the monks, being all of a subsequent date.

_____

CCLXXXX.[1]   **Carta Ricardi Walensis.**

[. . . . . . I, Richard Wallis, son of Henry Wallis, ... a bovate of land in the territory of Fryston . . . . . . To be held and possessed, &c. Paying annually . . . . . . sixpence. Seal. Witnesses.]

Sciant presentes et futuri quod ego Ricardus Walensis filius Henrici Walensis, pro salute anime mee et domine Alicie Haget avie mee, et omnium antecessorum et heredum meorum, concessi et hac presenti carta mea confirmavi deo et ecclesie sancti Johannis apostoli et evangeliste de Pontefracto et monachis ibidem deo servientibus, unam bovatam terre in territorio de Fristona, cum omnibus pertinentiis suis. Illam scilicet quam Nicholaus filius Ranulfi de Fristona dedit quondam Willelmo Marescallo et quam idem Willelmus postea dedit dictis monachis cum corpore suo. Tenendam et habendam prefatis monachis in perpetuam elemosinam, libere, quiete, pacifice, et honorifice, sine aliqua contradictione, gravamine vel impedimento mei vel heredum meorum, inperpetuum,

_____

(1) There is an abstract of No. 290 in *Lansdowne* 207 A, and another in *Dodsworth*, vol. 136.

cum omnibus aisiamentis, libertatibus, liberis consuetudinibus et pertinentiis ad dictam bovatam terre infra villam et extra et ubique pertinentibus. Reddendo inde annuatim heredibus predicti Nicholai sex denarios, medietatem ad Pentecosten et alteram medietatem ad festum sancti Martini pro omnibus servitiis secularibus et demandis. Et ut hec mea concessio et confirmatio perpetue firmitatis robur optineat presenti scripto tam pro me quam pro heredibus meis sigillum meum apposui. Hiis testibus, *domino Henrico Walensi patre meo, domino Henrico fratre meo, Gregorio de Camera, Roberto et Nicholao de Knaresburga, Johanne Vinetario, Ricardo Seman,* et aliis.

CCLXXXXI[1]   Carta Ricardi Walensis.

[. . . . . . I, Richard Wallis . . . . . . eighteen acres of land in the Fields of Ferry . . . . . which John of Batley formerly sold to them. To be held and possessed, &c. Paying yearly twenty-six pence. Warranty. Seal. Witnesses.]

Sciant presentes et futuri quod ego Ricardus Walensis, pro salute anime mee et domine Aliz Haget avie mee et omnium antecessorum et heredum meorum, concessi et hac presenti carta mea confirmavi deo et ecclesie sancti Johannis apostoli et evangeliste de Pontefracto et monachis ibidem deo servientibus, illas decem et octo acras terre in campis de Feria cum omnibus pertinentiis suis quas Johannes de Bateleya eis antea vendidit.[2] Quarum sex acre jacent in una cultura juxta Welleclif, scilicet in cultura Serlonis; et decem acre in ·Puthale in cultura Serlonis abuttantes super montem de Knottinglay; et due acre abuttantes super limpit. Tenendas et habendas dictis monachis de me et heredibus meis in perpetuam elemosinam, libere, quiete, pacifice et honorifice, cum omnibus pertinentiis suis infra villam et extra, sine aliquo retenemento vel contradictione, gravamine vel impedimento mei vel heredum meorum. Reddendo inde annuatim mihi et heredibus meis viginti et sex denarios, scilicet ad Pentecosten tresdecem denarios et ad festum sancti Martini tresdecem denarios pro omnibus servitiis, sectis, consuetudinibus, et secularibus demandis. Ego vero Ricardus et heredes mei predictas decem et octo acras terre cum omnibus pertinentiis, libertatibus, et aisiamentis suis dictis monachis contra omnes homines warantizabimus et per predictum servitium adquietabimus in omnibus et defendemus inperpetuum. In cujus rei testimonium huic scripto tam pro me quam pro heredibus

---

(1) There is an abstract of No. 291 in *Lansdowne* 207 A, and in *Dodsworth*, vol. 136.

(2) See No. 288 *ante*.

meis sigillum meum apposui.   Hiis testibus, *domino Waltero de Ludham tunc senescallo de Pontefracto, domino Henrico et Roberto*[3] *fratribus meis, Johanne de Bateleya, Gregorio de Camera, Willelmo filio Helye, Ricardo Seman,* et aliis.

(3) The future vicar, on the presentation of the lady Alice his grandmother, instituted in October, 1248, after her death, and six months after the execution of this deed. See *ante,* p. 320. It is noteworthy that in No. 291 he makes no claim to be vicar.

CCLXXXXII.[1]   **Carta Alani de Thornhil.**   **Cir. 1240.**

[. . . . . . . I, Alan of Thornhill, ... have confirmed to Hugh Parker· of Pontefract and Alice ¯his wife two acres of land with the appurtenances in the Fields of Featherstone. . . . . To be held and possessed, &c.   Paying thence . . . . six pence yearly. . . . . Two marks of silver in hand.   Warranty. Seal.   Witnesses.]

Sciant presentes et futuri quod ego Alanus de Thornhilla, dedi, concessi, et hac presenti carta confirmavi Hugoni Parcario de Pontefracto et Alicie uxori sue duas acras terre cum pertinentiis in campis de Fetherstana, que quidem jacent in[ter] terram Willelmi filii Hode et terram meam, extendentes a via de Fetherstana versus parcum de Pontefracto.   Tenendas et habendas de me et de heredibus meis eisdem Hugoni et Alicie et eorundem heredibus vel assignatis, et maxime predicte Alicie et heredibus suis vel cuicumque assignaverit, si Hugo vir ejus ante ipsam in fata[2] discesserit, libere, quiete, integre, honorifice et pacifice inperpetuum.   Reddendo inde annuatim mihi et heredibus meis sex denarios ad duos terminos, videlicet tres denarios ad Pentecosten et tres denarios ad festum sancti Martini, pro omni seculari servitio et demanda.   Pro hac autem donatione, concessione, et presentis carte confirmatione, dederunt mihi predicti Hugo et Alicia duas marcas argenti pre manibus.   Ego vero Alanus et heredes mei predictam terram predictis Hugoni et Alicie et eorum heredibus vel assignatis secundum quod superius dictum est pro predicto servitio in omnibus et contra omnes warantizabimus et adquietabimus inperpetuum.   In cujus rei testimonium presens scriptum sigilli mei appositione roboravi.   Hiis testibus, *Roberto filio Ernisii, Roberto de Knarisburga, Willelmo filio Helye, Ricardo filio Radulfi, Roberto Mariscallo,*[3] *Reginaldo clerico,* et aliis.

(1) No. 245, a charter from Henry Fresel, is built upon the same lines as No. 292, though the quantity of land, the amount paid, and other particulars vary curiously.   The two apparently refer to different portions of the same property.   (2) *Sic ;* "fatis" in No. 300.   (3) *Sic.*

FETHERSTAN.

CCLXXXXIII.[1]   Carta Tibbe filie Johannis de Fetherstana.   Cir. 1235.

[. . . . . I, Tibba, daughter of John of Featherstone, ... have confirmed
. . . . . to Alice my sister . . . . . my right and claim . . . . . in a toft . . . . in the
town of Featherstone. . . . . . Half a mark of silver. Seal. Witnesses.]

Sciant presentes et futuri quod ego Tibba filia Johannis[2] de
Fethirstana dedi, concessi, quietum clamavi de me et heredibus
meis, et hac presenti carta mea confirmavi Alicie sorori mee et
heredibus suis, vel cuicumque assignare voluerit, totum jus et clamium
quod habui, et quod habere potui, in uno tofto cum pertinentiis
in villa de Fetherstana, continente in latitudine tres perticatas et in
longitudine undecim perticatas, quod quidem toftum jacet inter
croftum Nicholai de Fethirstana et toftum Johannis quondam
patris mei. Pro hac autem donatione, concessione, quieta clamatione,
et presentis carte confirmatione, dedit mihi dicta Alicia dimidiam
marcam argenti pre manibus. Et ne ego Tibba nec heredes mei in
dicto tofto nec in suis pertinentiis aliquid juris vel clamii de cetero
vendicare possimus, hoc presens scriptum sigilli mei appositione
corroboravi. Hiis testibus, *Jacobo de Medelay, Henrico de Medelay,
Radulfo de Fethirstana, Henrico Fresel, Willelmo de Fethirstana,
Radulfo filio Ricardi, Petro filio Godefridi, Nicholao de Fethirstana,
Henrico fratre suo*, et aliis.   ———

(1) The group of Durward charters is continued in No. 308.
(2) Son of Durward. See No. 280, No. 308, and No. 309.

FRISTONA.

CCLXXXXIIII.[1]   Carta Nicholai filii Radulfi.   Cir. 1226.

[Heading supplied by a modern hand.]

[. . . . I, Nicholas son of Ralph of Frystone, ... have confirmed to Ralph
chaplain of Rawcliffe, a bovate of land in the town of Frystone . . . . To be
held, &c. Paying . . . . . . six pence for all service. . . . . Three marks and a
half, and to Alice my wife three shillings. Warranty. Witnesses.]

Sciant presentes et futuri quod ego Nicholaus filius Radulfi de
Fristona dedi et concessi et hac presenti carta mea confirmavi
Radulfo capellano de Radeclive unam bovatam terre in villa de
Fristona cum pertinentiis. Scilicet talem bovatam qualem ecclesia
de Friston tenet excepto tofto. Tenendam sibi vel cui assignare
voluerit, in feudo et hereditate, libere, quiete, pacifice, et integre.
Reddendo inde annuatim mihi et heredibus meis sex denarios pro

(1) This charter, which gives a not unusual instance of a married woman having a separate purse,
is a confirmation of the original grant, which we shall come to directly, in No. 298.

omni servitio, scilicet tres denarios ad Pentecosten et tres denarios ad festum sancti Martini, faciendo forinsecum servitium quantum pertinet ad unam bovatam terre in villa de Fristona. Pro ista vero donatione et confirmatione dedit mihi predictus Radulfus de recognitione iij marcas et dimidiam et Alicie uxori mee iij solidos. Et ego Nicholaus filius Radulfi et heredes mei predicto Radulfo capellano vel assignatis ejus predictam bovatam terre cum pertinentiis contra omnes homines warantizabimus. Hiis testibus, *Johanne de Byrkin, Jordano de Sancta Maria, Marmeduc Darel, Henrico Walensi, Ricardo de Sancta Maria,*[2] *Ricardo filio Astini, Willelmo filio Uchredi, Willelmo proph'a,*[3] *Petro de Feria, Symone Marescallo, Roberto Camerario,* et aliis.   ———

(2) See No. 298, note (5).

(3) See No. 298. There was a William chaplain of Frystone and a William chaplain of the chapel (of Wheldale), and a William, clerk of St. Andrew's (Frystone). The title "propheta" occurs also in No. 333.

———

CCLXXXXV.[1]   Carta Willelmi filii Hamerici de Withewode.   Cir. 1230.

[. . . . . . I, William son of Hameric of Whitwood, ... have confirmed . . . . . . Robert son of Robert Moses, my native, of the Mere, ... Warranty. Witnesses.]

Sciant presentes et futuri quod ego Willelmus filius Hamerici de Withewode dedi, concessi, et presenti carta mea confirmavi deo et sancto Johanni de Pontefracto et monachis ibidem deo servientibus in puram et perpetuam elemosinam Robertum filium Roberti Mose nativum meum de Mara cum tota sequela sua que de eo iam exiit vel postea exire poterit, et cum catallis suis. Et ego prefatus Willelmus et heredes mei warentizabimus prefatis monachis predictum Robertum cum tota sequela sua et catallis suis ubique et contra omnes homines. Hiis testibus, *Willelmo filio Everardi, Ricardo Lond',*[2] *Jacobo de Medeley, Ranulfo de Castelforda, Ada filio Serlonis, Johanne filio Michaelis, Johanne filio Ricardi de Stagno, Ricardo de Martona, Willelmo Cusyn,* et aliis.

———

(1) No. 295, in conjunction with No. 252, affords a singular and striking illustration of the condition of a "nativus adscriptus glebæ"—a slave born and belonging to the land,—and of the manner in which his servile condition was being ameliorated. This charter shows the condition of Robert son of Robert to have been absolutely servile, for he was handed over like a bale of goods; while No. 252 shows both himself and his brother Peter as holding land and capable of selling his right thereto to the monks. It shows, moreover, how a paternal name was gradually becoming a surname, for in the body of No. 252 itself the grantor is called Robertus filius "Roberti filii Mose;" but in its somewhat later heading he is styled Robertus filius "Roberti Mose."

(2) Lond' in Chartulary, but extended to "de Londoniis" in No. 260.

STUBBS.

CCLXXXXVI.[1]   Carta Theobaldi de Stubbis.   **Cir. 1240.**

[. . . . . I, Theobald de Stubbs, ... have confirmed . . . . . . a site in the town of Stubbs which lies next the land which Otto my uncle formerly gave to them and my culture which is called Athelstan's croft ; having in length 114 feet, and in breadth at one head 62 feet and at the other head 18 feet. Moreover I confirm to them the gift of O., my uncle, ... with common, &c. To be held and possessed, &c. Witnesses].

Sciant presentes et futuri quod ego Theobaldus de Stubbis dedi, concessi et hac presenti carta mea confirmavi deo et ecclesie sancti Johannis de Pontefracto et monachis ibidem deo servientibus quandam placiam in villa de Stubbis que jacet juxta terram quam Otto avunculus meus eis prius dederat et culturam meam que vocatur Adelstancroft, habentem in longitudine centum et xiiij pedes et in latitudine ad unum capud lx et duos pedes et ad aliud capud xviij pedes.   Insuper confirmo eis donationem illam quam prefatus O. avunculus meus eis prius dederat, pro salute anime mee et omnium antecessorum meorum, cum communis et aliis aisiamentis predictis terris pertinentibus.   Tenendam et habendam de me et heredibus meis in puram et perpetuam elemosinam inperpetuum.   Hiis testibus, *domino Jordano Folioth, Ricardo filio suo,*[2] *Gaufrido de Nortona, Symone filio suo, Henrico Butel', Roberto filio Ottonis, Alano filio Josien, Alano filio Ranulfi, Ricardo de Martona,* et aliis.

---

(1) Theobald was the son of Henry, son of William the soldier, son of Walding ; and of the third generation from the time of King Stephen, to which Walding belongs. As Otto also was the son of William (see pedigree under No. 101), Theobald the grantor and Robert the witness were cousins.

(2) There were probably two Richards, this being the father of the Richard on the pedigree facing Fasciculus Four.

SWINLINGTONA.

CCLXXXXVII.   Carta Thome Campiun.   1192.

[. . . . . I, Thomas Campion, have confirmed . . . . . an acre of land and half a rood in Swillington . . . . and a rood and a half at Millcliff, and another rood and a half before the gate of Matilda Painel. . . . . . Warranty. Witnesses.]

Omnibus sancte matris ecclesie filiis Thomas Campio salutem. Sciatis me concessisse, dedisse, et presenti carta mea confirmasse deo et sancto Johanni et monachis de Pontefracto ibidem deo servientibus, in puram et perpetuam elemosinam, unam acram terre et medietatem unius rode in Swinlingtona, quas Henricus Kalz tenuit, et unam rodam et dimidiam ad Milneclif, et aliam rodam et dimidiam ante ostium Matildis Painel, sicut pura elemosina melius et liberius potest dari.   Et ego et heredes mei de omnibus servitiis secularibus adquietabimus et warentizabimus predictam terram prefatis monachis de Pontefracto erga dominum regem et erga dominos meos et erga omnes homines. Hiis testibus, *Ivone tunc senescalio domini Roberti de Lasci, Thoma filio Petri, Petro de Ardingtona, Willelmo filio Everardi, Johanne de Kellingtona, tunc decano de Pontefracto,*[1] *Thoma et Ada filiis suis, Moyse fratre predicti Johannis, Symone de Rughal, Ada de Birum, Ricardo de Suttona, Radulfo fratre Baldewini de Bramhope,* et aliis.

(1) Formerly vicar of Kellington. His brother Henry had probably succeeded him in that vicarage, to be followed later on by Thomas and Alexander. The following seems to be the line of descent of this family:—

? John   KELLINGTON.

Ralph=Amabel	John rector [1185] of	Henry	Simon	Alexander	Roger	Moses
Fines, 3 John	Kellington 107; dean	107, 228,	107, 271	228	216, 226,	107, 228,
(1202)	of Pontefract [1192]	[1189] 248,			231, 232	271, 297
	208, 228, 271, 297	271				

Thomas [1202] S 925, 220, 232

Alexander S 381, 232, 550

Adam vicar of Darrington [c. 1200], 28, 99, 220; Master, 95, 98, 100, 179, 212, 525

DE FRISTONA.

CCLXXXXVIII.[1]   **Carta Willelmi Marescalli de Fristona.**   Cir. 1230.

[. . . . . I, William Marshall, of Frystone, have . . . . confirmed, &c., with my body, a bovate of land in the town of Frystone. That is to say, that which Nicholas son of Ralph of Frystone gave to me for my homage and service. To be held and possessed, &c. Paying, &c., six pence for every secular service or demand . . . . And I have assigned this bovate of land to the said monks to make my anniversary, which Sigereda of Frystone shall hold from the said monks, only for her life and not hereditarily, paying them yearly four pence. Seal. Witnesses.]

Sciant presentes et futuri quod ego Willelmus Marescallus de Fristona dedi, concessi et hac presenti carta mea confirmavi deo et ecclesie sancti Johannis de Pontefracto et monachis ibidem deo servientibus, pro salute anime mee et omnium antecessorum meorum, cum corpore meo, unam bovatam terre in villa de Fristona; illam scilicet quam Nicholaus filius Ranl' de Fristona dedit mihi[2] pro homagio et servicio meo. Tenendam et habendam prefatis monachis in perpetuam elemosinam cum omnibus pertinentiis suis, salvo forinseco servitio, domino capitali pertinenti. Reddendo inde annuatim heredibus dicti Nicholai sex denarios pro omni servitio seculari vel demanda, medietatem ad festum sancti Martini et alteram medietatem ad Pentecosten. Hanc vero bovatam terre assignavi dictis

(1) No. 298, read with No. 290 and No. 294, shows how the monks profited by the right of sepulture granted to them (No. 65) by Pope Celestine III, about 1192. It was evidently a valuable privilege and the means of their obtaining valuable grants. The hint contained in the second clause of No. 290 indicates how the "church of Fryston" was induced to permit a parishioner of that parish to be removed for burial with the monks at Pontefract.   (2) See No. 294.

monachis ad anniversarium meum faciendum, quam Sygereda de Fristona[3] tenebit de predictis mónachis tantummodo in vita sua et non hereditarie, reddendo eisdem annuatim iiij*or* denarios in die sancti Johannis ewangeliste infra Nathale domini.   In hujus vero rei testimonium huic scripto sigillum meum apposui.   Hiis testibus, *Domino Willelmo persona de Helaga, Johanne*[4] *persona de Fristona, Nicholao de Queldala, Willelmo capellano de Fristona, Willelmo capellano de capella, Willelmo dispensatore, Willelmo filio Huctredi, Ivone de Frikel', Willelmo clerico, B' Ricardo de Sancta Maria,*[5] *Radulfo de Helaga, Willelmo clerico de S. Andrea,*[6] et aliis.

---

(3) The wife of William Marshall. No. 511 will inform us that this Sigereda, who retained a life interest in the bovate, was the widow of the donor William Marshall and that she re-married with Roger son of Matilda of Frystone.

(4) A subsequent William de Feugers was instituted in 1238. See *ante*, page 320.

(5) He would appear to have died between the grant and this confirmation. Richard de St. Mary, apparently the only son of Jordan de St. Mary and his wife Alice Haget, witnessed No. 333, and No. 294 also, but not No. 290, the latest of the group. The B' may be a clerk's error, but looks as if he actually witnessed the present document and died so immediately after the transaction as to lead the clerk to prefix B' for Beatus to his name. I have met with no similar example. As an only son, this young man, like his grandmother's brother Bertram, must have had great hopes centred in him, and his early death, like that of Bertram, passed the manor into another name. He must, however, have been soon forgotten, for he is not even catalogued in the genealogical scheme on the first page of the Healaugh Chartulary to which I have before made reference, in note (2) to No. 289 ; like Thomas de Reineville son of Adam Vetus, he passed, with his death, beyond the horizon of the monks. The Hagets had lands at Towton also, for on 27 June, 1196, there was a fine at Westminster between Ralph Haket, p., and Oliver Haket and Baldwin Haket, his brother-tenants, of three virgates of land with their appurtenances in Towton. Ralph granted to the tenants by paying a "nisus sorus," or "sore hawk," at the Feast of St. Kenelm (*Pipe Rolls*, vol. xvii.). See also No. 334.

(6) William, clerk of St. Andrew, was clerk of Frystone, that church being dedicated to St. Andrew. He was William de Feugers, instituted on the ides of January, 1238, on the presentation of Alice Haget. It may be noted that at least five clerical Williams witnessed the document.

FETHERSTANA.

CCLXXXXIX.[1]   Carta Alicie filie Johannis de Fetherstana.   Cir. 1235.

[. . . . . I, Alice, daughter of John of Featherstone, have . . . . . confirmed to Hugh, son of Ralph of Methley, a toft in the town of Featherstone, containing in breadth three perches of land and in length eleven perches. To be held and possessed, &c.   Paying, &c.   Twenty four shillings in hand.   Warranty.   Seal. Witnesses.]

Sciant presentes et futuri quod ego Alicia filia Johannis[2] de Fetherstana dedi, concessi, et hac presenti carta mea confirmavi Hugoni filio Radulfi de Medeleia unum toftum in villa de Fetherstana jacens inter toftum Johannis quondam patris mei et toftum Nicholai de Fetherstana, continens in latitudine tres perticatas terre et in longitudine undecim perticatas.   Tenendum et habendum illi et heredibus suis vel cui assignare voluerit de me et heredibus meis libere, quiete, plenarie, et integre, cum omnibus pertinentiis suis

---

(1) I have met with neither abstract nor copy of any charter from No. 290 to No. 299.
(2) Son of Durward. See No. 293.

et aisiamentis, in campis, pratis, pascuis, et turbariis, infra villam et extra. Reddendo inde annuatim mihi et heredibus meis unum denarium ad Nathale domini, pro omni servicio seculari, exactione et demanda. Pro hac autem donatione, concessione et presentis carte confirmatione, dedit mihi dictus Hugo viginti quatuor solidos pre manibus. Ego vero Alicia et heredes mei predictum toftum cum pertinentiis suis predicto Hugoni et heredibus suis vel suis assignatis pro predicto servitio, in omnibus et contra omnes homines, warantizabimus inperpetuum et defendemus. Ut autem hec mea donatio, concessio et presentis carte confirmacio robur perpetue firmitatis optineat, hoc presens scriptum sigilli mei munimine corroboravi. Hiis testibus, *Jacobo de Medelaya, Henrico de Methelaya, Radulfo de Fetherstana, Willelmo de Fetherstana, Radulfo filio Ricardi, Petro filio Godefridi, Nicholao de Fetherstana, Henrico Fresel,* et aliis.

CCC.[1]   **Carta Pigoti de Brettona.**   **Cir. 1210.**

[. . . . . I, Pigot de Bretton, have demised [and] granted to Serlo de Bretton the land which I had given to my daughter Agnes in marriage, in the town of Bretton, namely 7 acres and a half, to be held for his life, from me and my heirs as long as he shall live. Paying yearly six pence, for every service, &c. He shall do forinsec service, namely a half-penny when the scutage shall happen. Witnesses.]

Sciant presentes et futuri quod ego Pigotus de Brettona demisi, concessi Serloni de Brettona terram quam dederam filie mee Agneti in maritagium in villa de Brettona, scilicet vij acras et dimidiam, in vita sua tenendam de me vel de heredibus meis quamdiu vixerit. Reddendo annuatim vi denarios pro omni servitio mihi vel heredibus meis, scilicet tres denarios ad Pentecosten et iij denarios ad festum sancti Martini ; forinsecum autem servitium faciet, scilicet obolum cum scutagium advenerit. Et sciendum est quod cum prefatus Serlo in fatis[2] discesserit hec eadem terra redibit et quieta remanebit in perpetuum mihi vel heredibus meis de predicto Serlone et de heredibus suis. Hiis testibus, *Johanne de Birkina, Hugone de Stivetuna, Ricardo de Hudlestuna, Ottone de Barkestuna, Willelmo de Rither, Johanne filio ejus, Willelmo de Reinevilla,*[3] *Osberto de Brettona, Jordano de la Landa, Willelmo de Lasci,* et multis aliis.[4]

---

(1) There is an abstract of No. 300 in *Dodsworth*, vol. 136, where, however, it is miscalled No. 310. But this charter seems to have been altogether misplaced. It belongs to the series No. 332, &c., in the Eighth Fasciculus.   (2) " Fata " in No. 292.

(3) The first-born of Adam Vetus, according to the Kirkstall Chartulary. See pedigree facing this Fasciculus.   (4) See forward, No. 333 and others.

De Lincoln.

CCCI.[1]   Carta Eue filie Hugonis de Bobi.[2]   1218.

[. . . . . I, Eva, daughter of Hugh de Boby, widow of Thomas de Reineville, in the full and free power of my widowhood, have . . . . . confirmed, for the good of my soul and that of my lord Thomas de Reineville . . . . a rent of ten shillings yearly . . . . . . To be held and possessed, &c. And this rent I the said Eva have specially assigned to the infirmary of the monks for the healing and curing of those who suffer in health of body, that by the oversight of the subprior of the said house, as much as may suffice may be distributed discreetly to those who have need. Warranty. Seal. Witnesses.]

Sciant presentes et futuri quod ego Eva filia Hugonis de Bobi, quondam uxor Thome de Reinevilla, in viduitatis mee plena et libera potestate, dedi, concessi, et hac presenti carta mea confirmavi, pro salute anime mee et domini mei Thome de Reinevilla et omnium antecessorum et heredum meorum, deo et ecclesie sancti Johannis de Pontefracto et monachis ibidem deo servientibus, redditum decem solidorum annuatim ad duos terminos per manus Petri de Wikeford[3] et heredum suorum percipiendorum, medietatem ad festum sancti Michaelis et medietatem ad Pascha, videlicet de terra quam Gillebertus Le W. . .der[4] tenuit de me in parochia sancti Johannis apostoli et evangeliste in Lincolnia, de feodo comitis d'd',[5] que jacet inter vicum domini regis[6] et terram Johannis de Mere. Tenendum et habendum prefatis monachis de me et heredibus meis in liberam, puram et perpetuam elemosinam. Hunc vero redditum ego dicta Eva specialiter assignavi infirmario monachorum ad illorum reparationes et curationes qui corporis in valetudine laborant ut per visum supprioris dicte domus hiis qui necesse habent in quantum sufficere potest discrete distribuatur. Et ego prefata Eva et heredes mei predictum redditum x solidorum contra omnes homines warantizabimus inperpetuum ac defendemus. In cujus rei testimonium huic scripto sigillum meum apposui. Hiis testibus, *Henrico Walensi tunc*

---

(1) There is a copy of No. 301 in *Dodsworth*, vol. 151. This charter is not earlier than 1218, for at its date Thomas de Reineville was dead, and he died that year. Moreover, as Henry Wallis, who here signs as seneschal, had been succeeded by Robert de Kent in the summer (for the latter was then so acting for his lord at Damietta), this charter may safely be assigned to the early part of the year.

(2) Hugh de Boby, the father of Eva, was of Boothby, in Lincolnshire. He had been vice-sheriff of Yorkshire, 4-6 Richard I (1192-4), and sheriff of Lincolnshire in part of 1 John (1199).

(3) "Ballium" in No. 302.

(4) The word "W...der" is written over a defect in the membrane, but in No. 151 the two omitted letters are supplied as "ar" with no hesitation.

(5) The earl is described as "dd',"—a symbol which has occurred in No. 265, and seems to stand for David. The charter appears to belong to the short vacancy after Gilbert de Gaunt the younger. There was no earl David of Lincoln.

(6) Miscopied "Rogeri" in 151.

senescallo, Johanne de Rowecestre[7] tunc constabulario, Gregorio de Camera, Willelmo de Alretona, Johanne filio Michaelis, Henrico filio Ranulfi, Ricardo de Martona, et aliis.

(7) In Staffordshire. There was at Rocester a convent of Augustinian canons, founded by Richard de Bacon, a nephew of Ranulf, earl of Chester.

LINCOLN.

CCCII.[1]   Carta Ade de Rainevill filii Eve de Boby.   1232-8.

[. . . . . . I, Adam de Reineville, son of Eva de Boby, have . . . . . confirmed . . . . . a rent of ten shillings in the town of Lincoln; namely in Wickford in the parish of St. John the Evangelist . . . . . Warranty. Seal. Witnesses.]

Sciant presentes et futuri quod ego Adam de Rainevilla filius Eve de Boby[2] concessi et hac presenti carta mea confirmavi deo et ecclesie sancti Johannis ewangeliste de Pontefracto et monachis ibidem deo servientibus pro salute anime mee et omnium antecessorum et heredum meorum redditum decem solidorum in villa Lincolnie, scilicet in Wikeford in parochia sancti Johannis evangeliste, annuatim percipiendorum per manus Petri de Ballio[3] et heredum suorum, medietatem ad pascha et medietatem ad festum sancti Michaelis. Quem redditum Eva de Boby predicta mater mea in sua viduitate et plena potestate eisdem monachis in puram et perpetuam elemosinam antea dederat. Ego vero Adam et heredes mei dictum redditum decem solidorum dictis monachis contra omnes homines inperpetuum warantizabimus ac defendemus. Et ne ego vel heredes mei contra tenorem huius carte in posterum venire possimus eam sigilli mei munimine roboravi. Hiis testibus, *domino Ada de Neirforda tunc[4] senescallo de Pontefracto, domino Roberto de Stapiltona, Willelmo de Longo Campo, Ricardo fratre ejus, Roberto Walensi, Johanne de Lowain, Johanne Vinitore, Roberto filio Ernis, Willelmo filio Helye,* et aliis.

(1) There is an abstract of No. 302 in *Lansdowne* 207 A ; and another, in some respects fuller, in others not so full, in *Dodsworth*, vol. 136.

(2) The *inq. p. mort.* of Thomas de Reineville, the deceased husband of Eva, was taken in 1218, so that these two charters are of at least a later date ; the second probably either at the death of Eva the grantor, his widow, or at the coming of age of Adam their son. Thomas de Reineville was the eldest son of Adam (Vetus), and for a long series of years was his constant attendant and co-witness, but as he died before his father he never succeeded to the inheritance or to a share in it, and his personality came to be almost entirely overlooked by the genealogists. Of this I have met with many very curious instances.   (3) "Wickford" in No. 301.   (4) 1232-8.

ALRETON.

CCCIII.[1]   Carta Rogeri de Tornetona.   Cir. 1246.

[. . . . . . I, Roger de Thornton, have . . . . . . confirmed . . . . . all my right and claim . . . . . . in all the tenement which Robert, brother of Robert the Smith,

(1) There is an abstract of No. 303 in *Dodsworth*, vol. 136.

has held of me in the territory of Allerton, namely that assart which lies between Clitheroegate and Foxroyd, and between Murewell and Esterlick.   And the aforesaid Robert and his heirs shall hold of the monks, &c.   Paying thence yearly to the aforesaid monks 12 pence . . . . . Warranty.. Eight shillings of silver.   Seal.   Witnesses.]

Sciant presentes et futuri quod ego Rogerus de Tornetona dedi, concessi, et hac presenti carta mea confirmavi deo et sancto Johanni evangeliste et monachis de Pontefracto, in puram et perpetuam elemosinam, pro salute anime mee et Aliz uxoris mee et omnium antecessorum et heredum meorum, totum jus et clamium quod habui vel habere potui ego vel heredes mei in toto tenemento quod Robertus frater Roberti Fabri de me tenuit in territorio de Alretona,[2] videlicet illud assartum quod jacet inter Kliderowgate et Foxrode et inter Murewelli et esterlic.   Predictus vero Robertus et heredes sui totum predictum tenementum de predictis monachis tenebunt in feudo et hereditate, libere et quiete, in bosco et plano, in pratis et paschuis, et in omnibus aisiamentis, libertatibus, et communibus[3] predicte ville de Alretona pertinentibus.   Reddendo inde annuatim predictis monachis xii denarios, scilicet vi denarios ad festum sancti Martini et vi denarios ad Pentecosten, pro omni servitio et exactione et demanda.   Ego vero Rogerus et heredes mei warantizabimus predictis monachis totam terram prenominatam cum omnibus libertatibus predictis et pertinentiis contra omnes homines.   Pro hac vero donatione et concessione et confirmatione dederunt mihi predicti monachi viii solidos argenti de recognitione.   Et ne ego Rogerus de Tornetona vel heredes mei contra hanc meam donationem, concessionem et firmationem in posterum venire possimus, presenti scripto sigillum meum apposui in testimonium.   Hiis testibus, *Hugone Pincerna tunc temporis senescallo, Roberto de Stapiltona, Willelmo de Swinlingtona, Symone Wart, Willelmo Scoto,*[4] *Ivone de Madeley, Roberto de Hortona,*[5] *Helia de Oxenope, Jordano de Hawrthe, Ricardo de Martona,* et aliis. ———

(2) Near Bradford.   (3) *Sic.*

(4) Of Calverley.   He married Insella, a second cousin half removed from this grantor.   See pedigree under the next charter.

(5) Son of Hugh de Stapleton, who assumed the name of Horton.   He died in 1246.   See his inquisition under No. 304.

CCCIIII.[1]   Carta Rogeri de Tornetona.[2]   1240-6.

[. . . . . I, Roger de Thornton, ... have confirmed to Robert, brother of Robert the Smith, an assart in the territory of Allerton, ... To be had and

(1) There is an abstract of No. 304 in *Dodsworth*, vol. 136, but it is numbered No. 305.

(2) Thornton was a very common Yorkshire place-name, and there are in Domesday nearly twenty different manors so called, in some variety of form.   But the Thornton near Allerton, Horton, Bolling,

held, &c. Paying thence, &c. And the aforesaid Robert and his heirs shall grind at my mill for the sixteenth measure. Warranty. Eleven shillings in acknowledgment. Witnesses.]

Sciant presentes et futuri quod ego Rogerus de Tornetona dedi et concessi et hac presenti carta mea confirmavi Roberto, fratri Roberti Fabri,[3] unum assartum in territorio de Alretona, illud videlicet quod jacet inter Kliderowgate et Foxerode et inter Merewelle et esterlik. Habendum et tenendum illi et heredibus suis de me et heredibus meis, in feodo et hereditate, libere et quiete, solute et honorifice, in bosco et plano, in pratis et pascuis et pasturis, et in omnibus aisiamentis, libertatibus et communibus[4] predicte ville de Alretona pertinentibus. Reddendo inde annuatim mihi et heredibus meis xii denarios, scilicet vi denarios ad Pentecosten et vi denarios ad festum sancti Martini pro omni servitio et exactione et demanda. Predictus vero Robertus et heredes sui molabunt[4] ad molendinum meum ad sextum decimum vas.[5] Et ego prefatus Rogerus et heredes mei warentizabimus predicto Roberto et heredibus suis terram prenominatam cum libertatibus predictis ubicunque et contra omnes homines. Pro hac vero donatione et concessione dedit mihi predictus Robertus undecim solidos de recognitione. Hiis testibus, *Thoma de Tornetona, Roberto de Hortona, Willelmo de Bolling, Alano de Scypedene, Jordano de Crosley, Johanne de Lowintorph, Alexandro de Wlsyndene, Matheo de Mainghama, Willelmo de Bateley, Helya de Tornetona, Hugone senescallo domine de Braford,*[6] et aliis.[7]

Crossley, Wilsden and Manningham, each of which contributed a witness or witnesses to these charters, is evidently the Thornton near Bradford, which is entered in duplicate in the Norman record, with a small variation which contributes to the meaning. The second of these entries is now quite obliterated by the use of nutgalls ; but is said in the printed vol. of 1783 to have been as follows :—

First Entry. 318 ; xli, col. 1.

Ad hoc manor [Bodeltone] pertinet hec terra. Celeslau, Alretone, Torentone, Claitone, Wibetese. Simul ad geldum x carucate terre, & vi caruce possunt ibi esse. Wasta est. T.R.E. valuit xl solidos.

Second Entry. 318 ; xli, col. 2.

In Celeslau & Alretune & Torentune & Claiton & . bet . es x carucate terre ad geldum. Terra est vi carucatis. Archil tenebat (*sic ;* not the usual "tenuit") T.R.E., & valebat xl solidos. Modo nil est.

(3) "Fabri" is written on an erasure.

(4) *Sic* in each case.

(5) The multure, or perquisite of the miller, was thus fixed at a sixteenth. This was also the custom at some of the Guisborough mills (G 590), but at Whitby (W 406) it was as much as a thirteenth, "ad tertium decimum vas."

(6) The "lady of Bradford" would appear to be the Margaret de Quency, widow of John de Lascy, who was earl of Lincoln in her right, and who died in 1240. His inquisition seems not to have been preserved, but it is probable that his widow possessed Bradford and other manors as dower, and was thus styled "lady of Bradford." I have not met with a second instance of that title having been applied to her. As Robert de Horton, another of the signatories to No. 304, died in 1246, the date of this charter must have been between 1240 and 1246. The following is his *inq. p. mort.* (Chancery *Inq. p. m.* 30 Henry III [1246], No. 22):—

This Inquisition was made by instructions of the lord king, concerning the manors of Robert Horton ; namely by Roger de Thornton, Elias de Oxenhope, John de Howrde, Henry de Ocwrde,

Robert de Bolling, Godfrey de Wylsindene, Hugh de Clayton, Adam de Clayton, Simon de eadem, Henry de Clayton, Swain de Horton, and William son of William de Braforde, who say by their oath that—

	s.	d.
Robert de Horton had in demesne in Horton, and in Clayton, liiij acres (value of the acre 4*d*.). Whence sum	18	0
He had in villenage xxv [should be xxvii] acres of land (value of the acre 4*d*.). Whence sum	9	0
He had in service of free men xi bovates of land and v score and viii acres, worth	37	5

And he held his land of J. de Lascy, formerly earl of Lincoln, by the service of the third part of one knight's fee.

And Hugh de Horton is the next heir, and of full age.

With reference to this mention of the "lady of Bradford," it may be noted that Joan, the second wife and widow of Henry, earl of Lincoln, had Bradford similarly as part of her dower, and that Nicholas d'Audley, her second husband, is returned as lord of Bradford in the Nomina Villarum of 9 Edward II, (1316) (*Kirhby's Inquest* 316, and note *n*). Joan died three years afterwards.

(7) The local character of all the witnesses to No. 304 (Bolling in Bradford, Crossley and Wilsden in Allerton, Leventhorp in Thornton, &c.) shows that these charters belong, not to the Allerton (Bywater) near Castleford and Pontefract, but to the Allerton near Bradford; though the grantor, Roger de Thornton, came of a family that had made several matrimonial connections with landowners in the neighbourhood of the former Allerton. The following is an illustration :—

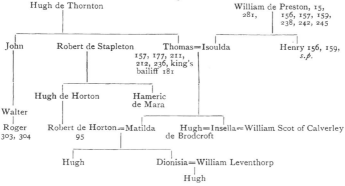

STUBBIS.

CCCV.[1] Carta Roberti filii Ottonis.[2]

[. . . . . I, Robert son of Otto of Stubbs, ... have confirmed . . . . a plot in the town of Stubbs in increase of the alms of Sir Otto my father . . To be held and possessed, &c. Witnesses.]

Sciant presentes et futuri quod ego Robertus filius Ottonis de Stubbis dedi, concessi, et hac presenti carta mea confirmavi deo et ecclesie sancti Johannis de Pontefracto et monachis ibidem deo servientibus, quandam placiam in villa de Stubbis in augmento elemosine domini Ottonis patris mei, pro animabus ipsius Ottonis et matris mee et omnium antecessorum et heredum meorum, habentem

---

(1) I have met with no transcript or abstract of No. 305.

(2) Otto, the father of this grantor, was a grandee of Stubbs; the second son of William, son of Walding. Another Alan, the son of Josiana, has appeared as a witness to No. 205, and was one of the jurors in the *inq. p. mort.* of Roger de Quency in 1246 (see *Record Series*, vol. 12, p. 97). He is, however, correctly indexed in that volume as son of Josiana, who was his mother, as we have already learnt from No. 205 and No. 269; in which latter, in the body of the charter, Alan, son of Robert, son of Oliver, speaks of "the land of Josiana his mother," as if she were still living. See pedigree under No. 101. It may be noted that No. 305 is tested by each of the Alans, and that the Walding Alan takes precedence.

2 F

in longitudine lx et iiij^or pedes, et in latitudine xl duos pedes, que jacet inter terram Ricardi hominis predictorum monachorum versus suth et terram domini Theobaldi militis de Stubbis. Tenendam et habendam prefatis monachis in liberam, puram et perpetuam elemosinam, in perpetuum. Hiis testibus, *Alano de Smythetona, Gaufrido de Nortona, Symone filio suo, Alano filio Josien, Henrico Burel, Thoma de Stagno, Thoma Molend', Ricardo de Martona, Hugone de Bylam, Gaufrido de Ledeshama, Rogero Pateman, Jordano fratre suo*, et multis aliis.

DE FERIA.

CCCVI.[1]   Carta Alicie Haget quondam uxoris Jordani
                           de Sancta Maria.   Ante 1239.

[. . . . . . . I, Alice Haget, widow of Jordan de St. Mary, in free widowhood, ... have confirmed . . . . . three plots of land in the Fields of Ferry . . . . . To be held and possessed, &c., as pure and perpetual alms. Warranty. Witnesses.]

Sciant presentes et futuri quod ego Alicia Haget, quondam uxor Jordani de Sancta Maria, in libera viduitate et in mea plena potestate, dedi, concessi, et hac carta mea confirmavi deo et ecclesie sancti Johannis de Pontefracto, et monachis ibidem deo servientibus, in puram et perpetuam elemosinam, pro salute anime mee et domini Jordani quondam viri mei et patris et matris mee, et omnium antecessorum et heredum meorum, tres culturas terre in campis de Feria, quarum una buttat super viam occidentalem que tendit versus Mundgoie et super - Wluedale versus est. Et culturam que buttat supra Torndic versus north et super Heirthesti versus sud.[2] Tenendas et habendas prefatis monachis de me et heredibus meis, libere, quiete, et integre, sicut puram et perpetuam elemosinam. Et ego prefata Alicia Haget et heredes mei predictas culturas sepedictis monachis contra omnes homines inperpetuum warantizabimus et defendemus. Hiis testibus, *Hugone Pincerna, tunc senescallo, Hereberto de Archis, Willelmo de Federstana, Simone clerico de Nortona,*[3] *Willelmo persona de Helage, Johanne persona de Fristona,*[4] *Willelmo dispensatore, Willelmo Mariscallo.*[5] *Johanne Vinitore, Henrico filio Matildis*, et aliis.

---

(1) There is a slightly abbreviated copy of No. 306 in *Lansdowne* 207 A, and an abstract in *Dodsworth*, vol. 136.

(2) There is no present trace of the names Munjoy, Thorndike, or Hirdesty. The "via occidentalis" is probably a comparatively late road, which leads diagonally through the plots, from Monkhill to Hamelin's mill, and the westerly road would clearly be that lower road, from Ferrybridge to Castleford, which has Wheldale to the right.   (3) This might be the Simon de Notton of No. 114.

(4) The witness of "John parson of Fristone" to this charter shows that it belongs to a date before January, 1238-39, when William de Fewgers was instituted to the position and office of parson.

(5) No. 298 is the original deed of gift of William Marshall of the bovate in Fristone.

De Feria.

CCCVII.[1]   **Carta Alicie Haget.**   **1238-40.**

[. . . . . . I, Alice Haget, in my widowhood, ... have confirmed . . . . . . the gift which my late husband, Sir Jordan de St. Mary, gave for the good of our souls and of all our ancestors and heirs, all our meadow which we have had in the territory of Ferry. That is to say, &c. And also I have given and confirmed . . . . . the headlands of my meadow of Frystone which extend on the one side to Frystone brook, and on the other to the meadow of Agnes de Merston . . . . Warranty. Seal. Witnesses (blank, with no space left for names)].

Sciant presentes et futuri quod ego Alicia Haget, in viduitate mea et in plena potestate, dedi et donationem quam quondam vir meus dominus Jordanus de Sancta Maria pro salute animarum nostrarum et omnium antecessorum et heredum nostrorum dedit presenti carta mea confirmavi deo et ecclesie sancti Johannis de Pontefracto et monachis ibidem deo servientibus, in puram et perpetuam elemosinam, totum pratum nostrum quod habuimus in territorio de Feria. Illud scilicet pratum quod jacet inter pratum quod fuit terri[2] de Feria versus suth, et pratum Ade Russel versus north. De quo unum capud percutit super Langelathe et tendit usque ad magnam aquam de Air, et unam aliam partem prati versus heliwelle ultra rivulum qui venit de Pontefracto in pratum abbatis et monachorum de Fontibus versus north, et pratum terri de Feria versus suth. De quo prato unum capud percutit supra pratum hospitalis de Fulsnap, et tendit usque ad magnam aquam de Ayr et fordales ejusdem prati quod[2] percutiunt ex una parte super pratum hospitalis de Fulsnaph, et ex alia parte super magnam aquam de Ayr et ex tercia parte super pratum quod fuit Roberti de Hykeltona. Et insuper dedi et confirmavi eisdem monachis fordales prati mei de Fristona que percutiunt ex una parte super rivulum de Fristona et ex alia super pratum Agnetis de Merstona. Hec omnia prefata habebunt et tenebunt predicti monachi libera, quieta et soluta ab omni servitio et consuetudine seculari. Et ego A. et heredes mei warentizabimus omnia predicta prefatis monachis ubique et contra omnes homines. Et ut hec mea donatio et confirmatio firma sit et stabilis huic scripto sigillum meum pro me et heredibus meis in testimonium apposui perpetuum. Hiis testibus.[3]

---

(1) There is an abstract of No. 307 in *Lansdowne* 207 A, but the *Monasticon* gives only No. 333, which is the original gift of Jordan de St. Mary referred to in the opening clause of No. 307.

(2) *Sic*, in each case.   (3) *Sic ;* carent.

FETHERSTANA.

CCCVIII.[1]   Carta Tibbe filie Johannis Durward.   Cir. 1236.

[. . . . . I, Tibba, daughter of John son of Durward, of Featherstone, ... to Hugh son of Ralph of Methley and his heirs, or to whom he will assign, all the gifts which Alice my sister has given to him in her free virginity and has by charter confirmed an l all the agreements which have been made between him and her. . . . . . . three shillings in hand. Seal. Witnesses.]

Sciant presentes et futuri quod ego Tibba, filia Johannis filii Durward de Fetherstana, concessi et hac presenti carta mea confirmavi, in libera virginitate mea, Hugoni filio Radulfi de Methelay, et heredibus suis, vel cui assignare voluerit, omnes donationes quas Alicia soror mea ei dedit in libera sua virginitate et carta confirmavit, et omnes conventiones que sunt facte inter ipsum et ipsam.[2] Pro hac autem concessione et presentis carte me^u confirmatione dedit mihi predictus Hugo tres solidos pre manibus. Et ut hec concessio rata et stabilis permaneat, sigillum meum huic scripto apposui in testimonium. Hiis testibus, *Jacobo de Methelay, Radulfo de Fetherstana, Henrico Fresel, Willelmo de Fetherstana, Ricardo filio Ricardi, Petro filio Godfrido, Nicholao de Fetherstana, Henrico fratre suo, Ricardo de Daneport,* et aliis.

---

(1) The land referred to in these Durward charters must be one of the plots in the east of Featherstone between what is still called Park Field Lane and the portion of the ancient Pontefract Park which is now converted into farms. "Park Cottage," as it is still called, seems to be on the site of an ancient Park Lodge, perhaps that of which the original Durward had charge. Durward's son was called indifferently "John son of Durward" and "John Durward," illustrating the fashion in which a certain class of paternal names was being adopted as surnames.

(2) See No. 299.   (3) *Sic.*

CCCIX.   Carta Alicie et Tibbe de Fetherstana.   Cir. 1236.

[. . . . . I, Alice of Featherstone and Tibba my sister, daughter of John Durward, ... to Hugh son of Ralph of Methley and his heirs or his assigns, an acre of land with all appurtenances . . . . in the Fields of Featherstone. . . . . . To be held, &c. Paying . . . . . eight shillings in silver. Warranty. Seal. Witnesses.]

Sciant presentes et futuri quod ego Alicia de Fetherstana et Tibba soror mea, filia Johannis Durward, dedimus et concessimus et presenti carta nostra confirmavimus Hugoni filio Radulfi de Methelay et heredibus suis vel suis assignatis unam acram terre cum omnibus pertinentiis ad illam pertinentibus in campis de Fetherstana jacentem inter terram Nicholay de Fetherstana et terram Hervei de eadem villa et abuttantem super domum predictarum sororum et tendentem versus occidentem et orientem. Tenendam et habendam de nobis et heredibus nostris sibi et heredibus suis vel suis assignatis libere et quiete, pacifice et integre. Reddendo inde annuatim nobis et heredibus nostris i denarium ad Nathale domini pro omnibus servitiis et demandis. Pro hac autem donatione et concessione dedit predictus Hugo nobis viii solidos de argento pre manibus de recognitione. Et ego vero Aliscia et soror mea Tibba et heredes nostri predicto Hugoni et heredibus suis vel suis assignatis predictam terram cum pertinentiis ubique et contra omnes gentes warantizabimus et defendemus. Ut hec nostra donatio et carte nostre[1] confirmatio robur perpetue firmitatis optineat inperpetuum, hanc cartam sigilli mei inpressione corroboravimus. Hiis testibus, *domino · Adam de Neirford tunc senescallo,*[2] *Waltero clerico, Jacobo de Medelay, Willelmo de Fetherstana, Gregorio de Camera, Roberto filio Hernisis, Willelmo filio Helye,* et aliis.

---

(1) On an erasure, as if " mea " had been first written.   (2) 1232-8.

De Ledeshama.
CCCX.[1]   Carta Symonis de Cliftona.

[. . . . . I, Simon de Clifton, at the request of Cecilia my wife, ... have confirmed to Nigel son of Peter of Ledsham, ... that bovate of land in Ledsham which Robert son of Rahenilda has held. To be held, &c. Paying to us yearly only eight shillings. . . . . Warranty from Simon and Cecily, and from Geoffrey, father of Cecily, and from Walter his son. Witnesses.]

Sciant presentes et futuri quod ego Symon de Cliftona ad petitionem Cecilie spouse mee dedi et concessi et hac presenti carta mea confirmavi Nigello filio Petri de Ledeshama pro homagio et servitio suo et pro tribus marcis argenti quas nobis dedit illam bovatam terre in Ledeshama quam Robertus filius Rahenilde tenuit. Scilicet tenendam sibi et heredibus suis de nobis et heredibus nostris, in feodo et hereditate, libere, integre, honorifice, et quiete ab omni servitio et ab omni exactione. Reddendo nobis annuatim et tantummodo octo solidos, iiij[or] ad Pentecosten et iiij[or] solidos ad festum sancti Martini. Et ego Symon et ego Cecilia predicti warantiza-bimus et adquietabimus, et heredes nostri similiter, predicto Nigello et heredibus suis predictam bovatam terre cum omnibus liberis aisiamentis, et liberis pertinentiis suis, infra villam et extra, inperpetuum contra omnes homines. Et ego Gaufridus de Michelfeld[2] pater predicte

---

(1) I have not met with transcripts or abstracts of either of these three charters. This last document belongs to the series commencing with No. 200,—the Geoffrey named in it being the Geoffrey son of Walter, who was a party thereto.

(2) The husband successively of Agnes de Parlington and Cecily the elder. The Cecily named in the charter was the issue of Geoffrey's second marriage.

Cecilie et advocatus predicte bovate terre et heredes mei warentizabimus et adquietabimus predicto Nigello et heredibus suis predictam bovatam terre cum omnibus liberis pertinentiis suis in perpetuum contra omnes homines. Si Symon vel Cecilia predicti in aliquo indefecerint vel heredes eorum, et hoc Nigello predicto et heredibus suis tenendum pro me et pro heredibus meis affidavi, et presenti sigillo meo confirmavi, et ego Walterus filius et heres predicti Gaufridi hoc legitime tenendum et warantizandum quod pater meus hic concessit similiter affidavi pro me et pro heredibus meis et presenti sigillo meo confirmavi. Hiis testibus, *Hugone de Stivetona, Ricardo de Hudlestuna et Jordano de Lalande, Ricardo de Luttringtona, Roberto le Walleis, Osberto de Brettona, Henrico de Fareburne, Henrico de Ledestona, Nicholao de Barkstona, Nicholao de Leuenadtona, Gaufrido de Waldebi, Henrico de Thalamo,* et multis aliis.

No. 310 concludes the Seventh Fasciculus of the Chartulary at the close of fo. 55, which is completely filled, leaving but a line as vacant space at the foot.

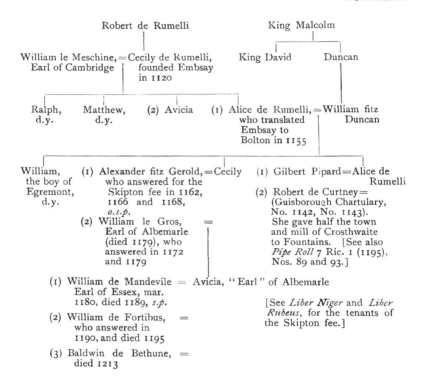

Robert de Rumelli   King Malcolm

William le Meschine, = Cecily de Rumelli,   King David   Duncan
Earl of Cambridge   founded Embsay
        in 1120

Ralph,   Matthew,   (2) Avicia   (1) Alice de Rumelli, = William fitz
d.y.   d.y.   who translated   Duncan
                              Embsay to
                              Bolton in 1155

William,   (1) Alexander fitz Gerold, = Cecily   (1) Gilbert Pipard = Alice de
the boy of   who answered for the   Rumelli
Egremont,   Skipton fee in 1162,   (2) Robert de Curtney =
d.y.   1166 and 1168,   (Guisborough Chartulary,
               o.s.p.   No. 1142, No. 1143).
        (2) William le Gros,   =   She gave half the town
             Earl of Albemarle   and mill of Crosthwaite
             (died 1179), who   to Fountains. [See also
             answered in 1172   *Pipe Roll* 7 Ric. 1 (1195),
             and 1179   Nos. 89 and 93.]

      (1) William de Mandevile = Avicia, " Earl " of Albemarle
           Earl of Essex, mar.
           1180, died 1189, *s.p.*   [See *Liber Niger* and *Liber*
      (2) William de Fortibus,   =   *Rubeus*, for the tenants of
           who answered in   the Skipton fee.]
           1190, and died 1195
      (3) Baldwin de Bethune,   =
           died 1213

Fasciculus VIII.

THE EIGHTH FASCICULUS commences on folio 56 with an important document. It is a very early specimen of a Fine or Final Concord.

The mention of "Rainer dapifer" as presiding at this Court opens up a remarkably interesting piece of history; for, except on the circuit of this year 1184, he seems to be mentioned only in witnessing the cyrograph R 112, which was of 1181, though the date is inaccurately copied as 1188. That he should have presided at this York Assize as deputy to Ralph de Glanville, the Chief Justiciary, is an indication of the position to which he might have attained had it not been for what followed during this summer and this assize. At York Sir Gilbert de Plumpton was taken into custody on a capital charge and carried by the chief justice to Worcester, where, the assize being opened, he was tried and condemned to death. The king was then at Worcester, on the occasion of his last visit to that city, and the day being Sunday (July 22, St. Mary Magdalene's Day) Baldwin, bishop of Worcester (the king's nominee for the primacy a few weeks afterwards), was on that account emboldened to intercede with the king for the life of the condemned man. This led to a reprieve, but as Sir Gilbert was retained in prison for some years, it is probable that he was not altogether innocent of the offence of which he was accused, though he might have been hardly pressed, and with a sinister purpose.

For the charge against the fair fame of Ralph de Glanville,—the solitary charge, almost at the close of a long and eminently public life,—was that this Rainer, generally named only as the "friend of the chief justiciary," now proving to be his dapifer and deputy, had had designs upon the wife of Sir Gilbert (the daughter of one Roger Gulewast) and that he intended to marry her and obtain her fortune if he could compass the death of her young husband; that the chief justiciary was privy to those designs; and that, by this harsh treatment of the successful suitor, he was helping forward the sordid schemes of his friend Rainer.

But there is not a particle of evidence of the complicity of Ralph de Glanville; while had the charge against him been in the smallest degree probable to the eminently just King Henry, there can be no moral doubt that the justiciary would not have retained the king's favour as he did, nor been made executor to the king's will. On the other hand, after this transaction, Rainer, the dapifer and vice-sheriff, absolutely and at once disappears from public life; so absolutely that, except in the document before us and the cyrograph R 112, there is no solitary evidence that he ever held the high office which this Fine proves that he did indeed possess.

The circumstances are well and graphically related by Benedict Abbas, and repeated, though hardly with accuracy, by Roger de Hoveden, and from the narrative we learn that at the moment of the interposition of the bishop, Sir Gilbert had the "iron chain" (not a rope) round his neck and was about to be "hoisted"; thus giving us a. graphic picture of the method of execution in the time of Henry II.

As "dapifer of Ralph de Glanville" Rainer witnesses R 113 before the justices of the lord the king, then at Doncaster, in 1181; and as Rainer, "vice-sheriff of Yorkshire," that is deputy to Ralph de Glanville, who locally was the sheriff, this officer appears in a charter of Richard Malebise to Byland (Guisborough Chartulary, ii, 61, *note*), but his name is not on the official list of vice-sheriffs, possibly because he made no return, having held the office during part only of the course of a single year; entering upon his duties after the year had begun, ceasing from them in July before it had concluded. For it can hardly be doubted that the Plumpton episode was the cause of the immediate withdrawal from him of the confidence of the great justiciary, and that his disgrace too soon followed his accession to dignity to allow of the appearance of his name at the foot of even a single roll; that is, he did not hold the office in the September of any year.

With reference to the "Marsh which is called the Soke" in No. 312, it may be noted that a soke is generally a "jurisdiction," and the word is likewise applied to the territory in which the jurisdiction is exercised. In this case there was no such separate jurisdiction; but "soke" appears to be a variant of "syke,"—a fountain or stream of water. A similar marshy strip between two streams at Kippax was also called "the soke," the water-mill thereon being called the "soke mill," and thus giving colour to the idea that the mill was a manorial mill, of which there is no evidence.

In No. 313 there is a clear indication that a member of a monastery was by no means necessarily a priest; he might be or he might not; though the priestly section gradually became the preponderating element. Such, however, was not the original intention of the institution; a large proportion of the professed monks were intended to be lay-brothers, given up to study or to labour. Hence monasticism in its original constitution appealed to all classes; priestly or lay, high or low, rich or poor, learned or unlearned. As in this charter, each could do his own special service; the priest could say masses, the lay-brother, in addition to his bodily labour, could sing psalms.

This and the two following—all charters of William, eldest son of Hervey, eldest son of the great Jordan of Ledstone,—together with No. 262, No. 263, and No. 264, show how the grandson was gradually alienating his share of the large patrimony.

No. 317 and No. 318 represent the original gifts of Peckfield and of the commonage of Micklefield. They belong to the reign of King Stephen, and were confirmed by King Henry II in the two charters given by him at the opening of his reign, at the Council of Northampton in January, 1155 (see No. 71 and No. 73), and by archbishop Theobald (see No. 57).

The Thomas, provost of the monks, and William his brother, sometimes called William the baker, were younger brothers of the father of the next grantor, Adam fitz Peter.

The group of seven Birkin charters helps materially to illustrate the fortunes of the widespread family of the descendants of Asolf, probably a monied trader, who aided King Stephen in some of the financial difficulties of the earlier part of his reign, and who received in payment, or perhaps bought by his action, a vast tract of country in the centre of Yorkshire, it is hard to say how far towards Liverpool and how far towards Goole. The steadfast policy of Henry II to ignore King Stephen's acts eventuated in the total destruction of all the fiscal records of the reign of the Usurper (as he was persistently called by the partizans of the son of the empress), so that the name of Asolf, in the person of his sons, emerges out of the thick darkness only in the *Pipe Rolls* of Henry II. Their names, in the order of their seniority, may be found *ante*, pp. 254-5, and it seems to have been the policy of the astute Asolf to divide his large booty among his children as early as possible, so as to separate the interests, and thereby lessen the risk of all being resumed by the crown at some perhaps unexpected change of national policy.

This process of subdivision was, I think, completed by 1140, if not before; and the remaining fourteen years of King Stephen's reign, and the remainder of the life of the original grantee, was long enough to enable each of the sons of Asolf to come of age and consolidate his power in his own estate. This was done so thoroughly that it has seldom been suspected how closely these lordly tenants were allied, especially when the process was aided by the practice which shortly afterwards sprang up of designating the owner of an estate by its territorial name.

But to confine ourselves at present to the line of the eldest son of Asolf, Peter fitz Asolf, who was the large local tenant of this district and much beyond, Peter and his father seem to have died within a few months of each other; at least their names appear together on the *Pipe Roll* of 12 Henry II (1165), when the following royal claims were made :—

Ada' fil' Pet' fil' Essulfi	deb' xl*s*.
Helias fil' Assulfi	deb' l*m*.
Hug' fil' Essulfi	deb' l*m*.
Thoma Pinc'na	deb' l*m*.

The second and third indicate the death of Asolf, the allegation being that Elias and Hugh had concealed their liability at the devolution of the property; but the first implies that Peter also was dead, and that Adam was inheriting from him probably the Birkin property and its appurtenances. He has already appeared in the Pontefract Chartulary as Peter de Flockton (No. 86), which manor probably belonged to a property which his father was placing in his possession, and was rightly his. But he is erroneously called Peter de Leeds, Peter de Midgley, and Peter de Birkin ; the first from Gipton which is in Leeds, the second and third from Little Midgley in Shitlington, and Birkin, each of which appears to have belonged to his son Adam, if not to himself. Similarly Adam was called, and calls himself at different times, de Birkin, de Falthwaite, de Flockton, de Middleton, de Midgley, de Shitlington, and de Stainburgh, for he had interests in all those places, most of which he had received with his wife.

Adam was Adam de Birkin or Adam fitz Peter de Birkin for nearly forty years ; and it can hardly be doubted that his friendship, goodwill, and benevolence towards the monks of Pontefract were fostered and furthered by his uncle Thomas, at different times their prepositus, dapifer, seneschal, and pincerna,—also known as Thomas of Monkhill.

But as Adam fitz Peter (de Stainburgh), he and his wife Matilda made large and important grants to the monks of Rievaux ; in one of the charters connected with which, probably with a remembrance of their patron's connection with Pontefract and the influences under which he might there be placed, the Helmsley monks took care to obtain exclusive rights and a special engagement that no other monastery should have a grant in any manor in which they had received a donation. This was a singular instance of their farseeing astuteness, stimulated by the determination to do all possible to prevent competition with the mineral interests which their property gave them in these manors.

Moreover, it is observable that Adam's brothers Thomas, William, and Roger, witness his grants to Rievaux in Shitlington and Flockton, as if they also had interests there ; while Adam's eldest son Robert witnesses those of Midgley, probably for a similar reason. He seems to be afterwards known as Robert de Midgley, while John, the third son, became John of Birkin.

No. 330 and No. 331, read with No. 228*, enable us to construct the following small genealogy of the Muhalt, Mohaut, Muhaut, Mont Alto, or Maude family between 1150 and 1250 ; and as several other interesting points are indicated in the documents, it may be worth while to linger and discuss them.

The property concerned was two bovates in Keswick, near Leeds, which are described as being of 20 acres each, thus making a carucate to consist of 160 acres, a fourth of a knight's fee, a modern square mile. It was first granted by Simon de Muhaut the elder (No. 331), and as his charter was witnessed not only by Jordan of Ledstone and his three brothers, but by Thomas fitz Asolf, the steward, and as (under the name of Coshist or Coshirst) it was confirmed by archbishop Theodore as papal legate, the gift was probably early in the decade 1160-70. A generation afterwards, the son and namesake of his father confirmed the gift (No. 330), and made a curious exchange of it for other two bovates in the same manor, which should be between his own land and that of his brother Robert, engaging that if two bovates conterminous with his brother's land, and good in measure, could not be completed in that peculiar position, he would make it up to the monks by so much from his demesne lands. This was surely a sensible exchange, designed, like that of the patriarch of old, to prevent his servants from quarrelling with those of his brother; which compels the reflection that if these men were not able to read the Scriptures, they practised their precepts and copied their examples.

The transaction was witnessed by as many as nineteen witnesses, and as the usual "and others" or "and many others" is not appended, it is probable that all are recorded. This serves as indication as to the usual number of witnesses to similar deeds.

No. 228* shows the grandson of the original donor (who tests No. 331 under his local name, but in the later deed uses his patrimonial appellation) dealing with the substituted two bovates, his charter being cancelled in the Chartulary, with the intimation that the monks had once more exchanged the land, that they had been accustomed to receive 2s. 6d. yearly from it, but that in exchange they had obtained a messuage in Bondgate, Pontefract (only a few yards from their house, and therefore more convenient), and that they now received from their new property 2s. 8d. a year. A satisfactory exchange in every way for the businesslike monks of Pontefract.

The following is the genealogy :—

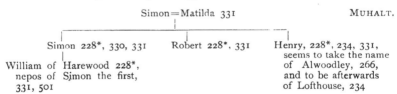

Simon = Matilda 331   MUHALT.

Simon 228*, 330, 331   Robert 228*, 331   Henry, 228*, 234, 331,
                                                    seems to take the name
William of Harewood 228*,   of Alwoodley, 266,
nepos of Simon the first,   and to be afterwards
331, 501   of Lofthouse, 234

It must be the second Simon de Muhalt who by Fine of 9 Richard I (*Yorkshire Archæological Journal*, xi, 183) gave to Warin Fitzgerold son of Warin 40 silver marks, and to his wife, Alice de Curzi, 5 marks, that he might have 8 carucates of land in Wike and Kisewik.

Between No. 333, the original charter, and No. 307 and No. 289, the professed copies embodying confirmations of subsequent generations, there are small differences, and these are not to the advantage of the later documents, but tend rather to obscure their sense. A very singular misreading of "parti' for "prati" appears in Dodsworth's copy of this charter in the original edition of the *Monasticon* of 1655, which he discovered in time to schedule it among the errata ; and when the volume was reprinted in 1682, to make it uniform with the two others issued by Dugdale, the error was corrected.

When, however, the *New Monasticon* was being compiled, the editors seem to have printed from the original volume and altogether disregarded the repeated correction, rehabilitating the old error which Dodsworth had done his best to amend, so that "aliam partem parti" has resumed its position and again mars the text (*Monasticon*, v, 126). See *Yorkshire Archæological Journal*, x, 548.

The gift which passed by this charter was a piece of about nine acres.

The position of No. 334, immediately following No. 333, tends to show that there was some connection between the two grantors, but there is no evidence of its character. Neither has it been ascertained how Roland Haget had a foothold in Skelbrook. His charter, which was in any case witnessed by very distinguished persons, appears to belong to about the middle of the reign of Henry II, for as it is not named in either No. 57, No. 71, or No. 73, the gift had not been made when those confirming charters, lay and ecclesiastical, were granted.

With this charter of Roland Haget the Osgoldcross documents conclude, and those of Staincross commence. These latter include the properties dealt with in No. 2, No. 7, and No. 72, parts of Silkstone, Dodworth, Monk Bretton, and Barnsley, with a small property in Barugh and Notton. The six manors border each other, Notton, Bretton, Barnsley, and Barugh having so to say a common centre, as if the point at which they meet had once been a common Field, subsequently divided rather capriciously among the four townships.

There seem to have been two contemporary Hugh Butlers, belonging to the early part of the thirteenth century.

The first was Hugh Buticularius, who at the date of No. 23 was seneschal to John de Lascy the constable, before he became earl; otherwise Hugh Pincerna, seneschal, who in that capacity tested No. 118, No. 123, No. 165, No. 166, No. 209, No. 225, and No. 227. He is called "Sir Hugh the seneschal" in No. 189, "Sir Hugh Pincerna the seneschal" in No. 210, and perhaps "seneschal to the lady of Beal" in No. 229. But this Hugh was clearly connected officially (though perhaps only officially) with the Lascy fee, in the Pontefract part of which he does not seem to have had any property, and in which he announced no relationships. He is also probably that Hugh Pincerna who appears in 3 John [1202] as Hugh son of Alan, and who, as "son of the elder brother" (that is Alan, possibly the headman who succeeded Adam fitz Swain in 1156), is admitted to the town and advowson of Armthorpe. But Hugh appears to have fallen under the royal displeasure, for in 17 John [1216] his lands in Armthorpe and in Skelbrook were given to Robert Talbot. [South Yorkshire I, 87.]

The second Hugh referred to in No. 335 was of Sandal, connected with the Warren fee, and he had three sons and two daughters, three of whom had their inheritance in Silkstone. We shall learn much more of Richard, the grantor of the present charter; and when we come to No. 354 we shall find that he is called Richard de Seville. His descendants have always held highly important positions in this and other counties; and there can be little doubt that he or his father was the progenitor of all the numerous branches of the Savile family.

There was also a third Hugh Pincerna who, later in the century, between 1240 and 1246, tested No. 304 as "seneschal to the lady of Bradford," Margaret de Quency, widow of John de Lascy, who had been Earl of Lincoln in her right.

No. 336 testifies to the existence of a church at Silkstone, which was (at the time of the Domesday Survey) the only one in the whole wapentake of Staincross. All the rest have been built and endowed subsequently by private persons; thus showing the falsity of the claim that the English Church was state endowed, and illustrating the fact that it extended with a gradual growth, and by no means with that uniformity which the "state-endowment" theory would require.

No. 340 is interesting, not only as being dated, but as illustrating a custom of the monks, as practical and improving farmers, to take into their hands on lease the lands of an heir. Doubtless in this case the term of the lease was calculated with reference to his age.

Nothing is more striking in collating and comparing these charters than the fact that the younger branches of even the more wealthy middle class families came to "great necessity" in the third or at latest the fourth generation. But they always had the wealthy convent to fall back upon as a purchaser of their small patrimony. Thus we shall learn from No. 376 that the Matilda of No. 350 and No. 351, apparently the younger daughter of the wealthy steward of Barnsley, married the Richard de Craven who tests so many of these charters. She was unfortunate in her marriage, or at least was early left a widow with two daughters, and therefore was compelled to capitalise a small annuity which she held from the monks, but of the origin of which we learn nothing; yet in this charter, even "in her great necessity" she says nothing of her widowhood.

No. 349 and No. 350 seem to represent an early stage of the separation of a born thrall· from the land to which he was native, inasmuch as the land itself and its tenant were transferred by two distinct deeds, though the deeds were tested by (with only one exception) the same witnesses, and therefore may be assumed to have been granted at the same date. Or it might have been that they were only preliminary to a grant of his freedom to the native.

No. 354 is one of a remarkable series of charters which dispose of land with natives attached to the soil and sold with it. In this instance, Rainer, son of Hugh the reeve, was sold with the land, but it is asserted that Hugh his father formerly held it, showing that, although he was a "nativus," his inferior and servile birth had not precluded him from the tenancy of office. (See also No. 370, No. 373, No. 381, No. 388, and No. 389.)

No. 388 shows the wife of the grantor of No. 354, Hugh Pincerna, to have been Avicia de Savile, a name not adopted by her husband, but used by all her children, as we shall see in many instances. The family of Savile is still in possession of estates in various parts of the West Riding, and has been several times ennobled. The present owner of Methley (the Earl of Mexborough) is a Savile. Hugh Pincerna and the lady Avicia de Savile (whom we shall find a widow in No. 370) had at least five children, William, John, Richard, Dionis, and Idonea who married Michael of Doncaster There were also a Ralph de Savile and Sir Henry de Savile, who both sign No. 340, and were probably brothers of the lady Avicia.

Brian fitz Alan, who witnesses No. 357, was sheriff of Yorkshire for three years, the last half of the 20th year, the 21st year, the 22nd year, and the first half of the 23rd year of King Henry II, during which time the deputyship was fulfilled by Roger de Stapleton, who follows him as witness. Roger is presumably one of the North Riding Stapletons; for the name of Roger does not appear among the Stapletons of Darrington, in the West Riding.

The elder male line of Ailric failed in the person of his grandson Adam fitz Swain, after which there was a succession of similar failures.

Adam had two co-heirs, Amabel and Matilda. The former whose seat was at Cawthorn, married firstly William de Nevile, and their heir Sarah married Thomas son of Philip de Burgh, whose line was continued through the thirteenth century. Amabel married secondly Alexander de Crevequer, to whom also she had daughters only, Matilda who married Hugh de Cheney, and Cecilia who married another Nevile. The first had no children, and the line of the second failed in the third generation, leaving four co-heirs.

Matilda, the younger daughter of Adam fitz Swain, was seated at Brierley, and to her and her descendants the Silkstone property fell. She was married three times—(1) to Adam de Montbegon, (2) to John Malherbe, from whom there is a charter, R 107, of two acres of land at Worsborough to Rievaux, (3) to Gerald Glanville; but the descendants of only the first two were interested in Silkstone. Her first husband, Adam de Montbegon, was lord of Hornby, a princely Lancashire property, and his son Roger would have been the heir to whom the monks had to look for confirmation of their title. This confirmation they obtained by No. 379, in the time of Roger de Lascy. Roger de Montbegon, however, having died in 12 Henry III (1227) without issue, the property descended to his half-sister Clemence, the elder co-heir of her mother's second marriage to Malherbe. But in her charter No. 357, Clemence gives no hint of the relationship, and uses the surname of her deceased husband, Eudo de Lungvilers, a former seneschal to Robert de Lascy; so that reading the charters together it cannot be gathered that they were given by two who bore the relationship of brother and sister.

The charter of Clemence de Lungvilers is remarkable as invoking a curse from the grantor and "all women" upon any of her heirs who should infringe its provisions.

No. 358 and No. 359 refer to the same land, but at a considerable interval of time. For John the chaplain, son of Hugh, priest of Barnsley, has become John, chaplain of Silkstone, with a daughter Matilda married to Adam son of Gilbert, whom (probably to avoid the questions arising in this first half of the thirteenth century with regard to married clergy) John of Silkstone made his heir. We saw a similar expedient adopted in No. 190 with regard to Germanus son of Adam, son of Richard, son of Lesing, of Ledstone, who was made heir to his father under the title of Germanus son of Milisanda of Kippax (his mother).

Hugh, parson of Silkstone, who tests No. 359, was probably Hugh, priest of Barnsley, named in it; but it contains mention of three clerical Johns, John the chaplain, John clerk of Stainbrough, and John clerk of Hoyland.

No. 360 is a little later than No. 359. It is tested by the same witnesses, with one addition, namely Nicholas son of Walter of Eastfield.

In No. 361 we evidently have the land referred to in No. 347, and its confirmation. It is noticeable that the half acre is occasionally included in the term "toft"; so that the "toft" implies not only the toft but the half acre of meadow-land which went with it.

No. 347 and No. 361 are clearly contemporary, but in No. 347 one of the witnesses is called "Robert, chaplain of Barnsley"; in No. 361, probably with more accuracy, he is called "Roger."

Similarly No. 362 belongs to the same transaction as No. 355; the monks were gradually acquiring and absorbing the estates of the smaller tenantry of Dodworth.

No. 365 appears to have been a mutual concession between the grantors and the convent, owing to some dispute, after the death of their father, concerning their rights to his property at Dodworth. For according to No. 45, the Bernard of Silkstone herein named was the tenant from the monks of the whole town of Dodworth, for his life. At his decease or "change of life"—that is, if he should become a monk,—the convent was to succeed to the full possession. The date given in the charter was probably that of his death. It will be noticed that the signatories were in a large proportion men of Osgoldcross, and it indicates his social position that among many other grandees, and almost at the head of them, Bernard of Silkstone witnessed that early charter No. 206, which was a grant of a bovate of land at Slepehill.

The two charters numbered 366 and 367, from the same man, with a different description, refer to the same property, the "Hugh my brother" mentioned in each being the "Hugh de Baghill" mentioned in No 340 as being dead in 1222.

John de Oldfield, otherwise John son of Adam de Oldfield, otherwise (see No. 374) John son of Adam of Shepley, granted this land first to his brother Hugh, and then, after Hugh had surrendered it, to the monks. Adam his father was an important man, who really owned these many names. He was Adam son of Roger de Barnsley in No. 345, No. 374, and No. 392; Adam de Oldfield in No. 342, No. 345, No. 349, No. 367, and No. 375; Adam de Shepley in No. 345, No. 374, and No. 375; and Adam, steward of Barnsley, in No. 376. He had married a daughter of the Hugh de Barugh who tests the charter (see No. 375).

No. 369 is an important charter, and its wording is typical. Read by itself, it contains nothing to show but that Adam fitz Swain was the original grantor of the church of Silkstone to the monks of Pontefract. Such, however, was not the case; the original grant was made by Swain his father, as appears by No. 378.

This confirmation is moreover tested by Henry his brother, who witnesses No. 45 as Henry fitz Swain. He was of Denby; and as already stated (*ante*, p. 66), there is still extant an original charter from him, which is numbered as 7416 of the Additional Charters in the British Museum.

No. 370 is a correlative of No. 354, from a younger brother Richard, who tests the present charter and No. 373 as Richard Pincerna. Thus he was known by three names, Richard Pincerna from his father, Richard de Savile from his mother, and Richard son of Hugh. There are also other charters, No. 373, No. 381, No. 388, and No. 389, by means of which the monks made their title sure.

In the case of No. 372 (the date of the charter being before 1218, the year in which the *post mortem* of Thomas son of Adam de Reineville was issued) the "natives" were transferred separately from the land to which they belonged; another illustration of the manner in which the old land system was breaking up.

No. 373 gives us the most complete list of "natives" in the series, and is remarkable as containing the names of three females, though it does not say to what family they belonged, other than that they ranked with this good lady's "homines et nativos."

No. 370 and No. 373, the charters from William son of Hugh and Dionisia his sister, are identical in terms and witnesses, though the second has in addition to all the names in No. 370, one other, John de Thurgoland. But as the name of the native is different, it is probable that this grant was not of the same bovate, but of another of similar character which Dionisia had received from her mother under similar conditions to those which had been imposed on her brother William.

No. 374 is practically a duplicate of No. 345, except that it prescribes the place at which the payment should be made, that it has two clauses which were superseded in No. 345, and that it contains the names of two additional witnesses, Henry de Savile and Adam de Hoyland. This charter is the earlier, but probably not very much the earlier of the two. The six acres of No. 366 and No 367 seem to have been a portion of this larger property. Here also Henry de Tankersley (lord of Tankersley, according to No. 342) is clearly distinguished from Henry de Savile; for each signs No. 374. This could not have been said of No 345, as the Chartulary copy of that charter did not contain the name of Henry de Savile.

The "Hugh son of Robert" in No. 375 was the elder son, whose daughter married Adam the steward, the son of Roger de Barnsley, and the only male heir to his father. From this Hugh, his grandson Hugh of Baghill, the husband of Edusa (No. 340), would have acquired his name. The following is the line:—

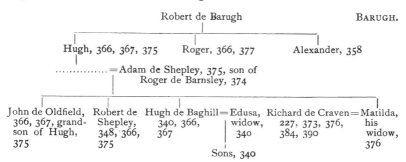

Robert de Barugh   BARUGH.

Hugh, 366, 367, 375   Roger, 366, 377   Alexander, 358

.... = Adam de Shepley, 375, son of
                    Roger de Barnsley, 374

| John de Oldfield, 366, 367, grandson of Hugh, 375 | Robert de Shepley, 348, 366, 375 | Hugh de Baghill = Edusa, 340, 366, 367 | widow, 340 | Richard de Craven = Matilda, 227, 373, 376, 384, 390 | his widow, 376 |

Sons, 340

No. 378 is the only early charter to the monks of Pontefract, granted by a tenant, that has survived. The earlier gifts of the William Foliot, who gave a carucate at Baghill, and of Ailsi (the Domesday tenant of Silkstone and of one of the manors of Darfield), who gave six bovates in the former place; of Ascelin de Dai and of Henry de Campels, who each gave tofts in Pontefract; and of Ailsi Bacun, who gave a bovate of land in Ravensfield, were either made without charter, or the charter is not extant. That of Paganus the son of Bucardus, who gave 30 acres in Pontefract, has also perished, as have those of Ralph de Catwick and Simon his son. That, of all the charters of these eight grandees, only one should have escaped the oblivion which befell each of the others, is at best a suspicious circumstance which incites us to investigation, lest it may be found that the apparent survival is due to some active imagination. But let us first consider the charter as if indubitably trustworthy, and as we should view it if it were a thoroughly authentic document.

The date of this charter of Swain cannot be fixed with certainty. It was before 1122, for Hugh de Laval names it in his confirmation charter; though how much before that date it is impossible to say. It was witnessed (perhaps out of respect to the former tenant Ailsi) by Edwin the priest and parson of Darfield, and by Ulf the priest and parson of Adwick, which implies the existence of churches at each of those places, where neither had been provided at the time of the Survey. But the mention of Edwin would also imply that there was but one parson there, while as a matter of fact the church was always held in medieties, a remarkable condition of things which has unfortunately survived till the present day. Here is at once a discrepancy which requires reconcilement. For this mention of a single parson where two might have been expected is a very suspicious circumstance, which must carefully be taken into account when considering the authenticity of the document.

The name of Saxe of Horbury, who signs last of those witnesses whose names have been preserved, would tend to show that the charter was not of much earlier date than 1120. Saxe's name is of unusual occurrence. He was tenant of a very large district west of Wakefield, and according to this charter, and to make him contemporary with its grantor, he must have been in possession of at least some of the holding about the middle of the reign of Henry I. Swain fitz Ailric died some time before 1130, in which year (as we gather from that very interesting *Pipe Roll*, 30–31 Henry I, the only document of the class which has survived from the reign of that king, and indeed of his successor also) his widow likewise had deceased; for Adam fitz Swain, who enjoyed his possessions till 1158, was in 1130 charged with a death-duty of five marks as inheritor of the dowry of his mother. Swain had been the tenant of both Kexborough and Dodworth before Robert de Lascy gave the latter manor to the monks of Pontefract, as his father had been the tenant of Silkstone, Cawthorn, Hoyland, Clayton, Peniston, Brierley, and Hiendley, all in Staincross, and had moreover held in fee, direct of the king, one of the Darfield manors. After Ailric's death, which must have occurred between 1086 and 1090, Swain would have been a very important personage, and though Dodworth was given to the monks in the name of the lord, it is probable that the gift was practically the outcome of Swain's own generosity. In any case his gifts were twice confirmed by Robert de Lascy, by No. 2 (1090), and by No. 7 (about 1114); by Henry I (No. 72), and by Hugh de Laval (No. 3), about 1122; by the two charters of King Henry II (No. 71 and No. 73) in January 1155; and by that of archbishop Theobald (No. 57) a little later.

Collating all these charters and confirmations, we meet with another extraordinary discrepancy. Neither in No. 2 nor in No. 7 was there any mention under Cawthorn or anywhere else of the two-thirds of the tithe of the lordships, which Swain's charter, as now presented, professes to grant; but in No. 3 there is an insertion of " cum duabus partibus decimarum totius dominii sui " —" with two-thirds of the tithes of all his lordship"—in the singular number.   In No. 71 and No. 73, the royal confirmations, the expression is exactly repeated, with the omission of "sui." This was, however, reinstated in No. 57, the ecclesiastical confirmation, although this latter may be imagined not to have been guided by such fixed rules as the royal confirmations, and although in other respects it is not remarkable for verbal accuracy.

Moreover, in the charter we are considering, No. 378 (copied into the Chartulary, as it must be borne in mind, above a hundred years after date), the phrase appears as "omnium dominiorum meorum"— "all my lordships,"—plural; while its force is so amplified and extended that it is impossible to believe that such an important enlargement, if it really existed, could have been ignored by subsequent confirmations.

But not content with having thus added to what must be considered the meaning of the original charter as represented in its confirmations, a still further expansion was made at a still later date, in a charter professedly by Adam fitz Swain, the founder of Monk Bretton. This appears as No. 60 in the Chartulary, among the ecclesiastical documents, and is given in the *Monasticon* as No. vii. As, however, it was a much later addition to the collection, and as it was inserted only on a vacant page, it does not fall within our present scope, and we have accordingly omitted it (see *ante*, p. 52).

Thus the facts by which these charters are surrounded are altogether so discordant that hardly any one set can be reconciled with any other; and when we remember the difficulty of harmonising No. 2 and No. 1, to which allusion has already been made (pp. 8–9), it is impossible not to see that the series has been tampered with, and that before the documents were registered in the Chartulary, perhaps small, but certainly important, alterations were made in each.

For instance, on their face No. 2 is represented as confirming No. 378; that is, it makes out No. 378 to be the older document. But while No. 2 is tested by men of the age of the Survey, No. 378 (by the conditions supposed to be the older) is tested by priests of both Darfield and Adwick, at neither of which places is there any record of a church in the Survey.

On the whole, therefore, balancing the evidence as carefully as possible, we cannot but feel that the claims of the monks with regard to the tithes of Swain's lordships can never have been legally tested, or the weakness of the claim as registered in this No. 378 would have been apparent.

No. 381 is a confirmation of No. 354, and is witnessed by persons of greater rank, though No. 354 bears the names of many honourable witnesses. The comparative value of the two interests which the monks acquired by the two charters may be fairly valued by setting the one purchase money against the other. Though the monks paid Richard 66s. 8d. for his interest, only 20s. sufficed to purchase that of his sister.

No. 382 and No. 383 complete the alienation of Millholm and Milcarr, "by Barnsley mill," "to the length of the water."

The one that follows (No. 384) is the last, in order of time, of eight charters by which the right to two bovates in Dodworth, with the dependent assart in Hugset and the natives thereto belonging, finally centred in the monks.

The land seems to have been originally—perhaps when the monks obtained their grant of the manor—in the possession of one Ulf, of whom we learn no more than that he had two sons, Richard and William, with whom the dealings in respect of these lands commence. As Richard died early, without children, the property came to his younger brother William.

The following are the charters regarding the property:—

No. 359.   Lease at 2s. rent from William son of Ulf to John the chaplain, son of Hugh the priest of Barnsley : a bovate in Dodworth which belonged to Bared Ruffus and its meadow, and that assart in Hugset which was Ulmer's.

No. 360.   Confirmation of No. 359 by Richard, William's elder brother.

No. 358.   Grant of the same by John the chaplain to Matilda his daughter, and Adam her husband.

No. 336.   Warranty by John son of John the chaplain, and brother of Matilda.

No. 384.   Sale of the same to the monks by Matilda widow of Adam, for 9s. purchase money.

No. 339.   Release by William son of Ulf, at a chief rent of 4d., of a bovate which he had held of Richard his brother.

No. 372.   Confirmation by both brothers, to the monks, of the natives belonging to their land in Dodworth.

No. 397.   Release from William son of Ulf of two bovates which he had held from Richard his brother, now deceased.

No. 385 furnishes a hint of one method adopted by the early monks to subdue the waste places of their manor.   In this case they seem to have given 32 acres into the hand of Hugh son of Herbert, that he might assart, or clear them of their wood; his remuneration being the possession of the cleared land for his life.

The two charters, No. 386 and No. 387, are of son and father, the earlier being granted in the latter part of the reign of King Stephen. It shows Henry de Lascy in possession and with Matilda his mother still alive.   The witness William being described simply as "brother of Thomas" perhaps implies that the date of the charter was before William had become almoner, and therefore before No. 11, No. 14, No. 15, No. 17, No. 18, and No. 48.

The value of the gift concerned was large, if not in the present, at least in the future, as may be judged by an enumeration of what the monks gave in exchange.   No. 386 is a generation later than No. 387; of all the witnesses to the early charter only Henry de Lascy himself remains, but William the almoner, brother of Thomas the steward, is represented by his son.

The early charter gives some interesting particulars as to the businesslike method with which these monks of the middle of the twelfth century—just recovering from the effects of the civil war between the Gaunt and the de Lascy—laid the foundation for the future prosperity of their house, by giving large present gifts for that which had much larger possibilities.   Those gifts were but a small mortgage on the future, and when the few payments had run out the monks would continue to hold in possession a manor of exceptional value, though at an early stage of its productiveness.

Jordan seems to have received ten marks twice; once at the time his father granted No. 387, and a second time when he himself granted No. 386; while the robe and boots, which were an annuity for his father, seem to have been continued to him; as was the permission to become a monk when he would.

Ralph de Caprecuria granted No. 387 at the time that seals were coming into use by the tenant or squire class, and accordingly he speaks of his "present seal."

From these charters we thus obtain a small pedigree :—

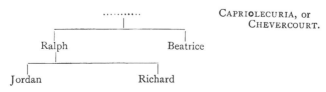

To this is added in a charter of Wallingwells that Ralph had three grand-daughters, of whom one married a Newmarch and another a St. Quentin. No trace, however, of either occurs in the Pontefract Chartulary, though so late as the fifteenth century the advowson of Campsall, which belonged to the Newmarch family, was given to the monastery of Wallingwells, founded by this ancestor.

Richard Bagot, who signs each of these charters, was probably a monk of the house. He also witnessed No. 11, No. 222, and No. 223, gradually rising in position, but never giving any hint as to that position, or as to either his family or his property; probably he had neither of these last-named. In signing No. 11, No. 386 and No. 387, he immediately precedes the officials of the monastery, whether steward, or treasurer, or almoner; but in No. 222 and No. 223 he takes a higher position.

No. 386 was confirmed with very considerable solemnity in the presence of the royal justiciary, Richard de Lucy, and in the chapel of St. Mary Magdalen in Doncaster.

In an earlier stage of his career, Richard de Lucy had witnessed No. 70, the charter by which King Stephen gave to the monks the two York churches of St. Sampson and St. Benedict. When peace was made between King Stephen and the Empress, he seems to have heartily accepted it, and on the death of Stephen he at once ranged himself on the side of the new king, who probably owed much to de Lucy's talents for government. Less than three months after the succession of Henry II, Richard de Lucy tested the two charters of that monarch to the Pontefract monks (No. 71 and No. 73), accompanied in the latter, as he had been preceded in No. 70, by Henry de Lascy, a slight indication of his advancing fortunes which is worthy of notice. In No. 386 he had advanced another stage, being justiciary, though not yet chief justiciary, which he became in 1168 in succession to Robert Bossu, Earl of Leicester, whom he followed in No. 73. We have no data at hand by which the date of Jordan's charter can be more nearly fixed than 1155–1168. Ralph and Beatrice would seem to have been dead at its date.

It is curious that in neither of these charters is there any allusion to the fact named in No. 15, that Henry de Lascy was a joint donor of Barnsley. The claim to joint donorship was probably intended only to indicate the formal consent of the holder of the fee.

The two next charters complete the transference of all the property in the Silkstone bovates which had belonged to Hugh

Pincerna and his wife, with their respective natives. The final vestige of ownership is absolutely alienated and transferred to the monks by Avicia de Savile in the full power of her widowhood. The various charters complement each other in the information they deal out to us, and it is only by collating them that we ascertain how much can be gleaned. For instance, we should not learn from either of these two that Hugh Pincerna was this lady's deceased husband, though that such was the case is made abundantly clear by statements in No. 370. In one small point, however, every one of them fails us. Not one informs us of the exact relation which was borne by John de Savile to the others of the name. He appears in No. 346, No. 363, and No. 364 as an independent witness, in the two last-named having the knightly prefix, and in No. 388 immediately preceding Richard Pincerna as an elder brother would do ; and in No. 389 he is a grantee as if he were one of the sons of Avicia, though neither of the documents so styles him. Assuming that such was the relationship, we thus arrive at the following :—

Hugh Pincerna, = The Lady Avicia de Seyville,
   of Sandal   (a widow) 370, 388

William,	(Sir) John,	Richard,	Dionis,	Michael, = Idonea
335, 370,	346, 363,	335, 354,	335, 373	of Don- (a widow),
388, 389	364, 388,	370, 373,		caster 381
	389	381, 388		

Besides these, the following occur, but there is no indication where they should be placed. They were probably relatives of the Lady Avicia, perhaps brothers or cousins, but the Pontefract Chartulary is silent : Ralph de Savile No. 340, and Henry de Savile No. 227, No. 267, No. 336, No. 340, No. 347, No. 355, and No. 390.

It may be added that Seyville or Savile, from which this family are thought to have sprung, was a place in Anjou ; so that their arrival in England may be connected with the reign of Henry II, Earl of Anjou.

They seem to have held this property in Silkstone at the time it was acquired by the monks.

With regard to the Gerard who made so large a conveyance to the monks by No. 393, we learn from that charter that he was Gerard of Barnsley, and that his elder son was named Adam ; from

No. 394 we learn that he was the greave of Roger of Barnsley, the steward of the monks (see No. 382 and No. 383); and from No. 395 we learn that he was the son of Alured. Since No. 356 has already informed us that he had a son Robert, we thus obtain the following pedigree of three generations :—

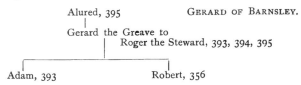

Alured, 395   GERARD OF BARNSLEY.
    |
Gerard the Greave to
            | Roger the Steward, 393, 394, 395

Adam, 393   Robert, 356

Of the second Gerard nothing can be said more` than that he was the son of a Thomas, by which name he tests this charter.

Very peculiar interest in many directions attaches to No. 396, which seems to be of about 1155. Broughton is in Craven, and perhaps as a consequence of the condition of civil disturbance through which the district had lately passed, the charter before us is tested in a manner of which we have had no previous example ; for out of eleven witnesses six, and perhaps indeed eight, are the lords and the heirs presumptive, or apparent, of three (or four) manors in its immediate neighbourhood, whose witness was especially requisitioned by the grantor, and stated on the face of the document so to be.

These witnesses, perhaps eight out of eleven, are Peter de Marton and William his son, Roger Tempest and Richard his brother, of Bracewell, Simon de Mohaut and Simon his son ; to which may be added Rainer of Fernhill and Adam his grandson. The second of these names (Latinized Tempestas) is that of a still existing family, and it is a matter of some interest to know that the Roger who tests No. 396 is the earliest known ancestor of the family, who thirty or forty years previously had acquired Bracewell, and who as early as 1120 had been a witness to the foundation of Embsay, the predecessor of Bolton.

During the century preceding the grant conferred by No. 396, Broughton and its neighbouring manors had been subject to many vicissitudes. In pre-Norman times they had belonged to Earl Edwin, and after his deprivation in 1069 had been part of the large possessions of Roger Pictavensis, third son of Roger Montgomery, Earl of Shrewsbury. Pictavensis also had been deprived before the Domesday Survey was taken in 1086 ; for at that time all the manors of North-Western Yorkshire between Ribble and Wharfe were in the hands of the king. But even while the Survey was in progress and before it was completed Roger Pictavensis obtained a re-grant of much of his former holding, including both Broughton and Bracewell.

It was probably during the second possession of this district by Roger Pictavensis that Robert de Rumelli became the tenant of Broughton and Roger Tempest of Bracewell, each holding at least as early as 1120. But such are the apparently capricious contrasts afforded by history, that while Roger Tempest himself survived till the date of No. 326, and his family has continued in male heirs to the present day, that of Robert de Rumelli failed in the first generation; he himself died comparatively early; and it was his daughter's daughter who granted the charter thus witnessed by the aged contemporary of her maternal grandfather. But although the name of the father and founder of their race had each died out, both she and her mother seem to have had such reverence for their paternal cognomen that they never really abandoned it, Cecily de Rumelli being always so known, notwithstanding her fruitful marriage with William le Meschine; while her granddaughter, Alice de Rumelli, even so late as 1195, notwithstanding two marriages, was under that name the defendant in two Final Concords with regard to land in Oxfordshire and Cumberland. These transactions arose out of her third or fourth marriage, namely, with Robert de Curtney.

As has been said, Robert de Rumelli had no male heirs; but his daughter Cecily made an illustrious marriage with William le Meschine, one of the sons of the powerful Earl of Chester and himself Earl of Cambridge. They were in full possession at Skipton in 1120, in which year they founded the Augustinian priory of Canons at Embsay, near the head of their fee, which continued rather more than thirty years, when it was transferred to Bolton. They had then no male heir, though they had had two sons, Ralph and Matthew, who had both died young; but Alice their eldest daughter was married to William fitz Duncan, who was treated as their heir, and as William, son-in-law of Cecily and grandson of Malcolm king of Scots, he joined his wife's mother in a grant of the manor of Kildwick to the monks of Embsay. The date of this grant is not clear, neither is his description in the charters connected with it uniform, but it is tested among others by Adam fitz Swain, Roger Tempest, and Richard fitz Asolf, the brother of Peter and one of that numerous family of sons, of which we have made mention, *ante*, pp. 254–5. There is a later charter copied *(Monasticon Anglicanum,* ii, 101) as from William himself to Archbishop Thurstan, by which, under the title of "son of Duncan and grandson of the king of Scotland," he notified that he had given the church of Broughton to the canons of Embsay. This was evidently later than 1147, for it was tested by Alexander Abbot of Kirkstall and Benedict Abbot of Sallay.

Now this William fitz Duncan, as he was called in England, or William Mac Donochy, as was his Scottish name, was that Scottish prince who in 1138 was leader of the Galloway contingent that acted with such truculent brutality towards the unhappy people upon whom the army of his uncle David king of Scots made a raid, described in most harrowing terms by the historians of the period. The northern forces were ultimately defeated and driven home by the victory of Northallerton, where the invading Scots, under this William fitz Duncan, were crushed by the manhood of the north, incited by Archbishop Thurstan and his assistant-bishop Ralph Noel or Novellus, and led by every nobleman of consequence in Yorkshire. And considering this, it is (to say the least) remarkable that none of the historians who narrate the circumstances of the battle of the Standard hint at the fact that this very William fitz Duncan became, by his marriage with Alice de Rumelli, the presumptive lord of the Skipton fee, and that he was joined in the gift first of the church of Broughton and afterwards of the manor to the canons of Embsay. There is nothing to show how his married life was spent till 1152, when (perhaps at the death of Cecily de Rumelli, the mother of his wife, and his consequent accession to the property) William fitz Duncan appears as a claimant for his wife's inheritance, the Skipton Fee, and is stated to have been forcibly put in possession there by his uncle David, king of Scotland.

But it should be stated that all the documents relating to the Skipton transactions are fourteenth century copies only; and though authenticated by exemplification on the patent rolls, and probably true witnesses of actual fact, there are yet evidences that they have been carelessly and perfunctorily transcribed, and that important errors have been made in what were only subsidiary details from the cartographer's point of view. We have shown how William fitz Duncan was mis-described, being correctly stated in one case to have been "filius Dunecani, nepos regis Scotiæ," and in another to have been "nepos regis Scotæ Dunecani," thus confusing William's father Duncan, who was never king, with his grandfather Malcolm; and in still one other important instance it is evident that Archbishop Thurstan's name has been substituted for that of a subsequent archbishop (perhaps Murdac [1147–53], which, with an initial much elaborated, would bear a superficial resemblance to Thurstan, and without close examination might deceive even a practised eye); while the document was tested by an abbot of Kirkstall, and one of Sallay, although neither of those monasteries was founded till some years after the death of Thurstan.

Still one other of these documents (all quoted as taken from Rolls 33 Edward I, and 5 Edward II, part 2) asserts that at the impossible date of "1 Henry II, 1151," Alice de Rumelli, with the consent of William her son, had exchanged with the canons of Embsay the manor of Bolton for certain lands which they possessed. Doubtless the exchange was made, but the date was impossible; for 1 Henry II was 1155, not 1151. And the exchange was otherwise impossible at the earlier date; for Alice de Rumelli was not then in possession, but, as we have said, obtained her seisin at the hands of the Scottish king, her uncle David, only so late as 1152.

But the two dates represent very different conditions of affairs; for the few years 1151-5 had effected a complete revolution. In 1151, the date incorrectly given in the document to which we have referred, there was open civil war, and it was by no means certain what would be the result. The death, however, of Eustace fitz Stephen in 1152, of King David of Scotland in 1153, and of King Stephen himself in 1154, closed the period of anarchy. The year 1155 was therefore the most likely date for this exchange, which was certainly confirmed by the new king (Henry II) in February, 1155, when he had been but three months on the throne.

The charter No. 396 may likewise be safely assigned to the same year. For there had been an anarchical period in Pontefract also, owing to that fee having been, on the death of Ilbert de Lascy in 1141, conferred upon William de Romare, Earl of Lincoln. When he died, his son-in-law claimed the fee in right of his wife, on which Henry de Lascy felt himself strong enough to put in his claim, and there was open war between the two claimants, during which the monastery was so injured as to necessitate a rebuilding. While that was being effected, the monks were homeless, and Alice de Rumelli made this grant, having probably in view not only the destitute condition of the Pontefract monks but the desirability of introducing them for its protection to her Skipton fee.

The William, her son, with whose consent the grant was made, was the "Boy of Egremont," whose presumed death at the Strid, while leaping the stream, has inflamed so many poetical imaginations. Into the exact truth of the tradition this is hardly the place to enquire, though it seems probable that the circumstance has been fixed on the wrong hero, and that it was one of the sons of Cecily (who both died young) who was the subject of the "bootless bene."

No. 397, the last of the series, is a more inclusive and a later charter than No. 339. It appears to have been granted while the Chartulary was in compilation, and so to have been made to follow the rest, not to precede them. William had at its date "succeeded by hereditary right," that is to say his brother Richard was dead without male heir.

At this point (folio 65 of the Chartulary, the last of the Eighth Fasciculus) the difference in character of the parchment of the eighth and ninth, though not very pronounced, is much more marked than in any other part of the volume ; and the retro of folio 66, the first folio of the Ninth Fasciculus, is worn thin by the abrasion to which it was subjected, probably while yet the fasciculi were separate sections of the projected volume.

No. 396 and No. 397 were evidently inserted rather later than the previous documents, though written by a nearly, if not quite, contemporary hand, and they complete the recto of folio 65. The dorse of the folio has never been filled.

De Peckefeld.

CCCXI.[1]   1184.

[Agreement made at York . . . . before Rainer the steward of Ralph de Glanville, then sheriff of Yorkshire, and the barons of the lord king . . . . between Hugh, prior of Pontefract, and the monks, and Hugh and Geoffrey, sons of William de Bolton, concerning the half part of Peckfield. . . . . . The prior and monks have given Geoffrey a bovate of land in Ledsham, with its appurtenances, and the toft of Richard, with Richard himself and his belongings, ... by the service of 6 pence yearly. . . . . . Also the aforesaid Hugh and Geoffrey . . . . . have quit-claimed to H. prior and the monks of Pontefract all their aforesaid part of Peckfield, ... Warranty. Witnesses.]

Hec est Concordia (. . . . .)[2] facta in primo comitatu apud Ebor' post festum sancti Johannis baptiste anno xxx° regni Regis H. secundi coram Rainero[3] dapifero Ranulfi de Glanvill', tunc vicecomite Ebor', et baronibus domini Regis qui tunc ibi aderant, inter Hugonem Priorem de Pontefracto et monachos, et Hugonem[4] et Gaufridum filios Willelmi de Boeltona, de media parte de Pechfeld, unde placitum fuit inter eos. Scilicet quod predicti H. Prior et monachi dederunt predicto Gaufrido unam bovatam terre in Ledesham'[4] cum omnibus pertinentiis suis et toftum Ricardi cum ipso Ricardo et secta sua, in feudo et hereditate, de se tenenda per servitium vi denariorum, iii ad festum sancti Martini et iii ad Pentecosten inde reddendorum annuatim, consentiente et consedente[5] predicto Hugone[4] fratre suo, qui totum jus suum quod habuit in Pekefeld eidem Gaufrido quietum clamavit. Predicti quoque Hugo[4] et Gaufridus filii Willelmi de Boeltona clamaverunt H. priori et monachis de Pontefracto totam predictam partem suam de Pekfeld quietam imperpetuum de se et de heredibus suis. Istam excambiam warantizabunt prior et monachi Gaufrido et heredibus suis, et Gaufridus et heredes sui monachis contra omnes homines. Hiis testibus, *Osberto de Baius,*[4] *Adam filio Petri et Thoma fratre suo, Ada de Rainevill, Petro filio*[6]

---

(1) This Fine (which it was, though it does not bear the name—see next note) was very badly copied for the *Monasticon*, in which it appears as one of the additional documents in the new edition (vol. v, p. 129, No. 34). Stevens originally printed it, with the statement that he had obtained it from an original in the possession of Ralph Thoresby. But Thoresby's document was probably only a copy imperfectly transcribed from the original Court Roll. The mis-spellings, especially of names, are numerous ; and some of them, so to say, ingeniously bad. See note (4). Dodsworth had no copy of it for the original *Monasticon* of 1655.

(2) The first three words constitute a line, the cartographer having left a blank, either for the reception of the word "finalis" or for a more elaborate rubrication, which was never inserted.

(3) Possibly the Rainer de Waxtonsham of No. 422.

(4) In *Monasticon Anglicanum* Hugo appears as Hubert, Ledesham as Ledegham, Baius as Bains, Stivetona as Stiveter, Luttringtona as Luquetuna. In No. 427, as in S 463 and S 466, Osbert de Baius was a tenant in Middle Haddlesey.   (5) *Sic.*

(6) There seems to be some omission between this word and the next.

Hauterive, Maugero de Stivetona,[4] et Hugone filio suo,[7] Ricardo de Luttringtona,[4] Henrico clerico de Kellingtona,[8] Ada filio Ormi, Ricardo filio Laising, et aliis. _____

(7) As Hugo de Stiveton he tests No. 310, while Robert his brother tests No. 320, No. 323 and No. 324.   (8) He was next brother to John the rector.

BURTON [SALMON].
CCCXII.   Carta Galfridi Pigot de Brettona.

[. . . . . I, Geoffrey, son of Pigot, of Bretton, have . . . . . confirmed to Herbert Sele of Brotherton, ... an acre of land in the territory of Bretton, whereof half an acre lies in the Broad Assart, and half a rood at the fourth, and a rood and a half next the marsh which is called soke, and a toft from my toft, ... and to make a garden . . . . . To be held and possessed . . . . . . Paying thence yearly to me and my heirs 2 pence, ... Warranty. Witnesses.]

Sciant presentes et futuri quod ego Gaufridus filius Pigot de Brettona dedi et concessi et hac presenti carta mea confirmavi Hereberto Sele de Brotherton, pro homagio suo et servitio suo unam acram terre in territorio de Brettona, unde dimidia acra jacet in lato essarto et dimidia perticata ad quartum, et perticata et dimidia juxta mariscum qui vocatur soke, et unum toftum de tofto meo in occidentali parte tofti, habentem xx*ti* et novem pedes de latitudine et sexaginta et duodecim de longitudine, et ad ortum faciendum xx*ti* pedes de latitudine, et de longitudine quantum totus ortus durat. Tenenda et habenda sibi et heredibus suis de me et heredibus meis, libere et quiete, in bosco et plano, in prato et pastura, et in omnibus aisiamentis et communitatibus ad tantum tenementum pertinentibus. Reddendo inde annuatim mihi et heredibus meis ij denarios, pro omni servitio seculari et exactione. Scilicet unum denarium in Nathale domini, et unum denarium in die pasche. Et ego prefatus Galfridus et heredes mei warentizabimus predictam terram predicto H. et heredibus suis cum omnibus pertinentiis contra omnes homines. Hiis testibus, *domino Osberto de Brettona, Serlone fratre suo, Galfrido de Ledeshama, Waltero de Byrum, Jordano Pateman, Willelmo filio Petri,*[1] *Thoma fratre suo, Willelmo clerico, Adam de Brettona,*[2] et multis aliis. _____

(1) See No. 447 and pedigree in connection with No. 505.   (2) See No. 265.

DE DARDINGTONA.
CCCXIII.   Carta Willelmi filii Hervei.

[. . . . . . I, William, son of Hervey, have . . . . confirmed . . . . four shillings of rent from that land which Jordan of Ledston holds of me in Darrington, that is to say from two bovates and their assarts . . . . . to provide for the monks with three shillings, and to buy wine with 12 pence for masses. Every priest shall sing one mass for the souls of my relations and ancestors, and the other monks, who are not priests, 50 psalms while I live, and after my death by name for my soul and for all the faithful departed. Witnesses.]

Notum sit omnibus qui viderint vel audierint hanc cartam quod ego Willelmus filius Hervey concessi et donavi et hac eadem carta mea sigillata confirmavi ecclesie sancti Johannis et monachis de Pontefracto pro salute anime mee et patris mei et matris mee et antecessorum meorum, in puram elemosinam et perpetuam, quatuor solidos redditus de terra illa quam Jordanus de Ledestona tenet de me in Dardingtona; scilicet duabus bovatis et sartis ad bovatas pertinentibus. Quos quatuor solidos secretarius recipiet annuatim de Jordano et de heredibus suis in media quadragesima, ad procurandum monachos de tribus solidis et ad emendum vinum de xii denariis ad missas. In die vero qua procuratio fiet, cantabit unusquisque sacerdos missam unam pro animabus parentum et antecessorum meorum et alii monachi qui non sunt sacerdotes L. salmos dum ego vixero et post obitum meum nominatim pro anima mea et pro omnibus fidelibus defunctis. Testibus, *Roberto de Stapiltona, Adam filio Orm, Gervasio de Milleford, Everardo filio Jordani, Thoma de Monte monachorum, Ricardo de Ledestuna, Henrico filio Ricardi, Nicholao celerario de sancto Oswaldo, Helya de Hudlestuna, Rainaldo de Ledestuna, Rogero presbitero de Ledeshama, Gilleberto filio Rainaldi, Ricardo de Stapiltona, Hugone de Kercroft*, et aliis.

CCCXIIII.   Carta Willelmi filii Hervei.   117...

[. . . . . I, William, son of Hervey, have . . . . . confirmed . . . . . . those two bovates of land in Darrington which I hold of William son of Gerold, William son of Gerold himself granting, and with me upon the altar of St. John offering the same alms, saving forinsec service. Witnesses.]

Notum sit presentibus et futuris quod ego Willelmus filius Hervei dedi et concessi et per hanc meam cartam et meum sigillum confirmavi deo et sancto Johanni et monachis de Pontefracto illas duas bovatas terre in Dardingtona quas ego teneo de Willelmo filio Geroldi, in puram et perpetuam elemosinam, ipso Willelmo filio Geroldi concedente et mecum super altare sancti Johannis eandem elemosinam offerente, salvo forensi servitio. Testibus, *Roberto de Stapiltona et Hugone et Ricardo*[1] *fratribus suis, Gilberto constabulario,*

---

(1) Richard de Stapleton witnessed the Little Charter. See vol. i, page xl.

Ricardo Bagot, Thoma dapifero et Willelmo pistore, Asketillo et Ranulfo fratre suo, Jordano de Ledestuna et Rainaldo et Rogero et Waltero fratribus suis, Helya de Huddlestona, Haymerico de Stapiltona, Adam pistore, et aliis.

CCCXV.[1]   Carta Willelmi filii Hervey.

[. . . . . I the son of Hervey have granted . . . . . a bovate of land from the clearings of Byram, which Gilbert holds of me, paying yearly 16 pence. This same bovate Gilbert shall hold from the monks, paying them that amount. And when he is dead, the monks shall do with that land what they please. These being witnesses, &c.]

Notum sit omnibus fidelibus tam presentibus quam futuris quod ego filius Hervei dedi et concessi deo et sancto Johanni et monachis de Pontefracto in puram et perpetuam elemosinam unam bovatam terre de sartis de Byrum quam Gillebertus tenet de me, reddendo per annum xvi denarios in die sancti Martini. Hanc ipsam bovatam tenebit ipse Gillebertus a monachis de Pontefracto, eundem censum in die sancti Martini unoquoque anno reddendo ipsis monachis quam diu vixerit. Cumque mortuus fuerit ipse Gillebertus facient monachi de ipsa terra sicut de sua propria quod eis placuerit. Hiis testibus, *Johanne presbitero de Sancta Trinitate,*[2] *Rogero Grosso presbitero, Roberto capellano, Gaufrido Pullano, Roberto de Stapiltona, Willelmo*[3] *et Roberto fratre ejus, Roberto dispensatore, Waltero Blundo de Ebor', Helya de Hudlestona, Bartholomeo Scirmatore, Jordano, Rainaldo et Waltero filiis Ailrici de Ledestona, Willelmo et Adam pistoribus, Roberto brasatore, Jollando janitore, Willelmo filio Giroldi de Dardingtona,* et aliis.

(1) Not one of these four charters appears in any of *Dodsworth's MSS.*, or in *Lansdowne MS.*
(2) Possibly of York.   (3) There seems nothing to tell us who this William was.

DE LEDESHAM SUPER PEKKEFELD.
CCCXVI.   Carta Jordani de Lalanda.[1]   1205-10.

[. . . . . . I, Jordan de Laland, ... have confirmed . . . . . . two parts of Peckfield, which Paganus, my grandfather, gave to them. I have also . . . . confirmed . . . . . to all their tenants of Ledston and of Ledsham, full, free, and entire commonage of all the whole pasture of my land at Micklefield, except grain

(1) De la Land is the usual way of spelling this name. The Lalands became a good Lincolnshire family, and Ashby de la Land was named from them. A reference to No. 260 will show how the name had become "de Land" in the time of the great-grandson.

and meadow. The monks shall pay to me and my heirs, from Ledston, two skeps of wheat yearly, ... and from Ledsham two old measures of wheat, as contained in the charter of Paganus, my grandfather. Warranty. Witnesses.]

Omnibus sancte matris ecclesie filiis Jordanus de Lalanda salutem. Noverit universitas vestra quod ego Jordanus de Lalanda pro salute anime mee et antecessorum et heredum meorum concessi et hac presenti carta confirmavi deo et sancto Johanni et monachis de Pontefracto, in puram et perpetuam elemosinam, duas partes de Pekefelda quas Paganus avus meus eis dedit et confirmavit. Insuper concessi et hac presenti carta confirmavi predicte ecclesie sancti Johannis et prefatis monachis ejusdem loci et omnibus hominibus suis de Ledestona et de Ledeshama plenam, liberam, et integram communam totius pasture universe terre mee de Mikelfeld, extra bladum et pratum. Predicti vero monachi reddent mihi et heredibus meis annuatim de Ledestona duas sceppas frumenti infra festum sancti Martini et Nathale domini pro libera communa predicte pasture, et de Ledeshama duas veteres melas frumenti ad eundem terminum prout continetur in carta predicti Pagani avi mei. Ego autem Jordanus de Lalanda et heredes mei predictam elemosinam de Pekefeld et communam pasture de Mikelfelde warentizabimus prefatis monachis contra omnes homines. Hiis testibus, *Roberto Walensi, tunc vice-comite Ebor',*[2] *Johanne de Byrkin, Willelmo de Stapiltona, Ricardo de Hudlestuna, Ricardo et Roberto filiis suis, Osberto de Brettona, Ada de Stiuetona, Rogero decano de Ledeshama, Magistro Johanne Wakring-hama, Hugone de Bateleya, Johanne filio Langus,*[3] et aliis.

---

(2) The mention of Robert Wallis as sheriff of Yorkshire fixes the date of this charter as between 1205 and 1210 ; the probability is that it may be assigned to 1208 or 1209.   (3) *Sic.*

CCCXVII.[1]   Carta Pagani de Laland.

[. . . . . I, Paganus de Laland, by the consent and advice of my wife Alice, have . . . . . confirmed . . . . . two parts of Peckfield . . . . . And the monks have received me into their brotherhood, and have appointed me an anniversary, so that every priest shall celebrate a mass ; the rest sing psalms. Also I have . . . . confirmed . . . . commonage of all the pasture in all my land of Micklefield, except meadow and grain. And the monks shall pay to me yearly from Ledston two skeps of wheat, and from Ledsham two old measures of wheat. Warranty. Witnesses.]

---

(1) Abridged transcripts of No. 316 and No. 317 are copied into *Lansdowne* 207.

Universis sancte ecclesie filiis Paganus de Lalanda salutem. Noverit universitas vestra quod ego Paganus de Lalanda consensu et consilio uxoris mee Aliz dedi et hac presenti carta confirmavi deo et sancto Johanni et monachis de Pontefracto duas partes de Pechefeld in puram et perpetuam elemosinam pro salute anime mee et uxoris mee predicte Aliz et omnium antecessorum et heredum meorum. Predicti vero monachi receperunt me in monachum suum, et anniversarium pro me fieri unoquoque anno constituerunt, ita ut in die anniversarii mei unusquisque sacerdos unam missam celebret; ceteri salmos cantent. Insuper concessi et hac presenti carta mea confirmavi predicte ecclesie sancti Johannis et predictis monachis ejusdem loci et omnibus hominibus suis de Ledestuna et omnibus hominibus de Ledeshama, plenam, liberam et integram communam totius pasture universe terre mee de Mikelfelda extra pratum et bladum.[2] Predicti vero monachi reddent mihi annuatim de Ledestuna duas skeppas frumenti infra festum sancti Martini et Nathale domini pro libera communa predicte pasture et de Ledesham duas veteres melas frumenti ad eundem terminum. Ego vero Paganus et heredes mei hanc puram elemosinam, scilicet duas partes de Pekefeld et liberam communam totius pasture terre mee de Mikelfelda sicut prescriptum est, warentizabimus predictis monachis contra omnes homines. Hiis testibus, *Willelmo filio meo qui mecum hanc Kartam[3] super altare sancti Johannis de Pontefracto presentavit, et presentibus hiis testibus Willelmo filio Hervei, Herberto de Archis, Roberto de Stapiltona, Petro de Toulestuna, Jordano de Ledestuna, et Rainaldo fratre suo, Michaeli filio Thome, Johanne de Baldirtona, et W. fratre suo, Willelmo de Horbyre, Willelmo de Archis, Willelmo de Hoctona,* et multis aliis.

_____

(2) We have here in these two charters an indication of the threefold division of the land into arable, meadow, and field or common land. The exception of "pratum et bladum," common to these and to No. 260, is not specified in the complementary charter, No. 318.   (3) *Sic.*

CCCXVIII.[1]   Carta Maugeri de Stivetuna.

[. . . . . I, Mauger de Stiveton, have . . . . . . confirmed . . . . . all my part of Peckfield, that is to say, the third part of all Peckfield . . . . . . for sixteen pence yearly. And because the aforesaid monks have received me into their full brotherhood with my wife and my heirs, I have confirmed . . . . . free commonage of all the pasture belonging to the third part of Micklefield . . . . Warranty. Witnesses.]

_____

(1) I have not met with a copy of No. 318.

Omnibus fidelibus sancte matris ecclesie Maugerius de Stivetuna salutem in Christo. Sciatis quod ego Maugerius de Stivetuna dedi, concessi, et hac presenti carta mea confirmavi deo et sancto Johanni et monachis de Pontefracto totam partem meam de Pekefeld. Scilicet totam terciam partem totius Pekefeld cum omnibus pertinentiis suis. Tenendam de me et de heredibus meis inperpetuum. Reddendo mihi annuatim et heredibus meis sexdecim denarios, octo in Pentecosten, et octo in festo sancti Martini. Et quia predicti monachi receperunt me in plenariam fraternitatem suam et uxorem meam et heredes meos, concessi et hac presenti carta mea confirmavi predictis monachis et omnibus hominibus eorum, tam de Ledestuna, quam de Ledeshama, quietam et liberam communam totius pasture pertinentis tercie parti de Mikelfeld in puram et perpetuam elemosinam, pro anima mea et uxoris mee et omnium antecessorum et heredum meorum. Et hanc communam pasture ego et heredes mei warantizabimus contra omnes homines. Hiis testibus, *Arnaldo presbitero et Roberto socio ejus, Thoma filio Petri, Ricardo Bagoth, Hugone clerico de Calthorn, Roberto Norreis, Ailrico et Godefrido de Ledestuna, Ricardo filio Laising, Nigello filio Aldani, Thoma preposito monachorum et Willelmo fratre ejus, Michaele filio Thome prepositi monachorum,* et multis aliis.

CCCXIX.[1] Carta Ade filii Petri et Matildis uxoris sue. Cir. 1160.

[. . . . I, Adam fitz Peter and my wife Matilda de Caux have granted . . . . to amend their provision . . . . . . half the mill of Stainborough. Witnesses.]

Sciant presentes et futuri quod ego Adam filius Petri et uxor mea Matilda de Calz[2] concessimus et donavimus deo et sancto Johanni et monachis de Pontefracto ad procurationem eorum emendandam, pro remedio animarum mearum,[3] et antecessorum meorum, in puram et perpetuam elemosinam, medietatem molendini de Stainburch. Hiis testibus, *Thoma filio Petri, et Rogero filio Petri, fratribus meis, Roberto filio meo, Willelmo de Mungai,*[4] *Henrico de Suinlingtona, Widone de Aula, Radulfo et Willelmo de Mugai, Rogero de Capreolecuria, Helya filio Ricardi, Jordano et Rainaldo, et Rogero, et Waltero de Ledestona,* et aliis. _____

(1) No. 319 appears as No. xxiii in the *Monasticon*, with the omission of Henry de Swillington from among the witnesses. It was a somewhat early grant, probably 1160.

(2) Matilda de Caux was one of the co-heirs of Robert de Caux at Lexington; and Stainborough being in her patrimony, it was necessary that she should join in this donation to the monks of St. John.   (3) *Sic.*

(4) Some of the names of the witnesses to this charter seem not to have been carefully copied. Munjoie was misspelt in two different ways. "Rogero de Capreolecuria" is not met with elsewhere, though there is a Robert and a Ralph. It should be noticed that there were two Williams de Munjoie.

CCCXX.[1]   Carta Ade filii Petri.

[. . . . . I, Adam fitz Peter, ... have confirmed . . . . for myself . . . . . and for all who may have sinned by me or for me five acres from assarts in the territory of Birkin, next the assart of Richard son of Arnald, and three acres of meadow in Smeathalls, next to two acres of the hospital of Saint Michael, and sufficient pasture to keep 20 cows and a bull, with the young of the cows until two years old; and what may be necessary to build there, to make a fireplace there, and hedges. . . . . with the common easements . . . . Warranty. Witnesses.]

Sciant presentes et futuri quod ego Adam filius Petri, sponte, et in ligia mea potestate, dedi et concessi et hac presenti carta mea confirmavi deo et ecclesie sancti Johannis de Pontefracto et monachis ibidem deo servientibus, pro me et pro omnibus antecessoribus et heredibus meis et pro omnibus[2] qui me vel pro me aliquo modo peccaverint, in puram et perpetuam elemosinam, quinque acras de sartis in territorio de Byrkine[3] juxta sartum Ricardi filii Arnaldi ex parte del North sarti predicti Ricardi; et tres acras prati in Smethale proximas duabus acris hospitalis sancti Michaelis ex parte del West; et plenariam pasturam ad xx*ti* vaccas ibidem sustinendas et unum taurum, cum nurrina[4] predictarum vaccarum usque fuerint duorum annorum, et que necessaria fuerint ad ibi edificandum et ad focum ibidem faciendum, et ad sepes faciendas. Predictum vero sartum et pratum et pasturas dedi eis cum communibus aisiamentis ejusdem ville infra predictam villam et extra. Et hanc elemosinam warantizabimus eis ego et heredes mei contra omnes homines in puram et perpetuam elemosinam. Hiis testibus, *Thoma filio Petri, Ranulfo Hose, Roberto de Stiuetona, Rogero de Ledeshama, Johanne de Rorestona, Ricardo Wasp, Willelmo Coco, Radulfo de Broctona, Johanne de Knuctona,* et aliis.

(1) There is an abridgment in the *Lansdowne MS.*

(2) For a similar addition see also No. 323, where we have "causa mei" in place of the ungrammatical "me vel pro me."

(3) No. 322 confirmed the acres in Smeathalls but not those in Birkin.   (4) *Sic.*

CCCXXI.[1]   Carta Ade filii Petri.   Cir. 1160.

[. . . . . I, Adam fitz Peter, under the attestation of the present cartule, confirm a half bovate of land in Fairburn . . . . to make oblations and for wine at masses, for the redemption of my soul . . . . . . For this the monks have received me and all my friends into their brotherhood . . . . The witnesses of this donation are, &c.]

(1) It is No. xxiv in the *Monasticon.*

Sciant omnes presentes et futuri quod ego Adam filius Petri do et sub presentis cartule attestatione confirmo dimidiam bovatam terre in Fareburna deo et sancto Johanni et monachis de Pontefracto, ad oblata facienda et ad vinum ad missas, liberam et quietam ab omni seculari servitio et in puram elemosinam inperpetuum, pro redemptione anime mee, et uxoris, et patris, et matris mee, omniumque parentum meorum et amicorum.   Pro hoc beneficio receperunt me monachi et omnes amicos meos in fraternitatem et societatem omnium bene-ficiorum suorum que amodo in monasterio sancti Johannis agentur. Hujus donationis testes sunt, *frater meus Rogerus, Radulfus Figura, Robertus dispensator*[2] *Henrici de Lasci, Robertus butiler ejusdem, Willelmus pistor monachorum, Fossardus portarius, Symon prepositus de Fareburne.*[3]

(2) See No. 15 and R 98.   (3) Fairburn was then the seat of Adam fitz Peter.

CCCXXII.[1]   Carta Johannis filii Ade.[2]

[. . . . I, John son of Adam, ... have confirmed . . . . 13 acres of meadow in Smeathalls, namely, those which my father confirmed to them, and two oaks in my wood of Birkin, every year, against the Nativity of the Lord, and a doe in my park, at the feast of St. John at Port Latin, and half the mill of Stain-borough, with the profit of that half.   I have made this confirmation for the good of my soul, ... and for the care of our bodies.   Witnesses.]

Sciant presentes et futuri quod ego Johannes filius Ade dedi et concessi et hac presenti mea carta confirmavi deo et sancto Johanni et monachis de Pontefracto pro animabus patris et matris mee et omnium antecessorum meorum et successorum in puram et perpetuam elemosinam xiij*cim* acras prati in Smethala.   Illas scilicet quas pater meus eis dedit et confirmavit.   Et duas quercus in bosco meo[3] de Byrkin singulis annis contra Nathale domini et unam damam in parco meo in festo sancti Johannis ante portam Latinam, et dimidium molendini de Stainburga cum secta medietati ejusdem molendini pertinente.   Hanc concessionem et confirmationem feci ego Johannes predictis monachis, pro salute anime mee, et uxoris mee Johanne, et heredum meorum, et pro sospitate corporum nostrorum.   Hiis testibus, *Jacobo Canonico de Drakes, Osberto de Brettuna, Pigot de Brettona, Alano de Rorestuna,*[4] *Petro et Rogero et Willelmo fratribus meis,*[5] *et Martino capellano qui hanc cartam scripsit.*

(1) No. 322 is No. xxv in the *Monasticon*, and there is a transcript in *Lansdowne* 207.

(2) *I.e.*, John de Birkin, son of the preceding Adam fitz Peter.

(3) A comparison with No. 320 shows that a partition has now been made between park and wood, which did not then exist.   See also No. 325.

(4) "Rotestun" in the *Monasticon*.   (5) That is, John the grantor's

CCCXXIII.   Carta Ade filii Petri de Migelaya.

[. . . . I, Adam fitz Peter, have confirmed . . . . a bovate of land in Midgley, that is to say the eighth part of all Midgley, . . . for the healing of my soul, ... and for the souls of all who have sinned through my occasion, Robert, my son, witnessing and granting. Witnesses.]

Omnibus fidelibus sancte ecclesie filiis Adam filius Petri salutem. Sciatis me dedisse et concessisse et hac presenti mea carta confirmasse deo et sancto Johanni et monachis deo servientibus in Pontefracto unam bovatam terre in Migelaia,[1] scilicet octavam partem totius Migelie,[2] in bosco et plano, in paschuis et pratis, in viis et semitis, in molendinis, et cum omnibus pertinentiis suis, in puram et perpetuam elemosinam, liberam et quietam ab omni servitio et seculari exactione de me et de heredibus meis, pro remedio anime mee et patris mei et matris mee et uxoris mee Matildis et omnium antecessorum et heredum meorum et pro animabus omnium qui[3] causa mei peccaverint. Testante et concedente, *Roberto filio meo*, et testibus hiis, *Thoma filio Petri,[4] Willelmo Campiun, Rainero Flamingo, Petro filio Ade, Huctredo de Birkewait, Roberto de Stivetuna, Johanne de Rorestona, Ricardo filio Laising, Rogero fratre suo*, et aliis.

---

(1) This manor is "Little Midgley" in Shitlington, not Midgley near Halifax.   (2) *Sic.*
(3) See No. 320. There is a similar clause in a charter R 345 of this same Adam to Rievaux, "qui propter me vel per me peccaverunt."   (4) Of Leeds.

BYRKYN.
CCCXXIIII.[1]   Carta Ade filii filii[2] Petri.   Cir. 1170.

[. . . . . . . I, Adam fitz Peter, for the love of our Lord Jesus Christ and the good of . . . . . all those who through my evil occasion shall do ill, ... have confirmed . . . . . ten acres of my meadow of Smeathalls. Witnesses.]

Universis sancte matris ecclesie filiis tam presentibus quam futuris Adam filius Petri salutem. Notum sit universitati vestre quod ego Adam filius Petri, pro amore domini nostri Jh'u Christi et salute anime mee et Matildis uxoris mee, et patris et matris mee, et antecessorum et benefactorum meorum, et omnium illorum qui causa mei mali quibus delinquent, donavi et concessi et hac mea presenti carta confirmavi deo et sancto Johanni de Pontefracto et monachis ibidem deo servientibus decem[3] acras de prato meo de Smethala in liberam, puram et perpetuam elemosinam. Hiis testibus, *Paulino*[4]

---

(1) There is a transcript of each of these last charters in *Lansdowne* 207.   (2) *Sic.*
(3) Ten acres here and three in No. 320 (the earlier charter) make up the thirteen in No. 322.
(4) These were four brothers.

presbitero de Ledes, Magistro Albino de Hanepol, Turgisillo monacho de Sancta Trinitate, Petro[4] presbitero, Adam[4] presbitero, fratre ejus, Roberto de Gant,[5] Thoma filio Petri, Roberto filio[6] Ade filii Petri, Philippo de Alterive, Uctredo de Mirefeld, Roberto filio Mugeri[7] de Stivetona, Thoma[4] fratre Paulini, Roberto filio Hugonis de Pikeburna, et aliis.

(5) He died in 1192.   (6) Son and heir. See note to No. 325.   (7) *Sic.*

CCCXXV.   Carta Ade filii Petri de Birkin.[1]

[. . . . . . I, Adam fitz Peter, of Birkin, with the consent of John my son and heir, ... have confirmed . . . . . .ˑa buck or doe every year from my park of Birkin, and two old dry oaks every year against the Nativity of the Lord. Witnesses.]

Sciant presentes et futuri quod ego Adam filius Petri de Byrkin, concessione Johannis filii mei[2] et heredis, dedi et concessi et hac mea presenti carta confirmavi deo et sancto Johanni Apostolo et Evangeliste de Pontefracto et monachis ibidem deo servientibus unum damum vel damam singulis annis de parco meo de Birkin in commemoratione anime mee in die festo sancti Johannis, et duas veteres quercus infructuosas singulis annis ad ardendum contra Nathale domini. Hiis testibus, *Roberto le Vavasur, Thoma[3] filio Petri, Johanne[3] f[ilio] Petri, Petro et Rogero fratribus suis, Roberto de Stivetuna, Johanne[4] de Rorestuna, Martino capellano, Galfrido clerico de Cristecroft, Ricardo Waspe, Picot de Brettona,* et multis aliis.

---

(1) As he had now become.
(2) He was the second son, but Robert was now dead. See note (6) to No. 324.
(3) Thomas was "de Leeds," John was "de Byrkin." See No. 316 and No. 324.
(4) This may have been John Tyrol, the parson of Roreston.

LEDESHAMA.
CCCXXVI.   Carta Willelmi filii Johannis le Norreis.   Cir. 1250.

[. . . . . I, William, son of John the Norris of Ledsham, have surrendered and . . . . . quit-claimed . . . . all the land with its appurtenances and messuage which John my father held from the monks in Ledsham . . . . . to be held and possessed, &c. Seal. Witnesses.]

Sciant presentes et futuri quod ego Willelmus filius Johannis le Norreis de Ledeshama sursum reddidi et omnino de me et heredibus meis inperpetuum quietam clamavi deo et sancto Johanni Apostolo et ewangeliste de Pontefracto et monachis ibidem deo servientibus totam terram cum pertinentiis suis et mesuagio pertinente quam

Johannes pater meus antea tenuit de dictis monachis in territorio et villa de Ledeshama. Tenendam et habendam dictis monachis cum dicto mesuagio et cum omnibus pertinentiis suis, in bene[1] et pace, libere et quiete, pacifice et honorifice, sine contradictione, gravamine, vel molestia mei vel heredum meorum inperpetuum. Ita quod nec ego nec heredes mei in posterum aliquid juris vel clamii in dicta terra cum mesuagio et ceteris pertinentiis suis vendicabimus vel habere poterimus. In cujus rei testimonium huic scripto sigillum meum apposui. Hiis testibus, *domino Ricardo Wallensi, domino Henrico fratre ejus,*[2] *Hugone tunc vicario de Ledeshama, Willelmo de Fliggethorph, Adam Freman,* et aliis.

---

(1) *Sic.*

(2) The occurrence of the names of Sir Richard and Sir Henry, his brother, seems to place this charter in the decade ending 1250. Hugh, the vicar of Ledsham, and John, formerly reeve there (who might well be this John le Norreis), are mentioned in No. 54, a dated charter belonging to the year 1238. Adam Freeman also was of about that date. For Richard Wallis, see also No. 169.

CCCXXVII.[1]   Carta Roberti de Neutona.[2]   Cir. 1160.

[These witnesses were present when Robert of Newton surrendered . . . . . the meadow of Ledsham, which he and his have claimed . . . . . . by a staff upon the altar of St. Peter. Canons . . . . . priests . . . . . clerks . . . . . laymen.]

Hii testes interfuerunt ubi Robertus de Neutona pratum de Ledeshama quod ipse et sui calumpniati sunt, liberum et quietum a se, et ab omnibus suis heredibus, et ab omnibus suis, deo et sancto Johanni de Pontefracto, per baculum super altare sancti Petri reddidit inperpetuum : *Gerardus canonicus filius Osberti, Paulinus canonicus, Serlo canonicus filius Serlonis.* Sacerdotes hii, *Radulfus subcentor, Radulfus de Perci, Radulfus de Abbatia, Willelmus de Lincolnia, Robertus Morel, Normannus, Alexander, Herlewinus, Walterus Grevo, Serlo filius Gamelli, Robertus de Hospitali, Johannes de Silli, Heldanus.* Clerici hii, *Robertus Trenchebise, Petrus et Radulfus de Hospitali, Johannes filius Holdeberti, Suanus, Petrus, Philippus,* Diaconi. Laici hii, *Robertus de Grendala, Hedwinus, Fulco de Buthom, Ernaldus.*

---

(1) This deed is remarkable as witnessing a gift by a staff, and as having the names of the witnesses catalogued in order. The Hospital to which three of them belonged was St. Peter's, afterwards called St. Leonard's, of which Paulinus the canon (afterwards Vicar of Leeds) was Master.

(2) Robert of Newton (afterwards Newton Wallis) seems to be the Robert Wallis, who was dead in 1165, when his widow Alice, in Suffolk, made part payment for fines he had incurred. He was the then head of the Wallis family who possessed so much in the neighbourhood, and after whom the manors of Newton Wallis and Burghwallis were named. He was succeeded by Henry, who was returned in 1166 as possessing three knights' fees, and whose widow Agnes remarried with Hervey son of Jordan of Ledstone. No. 20 shows that this Henry was his son.

STUBBIS.

CCCXXVIII.[1]   Carta Ottonis filii Willelmi de Stubbis.

[. . . . . . I, Otto son of William de Stubbs, ... have confirmed . . . . . .
to make my anniversary, an assart in Stubbs which is called Rollescroft, and a
messuage on the other side of the road within sight of the messuage of William
Burnel, with its appurtenances and all town easements, and a rent of eighteen
pence from a toft in Pontefract, at Monkhill, which Thomas de Pool was accustomed to pay to me yearly. . . . . . Witnesses.]

Sciant presentes et futuri quod ego Otto filius Willelmi de Stubbis
dedi, concessi, et hac carta mea confirmavi deo et ecclesie sancti
Johannis de Pontefracto et monachis ibidem deo servientibus, in
puram et perpetuam elemosinam, pro salute anime mee et omnium
antecessorum meorum, ad anniversarium meum faciendum, unum
sartum in Stubbis quod vocatur Rollescroft et unum masagium[2] ex
altera parte vie, coram masagio Willelmi Burnel, cum pertinentiis suis
et omnibus aisiamentis ejusdem ville, et redditum decem octo
denariorum de quodam tofto in Pontefracto super montem monachorum, quem Thomas de Stagno mihi annuatim reddere solebat his
terminis, medietatem ad Pentecosten et medietatem ad festum sancti
Martini. Hiis testibus, *Henrico fratre meo et Theobaldo ejus filio,
Thoma de Bosevilla, Hugone filio Walteri, Alano filio Ranulfi, Willelmo
de Kamesala, Gaufrido de Nortona, Gaufrido Scorchebof, Thoma de
Tornetona,* et multis aliis. ⸻

(1) No. 328 must be read with No. 236, by which Otto's elder brother Henry granted him thi
assart and this messuage, "to be given in religion where he will."   (2) *Sic.*

⸻

LEDESHAMA.

CCCXXIX.[1]   Carta Germani clerici de Ledeshama.[2]   Cir. 1230.

[. . . . . I, Germanus, clerk of Ledstone, ... have confirmed to Katherine
my sister . . . . an acre of land in the territory of Ledstone. That is to say
one half acre in Waringreave and the other half acre in Scarcliffdale, ... To
be held and possessed . . . . . Paying thence yearly . . . . . three pence. Warranty.
Witnesses.]

Sciant presentes et futuri quod ego Germanus clericus de
Ledestona[2] dedi et concessi et hac presenti carta mei confirmavi
Katerine sorori mee et heredibus suis vel eius assignatis unam acram
terre[3] in territorio de Ledestona. Scilicet unam dimidiam acram in
Warinegreve et alteram dimidiam acram in Scartecliuedale in feudo
et hereditate pro humagio et servitio suo. Tenendam et habendam
de me et heredibus meis vel meis assignatis sibi et heredibus suis

(1) I have met with no copy of any of these five charters.   (2) *Sic* in each case.
(3) This is the acre referred to in No. 171 and No. 172, which latter is a deed of sale to the
monks in 1232, the consideration being eight shillings of sterling money.

vel eius assignatis, libere et quiete, pacifice, et integre, et honorifice. Reddendo inde annuatim mihi et heredibus meis vel meis assignatis tres denarios, scilicet medietatem ad Pentecosten et medietatem ad festum sancti Martini in hyeme, pro omni servitio et consuetudine. Ego vero Germanus et heredes mei vel me[2] assignati sibi et heredibus suis vel eius assignatis contra omnes homines warentizabimus inperpetuum. Hiis testibus, *Magistro Rogero persona de Kippeis, Rogero persona de Ledeshama, Henrico de Waleis, Jordano Pateman, Rogero fratre eius, Willelmo de Aluertona, Radulfo Painel*, et multis aliis.

CASEWICKA.

CCCXXX.[1]   Carta Symonis filii Symonis de Mohaut.   Cir. 1195.

[. . . . . I, Simon de Mohaut son of Simon de Mohaut, ... confirm . . . . . two bovates of land in Keswick, of twenty acres, with a toft of one acre, in exchange for those two bovates which my father had given to them, in order that those monks may have two bovates of land between my land in Keswick and the land of Robert my brother. . . . . If two bovates cannot be so made up, I will out of my demesne make up what is wanting. . . . . . in pure and perpetual alms, and with the common easement of the town of Keswick, and I will warrant it to them. Witnesses.]

Omnibus fidelibus sancte matris ecclesie filiis Symon de Mohaut filius Symonis de Mohaut salutem. Sciatis quod ego pro animabus parentum meorum et heredum meorum et mea do et concedo et confirmo hac mea carta deo et monachis sancti Johannis ewangeliste de Pontefracto duas bovatas terre in Casewic xx*ti* acrarum cum tofto unius acre, excambium illarum duarum bovatarum quas pater meus eis donaverat, ut ipsi monachi habeant duas bovatas terre inter terram meam in Casewic et inter terram Roberti fratris mei, et in longum et in latum ad mensuram terre predicti Roberti. Quod si due bovate non possint predictis monachis ita perfici, ego perficiam quod defuerit de meo dominio.[2] Hanc terram eis do et concedo et confirmo in puram et perpetuam elemosinam et liberam ab omni exactione seculari cum omnibus pertinentiis suis, et communi aisiamento ville de Casewic, et warentizabo eis contra omnes homines. Testibus, *Nicholao de Tathecastre vic*[? *ario*] *archidiaconi, Henrico priore de Boutuna,*[3] *Willelmo persona de Harewode, Gaufrido de Perci, Petro de Bramehama, Petro capellano de Birdesaia, Jordano clerico decani de Cravene, Willelmo de Lellaya, Willelmo filio Roberti, Petro de Arduntona, Willelmo de Witona, Ricardo de Stagno, Rogero de Ledestuna,*[4] *Willelmo filio Rogeri Gros, Thoma filio Henrici de Batelaia, Roberto Dust, Henrico Corf.*

---

(1) There is an incomplete transcript in *Lansdowne 207.*

(2) This may imply that he was lord.

(3) He appears to be now unknown, his name not being given in the list of priors in *Monasticon Anglicanum* or in " Monastic Notes."   (4) Son of Jordan.

CCCXXXI.[1]   Carta Symonis de Mohaut.   Ante 1160.

[. . . . I, Simon de Mohaut, for my salvation . . . . . have confirmed . . . . two bovates of land of twenty acres from my demesne in Keswick, together with one toft of one acre, with all appurtenances . . . . . And those monks have received me and all mine into their brotherhood and the prayers of their house and of all the order, and if it shall be needful will receive me as their brother. Witnessing, &c.]

Omnibus fidelibus sancte ecclesie Symon de Mohaut salutem. Sciatis quod ego pro salute mea et uxoris mee et antecessorum meorum et heredum meorum dedi et concessi et hac mea carta et hoc meo sigillo confirmavi, concedentibus predicta uxore Matilde et heredibus meis Symone et Roberto, deo et sancto Johanni et monachis de Pontefracto, libere et quiete, in puram et perpetuam elemosinam, duas bovatas terre viginti acrarum de meo dominio in Keswic simul cum uno tofto unius acre in eadem villa cum omnibus pertinentiis, videlicet in boscho et in plano, in pratis et paschuis, et aquis et viis et semitis, et in omnibus aisiamentis ejusdem ville. Et ipsi monachi me receperunt in fraternitate sua et orationibus domus et totius ordinis et omnes meos; et si necesse mihi fuerit me suscipient sicut fratrem suum qui me eis reddidi. Testantibus, *Willelmo de Harewde, nepote meo, Henrico filio meo, Nicholao de Fristona, Roberto filio Gilleberti, Jordano filio Bernardi; Jordano de Ledestuna et fratribus suis, Rainaldo, Rogero, Waltero; Roberto de Ledestuna*[2]*; Thoma dapifero et Michaele filio eius; Willelmo Pistore*[3] *et Alexandro filio eius; Thoma de Prestuna, Gaufrido de Pratis, Adam coco et Roberto fratre suo, Affrico de Keswic*, et aliis.

(1) No. 331 is No. xxvi in the *Monasticon.*
(2) Possibly son of the William who tested No. 222.
(3) William was brother of the preceding "Thomas dapifer."

BRETTONA.[1]
CCCXXXII.[2]   Carta Pigoti filii Hugonis de Brettuna.

[. . . . . I, Pigot, son of Hugh de Bretton, ... have confirmed . . . . all the land[3] in Bretton which Henry Neeloth gave and confirmed . . . Seal. Witnesses.]

Sciant presentes et futuri quod ego, Pigotus filius Hugonis de Brettuna, concessi et hac presenti carta mea confirmavi deo et sancto Johanni et monachis de Pontefracto, in puram et perpetuam elemosinam totam terram in Brettona cum pertinentiis suis, quam Henricus Neelot eis dedit et carta sua confirmavit, sicut continetur

(1) Burton Salmon.   (2) I have not found a copy of No. 332.
(3) The quantity of land here granted was two acres and three roods, as we shall learn from No. 505, a dated charter of 8 Richard I [1197], which included Beatrice Hill in Hillam.

in carta eiusdem Henrici. Et ne ego Pigotus vel heredes mei venire possimus contra predictam predicti Henrici donationem, illam presenti scripto et sigilli mei appositione roboravi. Hiis testibus, *Roberto Walensi, Henrico filio suo, Ada de Rainevilla, Thoma filio suo, Jordano de la Landa, Ricardo de Hudlistona, Rogero decano de Ledeshama, Willelmo filio Everardi, Thoma de Kellingtona,* et aliis.

DE FERIA.

CCCXXXIII.[1]   Carta Jordani de Sancta Maria.

[To all who shall see or hear this writing, Jordan de St. Mary and Alice his wife, of Frystone, greeting in the Lord. Know that we . . . . . have . . . . confirmed . . . . . all our meadow which we have had in the territory of Ferry. That is to say, that meadow which lies between the meadow which was of the territory of Ferry towards the south and the meadow of Adam Russel towards the north. One head abuts on Longlathe and extends to the great water of Aire, and another part of the meadow towards Halliwell beyond the brook which comes from Pontefract, between the meadow of the Abbot and monks of Fountains towards the north and the meadow of the territory of Ferry towards the south. Of which one head abuts upon the meadow of the hospital of Fulsnap, and extends even to the great river of Aire and to the headlands of the same meadow, which abut on one side upon the meadow of the hospital of Fulsnap, and on another side upon the great water of Aire, and on the third side upon the meadow which was Robert of Hickleton's. And, moreover, we have given to those monks the headlands of our meadow of Frystone, which abut on one side upon the river of Frystone and on another upon the meadow of Agnes de Merston. . . . . Release. Warranty. Seals. Witnesses.]

Universis hoc scriptum visuris vel audituris Jordanus de Sancta Maria et Aliz uxor sua de Fristona salutem in domino. Noveritis nos pro salute animarum nostrarum et omnium antecessorum et heredum nostrorum dedisse, concessisse, et presenti carta nostra confirmasse deo et sancto Johanni de Pontefracto et monachis ibidem deo servientibus, in puram et perpetuam elemosinam, totum pratum nostrum quod habuimus in territorio de Feria. Illud scilicet pratum quod jacet inter pratum quod fuit terre[2] de Feria versus Suth et pratum Ade Russel versus North. De quo unum capud percutit super Lengelathe et tendit usque ad magnam aquam de Ayr, et unam aliam partem prati[3] versus Heliwelle ultra rivulum qui venit de Pontefracto inter[4] pratum Abbatis et monachorum de Fontibus versus north et pratum terre[2] de Feria versus suth. De quo unum capud percutit super pratum hospitalis de Fulsnaph et tendit usque ad

---

(1) No. 333 is No. XXII of the *Monasticon* series, and there is an imperfect transcript in *Lansdowne* 207.   (2) In No. 289, "territi;" in No. 307, "terri."
(3) In *Monasticon Anglicanum,* "parti."   (4) "In" in No. 307.

magnam aquam de Ayr et fordales ejusdem prati que[5] percutiunt ex una parte super pratum hospitalis de Fulsnaph, et ex alia parte super magnam aquam de Ayr, et ex tertia parte super pratum quod fuit Roberti de Hikiltona. Et insuper dedimus eisdem monachis fordalas[6] prati nostri de Fristona, que percutiunt ex una parte super rivulum de Fristona et ex alia super pratum Agnetis de Merstona. Hec omnia prefata habebunt et tenebunt predicti monachi libera, quieta, et soluta ab omni servitio et consuetudine seculari. Et nos et heredes nostri warentizabimus omnia predicta prefatis monachis ubique et contra omnes.[7] Et ut hec nostra donatio et confirmatio firma sit et stabilis huic carte sigillorum nostrorum munimen apposuimus. Hiis testibus, *Ricardo filio nostro presente et concedente, Thoma de Kriggelestona, Waltero de Birum, Roberto Camberlano, Radulfo de Batelay, Ricardo de Stagno, Roberto filio Gaufridi,*[8] *Willelmo proph'a,*[9] *Willelmo dispensatore, Nicholao de Greve, Willelmo Marescallo,* et aliis.

---

(5) "Quod" in No. 307.   (6) *Sic.*   (7) "Homines" in No. 307.

(8) Possibly the Geoffrey de Reineville of No. 212.   (9) See No. 294.

CCCXXXIIII.[1]   Carta Rollandi Hageth.

[. . . . . Roland Haget has granted . . . . . a bovate of land in Skelbrook free and quit from all customs, blessings and prayers excepted. Which land Oliver his brother formerly gave and offered upon the altar by a clasped knife. The witnesses of this gift are, &c.]

Sciant presentes et futuri quod Rollandus Hagath[2] concessit monachis ecclesie sancti Johannis de Pontefracto unam bovatam terre in Scelebroch, liberam et quietam ab omnibus consuetudinibus inperpetuum, exceptis beneficiis et orationibus fratrum. Quam terram Oliverus frater eius prius donaverat, et super altare obtulerat per cultellum plicatum. Huius donationis testes sunt, *Willelmus presbiter de Hymelesword, Willelmus de Fristona, Henricus Walensis, Henricus de Burg, Willelmus filius Roberti de Burgo, Walterus filius Hugonis,*[3] *Rogerus presbiter, Robertus Norreis, Jordanus de Ledestuna, Ricardus*[4] *de Ledestuna, Willelmus*[5] *pistor,* et aliis.

---

(1) There is a bad copy of No. 334 in *Lansdowne* 207, and a brief abstract in *Dodsworth*, vol. 135.

(2) *Sic.*   (3) Afterwards of Swillington.   (4) Son of Lesing.   (5) Fitz Asolf.

SILKESTONA.

CCCXXXV.[1]   Carta Ricardi filii Hugonis Pincerne.

[. . . . . . I, Richard son of Hugh Butler of Sandal, have confirmed . . . . . . those two bovates of land with their appurtenances lying in the territory of Silkstone, which William my brother and Dionis my sister have surrendered to the said monks (together with Henry and William the sons of Ketel with all their following and their goods) . . . . and quit-claimed for ten marks of silver 4 shillings and 8 pence . . . . in hand. Warranty. Witnesses.]

Omnibus hoc scriptum visuris vel audituris Ricardus filius Hugonis Pincerne de Sandala salutem. Noverit universitas vestra me pro amore dei et salute anime mee et omnium antecessorum et heredum meorum concessisse et confirmasse deo et ecclesie sancti Johannis de Pontefracto et monachis ibidem deo servientibus illas duas bovatas terre cum pertinentiis suis in territorio de Silkestona jacentes, quas Willelmus frater meus et Dion[isia] soror mea, una cum Henrico et Willelmo filiis Ketil, cum tota secta sua et catallis suis, dictis monachis sine aliquo retenemento sui vel suorum sursum reddiderunt, et omnino eisdem pro decem marcis argenti iiij solidis et viij denariis[2] quos eis pre manibus pacaverunt quietas clamaverunt. Hanc vero confirmationem ego Ricardus filius Hugonis et heredes mei contra omnes homines inperpetuum warantizabimus ac defendemus. Hiis testibus, *Baldewino Theuton[ico], Willelmo de Brettona, Germano de Mortel', Ricardo de Crave',*[3] *Johanne de Hauch'k, Henrico Portebref, Willelmo de Golthorph,* et aliis.

(1) No. 335 is transcribed into *Dodsworth*, vol. 151.   (2) That is, £6 18s.

(3) In No. 336 it is "de Cravena."

DE DODDEWDA.

CCCXXXVI.[1]   Carta Johannis filii Johannis capellani.

[. . . . . I, John, son of John the chaplain of Silkstone, and my heirs ought to warrant . . . . . against Adam the son of Gilbert of Dodworth and against Matilda my sister, his wife, and their heirs, and against all men, ... an assart in the territory of Dodworth in Hugset which was Ulmer's, and a bovate of land with its appurtenances in Dodworth and without. That is to say the assart and the bovate which Adam and Matilda had of my father and sold to the prior and monks. Seal. Witnesses.]

Sciant presentes et futuri quod ego Johannes filius Johannis capellani de Silkestona et heredes mei debemus warantizare dominis meis priori et monachis de Pontefracto contra Adam filium Gilberti de de[2] Doddeword et contra Matildam sororem meam uxorem prefati

(1) This was twice copied into *Dodsworth*, vol. 151 ; firstly as a Dodworth charter, and secondly for its connection with the name of Savile. There is also a short abstract in vol. 133, which, however, is frequently better than those in vol. 151.   (2) *Sic.*

Ade et contra heredes qui de eis exibunt et contra omnes homines,
qui de nomine patris mei Johannis capellani de Silkestona aliquod
jus aut clamium poterunt clamare, unum assartum in territorio de
Doddeworda in Huggesside[3] quod fuit Ulmeri, et unam bovatam terre
cum omnibus pertinentibus ad eam in prefata villa de Doddeworda et
extra.   Quod scilicet essartum et quam bovatam terre prenominati
Ada et Matilda sponsa sua habuerunt ex dono patris mei Johannis
capellani de Silkestona et dictis dominis meis priori et monachis de
Pontefracto vendiderunt.   Et in huius warentizationis mee[4] testimonium, huic scripto pro me et heredibus meis sigillum meum apposui.
Hiis testibus, *magistro Roberto Wintoniensi, Willelmo de Brettona.*
Henrico de Tankesleia, Henrico de Siewilla, Ada de Hoylanda, Ricardo
de Martona, Ricardo de Cravena, Roberto filio Geraldi, et multis aliis.

---

(3) Huggesside is named in No. 2 and No. 72 as one of the bounds of Dodworth.   Its modern
name is Hugset.   (4) In vol. 133, "inde."

DE BRETTONA.
CCCXXXVII.[1]   **Carta Johannis de Celario de Brettona.**

[To all Christ's faithful . . . . . John de Cellario of Bretton greeting . . . .
With the consent of William my son I have . . . . . confirmed . . . . . a site in the
territory of Bretton, which is called Halrenesrebella, next the mill of Barnsley,
which I bought of Isoda daughter of Alexander son of Thomas of Bretton.   To
be held and possessed . . . . . Warranty.   Seal.   Witnesses.]

Universis Christi fidelibus presens scriptum visuris vel audituris
Johannes de Cellario de Brettona salutem in domino.   Noverit
universitas vestra me, assensu et voluntate Willelmi filii mei, dedisse,
concessisse et presenti scripto confirmasse de[2] et ecclesie sancti
Johannis ewangeliste de Pontefracto et monachis ibidem deo servientibus quandam placiam in territorio de Brettona que vocatur Halrenesrebella et jacet juxta molendinum de Berneslaya.   Quam quidam[2]
placiam ego emi de Isoda filia Alexandri filii Thome de Brettona.
Tenendam et habendam dictis monachis sine contradictione mei vel
meorum in liberam, puram et perpetuam elemosinam inperpetuum.
Ego vero et heredes mei dictam placiam cum omnibus suis pertinentiis
dictis monachis contra omnes homines warentizabimus ac defendemus.
In cujus rei testimonium presenti scripto sigillum meum apposui.
Hiis testibus, *domino Johanne de Hoderode, Adam de Holande, Roberto*
filio suo, Gregorio de Brettona, Roberto de Botlee, Henrico de Botlee,
Ada de Berneslaya, clerico, et aliis.

---

(1) I have not met with any transcript of No. 337.   (2) *Sic* in both cases,

DE BRETTONA.[1]
CCCXXXVIII.[2]   Carta Willelmi filii Ulfi de Berneslaya.

[. . . . . I, William son of Ulf, ... have confirmed to Gerard of Barnsley
 . . . . four pence, to be received yearly from the monks of Pontefract on St.
Andrew's Day, which those monks have paid to me for a bovate of land in Dodworth. . . . . . Gerard has given to me 32 pence in hand. Warranty. Witnesses.]

Sciant presentes et futuri quod ego Willelmus filius Ulfi dedi,
concessi, et presenti carta mea confirmavi Gerardo de Berneslaya, vel
ubicumque vel cuicumque assignare voluerit, quatuor denarios a
monachis de Pontefracto in die sancti Andree annuatim percipiendos,
quos ipsi monachi solebant mihi reddere pro una bovata terre in
Doddewrd.[3] Pro hac autem concessione et confirmacione dedit mihi
predictus Gerardus xxxii denarios premanibus. Et ego prefatus
Willelmus filius Ulfi et heredes mei warentizabimus predicto Gerardo
vel ubicumque vel cuicumque assignare voluerit prenominatos quatuor
denarios contra omnes homines. Hiis testibus, *Willelmo filio Everardi,*
Rogero diacono[4] *de Silkestuna, Ricardo de Stagno, Thoma de Stagno,*[5]
Adam de Berneslaya, Johanne filio Michaelis, et aliis.

---

(1) *Sic,* an obvious error for "Doddewd."
(2) No. 338 is twice transcribed into *Dodsworth,* vol. 151, there is an abstract in vol. 133, and
there is a copy in Jackson's *History of Barnsley.*
(3) Vol. 151 adds "videlicet duas bovatas terre."
(4) *Sic,* for "decano."   (5) Thomas de Pool is omitted in vol. 151.

DE DODDEWD.
CCCXXXVIIII.[1]   Carta Willelmi filii Ulfi.

[. . . . . I, William son of Ulf, ... have confirmed . . . . a bovate of land
in Dodworth with appurtenances, namely, that which I held of Richard my
brother. Paying at the feast of St. Andrew four pence for all service. Warranty.
Witnesses.]

Sciant presentes et futuri quod ego Willelmus filius Ulfi dedi,
concessi, et presenti carta mea confirmavi deo et sancto Johanni de
Pontefracto et monachis ibidem deo servientibus unam bovatam terre
in Doddewrth cum omnibus pertinentiis suis infra villam et extra.
Illam scilicet quam tenui de Ricardo fratre meo. Reddendo inde
annuatim mihi et heredibus meis ad festum sancti Andree quatuor
denarios pro omni servitio. Et ego Willelmus et heredes mei

---

(1) This charter is transcribed into *Dodsworth,* vol. 151, and there is an abstract in vol. 133.

warentizabimus prenominatam bovatam terre prefatis monachis contra omnes homines.   Hiis testibus, *Willelmo filio Everardi, Rogero diacono*[2] *de Silkestona, Gerardo de Berneslay, Ricardo de Stagno, Thoma fratre suo, Adam de Berneslay,* et aliis.

---

(2) As in No. 338, Roger is clearly described as "diaconus," but it is evident that the word should be "decanus," a description at this time applied to the parish priest of such parishes as Silkstone, Ledsham, Pontefract, Kellington, Darrington, &c.

CCCXXXX.[1] **Cyrographum de Berneslaya.** **1222.**

[At the Feast of St. Michael in the year 1222 . . . . . agreement made between the prior and monks and Edusa of Barnsley, widow of Hugh of Baghill. Edusa in her widowhood granted for six years her capital messuage with its buildings, and the land with appurtenances . . . . The prior and monks have given twenty shillings, and for the sake of good-will a quarter of wheat and a bushel of peas. And the six years ended the aforesaid land with appurtenances shall remain free to Edusa and her son ; saving to the prior and monks the service and rent which they ought to have. Edusa or her sons shall contribute towards the expenses incurred in the maintenance and repair of the houses. Seals. Witnesses.]

Anno ab incarnatione domini m⁰. cc⁰. xxii⁰., ad festum sancti Michaelis. Hec est conventio facta inter priorem et monachos de Pontefracto ex una parte et Edusam de Bernelay[2] que fuit uxor Hugonis de Baggehil[3] ex alia. Scilicet quod prefata Edusa in plena viduitate sua dimisit et concessit predictis priori et monachis usque ad terminum sex annorum capitale suum mesuagium cum omnibus edificiis et totam terram cum omnibus pertinentiis suis quam habuit vel eam contingere potest,[2] tam de dotario quam de custodia filii sui in territorio de Berneslaya. Pro hac autem concessione dederunt prefati prior et monachi predicte Eduse viginti solidos et karitatis intuitu unum quarterium frumenti et unum windel pisorum. Finitis vero sex annis predicta terra cum pertinentiis suis remanebit soluta et quieta prefate Eduse et filio suo sine impedimento vel contradictione prioris et monachorum, salvis predictis priori et monachis servitio et firma quam debent habere de eadem terra. Insuper prenominata Edusa vel filii sui[2] reddent in fine sex annorum versus expensas quas prior et monachi posuerint in sustentatione et reparatione domorum. Et ut hec conventio firma sit et stabilis, hoc scriptum sigillorum

---

(1) No. 340 is transcribed twice into *Dodsworth*, vol. 151, and there is an abstract in vol. 136. It is also transcribed into Jackson's *History of Barnsley*. One of the copies in *Dodsworth*, vol. 151, makes the year 1222, and adds a marginal note, "6 H. 3," which is correct. The second makes the date 1232, and with a double inaccuracy notes that year as 17 H. 3, which it was not ; for 17 H. 3 did not commence till 28 October, 1232, while, as the date of this charter was St. Michael's Day, the 16th year had then still four weeks to run.

(2) *Sic* in each case.   (3) See pedigree, page 405.

suorum appositione roboraverunt. Hiis testibus, *Gilberto de Nottona, Willelmo filio suo, Alano filio Rannulfi, tunc ballivo de Staincros et de Osgotecros, Radulfo de Saivile, Henrico de Saivile, Ricardo de Martona,* et aliis.

DE DODDEWRDA.

CCCXLI.[1]   **Carta Thome filii Ricardi de Stagno.**   **Ante 1218.**

[. . . . . I, Thomas son of Richard of Pool, have . . . . . foresworn . . . . . all the land which I have held in Dodworth, within the town and without, in wood and in plain. The Prior and monks have given me two marks of silver. Seal. Witnesses.]

Sciant presentes et futuri quod ego Thomas filius Ricardi de Stagno reddidi, quietam clamavi, et forisjuravi de me et heredibus meis priori et monachis de Pontefracto totam terram quam tenui in Doddeworda infra villam et extra, tam in boscho quam in plano. Pro hac autem quieta clamantia dederunt mihi predicti prior et monachi duas marcas argenti. Et ne ego vel heredes mei contra hanc quietam clamantiam in posterum venire possimus, hanc cartam sigilli mei appositione roboravi. Hiis testibus, *Johanne de Birkina, Roberto Walensi, Adam de Rainevilla, Thoma filio suo,*[2] *Willelmo de Stapiltona, Gilberto de Nottona, Hugone filio Walteri, Magistro Ricardo de Madelaya,*[3] *Willelmo de Kamesal,* et aliis.

(1) No. 341 was transcribed into *Dodsworth*, vol. 133, and there was an abstract in vol. 136.

(2) The presence of the name of Thomas, son of Adam de Reineville, fixes the date of this charter as not later than 1218, in which year Thomas died. See note (3) to No. 343.

(3) This name is given twice, the second occurrence being erased with a red line. It is probable that after "Hugone filio Walteri" the signatories should have been "Magistro Raimundo, Ricardo de Medelaya," &c., as in No. 343. In that case the error made could have been accurately corrected by the substitution of "Raimundo" for the first "Ricardo."

DE BERNESLAYA.

CCCXLII.[1]   **Carta Roberti de Bergha.**

[. . . . . I, Robert of Barugh, have . . . . . confirmed . . . . . . a rent of twelve pence which Roger of Barnsley used to pay me yearly at the feast of St. Oswald, and all the service . . . . from that land which Roger has held from me in Wilmersthorp. To be held and possessed, &c. Warranty. Seal. Witnesses.]

Sciant presentes et futuri quod ego Robertus de Berh[2] dedi et concessi et inperpetuum quietum clamavi de me et heredibus meis et confirmavi deo et sancto Johanni de Pontefracto et monachis ibidem deo servientibus, pro salute anime mee et antecessorum

(1) No. 342 was not transcribed or abstracted by Dodsworth, but there is a copy in Jackson's *History of Barnsley.*

(2) In both cases his name is given thus. He witnesses No. 351 and No. 352, and is possibly Robert son of Adam fitz Peter. See pedigree, page 405.

meorum, redditum duodecim denariorum quem Rogerus de Berneslaya solebat reddere mihi annuatim ad festum sancti Oswaldi.　Et preterea totum servitium plenarie sine retenemento mei vel heredum meorum de terra illa quam predictus Rogerus de Berneslaya tenuit de me in Wilmerstordh.[3]　Tenendam et habendam[4] predictis monachis in puram et perpetuam elemosinam, liberam et quietam ab omni servitio et consuetudine.　Ego vero Roberto de Berh[2] et heredes mei predictis monachis de Pontefracto predictum redditum et servitium contra omnes homines warantizabimus.　Et ne ego Robertus vel heredes mei contra tenorem huius carte venire possimus, huic scripto pro me et heredibus meis sigillum meum apposui.　Hiis testibus, *Nicholao de Wrthlay, Henrico de Tancreslay,[5] Radulfo de Turkerlanda, Ada de Aldefeld, Regner de Wambewelle.*

(3) This may be Ulmersthorp.　　　　(4) *Sic.*

(5) In Archbishop Gray's Register, under the date 4 nones April, 10th Pont. [1225], is a memorandum of the institution of William Tankerle to that moiety of the church of Tankersley, at the presentation of Henry de Tankerle, which Richard son of the said Henry had held.　This shows Henry de Tankerley, or Tankersley, as the lord of that fee.

DE BERNESLAYA.[1]

CCCXLIII.[2]　　　　**Carta Diane filie Rogeri.**　　　　**Ante 1218.**

[. . . . . . I, Diana daughter of Roger of Barnsley, have foresworn . . . . . . all the land which I have held in Dodworth, within the town and without, in wood and in plain.　For this quit-claim the prior and monks have given me two marks of silver.　Seal.　Witnesses.]

Sciant presentes et futuri quod ego Diana filia Rogeri de Berneslaya reddidi, quietam clamavi, et forisjuravi de me et heredibus meis priori et monachis de Pontefracto totam terram quam tenui in Doddeword infra villam et extra, tam in bosco quam in plano.　Pro hac autem quieta clamantia dederunt mihi predicti prior et monachi duas marcas argenti.　Et ne ego vel heredes mei contra hanc quietam clamantiam in posterum venire possimus hanc cartam sigilli mei appositione roboravi.　Hiis testibus,[3] *Johanne de Birkina, Roberto Walensi, Adam de Raineville, Thoma filio suo, Willelmo de Stapletona, Gilleberto de Nottona, Hugone filio Walteri, Magistro Raimundo, Ricardo de Madelaya, Willelmo de Kamesal,* et aliis.

(1) In No. 341, No. 342, and No. 343, the marginal headings, "de Doddewrd'," "de B'nesl'," and "de B'nesl'," are in red.　All previously and (with one or two exceptions) all subsequently are in black.

(2) No. 343 was abstracted in *Dodsworth*, vol. 133, and copied into Jackson's *History of Barnsley*.

(3) The witnesses are, with the addition of Master Raimond, the same as those to No. 341. Each was before 1218, the year of the death of Thomas son of Adam de Reineville, while Master Raimond and Richard the clerk of Methley (his brother in No. 255) witnessed the "little town charter" of Pontefract in 1194 (see page xl, vol. 1).

De Berneslaya.
CCCXLIIII. Carta Ade de Falthwait.[1]

[. . . . . . I, Adam de Falthwait, ... have confirmed . . . . a toft in Barnsley of half an acre, between the land of Gerard son of Bernard and the land of Paganus, on the east of the toft of Hugh de Baghill, and half an acre in Collegrimewelleroyds, and half an acre upon Kirk costes, and half an acre upon Longlands, and a rood upon Claylands. To be held and possessed . . . . Warranty. Witnesses.]

Sciant presentes et futuri quod ego Adam de Falthuuait, pro salute anime mee et omnium antecessorum et heredum meorum dedi, concessi, et hac presenti carta mea confirmavi in puram et perpetuam elemosinam deo et sancto Johanni de Pontefracto et monachis ibidem deo servientibus unum toftum in Berneslay de dimidia acra terre inter terram Gerardi filii Bernardi et terram Pagani in orientali parte tofti Hugonis de Baggehyl, et dimidiam acram in Collegrimewellerodes, et dimidiam acram super Kirke costes,[2] et dimidiam acram super Langelandes, et unam percatam[3] super Clailandes. Tenendum et habendum[3] prefatis monachis inperpetuum, libere et quiete, et absolute ab omni servitio seculari et consuetudine. Et ego prenominatus Adam et heredes mei warentizabimus prefatis monachis predictas acras terre contra omnes homines. Hiis testibus, *Johanne de Birkina, Rogero clerico de Silkestona, Roberto de Turs,*[4] *Rainero de Wambewelle, Adam de Aldefeld,* et aliis.

---

(1) This Adam de Falthwait (in Stainborough) was Adam fitz Peter of Birkin (died 1207), and his charter is witnessed by his brother, John de Birkin. See No. 512. Falthwait is in the west part of Stainborough, bordering on Thurgoland and Dodworth.

(2) In No. 512 this is "toftes." Here it is clearly either "costes" or "castes."

(3) *Sic* in each case.   (4) Possibly for "Thurgoland."

De Berneslaya.
CCCXLV.[1] Carta Johannis filii Ade de Sepelay.

[. . . . . I, John, son of Adam of Shepley, ... have confirmed . . . . . ten acres of land in the territory of Old Barnsley, namely, those ten acres which are called Oldfield. To be held and possessed . . . . with all buildings and other things belonging . . . . Paying thence yearly to the chief lords twenty pence. . . . . Also a corner adjoining to the aforesaid acres which I have held from Adam, son of Roger of Barnsley, for one penny yearly, which the monks are to pay to the heirs of the said Adam. Seal. Witnesses.]

---

(1) Neither No. 344 nor No. 345 was transcribed by Dodsworth, but there is a modern transcript of each in Jackson's *History of Barnsley*. No. 345 is almost a transcript of No. 374, but it changes the payees. In the earlier charter the rent was to be paid to John and his heirs in the church of Barnsley (probably because he held no court), and he himself was bound to render the amount to the chief lords. But by No. 345 his intervention was dispensed with, and the rent was to be paid direct to the chief lords themselves. There is a further and singular variant between the two charters, that in the earlier Alan de Smeaton is said to be bailiff of "Osgoldcross and Staincross."

Sciant presentes et futuri quod ego Johannes filius Ade de Sepelay, pro salute anime mee et omnium antecessorum et heredum meorum dedi, concessi, et hac presenti carta mea confirmavi deo et sancto Johanni apostolo et ewangeliste de Pontefracto et monachis ibidem deo servientibus, in perpetuam elemosinam, decem acras terre in territorio veteris Berneslaye. Illas scilicet decem acras que vocantur Aldefeld. Tenendas et habendas prefatis monachis inperpetuum, sine impedimento vel reclamatione mei vel heredum meorum, libere et quiete, integre et pacifice, cum omnibus edificiis, et omnibus aliis pertinentibus ad prefatas decem acras infra villam et extra. Reddendo inde annuatim capitalibus dominis viginti denarios ad festum sancti Martini pro omni servitio. Insuper dedi, concessi, et hac carta mea confirmavi predictis monachis in perpetuam elemosinam unum angulum adiacentem prefatis acris quem ego tenui hereditarie de Adam filio Rogeri de Berneslaya[2] pro uno denario annuatim ad festum sancti Martini pro omni servitio reddendo, quem denarium predicti monachi persolvent heredibus prefati Ade nomine meo. Et ut hec mea donatio firma sit et stabilis, huic carte sigillum meum pro me et heredibus meis apposui. Hiis testibus, *Alano de Smythetona tunc ballivo de Staincros et Osgotecros, Gilleberto de Nottona, Henrico de Tacreslay,[3] Willelmo de Brettona,* et aliis.

(2) This was his own father.   (3) *Sic.*

De Notton.
CCCXLVI.[1]   **Carta Rogeri de Notton.**[2]

[. . . . . . I, Roger de Notton, ... moved by divine piety, ... have quit-claimed . . . . . that land which is called Hulleroyd, which my father acquired from the monks, barely justly as I call to mind. To be held and possessed. Witnesses.]

Omnibus sancte matris ecclesie filiis ad quos presens scriptum pervenerit Rogerus de Nottona salutem in domino. Noverit universitas vestra me divine pietatis intuitu, pro salute anime mee et patris mei et matris mee et antecessorum et successorum meorum, dedisse et sursum reddidisse et quietam clamasse de me et heredibus meis deo

(1) No. 346 was transcribed into *Dodsworth*, vol. 151.
(2) This Roger de Notton, who appears here with his seneschal and his chaplain, was a younger brother of William de Notton the constable, of No. 100. Their father was Gilbert de Notton, the seneschal to John de Lascy, who about 1190 married Edith de Barton, and held property at Barton in right of his wife. In Lincolnshire Gilbert de Notton was known as de Barton, but when in Yorkshire he seems to have preferred the name he inherited from his father, William de Notton. Roger, the second son, adhered to the family name throughout, but there was a third son, John, who was a benefactor to Whalley, under the name of Bromyhurst.

et ecclesie sancti Johannis apostoli et evangeliste de Pontefracto et monachis ibidem deo servientibus terram illam que vocatur Hullerode. Illam scilicet quam pater meus ab eisdem monachis minus juste ut recolo adquisivit.   Tenendam et habendam libere, quiete, pacifice, et honorifice sine aliquo gravamine vel molestia mei vel heredum meorum inperpetuum, cum omnibus pertinentiis predicte terre pertinentibus. Hiis testibus, *domino Roberto de Stapiltona, domino Johanne de Hoderode, Johanne de Sevile, Radulfo de Rupe, Ada Cossardo tunc senescallo meo, Rogero capellano meo, Willelmo de Rorestona*, et aliis.

DE DODDWRDA.
CCCXLVII.[1]   **Carta Petri de Doddeworda.**

[. . . . . I, Peter of Dodworth, ... have confirmed . . . . . . for 4 shillings, ... in my great necessity, that toft with half an acre of land which I bought of Diana, daughter of John Blomer, which lies between the toft of Robert Bolehale, and the toft of Alan son of Mauger. This grant I have made with the assent of the aforesaid Diana. Seal. Witnesses.]

Sciant presentes et futuri quod ego Petrus de Doddeworda dedi, concessi, et hac carta mea confirmavi deo et sancto Johanni evangeliste de Pontefracto et monachis ibidem deo servientibus, pro iiij*or* solidis quos mihi premanibus in mea magna necessitate dederunt, illud toftum cum dimidia acra terre quam emi de Diana filia Johannis Blomer, qui[2] jacet inter toftum Roberti Bolehale et toftum Alani filii Maugeri.   Hanc vero donationem et concessionem feci per voluntatem et assensum predicte Diane.   Et ne ego vel heredes mei contra hoc factum meum venire unquam possimus huic scripto sigillum meum apposui.   Hiis testibus, *domino Symone capellano de Silkestona, Roberto capellano de Berneslay, Henrico de Sevilla, Henrico filio Rogeri, Henrico Portebref, Ricardo de Martona*, et aliis.

---

(1) No. 347 was transcribed twice into *Dodsworth*, vol. 151, and there is a rather faulty abstract in vol. 133.   (2) *Sic.*

CCCXLVIII.[1]   **Carta Johannis filii Ade de Sepelay.**

[. . . . I, John son of Adam de Shepley, ... have confirmed . . . . . twenty acres of land in Barugh. Namely, those acres which are called Waldefroyd and which lie between the land of the monks of Revesby towards the north and the boundary of the field of Barnsley towards the south, and the assart of Reginald, brother of Wuldef', which lies between the land of Robert son of Adam de Oldfield and the boundary of Barnsley. To be held and possessed . . . . as entirely . . . . . as I and my father have held them. Seal. Witnesses.]

---

(1) No. 348 should have been headed Bercht (Barugh), which here interposes a long narrow slip between Notton, Darfield, and Monk Bretton to the north, and Barnsley to the south.

Sciant presentes et futuri quod ego Johannes filius Ade de Sepelay, pro salute anime mee et omnium antecessorum et heredum meorum dedi, concessi, et hac presenti carta mea confirmavi deo et sancto Johanni Apostolo et ewangeliste de Pontefracto et monachis ibidem deo servientibus, in perpetuam et puram elemosinam, viginti acras terre in territorio de Bercht. Illas scilicet acras que vocantur Waldefrode et que jacent inter terram monachorum de Revesby[2] versus North, ex una parte, et divisam campi de Berneslaya versus suth ex altera, et essartum Reginaldi fratris Wuldef' quod jacet inter terram Roberti filii Ade de Holdefeld et divisam de Berneslaya. Tenendas et habendas prefatis monachis inperpetuum sine retenemento et sine reclamatione mei vel heredum meorum ita integre cum omnibus libertatibus et aisiamentis ad easdem acras pertinentibus infra villam de Brecht[3] et extra, sicut ego et pater meus tenuimus vel unquam habere potuimus aut debuimus. Et ut hec mea donatio predictis monachis firma sit et stabilis huic carte pro me et heredibus meis sigillum meum apposui. Hiis testibus, *Alano de Smythetona, tunc ballivo de Staincros et Osgotcros, Gilberto de Nottona, Henrico de Tancreslay, Willelmo de Brettona, Adam de Holand*, et aliis.

---

(2) Revesby was a monastery in Lincolnshire. Like Rievaux, it was founded by Walter Espec.

(3) *Sic.*

DE BERNESLAYA.
CCCXLIX. **Carta Henrici filii Willelmi de Portebref.**

[. . . . . I, Henry, son of William de Portbref, ... have confirmed . . . . . a bovate of land in the territory of Barnsley, ... which Roger son of Arnald held. Warranty. Witnesses.]

Sciant presentes et futuri quod ego Henricus filius Willelmi de Portebref, pro salute anime mee et omnium antecessorum et heredum meorum, dedi, concessi et presenti carta mea confirmavi, et inperpetuum quietam clamavi sine retenemento de me et de heredibus meis deo et sancto Johanni et priori et monachis de Pontefracto, in puram et perpetuam elemosinam, unam bovatam terre in territorio de Barneslaya, cum omnibus pertinentiis suis infra villam et extra. Illam scilicet quam Rogerus filius Arnaldi tenuit. Et ego Henricus et heredes mei warentizabimus predictam bovatam terre prenominatis monachis contra omnes homines. Hiis testibus, *Alano filio Rand' tunc ballivo, Willelmo filio Ade, Roberto de Deneby, Ada de Holand, Roberto filio Willelmi de Deneby, Ada de Holdefelda*, et aliis.

CCCL.   Carta Henrici filii Willelmi de Portebref.

[. . . . . I, Henry, son of William Portbref, have . . . . . quit-claimed William, son of Hugh, my man and my native, with all his goods and with all his following. Warranty. Witnesses.]

Sciant presentes et futuri quod ego, Henricus filius Willelmi Portebref, dedi, concessi et inperpetuum quietum clamavi de me et de heredibus meis priori et monachis de Pontefracto Willelmum filium Hugonis, hominem meum et nativum meum, cum omnibus catallis suis, et cum tota sequela sua. Et hanc donationem meam ego Henricus et heredes mei predictis priori et monachis warantizabimus contra omnes homines. Hiis testibus, *Alano filio Rand' tunc ballivo, Willelmo filio Ade, Roberto de Deneby, Ada de Holanda, Ada de Oldefelda,* et aliis.

CCCLI.[1]   Carta Matildis filie Ade dispensatoris.

[. . . . . I, Matilda, ... have quit-claimed . . . . . . two quarters of wheat, and two skeps of fine wheat, and half a mark of silver, in which the prior and convent were bound to me yearly. . . . . also three acres of land from their demesne, with a house in Barnsley, which they had granted to me for life. Sealed and surrendered with my own hands, along with the charter which I had from them. They have given me, in my great necessity, four silver marks. Witnesses.]

Omnibus Christi fidelibus ad quos presens scriptum pervenerit Matildis filia Ade dispensatoris de Berneslaya salutem in domino. Noverit universitas vestra me remisisse et quieta clamasse priori et conventui de Pontefracto duo quarteria frumenti et duas sceppas siliginis et dimidiam marcam argenti, in quibus idem prior et conventus annuatim michi in vita mea tantummodo per cartam suam tenebantur. Et insuper tres acras terre de dominico suo, cum una domo in Berneslaya, quas michi in vita mea similiter concesserant eisdem quietas clamavi Et ne ego Matildis in dictis quarteriis frumenti cum duabus sceppis siliginis, dimidia marca argenti, domo, et tribus acris terre, jus aliquod vel clamium in posterum vendicare possim, presens scriptum sigillo meo signavi. Et illud cum carta quam de dictis priore et conventui[2] habui propriis manibus sursum reddidi eisdem. Pro hac autem remissione et quieta clamatione dederunt michi dicti prior et conventus in magna necessitate mea quatuor marcas argenti pre manibus. Hiis testibus, *Roberto de Berche, Rogero capellano de Berneslaya, Adam de Berneslaya clerico, Henrico Portebref, Andrea Tinctore,* et aliis.

---

(1) No. 351 and No. 352 are, with two very slight differences, identical.   (2) *Sic.*

De Berneslaya.
CCCLII.   Carta Matildis filie Ade dispensatoris.

[. . . . . I, Matilda, have . . . . . . quit-claimed . . . . . two quarters of wheat and two skeps of fine wheat and half a mark of silver, in which the prior and convent were bound to me yearly . . . . . also three acres of land from their demesne, with a house in Barnsley, which they had granted to me for life. . . . . Sealed and surrendered with my own hands, along with the charter which I had from them. They have given me, in my great necessity, four silver marks. Witnesses.]

Omnibus Christi fidelibus ad quos presens scriptum pervenerit Matildis filia Ade dispensatoris de Berneslaya salutem in domino. Noverit universitas vestra me remisisse et quieta clamasse priori et conventui de Pontefracto duo quarteria frumenti et duas sceppas siliginis et dimidiam marcam argenti, in quibus idem prior et conventus annuatim mihi in vita mea tantummodo per cartam suam tenebantur. Et insuper tres acras terre de dominico suo, cum una domo in Berneslaya, quas mihi in vita mea similiter concesserant eisdem quietas clamavi. Et ne ego Matildis in dictis quarteriis frumenti, duabus sceppis siliginis, dimidiam marcam[1] argenti, domo, et tribus acris terre, jus aliquod vel clamium in posterum vendicare possim, presens scriptum sigillo meo signavi. Et illud cum carta quam de dictis priore et conventu habui propriis manibus sursum reddidi eisdem. Pro hac autem remissione et quieta clamatione dederunt michi dicti prior et conventus in magna necessitate mea quatuor marcas argenti pre manibus. Hiis testibus, *Roberto de Berch, Rogero capellano de Berneslaya, Adam de Berneslaya clerico, Henrico Portebref, Andrea Tinctore*, et aliis.   ——————

(1) *Sic.*

———————————

De Berneslaya.
CCCLIII.   Carta Raineri Marescalli.[1]   Cir. 1192.

[. . . . . . I, Rayner Marshall, have . . . . . . quit-claimed . . . . those two bovates of land in Barnsley which I held from them. . . . . . Likewise my mother Godith and my brother Adam have quit-claimed them . . . . The monks have given to me three marks of silver and have received in their prayers me and my

(1) This may be the grandfather of the Reginald le Ferrur of No. 169. There has been nothing to show how he became possessed of these two bovates, who was his wife, or what the name of his son. But there was a William Marshall who owned land in Frystone, and by No. 268 gave it to the monks as the price of his burial in the monastery. Several of the name are mentioned in the Selby Chartulary, though I cannot connect Rayner of Staincross with either the Marshalls of Barkston Ash or those of Osgoldcross. The following is the genealogical connection disclosed in the present charter :—

```
                 . . . . . . Marshall = Godith
                                |
         |----------------------------------------|
   Rayner Marshall                               Adam
        |
   ? Reginald le Ferrur, No. 169
```

wife and my son and my mother Godith and my brother Adam and the soul of my father. Warranty. The monks have given Adam my brother twelve pence in testimony. Witnesses.]

Sciant presentes et futuri quod ego Rainerus Marescallus reddidi deo et sancto Johanni et monachis de Pontefracto et quietas clamavi de me et de heredibus meis inperpetuum illas duas bovatas terre in Bernesleya cum omnibus pertinentiis suis, quas bovatas de eis libere tenebam, et hoc confirmavi hac mea carta et hoc meo sigillo. Similiter mater mea Godith et frater meus Adam eandam[2] terram quietam clamaverunt predictis monachis inperpetuum. Monachi vero propter hoc mihi dederunt tres marcas argenti et receperunt me et uxorem meam et filium meum et matrem meam Godith et fratrem meum Adam et animam patris mei in orationibus. Hoc autem sicut prescriptum est warentizabimus ego et heredes mei predictis monachis contra omnes homines. Ade vero fratri meo dederunt ipsi monachi in testimonium hujus rei duodecim denarios. Testibus, *Radulfo Figera*,[3] *Willelmo filio Hervei, Roberto de Lascy, Jordano de Ledestuna, Waltero de Tribus*,[4] *Ernis, Gundwino, Gilberto de Bagghil*,[5] *Widone de Aula, Rogero dispensatore*, et aliis.

(2) *Sic.*   (3) *Sic*, for Figura. He appears also in No. 148, No. 149, and No. 155.
(4) *Sic*, for Turribus.   (5) See No. 158.

DE SILKISTONA.
CCCLIIII.[1]   **Carta Hugonis**[2] **Pincerne.**

[. . . . . I, Richard de Savile, son of Hugh Pincerna of Sandal, ... have confirmed . . . . a bovate of land in the territory of Silkstone with its appurtenances, and Rainer son of Hugh the reeve, with all his following and all his goods, namely, that bovate which the said Hugh formerly held, and which lies in Bolehalt. To be held and possessed . . . . . . The monks have given me five marks of silver, which Ralph the chaplain has given to them by way of charity to buy the said land. Warranty. Seal. Witnesses.]

Sciant presentes et futuri quod ego, Ricardus de Sevilla filius Hugonis Pincerne de Sandala, dedi, concessi, et hac presenti carta mea confirmavi deo et ecclesie sancti Johannis de Pontefracto et monachis ibidem deo servientibus, pro salute anime mee et omnium antecessorum et heredum meorum, unam bovatam terre in territorio de Silkestona cum pertinentiis suis, et Rainerium filium Hugonis prepositi,[3] cum tota secta sua, et omnibus catallis suis. Illam scilicet

(1) Neither of the seven charters after No. 347 was transcribed by Dodsworth, but a copy of No. 349, No. 350, and No. 351 is to be found in Jackson's *Barnsley*.   (2) *Sic*.
(3) We see here the son of the reeve "adscriptus."

bovatam quam dictus Hugo prepositus prius tenuerat que jacet in Bolehaut.   Tenendam et habendam prefatis monachis de me et heredibus meis in liberam, puram et perpetuam elemosinam, cum omnibus pertinentiis suis infra villam de Silkestona et extra pertinentibus, sine aliquo retenemento mei vel heredum meorum inperpetuum. Pro hac vero donatione et concessione dederunt mihi prefati monachi quinque marcas argenti pre manibus, quas Radulfus capellanus ad dictam terram emendam eisdem caritative contulit.   Et ego Ricardus et heredes mei prefatam terram cum pertinentiis suis dictis monachis contra omnes homines, sicut liberam et puram elemosinam nostram, warantizabimus ac defendemus.   Et ne ego Ricardus vel heredes mei contra hanc meam donationem inposterum venire possimus, huic scripto sigillum meum apposui.   Hiis testibus, *Willelmo de Brettona, Henrico de Tancresleya, Ada de Hoyland, Hugone de Berhg, Rogero de Berh,*[4] et aliis.

(4) *Sic.*

De Doddewrda.
CCCLV.[1]   **Carta Diane filie Johannis Blomer.**

[. . . . . I, Diana, daughter of John Blomer, in my lawful power have . . . . . confirmed all my land of Dodworth . . . . for three and a half marks of silver to me and my mother and sister, and I have attorned to them all my tenants, that they shall render them their rent and service. Seal. Moreover I have sworn that I will keep this sale faithfully and without fraud for ever. Witnesses.]

Sciant presentes et futuri quod ego Diana filia Johannis Blomer in ligia potestate mea vendidi, concessi et presenti carta mea confirmavi totam terram meam de Doddeword cum omnibus pertinentiis infra villam et extra dominis meis priori et monachis de Pontefracto pro tribus marcis argenti et dimidia quas mihi et matri et sorori mee premanibus dederunt, et eis omnes tenentes meos attornavi, ut eis de omni redditu et servitio quod mihi et heredibus meis facere tenebantur de cetero inperpetuum eis satisfaciant.   Et ne ego vel heredes mei contra hanc venditionem venire possimus, hoc scriptum sigillo meo roboravi.   Et insuper affidavi et juravi quod hanc venditionem fideliter et sine dolo inperpetuum observabo.   Hiis testibus, *domino Henrico de Sewilla, Rogero capellano de Berneslaya, Ricardo de Cravene, Roberto de Veteri Villa, Henrico filio Rogeri, Henrico Portebref, Ricardo de Martona,* et aliis.

(1) No. 355 was transcribed twice into *Dodsworth*, vol. 151.

De Berneslaya.

CCCLVI.[1]   Carta Roberti filii Gerardi de Berneslaya.[2]

[. . . . . I, Robert, son of Gerard of Barnsley, have . . . . . quit-claimed . . . . all my right in two acres of land which I held from them in Barnsley, which lie in the hay ings, and which I received from them in exchange for the half of Gresroyd. And the monks have given me ten silver shillings. Seal. Witnesses.]

Sciant presentes et futuri quod ego Robertus filius Gerardi de Berneslaya sursum reddidi et de me et heredibus meis inperpetuum quietum clamavi dominis meis priori et conventui de Pontefracto omne jus et clamium quod habui vel unquam habere potui, in duabus acris terre cum pertinentiis suis quas de eisdem prius tenui in territorio de Berneslaya; que jacent in heyinges[3] et quas recepi de eisdem in excambium pro dimidietate de Gresroda. Pro hac vero quieta clamatione et sursum redditione dederunt mihi dicti monachi decem solidos argenti pre manibus. Et ne ego Robertus vel heredes mei in posterum aliquid juris vel clamii in dictis duabus acris terre et earum pertinentiis vendicare possimus, huic scripto sigillum meum pro me et heredibus meis inperpetuum apposui in testimonium. Hiis testibus, *Ricardo de Cravene, Andrea tinctore, Henrico Portebref, Roberto de Veteri Villa, Ricardo de eadem,* et aliis.

(1) I have met with no transcript of No. 356.

(2) There were two contemporary Gerards of Barnsley, one of whom was Gerard the greave to Roger de Barnsley, and it is not always easy to distinguish between them. The grantor here is apparently Robert son of Gerard the greave. According to No. 393 the two Gerards held adjacent plots.　　　　　　　　　　　　　　(3) "Hevening" in No. 393.

De Silkestona.

CCCLVII.[1]   Carta Clementie de Lungvilers.   1238.

[. . . . . . I, Clemence de Lungvilers, in my pure widowhood, having inspected the charters of my ancestors . . . . concerning the advowson of the church of Silkstone with the chapels thereto belonging, have confirmed those charters. . . . . . Moreover I have quit-claimed all my right . . . . in the patronage of the said church . . . . . And if any of my heirs presume to contravene this . . . . . he has incurred the malediction of God Almighty, and the indignation of His Mother the Blessed Mary, and the curse of myself and of all women. Seal. Given at York in full Court, on the first day after the feast of St. Michael, in the twenty-second year of the reign of King Henry, son of King John. Witnesses.]

Omnibus hoc scriptum visuris vel audituris Clementia de Lung-vilers salutem. Noverit universitas vestra me in pura viduitate mea inspectis carta[2] antecessorum meorum caritatis intuitu collatis deo et sancto Johanni de Pontefracto et monachis ibidem deo servientibus,

(1) No. 357 is No. VIII in the *Monasticon,* and there is a copy in both *Lansdowne* 207 and *Dodsworth,* vol. 151.　　　　　　　　　　　　　　(2) *Sic.*

super advocatione ecclesie de Silkistona cum capellis ad eandem ecclesiam spectantibus, easdem cartas confirmasse dictis monachis ob salutem anime mee et omnium predecessorum et heredum meorum. Quietum etiam clamavi dictis monachis totum jus meum et clamium quod habui vel unquam habere potui in jure patronatus dicte ecclesie cum ejus pertinentiis de me et de omnibus heredibus meis inperpetuum, ita quod de cetero nec ego nec heredes mei aliquod jus vel clamium habere possimus nec vendicare in dicta ecclesia vel ejus pertinentiis. Et si ita contingat quod aliquis heredum meorum contra hanc meam confirmationem et quietam clamationem ausu temerario venire presumpserit jus monachorum vel presentationem eorum impediendo in aliquo tempore cum dicta ecclesia vacaverit, maledictionem dei omnipotentis, et indignationem genetricis sue beate marie, et maledictionem meam et omnium mulierum se noverit incursum. Et ut hec mea confirmatio et quieta clamatio rata et stabilis perseveret omni tempore huic scripto pro me et heredibus meis sigillum meum apposui. Datum apud Eboracum in pleno comitatu et primo post festum sancti Michaelis, anno regni regis Henrici filii Johannis regis vicesimo secundo. Hiis testibus, *domino J. de Lascy, comite Lincolnie, domino Briano filio Alani, tunc vicecomite Eborascensi, Rogero de Stapiltona, Ada de Neirfort, Henrico Walensi, Roberto de Stapiltona, Rogero de Nottona,* et aliis.

DE DODDEWORDA.
CCCLVIII.[1]   Carta Johannis capellani de Silkestona.

[. . . . . I, John, chaplain of Silkstone, ... have confirmed to Adam son of Gilbert, as if to my heir, and to Matilda my daughter, his wife, and their heirs, the bovate of land with its appurtenances in Dodworth which I have held . . . . . Paying thence to the prior and convent 2 shillings yearly. Witnesses.]

Sciant presentes et futuri quod ego Johannes capellanus de Silkestona concessi et hac presenti carta mea confirmavi Ade filio Gilberti sicut heredi meo et Matildi filie mee uxori sue et heredibus eorum illam bovatam terre cum pertinentiis suis in Doddeworda, quam ego tenui in feudo et hereditate, libere et quiete cum omnibus libertatibus et liberis communibus sicut ego eam prius[2] tenui. Reddendo inde annuatim Priori de Pontefracto et conventui ejusdem domus ij solidos duobus terminis, scilicet dimidium ad festum sancti Johannis Baptiste, et dimidium ad festum sancti Andree, pro omnibus servitiis. Hiis testibus, *Matheo de Sepelay, Roberto de Deneby, Roberto de Berch, Alexandro filio suo, Roberto de Turs,* et aliis.

---

(1) No. 358 was transcribed into *Dodsworth*, vol. 151.   (2) Vol. 151 omits "eam prius."

2 J

DE DODDEWRDA.

CCCLVIIII.[1]   Carta **Willelmi-filii Ulf de Doddeworda.**

[. . . . . I, William son of Ulf of Dodworth, ... have confirmed to John
the chaplain, son of Hugh the priest of Barnsley, ... a bovate of land in Dodworth, with its meadow, namely, the bovate which belonged to Bared Ruffus,
and the assart which was Ulmer's in Hugset.   To be held, &c . . . . Paying
yearly two shillings . . . . . Warranty.   Witnesses.]

Sciant presentes et futuri quod ego Willelmus filius Ulf de
Doddeworda dedi et concessi et hac mea presenti carta confirmavi
Johanni capellano filio Hugonis sacerdotis de Berneslaya, et cuicumque
voluerit facere heredem suum, unam bovatam terre in Doddeworda,
cum prato quod pertinet ad predictam bovatam, scilicet illam que
fuit Baredi Ruffi, et illud sartum quod fuit Ulmeri in Huggeside, ad
tenendum de me et heredibus meis, ille et heredes sui,[2] cum libera
communione predicte ville de Doddeworda, libere et quiete, in feudo
et hereditate, annuatim reddendo mihi et heredibus meis, ille et
heredes sui,[2] duos solidos pro omni servitio, scilicet medietatem in
vigilia sancti Johannis Baptiste et medietatem in vigilia sancti Andree
Apostoli.   Et ego Willelmus et heredes mei warentizabimus prenominato J. et heredibus suis predictam terram contra omnes homines.
Hiis testibus, *Hugone persona de Silkestona, Johanne clerico de Stainburga, Rogero fratre suo, Johanne clerico de Holand, Roberto de Pul,
Waltero de Estfeld,* et aliis.   _____

(1) No. 359 was transcribed into *Dodsworth,* vol. 151, and into *Lansdowne,* vol. 207.   There is
also an abstract in *Dodsworth,* vol. 133.   (2) *Sic* in both places.

CCCLX.   Carta **Ricardi filii Ulf.**

[. . . . . I, Richard son of Ulf of Dodworth, ... have confirmed to John
the chaplain, son of Hugh the priest of Barnsley, ... all the land which William
my brother gave to him in Dodworth, namely, the bovate which belonged to
Bared Ruffus with its meadow, and the assart which was Ulmer's in Hugset.   To
be held &c. . . . . . . Paying two shillings yearly to the aforesaid William.   Seal.
Witnesses.]

Sciant presentes et futuri quod ego Ricardus filius Ulf de
Doddeworda concessi et hac mea presenti carta confirmavi Johanni
capellano, filio Hugonis sacerdotis de Berneslaya, et cuicumque
voluerit facere heredem suum, totam terram quam Willelmus frater
meus dedit ei in Doddeworda.   Scilicet illam bovatam terre que fuit
Baredi Ruffi, cum prato quod pertinet ad predictam bovatam, et illud
sartum quod fuit Ulmeri in Huggeside.   Ad tenendum de illo et de

heredibus suis, ille et heredes sui,[1] libere et quiete cum libera communione predicte ville in feudo et hereditate, annuatim reddendo duos solidos prenominato Willelmo et heredibus suis, ille et heredes sui,[1] pro omni servitio, scilicet medietatem in vigilia sancti Johannis Baptiste et medietatem in vigilia sancti Andree Apostoli. Et ut mea concessio et confirmatio firma sit et stabilis, istam meam presentem cartam sigilli mei inpressione corroboravi.   Hiis testibus, *Hugone persona de Silkestona, Johanne clerico de Stainburga, Rogero fratre suo, Johanne clerico de Holand, Roberto de Pul, Waltero de Estfield, Nicholao filio suo*, et aliis. ———

(1) Sic here also in both places.

CCCLXI,   Carta Diane filie Johannis Blomer.

[. . . . . I, Diana, daughter of John Blomer, have confirmed . . . . . . that toft in the town of Dodworth which Peter held of me and gave to the monks with my assent for four shillings . . . . . Seal.   Witnesses.]

Sciant presentes et futuri quod ego Diana filia Johannis Blomer concessi et presenti carta confirmavi deo et sancto Johanni evangeliste de Pontefracto et monachis ibidem deo servientibus, pro salute anime mee et omnium antecessorum et heredum meorum, in puram et perpetuam elemosinam, illum toftum in villa de Doddeworda quem Petrus tenuit de me et eisdem monachis per voluntatem et assensum meum dedit pro quatuor solidis, quos dicti monachi predicto Petro pro prefato tofto et dimidia acra terre pre manibus dederunt. Et ne ego vel heredes mei contra hanc concessionem et confirmationem meam in libera potestate factam unquam venire possimus, huic scripto sigillum meum apposui. Hiis testibus, *domino Symone capellano de Silkestona, Rogero capellano de Berneslaya, Henrico filio Rogeri, Roberto de Veteri Villa, Henrico Portebref*, et aliis.

CCCLXII.   Carta Sibilie filie Johannis Blomer.

[. . . . . I, Sybil, younger daughter of John Blomer, in my lawful power. . . . . have confirmed all my land of Dodworth, with its appurtenances, for three and a half marks of silver, given to me and my mother and sister. And I have attorned all my tenants . . . . . Seal. Moreover I have sworn that I will observe this sale faithfully and without fraud.   Witnesses.]

Sciant presentes et futuri quod ego Sibilia postgenita filia Johannis Blomer in ligia potestate mea vendidi, concessi et presenti carta mea

confirmavi totam terram meam de Doddeworda, cum omnibus pertinentiis suis infra villam et extra, dominis meis priori et monachis de
Pontefracto, pro tribus marcis argenti et dimidia, quas mihi et matri
et sorori mee pre manibus dederunt, et eis omnes tenentes meos
attornavi, ut eis de omni redditu et servitio quod mihi et heredibus
meis facere tenebantur de cetero inperpetuum eis faciant.[1] Et ne
ego vel heredes mei contra hanc venditionem unquam venire
possimus hoc scriptum sigillo meo roboravi. Et insuper affidavi et
juravi quod hanc venditionem fideliter et sine dolo inperpetuum
observabo. Hiis testibus, *domino Henrico de Sevilla, Simone capellano
de Silkestona, Rogero capellano de Berneslay, Ricardo de Cravena,
Roberto de Veteri Villa, Henrico filio Rogeri,* et aliis.

(1) In No. 355 this was "satisfaciant," but both there and here the "eis" is thus repeated.

DE BERNESLAYA.
CCCLXIII.[1]   **Carta Andree filii Willelmi de Holdtona.**[2]

[. . . . . I, Andrew, son of William of Oldtown, have . . . . . confirmed . . . . .
a bovate of land in Barnsley which William my father held. To be held and
possessed, with toft and croft, &c.   Seal.   Warranty.   Witnesses.]

Sciant presentes et futuri quod ego Andreas filius Willelmi de
Holdtona dedi et concessi et hac presenti carta mea confirmavi, in
puram et perpetuam elemosinam, pro salute anime mee et antecessorum meorum, deo et beato Johanni apostolo et evangeliste de
Pontefracto et monachis ibidem deo servientibus, unam bovatam terre
in territorio de Berneslaya. Scilicet illam bovatam quam Willelmus
pater meus quondam tenuit. Tenendam et habendam, libere, quiete,
pacifice, cum tofto et crofto et omnibus libertatibus et aisiamentis ad
unam bovatam terre pertinentibus, infra villam de Berneslaya et extra.
Et ut hec donatio et confirmatio rata sit et stabilis, ego predictus
Andreas sigillum meum huic scripto apposui. Et ego prenominatus
Andreas et heredes mei predictam bovatam terre cum pertinentibus
contra omnes homines warantizabimus et defendemus. Hiis testibus,
*domino Johanne de Saivile, domino Roberto de Holand, Roberto de
Bergh, Johanne de Rupe, Roberto de Turs, Andrea Tinctore, Ricardo
de Bergh,* et aliis.

(1) In the margin is the note, "Rob. de Bergh testis 2 K. Jo',—carta 365."
(2) Old Town was a district to the north-west of Barnsley, Old Field being still further away
in the same direction; and, as was the case with all "Fields," it was on the border of the neighbouring township, that of Barugh (Bergh as the monks called it).   This accounts for the appearance
of so many attesting witnesses of the name of Bergh.

CCCLXIIII.   Carta Henrici Portebref.[1]

[˙ . . . . I, Henry Portbref of Barnsley, ... have confirmed . . . . . a bovate of land in Barnsley, which Roger de Monte held. To be held and possessed, &c. Seal. Warranty. Witnesses.]

Sciant presentes et futuri quod ego Henricus Portebref de Berneslaya dedi et concessi et hac presenti carta mea confirmavi, in puram et perpetuam elemosinam, pro salute anime mee et antecessorum meorum, deo et beato Johanni apostolo et evangeliste de Pontefracto et monachis ibidem deo servientibus, unam bovatam terre in territorio de Berneslaya. Scilicet illam bovatam quam Rogerus de Monte quondam tenuit. Tenendam et habendam libere, quiete, pacifice, cum tofto et crofto et omnibus aliis libertatibus ad unam bovatam terre pertinentibus infra villam de Berneslaya et extra. Et ut hec donatio et confirmatio rata sit et stabilis sigillum meum huic scripto apposui. Et ego predictus Henricus et heredes mei predictam bovatam terre predictis monachis contra omnes homines warentizabimus et defendemus. Hiis testibus, *domino Johanne de Sevile, Rainero de Wambewelle, Roberto de Berh, Roberto de Turs, Roberto de Haltona, Andrea Tinctore,* et aliis.

---

(1) It may be noticed that in No. 349 this Henry is said to be son of William Portbref, while Roger de Monte is called Roger son of Arnald. The following seems to be the relationship of these Portbrefs :—

William Portbref, of Old Town

Henry   Andrew

DE DODDEWORDA.

CCCLXV.[1]   Carta Ricardi et Walteri.   1200.

[. . . . . I, Richard, and I, Walter, sons of Bernard of Silkstone, hold valid what the prior and monks may do within the common land of Dodworth, in assarting to the amount of ten shillings' rents from the day of the Blessed Peter Ad Cathedram in the second year of the reign of King John . . . . ˙. And all gifts which they have made we hold valid. Seals. Witnesses.]

Sciant presentes et futuri quod ego Ricardus et ego Walterus filii Bernardi[2] de Silkestona concessimus et ratum habemus quod prior et monachi de Pontefracto faciant probum suum infra communam de Doddeworda in sartando usque ad summam decem solidorum redditus a die Beati Petri ad cathedram[3] deinceps anni secundi regni regis Johannis sine omni querela et omni reclamatione juris quod

---

(1) No. 360 to No. 365 are all copied into *Dodsworth*, vol. 151.

(2) In vol. 151 this is miscopied "Ricardi."   (3) At Rome and Antioch, Feb. 22.

nos vel heredes nostri inde facere possimus. Et similiter omnia dona que prior et monachi fecerunt usque ad predictam diem rata habemus et super hiis querelam non movebimus. Et ne contra hoc factum nostrum nos aut heredes nostri venire possimus hoc scriptum sigillorum nostrorum appositione roboravimus. Hiis testibus, *Hugone decano de Silkestona, Rogero decano de Pontefracto, Roberto de Berch, Willelmo de Insula, Willelmo Gramatico, Rogero et Alexandro de Rugala,*[4] *Symone de Kellingtona,* et aliis.

(4) These may be of the Kellington family also. See p. 378 ; also No. 430.

DE OLDFELDA.[1]
CCCLXVI.   Carta Johannis de Hodfelda.[2]

[. . . . I, John de Oldfield, ... have confirmed to Hugh my brother six acres of land in Oldfield towards the south. To be held and possessed . . . . . . Paying yearly sixpence . . . . Warranty. Witnesses.]

Sciant presentes et futuri quod ego Johannis de Oldfelda dedi et concessi, et hac mea presenti carta confirmavi Hugoni fratri meo et heredibus suis vel cui assignare voluerit, pro homagio et servitio suo, sex acras terre in Oldfelda versus suth. Tenendas et habendas de me et de heredibus meis illi et heredibus suis vel cui assignare voluerit in feudo et hereditate, libere et quiete et honorifice. Solvendo inde annuatim mihi et heredibus meis sex denarios in die sancti Martini pro omni servitio et demanda. Ego autem et heredes mei warentizabimus ei et heredibus suis vel ejus assignatis predictam terram contra omnes homines. Hiis testibus, *Roberto de Sepelay, Hugone de Berch, Rogero fratre ejus,* et aliis.

(1) I have met with no transcription or abstract of No. 366.   (2) *Sic.*

CCCLXVII.[1]   Carta Johannis filii Ade de Oldfield.   Ante 1222.

[. . . . . I, John son of Adam de Oldfield, ... have confirmed . . . . . . all the land which Hugh my brother has held from me in Barnsley, and which in the court of the lord prior he surrendered to me . . . . It lies within the boundaries of the plot which formerly belonged to my father towards the south. To be held and possessed. Warranty. Witnesses.]

Sciant presentes et futuri quod ego Johannes filius Ade de Oldfelda dedi, concessi et hac presenti carta mea confirmavi, pro

(1) No. 367 is transcribed into *Dodsworth*, vol. 151.

salute anime mee et patris mei et matris mee et omnium antecessorum et heredum meorum, deo et ecclesie sancti Johannis de
Pontefracto et monachis ibidem deo servientibus totam illam terram
quam Hugo frater meus tenuit de me in territorio de Berneslaya,
et quam idem Hugo in curia domini prioris de Pontefracto mihi
sursum reddidit et omnino de se et heredibus suis quietam clamavit.
Illamque scilicet que jacet infra divisas culture que fuit quondam A.
patris mei versus australem partem. Tenendam et habendam prefatis
monachis in puram et perpetuam elemosinam. Hanc vero donationem
et concessionem ego Johannes et heredes mei prefatis monachis
contra omnes homines warantizabimus inperpetuum. Hiis testibus,
domino Willelmo de Bretton, Henrico de Sevile, Hugone de Berch,
Ricardo de Cravena, Henrico filio Rogeri, et aliis.

DE FLOCTONA.
CCCLXVIII.[1]   **Carta Ade filii Hervey.**[2]

[. . . . . I, Adam son of Hervey de Flockton, have . . . . . confirmed . . . . . .
Henry son of Edward and all his following. They have given me 20 shillings
sterling. Warranty. Witnesses.]

Sciant presentes et futuri quod ego Adam filius Hervei de
Floctona dedi et concessi et hac mea presenti carta confirmavi deo
et sancto Johanni de Pontefracto et monachis qui ibidem deo
servient[3] Henricum filium Edwardi et totam sequelam suam, in
perpetuam et puram elemosinam, pro anima mea et pro animabus
patris et matris mee et antecessorum meorum, et pro ista donatione
et concessione dederunt mihi xx*ti* solidos sterlingorum. Ego vero
Adam et heredes mei warantizabimus predictis monachis prefatum
Henricum et totam sequelam suam contra omnes homines. Hiis
testibus, *Jordano filio Edulf,*[4] *Thoma filio Edulf, Waltero filio Hugone,*
Johanne filio Harding,[5] et aliis. _____

(1) I have met with no transcription of No. 368.

(2) The grantor was Adam de Byram, by which name he was known in this neighbourhood
(see *ante,* p. 298).   (3) A variant of the usual phrase.

(4) The Chartulary has clearly E*d*ulf, but there can be little doubt that the name should be
Essulf, and that the witnesses are Jordan de Flockton and Thomas, sons of Essulf, the latter being
afterwards Thomas Pincerna and Thomas de Monte (*ante,* pp. 254-5)

(5) This John son of Harding tested one of Adam fitz Peter's charters to Rievaux (see
Chartulary R., p. 58), and both No. 263 and No. 264, *ante.*

De Silkistona.

CCCLXIX.[1]   **Carta Ade filii Suani.**   Cir. 1154.

[. . . . . I, Adam fitz Swain, ... have confirmed to the church of St. Mary of Charitè and to their sons of Pontefract the church of Silkstone, with six bovates of land and their appurtenances, with the chapels and lands and tithes, and all things belonging, for their maintenance and that of their guests, without any withholding. . . . . . . Warranty. Witnesses.]

Domino et patri R[ogero] dei gratia Eboracensi archiepiscopo et omnibus sancte matris ecclesie filiis presentibus et futuris Adam filius Suani salutem. Sciatis omnes quod ego Adam filius Suani pro amore dei et pro salute anime mee et patris mei et matris mee et omnium antecessorum et heredum meorum, concessi et presenti carta mea confirmavi deo et ecclesie sancte marie de Karitate et ejusdem ecclesie filiis, monachis de Pontefracto in ecclesia beati Johannis evangeliste deo ibidem servientibus, ecclesiam de Silkistuna cum sex bovatis terre et earum pertinentiis in eadem villa, cum capellis et terris et decimis et cum omnibus ad eandem ecclesiam pertinentibus, in puram et perpetuam elemosinam, ad suam et hospitum sustentationem, sine omni retenemento mei vel heredum meorum, liberam et quietam ab omnibus terrenis impedimentis. Et ego et heredes mei prefate ecclesie et prefatis monachis predictam ecclesiam warentizabimus per totum contra omnes homines. Hiis testibus, *Rogero archiepiscopo, Henrico de Lascy, Osberto archidiacono, Henrico fratre meo, Suano de Derefeld*, et aliis. _____

(1) No. 369 is transcribed into *Lansdowne* 207. The gift with which it deals was confirmed by No. 71 in January, 1155. Roger, who tests the charter, was archbishop from 1154 to 1181, and Osbert was archdeacon from 1153 to 1166.

_____

De Silkistona.

CCCLXX.[1]   **Carta Willelmi filii Hugonis Pincerne.**

[. . . . . I, William son of Hugh Pincerna of Sandal, have surrendered . . . . . all my right in the bovate of land which the lady Avicia my mother . . . . . gave me in Silkstone. It lies in Bolehall, and Henry son of Ketel has held it from me. I have quit-claimed to them Henry son of Ketel, my man and native, with all his following and his goods. The monks have given me five marks of silver. Seal. Witnesses.]

Sciant presentes et futuri quod ego Willelmus, filius Hugonis Pincerne de Sandala, sursum reddidi et de me et heredibus meis sine aliquo retenemento vel reclamatione quietum clamavi dominis meis priori et monachis de Pontefracto omne jus et clamium quod habui vel unquam habere potui in illa bovata terre quam domina Avicia mater mea in ligia et plena viduitatis sue potestate mihi dederat in territorio de Silkestona, que jacet in Bolehal', quam Henricus filius Ketel tenuit de me, cum omnibus pertinentiis et aisiamentis infra villam de Silkestona et extra pertinentibus. Insuper quietum clamavi eisdem Henricum filium Ketil hominem meum et nativum, cum tota secta sua et catallis suis. Pro hac vero sursum redditione et quieta clamatione dederunt mihi dicti monachi quinque marcas argenti premanibus. Et ne ego dictus Willelmus vel heredes mei contra tenorem huius carte inposterum venire possimus, huic scripto sigillum meum in testimonium apposui perpetuum. Hiis testibus, *Willelmo de Brettona, Germano de Morteleya, Ricardo Pincerna, Ricardo de Cravena, Willelmo de Goldthorph,* et aliis.

DE BERNESLAYA.

CCCLXXI.[1]   **Carta Gregorii de Altona.**

[. . . . . . . I, Gregory of Oldtown, have . . . . confirmed all my land in Barnsley which I have held from the monks.   To be possessed and held in perpetual alms.   Warranty.   Witnesses.]

Sciant presentes et futuri quod ego Gregorius de Altona dedi, concessi, et presenti carta mea confirmavi et quietam clamavi de me et heredibus meis, sine retenemento, deo et sancto Johanni de Pontefracto et monachis ibidem deo servientibus, totam terram meam in Bernesleia quam tenui de eisdem monachis in territorio de Bernesleia.[2] Habendam et tenendam prefatis monachis in perpetuam elemosinam, cum omnibus aisiamentis et libertatibus ad eandem terram pertinentibus. Et ego prenominatus Gregorius et heredes mei warentizabimus prefatis monachis predictam terram cum omnibus pertinentiis suis contra omnes homines. Hiis testibus, *Rogero clerico de Silkestona, Adam de Oldfelda, Ricardo de Martona, Gerardo de Berneslay, Henrico filio Rogeri, Andrea tinctore,* et aliis.

(1) I have met with no transcription of No. 371.

(2) Oldtown, Old Barnsley as it was sometimes called, was thus considered to be a part of the "territory" of Barnsley; that is to say, it was in the outlying district of that manor.

DE DODDEWORDA.

CCCLXXII.[1]   **Carta Ricardi**[2] **fil' Ulf de Doddeword.**

[. . . . . We, Richard son of Ulf of Dodworth and William his brother, have . . . . confirmed all the men whom we had in Dodworth, with all their following and goods.   The land also we will confirm for ever.   Witnesses.]

(1) No. 372 is published as No. xx in the *Monasticon*, and was copied int *Dodsworth*, vol. 151, with the substitution of "territorio" for "terra nostra."

(2) This word is interlined in black.

Omnibus sancte matris ecclesie filiis presentibus et futuris
Ricardus filius Ulf de Doddeword et Willelmus frater suus salutem.
Sciatis omnes nos dedisse, concessisse, et presenti carta nostra
confirmasse deo et sancto Johanni et priori et monachis de Pontefracto
omnes homines illos quos habuimus in terra nostra de Doddeword
cum omnibus sectis eorum et catallis, pro amore dei et pro salute
animarum nostrarum. Et tam terram ipsam quam etiam omnes
homines illos eis confirmabimus inperpetuum. Hiis testibus, *Roberto
Walensi, Johanne de Birkina, Adam de Rainevilla, Thoma filio suo,*[3]
Willelmo de Stapiltona, Hugone de Brettona, Rogero de Berneslaya,
et aliis.

(3) The name of Thomas de Reineville is absent from a subsequent confirmation (No. 397),
implying for it a later date.

DE SILKISTONA.
CCCLXXIII.[1] **Carta Dionisie filie Hugonis Pincerne de Sandale.**

[. . . . . . I, Dionisia, daughter of Hugh Pincerna of Sandal, have surrendered
. . . . . . all my right in the bovate of land which the lady Avicia my mother gave
me in Silkstone. It lies in Bolehall, and William son of Ketel has held it from me.
I have quit-claimed to them also William son of Ketel, Roger son of Thomas,
Mary, Matilda, Amicia, my folk and natives, with all their following and their
goods, and all the land in Silkstone which Thomas son of Geoffrey Lesurais has
held of me. The monks have given me six silver marks and four shillings and a
penny. Seal. Witnesses.]

Sciant presentes et futuri quod ego Dionisia, filia Hugonis
Pincerne de Sandale, sursum reddidi et de me et heredibus meis
sine aliquo retenemento vel reclamatione quietum clamavi dominis
meis priori et conventui de Pontefracto omne jus et clamium quod
habui vel unquam habere potui in illa bovata terre quam domina
Avicia mater mea in ligia et plena viduitatis sue potestate mihi
dederat in territorio de Silkestona, que jacet in Bolehala, quam
Willelmus filius Ketelli tenuit de me, cum omnibus pertinentiis et
aisiamentis suis infra villam de Silkestona et extra pertinentibus.
Insuper quietum clamavi eisdem Willelmum filium Ketil, Rogerum
filium Thome, Mariam, Matildam, Amiciam, homines meos et nativos,
cum tota secta sua et catallis suis, et totam terram illam in Silkistona
cum pertinentiis quam Thomas filius Gaufridi Lesurais de me tenuit.
Pro hac vero sursum redditione et quieta clamatione dederunt mihi
dicti monachi sex marcas argenti et quatuor solidos et unum
denarium pre manibus. Et ne ego Dionisia vel heredes mei contra

(1) No. 373 and No. 374 were both transcribed into *Dodsworth*, vol. 151, apparently with
reference to a genealogy of the Savile family, which he projected. John de Turgerland is there
omitted from among the witnesses.

tenorem huius carte inposterum venire possimus huic scripto sigillum meum in testimonium apposui perpetuum.   Hiis testibus, *Willelmo de Brettona, Germano de Morteleya, Ricardo Pincerna, Ricardo de Cravena, Willelmo de Golthorp, Johanne de Turgerland,* et aliis.

DE BERNESLAYA.

CCCLXXIIII.   Carta Johannis filii Ade de Sepelay.

[. . . . . . . I, John son of Adam of Shepley, ... have confirmed those ten acres of land in Old Barnsley, which are called Oldfield.   To be held and possessed . . . . . .   Paying me yearly at the church of Barnsley 20 pence on the feast of St. Martin.   Moreover, I have . . . . confirmed a corner adjoining those acres, which I have held from Adam son of Roger of Barnsley, for one penny to be paid yearly at the feast of St. Martin . . . . I and my heirs will answer to the chief lords concerning the aforesaid 21 pence.   Warranty.   Seal.   Witnesses.]

Sciant presentes et futuri quod ego Johannes filius Ade de Sepelay, pro salute anime mee et omnium antecessorum et heredum meorum, dedi, concessi, et hac presenti carta mea confirmavi deo et sancto Johanni apostolo et ewangeliste de Pontefracto et monachis ibidem deo servientibus, in perpetuam elemosinam, decem acras terre in territorio veteris Berneslaya.   Illas scilicet decem acras que vocantur Aldefeld.   Tenendas et habendas prefatis monachis inperpetuum, sine impedimento vel reclamatione mei vel heredum meorum, libere, quiete, integre et pacifice, cum omnibus edificiis, et omnibus aliis pertinentibus ad prefatas decem acras infra villam et extra.   Reddendo inde annuatim mihi et heredibus meis xx*ti* denarios ad festum sancti Martini ad ecclesiam de Berneslaya pro omni servitio.   Insuper dedi, concessi, et hac presenti carta mea confirmavi predictis monachis in perpetuam elemosinam unum angulum adjacentem prefatis acris quem ego tenui hereditarie de Ada filio Rogeri de Berneslaya[1] pro uno denario annuatim ad festum sancti Martini pro omni servitio reddendo, quem denarium predicti monachi persolvent mihi et heredibus meis.   Et ego et heredes mei capitalibus dominis de predictis xx*ti* et uno denariis respondebimus.   Et ego Johannes et heredes mei omnia supradicta prefatis monachis contra omnes homines inperpetuum warantizabimus.   Et ut hec mea donatio firma sit et stabilis, huic carte sigillum meum pro me et heredibus meis apposui.   Hiis testibus, *Alano de Smithetona tunc ballivo de Osgotecros et Staincros, Gilleberto de Nottona, Henrico de Tancrelaya,*[2] *Willelmo de Brettona, Henrico de Seiwilla, Ada de Holanda,* et aliis.

---

(1) His father.   (2) *Sic.*

De Berch.
CCCLXXV.[1]   Carta Hugonis filii Roberti.

[. . . . . . I, Hugh son of Robert de Barugh, ... have confirmed . . . . .
20 acres of land in Barugh, which John son of Adam of Shepley, my grandson, has
given to the monks, that is to say, those twenty acres which are called Waldefroyd
and which lie between the land of the monks of Revesby towards the north and
the boundary of Barnsley Field ; also the assart of Reginald brother of Waldef,
which lies between the land of Robert son of Adam of Oldfield and the boundary
of Barnsley. To be held and possessed . . . . . . as fully as Adam de Shepley and
John his son held them. Moreover, I have . . . . quit-claimed a rent of two
pence which I have been accustomed to receive yearly from the aforesaid acres.
Warranty. Seal. Witnesses.]

Sciant presentes et futuri quod ego, Hugo filius Roberti de
Brech, pro salute anime mee et omnium antecessorum et heredum
meorum, concessi et hac presenti carta mea confirmavi deo et sancto
Johanni apostolo et ewangeliste de Pontefracto et monachis ibidem
deo servientibus, in puram et perpetuam elemosinam, xx acras terre
in territorio de Brech, quas Johannes filius Ade de Sepelay nepos
meus prefatis monachis dedit et carta sua confirmavit. Illas scilicet
viginti acras que vocantur Valdefrode et que jacent inter terram
monachorum de Revesby versus north ex una parte et divisam campi
de Berneslaya ex altera ; et essartum Reginaldi fratris Waldef quod
jacet inter terram Roberti filii Ade de Holdefeld et divisam de
Berneslaya. Tenendas et habendas prefatis monachis inperpetuum
sine reclamatione mei vel heredum meorum, cum omnibus libertatibus
et aisiamentis ville de Brech ad predictas viginti acras pertinentibus,
ita integre sicut Adam de Sepelay et prenominatus Johannis filius
suus nepos meus unquam habuerunt vel habere potuerunt aut
debuerunt. Insuper dedi, concessi et presenti carta mea quietum
clamavi[2] de me et heredibus meis prefatis monachis redditum duorum
denariorum quem consuevi recipere annuatim de predictis xx*ti* acris
terre. Et ego prenominatus Hugo et heredes mei warentizabimus
predictas xx*ti* acras terre prefatis monachis contra omnes homines.
Et ut hec mea concessio et confirmatio firma sit et stabilis huic carte
pro me et heredibus meis sigillum meum apposui. Hiis testibus,
*Alano de Smythetona, tunc ballivo de Staincros et Osgotecros, Gilleberto
de Nottona, Willelmo de Brettona, Hugone de Tretona, Ricardo
Londoniensi,* et aliis.   ————————

(1) I have met with no transcription of No. 375.
(2) These two words are written on an erasure, and repeated in the margin.

BERNESLAYA.
CCCLXXVI.[1]   Carta Matildis filie Ade dispensatoris.

[. . . . . . I, Matilda, daughter of Adam, formerly steward of Barnsley, formerly wife of Richard de Craven, have . . . . . . surrendered all my tenement of Barnsley and of Oldtown, which Adam my father formerly held from the monks. To be held and possessed . . . . with all men, rents, escheats, and all liberties and easements. Seal. Witnesses.]

Sciant presentes et futuri quod ego Matildis, filia quondam Ade dispensatoris de Berneslaya, quondam uxor Ricardi de Cravena,[2] in mea ligia potestate, libera et licita viduitate, dedi, concessi, sursum tradidi, et quietum clamavi inperpetuum de me et heredibus meis deo et sancto Johanni apostolo et evangeliste de Pontefracto et monachis ibidem deo servientibus, pro salute anime mee et antecessorum meorum, totum tenementum meum de Berneslaya et de Veteri Villa, quod quidam[3] tenementum Adam pater meus de eisdem monachis quondam tenuit. Tenendum et habendum dictis monachis in puram et perpetuam elemosinam, libere, quiete, honorifice, pacifice et integre, sine ullo retenemento mei vel heredum meorum, cum omnibus hominibus, redditibus, aschaetis, et cum omnibus aliis libertatibus et aisiamentis ad dictum tenementum pertinentibus, in bosco, in plano, in pratis, et paschuis, et ceteris communis suis infra villam et extra, sicut dictus Adam pater meus et ego ipsum tenementum liberius et integrius unquam tenuimus vel de jure tenuisse debuimus vel potuimus. Ut igitur hec mea donatio, concessio, sursum datio, et quieta clamatio robur perpetue firmitatis optineat, presens scriptum sigilli mei appositione roboravi. Hiis testibus, *domino Ada de Everingham, domino Roberto de Stapiltona, domino Johanne de Hoderode, domino Johanne de Sevile, Adam de Holande, Johanne de Rupe, Roberto de Turs*, et aliis. _____

(1) No. 376 was transcribed into *Dodsworth*, vol. 151.
(2) By an earlier deed (No. 390) Richard de Craven himself had surrendered his rights in the Barnsley woods.   (3) *Sic*.

BERNESLAYA.
CCCLXXVII.[1]   Carta Henrici Rasur de Brettona.

[. . . . . I, Henry Rasur of Bretton, with the consent of Alice my wife . . . . . have confirmed . . . . . the land lying near Barnsley Bridge towards the north, which is called Stephen Crimhil, with all its liberties, as well as those belonging to our land which is called Lagelay. To be held and possessed . . . . Seals. Witnesses.]

Sciant presentes et futuri quod ego, Henricus Rasur de Brettona, concessione Alicie uxoris mee dedi et concessi et hac presenti carta

(1) I have met with no transcription of No. 377.

mea confirmavi deo et beato Johanni apostolo et ewangeliste de Pontefracto et monachis ibidem deo servientibus terram jacentem juxta Pontem de Berneslaya versus aquilonem que vocatur Stephene Crimhil, cum omnibus libertatibus[2] aisiamentis de quibus aliquo tempore saisiati fuerunt, tam ad terram nostram que vocatur Lagelay quam ad istam prenominatam terram pertinentibus. Tenendam et habendam in puram et perpetuam elemosinam pro salute animarum nostrarum et antecessorum nostrum. Et ne ego predictus Henricus vel Alicia uxor mea aliquod jus vel clamium contra tenorem istius carte revocare poterimus, sigilla nostra huic scripto apposuimus. Hiis testibus, *Roberto de Berch, Roberto de Turribus, Hugone filio Johannis de Brettum,*[3] *Henrico Portebref, et Ada clerico de Berneslaya,* et aliis.

(2) Here " et " has been omitted.   (3) *Sic.*

SILKISTONA.
CCCLXXVIII.[1]   **Carta Suani filii Ailrich.**[2]

[. . . . I, Swain son of Ailric, wish you all to know that I . . . . have given the church of Silkstone and six bovates of land there, with all that depend on it, and the chapel of Cawthorn with two bovates of land there, and with two parts of the tithes of all my lordships, that is to say of the sheaves . . . . If anyone who holds of me shall have wished to make them any alms from my fee, I permit it freely. I invoke God as witness of this gift. And these are witnesses, &c.]

Spirituali patri suo T.[3] archiepiscopo et cunctis sancte ecclesie filiis Swanus filius Ailrich salutem. Volo vos omnes scire qui nunc estis presentes et futuri quod ego, in remissione omnium peccatorum meorum et pro salute anime mee et omnium parentum meorum qui de hoc seculo transierunt et pro animabus omnium heredum meorum, donavi per istam meam cartam et sigillum ecclesie sancti Johannis de Pontefracto et monachis qui ibi deo serviunt ecclesiam de Silkistuna et sex bovatas terre in eadem villa et cum omnibus que

---

(1) No. 378 was transcribed into *Lansdowne* 207, and into *Dodsworth*, vol. 116. Hunter gives an abstract of it (*South Yorkshire*, ii, 221), not always exact, and he makes the first of the witnesses to be Godwin. The name is, however, clearly Edwin.

(2) The following is the pedigree of this Ailric :—

Ailric
|
Swain
|

Adam	Robert of Snydale (?)	Henry of Denby	Richard, No. 228, No. 238
Matilda			
	Simon	Jordan Alice	Walter Alan

(3) Either Thomas or Thurstan.

pendent ad illam in omnibus locis. Et capellam de Calthorn cum duabus bovatis terre in eadem villa. Et cum duabus partibus decimarum omnium dominiorum meorum, scilicet garbarum, in puram et perpetuam elemosinam, ita quod in predicta ecclesia et in predicta capella mihi nichil retinui vel alicui heredum meorum. Et si aliquis qui tenet de me aliquam elemosinam de feudo meo eis voluerit facere libenter concedo. Hujus donationis testem voco deum. Et isti homines testes sunt, *Edwinus presbiter et persona de Derefeld, Ulfus presbiter et persona de Adewic, Dolfin de Wolvlay, Saxi de Horbiri*, et multi alii.

CCCLXXIX.[1] Carta Roberti[2] de Monte Begonis. Ante 1197.

[. . . . . I, R[oger] de Montebegon . . . . . have confirmed . . . . . the church of Silkstone, with all its appurtenances, ... according to the tenor which they have from A. fitz Swain. And all the right and claim and liberty which I asserted in that church I have remitted to them, and I have surrendered to them the charters which I had thereof . . . . . . Seal. Witnesses.]

Omnibus sancte matris ecclesie filiis ad quos presens scriptum pervenerit R. de Monte Begonis salutem. Noverit universitas vestra me divine pietatis intuitu, pro salute anime mee et pro animabus antecessorum et heredum meorum, dedisse, concessisse, et presenti carta mea confirmasse in puram et perpetuam elemosinam deo et ecclesie sancti Johannis de Pontefracto et monachis ibidem deo servientibus ecclesiam de Silkestona, cum omnibus pertinentiis suis, sine omni retenemento vel impedimento de me vel de heredibus meis, secundum tenorem quem habent de A.[3] filio Suani. Et omne jus et clamium et omnem libertatem quam mihi et heredibus meis in eadem ecclesia de Silkestona vendicabam eis inperpetuum remisi, et cartas quas inde habui eis sursum reddidi. Et ne ego vel heredes mei possimus in posterum contra hanc donationem et concessionem et quietam clamationem venire, vel eosdem monachos de Pontefracto super eadem ecclesia de Silkestona aliquo modo vexare vel molestare, prefate donationis mee concessionem presentis scripti patrocinio et sigilli mei appositione confirmavi. Hiis testibus, *Rogero de Lasci constabulario Cestrie, Johanne de Birkina, Rogero fratre suo, Roberto le Waleis,*[4] *Henrico filio eius, Willelmo de Stapiltona, Willelmo filio Everardi*, et aliis.

---

(1) No. 379 is No. IX in the *Monasticon*, and there is a copy in *Lansdowne* 207. I have already explained (in connection with No. 357) that it is by far the earlier of the two charters which show the dealing of the co-heirs of that daughter of Adam fitz Swain to whom this portion of his inheritance fell.

(2) The rubricator has incorrectly named the grantor of this charter "Robert." It was Roger, son of Adam de Montbegon and of Matilda, daughter of Adam fitz Swain. The incorrect heading was copied into the *Monasticon*, and (so far as I have seen) it has continued to escape remark.

(3) Adam.   (4) He was not yet seneschal.

De Silkistona.

CCCLXXX.[1]   **Carta Ade filii Swani.**[2]   **Circa 1158.**

[. . . . . I, Adam fitz Swain, have given . . . . . for religion the house of St. Mary Magdalen of Lund which I have founded on my patrimony . . . . . . There is granted to me an obit yearly in their mother church of Charité, and an obit in their house of Pontefract, and my anniversary each year there, and in all their houses a trental, but in others as much as for a Cluniac monk. And Adam the prior and founder, when he shall depart from Pontefract, shall dwell in that house of Lund as long as he shall live, as keeper and prior. After his decease, the prior and monks, with my advice or my heirs', shall put in his place others who may be suitable. And if any brother from Pontefract come to me in a suitable season on the business of his house, he shall eat with me. In gratitude for this, there ought to be paid every year a silver mark from the house of Lund to the church of St. John. The witnesses are, &c.]

Domino Eboracensi archiepiscopo et omnibus fidelibus sancte matris ecclesie Adam filius Suani salutem. Sciatis quod ego donavi ecclesie sancti Johannis de Pontefracto ad religionem locum illum sancte Marie Magdalene de Lunda quem ego fundavi in patrimonio meo, ad opus monachorum qui ibidem deo regulariter servient, pro animabus patris et matris mee et pro salute mea et successorum meorum. Propter hoc beneficium concessum est mihi annuale pro me fieri in matre sua ecclesia de Karitate et in domo sua de Pontefracto unum annuale, et singulis annis ibidem anniversarium meum, et in omnibus locis suis ubi ordo tenetur tricennarium, in aliis vero quantum pro uno monacho Cluniacensi. Adam vero prior, ejusdem loci adquisitor et primus fundator, cum a Pontefracto discesserit, in eodem loco de Lunda manebit quamdiu vixerit custos et prior domus. Post cujus decessum prior de Pontefracto et monachi ejusdem loci, consilio meo et heredum meorum, alios qui idonei sint in loco ejus substituent. Et si forte aliquis frater de Pontefracto pro negotio domus sue in loco competenti ad me venerit, si honeste fieri possit, cibis quibus vescor et ipse mecum vescetur. Hujus rei gratia unoquoque anno marcam unam argenti a domo illa de Lunda ecclesie sancti Johannis de Pontefracto constitui debere persolvi ad recognitionem. Hujus conventionis testes sunt, *Osbertus archidiaconus*,[3] *Radulfus dapifer, Ernaldus et Robertus capellani, Thomas dapifer monachorum.*

---

(1) There is a copy of No. 380 in *Lansdowne* 207, and an abstract in *Dodsworth*, vol. 159.

(2) As Selby had been founded by the king, and Pontefract by the lord of the fee, so Monk Bretton was founded by the tenant. Adam had been in possession between thirty and forty years and was now declining in life, though the whole tone of this charter shows that he was still a hale man with no immediate expectation of death. But as a matter of fact he did not long survive this setting of his house in order.

(3) This is Osbert II ; Ralph was perhaps Ralph de Tilly, and Ernald the priest of Tadcaster.

DE SILKISTONA.

CCCLXXXI.[1] **Carta Idonee uxoris Michaelis de Donecastre.** Post 1240.

[. . . . . I, Idonea, formerly wife of Michael of Doncaster, ... have quit-claimed . . . . . all my right and claim in the bovate of land which Rainer son of Hugh the reeve held in Bolehale, in Silkstone, with all belonging . . . . . Richard de Savile, my brother, with the consent of Michael my husband and of myself, formerly sold it to the monks. The monks have given me twenty silver shillings. Seal. Witnesses.]

Sciant presentes et futuri quod ego Idonea, quondam uxor Michaelis de Donecastre, in ligia viduitate mea concessi et quietum clamavi deo et ecclesie sancti Johannis de Pontefracto et monachis ibidem deo servientibus totum jus et clamium quod unquam habui vel habere potui in illa bovata terre quam Rainerius filius Hugonis prepositi tenuit, que jacet in Bolehalt[2] in territorio de Silkestona, cum omnibus ad dictam bovatam terre infra villam de Silkestona et extra pertinentibus. Illam scilicet bovatam terre quam Ricardus de Sevile, frater meus, de consensu et voluntate dicti Michaelis quondam viri mei et mei, dictis monachis antea vendiderat. Pro hac autem concessione et quieta clamatione dederunt mihi dicti monachi viginti solidos argenti. Et ne ego Idonea vel heredes mei contra tenorem presentis scripti inposterum venire possimus presentem paginam pro me et heredibus meis sigilli mei munimine roboravi. Hiis testibus, *domino Waltero de Ludhama tunc senescallo Pontisfracti, domino Roberto de Stapiltona, Henrico Walensi, Adam de Prestona, Willelmo de Brettona,* et aliis.

———

(1) No. 381 is copied into *Dodsworth*, vol. 151. (2) *Sic.*

———

BERNESLAYA.

CCCLXXXII.[1] **Carta Ade filii Rogeri dispensatoris de Berneslaya.**

[. . . . . I, Adam son of Roger the steward of Barnsley, ... have confirmed . . . . . all the land which my father and I have had in Millholm and in Millcarr, saving eight acres next the mill of Barnsley to the length of the water. For which eight acres and other five acres of assart near the forge of Ralph the clerk I and my heirs will pay yearly 14 pence, half at Whitsuntide and half at the feast of St. Martin. Witnesses.]

Sciant presentes et futuri quod ego Adam filius Rogeri dispensatoris de Berneslaya, pro salute anime mee et patris mei et matris mee et omnium antecessorum et heredum meorum, dedi, concessi et hac presenti carta confirmavi deo et sancto Johanni de Pontefracto

———

(1) I have not found a copy of either No. 382 or No. 383 among the *Dodsworth* or *Lansdowne* MSS., but No. 383 is printed in Jackson's *Barnsley*, with the substitution of *carucas* for *curtas*. The first signatory, Rogerus "decanus," is there printed correctly, but an erratum says erroneously that the word should be "diaconus."

et monachis ibidem deo servientibus totam terram in Milneholm et in Milneker, quam pater meus et ego habuimus in eisdem locis. Salvis mihi et heredibus meis octo acris in eodem territorio propinquioribus molendino de Berneslaya in longum aque. Pro quibus octo acris et aliis quinque acris de essarto juxta forgiam Radulfi clerici ego et heredes mei reddemus annuatim eisdem priori et monachis xiiij denarios, medietatem ad Pentecosten et medietatem ad festum sancti Martini. Hiis testibus, *Willelmo filio Everardi, Willelmo de Kamesala, Waltero de Birum, Petro fratre suo, Ricardo de Stagno,* et aliis.

De Berneslaya.
CCCLXXXIII. **Carta Ade filii Rogeri de Berneslaya.**

[. . . . . I, Adam son of Roger of Barnsley, ... have confirmed . . . . . . eight acres of land with appurtenances in Millholm and in Millcarr in Barnsley; and the charters which my father has had thence I have surrendered . . . . Witnesses.]

Sciant presentes et futuri quod ego, Adam filius Rogeri de Berneslaya, dedi, concessi, et presenti carta mea confirmavi deo et sancto Johanni de Pontefracto et monachis ibidem deo servientibus in puram et perpetuam elemosinam, pro salute anime mee et omnium antecessorum et heredum meorum, octo acras terre cum pertinentiis in Milneholm et in Milneker in territorio de Berneslaya, et cartas quas pater meus inde habuit prefatis monachis sursum reddidi et quietas de me et heredibus meis inperpetuum clamavi. Hiis testibus, *Rogero decano de Ledeshama, Willelmo filio Everardi, Rogero de Silkistona, Roberto de Stainburge, Willelmo de Kamesal, Waltero de Byrum,* et aliis.

De Doddeworda.
CCCLXXXIIII. **Carta Matildis filie Johannis de Berneslaya.** **Cir. 1232.**

[. . . . . . I, Matilda, daughter of John the chaplain of Silkstone, ... have quit-claimed . . . . the bovate of land in Dodworth with all its appurtenances, which I have possessed from my father. Also I have quit-claimed the assart in Hugset which was Ulmer's. To be held and possessed . . . . The prior and monks have given me in hand nine silver shillings. Seal. Witnesses.]

Sciant presentes et futuri quod ego Matildis filia Johannis capellani de Silkestona, in viduitatis mee ligia et plena potestate, sursum reddidi et sine aliquo retenemento mei vel meorum dominis meis priori et monachis de Pontefracto inperpetuum quietum[1] clamavi illam bovatam terre in Doddeworda cum omnibus pertinentiis suis

---

(1) *Sic.*

infra villam et extra, quam habui ex dono Johannis capellani, patris mei. Insuper quietum clamavi prefatis priori et monachis illud essartum in Huggesida quod fuit Ulmeri. Tenendum et habendum prefatis priori et monachis sine reclamatione mei vel heredum meorum. Pro hac autem quieta clamatione et sursum redditione dederunt mihi prefati prior et monachi novem solidos argenti premanibus. Et ne ego Matildis vel heredes mei in posterum contra hanc meam quietam clamationem venire vel aliquod jus aut clamium in predictis terris vel eorum pertinentiis vendicare possim, huic carte pro me et heredibus meis sigillum meum apposui. Hiis testibus, *Henrico Walensi tunc senescallo,*[2] *Johanne clerico magistro hospitalis sancti Nicholai,*[3] *Ricardo de Cravena, Johanne filio Henrici de Berneslaya, Ricardo de Martona,* et aliis.

---

(2) He became seneschal *circa* 1232.
(3) We are not told what had become of Master Raimond. See No. 119.

BARNESLAYA.
CCCLXXXV.[1]   **Carta Hugonis filii Herberti.**

[. . . . . I, Hugh son of Herbert of Silkstone, hold from the prior and monks 32 acres of land from assarts in Barnsley, for my life. So that after my death the aforesaid acres will remain with the prior and monks, ... with all improvement which I shall have been able to make. Out of the aforesaid acres I have demised part to Roger of Barnsley, part to Thomas of Darton, to be held from me for my life only. Seal. Witnesses.]

Omnibus sancte matris ecclesie filiis Hugo filius Herberti de Silkistona salutem. Noverit universitas vestra quod ego teneo de priore et monachis de Pontefracto xxxij acras terre de sartis in territorio de Berneslaya tantum in vita mea et non hereditarie. Ita quod post mortem meam predicte acre predictis priori et monachis solute et quiete remanebunt, sine omni impedimento vel retenemento de me vel de heredibus meis, cum tota melioratione quam ibi potuero. Et quia de supradictis xxxij acris in territorio de Berneslaya partem dimisi Rogero de Berneslaya, partem Thome de Dertuna, ad tenendum de me tantum in vita mea, ne idem Rogerus et Thomas aut heredes sui in eodem tenemento post obitum meum jus aut clamium habere possint presentem cartam hujus rei veritatem continentem sigilli mei munimine roboravi. Hiis testibus, *Johanne de Birkina, Willelmo de Stapiltona, Ricardo de Fareburna, Willelmo de Brodecroft, Willelmo filio Everardi, Ricardo de Stagno,* et aliis.

---

(1) There is a copy of No. 385 in Jackson's *History of Barnsley.*

DE BERNESLAYA.

CCCLXXXVI.[1]   Carta Jordani de Caprecuria.[2]   **Ante 1168.**

[. . . . . I, Jordan de Capriolecuria, quit-claim . . . . . the claim which I have had in Barnsley. . . . . . . Also the gift of Barnsley with all its appendages, which Beatrice my aunt and Ralph de Capriolecuria my father have given, I confirm in all things. The monks have given me ten silver marks, and they shall give me yearly a monk's robe and boots, and they have made a monk for me, and shall make me a monk when I will. Whichever of my heirs shall wish to hinder this my gift, may he incur God's curse and mine. This treaty and composition between me and the monks was made in the chapel of St. Mary Magdalen in Doncaster before the King's justiciary. Witnesses.]

Sciant presentes et futuri quod ego Jordanus de Capriolecuria calumpniam quam habui in Berneslaya quietam clamo de me et heredibus meis inperpetuum deo et sancto Johanni et monachis de Pontefracto, pro salute mea et antecessorum meorum et uxoris mee et heredum meorum. Insuper donationem ejusdem ville de Berneslaya cum omnibus appendiciis suis quam donaverunt eis Beatrix amita mea et Radulfus de Capriolecuria pater meus concedo et dono et hac mea carta confirmo in omnibus. Ipsi autem monachi sancti Johannis de Pontefracto pro gratia hujus concessionis et donationis decem marcas argenti mihi dederunt, et annuatim dabunt pelliceam mihi et botas monachi, et unum monachum pro me fecerunt et me monachum facient quando voluero. Quicumque heredum meorum aliquod impedimentum facere voluerit de hac mea donatione et elemosina, maledictionem dei incurrat et meam. Hec pax et compositio inter me et eosdem monachos facta est in capella sancte Marie Magdalene in Donecastria coram justiciario regis, Ricardo de Lucio.[3] Testibus, *eodem Ricardo, Rogero archiepiscopo Eboracensi, Henrico de Lascy, Willelmo de Vesci, Roberto clerico vicecomitis, Turstano de Suttona, Magistro Roberto Morel, Willelmo Vavasore, Jordano Foliot,*[4] *Ricardo Bagot, Roberto dispensatore,*[5] *Johanne filio Willelmi elemosinarii.*

<hr>

(1) No. 386 is No. xxx in the *Monasticon;* and there is a copy in Jackson's *Barnsley.*
(2) *Sic.*   (3) In 1168 he became chief justice.   (4) Jordan Foliot I.
(5) Possibly Robert Wallis.

<hr>

DE BERNESLAYA.

CCCLXXXVII.[1]   Carta Radulfi de Caprecuria.   **Cir. 1150.**

[. . . . . . I, Ralph de Caprecuria and my sister Beatrice have given the town of Barnsley, in wood, in plain, in mill, in waters, in meadows, and in all belonging to it, ... my sons Jordan and Richard assenting. The monks will appoint a monk for our mother, and another for my sister, and a third for me when I die,

<hr>

(1) No. 387 is No. xxix in the *Monasticon.*

that they may pray for us by name. To me also they have granted a monk's place whenever I will. In acknowledgment, the monks have given my sister ten silver marks, and to me three, and a monk's robe and boots yearly; they have also given to my son Jordan a palfrey, and to my son Richard 5 marks. Seal. If any of my heirs, by presuming to infringe it, attempt to lessen the advantage of my soul and of my sister's, may God blot him from the book of life. Witnesses.]

Sciant presentes et futuri quod ego Radulfus de Caprecuria et soror mea Beatrix concessimus et dedimus deo et sancto Johanni et monachis de Pontefracto villam de Berneslaya, in boscho, in plano, in molendino, in aquis, in pratis, et in omnibus qui² ad eam pertinent, in puram et perpetuam elemosinam, pro animabus nostris et antecessorum nostrorum et heredum, annuentibus filiis meis Jordano et Ricardo. Concesserunt etiam nobis predicti monachi de Pontefracto propter hanc elemosinam quod facient unum monachum pro matre nostra et alium pro sorore mea et tercium pro me cum obiero, qui nominatim orent pro nobis. Mihi etiam concesserunt monacatum quandoque voluero. Ad recognitionem hujus rei dederunt monachi eidem sorori mee decem marcas argenti et mihi tres et annuatim pelliceam monachorum et botas; dederunt etiam Jordano filio meo pro concessione hujus rei palefridum unum, et filio meo Ricardo v marcas. Hanc donationem ego Radulfus de Caprecuria meo presenti sigillo confirmo. Quod si quis heredum meorum infringere presumendo commodum anime mee et sororis mee in hoc minuere temptaverit, deleat eum deus de libro vite. Testibus, *Henrico de Lascy, in cujus presentia hec donatio facta est, et Matilde matre sua, Arnaldo presbitero, Roberto presbitero, Henrico le Gwalers,³ Ricardo Bagot, Thoma dapifero et Willelmo fratre ejus, Ricardo filio Leising et Ricardo Franceis.*

(2) *Sic.*

(3) He was not the seneschal but the son of Robert, who died in 1165.

CCCLXXXVIII.   Carta Avicie de Sevile.

[. . . . . . I, Avicia de Savile, in my widowhood and free power, ... have confirmed to William my son and his heirs or his assigns, for his homage and service, the bovate of land in Bolhalch, which Henry son of Ketel, my native, has held, with Henry and all his goods and his whole following. To be held and possessed . . . . . . Paying yearly a pair of white gloves at the Nativity of the Lord. Saving forensic service. Warranty. Witnesses.]

Sciant presentes et futuri quod ego Avicia de Seyvile, in viduitate et libera potestate mea, dedi et concessi et hac presenti carta mea confirma confirmavi[1] Willelmo filio meo et heredibus suis vel assignatis suis, pro homagio et servitio suo, illam bovatam terre in Bolehalch cum pertinentiis quam Henricus filius Ketil tenuit, cum predicto Henrico et omnibus catallis suis et tota sequela sua qui fuit nativus meus. Tenendam et habendam de me et heredibus meis sibi et heredibus suis vel assignatis suis, in feodo et hereditate, libere et quiete, pacifice et honorifice, cum omnibus liberis communis[1] libertatibus et aisiamentis ad predictam bovatam terre pertinentibus. Reddendo inde annuatim mihi et heredibus meis unum par albarum cyrotecarum ad Nathale domini pro omni servitio et exactione. Salvo forinseco servitio. Et ego et heredes mei warentizabimus predicto Willelmo et heredibus suis vel assignatis suis predictam bovatam terre cum pertinentiis, et predictum Henricum cum omnibus catallis suis et tota sequela sua, sicut predictum est, contra omnes homines in perpetuum. Hiis testibus, *domino Baldewino Teutonico, domino Willelmo de Brettona, Jeremia de Leysers, Johanne de Midehope, Ada de Holanda, Johanne de Seivile, Ricardo Pincerna,* et aliis.

(1) *Sic* in each case.

CCCLXXXVIIII.[1]   Carta Willelmi filii Avicie de Sevile.

[. . . . . . I, William son of Avicia de Savile, ... have confirmed to John de Savile and his heirs or his assigns the bovate of land in Bolhalch which Henry son of Ketel, my native, has held, with Henry and all his goods, and his whole following. To be held and possessed . . . . . . Paying yearly to me and my heirs a pair of white gloves at the Nativity of the Lord. Saving forensic service. Warranty. Witnesses.]

Sciant presentes et futuri quod ego, Willelmus filius Avicie de Saivile, dedi et concessi et hac presenti carta mea confirmavi Johanni de Saivile et heredibus suis vel assignatis suis illam bovatam terre in villa de Bolhalch cum pertinentiis quam Henricus filius Ketil tenuit, cum predicto Henrico et omnibus catallis suis et tota sequela sua, qui fuit nativus meus. Tenendam et habendam de me et heredibus meis sibi et heredibus suis vel assignatis suis, in feodo et hereditate, libere et quiete, pacifice, honorifice, cum omnibus liberis communis,[2] libertatibus et aisiamentis ad predictam bovatam terre pertinentibus pertinentibus[2] inter divisas de Silkestona. Reddendo inde annuatim mihi et heredibus meis unum par albarum cyrotecarum ad Nathale

(1) There is an abstract of both No. 388 and No. 389 in *Dodsworth,* vol. 136, and each was copied into vol. 151.   (2) *Sic* in each case.

domini pro omni servitio et exactione.   Salvo forinseco servitio.   Et
ego et heredes mei warentizabimus predicto Johanni de Seyvile et
heredibus suis vel assignatis suis predictam bovatam terre cum
pertinentiis, et predictum Henricum cum omnibus catallis suis et tota
sequela sua, sicut predictum est, contra omnes homines inperpetuum.
Hiis testibus, *Willelmo de Brettona, Johanne de Hetona, Jordano fratre
suo, Ada de Holanda, Radulfo de Rupe, Willelmo de Goldtorph,* et aliis.

DE BERNESLAYA.
CCCLXXXX.[1]   **Carta Ricardi**[2] **de Cravena.**

[. . . . . . I, the son of Richard de Craven, and Matilda my wife, have quit-
claimed . . . . all the right which we had in the woods of Barnsley, with all
oaks everywhere standing and growing throughout the whole territory of Barnsley,
as well in our own land as in that of holders from us . . . . . Saving free common
of way abroad to the boundaries of Keverford towards the west and common
pasture through all the boundary of Barnsley, without the closes of the aforesaid
prior and convent . . . . For this the prior and convent have given us a mark
of silver, and by their grace have granted that, when the herbage shall come, our
hogs of the demesne, having been fed in our own court without any hindrance,
shall be free of pannage.   Warranty.   And if by chance (which God forbid) we or
our heirs shall wish to contravene this quit-claim, we pledge all our goods, within
the town of Barnsley and without, to our lords the prior and monks, until we shall
have given satisfaction ; and we will give as a fine to the work of the church of
the blessed John of Pontefract 40 silver shillings.   Witnesses.]

Sciant presentes et futuri quod ego filius Ricardi de Cravena et
Matildis uxor mea inperpetuum quietum clamavimus de nobis et
heredibus nostris dominis nostris priori et conventui de Pontefracto
omne jus et clamium quod habuimus vel aliquo modo habere
potuimus in boscis de Berneslaya cum omnibus quercubus ubique per
totum territorium de Berneslaya stantibus et crescentibus, tam in
terra nostra quam tenentium de nobis, libere et quiete, integre et
honorifice, cum omnibus libertatibus et aisiamentis ville de Berneslaya
pertinentibus.   Salva nobis et heredibus nostris libera communa de
via fori usque divisas de Keverford versus West et communa pastura
per totam divisam de Berneslaya, extra clausturas predicti prioris et
conventus de Pontefracto.   Ita quod nec nos nec heredes nostri de
cetero aliquod jus vel clamium vel demandam in predictis boscis et
quercubus habere vel exigere possimus.   Pro hac autem quieta
clamatione dederunt nobis prior et conventus de Pontefracto unam
marcam argenti premanibus, et sua gratia concesserunt quod quando
pessona advenerit, dominici porci nostri in propria curia nostra

---

(1) There is a copy of No. 390 in vol. 151.   (2) *Sic.*

nutriti sine contradictione aliqua quieti erunt de panagio. Et ego antedictus Ricardus de Cravena et Matildis uxor mea et heredes nostri hanc quietam clamationem predicto priori et conventui contra omnes homines inperpetuum warentizabimus. Et si forte, quod absit, contigerit quod nos aut heredes nostri huic quiete clamationi contraire voluerimus, obligimus omnia bona nostra infra villam de Berneslaya et extra dominis nostris priori et monachis de Pontefracto donec eisdem monachis satisfecerimus de predicta marca argenti; et nichilominus dabimus nomine pene ad opus ecclesie beati Johannis de Pontefracto xl solidos argenti. Hiis testibus, *Henrico Walensi*[3] *tunc senescallo, Jordano Folioth, Roberto de Stapiltona, Willelmo de Brettona, Henrico de Sevile, Galfrido de Ledeshama, Ricardo de Martona*, et aliis.

---

(3) Henry Wallis being seneschal, this charter is of the date of about 1200, or perhaps somewhat later, when the monks had possessed the manor of Barnsley for about forty years. From it we gather that works were then proceeding at the church of the monastery, towards the expenses of which, in a certain contingency, Richard de Craven would have had to contribute by fine.

CCCLXXXXI.[1]　　　Carta Gerardi[2] de Berneslaya.

[. . . . . . . I, Gerard of Barnsley, hold of the prior and monks, as long as it shall please them and not hereditarily, a bovate in Barnsley which William son of Ralph formerly held. Paying yearly to the prior and monks 4 shillings, half at the feast of St. Martin and half at Whitsuntide. Again, I hold of the same prior and monks, as long as it shall please them and not hereditarily, a half bovate which Thomas of Milnthorp and Hugh son of Luke held before me. Paying yearly to the prior and monks 15 pence, half at the feast of St. Martin and half at Whitsuntide. The monks shall take the bovate and a half when they will, without hindrance from me or my heirs, saving the crop of my grain. Seal. Witnesses.]

Sciant presentes et futuri quod ego, Gerardus de Berneslaya, teneo de priore et monachis de Pontefracto unam bovatam in territorio de Berneslaya tantum modo quamdiu illis placuerit et non hereditarie. Illam scilicet quam Willelmus filius Radulfi ante me tenuit. Reddendo inde annuatim prefatis priori et monachis iiij solidos, medietatem ad festum sancti Martini, et medietatem ad Pentecosten. Iterum teneo de eisdem priore et monachis in eadem villa de Berneslaya unam dimidiam bovatam terre, tantummodo quamdiu illis placuerit et non hereditarie. Illam scilicet quam Thomas de Milnethorp et Hugo filius Leuke ante me tenuerunt. Reddendo inde annuatim prefatis priori et monachis xv denarios, medietatem ad

---

(1) I have met with no transcription or abstract of No. 391.

(2) There are here two Gerards, each from Barnsley, the grantor being apparently that Gerard who was greave to Roger the steward, and so named in No. 394. More will be said of him when we reach the next group of charters.

festum sancti Martini et medietatem ad Pentecosten.   Prefati vero monachi capient quando voluerint predictas bovatam terre et dimidiam sine impedimento mei vel heredum meorum.   Salvo mihi et heredibus meis croppo bladi mei.   Et ne ego Gerardus vel heredes mei post mortem meam aliquod jus aut clamium in predictis bovata terre et dimidia, nisi de accommodatione, vendicare possimus, hanc cartam sigilli mei appositione roboravi.   Hiis testibus, *Johanne Tyrel,*[3] *Rogero clerico, Waltero de Byrum, Ricardo de Martona, Gerardo de Berneslaya, Adam de Oldtona, Roberto dispensatore,* et aliis.

(3) John Tyrel, who heads these witnesses, was the parson of Royston, a large parish which includes also Notton, Cudworth, and Woolley.

CCCLXXXXII.[1]   Carta Gerardi filii Thome de Berneslaya.

[. . . . . I, Gerard, son of Thomas of Barnsley, ... have confirmed . . . . . a plot of land in Barnsley, which lies next the court of the monks towards the west; seventeen perches and five feet in length, and two perches in breadth. A head of it abuts upon the burial ground and another upon my orchard.   To be held and possessed . . . . . Seal.   Witnesses.]

Sciant presentes et futuri quod ego Geraldus[2] filius Thome de Berneslaya dedi, concessi, et hac presenti carta mea confirmavi, pro salute anime mee et omnium antecessorum meorum, deo et ecclesie sancti Johannis de Pontefracto et monachis ibidem deo servientibus, quandam placiam terre in villa de Berneslaya, que jacet juxta curiam eorundem monachorum versus west, habentem decem et septem percatas et quinque pedes in longitudine et duas percatas in latitudine. Cujus capud buttat super cimiterium et aliud super ortum meum. Tenendam et habendam prefatis monachis in puram et perpetuam elemosinam inperpetuum.   In hujus rei testimonium pro me et heredibus meis sigillum meum huic scripto apposui.   Hiis testibus, *Henrico de Sevile, Hugone de Berch, Ricardo de Cravena, Ricardo de Martona, Henrico Portebref,* et aliis.

(1) There is a copy of No. 392 in *Dodsworth,* vol. 151, and the charter is printed in Jackson's *Barnsley.*   (2) *Sic.*

BERNESLAYA.
CCCLXXXXIII.   Carta Gerardi de Berneslaya.

[. . . . . . I, Gerard of Barnsley, with the assent of Adam, my first-born son, ... have confirmed . . . . . . a bovate of land with appurtenances in Barnsley, which Richard of Milnthorp has held, and four acres of land in Milncarr, with appurtenances, and all the land with appurtenances which I have held in Hevening, one head of which strikes upon the wood towards the river Dearne, and another strikes upon Swinhill and the land of Richard son of Eda. Also a toft in Barnsley which Henry de Mora and Matilda the widow have held of me during their life. And the land called Crimbles, which I have held of John de Cellario and his heirs for three pence, to be paid yearly, according to the custom of the manor. Which threepence the monks shall pay. Also two acres and a half, with their buildings, which I have held of Adam son of Roger and his heirs for 12 pence to be paid yearly, half at Whitsuntide and half at the feast of St. Martin, which 12 pence the monks shall pay. These two acres and a half lie between the land of Richard de Marton towards the north, and the land of Gerard son of Thomas towards the south, and the land where my grange was established which I have held from Gerard son of Thomas, for a penny to be paid yearly, which the monks shall pay. All these the monks shall hold freely and quietly for ever. Warranty. Witnesses.]

Sciant presentes et futuri quod ego Gerardus de Berneslaya, assensu et voluntate Ade primogeniti filii mei, pro salute anime mee et omnium antecessorum meorum et heredum meorum, dedi, concessi, et presenti carta mea confirmavi deo et sancto Johanni de Ponte-fracto et monachis ibidem deo servientibus in perpetuam elemosinam unam bovatam terre cum pertinentiis suis in territorio de Berneslaya, illam scilicet quam Ricardus de Milnetorph tenuit. Et quatuor acras terre in Milneker cum pertinentiis suis, et totam terram cum pertinentiis suis quam ego tenui in Hevening, de qua terra unum capud percutit super boscum versus aquam de Dirne, et aliud capud percutit super Suimhil[1] et terram Ricardi filii Ede. Et unum toftum in Berneslaya quod Henricus de Mora et Matildis vidua tenuerunt de me tantummodo in vita sua et non hereditarie. Et terram que vocatur Grimblis quam ego tenui de Johanne de Cellario et heredibus suis pro tribus denariis annuatim dominice solvendis, pro omni servitio. Quos tres denarios prefati monachi reddent predicto Johanni et heredibus suis. Et duas acras et dimidiam cum omnibus edificiis quas tenui de Adam filio Rogeri et heredibus suis pro xij denariis annuatim reddendis, medietatem ad Pentecosten et medietatem ad festum sancti Martini, quos xij denarios dicti monachi reddent annuatim heredibus prenominati Ade. Illas scilicet duas acras et dimidiam que jacent inter terram Ricardi de Martona versus north, et terram Gerardi filii Thome versus suth, et terram ubi grangia mea fundata fuit quam tenui de Gerardo filio Thome, pro uno denario

---

(1) *Sic.*

annuatim reddendo, quem denarium prefati monachi persolvent heredibus predicti Gerardi.   Hec omnia supradicta habebunt prenominati monachi et tenebunt libere et quiete in perpetuum, cum omnibus ad prefatas terras infra villam et extra pertinentibus.   Et ego prenominatus Gerardus et heredes mei omnia predicta prefatis monachis warentizabimus contra omnes homines.   Hiis testibus, *Alano de Smythetona, Nicholao de Wrthlay,*[2] *Henrico de Tancreslaya, Willelmo de Brettona, Radulfo de Rupe, Ricardo de Martona,* et aliis.

(2) *Sic.*

BERNESLAYA.
CCCLXXXXIV.   Carta Gerardi filii Thome de Berneslaya.

[. . . . . . I, Gerard son of Thomas of Barnsley, ... have confirmed to Gerard the greave of Roger of Barnsley and his heirs all the land with buildings which he has held of my father in Barnsley. It lies between the land which that Gerard has held from the church in which it has remained and Newcroft, whence one head abuts upon the way which goes through the middle of the town towards the north, and another head upon my land which I have held from the lord prior. To be held and possessed . . . . . . Paying thence yearly to me and my heirs one penny, one halfpenny at Whitsuntide and one halfpenny at the feast of St. Martin. Warranty. Gerard has given me 2 shillings in acknowledgment. Witnesses.]

Sciant presentes et futuri quod ego Gerardus filius Thome de Berneslaya concessi et hac mea presenti carta confirmavi Gerardo greve Rogeri de Berneslaya et heredibus suis totam illam terram cum edificiis quam tenuit de patre meo in villa de Berneslaya.   Scilicet que jacet inter terram quam idem G. tenuit de ecclesia in qua mansit et Neucroft, unde unum capud buttat super viam que vadit per mediam villam versus north, et aliud capud super terram meam quam tenui de domino priore.   Tenendam et habendam de me et heredibus meis sibi et heredibus suis, in feudo et hereditate, libere et quiete et honorifice, solvendo inde annuatim mihi et heredibus meis unum denarium pro omni servitio et demanda.   Scilicet unum obolum ad Pentecosten, et unum obolum ad festum sancti Martini.   Ego autem et heredes mei warentizabimus illi et heredibus suis predictam terram cum edificio[1] contra omnes homines.   Pro hac autem concessione et confirmatione dedit mihi idem G. ij solidos de recognitione.   Hiis testibus, *Rogero de Keverford, Ada de Oldefelda, Johanne filio ejus, Symone filio Arnaldi, Henrico filio Rogeri de Brettona,* et aliis.

(1) *Sic.*

BRETTONA.[1]

CCCLXXXXV.[2]   Carta Johannis de Cellario de Brettona.

[. . . . . . . I, John de Cellario of Bretton, ... have confirmed to Gerard of Barnsley, son of Alured, and his heirs, or to whom he will assign it, two crimbles in the fields of Bretton, which belong to my two assarts, Lammeroyd and Langley, which I hold of the lord prior of Bretton, and which lie near the mill of Barnsley. One crimble abuts upon the mill, and another head upon the water, and one head of one crimble abuts upon the Dearne, and another upon the bridge. To be held and possessed . . . . Paying thence yearly to me and my heirs threepence at the Annunciation of the blessed Mary. Warranty. Gerard has given me two shillings in hand. Witnesses.]

Sciant presentes et futuri quod ego Johannes de Cellario de Brettona dedi et concessi et hac mea presenti carta confirmavi Gerardo de Berneslaya filio Alveredi et heredibus suis, vel cui assignare voluerit, duos crimblos[3] in campis de Brettona, illos scilicet qui spectant ad duas essartas meas scilicet Lammeroda et Langelaya[4] quas teneo de domino priore de Brettona que jacent juxta molendinum de Berneslaya, unum crimble buttat super molendinum, et aliud capud super aquam, et unum capud unius crimble buttat super dirne, et aliud capud super pontem. Tenendos et habendos de me et de heredibus meis illi et heredibus suis, in feodo et hereditate, libere et quiete et honorifice, solvendo inde annuatim mihi et heredibus meis tres denarios ad annunciationem beate Marie pro omni servitio et exactione. Ego autem et heredes mei warentizabimus predicto G. et heredibus suis vel cui assignaverit predictas crimbles contra omnes homines. Pro hac autem donatione et concessione dedit mihi idem G. duos solidos de gersumma. Hiis testibus, *Johanne filio Hugonis de Brettona, Roberto de Pul, Henrico filio Rogeri de Berneslaya, Roberto filio Thome, Gerardo filio Thome, Ricardo de Cravena*, et aliis. ————

(1) That is, Monk Bretton.
(2) I have met with no transcript of No. 393, No. 394, or No. 395.
(3) The varying forms of this word, and its varying genders, will be noted.
(4) In No. 377 this is Lagelay.

————

BROCTUNA.[1]

CCCLXXXXVI.[2]   Carta Alicie de Rumelli.   Circa 1156.

[. . . . . I, Alice de Rumelli, with the consent of William my son, have granted, ... free from all custom and from all human service for ever, a carucate of land in Broughton. And beside the carucate a place in that town where the monks may entertain, for the soul of my lord William son of Duncan. . . . . . . Lest it should be doubted hereafter what carucate it is, it is that of which Ralph has held 3 bovates, and William his brother one, and Waltef 2, and Anketil

(1) That is, Broughton-in-Craven.
(2) No. 396 is XIV in the *Monasticon*, and there is a copy in *Lansdowne* 207.

2, whose homage, together with the land, I have given and granted, and I have seised and corporally inducted the monastery in the afore-named land and in all belonging to it, and Robert the monk of Oldtown has received the seisin in the name of the monastery and convent.   The monks and the tenants who shall hold from them ought to have commonage of that town with their herds . . . . . . The witnesses are, &c., at my request.   My seal is the testimony.   The monks have received me and my son and all my relations into fraternity, and they have made me and all mine partakers of all the benefits of their church for ever.]

Notum sit omnibus legentibus et audientibus has literas quod ego Aaliz[2] de Rumelli, consensu et concessione Willelmi filii mei, donavi et concessi deo et sancto Johanni de Pontefracto· et monachis ejusdem loci, in puram et perpetuam elemosinam, et liberam, et solutam, et quietam ab omni terrena et laicali consuetudine, et ab omni humano servitio inperpetuum, unam carucatam terre in Broctuna.   Et preter carucatam unam mansuram in eadem villa, ubi monachi hospitari possint, pro anima domini mei Willelmi filii Dunecan et pro animabus omnium predecessorum meorum et pro salute anime mee et omnium parentum meorum.   Et ne in dubium posteris veniat que carrucata illa sit, illa est nominatim de qua Radulfus tenuit iij bovatas, et Willelmus frater ejus unam, et Waltef ij, et Antkil ij, cujus humagium simul cum terra donavi et concessi deo et sancto Johanni et monachis, et saisiavi et corporaliter induxi monasterium sancti Johannis de eadem terra prenominata et de omnibus ad eam pertinentibus, et Robertus monachus de Hold' recepit eam saisinam nomine monasterii et totius conventus.   Ex hac etiam donatione et concessione mea debent ipsi monachi et homines qui de eis tenebunt simul cum pecunia sua habere communionem ejusdem ville, libere et quiete et honorifice, in paschuis, in pratis, in aquis, viis et semitis, in eundo et redeundo, et ibidem remanendo. Hujus donationis testes sunt, *Osmundus capellanus, Walterus filius Willelmi, Petrus de Martona et Willelmus filius ejus, Rogerus Tempestas, et Ricardus frater ejus, Symon de Mohaut et Symon filius ejus, Gaufridus Mori, Reinero de Fernhil et Adam nepos ejus.*   Omnes isti peticione mea testes sunt hujus rei.   Insuper hoc meum sigillum est testimonium istius carte.   Pro hujus rei beneficio susceperunt me monachi et filium meum et omnes parentes meos in fraternitatem, et participem me fecerunt et omnes meos omnium beneficiorum ecclesie sue inperpetuum.

----

(2) *Sic.*

DE DODDEWORDA.
CCCLXXXXVII.[1]   **Carta Willelmi filii Ulfi.**

[. . . . . . . I, William son of Ulf of Dodworth, ... have confirmed and
quit-claimed all the land which I had and held from Richard my brother in the
territory of Dodworth, namely, two bovates of land with adjacent assarts and all
other appurtenances.   Also I have confirmed . . . . those two bovates of land
with assarts and all other appurtenances which Richard my brother gave to them,
and all the claim which I and my heirs have had of succeeding to the aforesaid.
Warranty.   The monks have given me two and a half marks of silver, and they
will give to me and my heirs yearly four pence within the octave of St. Andrew.
Witnesses.]

Omnibus sancte matris ecclesie filiis tam presentibus et futuris
Willelmus filius Ulf de Doddeworda salutem.   Noverit universitas
vestra quod ego Willelmus pro amore dei, et pro salute anime mee
et omnium meorum vivorum et mortuorum, dedi, concessi, et presenti
carta mea confirmavi et sursum reddidi et quietum[2] clamavi de me
et de heredibus meis inperpetuam elemosinam deo et sancto Johanni
et priori et monachis de Pontefracto totam terram meam quam habui
et quam tenui de Ricardo fratre meo in territorio de Doddeworda,
videlicet duas bovatas terre cum sartis adjacentibus et omnibus aliis
pertinentiis sine omni retenemento mei et heredum meorum.   Hac
etiam presenti carta mea confirmavi prefatis monachis et quietum[2]
clamavi inperpetuum illas duas bovatas terre cum sartis et omnibus
aliis pertinentiis quas idem Ricardus frater meus dedit eis pro salute
anime sue et suorum, et totum jus et clamium quod ego Willelmus
et heredes mei habuimus succedendi prefato Ricardo et suis jure
hereditario.   Et hanc donationem et concessionem et confirmationem
et quietam clamationem ego Willelmus et heredes mei warentizabimus predictis monachis contra omnes homines.   Pro hac donatione,
concessione, confirmatione, et quieta clamatione, dederunt mihi prefati
monachi premanibus duas marcas argenti et dimidiam et dabunt mihi
et heredibus meis annuatim quatuor denarios infra octavas sancti
Andree.   Hiis testibus, *Roberto Walensi, Johanne de Birkina, Adam de
Rainevilla, Willelmo de Stapiltona, Gilleberto de Nottuna, Berardo*[2] *de
Berch, Hugone de Brettona, Roberto de Berneslaya,* et aliis.

---

(1) I have met with no copy of No. 397.   (2) *Sic* in each case.

DE GAUNT.

Baldwin, Earl of Flanders = Matilda, sister of the Conqueror

Gilbert de Gaunt, = Alice, daughter of Hugh de Montford; founded the abbey of Bardney, and died a monk there

- Walter de Gaunt, = Maud, daughter of Alan, Earl of Brittany; founded Bridlington 1114, died 1139
- Emma = Alan, lord Percy
- Robert de Gaunt,[1] provost of Beverley 1142, dean of York 1148, chancellor of England 1153, died 1154
- Nigel de Albini = Gundred de Gournay, 16

Gilbert de Gaunt, = Rohais or Avicia, niece of his captor at Lincoln, and daughter of Wm. de Romare; Earl of Lincoln, prisoner at Lincoln in 1141 to Ranulph, Earl of Chester; founded Rufford 1148; died 1156

Robert de Gaunt = Adelicia Paynell, died 1182; died 1192
- Robert
- Maurice de Gaunt of Leeds; deprived 1216; died 1230

Otho Fitzwilliam = Margaret

Ilbert de Lascy; dead in 1141 = Alice de Gaunt,[2] called Adelicia in *Mon. Ang.*, ii, 97 — , 2 = Roger de Mowbray
- Nigel de Mowbray
- William de Mowbray

Alice, died in 1185 = Simon St. Liz, Earl of Huntingdon, died 1184

(1) This was he who was so staunch a friend of Archbishop William. He is frequently confused with Robert de Butivelain, his successor, who tested No. 46, and who on 9th May, 1154 [*ante*, pp. 51-2], went from York to meet him and protest against his entrance into the archiepiscopal city.

(2) There is a haziness in the various statements as to who this Alice de Gaunt is, one writer calling her the daughter of Gilbert de Gaunt, earl of Lincoln, and thereby confusing her with her niece, who married Simon St. Liz. She was, however, the sister of Gilbert de Gaunt, as the above sketch will show.

ℐasciculi IX and X.

WE group these two Fasciculi together, because (as will be seen presently) in their case only there is in the Chartulary no division.

The Ninth opens with charters of the Earls of Lincoln, or so-styled Earls of Lincoln; and, as was the case with the Eighth Fasciculus, important documents, or documents considered important, were placed at the opening, as it were to give a tone to the contents.

It is not a little remarkable that the title "Earl of Lincoln," which does not occur in the body of No. 398, is introduced into its heading; for the rubricator had no hint from the document itself that Simon was presumptive claimant to that earldom. As a matter of fact he never obtained the dignity, so that the rubricator must, in this case, have brought his own personal knowledge to bear upon his work and introduced a title for which he had no real authority. The history itself is interesting, and throws much light upon various passages in the Chartulary.

Edwin and Morcar, the Saxon earls, had a sister Lucy, who married Ivo Tailbois; but, being left a widow with no children, she remarried with Roger de Romare, by whom she had William de Romare, created first Earl of Lincoln by King Stephen. On the death of this second husband, she again married, her third husband being Randolph le Meschine, who received the grant of the earldom of Chester in 1120, after the decease of his cousin Richard (his mother's nephew) in the White Ship, from which disaster William de Romare himself had a remarkable escape, since being an intending passenger he refused to go on board almost at the last moment.

By her third husband the Countess (though some think there were two Lucies, mother and daughter) had for heir Ralph de Gernoniis, who thus was half-brother to William de Romare. The two were against Stephen at Lincoln, but on his release they submitted to him, William de Romare being created Earl of Lincoln and even endowed with the land and fee of Ilbert de Lascy, an old supporter of the king, who had perished either in the siege or in his subsequent captivity, for nothing certain is known of him after 1141.

The most particular account of this gift appears in Yorke's *Union of Honour*, which says of William de Romare that he "was

2 L

by King Stephen, in the sixth year of his reign, created the first Earl
of Lincoln; and also the said king gave him the manor of Chirchecon
[Tickhill], the castle of Gainsborough [Conisborough] and the castle
of Pontefract." His son William dying before his father and leaving
only an infant son, the earldom was on the death of the first earl,
in 1148, conferred upon Gilbert de Gaunt, husband of Avicia his
daughter, who, attempting to take possession of the Pontefract estates,
was successfully resisted by Henry de Lascy, the rightful heir, who
had just come of age. The church and monastery seem to have so
suffered in the contention as to require rebuilding, to compensate
for which Gilbert de Gaunt promised the monks six librates of
land, redeeming his promise by the gifts named in the three charters
before us.

When Earl Gilbert died in 1156, the lands similarly went to the
husband of his daughter Alice, Simon de St. Liz, Earl of Huntingdon,
who however did not succeed in obtaining the earldom of Lincoln;
although, in the popular mind, he was perhaps considered entitled
to it by the rule which had obtained in the case of his father-in-
law. Thus in No. 398 he was correctly described as Earl Simon, for
he was Earl of Huntingdon, though the rubricator was inexact in
particularising the earldom.

The following genealogy, in which only essential names are
included, will perhaps assist in making all this clear:—

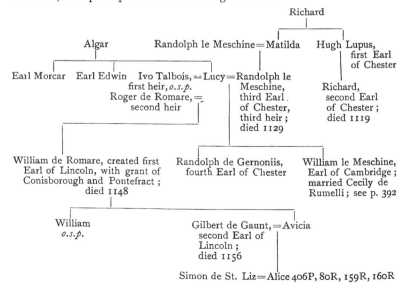

The Saxe referred to in No. 401 was an important tenant of the second class, who signed No. 378 as Saxe of Horbury.   He seems to have had much property to the west of Wakefield, at Horbury, Flockton, Midgley and Shitlington, and to have divided his lands among his children somewhat after the plan adopted by Asolf and Peter his son, a parallel personage.

The elder sons of Saxe were more concerned with the property possessed by the monks at Rievaux, while the interests of his younger sons were in a larger degree identified with that owned by the monks at Pontefract, as will be more clearly gathered from the following genealogy, where R=Rievaux and P=Pontefract :—

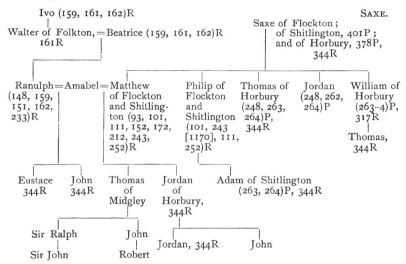

NOTE 1.—Ranulph fitz Walter granted large rights in Folkton to Rievaux (80, 82, 161)R, which were confirmed by Alice de Gaunt, the wife of Simon, Earl of Lincoln, grantor of 398P ; Ranulph was the first husband of Amabel, wife of Matthew de Flockton.

2.—Jordan's grant of a culture in Folkton (344R) was witnessed by Eustace fitz Walter and John his "brothers"; they were his half-brothers.

The concurrence of the Countess Isabel (or Elizabeth) in No. 401 seems to imply that it was by his wife that the Earl of Warren possessed the property thus charged, but there is nothing to favour that supposition, and enquiry into her antecedents throws no light upon our history.   She was the daughter of Hugh, Earl of Vermandoise, son of Henry, king of France, and had had for her first husband Robert de Beaumont, Earl of Leicester, by whom she had Walleran, Earl of

Worcester, and Robert, second Earl of Leicester. Her first husband died in 1118, so that any trace of her early connection with this neighbourhood must be sought for previous to that date. There is none; and the only conclusion open is that one or more of the three manors of Shitlington, which, like Wakefield, was at the Survey in the hands of the king, was granted, together with Wakefield, to de Warren, when he received the earldom of Surrey in 1086.

Isabel's second husband, the second Earl of Warren and Surrey, like Robert de Lascy, was on the unsuccessful side in 1120, but having been deprived of his earldom and estates he submitted and was restored, though no such place of repentance was found for Robert de Lascy, perhaps because he had previously offended in a similar way. Besides the three shillings of rent named in No. 401, the earl gave to the Pontefract monks six carucates from Shitlington (see No. 57 and No. 73, with their collation on pp. 305–9), Hugh de Laval giving other six. But he did not join in the charter to the monks from Hugh de Laval (No. 3), and no trace of him other than this can be found on the Pontefract side of Wakefield, unless it be indeed that (the Warren arms being *Checky*, *or* and *azure*) the moor between Pontefract and Carleton may be indebted to him for its name, The Chequers.

In No. 407 we find a mention of Bradley. There were two Bradleys, which have been occasionally confused. The only one which took township rank was Bradley in Kildwick, near Skipton, and in the Skipton Fee; which, as part of Kildwick, Cecily de Rumelli in 1120 gave to Embsay, the predecessor of Bolton. But the Bradley here referred to as bordering on the Calder was a manor of that name, now absorbed in Huddersfield, which before the Conquest had been held in moieties, but was waste (that is unfarmed) at the time of the Survey. Both moieties were then in the hand of Chetel, the Saxon owner of Almondbury. The capability of the manor was, however, soon ascertained, and, as No. 407 informs us, both Fountains and Pontefract had early metal-works there.

Ralph son of Nicholas, the owner of the manor, had given to Fountains that part of his wood of Bradley which lies near the Calder, and all the dead wood, to make charcoal for the forges, the iron-ore of the woodland, and other privileges that would have made the possession an exceedingly valuable holding. All was confirmed, and additions made, by Adam his son; after whose death it was confirmed by Alice the widow of Adam (she lived till 1219) and by Richard his brother.   And thus we obtain the following pedigree :—

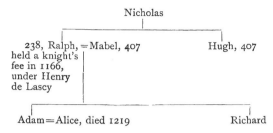

The mention in No. 407 of Ralph's wife Mabel rather implies that he owned Bradley by her right.

It will be observed that this charter was tested, among others, by Robert, priest of Darrington, Robert de Triberg, as he is called in No. 28 ; and this leads to the mention that Cridling, once owned by Adam, son of Ralph, is in the parish of Darrington, and that Adam parted with the manor by the following deed, which is extracted from the Duchy of Lancaster Great Coucher, in the Public Record Office :—

Duchy of Lancaster.—Great Coucher.—I. 174d.

[. . . . . I, Adam de Cridling, son of Ralph, son of Nicholas, have quit-claimed . . . . to Roger de Lascy, Constable of Chester, and his heirs, all the town of Cridling and all the town of Stubbs, which I have held from the aforesaid Roger de Lascy, Constable of Chester, by the free service of a fourth part of a knight, with all their appurtenances . . . . . . within the town and without, ... for a hundred and ten marks of silver and a charger worth 15 marks. . . . . This sale . . . . . . I have confirmed.   Witnesses.]

Sciant omnes presentes et futuri quod ego, Adam de Cridling, filius Radulphi filii Nicholai vendidi et quietam clamavi de me et de omnibus heredibus meis imperpetuum Rogero de Laci, Constabulario Cestrie, et heredibus suis, totam villam de Cridling et totam villam de Stubbes, quas ego tenui de predicto Rogero de Laci, Constabulario Cestrie, per liberum servicium quarte partis unius militis, cum omnibus pertinenciis earum, in bosco et plano, in pratis et pasturis, in viis et semitis, in moris et mariscis, in aquis et molendinis, infra villam et extra, et in omnibus locis ubique sine ullo retenemento, pro centum et decem marcis argenti et uno destrario sor' xv marcarum, que predictus Rogerus de Laci, Constabularius Cestrie, dedit mihi pro prenominatis terris.   Et hanc vendicionem predictaram terraram cum pertinenciis earum ego Adam per hanc meam presentem cartam confirmavi.   Testibus, *Petro de Brus, Eustachio de Vesci, Johanne de Birkin, Roberto Walensi, Adam de Rainville, Jordano de Sancta Maria, Willelmo de Stapleton, Hugone de Thouleston, Thoma de Ranville, Henrico Walensi.*

The name of Thomas de Reineville attached to this charter shows that its date is at least before 1218, when the *inq. p. m.* of Thomas de Reineville was taken. It is, however, much earlier than 1218, as Roger de Lascy died in 1211, and possibly it was given after he entered upon his inheritance in 1194.

In No. 461 is a notice that certain lands to the west of the Castle were of the fee of Cridling, and held of the brethren of the hospital of St. Michael.

The Rumelli family, to which we again come in No. 412, affords a remarkable illustration of one of the phases in the history of that evolution of personal surnames which was taking place during the twelfth century. In their case the line was carried on for five generations with but one male head. The founder was Robert de Rumelli, who, in the next generation to the Conquest, had a large grant of manors, which at the time of the Survey had been in the hands of the king, including the Skipton Fee. His heir was Cecily, who retained her paternal name though she married William le Meschine, Earl of Cambridge, the second son of the Earl of Chester. They founded Embsay, but left no male heirs, and there were three daughters, among whom the estates were apportioned. Of these, Alice de Rumelli had the Skipton Fee, and once more retained the paternal name, although married to William Fitz Duncan; and, jointly with him, she granted several charters.

William fitz Duncan and Alice de Rumelli also had co-heirs, a second Cecily and a second Alice (see p. 392), each of whom kept the name of Rumelli, though each married at least twice. Cecily's second husband was William le Gros, Earl of Albemarle, and again there was a failure of male heirs, their daughter Avice being Earl of Albemarle in her own right. She married (1) William de Mandeville, Earl of Essex, (2) William de Fortibus, (3) Baldwin de Bethune, each of whom was earl in right of his wife. Only the second had children by her, and, at the death of the third husband, in 1213, another William de Fortibus, son of the second husband and not long come of age, succeeded to the earldom. Meanwhile Alice de Rumelli, aunt to this Avice, maintained the paternal name in Cumberland, and this younger Alice has been overlooked by the genealogists.

No. 413 deals with the church of Catwick. In the time of King Edward the Confessor, Catwick had been held as two manors by Swein and Murdoc, and at the time of the Domesday Survey the whole was still held in medieties. As there was a church at the latter date, while there were two lords, the inference is that it had been built and endowed jointly by them, as were the churches at Campsall, Darfield, and Mexborough.

One moiety of Catwick Church early found its way into the possession of the monks of Pontefract by the gift of Ralph de Catwick, whose grant was confirmed by this No. 413, which is a charter of Earl Stephen of Albemarle. This we shall learn from No. 424, by which William le Gros (the son of Stephen) again confirmed the grant, referring to the charter of his father. It was an important grant, and it was confirmed by Archbishop Thurstan in No. 39, by King Henry II [1155] in No. 71 and No. 73, by Archbishop Theodore as papal legate in No. 57, and by Archbishop Roger in No. 48.

But it is remarkable that while each of these charters speaks of the moiety that had been granted by Ralph de Catwick, No. 73, the second charter of Henry II, speaks of both a bovate there, the gift of Simon son of Ralph, and of the whole church, as if the monks had at its date obtained possession of both medieties.

No. 539, which is a lease of the bovate by Prior Bertram to William the priest of Catwick, contains some curious particulars.

Of the two witnesses to No. 413, William Biset was the predecessor of Manasser Biset, probably his father; and Gerold was the father of the first husband of Cecily de Rumelli. The grantor was the father of her second husband.

The second moiety of Catwick Church was given to the priory by Peter de Falkenberg for the good of his own soul, that of Beatrice his wife, and of his sons William, Walter, and Stephen. The date of his gift is well ascertained to have been during January, 1155, by its non-record in No. 71 and its enrolment in No. 73.

It is somewhat noticeable that this gift of the first moiety of Catwick Church by Ralph de Catwick to the monks of Pontefract has almost escaped recognition. The gift of the second by Peter de Falkenberg and its confirmation by his grandson and son will be found to be referred to in No. 444, No. 445, and No. 446 of the Chartulary, while the charter itself is No. xvi in the *Monasticon*.

The distinction between "c" and "t" in the caligraphy of the Chartulary is very slight, but in No. 415 the name of the place is clearly Brocton, that is Broughton, which in No. 249 and No. 416 is as clearly Bretton, with but one minim between "e" and the second "t." This should be Burton [Salmon]; but the two are widely different places. The solution seems to be that the charters are from Alice the wife, and William the son, of Peter of Bretton, and that the land was at Broughton.

The name of no witness is common to any two of the charters, but there is a link connecting those of the two Alices. In No. 415 John de Louvain witnessed the charter of Alice, widow of Peter, the father; in No. 259 he lends his seal to Alice, widow of William the son.

A reference to No. 507 will show that the plot, described as being in New Scarborough, was afterwards leased to Robert Fareman, one of the witnesses to No. 419; for in the next generation the monks found it to be their better policy to lease out the smaller properties and not to retain them in their own holding. Robert Fareman is then described, as William Gamel has been, as a burgess of Scarborough.

No. 423 introduces us to William Maltravers. On the death of Hugh de Laval in 1130 this William Maltravers (sometimes erroneously called Henry Travers) had had a grant (1) of all de Laval's land for fifteen years, for which he paid a thousand marks of silver; and (2) of the marriage of the widow, for which he was fined £100, to be given to whom the king would. All this is recorded in the Pipe Roll of 1131, the solitary specimen extant of that series for the two reigns of Henry I and Stephen.

There is no concealing the fact that, till the last two or three generations, both the perfunctory discharge of duty and the absolute ignorance of the officials who had charge of the various Records was something appalling. It meets the enquiring student at every turn, and in no way is it better illustrated than in the history of this Roll. At one time, some hundreds of years ago, the Great Roll of 31 Henry I [1131] was actually thought to have been 1 Henry II [1155], and that date was endorsed upon it. This must have been done on the merest assumption that because the next extant Roll was 2 Henry II, this must necessarily be 1 Henry II. But that the mistake should have been possible tends to prove that the loss of the earlier Rolls had then already occurred; and, directly there was any pretence at investigation, it was ascertained that the names of none of its sheriffs tallied with those in the Red Book, while many of the persons named on the Roll had been dead long before its presumed date. About three hundred years ago Sir Simonds d'Ewes assigned the Roll to 5 Stephen [1140], and on his authority that date was endorsed upon it as a correction of 1 Henry II. Dugdale in his *Baronage*, published rather more than two hundred years ago, invariably quotes the Roll as 5 Stephen, notwithstanding that Prynne had some years before proved that it was of Henry I's reign. He thought, however, that it belonged to the 18th year of that king, because it contained an entry of an allowance to the sheriffs of London for oil to burn at the Queen's sepulchre, which he considered must refer to the burial of Queen Matilda, as it had taken place that year.   Its assignment to the reign of Henry I was accepted by Maddox, though he also continued to call the Roll, as it had so long been called, 5 Stephen, because, while rejecting 18 Henry I as incorrect, he was unable to assign to the document a date which he could assert to be absolutely accurate.   That was, however, done in 1835 by the late Mr. Joseph Hunter, who, after investigation, had no hesitation in dating the Roll as 31 Henry I, which date has proved to be perfectly accurate and reconcileable with all other known dates.   The year 1131 is, in fact, absolutely fixed as that of the death of an abbot of Abingdon who, certainly alive at the beginning of the Roll, had a discharge entered against his name during its currency, "because he was dead."

The not unnatural desire of William Maltravers under the circumstances was for peace.   As we now know from the Great Roll of 1131, if the monks of Pontefract themselves did not know it, his holding was but temporary; and he was therefore quite willing to contract by No. 423 to give the monks yearly the value of a mark, if they would postpone the litigation which they threatened with regard to the advowson of the church of Whalley; and they themselves were careful that the temporary compromise which they made should be acknowledged to be "without prejudice."

The church of Whalley had been originally given to the monks by Hugh de Laval, and William Maltravers seems to have believed that they had also the charter of the king confirming it ; but if so, it would have been by an independent charter not preserved, for the confirmation is not mentioned in Henry I's charter, No. 72.   Indeed, the only royal confirmations of the church of Whalley extant in the Chartulary are those of King Henry II in 1155 (No. 71 and No. 73), while neither of the de Lascies confirmed the gift.   This absence of confirmation by the de Lascies might, indeed, have been because the original grants had been made from the de Laval property held by Hugh prior to his acquisition of the Pontefract fee, a property in which the de Lascies had no interest.   In any case, the dispute seems to have fallen somewhat into abeyance during the remainder of the twelfth century, during which time the rectors or deans of Whalley had practically established their right to the living in lineal descent, so that it descended from father to son as many as ten times (*Whalley Chartulary*, pp. 188 and 1074). This state of things was absolutely terminated by Roger, the last dean, who not only abstained from marriage, but who ceded the living itself to John de Lascy, his great uncle (his grandmother being sister to Roger de Lascy, father of John). John de Lascy, the new patron, presented a young man, Peter de Cestria, who was probably his own illegitimate brother, and this Peter held the rectory for close upon sixty years. At his death the monks of Pontefract revived their claim, but did not persist in it; and the advowson was given to Stanlaw, which had permission to appropriate it.

It may be remembered that William Maltravers and his wife Dameta are stated by Archbishop Theodore (No. 57) to have given to the monks a bovate of land in Thorp [Audlin], which gift is not on record elsewhere.

Stotfield, referred to in No. 418 and again in No. 433, is a small member of the parish of Hooton Pagnell and a manor to the south-west of Bilham. It has but one house, presumably the "chief toft" which is here referred to and which was to be retained in the hands of William of Bilham and his heirs. The holding is still embanked; it is well defended with its hedge and ditch; and its general appearance can differ little from that which it has exhibited for some centuries. The house has been rebuilt within the last half century, and now occupies a site slightly to the east, while the old house has been converted into farm buildings.

William de Bareville, the grantor of No. 435, was the sub-infeudatory of the Luterels. There was also a Sir William de Bilham, who witnesses most of the Bilham charters; his position is not defined, but he precedes William de Bareville in No. 272 and No. 273. Almost all that is certain is that, at the time of *Kirby's Inquest* (13 Edward I), Bilham was held by a Robert de Bareville, so that, although William de Bareville had at one time such "great necessity" that he was compelled to sell to the monks for thirty shillings 16½ acres of his land in Bilham, there must have been at least three generations of that family holding the fee; but their history is not clear. In *Testa de Nevill*, Andrew Luterel is given as the head of the fee, and there is no reference in that document either to the subinfeudatory Bareville or to any of the Bilhams.

Bilham Grange, the former holding of the monks of Pontefract, still exists, but the hall has been demolished within recent memory.

The William Foliot who witnessed No. 436 was the eldest son of the original William, of Pontefract, who gave the carucate on Baghill at the foundation of the monastery. This second William was now of the East Riding, his next younger brother being the Jordan who inherited the Foliot property at Pontefract and its neighbourhood (see p. 117). He was the third husband of Agnes de Arches, widow successively of Herbert St. Quintin and of Robert de Falkenberg.

This charter gives also an Andrew, brother of Peter de Falkenberg, who is unknown to the genealogists.

The relationship does not appear, but evidently Ralph de Wick, the grantor of No. 437, was the representative (probably son or grandson) of the Ralph de Catwick who originally granted to the monks his mediety of the church there. That charter furnishes the name of a brother of Walter de Falkenberg, who is not named in the genealogies, but who is mentioned in No. 446 also. The three brothers here named were three of the six (hitherto considered to have been only five) sons of Peter de Falkenberg, who gave the second moiety of the church of Catwick to the monks (see No. 413).

It is thus not a little remarkable that each of these two charters supplies a name to the early part of the Falkenberg pedigree, which has been, I think, entirely overlooked. Its three early generations would thus be as follows, the new names furnished by the Pontefract Chartulary being distinguished by italics :—

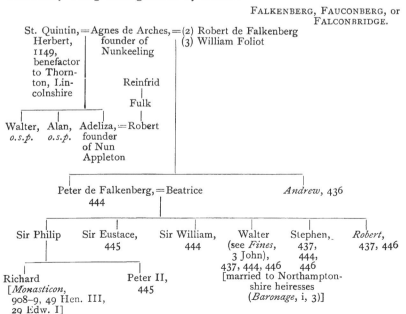

FALKENBERG, FAUCONBERG, or FALCONBRIDGE.

St. Quintin, = Agnes de Arches, = (2) Robert de Falkenberg
Herbert,   founder of   (3) William Foliot
1149,   Nunkeeling
benefactor
to Thorn-
ton, Lin-   Reinfrid
colnshire
     Fulk

Walter,   Alan,   Adeliza, = Robert
o.s.p.   *o.s.p.*   founder
     of Nun
     Appleton

Peter de Falkenberg, = Beatrice   *Andrew*, 436
444

Sir Philip   Sir Eustace,   Sir William,   Walter   Stephen,   *Robert*,
    445   444   (see *Fines*,   437,   437, 446
               3 John),   444,
Richard   Peter II,   437, 444, 446   446
[*Monasticon*,   445   [married to Northampton-
908–9, 49 Hen. III,   shire heiresses
29 Edw. I]   (*Baronage*, i, 3)]

The younger brethren of each generation, if they survived, probably hived out and assumed the names of the places at which they settled. That Stephen was junior to Walter is clear from their order in the attestation clause of both No. 444 and No. 446, which we shall shortly come to; while this No. 437 shows clearly that Robert was junior to both.

But, whatever might have been the case with Andrew and his nephew Robert, the bulk of the Falkenbergs (as the Pontefract Chartulary gives the name, differing from all the usual orthographies and maintaining a special rule) adhered to the family cognomen and ennobled it; though most of these six brothers, sons of Peter, had, it must be confessed, a keen and successful scent for lands by way of the spindle.

Rise, the seat of the family, had been originally held as two manors, one of them being owned by Franco de Falconberg, a vassal of the Domesday lord, Drogo de Bevere. His son or grandson (it is not clear which), Robert de Falkenberg, married Agnes de Arches, widow of Herbert St. Quintin; and their son was the Peter de Falkenberg whose wife Beatrice I have not been able to trace. The coincidence that they should have had a younger son, by name Andrew, the traditional brother of Peter, has been hitherto missed, Andrew having made no name in the world, at least as a Falconberg. Peter had a brave family of boys—certainly six, though he has been usually credited with five only—and of these at least three married heiresses. His eldest son, Sir Philip, seems to have had the bulk of the original property; and he added to it considerably by his marriage with Cecily, co-heir of William Scotney. He had descendants who all retained the family name, or its equivalent Falconbridge. The descent of this elder branch was carried on through Peter, who, as if inheriting owing to the death without issue of his brother Richard, made a claim in No. 445 on the mediety of Catwick. Another son seems to have become a monk; at least, he surrendered a competent estate for a specified corrody, the particulars of which are most interesting. [See Dodsworth's *Monasticon*, page 906 (49 Henry III), and page 908 (29 Edward I).]

Sir Eustace, the second son of Peter, took orders and was presented to the mediety of Catwick (see No. 445). But he entered into public life, being one of the justices itinerant throughout the reign of King John, and becoming bishop of London early in the reign of his successor. In 16 John, however, he married a wealthy widow, Childone, relict of Alverd de Cotes, though he does not appear to have had any family.   Foss was doubtful of his birth-place, though the incidental mention in No. 445 of his being presented to Catwick would be a natural outcome of his hereditary relations to that manor, and might have furnished a hint for at least enquiry.

Nothing is recorded of the marriage or career of the third son, William.

The fourth son, Walter, married Agnes, one of the co-heirs of Simon fitz Simon, and this branch obtained perhaps the highest share of wealth and honour.   For the grandson of the marriage—another Walter—married another heiress, one of the daughters of Peter de Brus, of Skelton,. and inherited Skelton through her.   He died 12 Edward II, and No. 51 of the Inquisitions for that year contains a lengthy enumeration of his manors, among which were Rise, Skelton, Ingleby, Marske, and Arncliffe.   Burke, in his *Extinct Genealogies*, treats these two Walters as one, his confusion arising from the circumstance that in each case, grandfather and grandson, the husband was a Walter and the wife an Agnes.   He thus misses two generations.

The fifth son, Stephen, married Parnel, another of the co-heirs of Simon fitz Simon, of Brixworth, Northampton, and with her he received Cuckney, in Lincolnshire, which remained in their family for many generations, their great-grandson being summoned to Parliament in 29 Edward I as lord of Cuckney.   Stephen and his father Peter jointly witnessed a charter concerning the foundation of Meaux, which is preserved in Dodsworth's *Monasticon*, 799.   He was dead in 1194 (Rot. Cur. Regis 6 R.I.), and it may be interesting to know that Simon de Kyme (in 1 John) offered to the lord king £100 sterling for her, that she might marry whom she pleased, "with the advice of her friends," and the sheriff of Nottinghamshire was instructed thereupon.

Of the sixth son, Robert, I have traced nothing except his mention in these Pontefract charters, No. 437 and No. 446.   He was the youngest, and there is no reason to identify him with the Robert "son of old Sir Robert" of Shakespeare's *King John*.   The poet, it will be remembered, makes Philip, the elder, renounce his lands in favour of his brother Robert, and it is curious that this discovery in the Pontefract Chartulary rehabilitates a Robert as brother to the Philip, *temp*. Richard.   Their relations towards each other do not, however, agree with those depicted by Shakespeare; and as a matter of fact the real Sir Philip retained his land in Yorkshire, and had nothing to do with Northamptonshire, but led the life of a useful country gentleman in the East Riding. He had a grant of free warren at Nun Appleton in 10 Henry III.

The family who thus called themselves "of Bilham" were strongly seated in the manor before the Barevilles, who ultimately displaced them, though for a time they signed concurrently, Bilham having the precedence.

I have collated the names of the members of this family, to produce the following scheme of relationship :—

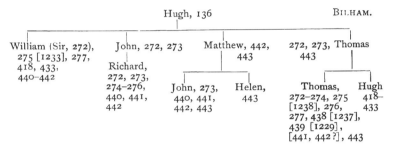

No. 440 has for witness Jordan de Insula de Brodsworth, while No. 443 has Jordan de Insula de Hooton, and No. 442 had simply Jordan de Insula; but there can be little doubt that all these were the same person, that he was of both Brodsworth and Hooton, and that he is also the Jordan de Insula "de Preston," who tests No. 244 and No. 273. He derived from Godwin de Insula of Heck. (Harl., 800.)

The use by this Jordan of both place-names, Brodsworth and Hooton, adjoining manors, and of Preston also, is an illustration of the way in which, in this century, such names were acquired as surnames. It was the merest chance which of them were to be perpetuated in that character, and by which descendant of the original owner. But as a matter of fact neither of those we are now considering was continued; for this Jordan died without heir, as did the heir of his elder brother Henry. His father William, the youngest of three brothers (No. 101 and No. 206), had been a cadet, and does not appear as a benefactor; though, as the family were more connected with Nostell than with Pontefract, their benefactions went in that direction, and it was to Nostell that Hugh de Dai (the husband of Alice de Insula, aunt to this Jordan) retired when stricken with leprosy.

Foss mentions as many as six justiciaries of this name during the twelfth century, one of whom occurs in the Pontefract Chartulary and one in that of Selby; but, though each had certainly a Yorkshire connection, I fail to affiliate either on the Yorkshire de Insulas. The six justiciaries given by Foss are:—

1.   Brian, who held office from 2 John (1200) till his death in 1234, in which year he was sheriff of Yorkshire. He was one of the justices before whom the Final Concord (No. 243, *ante*) was made at York in 1226.

2.   Godfrey. 10 Richard I (1199) to 13 John (1211).

3 and 4.   John de Insula (1290 to 1320, and 1307 respectively).

5.   Simon de Insula (John and Henry III).

6.   William de Insula [6 John (1204)—18 Henry III (1233)]. He was among the judges before whom the fines S[elby] 598 and S 1284 were made on June 17, 1231.

Whatever became of the elder brothers, Ralph and Jordan,— whether they died heirless, or adopted some local name and so lost that which they had hereditarily,—the property and name centred upon the youngest brother William, who, as we learn from No. 185, was living in 1201. William's eldest son Henry, his grandson William, and his second son Jordan, inherited successively; so that, to satisfy the various rights of the female members of the family, widows or spinsters, the manor of Pollington was theoretically divided into fifteenths, three of which were in 1330 transferred by Final Concord from Peter de Wendover and his wife Agnes to Thomas de Metham. (See *Yorkshire Archæological Journal*, xi, 459.)

The Jordan Folioth who witnesses No. 444 was possibly the grantor of the West Mill at Norton to the monks. (See the Foliot pedigree, page 114.) But that family were early on this ground. William Foliot, eldest son of William Foliot of Pontefract, is mentioned in the *Pipe Roll* of 31 Henry I as even then having some interest in Holderness; and he afterwards became third husband to Agnes de Arches, the grantor of this charter being her great grandson by her second husband. A third William and his brother Hugh are named in a charter of Archbishop William to the nuns of Keeling (*Monasticon*, 475), and one of these brothers was probably father or grandfather of William, the witness to No. 445.

No. 446 shows us how Walter de Falkenberg and Ralph de Wick reciprocate. Each witnesses the other's grant of their respective moieties of the church of Catwick, the advowson of which remained in the monks of Pontefract until the Dissolution. But Walter's grandson, the young Eustace de Falconbridge, the future justiciary, obtained the presentation from the monks.

As we have seen (No. 51), when Archbishop Gray settled the rights of the various parties interested in benefices in which vicarages had been ordained, the monks' share of the value of Catwick was fixed at three marks (£2) yearly, which was only two-sevenths of the full value of the benefice. The vicar took the remaining £5, a far larger proportion than usual, the benefice itself being but poor.

The Ninth Fasciculus closes and the Tenth begins in the middle of the charter numbered 450. The two together make a section, the only instance of the sort in the Chartulary. The word "perticatas" marks the junction, and is written as a catch word at the foot of the second column of the dorse of fo. 70, in addition to coming as the first word of fo. 71. This is a very early instance of the use of such a device, which is sometimes said to have originated with Caxton.

Of the charter numbered 454 and the preceding one (which is not numbered), No. 454 was the earlier, as is evidenced by the presence as witnesses of the names of Jordan and his three brothers, who were in so constant an attendance upon him that it seems to have been considered almost a work of supererogation to name them individually.

By his marriage with Eva de Dai, the daughter of Hugh the leper, Peter de Toulston acquired a high position, for he became a holder of the share of the knight's fees which belonged to her father (whose leprosy excluded him from social, not to say public, life), and appears in *Liber Niger* as holding them in 1166. But the name of Toulston perished with him and his elder son; for his second son Rayner acquired that of Aketon, and his granddaughter lost it by becoming wife to Henry de Huntwick.

The following was the family of this Robert de Toulston, thus mentioned so accidentally (see page 188):—

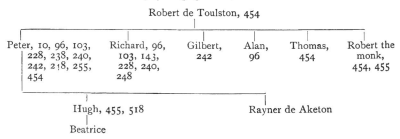

Robert de Toulston, 454

| Peter, 10, 96, 103, 228, 238, 240, 242, 218, 255, 454 | Richard, 96, 103, 143, 228, 240, 248 | Gilbert, 242 | Alan, 96 | Thomas, 454 | Robert the monk, 454, 455 |

Hugh, 455, 518   Rayner de Aketon

Beatrice

Rayner, clerk of Darfield, who had been, as we learn from No. 456*, a tenant of the monks for land at Menton, was the holder of one of the medieties at Darfield.   He was a Rayner Fleming and has occurred before as a witness to No. 96, No. 207, and No. 238. In No. 207 Ralph his brother also is named, who is clearly to be identified with the "Ralph de Wath, my uncle" of No. 456*.

(Wath and Darfield were adjoining manors, each held ecclesiastically in mediety.)

But although (as we shall see from Archbishop Gray's Register) this Rayner the clerk was of the family of Fleming, which occupied so large a position in West Yorkshire, if not in our immediate district, yet he was not the head of the family, which was another Rayner, the founder of Kirklees.   This is evident since they both test No. 238.

The Flemings long owned Sharlston Hall, which (in the time of Queen Elizabeth) Cuthbert, the last of the race, rebuilt much as we see it now.   The front of the house still bears an inscription recording the fact of its having been rebuilt by Cuthbert Fleming.

At the time of the Great Survey in 1086, four centuries and a half after the mission of Paulinus into Northumbria, the West Riding of Yorkshire was still very sparsely supplied with buildings dedicated to the worship of God.   York, the ecclesiastical centre of the diocese, had many; Pontefract and its neighbourhood, its civil centre, was also very fairly provided; but the greater part of the West Riding was still a spiritual waste.   Churches had been built in Pontefract; and most of the adjoining manors—Darrington, Ackworth, Womersley, South Kirkby, Featherstone, Kirk Smeaton—had been provided with its church and its priest, but this was not the case further from the centre, Staincross and that part of Strafford immediately adjoining being almost destitute.   The church accommodation of the portion of Staincross which was given to the Earl of Morton was represented by one at Tankersley, while the much larger portion granted to Ilbert de Lascy had but the building at Cawthorn (then itself reckoned with Silkstone), which, however, seems in reality to have been only for the more especial accommodation of the lord and his immediate retainers.   But among the very earliest of the churches built when the district had passed under the sway of the Normans—a great church-building race—was that of Darfield, which must have followed almost immediately after the Norman irruption, while, indeed, it was practically in progress and before the settlement had been fully effected.

2 M

However lightly we may talk about the erection and endowment of a church, it was then, as now, no light undertaking; and the early buildings were generally rough and perhaps in many cases tentative, though in some few cases they were strong and substantial, if with little pretence at the structural adornment which was provided at a later date.

But generally a great advance in architectural refinement had been made when the building was renewed, which required to be done in almost every instance within the first century after the Conquest. I may, indeed, say that the church at Adwick-on-Dearne —restored within the last ten or fifteen years, but so as still to retain its original Norman nave and chancel, with no aisles, and but a turret for a bell—is the single such building which I can call to mind in this part of Yorkshire as surviving from before 1100. Every other, built between 1080 and the time of Stephen's wars, succumbed very speedily, generally requiring to be renewed in that great era of church organization, the thirty years of the second half of the twelfth century, when Roger was archbishop and Henry Plantagenet was king.

There was a fashion in church endowment as in so many other things, and at the particular time when Darfield was founded (*temp.* William II and Henry I) the fashion set in strongly to endow churches by halves. It may have been, and perhaps generally was the case, that two owners who each held part of a manor combined for this necessary work; but, however that may be, most of the churches built about 1100 were endowed in medieties. I instance Campsall, Wath (where, indeed, there were three lords, and the living was therefore held in thirds, each belonging to one particular lord, and perhaps each for the special benefit of one set of tenants, but all using the same church), Tankersley, Penistone, and Darfield; and when this was the case the presentation (which the founder always retained till he or a successor voluntarily parted with his interest, generally by surrender to a monastery) was either alternately to the whole, or each lord presented to his own half. Of these medieties few survive; they mostly merged into one hand within the next hundred years. At Campsall, for instance, each soon fell to the Lascies; but that at Darfield has existed with its separate interests until this present day, and with a singular complication which in itself furnishes a very profitable lesson in Church history.

From the very earliest times Darfield had been held as two manors, and in the time of Edward the Confessor their lords were

Alsi or Ailsi and Chetelber, each a very considerable owner in other parts of this great county. Chetelber seems to have been dispossessed in Darfield—if not, he was not named—and, at the time of the Domesday Survey, Alsi appears to have held both manors as the temporary tenant of the king, with no intermediate lord, for Darfield had not yet been granted out. There were then four carucates of taxable land, valued in King Edward's time at 40*s.*, and under Alsi they continued to pay the large proportion of four-fifths of the former amount; after which a veil of thick obscurity descends; Domesday gives us a glance of Alsi in possession as king's tenant and apparently prospering, and reveals no more. How long he maintained what he must have felt to be a precarious tenure there is nothing yet to show; and, since it is possible more may still be learnt of the method by which the original Saxon owner was finally supplanted by his Norman successor, I refrain from a premature guess. It is sufficient to say that the process was not entirely completed at the close of the time of the Conqueror, for Domesday shows Alsi and others still in possession of their former lands. Nor is it clear on what terms he continued his tenure, whether as a life-holding and intended so to be by mutual consent (a possible case, analogous to the agreement come to half a century afterwards between King Stephen and Queen Matilda at the treaty of Wallingford), or whether till he offended either the new king or the new de Lascy (and the throne and the castle each received a new occupant almost contemporaneously), cannot yet be said. We must be content that Domesday gives us a glance of Alsi in possession and apparently prospering. His lands at Campsall, Darrington, Stubbs, Thorp, Elmsall, and Kinsley, had with others gone to Ilbert de Lascy, while Roger de Busli had obtained those at Brodsworth, Ecclesfield, Kimberworth, and Tickhill. But he himself remained settled at Darfield, as his neighbour Ailric did at Cawthorn. Neither, however, retained his position long. Ailric was dead before 1090, and, when next after that date the curtain lifts at Darfield, we find the manor there once more in two fees.

But in that year we are able to gain a slight and almost accidental glimpse of a church, or the preparations for the foundation of a church, enough to establish the fact of their existence, though not enough to reveal any particulars. For in 1090 or shortly before, Swain fitz Ailric, who had come into possession of Silkstone, was placing the church there under the protection of the monks of Pontefract, and No. 378, by which this was effected, was witnessed, among others, by the priest and parson of Darfield, one Edwin (not Godwin, as mis-stated by Hunter, and repeated, sometimes without acknowledgment, by the usual copyists). Of which half Edwin was parson it is bootless now to enquire; nor, indeed, whether the re-division of the manors had really taken place so soon. Mere speculation is profitless; we must wait till time and circumstance throw light on the obscurity by means of some fortunate discovery. It is enough at present to state that Archbishop Gray's Register, No. 130, shows that on 5 (*sic*, but?) Nones, Dec xiv, *i.e.* 1229, on the presentation of William Fleming, he instituted Richard son of Robert to that mediety of the church of Darfield which Rayner Fleming had held. This shows the Flemings in possession of at least one half of the manor; but the two moieties were shortly in the hands respectively of Fitzwilliams and Bosviles, the former at Wood Hall, the latter at New Hall.

I do not intend to follow out the fortunes of the two medieties, indeed I have not the materials at hand; but it is amply sufficient for my present purpose to say that the two parsons remained in concurrent possession, separate rectors being appointed to each mediety till October, 1363, when the lord Grey of Rotherfield, who was the patron of the second, "appropriated" it, as the phrase went, to the Priory of St. John of Jerusalem. As a consequence of this "appropriation," the Knights Hospitallers took the living into their own possession, absorbed the revenues, and (acknowledging that the provision of divine service was "incumbent" upon them) appointed a vicar, a *vice* that is to say to themselves, to perform the clerical duties and to receive as remuneration the fees and a fixed stipend. In their hands, and under these conditions, the mediety remained until the Reformation, when so many monastic possessions fell to the king, among them that at Darfield. In this case, however, the properties were not sold at a cheap rate to some grasping courtier, but they became a monument of what might have been, and doubtless of what, in the mind of many, should have been, when the Dissolution of the Monasteries came.

No one seems to have had a thought of converting them to their original purpose and restoring the endowments to the parish to which they belonged, to be devoted to the spiritual good of the people, for which purpose they were at first destined; in which case this impoverished vicarage would have been again enriched. But perhaps the next best thing was done. The king used them still for the purposes of religion and learning, and gave them towards the endowment of Trinity College, Cambridge, then in course of foundation. And thus that college acquired the right of presentation to the second mediety of Darfield Church, the endowment of which is something under £100, now that the bulk of what should have been the value of the living goes towards the maintenance of Trinity College.

In the case of the first mediety, the patronage descended in the usual way in the family of the founder; and the living is now of the yearly value of some £1,500. The holder is called the rector (which he is) of the first mediety; but there is nothing common between the rector of the first mediety and the vicar of the second, such as naturally springs to the mind when we hear of the rector and the vicar of the same place. As I have shown, except that they have a church in common, these medieties are as distinct as if they formed separate parishes; and the value of the first is only an illustration of what the value of the second might have been had it not been "appropriated" five hundred years ago. But now, especially when thus contrasted with its co-ordinate mediety, it shows in a manner which cannot be gainsaid how so many vicarages have been impoverished.

No. 456* affords also a side illustration of the carelessness which accompanied the latter part of the reign of Henry III. The abrupt ending, "et cetera," the general slovenly appearance of the writing, and the absence of the names of the witnesses, are all in marked contrast to the careful, punctilious manner in which the original scribe and his immediate follower performed their work. One feels that the hours of leisure which permitted of the stately self-respecting reverence characterising the first half of the century had passed away, and that their place had been supplied by features which were characteristic, not only of the impatience and rebelliousness of the third quarter of the century, but of that utter feebleness which in the end prepared so grand a field for the labours of the "Greatest of All the Plantagenets."

The four charters No. 457 to No. 460 refer to land in the North Field, as it had been called. North Field was a common arable land, which at the time of these charters had, within comparatively recent memory, been reduced to severalty. When common, it had belonged partly to Pontefract and partly to Ferrybridge, but there was now a good, well-defined boundary line. In these charters the land that had once been this North Field is never so styled; but the landmarks by which it is described are "The Waterfall," "The Gallows," and "The Thieves' Gallows."

The Waterfall is still known by that name, but the Thieves' Gallows is not recognizable. "Gallows Hill" is indeed marked on the 6in. Ordnance Map as being at the extreme north of the manor; and probably that elevation at one time bore a gallows, for this last charter, No. 460, points to the existence at this date of a "thieves' gallows" at the termination of "the great road leading from Monk-hill," which can only be that passing St. Ive's Well.

On the other hand, No. 121 grants half an acre "which lies near the Gallows." And this must be in another direction, perhaps on St. Thomas's Hill; certainly not at Gallows Hill, which never had so small a patch as a half-acre.

Thus it is clear that in the last quarter of the twelfth century and the first quarter of the thirteenth,—the half century to which these charters refer,—there were two sites in the eastern portion of the manor, each of which contained a gallows. These were Gallows Hill, overlooking Frystone and the Aire valley to the north, and St. Thomas's Hill, overlooking Ferrybridge and the Aire valley to the east, with Knottingley in the further distance. According to this theory, the latter, the site of the execution of Thomas, Earl of Lancaster, would have been an old place of execution on the boundary of the manor, and not made use of for the occasion only of the decapitation of the earl.

In connection with the Gallows Hill site, it may be recorded in this place that on Monday, 25 March, 1822 (Lady Day), a large stone coffin, weighing about a ton and a half, was found in the Paper Mill Garth (Hepworth's Survey, No. 365). This was a plot which was a part of the manor of Spital Hardwick, and therefore belonged to St. Nicholas' Hospital, and was included in the grant of the hospital estates which Mrs. Milnes, of Frystone Hall, possessed at the time in their entirety. The coffin contained the decapitated skeleton of a full-grown man, whose remains, being supposed to be those of Thomas, Earl of Lancaster, were taken into the grounds of Frystone Hall, where they are still preserved. There can, however, be no doubt that the supposition that they were the remains of the unfortunate Earl of Lancaster was the result of an entire misapprehension. For the earl is well known to have been buried on the right hand of the altar of St. John's Church by the monks of that place, who had begged his body from the king, and who for some generations maintained his place of sepulchre there as a popular resort for pilgrims.

Besides these two gallows-sites, there was one other in the centre of the town, the present Wool Market, styled in Jollage's map "Hemp Cross." Hemp Cross is within a few yards of the Moot Hall and of the Tanshelf boundary of the manor; but I have met with no recorded instance of its use as a place of execution.

The name "Waterfall" is still applied to the plot referred to in No. 460, which was numbered 519 on Hepworth's Survey. At the present day its boundaries are extended to include several smaller enclosures between the Waterfall and New Hall Orchard, which are now thrown into one and locally known as "The Waterfall." But the Ordnance 6in. Survey has transferred the name to an acre plot to the west, which also belonged to the monks and which is No. 337 on Hepworth's Survey. There it is incorrectly called "Waterfall or Drunken Flat."

Now "Drunken" or "Duncan" Flat was a nine-acre plot to the north, which will be found to be the subject of the charter No. 471. It contains the outcrop and termination of that contour which seems to have given to the more easterly incline the picturesquely descriptive name of "Waterfall." The two are, however, perfectly distinct, and should not have been confused. Still less should the names have been jointly transferred to another plot with which they had no connection.

The Waterfall is a remarkable geological formation. To the wayfarer on the road to Spital Hardwick, it justifies its name, being as clearly to him in the shape of a waterfall as is a simple daisy (day's eye) like the sun. The name is as truly and poetically descriptive. Geologically the northerly portion is lower magnesian limestone, and the more southerly is sandstone of the coal measures. But between the two was a strip of sand, which has been to a considerable extent excavated. This extended into Drunken Flat also, from which plot it was carried away bodily about twenty-five years ago. In the course of the excavation from Drunken Flat, the workmen exhumed some fossil sponges and some bones of a *Bos Longifrons*. These I carried up to London for identification by Professor Owen, who thought they were no earlier than the Roman period.

The original Waterfall extended northward to one of the triangular reservations, entered at the three corners, of which those were so liberal who originally planned the Angle settlements, and which are so numerous in Pontefract, and indeed throughout the district. In the instance before us, population never settled upon this spot so reserved, and to this day it remains an indication of what "might have been,"—the Market Place of a hive of industry, on an elevated plateau; the anti-type of the Market Place of the borough town, which to the south-west occupies a neighbouring summit, at exactly the distance of a mile as the crow flies.

It will be noticed that Master Raimond and Walter the receiver were contemporaries of different generations; Master Raimond would have been in his prime in the decade before 1200, that is to say in the reign of Richard I, and Walter in that of his successor John. Master Raimond was one of the witnesses to Roger de Lascy's charter to his burgesses of Pontefract, and must have been a man of the very highest local influence, arising from his great wealth, the public-spirited uses to which he put it, and the position which he had inherited from his father. He was a University man, as was his father; and, like him, he held the degree of "Master," by which title, however, he was not described when he gave the next charter. This, therefore, might be considered to antedate the Borough Charter, except that the names of the witnesses are clearly of a later date, and probably about 1220. Master Raimond appears to have been ultimately the Rector of Methley (see *ante*, p. 165).

There is much interest connected with a few words in the first clause of No. 461, in which its subject is said to be—(1) Land to the west of the Castle; (2) Which is of the fee of Cridling; (3) Which I have held from the brethren of the Hospital of St. Michael.

(1) The "land to the west of the Castle" is clearly part of the plot outside the Porter's Lodge, which became the Bede House, the poor man's house at the rich man's gate. And we learn that there were here at least two estates, held respectively by Raimond the clerk, Master Raimond the subsequent parson of Methley, and by William Campion.

(2) This land to the west of the Castle was of the "fee of Cridling," which with all its interests had been purchased by the lord of the honour, Roger de Lascy. This has been already ascertained from a charter in the Great Chartulary of the Duchy of Lancaster, now in the Record Office (see *ante*, p. 485).

(3) Raimond the clerk had held this land from the brethren of St. Michael's Hospital. This shows a connection between those brethren, the Bede House, and the fee of Cridling, which may account for the existence in the wall at Cridling Park of a remark-able crucifix. (See my paper upon it in the *Yorkshire Archæological Journal*, vol. xi, p. 23, &c.) For it may well be that the Foulsnape brethren, the hospitallers of St. Michael's, had been early tenants of Cridling, before even Roger de Lascy possessed it, and had there placed this their mark, with their distinguishing double cross; a

crucifix which, moreover, shows the reason (not always understood) for this use of a cross with two arms, to support both the shoulders and buttocks.

Peter the chaplain, as we learn from No. 463, was priest of St. Clement's. It may be he who witnessed No. 100 and No. 221, and who by No. 463 acquired the ownership of another plot in this neighbourhood, just outside the Castle curtilage and on the other side of the Porter's Lodge, with, moreover, the definite statement that it was the central piece of three, and that it had a frontage measurement of 54 feet. This is a clear identification. A third plot, called in No. 463 the "house of Richard Lorimer," in No. 472 that of Hugh son of Richard, and in No. 135 that of Hugh Lorimer, seems as clearly to be a "Lorimer" possession, first in the hands of Richard the father, and afterwards in the possession of Hugh his son. The plot assigned to Peter the chaplain is now a maltkiln, while the site of Hugh Lorimer's house is occupied by cottages. Each of these properties, together with the building at the corner of Spink Lane, which was now the house of Lisiard (No. 463), and at a later date became the Outer Lodge, where applicants for admission to the Castle were received before the drawbridge was lowered, is still considered without the Castle precincts and within the township of Pontefract.

We have already had to deal with the 18 acres in the Ferry Fields (see No. 284 to No. 288); but No. 462, the sixth charter concerning the property, enables us to collate and compare all. As they appear to be nearly contemporaneous, they illustrate very well the passion which possessed these monks for piling up legal documents. Possibly they obtained this department of their law at a cheap rate, owing to their having juridical monks among their body.

No. 287 and No. 288 are practically duplicates, the latter having an additional clause, enunciating that John of Batley had made the monks his assigns concerning the property, though there was no such clause in the deed by which he obtained it.

With regard to the witnesses, Hugh Butler tests each, except No. 284, and William the chaplain of Pontefract appears in one instance as parson of Healaugh, leading to the inference that he had received that presentation, even while the charters were being granted. John, rector of St. Nicholas' Hospital, appears twice, Walter the receiver three times, and John of Louvain four times; while Henry tests each, sometimes as the son of Ralph, sometimes as the son of Matilda (he being their second son); and as Alan, his elder brother, the bailiff of Staincross and Osgòldcross, never appears, he was probably dead.

The order and position of the name of John son of Michael (son of Thomas fitz Asolf, of Monkhill) leads to the inference that he was now becoming John of Baghill, and that he was the progenitor of the family that bore that name and survived till the fifteenth century, leaving their arms (*Argent, on a bend sable, three eagles' heads erased*) on the font at Featherstone. An Ussher married the heiress, so that John of Baghill is thus the connecting link with the family of the Usshers and the princely Asolf.

The order of the six charters appears to be thus :—

No. 284 and No. 462 are complementary. By No. 284, Agnes, daughter of Roger of Ledstone, interchanges her rights with those of Emma her sister (described in No. 462 as daughter of Beatrice daughter of Hugh, and now in widowhood; that is to say, that William de Calne, her husband, was dead) and William her son. By these deeds, Emma and William her son acquired the 18 acres.

No. 286. William, son of William de Calne, with the assent of Emma his mother, grants the 18 acres to John, described as "de Batley."

No. 285. Agnes approves the sale made by Emma her sister and William her son to John, whom she calls by his old name of Vintner.

No. 287. John de Batley grants the estate to the monks.

No. 288. He renews the grant to them as his assigns.

The following pedigree of Roger, third son of Ailric, will illustrate not only the various phases of this transaction but many other interesting points. A similar pedigree of the youngest son (Walter) will follow.

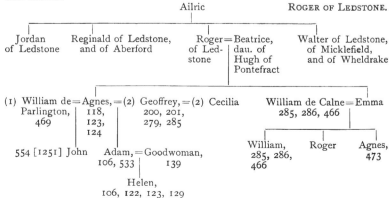

The Hugh of Pontefract, father to Beatrice wife of Roger, was an important and a wealthy man, of a grade above the burgess-tenants named in the "Little Charter;" though later on, in No. 148, he was called emphatically Hugh the Burgess, and is frequently named as joint bailiff with his son Gilbert.   He was grandfather of the Walter who assumed the name of Scot, perhaps from some tradition that the name of his great-grandfather, Ailbern the father of Hugh, was in some way derived from Scotland.   It is very curious that, while in the body of No. 169 (the deed by which, in 1253, he made such large exchanges with the monks, and received from them Monkroyd, which has even till now retained their name) he was styled Walter son of Gilbert son of Hugh, the rubricator gave him simply the name of "Walter Scot of Pontefract."

The following is the pedigree so far as these documents reveal it :—

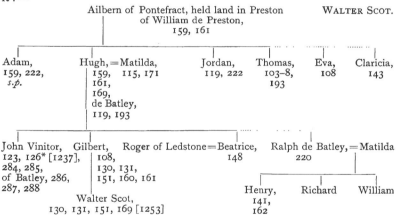

Thus Adam was the heir; but Hugh hived out, acquiring the surname of de Batley, with which he returned on the death of Adam.

No. 470 [468] stands by itself; and there is nothing more concerning its grantor, of either of the persons mentioned in it, or of either of the subjects of the grant.   Ferry is, of course, Ferrybridge; but ecclesiastically the manors of Ferry (Ferrybridge) and Frystone were united as a parish under the name of Ferry Frystone and Water Frystone, to distinguish it from Monk Frystone.   The church is frequently called Ferrybridge Church, but it is locally in Frystone, and, like almost all that were founded during the twelfth and thirteenth centuries, it is built upon a corner of the park.   Such churches are thus shown to be squire-founded, not state-founded ; their erection was due to the self-sacrificing, unostentatious philanthropy of the owner of the land, acted upon by the rage for church-building which possessed to so large a degree the early Norman possessors of these Yorkshire lands.

The plot granted by No. 471 [469] is known as Drunken or Duncan Flat and is No. 358 on Hepworth's Survey, where it is said to contain 8a. 2r. 23p. It is the last plot in Pontefract adjoining (separated by a road) St. Ive's closes, which contain St. Ive's Well and are in the manor of Hardwick, called Spital, as belonging to the Hospital of St. Nicholas. The actual boundary is not given on Hepworth's Survey (which treated Spital Hardwick as a part of Pontefract), but it can be easily traced.

Spital Hardwick contains the whole of the watershed of the Frystone Beck to the north, and sufficient on the south to give the full manorial rights over the brook to its possessors. Its extreme closes to the south of the brook are No. 392, No. 397, No. 395, No. 369 and No. 368 (Fairy Hill Closes, which include within their area a narrow strip to the south of the stream), No. 366 (Batley Close), and No. 365 (Paper Mill Garth), in which were found the human remains referred to on page 502. The manor now belongs by inheritance to the Earl of Crewe ; its whole extent is slightly under 440 acres ; and since the poor-rate settlement made in the time of Queen Elizabeth it has been legally reckoned as part of Pontefract township, to which it pays rates.

Spital Hardwick, called also Blind Hardwick, because it has no thoroughfare, was evidently the seat of an old civilization, and even Roman remains have been found there. The site of the building is sheltered from the north winds by the higher lands in that direction, and it is a few yards from a brook which brought pure water from the west, while the buildings were situated just at so convenient a distance as to allow their drainage to run into it towards the east, without occasioning any subsequent annoyance to the inhabitants.

The inclusion of both sides of a stream within the boundary of a manor is, moreover, one special mark of the seventh and eighth centuries ; and, in just those centuries during the early Saxon or Angle domination, Spital Hardwick was probably a place of considerable importance. A well, which is marked on Hepworth's Survey in No. 397 (a close since subdivided) and which is fed by a spring some twelve or fourteen feet below the general level, recalls the description given by the Venerable Bede of King Edwin's practice of establishing such wells for the use of wayfarers. It is still called St. Ive's Well, and thus gives colour to the surmise that the place was the site of one of the many religious communities founded by St. Hiva. The well itself is in a small sequestered dell, open only to the north and west, being sheltered to the south and east by a natural bank from fifteen to twenty feet high. The fount of water welling up from the rock is of delightful coolness, of steady abundance, of perennial continuance; and it has probably for nearly thirteen hundred years never ceased to project its clear cold stream, though not one-thousandth part of its produce has been utilised.

In the early times of the establishment of Christianity in Yorkshire, St. Ive [Hiva, Heiu, or Eve], the predecessor of St. Hilda at Hartlepool, had exercised a vast and widespread influence throughout the whole kingdom of Northumbria, the land between the Humber and the Forth; and her name, and that of St. Hilda, in some form or other, frequently attaches itself to lands where she had possessions or where there were monasteries under her jurisdiction. Healaugh near Tadcaster, this St. Ive's Well near Pontefract, another St. Ive's near Bingley, to which the Ivegate of Bradford so long pointed, are instances; while Ewecross, or Ivecross, the name of one West Riding wapentake, seems to have been an antithesis to Osgoldcross or Oswald's Cross, the name of another.

St. Hiva was probably of the royal blood, and seems to have been imbued with the strongest missionary impulses. She gathered around her at a place called Heret-eu, afterwards and now Hart-le-pool, a band of devoted women, of whom she became the abbess. She was beloved and venerated in the highest degree, and when, in 650, after some years' rule at Hartlepool, inspired by the wish to spend and be spent to further the progress of Christianity but to the great grief of her devoted friends and followers, she resigned that important charge, it was to be succeeded by the historical Hilda, whose fame as an abbess in her later career at Whitby was destined ultimately to far transcend that of Hiva.

Hiva came southward to found and establish another religious community, of which she continued the head for some years, and with which her name became so identified that the manor she owned, and where she ruled, was called "Hiva's lowy," or domain. This name was, however, soon softened into Hailaga and Helagh, thus losing somewhat of its original sound, which is an effective illustration of the way in which, in the course of some dozen generations, such a name becomes worn away by attrition. The modern use is Healaugh, two vowels having been inserted since the time of Domesday.

In Hiva's day what we now call parish churches were unknown. They were an aftergrowth, springing from subsequent needs. When, in the middle of the seventh century, Hiva's lowy was founded, the idea was to evangelise the people by means of monasteries—houses inhabited by communities of religious men or women bound by vows; and soon after Hiva's establishment of Healaugh the foundation of monasteries received a very considerable impulse in these northern parts. For in order to commemorate his victory in 655 over Penda, the great heathen king of Mercia, a munificent gift was made by Oswiu, the then ruler of Northumbria. He was. successor to his brother Oswald, whose name is perpetuated in Osgoldcross, the wapentake in the eastern part of the Riding, as I think Hiva's was intended to be at Ewecross in the west, though, her name having proved very susceptible of change, it is now indicated only obscurely. The gift of Oswiu was of twelve estates, or farms, or manors, as such came to be called, six in Deira and six in Bernicia; these estates were intended to be sites of monasteries such as Hiva had ruled at Hartlepool and Healaugh (very different establishments, by-the-bye, from the Norman houses of the twelfth century); and Hiva's name, which would doubtless have been connected with one or more of the twelve, may serve as a director and guide thereto.

These monastic institutions flourished and had their day; some were probably destroyed by marauding Danes, others perished from various accidents, but neither the memory nor the local habitation of even one of them has been preserved. It is, indeed, quite possible that some may still be in existence as parish churches, carrying on their religious work to the present day; but I suspect that in most instances the form of development taken by them was that of hospitals, in which case, being probably on low lands by the bank of a stream, they would differ from those of the eleventh and twelfth centuries, which were on high lands, and at the hilly extremities of manors. As hospitals they would hardly have escaped the Dissolution wave of the sixteenth century, when the links which might have bound the past to the present would have been rudely snapped and disconnected. In a word, with respect to the past, we know that such institutions were founded, though we cannot say where, for we cannot trace their continuance; while, with respect to the present, where such institutions survive, it is with an unknown past; the connecting link has perished, or been lost sight of. Probably in some cases the evidence of the connection still exists, though no one has had the good fortune to interpret the indications,

Spital Hardwick I think to be one of these manors of Oswiu, and that it was an approximate tithe of Pontefract I gather from its Domesday extent, two carucates out of eighteen (*Domesday*, i, 316, 379), a tithe dedicated to religious service, to God and the poor. It had probably originally belonged to Queen Ethelburga, the Kentish princess who came northward under the care of Paulinus to wed the Northumbrian King Edwin, with a guarantee that her religious rights should be respected. The story is well known ; her royal husband was converted, but Edwin having been attacked, defeated, and slain in battle at Winwoodfield by Penda the heathen king of Mercia, Ethelburga returned to Kent, still in the guardianship of Paulinus, taking with her her infant daughter Eanfleda, who had been under the charge of St. Hilda at Whitby, but leaving at Pontefract in two forms (Tateshale and Taddenscylf) her pet name Tadae ; as perhaps she did at Adwick and at Tadcaster.

The land would on her departure have reverted to the new king Oswiu, and been dedicated by him (one of the joint founders of Peterborough Cathedral) to God and the poor, the Hospital of St. Nicholas for thirteen poor people being the ultimate result.

That these two carucates, here 440 acres, have preserved much of their original appearance is due to the manor never having been subdivided or built upon, except on the top of one of the hills, there called Fairy (that is Ferry) Hill. Thus, in its natural features and in the compactness of its ownership, the nineteenth century sees it almost exactly as the ninth century may have done, or the eighth, or the seventh. It is situate on the very borders of sandstone and magnesian limestone, where the intervening sand gives frequent indications of its presence and crops out in such a manner that the limestone hills to the north and east are separated from the sandstone valleys to the south and west by a serpentine line of sand alternately west, north and east ; with moreover the coal outcrop, which extends from the north-east to the south-west throughout this district, similarly cropping up even in the very close in which the present farmstead is situate, and causing it to receive the name of Coal Pit Close. The surface, as may therefore be expected, displays in many parts marks of the attempts which succeeding generations have made to search for stone and coal and sand, attempts which here and there have left their evidence in the shape of a roughened surface. For the practice is to mine in search of the sand, extract what is easily obtainable, and when no more can be had, to retire, break down the props and pillars which have till the last supported the headway, and so to allow the thin roof of the excavation to fall in, with an irregular surface as the result.

This charter, No. 471 [469], is evidently the production of a stranger or of someone not intimately acquainted with the locality. As has been mentioned, its subject is the last plot in Pontefract proper, which is here described as "in the Field of Hardwick, lying near the way by which we go from Pontefract to the mill of Hardwick towards the east." Now here are two false descriptions, which could not have been written by anyone who knew the locality. In the first place, there never were any "Hardwick Fields." The districts described in the eleventh and twelfth centuries as Fields had been the outlying unappropriated moors between two Angle settlements; and Hardwick never had such, because the whole land to the utmost of its extent had been appropriated and brought into cultivation before the time of the Angles and their peculiar subdivision of the land. Thus throughout the manor of Spital Hardwick there is not the smallest trace of that Field system, with its long curving plots, which a reference to the map will show to be so marked a feature in the division of the land both in Ferrybridge and Pontefract on the southern side of the border. The difference in the method of the subdivision of the land is indeed most distinct. Moreover, in the neighbourhood of neither of the groups of buildings at Spital Hardwick, or on Fairy (Ferry) Hill, are there any of those strips so general in the neighbourhood of an Angle settlement.

Drunken Flat belonged to the North or Ferry Field—to the Field which had been divided between the two settlements of Ferry and Pontefract; for the term North Field was applied to the whole northern breadth of the Pontefract manor to the south of Hardwick; never, except in this instance, is any part of it called Hardwick Field.

But again the Hardwick group of buildings is, in this charter, called a mill, which there is no other evidence that it ever was. Nor has it now the appearance of having been such at any time. It is thus clear that this formal document was drawn up on the basis of inaccurate information.

The owner, as we learn, had been Agnes, co-heiress of Roger de Ledstone, whose pedigree will be found on page 506. She was at its date in her first widowhood; and as there is no mention of her son John, whom in No. 554, under date 1251, we shall find confirming this deed, it is probable that the Drunken Flat was dower land, and that it was hers out of the estate of her deceased first husband, William of Parlington, by right of her widowhood.

No. 472 [470] has been already considered under No. 461 ; but, as has been said, No. 96 shows a gift to the monks by Robert de Stapleton I (*cir*. 1170) of "a toft above the Pool," which may perhaps be of this property, for no other indication of it has yet emerged.

No. 457, No. 460, and No. 473 [471] refer to the same acre and a half, part of the same North Field as that called the "Field of Hardwick" in No. 471 [469]. The Waterfall lies between two roads leading from Monkhill, and, while it can be reached from the road to [Spital] Hardwick, it is directly approached only from the road leading from St. Thomas's Hill. The former route, as that used by the monks, seems to have been in the mind of the writers of these charters, and a glance at the map will show how much more convenient it was to them, at least for access on foot.

In No. 473 [471] the ground rent was increased from the former eighteen pence to two shillings, but probably the culture of this last charter contained an addition to the acre and a half which was leased in No. 457 and which William son of Geoffrey (the second husband of Agnes daughter of Roger de Ledstone) had in No. 460 assigned to Hugh son of Gilbert.

In No. 130 and No. 131 we saw the Matilda of No. 474 [472] and Isabel her sister assigning to Jordan Campion their interest in a half acre in the Fields near the land of Thomas son of Edwin, which half acre Jordan subsequently assigned to the sacristan of the monks "to promote the works of the church." Of Isabella we hear no more ; nor do we discover anything of the unnamed husband of Matilda, who at some little interval of time (she had been married and become a widow; the earlier charter had been tested by Simon Butler, this by Simon's son as seneschal) is thus parting with other two acres, in, however, separate plots.

No. 475 [473] has a nearly contemporary marginal note, " Ponsf': De quodam mesuagio et una acra terre pro vj denariis," thus altogether omitting mention of the two acres and a half behind the Hospital. There is also a late note, apparently by Dodsworth himself, calling attention to the notice of " Hospitalis sancti Michaelis." He does not, however, appear to have localized it. The site was facing the Darrington road, No. 181 on Hepworth's Survey, the area of the whole plot, including the site of the buildings, being 3 a. 1 r. 30 p. The "messuage which belonged to Robert White, the weaver," is No. 300 on Hepworth's Survey. It was for some generations in the ownership of Matthew Hutchinson and his ancestors. The "acre of land between two roads" was No. 213 on

2 N

the same Survey. This acre had belonged by right of marriage to William de Calne (see No. 464), whose daughter Agnes, claiming through her mother Emma, co-heir of Roger third son of Ailric, made this grant. It remained in the possession of the monks at the Dissolution, and till then had not been granted away. (See a paper by myself in the *Yorkshire Archæological Journal*, vol. x, 533, when, however, I had not had the advantage of access to this, Chartulary.)

I do not identify either of the properties mentioned in No. 476 [474].

No. 477 [475] is clearly the root of the title of No. 469 [467], and that Beatrice the wife was joined in the conveyance infers that the plot was part of her dowry. No. 103 shows the Astin land to have been near St. Thomas's Hill.

No. 458 was the root of the title of William son of Hervey to the land mentioned in No. 478 [476], but the two documents exhibit some differences. "Kaskin" is in the later charter "Kaskan," and Butellarius has become Pincerna. Moreover, the rent is made payable at St. Michael's Day (as usual for the lord's rent) instead of Easter, as in No. 458, and it is reduced from fourteen pence to thirteen, perhaps because the net content of the plot had been ascertained more accurately.

In the "little charter," p. xl, the holding was said to have been one of seven acres; on Hepworth's Survey it is No. 531 and measured as 6 a. 2 r. 20 p. Probably in the former valuation, the balk (now made into a lane and called, with the usual tautology, "Lady Balk Lane"), or part of it (between what appears to have been No. 530, one of the possessions of Simon Butler, and the assart here granted), was reckoned with it, to complete the seven acres of the "little charter."

William de Daneport was the only common witness.

No. 479 [477] and No. 480 [478] are complementary and apparently contemporary, though only the second is dated, and only the last-named witnesses to the second charter are common to both. In the first charter all the witnesses are lay, but in the monastic document securing the corrody the names preserved are those of the seneschal, three ecclesiastical witnesses, and finally the three laymen common to both.

Each of the documents is written in a fine hand, which, though not the same, was evidently modelled on, and very nearly contemporary with, the original. Each charter is fully rubricated and has the usual alternate red and blue initial which belonged to the bulk of the documents of the Chartulary.

No. 480 [478] contains a very early dated example of the details of a corrody, and it is interesting to have on record such full particulars of the bargain.

Of all the lands which Walter the receiver had accumulated with such anxious care during the course of so many years, and the particulars of which are to be gathered from the deeds immediately preceding, that portion which fell to Hugh, probably his youngest son (who in the next charter is called "Hugh the clerk"), are in No. 479 [477] and No. 480 [478] being exchanged away for a simple maintenance for life—a corrody consisting of bread, beer, and cooked food, with an additional yearly gift of ten shillings in silver, no provision being made for clothing.

It might have been wished that the lands had been enumerated in more particular terms, and that a copy of Walter's charter to his son had been entered in the Chartulary; but the monks must have thought that sufficient record was being made by the enrolment of the string of charters with that special heading which preceded No. 457.

It may be noted that the word used for the allowance of beer is galonem; in such documents it is generally lagonem. I have not met with the word galonem in any other document, but there can be no mistake about it in this instance. It is most clear.

There have been other instances of similar corrodies in No. 146, No. 171, and No. 207, those of a server, of a porter, and of a monk respectively; but the details, even in No. 146, though fairly full, are by no means so clearly particularised as in the document before us, which is of twenty or thirty years later date than any of them.

Indeed, I have met with no earlier instance of the gift of a corrody than those in this Chartulary. One was published by the late Mr. Albert Way in the *Archæological Journal* of 1862, vol. xix, 335, but that was only of the year 1345, and he instanced others of 1280 and 1307, apparently with the impression that they were phenomenal; but even this No. 480 [478] is one, two, or three generations earlier than any of those; while each of the other Pontefract corrodies is of a generation still earlier. In vol. xciv of the Surtees Society (*Fines, John*), p. 25, No. LIX, we have the corrody "unius servientis," but without particulars; while p. 101, No. CCLVII, gives a corrody consisting of "panem et cervisiam et pulmentum unius canonici,"

The document, No. 480 *bis*, concludes the transactions of three generations of secular clerks, all good friends to the monastery:— Master Ciprian (see No. 22 and No. 92); Walter the receiver, his son, the sedulous accumulator; and Hugh the clerk, son of Walter, who by this charter both confirmed what his elder brother John had given, and renounced all contingent rights which he might have in the property. It might be thought that this Hugh, son of Walter, was Hugh the vicar or dean of Pontefract, who makes a frequent appearance in the Chartulary; but there is nothing to prove the identity, and something against it. Hugh the vicar seems to have held the appointment before the commencement of the register of Archbishop Gray and till after its close; thus his name does not occur in that record, and we are therefore altogether cut off from the fount to which we should instinctively look for the information. In Torre's list the earliest vicar is Hugh de Birkesborough, and he without a date, whose successor was instituted in 1263, *i.e.* in the archiepiscopate of Godfrey de Ludham. And this was probably the Hugh, vicar of Pontefract, who tested No. 153.

No. 480 *bis* is in that finer and slightly later hand in which nearly contemporary additions were made to many of the fasciculi of the Chartulary, and these additional documents were generally, as in this case, without rubricated headings. A blank half column followed, in which was afterwards inserted, in a coarse fourteenth century hand and bad ink, so that in parts it is almost illegible, a Final Concord of Michaelmas, 35 Henry III [1251], between Prior Dalmatius, querant, and Hugh son of Walter, impediant, which ratifies the transaction. In this Final Concord the property concerned is said to consist of two messuages and thirty-eight acres. It is numbered 480 (*ter*), but is really No. 480, and completes the recto of fo. 74.

There was further application to the Court with regard to this property, for Mr. W. Paley Baildon (Y.A.S. Record Series, xvii, 168), though without any reference to the Fine of 1251, publishes the following :—

1263. Hugh fil' Walter *v.* the Prior of Pontefract, to hold to a fine made between Dalmatius, formerly Prior of Pontefract, plaintiff, and the said Prior, defendant, concerning two messuages and 38 acres of land in Pontefract.

And the "said Prior" being defendant in the case appealed to, this last-named must have been an intermediate action, between 1251 and 1263.

It may be noted that the regnal year of Henry III commenced on 28 October; so that 12 November, 1250, and Michaelmas term, 1251, were each within the limits of 35 Henry III, the one a fortnight from its commencement, the second a fortnight from its close. And also that "Walter receptor" is in No. 480 *bis* [479] "Walter le recevour"; while Hugh his son is "Hugh le clerc," showing the change which was passing over the language.

No. 483 [481] is in that finer hand which succeeded to the original. It was perhaps more artistic, but it introduced many abbreviations of a more abstruse character, which are much more difficult to decipher by any but the initiated. It embraces also some subtle distinctions which are not to be found in the older writing; for instance, Sir William Vavasour was constable of "the Castle of Pontefract," while Peter de Santon was seneschal "of Pontefract," Foliot has become Folyot in the text, while it remains Folioth among the signatories, and Swillington has become Swinlington, perhaps from an attempt to throw the etymology up to Swain, son of Ailric, who, as we have seen in No. 238 and No. 297 and as this scribe evidently knew, had once owned land there.

The chapel of St. Nicholas, Cobcroft, granted by No. 484 [482], can hardly have been considered a successful foundation. It was one of many attempts made in the twelfth and thirteenth centuries to establish a chapel in an outlying district. Some few succeeded and exist to the present day as parochial chapels, chapels of ease, or parish churches. But the far larger number, having been established to furnish only a temporary convenience, were neglected when the temporary want ceased to be felt. They then fell into decay, their buildings generally reverting to the lord, perhaps in the very manner provided for in this charter, and being given over to secular uses. Or if they survived till the Reformation, they were for the most part treated as chantries dedicated to superstitious uses, and abolished under the searching *régime* of the times of Edward VI. The chapel of Cobcroft was of the former class, and Prior Stephen of Pontefract, instituted 5 ides November, 1230, seems to have been the only incumbent; at least he is the only one of whom I have met any trace.

As was generally the case with these chapels, that of St. Nicholas, Cobcroft, was a simple rectangular building, with no chancel and no aisles. It is now a stable; or, rather, a stable of two compartments is built upon its foundations.

Cobcroft is in Womersley parish, in an outlying part of the township of Cridling Stubbs, and within a short distance both of the parish of Kellington and of the extremity of Knottingley, which is in the parish of Pontefract.

It is curious that the phraseology of this charter would imply that a monk was necessarily ordained, and that any monk could celebrate. Such is a very common mistake, but of course it was not the case; the celebrant would be one of those monks who were in priests' orders.

Edwin son of Walter, whom we meet in No. 486 [485], was one of the holders of land "in the moor" by the "little charter." He was nearly the largest holder, having as much as 11½ acres. His father Walter was the youngest son of Ailric and the youngest of the troop of brothers that so frequently followed Jordan of Ledstone. The pedigree of the family will be found facing Fasciculus V.

The grant here made to him consists of the two bovates of land at Flockton which were given to the monks by No. 263, and their history is worth tracing.

(1) William son of Hervey had given them to William de Hotton.

(2) By No. 263 William de Hotton gave them to the monks "to possess in peace," and this with no apparent reservation.

(3) By No. 264 Adam de Byram (brother of William son of Hervey, the original grantor,) confirms them to the monks, again "to possess in peace."

(4) But from the present charter we learn that the grant was really on condition that Edwin son of Walter, and his heir, should hold them in fee and heirship: a limitation doubtless justified, but one which is not warranted by anything which appears on the original charters.

The Chartulary contains no No. 486, and No. 487 is a form of presentation to the church of Kippax. This is under date 1397, and is from H., prior. . It names M., late rector of the church of Kippax, Thomas [Arundel], then Archbishop of Canterbury, recently promoted from York, and W. P., rector of the church of Harweonhull [Harrow-on-the-hill], the presentee, as the incomer. It is thus remarkable that this document indicates a prior of Pontefract, of whom nothing else is known, and two rectors of Kippax, neither of whose names occurs even in that most painstaking compilation, Torre's list.

This last omission is to be accounted for, however, by the presentation having been made during the vacancy of the Archi-episcopal see, after the death of Robert Waldby, when the dean and chapter had possession of the spiritualities, and the various transactions were entered not on the archbishop's books (for the see was vacant and there was no archbishop), but on those of the dean and chapter. These Mr. Torre does not seem to have examined. This therefore is an instance of the many defects and lacunæ in the wonderful amount of information which that painstaking investigator accumulated.

The Tenth Fasciculus concludes with a blank of rather more than half of the first column of the retro of fo. 75, the presentation to Kippax (No. 487) occupying the whole of the second column.

The documents thus far given complete the body of the Chartulary, as that word is generally understood,—the collection, that is to say, of the charters granted to the monks during the 160 years that preceded the middle of the thirteenth century by their lords—royal, episcopal and lay—and by their numerous benefactors of every degree.

The next and last Fasciculus, which we now approach, contains a copy of the charters (mainly leases) from the monks to their tenantry, which were in force at that time, though some few, as for instance No. 500 and No. 505, have come astray into it, which should have found a place in one of the earlier sections; and similarly, some that should have been reserved for this last Fasciculus appear in earlier sections of the volume. Such are No. 135, No. 146, No. 152, No. 156 and No. 161; after which the method of the compiler was always to reserve such leases for the final Fasciculus.

In this last Fasciculus the documents seem to have been entered indiscriminately as they came to hand; or, if there is any method in their arrangement, it is difficult to supply the key to it. For the most part, though even so far as this is concerned there is no uniformity, the rents were payable half-yearly, at the ecclesiastical terms of Whitsuntide and St. Martin; and the documents are all, except one (No. 539, from Prior Bertram), of the five priors, Hugh, Walter, Fulk, Stephen and Dalmatius. Peter, who ruled between Stephen and Dalmatius, does not appear to have granted any lease that has been here preserved.

FERIBY: DE PASSAGIO ET TRIBUS BOVATIS TERRE ET DIMIDIA
CUM XIIII MANSURIS.

CCCLXXXXVIII.   Carta Symonis comitis Lincolnie.

[Simon the earl to all his men and all the faithful of Holy Church, greeting.
I have confirmed . . . . the ford of South Ferriby, as the charter of my predecessor
Gilbert de Gaunt witnesses, and three bovates and a half of land, with 14 houses,
in the same town . . . . . . Witnesses.]

Symon comes omnibus hominibus suis et omnibus fidelibus sancte
ecclesie salutem.   Sciatis me concessisse et confirmasse hac carta
mea ecclesie sancti Johannis de Pontefracto et monachis qui ibidem
deo serviunt passagium de Suthferiby, sicut carta antecessoris[1] mei
Gilleberti de Gant testatur, et iij bovatas terre et dimidiam cum xiiij
mansuris in eadem villa in puram et perpetuam elemosinam et
liberam ab omni seculari exactione de me et de heredibus meis.
Testibus, *Willelmo de Mundevilla, Herberto de Horbiri, Thoma Pilato,
Safrea, Hugone de Bartona, Johanne filio Yvonis, Saxelino de Hesala.*

---

(1) There is a clear distinction here between ancestor and antecessor. Simon de St. Liz was
not of the blood of Gilbert de Gaunt, but was his son-in-law, having married his daughter Alice.
He thus possessed the property in right of his wife, and Gilbert was his antecessor, not his
ancestor.

SUTTH FERIBI : ET DE PASSAGIO ET ALIIS.

CCCLXXXXIX.   Carta Gilleberti comitis Lincolnie.

[. . . . . . I, Gilbert, Earl of Lincoln, have granted . . . . . . the ford of South
Ferriby, and three bovates of land and a half, with three houses in that town, and
besides them eleven other houses there, ... free and quit from all earthly
service, for six librates of rent, which I have pledged to them for the damage
which I brought upon them and their church through the war between me and
Henry de Lascy; and they have taken me into their fraternity and into the
participation of all the benefits of all their houses. Witnesses.]

Gillebertus comes Lincolnie universis matris ecclesie filiis salutem.
Notum sit omnibus tam presentibus quam futuris me dedisse et
concessisse in perpetuam elemosinam deo et ecclesie sancti Johannis
de Pontefracto et monachis ibidem deo servientibus passagium de
Suthferibi et tres bovatas terre et dimidiam, cum tribus mansuris in
eadem villa, et preter hec undecim alias mansuras ibidem. Hanc
vero elemosinam dedi et concessi ecclesie et fratribus predictis
liberam et quietam ab omni terreno servitio pro sex libratis redditus
quas pepigi eisdem pro dampno quod intuli eis et ecclesie eorum de
guerra illa deinter me et Henricum de Lascy, et ipsi me susceperunt

in fraternitatem suam et participationem omnium beneficiorum universarum domorum suarum.   Hiis testibus, *Gaufrido de Gant, Baldewino de Gant, Philippo de Kyme, Abbate de Rugford, Rogero canonico de Bredlingtona, Radulfo filio Gilleberti, Herberto de Horreby, Waltero clerico, Radulpho de Feriby.*

SUTH FERIBI, ET DE PASSAGIO ET ALIIS.

CCCC.   **Carta Gilleberti comitis de Lincolnia.**

[. . . . . I, G., Earl of Lincoln, have . . . . . confirmed to God and St. Mary and the church of St. John, &c., ... the ford of South Ferriby and three and a half bovates of land, with fourteen houses in that town, and six acres in the Fields of Barton, and nine acres in the territory of Hawkstowe, ... for six librates of rent yearly, which I had covenanted to pay the monks, ... for the very great injuries which I have brought upon the aforesaid church and monks in the war between me and H. de Lascy.   The monks have had me absolved from the excommunication with which they had me excommunicated, and have taken me into full fraternity.   They shall hold the aforesaid ford and lands, with all liberties, &c. Warranty.   If any of my heirs shall diminish or disturb this my alms, may he have God's curse and mine, till he shall have won suitable pardon.   Witnesses.]

Omnibus sancte ecclesie filiis presentibus et futuris Gillebertus comes Lincolnie salutem.   Noverit universitas vestra quod ego G. comes Lincolnie dedi et concessi et hac mea presenti carta confirmavi deo et sancte Marie et ecclesie sancti Johannis evangeliste de Pontefracto et monachis ibidem deo servientibus, in puram et perpetuam elemosinam, solutam et quietam ab omni seculari exactione, passagium de Suthferibi et tres bovatas terre et dimidiam, cum quatuordecim mansuris in eadem villa, et sex acras in Bartunie campis, et ix acras in territorio de Horkestoue.   Hoc passagium et has terras dedi predicte ecclesie et predictis monachis pro sex libratis redditus per annum quas pepigeram et affidaveram sepedictis monachis persolvere pro salute anime mee et omnium antecessorum meorum et heredum, pro maximis dampnis que predictis ecclesie et monachis, culpis meis exigentibus, intuli in guerra illa que fuit inter me et H. de Lascy.   Et ipsi monachi fecerunt me absolvi de excommunicacione qua fecerunt me excommunicari et susceperunt me in plenariam fraternitatem ecclesie sue et totius ordinis sui.   Predictum passagium et predictas terras cum omnibus libertatibus et pertinentiis et aisiamentis tenebunt et habebunt predicti monachi in bene et pace sicut decet puram elemosinam et perpetuam.   Hanc vero elemosinam ego et heredes mei warentizabimus predictis monachis contra omnes homines.   Siquis vero heredum meorum hanc elemosinam meam in aliquo minuerit vel perturbaverit, maledictionem dei et meam habeat donec de presumptione sua condignam veniam promoverit. Hiis testibus, *Galfrido de Gaunti*,[1] *Baldewino de Gant, Phillippo de Kime, Abbate de Rugford, Rogero canonico de Bridlingtona, Radulfo filio Gilleberti, Willelmo filio Walteri, Waltero clerico, Radulfo de Ferriby.*

---

(1) *Sic.*

DE SCITHLINGTONA : DE QUADAM TERRA PRO III SOLIDIS.

CCCCI.   **Carta Willelmi comitis Warena.**[1]   Ante 1139.

[. . . . . I, W., Earl of Warren, and I, Ysabel, countess, have granted . . . . . from the land of Saxe, which he possesses in Shitlington, three shillings every year until we otherwise give charge. Witness.]

Notum sit omnibus hominibus qui sunt et qui venturi sunt quod ego W. comes de Warena et ego Ysabel comitissa concedimus monachis de sancto Johanne de terra Sacsi, quam idem Sacse habet in Silintona, tres solidos unoquoque anno donec inde aliud precipiamus. Teste, *Waltero presbitero.*[2]

---

(1) As he died in 1138, this charter must be of a date not later.

(2) Walter the priest may be the Walter who signed the record of the foundation of St. Clement's Chapel.

SCARDEBURGA : DE REDDITU IIII SOLIDIS ET IIII DENARIIS.

CCCCII.   **Carta Symonis de Scardeburga.**

[. . . . . I, Simon, son of William Gamel of Scarborough, ... have granted . . . . a rent of four shillings and four pence in Scarborough, that is to say, forty pence from a toft near the chapel of St. Thomas which Richard Redking holds, to be received . . . . . . half at Whitsuntide and half at the feast of St. Martin, and the said Richard shall pay yearly to the lord king from that toft four pence ; and from three roods of land which lie above Ramsdale, between the land of William de Boston and the land of Margaret de Pa', twelve pence, which pence Richard, the son of Ralph, who holds the acres, shall pay, half at Whitsuntide and half at the feast of St. Martin, and to the lord king four pence. Also I have . . . . granted a toft in Scarborough, where my father's barns were built, and two crofts in Burtondale, out of which toft the monks shall pay to the lord king four pence, and for the crofts eight pence. The monks shall hold all in perpetual alms, &c., for all which belong to me or my heirs. Seal. Witnesses.]

Sciant presentes et futuri quod ego Symon filius Willelmi Gamelli de Scardeburga, pro salute anime mee et patris mei et matris mee et omnium antecessorum meorum, dedi, concessi, et presenti carta mea

confirmavi deo et sancto Johanni apostolo et ewangeliste de Pontefracto et monachis ibidem deo servientibus, in liberam, perpetuam
elemosinam, redditum iiij*or* solidorum et iiij*or* denariorum in villa de
Scardeburga.   Scilicet quadraginta denarios de uno tofto juxta
capellam sancti Thome quod Ricardus Redking tenet, recipiendos
prefatis monachis de eodem Ricardo, medietatem ad Pentecosten et
medietatem ad festum sancti Martini, et de quo tofto idem Ricardus
reddet annuatim domino Regi iiij*or* denarios.   Et de tribus percatis
terre que jacent super Ramisdale, inter terram Willelmi de Bostun et
terram Margarete de Pa'[1] duodecim denarios, quos denarios Ricardus
filius Radulfi qui tenet predictas acras prefatis monachis persolvet,
medietatem ad Pentecosten et medietatem ad festum sancti Martini ;
et insuper domino regi iiij*or* denarios.   Item dedi, concessi, et
presenti carta mea confirmavi prefatis monachis unum toftum in
predicta villa de Scardeburga ubi grangia patris mei fundata sunt, et
duos croftos in Burtundale, de quo tofto predicti monachi reddent
domino regi iiij*or* denarios et pro croftis octo denarios.   Hec omnia
habebunt et tenebunt prefati monachi in perpetuam elemosinam,
pacifice, integre, libere et quiete, pro omnibus que ad me vel heredes
meos pertinent.   Et ut hec mea donatio et concessio firma et stabilis
perseveret predictis monachis inperpetuum, huic carte pro me et
heredibus mèis sigillum meum apposui.   Hiis testibus, *Roberto
Fareman, Ucctredo de Wiverdethorph, Rogero filio ejus, Henrico de
Haverforda, Ernisio fratre ejus, Waltero filio Willelmi Gamel, Ricardo
Redking,* et aliis.

(1) *Sic.*

SCARDEBURGA : DE CLAMEQUITANCIA UNIUS CORREDII.

CCCCIII.[1]   **Carta Symonis de Scardeburga.**

[. . . . . I, Simon Gamel of Scarborough, have quit-claimed . . . . the
corrody which I have been accustomed to receive, for half a mark of silver. . . . .
I have promised also and have sworn, touching the gospels, that as to the rents which
they possess in Scarborough . . . . . . the monks shall hereafter incur no hindrance
or burden.   Seal.   Witnesses.]

Notum sit omnibus hoc scriptum visuris vel audituris quod ego
Symon Gamel de Scardeburga quietum clamavi deo et sancto Johanni
apostolo et ewangeliste de Pontefracto et monachis ibidem deo

---

(1) These two charters are supplemented by No. 419 (which is somewhat earlier in date than
No. 402), and also by No. 432 (from Walter the brother of this grantor), which confirms it. This
last gives some further particulars of the site. No. 499, No. 507, and No. 543 are subsequent leases.

servientibus illud corredium quod ab eis percipere solitus eram, pro dimidia marca argenti, quam mihi in magna necessitate mea contulerunt. Promisi etiam bona fide et tactis sacrosanctis juravi quod de redditibus, quos in supradicta villa de Scardeburg ex collatione doni mei et carte mee confirmatione possident, quam quidem cartam penes se habent, prefati monachi nullum de cetero per me vel per alium aliquem ex parte mea impedimentum vel gravamen incurrent. In cujus rei testimonium huic scripto sigillum meum apposui. Hiis testibus, *Thoma filio Willelmi capellani, Johanne Sanfal, Petro Janitore, Ada Lefranceis, Jordano de Kelingley,* et aliis.

BRETTONA: DE CLAMEQUITANCIA IIII DENARIORUM VEL DIMIDIE LIBRE PIPERIS, ET DE SERVITIO FORINSECO ACQUIETANDO PRO UNA CARRUCATA TERRE.

CCCCIIII.   Carta Radulfi filii Rogeri de Newby.

[. . . . . I, Ralph, son of Roger of Newby, have quit-claimed to Henry Neeloth all the service which I have in that carucate of land in Bretton which he has there held of me, that is to say, four pence a year, or half a pound of pepper. Warranty. Acquittance. Witnesses.]

Sciant omnes tam presentes quam futuri quod ego Radulfus filius Rogeri de Neuby dedi et quietum clamavi Henrico Neeloth totum servitium quod habui in illa carrucata terre in Brittona quam ipse ibi de me tenuit hereditarie, scilicet quatuor denarios per annum vel dimidiam libram piperis. Et ego et heredes mei warentizabimus ei et cuicumque ipse eam assignare voluerit et defendemus et adquietabimus eam de forinseco servitio. Hiis testibus, *Johanne de Distefalding, Thoma de Langwada, Magistro Willelmo de Shelduna, Alano de Onapetuna,*[1] *Willelmo Baska,* et aliis.

---

(1) This may be Snapeton.

BROCTONA: DE UNA CARUCATA TERRE CUM PERTINENTIIS.

CCCCV.[1]   Carta Henrici Neeloth. .

[. . . . . . I, Henry Neeloth, ... have confirmed . . . . . a carucate of land with appurtenances, which I have possessed in Bretton. To be possessed and held, &c., as is contained in the charters which I had from my patrons, as well in men as in rents and lands. Seal. Witnesses.]

Sciant presentes et futuri quod ego Henricus Neeloth, pro salute anime mee et antecessorum meorum, concessi et dedi et presenti

---

(1) I have met with no transcript of any of the last five charters.

carta confirmavi deo et sancto Johanni ewangeliste de Pontefracto et monachis ibidem deo servientibus unam carrucatam terre cum pertinentiis, sine aliquo retenemento, quam habui in Brettona.[2] Habendam et tenendam in puram et perpetuam elemosinam, adeo libere- et quiete sicut ego eam unquam melius habui et liberius, et sicut in cartis quas de advocatis meis inde habui continetur, tam in hominibus quam redditibus et tefris quibuscumque.   Ut autem hec mea concessio et donatio firmum robur et inconcussum optineant presens scriptum sigilli mei munimine roboravi.   Hiis testibus, *domino Johanne de Byrkina*,[3] *Rogero fratre suo, Ada de Bella aqua, Ricardo de Hudlistona, Jordano de Landa*, et aliis.

---

(2) There is no internal evidence to indicate with certainty in which Bretton these lands were situate, but a marginal memorandum to No. 505 in *Dodsworth*, vol. 151, says that Neeloth's land was in Bretton-juxta-Brotherton, which would be Burton Salmon.   In No. 421 we have a transaction between the same parties concerning a carucate of land in Bretton which Pigot son of Hugh had held.   It may have been one and the same.

(3) He was the brother of•Adam.

SUTH FERIBY : DE PASSAGIO ET ALIIS NOMIN . . .[1]

CCCCVI.[2]   Carta Alicie[3] comitisse filie Gilleberti de Gaunt.

[. . . . . I, Countess Alice, daughter of Gilbert de Gaunt, ... have confirmed . . . . . . the ford of South Ferriby, as the charter of my father Gilbert de Gaunt witnesses, and three bovates of land and a half with 14 houses. . . . . . Witnesses.]

Aliz comitissa, filia Gilleberti, de Gant, omnibus hominibus suis et omnibus fidelibus sancte ecclesie salutem.   Sciatis me concessisse et confirmasse hac carta mea ecclesie sancti Johannis de Pontefracto et monachis qui ibi deo serviunt passagium de Suthferibi, sicut carta patris mei Gilberti de Gant testatur, et iij bovatas terre et dimidiam cum xiiij mansuris in eadem villa, in puram et perpetuam elemosinam, et liberam ab omni seculari exactione de me et de heredibus meis. Testibus,[4] *Willelmo de Mundevilla, Hereberto de Horriby, Thoma Pilato, Safray, Hugone de Bartona, Johanne filio Yvonis, Saxelino de Hesala.*

---

(1) The end of the line is obscured in the binding.   Without opening the binding it is quite impossible to ascertain it.   As so many of these marginal headings are henceforth similarly obscured, they have been generally omitted.

(2) There is an abstract of No. 406 in *Lansdowne* 207.

(3) After her father's death she was titular " Earl " of Lincoln.

(4) No. 406 is signed by the same witnesses as No. 398, with which it seems to have been contemporary; indeed, the two charters may be considered to have represented parts of the same transaction,

CCCCVII.[1]   Carta Radulfi filii Nicholaya.

[. . . . I, Ralph, son of Nicholas, ... have confirmed . . . . . the rent of my workshops in Bradley, that is to say, ten shillings yearly, which the monks of Fountains shall pay to the monks of Pontefract at the accustomed terms. This alms I have given for the good of my soul, &c. The witnesses are, &c. I have made this gift with the advice and consent of my wife Mabel.]

Omnibus filiis sancte matris ecclesie Radulfus filius Nicholaye salutem. Noverit universitas vestra me concessisse et in perpetuam elemosinam donasse et hac mea carta confirmasse deo et sancto Johanni et monachis de Pontefracto redditum fabricarum mearum in Braddeleya, scilicet decem solidos annuatim quos persolvent eisdem monachis de Pontefracto monachi de Funtaines eisdem terminis quibus mihi persolvere consueverunt. Hanc elemosinam dedi eis pro salute anime mee et uxoris mee Mabilie et patris et matris mee et omnium antecessorum et heredum meorum. Hujus pure et perpetue elemosine testes sunt, *Robertus presbiter de Dardintona et Thomas capellanus suus, Hugo frater meus de Danefelda, Ricardus Vavasur, Ricardus de Barneby, et uxor mea Mabilia,* cujus consilio et concessione hanc donationem feci. ———

(1) I have met with no copy of No. 407.

———

CCCCVIII.[1]   Carta Thome presbiteri de Harewode.

[. . . . . I, Thomas the priest, have granted to Gilbert de Lasci and his heirs two bovates of land in Harwood. To be held in wood and in plain, &c., paying yearly three shillings and spurs of the price of three pence. . . . . . The bovates are those which Thomas holds of Henry de Eland in Great Harwood, and of which he has his charter. Witnesses.]

Sciant presentes et futuri quod ego Thomas presbiter dedi et concessi Gilleberto de Lasci et heredibus suis duas bovatas terre in Harewode, in feodo et hereditate. Tenendas de me et heredibus meis in bosco et in plano, in pratis et paschuis et in aquis, cum omnibus pertinentiis, libere et quiete, reddendo annuatim tres solidos et calcaria pretii trium denariorum pro omni servitio preter forinsecum servitium. Et sciendum est quod ille bovate sunt quas Thomas

(1) There is a copy of No. 408 in *Dodsworth*, vol. 151. It is the correlative of No. 240, and contains some curious and instructive differences in the names of the two first witnesses. Eudo de Lungwils of the former charter is here Ivo de Lungvilla; Alan the sheriff is here Alan of Kippax. Moreover, Harwood is definitely stated to be Great Harwood. The wapentake is Clitheroe,

tenet de Henrico de Elandia in magna Harewod et de quibus suam cartam habet. Testibus, *Yvone de Lungvilla, Alano de Kippes, Ricardo de Lewes, Waltef capellano, Willelmo de Mitton, Ricardo pistore, Hugone de Mittona, Nicholao clerico, et Willelmo filio Roberti, et toto wapentakio.*

CCCCIX.   Carta Alicie de Gaunt.

[. . . . . . I, Alice de Gaunt, ... have granted . . . . . a carucate of land in Ingolvesmeles, for the soul of my former lord, Ilbert de Lascy, who gave it to me in dower . . . . . . Henry de Lascy granted it to them. The witnesses are, &c.]

Omnibus sancte matris ecclesie fidelibus Aliz de Gant salutem. Notum vobis facio me concessisse et dedisse in puram et perpetuam elemosinam ecclesie sancti Johannis ewangeliste de Pontefracto et monachis in ea deo servientibus unam carrucatam terre in Ingolvesmeles, pro anima prioris domini mei Ilberti de Lascy qui mihi illam in dotem dedit, et pro salute mea. Quam etiam Henricus de Lascy illis concessit et carta[1] sua confirmavit. Hujus donationis testes sunt, *Willelmus filius Walteri de Wella, Salomon filius ejus, Gocelinus de Aufort, Ricardus de Smythetona, Ranulfus frater ejus, Willelmus pistor monachorum, Rainaldus filius Anketilli de Dardingtona.*

---

(1) See No. 16.

CCCCX.[1]   Carta Rogeri de Molbrai.

[. . . . . . I, Roger de Mowbray, ... grant . . . . . . a carucate of land in Ingolvesmeles, which my wife has given to them . . . . free and quit from all services. The witnesses are, &c.]

Rogerius[2] de Molbrai omnibus hominibus suis cunctisque sancte matris ecclesie fidelibus salutem. Sciatis quod confirmo et concedo monachis de Pontefracto carrucatam terre in Ingolvesmeles, quam uxor mea dedit eis, pro salute corporum et animarum nostrarum et pro anima prioris domini sui Ilberti de Lasci, liberam et quietam ab omnibus servitiis, sicut decet elemosinam, in plano, in aquis, in pratis, et in omnibus adjacentibus predicte terre. Hujus donationis testes sunt, *Samson capellanus ipsius Rogerii, Willelmus Peverel, Ricardus Burdet, Turgis de Molbrai, Henricus de Waeprez, Walterus de Daivilla.*

---

(1) No. 409 and No. 410 are No. XII and No. XIII in the *Monasticon,* and there is a transcript of the latter in *Lansdowne,* vol. 207.   (2) *Sic.*

CCCCXI.[1]   Carta Johannis de Builli.

[. . . . . . I, John de Busli, have given . . . . . half an acre of land with its toft in Kimberworth, which Godwin of Hillam holds, for a light in the chapel of St. Victor the Martyr, and the aforesaid Godwin with all that belong to him. Witnesses.]

Sciant presentes et futuri quod ego Johannes de Builli dedi et hac mea presenti carta confirmavi deo et sancto Johanni apostolo de Pontefracto et monachis ibidem deo servientibus dimidiam acram terre cum tofto ejusdem terre pertinente in Kymberwordia,[2] quam Godwinus de Hillum tenet, in liberam et puram et perpetuam elemosinam, ad luminare in capella sancti Victoris martiris, et predictum Godwinum cum omnibus que ad eum pertinent, pro remedio anime mee et pro animabus antecessorum meorum. Hiis testibus, *Hugone de Scauceby, Roberto filio Ricardi de Crokestune, Alano capellano, Hugone capellano de Roderame, Ricardo Pistore, Johanne de Curci, Radulfo Coco.*

---

(1) There is an inaccurate copy of No. 411 in the *New Monasticon*, No. xxxv. There was no copy in Dodsworth's *Monasticon*, that of 1655, but the editors of the new volume copied it from Stevens, to whom Thoresby, the Leeds historian, supplied it, professedly from the original deed. He did the same with No. 311, and in each case his copy was blundered. Here, however, it furnishes three additional names of witnesses, which were omitted in the copy preserved in the Chartulary, showing that the latter was independent of Thoresby's copy. In Thoresby's copy the last seven names are "Hugone de Monkesburgo, Hugone capelano de Roderham, Radulpho de Aigrano, Richardo Pistore, Willielmo de Monkesburgo, Johanne de Curci, Radulpho Coco." The first, third and fifth of these were omitted in the Chartulary.

(2) The *Monasticon* spells it Kingberwordia and has the correct form, "eidem terre," instead of "ejusdem terre."

CCCCXII.[1]   Carta comitis Albemarlie.   1190-5.

[. . . . . . I, William de Fortibus, Earl of Albemarle, ... have granted . . . . . . the carucate of land in Broughton, and the house with appurtenances, which the lady Alice de Rumelli gave to them, as contained in her charter. Witnesses.]

Omnibus sancte matris ecclesie filiis presentibus et futuris Willelmus de Forz comes Albemarlie salutem. Noverit universitas vestra me pro amore dei et pro salute anime mee et omnium meorum concessisse et presenti carta mea confirmasse deo et sancto Johanni et monachis de Pontefracto illam carrucatam terre in Broctuna et mansuram in eadem villa cum pertinentiis suis in puram et perpetuam elemosinam, quas eis dedit et carta sua confirmavit domina Aaliz de Rumelli, sicut continetur in carta ipsius domine Aaliz. Hiis testibus, *Willelmo Britone, tunc dapifero, Willelmo Painel, Magistro Michaele, Willelmo de Scalleby, Rainero Flemang,* et aliis.

---

(1) No. 412 is No. xv in the *Monasticon*, and there is a transcript in *Lansdowne*, vol. 207. It was clearly from the first William de Fortibus, who was Earl of Albemarle from 1190 to 1195.

CCCCXIII.[1]   Carta comitis Albemarle.

[The Earl of Albemarle to his steward and his barons of Holderness greeting. I grant . . . . . . half the church of Catwick, which Ralph of Catwick gave, and I ordain that they hold it in peace. Witnesses. Farewell.]

Comes de Albemarla dapifero suo et baronibus suis de Holdernessa salutem. Sciatis quod ego concedo monachis sancti Johannis de Pontefracto dimidiam ecclesiam de Cattewic, quam dedit eis Radulfus de Cattewic, et volo et precipio ut eam in pace teneant. Teste,[2] *Willelmo Biseth et Giroldo* et aliis baronibus meis multis. Valete. ————

(1) There is a copy of No. 413 in *Lansdowne* 207.   (2) *Sic.*

CCCCXIV.   Carta Radulfi filii Gilleberti.

[. . . . . . I, Ralph son of Gilbert, and my wife Constance, grant, ... in alms for us and our ancestors, the land which is between Cunelund and the river Nidd and the old road which is called Steinrig even to Omatum, the head of the pool which is called Blather, and the meadow which is called Flather, and the wood which is between the meadow and the pool, and a half acre of land which belonged to my demesne between the river and the pool. Witnesses.]

Radulfus filius G. omnibus fidelibus sancte dei ecclesie tam clericis quam laicis in Christo salutem. Notum sit vobis omnibus quod ego et uxor mea Constantia damus et concedamus[1] deo et sancte Marie et sancto Johanni de Pontefracto in elemosinam pro nobis et antecessoribus nostris, scilicet terram que est inter Cuneland[2] et aquam que vocatur Nid et via antiqua[1] que vocatur Steinrig usque ad Omatum, caput stagni quod vocatur blather, et pratum quod vocatur flattether, et nemus quod est inter pratum et stagnum, et dimidiam acram terre que pertinebat ad meum dominium que est inter aquam et stagnum. Teste,[1] *Willelmo filio G. et Radulfo Rustico fratre ejus, et Benedicto de Fenne, et Roberto Bone et Galfrido clerico suo, et T. de Tuschet, et Reinero de Willetonia.* ————

(1) *Sic* in each case.

(2) The names are so debased and obscured that, in the absence of any other charter to throw light upon them, it is difficult to do more than guess at the locality to which they refer. It seems to be somewhere north and east of Pateley Bridge, in the upper course of the Nidd, and "Cuneland" is possibly the neighbouring township which borders to the west the two Steinbecks (Upper and Lower).

CCCCXV.   Carta Alicie quondam uxoris Petri de Broctona.

[. . . . . I, Alice, formerly wife of Peter de Broughton, have quit-claimed to the prior and monks and my sons, William and Adam, the third part of four bovates of land in Broughton which fell to me as dower, and which William and

Adam my sons hold. Neither I nor anyone on my part shall have or demand any right or claim in it. The prior and monks have granted to me, for my life, those two bovates of land in Broughton which Ulchel has held. For five shillings and four pence, to be paid yearly to the secretary of the monks, half at the feast of St. Martin and the other half at Whitsuntide. Witnesses.]

Omnibus has litteras visuris vel audituris Alicia quondam uxor Petri de Broctona salutem in domino. Noverit universitas vestra me quietam clamasse in tota vita mea dominis meis priori et monachis de Pontefracto et filiis meis Willelmo et Ade totam terciam partem quatuor bovatarum terre cum pertinentiis - in villa de Broctona que mihi contigit nomine dotis, et quas Willelmus et Adam filii mei tenent. Ita quod nec ego nec aliquis ex parte mea in tota vita mea aliquod jus vel clamium in tercia parte predictarum quatuor bovatarum terre habeamus vel exigamus. Pro hac autem quieta clamantia predicti prior et monachi dimiserunt et concesserunt mihi tantum in vita mea illas duas bovatas terre cum pertinentiis in villa de Broctona quas Ulkel tenuit. Tenendas et habendas libere et quiete, pro quinque solidis et iiij*or* denariis secretario predictorum monachorum annuatim solvendis, medietatem ad festum sancti Martini et aliam medietatem ad Pentecosten. Hiis testibus, *Willelmo capellano, Johanne de Lovain, Johanne filio Hugonis de Batelay, Henrico filio Randolfi, Johanne filio Symonis, Ricardo de Martona*, et aliis.

416.[1]   Carta Willelmi filii Petri de Brettona.

[. . . . . I, William son of Peter de Bretton, ... have quit-claimed . . . . . half an acre of meadow in east Hallstead, in the territory of Bretton. That is to say, a fifth rood and a sixth which lie next the pasture towards the north, on one side, one acre excepted ; and on the other side next my meadow towards the south. To be held and possessed, &c. . . . . . . Warranty. Witnesses.]

Sciant presentes et futuri quod ego Willelmus filius Petri de Brettona, pro salute anime mee et omnium antecessorum et heredum meorum, dedi, concessi, et hac presenti carta mea confirmavi, et inperpetuum de me et heredibus meis quietam clamavi deo et sancto Johanni de Pontefracto et monachis ibidem deo servientibus dimidiam acram prati in este hallestede in territorio de Brettona. Scilicet quintam perticatam et sextam que jacent propinquiores pasture versus

---

(1) From this point onwards the use of Roman numerals is almost entirely dropped.

north ex una parte, excepta una acra prati, et ex alia parte juxta pratum meum versus sud.   Tenendam et habendam prefatis monachis inperpetuum in liberam; puram et perpetuam elemosinam.   Et ego prenominatus Willelmus et heredes mei warentizabimus, defendemus et adquietabimus prefatis monachis predictam dimidiam acram prati contra omnes homines.   Hiis testibus, *Johanne de Birkina, Roberto de Barkestuna, Ricardo de Hudlestuna,*[2] *Roberto de Lalanda, Waltero de Byrum, Ricardo de Suttona, Serlone de Brettona,* et aliis.

---

(2) Possibly this was the son of Hugh fitz Asolf (see pp. 254-5).

---

417.   **Carta Ricardi**[1] **filii Alicie de Martona.**

[. . . . . . I, Richard son of Alice de Marton, have granted . . . . my homage and service and that of all my heirs for ever, and when I shall have passed from this life the monks shall have all my goods, as well on my lands and in my houses as in all other things or beasts.   In acknowledgment I will give four pence yearly, on Whit-Sunday.   And they have received me into their full protection in life and limb; and at the last they have granted me burial in their cemetery.   Seal. I have offered it on the high altar of the aforesaid church.   Witnesses.]

Sciant presentes et futuri quod ego Ricardus filius Alicie de Martona dedi, concessi, et hac presenti carta mea confirmavi deo et ecclesie sancti Johannis de Pontefracto et monachis ibidem deo servientibus homagium meum et servitium et omnium heredum meorum inperpetuum, et cum ex hac vita migravero habebunt predicti monachi domini mei omnia catella mea que ad me in die obitus mei pertinebunt, tam in terris et domibus quam in omnibus aliis rebus vel bestiis.   Et ad recognitionem omnium predictorum dabo predictis dominis meis annuatim iiij*or* denarios, in die Pentecostes.   Et ipsi in plenariam protectionem suam me tanquam hominem suum in vita et membris receperunt, et ad ultimum in cimiterio suo mihi sepulturam concesserunt.   Et ne ego vel aliquis alius contra tenorem hujus carte inposterum venire possimus, eam sigilli mei munimine roboravi et super majus altare predicte ecclesie optuli.   Hiis testibus, *Serlone de Brettona, Salomone de eadem, Gaufrido Pigot, Ada de Aula,* et aliis.

---

(1) The grantor of this charter, occasionally known as Richard de Pontefract, Richard de Marton, and Richard de Aula, was for a considerable time an official witness for the monks, as he is in No. 418; he was afterwards their porter, and appears, from No. 171, to have died while holding that office.

418.   Carta Hugonis filii Thome. [1]

[. . . . . . I, Hugh son of Thomas of Bilham, have granted . . . . . . a bovate
of land in Stotfold with a toft, next the toft of Robert Pore, lying towards the
west, which William son of Hugh of Bilham gave me.   To be held and possessed,
&c.   Paying yearly to the aforesaid William or his heirs twelve pence, six pence
at the feast of St. Martin and six pence at Whitsuntide . . . . . . I have made the
monks my assigns.   Seal.   Witnesses.]

Sciant presentes et futuri quod ego Hugo filius Thome de
Bilam dedi, concessi, et hac presenti carta mea confirmavi deo et
ecclesie sancti Johannis de Pontefracto et monachis ibidem deo
servientibus, pro salute anime mee et omnium fidelium, unam bovatam
terre in territorio de Stodfold cum tofto juxta toftum Roberti Pore[2]
jacente versus west.   Illam scilicet bovatam quam Willelmus filius
Hugonis de Bilam michi dedit pro homagio et servitio meo.   Tenendam et habendam predictis monachis in perpetuam elemosinam,
libere, quiete, pacifice et integre, cum omnibus libertatibus et aisiamentis predicte terre infra villam de Stodfold et extra pertinentibus.
Reddendo inde annuatim predicto W. vel heredibus suis xij denarios,
scilicet vj denarios ad festum sancti Martini et sex ad Pentecosten,
pro omni servitio seculari vel demanda, faciendo forinsecum servitium
quantum pertinet ad unam bovatam terre de eodem feodo.   Ad hanc
vero meam donationem et concessionem firmiter roborandam predictos
monachos assignatos meos feci et hoc scriptum sigillo meo in
testimonium roboravi.   Hiis testibus, *domino Hugone Pincerna, domino
Henrico Walensi, Ricardo de Lund, Waltero receptore, Thoma de Bilam,
Johanne Vinitore, Ricardo de Mariona*, et aliis.

(1) He witnessed No. 136.   (2) This name is partially blotted.

---

419.   Carta Symonis de Scardeburga.

[. . . . . . I, Simon son of William Gamel, burgess of Scarborough, ...
have granted . . . . a plot which I have in Scarborough, which lies next
the wall of the lord king, towards the sea, and adjoins on one side to land of
Roger son of Uctred, and on the other to the public street.   To be held and
possessed, &c.   Paying yearly to the lord king four pence at the feast of the blessed
apostles Peter and Paul.   Warranty.   Seal.   Witnesses.]

Sciant presentes et futuri quod ego Symon filius Willelmi Gamel,
burgensis de Scardeburga, pro salute anime mee et antecessorum et
heredum meorum, dedi, concessi, et hac presenti carta mea confirmavi
deo et ecclesie beati Johannis apostoli et ewangeliste de Pontefracto

et monachis ibidem deo servientibus, in perpetuam elemosinam, unam placiam quam habui in territorio de Scardeburga. Illam scilicet que jacet juxta murum domini Regis versus mare, et adjungitur ex una parte terre Rogeri filii Uctredi, et ex alia publice strate. Tenendam et habendam libere et quiete, pacifice et honorifice, cum omnibus libertatibus et aisiamentis ad eandem placiam infra villam de Scardeburga et extra pertinentibus. Reddendo inde annuatim domino regi quatuor denarios ad festum beatorum apostolorum Petri et Pauli pro omni servitio seculari, exactione et demanda. Hanc autem donationem et confirmationem ego Symon et heredes mei prefatis monachis contra omnes homines warantizabimus inperpetuum. Et ut hec mea donatio et confirmatio firma sit et stabilis presens scriptum sigilli mei appositione roboravi. Hiis testibus, *Thoma de Linberch*,[1] *Henrico de Haverford, Roberto Fareman, Rogero Haldam, Symone Birger*, et aliis.

(1) "Thomas de Lingeberge" witnesses No. 499.

---

420. Carta Salomonis de Brettona.[1]

[. . . . . . I, Solomon de Bretton, have sold, granted and confirmed . . . . a bovate of land in Bretton . . . . which I bought of Geoffrey Pigot. To be held and possessed, &c. All the right and claim which I had, or could have, I have quit-claimed to the monks. For this the monks, in my great necessity, have given me seven and a half silver marks. Warranty. Seal. Witnesses.]

Sciant presentes et futuri quod ego Salomon de Brettona vendidi, concessi, et hac presenti carta mea confirmavi dominis meis priori et conventui de Pontefracto unam bovatam terre in territorio[2] de Brettona cum omnibus pertinentiis suis, libertatibus, et aisiamentis, tam infra villam de Brettona quam extra, ad dictam bovatam terre pertinentibus. Illam scilicet bovatam quam emi de Galfrido Picot. Tenendam et habendam dictis monachis in liberam, puram, et perpetuam elemosinam, sine aliqua contradictione vel impedimento mei vel heredum meorum inperpetuum. Et insuper totum jus et clamium quod habui vel unquam aliquo modo habere potui in dicta bovata terre vel in ejus pertinentiis dictis monachis de me et omnibus heredibus meis vel assignatis sine aliquo retenemento quietum clamavi. Pro hac vero vendicione, concessione, et confirmacione et quieta clamacione dederunt mihi monachi in mea

---

(1) It is probably from this Solomon, or from one of the same name, that the distinctive appellation of Burton "Salmon" was derived. But in No. 417 it would appear that Bretton was only a descriptive name, so far as Solomon was concerned. For he is there called Solomon "de eadem."

(2) No. 528 describes the Fields of Bretton as lying between Bretton and Fairburn.

magna necessitate septem marcas argenti et dimidiam in manibus. Et ego Salomon et heredes mei vel mei assignati totam predictam bovatam terre cum omnibus pertinentiis suis predictis monachis contra omnes homines inperpetuum warentizabimus ac defendemus. In cujus rei testimonium tam pro me quam pro heredibus meis huic scripto sigillum meum apposui. Hiis testibus, *domino Henrico Walensi, Adam de Prestona, Waltero de Ludham, Serlone de Brettona, Galfrido de Mercam, Willelmo de Byrum*, et aliis.

421.   Carta Rogeri de Neubi.[1]

[. . . . . . I, Roger de Newby, have granted . . . . . to Henry Neeloth and his heirs, for his homage and service, a carucate of land in Bretton, which Pigot son of Hugh held, with all Pigot's service. To be held, &c., paying to me and my heirs yearly . . . . half a pound of pepper, within the octave of the apostles Peter and Paul, and doing to the lord king free forinsec service, as much as belongs to a carucate of land where twenty carucates make a knight's fee. I have granted them the said carucate of land, in tofts and crofts, in land arable and non-arable, in wood and plain, &c. Witnesses.]

Sciant presentes et futuri quod ego, Rogerus de Neuby, concessi et dedi et presenti carta mea confirmavi Henrico Neeloth et heredibus suis in feodo et hereditate, pro homagio et servitio suo, unam carrucatam terre in Brettona. Illam scilicet quam Pigotus filius Hugonis tenuit, cum toto servitio Pigoti integre sine ulla retentione. Tenendam de me et de heredibus meis hereditarie, libere, quiete, et pacifice, reddendo mihi et heredibus meis annuatim pro omni servitio et exactione que ad me pertinent vel ad heredes meos dimidiam libram piperis infra octavam apostolorum Petri et Pauli, et faciendo liberum forinsecum servitium domino Regi, quantum pertinet ad unam carrucatam terre, unde viginti carrucate terre faciunt feodum unius militis. Dictam carrucatam terre eis concessi et dedi in toftis et croftis, in terra arabili et non arabili, in bosco et plano, in pratis et paschuis, in moris et mariscis, in viis et semitis, in introitibus et exitibus, et in omnibus aliis pertinentiis et aisiamentis que ibidem habere poterint. Hiis testibus, *Magistro Rogero Arundel, Magistro Radulfo de Kyme, Magistro Willelmo de Gilling, Alano canonico de Rip', Gilberto capellano, Roberto de Lanum, Adam de Byrum*, et aliis.

---

(1) In No. 404 his son Ralph confirms the grant, and in No. 405 Henry Neeloth grants it to the monks. This Henry was last on the list of witnesses to No. 91, the charter of Jordan son of Jordan Foliot, and was also a purchaser by No. 505.

422.[1]   Carta Roberti filii Bernolfi.

[To all his friends, &c., Robert son of Bernolf greeting. I have granted to Rainer de Waxtonsham all the toft which belonged to Alwin my grandfather in Doncaster, which Richard the chaplain has held. To be held, &c., paying to the lord king 12 pence yearly, and to me and my heirs two pence yearly, a penny at Easter and a penny at the feast of St. Michael. Witnesses.]

Omnibus amicis suis et omnibus litteras istas audientibus, tam presentibus quam futuris, Robertus filius Bernolf salutem. Sciatis me dedisse et concessisse et hac presenti carta confirmasse Ranerio de Waxtunesham[2] totum toftum[3] quod fuit Alwini avi mei in Donecastre quod Ricardus capellanus tenuit. Tenendum de me et de heredibus meis in feodo et hereditate, libere, et quiete, faciendo domino regi servitium suum, scilicet reddendo ei xij denarios annuatim et reddendo mihi et heredibus meis annuatim ij denarios pro omni servitio. Scilicet unum denarium ad pascha et unum denarium ad festum sancti Michaelis. Hiis testibus, *Rogero clerico de Triberge, Willelmo Prat, Adam de Evervic, Hugone de la Marais, Gerardo le Tanur*, et aliis. ————————

(1) I have met with no transcript of any of the last nine charters, from No. 414 to No. 422.
(2) This may be the Rainer of No. 311, who was steward to Ralph de Glanvill.
(3) There is no clue as to its locality in Doncaster.

CCCCXXIII.[1]   Carta Willelmi Maltravers.

[William Maltravers to all his men and friends greeting. . . . . For the deferring of their claim concerning the church of Whalley, I give . . . . . . a silver mark from my rents in assarts, to ·be paid every year on the festival of St. Michael, as long as I shall hold the honour of Pontefract, my wife Dameta assenting. Afterwards if they wish to assert their claim, either by the king's charter or by any other way, let not their claim be damaged on account of this. Witnesses.]

Willelmus Maltravers omnibus hominibus et amicis suis salutem. Notum vobis esse volo quod ego do monachis sancti Johannis de Pontefracto pro anima mea et pro exspectatione calumpnie sue de ecclesia de Walleya unam marcam argenti de redditibus meis in essartis, unoquoque anno reddendam in festivitate sancti Michaelis, laudante hoc et volente uxore mea Dameta; et hoc quamdiu tenebo honorem Pontisfracti. Postea autem si voluerint agitare calumpniam suam, vel per cartam regis quam inde habent vel per aliud, non sit calupnia[2] eorum pejorata propter istud factum. Testibus, *Hugone filio G.*,[3] *et Mengi, et Reginaldo, et Waltero filio Hugonis, et Rand' filio Orm.* ————————

(1) No. 423 is No. xxvii in the *Monasticon*. There is also an imperfect transcript in *Lansdowne*, vol. 207, and an abstract in *Dodsworth*, vol. 159.   (2) *Sic*.
(3) Possibly Gilbert of Stapleton.

CCCCXXIIII.[1]　　　　Carta comitis Albemarl'.

[W., Earl of Albemarle, to the Archbishop of York, and every clerk, and all barons, and all his ministers, greeting. I have granted . . . . . . half the church of Catwick which Ralph de Catwick has given them, and as Earl Stephen my father granted, and I command all mine that they do no injustice to the monks concerning its tenure. Witnesses. At Hornsea.]

W. comes Albemarl' archiepiscopo Eboracensi et omni clero et omnibus baronibus et omnibus ministris suis salutem. Sciatis me concessisse et confirmasse monachis sancti Johannis de Pontefracto dimidiam ecclesiam de Catewic quam dedit eis Radulfus de Catewic, et sicut Stephanus comes pater meus concessit et confirmavit. Et precipio omnibus meis quod predictis monachis de predicta tenura nullam faciant injuriam. Testibus, *Rogero de Toleha', Roberto constabulario, Radulfo Venatore, Benedicto Camerario, Agnete de Albemarl'.* Apud Hornesel.

(1) There is a copy of No. 424 in *Lansdowne* 207. It is the confirmation of No. 413, the grantor of which it specifies for the first time.

425.　　　　　Carta Willelmi de Welleken.[1]

[To all the faithful of Holy Church, William de Welleken greeting. I have granted . . . . . . a house in Barneby which was Brictina's, with a toft of half an acre, and a half acre in Oldfield, and another half acre in Rylands, with all common easements, ... for a conventual pittance at the hand of the sub-prior on Whit-Sunday. Witnesses.]

Omnibus fidelibus sancte ecclesie Willelmus de Welleken salutem. Sciatis quod ego concessi et donavi et hac mea carta confirmavi deo et sancto Johanni de Pontefracto et monachis ejusdem loci unam domum in Barneby que fuit Brictine cum tofto dimidie acre et unam dimidiam acram in Aldefeld et alteram dimidiam acram in Rilandis, cum omnibus communibus aisiamentis predicte ville in puram et perpetuam elemosinam de me et de heredibus meis, pro salute anime mee et uxoris mee et heredum meorum et patris mei Gaufridi et patrui mei Roberti et omnium antecessorum meorum, ad pitantiam conventus in manu supprioris in Pentecosten. Hiis testibus, *Ricardo de Stagno et filiis ejus Ricardo et Adam, Jordano de Ledestuna, Waltero fratre suo, Thoma senescallo,*[2] et aliis.

(1) There is no clue to the personality of this William de Welleken. The places named in the charter belong to the Barnsley district, but the witnesses to that of Pontefract.

(2) Thomas the seneschal is the monk's dapifer, father of Michael of Monkhill. The names of "dapifer" and "seneschal" were at this time often interchangeable, of which there is an instance in Guisborough Chartulary, where Edmund Seneschal witnesses No. 305, a charter of Richard Cumin, and is called Edmund Dapifer shortly afterwards in No. 306, a confirming charter from the widow.

426. Carta Jordani de Keswic.

[. . . . . . . I, Jordan de Keswick and Odierna my wife, owe to the prior and convent two silver marks to be paid half on the day when "Letare Jerusalem" is sung and half at Whitsuntide. In the meantime the prior and convent have delivered to us a bovate of land with appurtenances in Keswick, which Agnes, the mother of Hodierna, has held. If it should happen that at the appointed terms we have not paid the aforesaid debt, we will that that bovate revert to the prior and convent, so that neither we nor our heirs can hereafter have any right therein. Seals. Witnesses.]

Omnibus has litteras visuris vel audituris Jordanus de Keswic et Odierna[1] uxor ejus salutem in domino. Noverit universitas vestra nos debere dominis nostris priori de Pontefracto et ejusdem loci conventui duas marcas argenti solvendas ad duos terminos, scilicet medietatem ad diem qua cantatur Letare Jerusalem[2] et medietatem ad Pentecosten. Et interim domini prior et conventus nobis tradiderunt unam bovatam terre cum pertinentiis in villa de Keswic. Illam scilicet quam Agnes mater predicte Hodierne[1] tenuit. Si vero contigerit quod ad terminos statutos debitum predictum non solverimus, volumus et concedimus ut predicta illa bovata terre cum pertinentiis antedicto priori et conventui sine contradictione aliqua revertatur, ita quod nos nec heredes nostri in posterum aliquod jus vel clamium in illa bovata terre cum pertinentiis habere vel exigere possimus, et ad maiorem hujus rei securitatem huic scripto sigilla nostra apposuimus. Hiis testibus, *Willelmo capellano, Johanne Lovain, Johanne de Batelay, Thoma fratre ejus, Henrico filio Matildis, Roberto Haraldo, Ricardo de Martona,* et aliis.

(1) The name appears thus, both with the aspirate and without. What could be the special reason for her parents naming her "To-day's"?

(2) "Letare Jerusalem" is Mid-Lent Sunday. See No. 93 and note there.

---

427. Carta Osberti de Baius.[1] Circa 1180.

[. . . . . I, Osbert de Bayeux, grant . . . . a bovate of land in Middle Haddlesey, with Roger, the son of Gamel, dwelling thereon, with all his following, freely and quietly, &c. This I give for the good of my soul and that of my lord Thurstan, the archbishop, and the lord Henry de Lascy, &c. Warranty. Witnesses.]

(1) This is probably the Osbert Baiocensis who is the first witness to No. 311, and who gave to the monks of Guisborough a half carucate of land in Bradley near Grimsby and common of pasture in that town for sixty cows and sixty horses. His charter to Guisborough has not been preserved, but the confirmation of the gift by King Henry II in 1182 is given as No. 17 in the Guisborough Chartulary (page 17), from which the bare fact may be ascertained.

Sciant presentes et futuri quod ego Osbertus de Baius do et concedo et hac mea carta confirmo deo et sancto Johanni de Pontefracto et monachis ibidem deo servientibus unam bovatam terre in media hatelsaia, cum Rogerio filio Gamelli manente super eandem bovatam, cum omni secta sua et cum omnibus catallis suis, libere et quiete, in bosco, in plano, in pratis, in paschuis, in viis, in semitis, in aquis, et in omnibus libertatibus, in puram et perpetuam elemosinam. Hanc bovatam do predictis monachis pro salute anime mee et domini mei Turstini archiepiscopi et domini Henrici de Lascy[2] et omnium antecessorum meorum et heredum meorum. Quam bovatam ego Osbertus et heredes mei warentizabimus predictis monachis contra omnes homines. Hiis testibus,[3] *Adam de Reinevilla dapifero, Adam filio Petri, Thoma fratre suo, Roberto*[4] *filio predicti Ade, Maugero de Stivetona, et Hugone filio suo,* et aliis.

(2) It must not be supposed that "my lord Thurstan the archbishop" and "the lord Henry de Lascy" were in any sense contemporaries (which indeed is not here claimed for them); for Thurstan died in 1141, before Henry de Lascy had attained his lordship.

(3) The grantor and five out of these six witnesses test No. 311, though it may have been an earlier Hugh de Stiveton who gave the third of Peckfield to the monastery; for his grant was confirmed by Henry II as early as 1155 (No. 71 and No. 73).   (4) He died about 1185.

CCCCXXVIII.   Carta Roberti abbatis Sancte Marie Eborascensis.

[To all the sons of Holy Mother Church, &c., brother Robert, by the grace of God abbot of St. Mary of York, greeting in the Lord. . . . . Robert son of Roger Wallis, of Ledsham, formerly our serjeant, has in our presence given to the house of Saint John, &c., a rent of two shillings yearly in the town of Pontefract, to be received from that messuage which Walter the baker has held, which is between the land late of Sir William de Vescy, and the land late of John Langovinus. Because the said Robert had not his own seal then with him, we made this letter at his request and sealed it with our seal. And in witness we have given this letter to the monks. Witnesses.]

Omnibus sancte matris ecclesie filiis ad quos presentes littere pervenerint frater Robertus[1] dei gratia abbas sancte marie Eborascensis salutem in domino. Universitati vestre notum facimus quod Robertus filius Rogeri Wallensis de Ledeshama,[2] quondam serviens noster, in

(1) It is not clear which Robert, abbot of York, did this friendly service for Robert son of Roger Wallis. There were two abbots of that name in the time covered by the Chartulary; Robert de Harpham from 1184 to 1189, and Robert de Longchamp, who succeeded and presided till his death in 1239, having been abbot for fifty years. The latter is probably the grantor of this charter, and it was probably he also who as Sheriff of Yorkshire would have appointed Alan de Kippax as vice-sheriff (see p. 43).

(2) Newton Wallis being a hamlet of Ledsham, it is not improbable that in Roger Wallis, "formerly our serjeant," we have the hitherto unnamed father of Robert Wallis, and may identify the real grantor of this charter with the oft-named seneschal to Roger de Lascy and sometime vice-sheriff.

presentia nostra dedit domui sancte Johannis Ewangeliste de Pontefracto et monachis ibidem deo servientibus, in puram et perpetuam
elemosinam, redditum duorum solidorum annuatim in villa Pontisfracti
percipiendorum de illo mesuagio quod Walterus pistor tenuit, quod
scilicet mesuagium est inter terram quondam domini Willelmi de
Vescy et terram quondam Johannis Langovini.[3] Et quia[4] predictus
Robertus sigillum suum proprium tunc secum non habuit, ad preces
ipsius has litteras fecimus et eas sigillo nostro sigillavimus. Et in
predicte donationis testimonio has litteras nostras sigillo nostro
sigillatas predictis monachis tradidimus. Hiis testibus,[5] *domino Roberto
de Skegnesse, tunc senescallo nostro, magistro Rogero Pepin, Willelmo
Cervo, Walt'o pistore de Pontefracto,* et aliis.

---

(3) In No. 97 this appears as Lang', in No. 119 and No. 143 as Langevinus, and here as Lango'.

(4) This, like the instance in No. 259, is an illustration of the inherent value then attaching to a seal. It seems as if any seal would have answered the purpose, because any seal was supposed to add to the value and validity of the deed to which it was attached.

(5) None of the witnesses seems to have been a local man, except Walter the baker. Each was probably in the train of the Abbot of York.

---

429.   Carta Roberti filii Dd' de Poles.[1]   Circa 1231.[2]

[. . . . . . I, Robert, son of Dd' de Pollington, have granted . . . . an acre
of land in the Fields of Bretton, namely two roods and a half in the Furthest
Intake, near the ginnel towards the south, a half rood between the lord's land and
the Prior's land, a half rood in the Fields towards the west, and a half rood in
Reginald's croft. To be held and possessed, &c. They have given me in hand
four shillings. Seal. Witnesses.]

Sciant presentes et futuri quod ego Robertus filius Dd' de Poles
dedi, concessi et hac presenti carta mea confirmavi et omnino de
me et heredibus meis quietum[3] clamavi deo et ecclesie sancti Johannis
apostoli et ewangeliste de Pontefracto et monachis ibidem deo
servientibus unam acram terre in campis de Brettuna. Scilicet duas
perticatas et dimidiam in extremo Jnthac juxta venelam versus suth,
et dimidiam perticatam inter terram domini et terram prioris de
Pontefracto in rodis, et dimidiam perticatam in campis versus west,
et dimidiam perticatam in crofto Reginaldi. Tenendas et habendas
predictis monachis in perpetuam elemosinam. Pro hac vero donatione
et concessione dederunt michi pre manibus iiij*or* solidos. Et ne ego

---

(1) This charter is a sequel to No. 265, by which Robert, son of David, bought the acre of
Geoffrey, son of Pigot, for three shillings in hand and a rent of three half-pence. By No. 429 he
sells all his rights in the land for four shillings. The acre was in four different parts of the manor.
Poles is probably Pollington, and this David may possibly be David the son of Harvey Kaskin.

(2) A dated charter (No. 178), which contains the names of Henry Wallis, Jordan Pateman, and
Richard de Marton, serves to fix this date.   (3) *Sic.*

Robertus vel heredes mei contra hanc donationem et concessionem venire possimus huic scripto sigillum meum apposui in testimonium. Hiis testibus, *Henrico Walensi, Serlone de Brettona, Waltero de Birum, Salomone de Brettona, Jordano*[4] *Pateman, Ricardo de Martona,* et aliis.

---

(4) Jordan Pateman is frequently accompanied by Roger Pateman, but with no indication of relationship.

---

430.   Carta Walteri de Evermu.[1]

[To all the sons of Holy Mother Church, &c., Walter de Evermu greeting. I have granted . . . . to God and St. Mary, &c., a bovate of land in Middle Haddlesey, with all its liberties and appurtenances, &c., with the wife of Roger, son of Gamel, living upon that bovate, with all her following . . . . . . Witnesses.]

Omnibus sancte matris ecclesie filiis presentibus et futuris Walterus de Evermu salutem. Sciatis me concessisse et presenti carta mea confirmasse deo et sancte marie et ecclesie sancti Johannis evangeliste de Pontefracto et monachis deo ibidem servientibus unam bovatam terre in media Hatelsaia, cum omnibus libertatibus et pertinentiis suis, in boscho et plano, in pratis et pascuis et viis et semitis, cum uxore Rogeri filii Gamelli manente super eandem bovatam terre, cum tota secta sua, in puram et perpetuam elemosinam. Hiis testibus, *domino Henrico de Putheaco,*[2] *Johanne de Birkin, Rogero et Symone de Rugala,*[3] et aliis. ————

(1) Walter de Evermu was Sheriff of Lincoln in 1230-2.

(2) Sir Henry de Putheaco was the son of the great Bishop of Durham, so frequently miscalled Hugh de Pudsey. This bishop, properly Hugh de Puiset, was the sister's son of King Stephen and of Henry de Blois, Bishop of Winchester, and cousin of Archbishop (Saint) William. His eldest son, Sir Henry de Puiset, was a prominent man in this district, having married Dionysia de Tilli, co-heiress of Otto de Tilli of Conisborough and Doncaster.   (3) See No. 365, note (4).

---

431.   Carta Thome de Tornetona.[1]

[. . . . . . I, Thomas de Thornton, have granted . . . . . . a bovate of land in Denby, with toft and croft and with all appurtenances and easements, which I have held from Helias, son of Henry, and which lies nearest to the east of the bovate which Robert, son of Richard, holds from me . . . . Warranty and acquittance. Witnesses.]

Sciant presentes et futuri quod ego Thomas de Thornethona dedi, concessi et hac carta mea confirmavi deo et sancto Johanni et

---

(1) Thomas de Thornton had extensive possessions in Thornton, its hamlet Denby, and beyond Pontefract. He married Isolda, daughter and, after the death of her brother Henry (see No. 156 and No. 159), heir of William de Preston, whose charter (No. 157) he witnessed. He had no male heir, and his eldest daughter and co-heir, Matilda, married Robert de Horton, while the younger, Incella, married twice: (1) Hugh de Brodcroft and (2) William Scot of Calverley. (See page 385.)

monachis de Pontefracto unam bovatam terre in Deneby cum tofto et crofto et cum omnibus pertinentiis suis et aisiamentis ejusdem ville. Illam scilicet quam tenui de Helia filio Henrici et que jacet proxima versus orientem juxta bovatam quam Robertus filius Ricardi tenet de me, pro anima mea et pro animabus patris et matris mee et omnium antecessorum et heredum meorum, in puram et perpetuam elemosinam, liberam et quietam ab omni servitio seculari et exactione. Et ego Thomas et heredes mei hanc predictam bovatam terre cum pertinentiis warentizabimus et adquietabimus prefatis monachis contra omnes homines. Hiis testibus, *Robert Wal', tunc vicecomite Eborascensi, Johanne de Birkine, Roberto Wavasore, Willelmo de Stapiltona, Willelmo Gramatico, Rogero Scotto, Raimundo clerico,* et aliis.

432.[1]   Carta Walteri filii Gamel. [2]

[. . . . . . I, Walter, son of William Gamel, of Scarborough, ... have granted . . . . . . a rent of four shillings and four pence in the town and territory of Scarborough, and two crofts in Burtondale, which Simon my brother has given to the aforesaid monks, namely 40 pence from a toft next to the chapel of St. Thomas, which Richard Redking holds hereditarily, and twelve pence from three roods which Richard, son of Ralph, holds hereditarily. Seal. Witnesses.]

Sciant presentes et futuri quod ego Walterus filius Willelmi Gamel de Scareburg, pro salute mee[2] et omnium antecessorum meorum et heredum, concessi et presenti carta mea confirmavi deo et sancto Johanni apostolo et evangeliste de Pontefracto et monachis ibidem deo servientibus, in liberam et perpetuam elemosinam, redditum quatuor solidorum et quatuor denariorum in villa et territorio de Scardeburg, et duos croftos in Burtunedale quos Symon frater meus predictis monachis dedit et carta sua confirmavit. Scilicet de uno tofto juxta capellam sancti Thome quod Ricardus Redking tenet hereditarie xl denarios, et de tribus percatis quas Ricardus filius Radulfi tenet hereditarie xij denarios. Et ut hec mea concessio et confirmatio prefatis monachis firma et stabilis perseveret, huic carte sigillum meum apposui. Hiis testibus, *Roberto Fareman, Uctredo de Vivertorp, Rogero filio suo, Henrico de Haverford, Symone Biger,* et aliis.

---

(1) No. 432 is the correlative of No. 402, the charter of Simon, son of William, the brother of this Walter. Practically the names of the same witnesses are appended to the two charters. No. 402 seems to be a revised edition made at the death of Walter, its grantor.

(2) *Sic* in each case.

433.   Carta Willelmi de Bilam.

[. . . . . . I, William of Bilham, have granted . . . . . to Hugh, son of Thomas
of Bilham, my grandson, for his homage and service, one of the two bovates of land
which I have held of William Bareville in the territory of Stotfold, namely, that
which lies next the land of Robert Pore towards the south part, and a toft which
lies next the tóft of R. Pore towards the east, with all the liberties, &c., the
chief toft being retained for me and my heirs. To be held and possessed, &c.
Paying yearly to me or my heirs twelve pence, six pence at the feast of St. Martin
and six pence at Whitsuntide, saving forinsec service, as much as belongs to a
bovate of land of that fee. Warranty. Witnesses.]

Sciant presentes et futuri quod ego Willelmus de Bilham dedi,
concessi, et hac presenti carta mea confirmavi Hugoni filio Thome
de Bilham nepoti meo, pro homagio et servitio suo, unam illarum
duarum bovatarum terre quas tenui de Willelmo Bareville in territorio
de Stodfold. Illam scilicet que jacet propinquior terre Roberti Pore
versus australem partem, et unum toftum quod jacet juxta toftum
predicti R. Pore versus est, cum omnibus libertatibus et aisiamentis
ad eas infra villam et extra pertinentibus, retento mihi et heredibus
meis tofto capitali. Tenendam et habendam predicto Hugoni et
heredibus suis vel cui assignare voluerit in feudo et hereditate, libere,
quiete, integre, et pacifice, de me et heredibus meis. Reddendo inde
annuatim mihi vel heredibus meis xij denarios, scilicet vj denarios
ad festum sancti Martini et vj denarios ad Pentecosten, pro omni
servitio seculari vel demanda mihi vel heredibus meis pertinentibus.
Salvo forinseco servitio quantum pertinet ad unam bovatam terre de
eodem feudo. Et ego predictus Willelmus et heredes mei predictas
terras cum pertinentiis suis prefato Hugoni et heredibus suis vel suis
assignatis contra omnes homines imperpetuum warentizabimus. Hiis
testibus, *Johanne de Rokel', Jordano de Insula, Thoma de Bilam,
Henrico de Camera, Roberto Pore, Willelmo Barevilla*, et aliis.

434.   Carta Radulfi filii Rogeri Neuby.

[. . . . I, Ralph, son of Roger de Newby, ... have granted all that carucate
of land, with appurtenances, in the territory of Bretton, which Henry Neeloth
formerly conveyed to them. To be held and possessed, &c., with the tofts and
crofts and all other appurtenances, in wood and plain, &c., without anyone's
contradiction. Warranty. Seal. Witnesses.]

Sciant presentes et futuri quod ego Radulfus filius Rogeri de
Neuby, pro salute anime mee et omnium antecessorum et heredum
meorum concessi et hac presenti carta mea confirmavi deo et ecclesie

sancti Johannis apostoli et evangeliste de Pontefracto et monachis ibidem deo servientibus totam illam carrucatam terre cum pertinentiis suis in territorio de Brettona[1] quam Henricus Neeloth eis antea contulit et carta sua confirmavit.[2] Tenendam et habendam dictis monachis, in liberam, puram, et perpetuam elemosinam, cum toftis et croftis et ceteris pertinentiis suis, in bosco et plano, in pratis et paschuis, in moris et mariscis, in aquis et molendinis, in viis et semitis, in introitibus et exitibus, et in omnibus aliis aisiamentis et libertatibus, ad dictam villam de Brettona pertinentibus, sine alicujus contradictione, gravamine vel impedimento. Ego vero dictus Radulfus et heredes mei totam predictam carrucatam terre cum omnibus prenominatis pertinentiis et libertatibus et aisiamentis suis dictis monachis contra omnes homines inperpetuum warentizabimus inperpetuum warentizabimus[3] et defendemus. Et de forinseco servitio et de omnibus aliis exactionibus, sectis et demandis adquietabimus. In cujus rei testimonium huic scripto tam pro me quam pro heredibus meis sigillum meum apposui. Hiis testibus, *domino Thoma de Beleu,*[4] *demino Ricardo de Bereley, domino Jordano de Lalanda, Hugone de Lascy, Thoma de Barkestuna, Johanne de Aquila, Serlone de Brettona,* et aliis.

(1) That is, Burton Salmon. The history of this holding is given more clearly in the earlier charter, No. 421, that of the father Roger. (2) See No. 405. (3) *Sic.*
(4) In No. 405 it is Bella Aqua.

435. Carta Willelmi de Barevilla.

[. . . . . . I, William de Bareville, ... have given . . . . sixteen acres and a half of arable land in the territory of Bilham, with reliefs and wards and all other appurtenances. Five acres lie in East Field, five in Middle Field, five in West Field, three roods are called Riding, a rood abuts upon Hickleton Cross, and a half acre in East Field abuts upon the river Hoton. I have also given the toft with adjoining croft which lies before the gate of Robert de Aynesford, on another part of the way, as closed in by a ditch. These lands Robert de Aynesford formerly held from me for a yearly rent of forty-two pence. Which rent the monks shall receive yearly at the hands of Robert de Aynesford and his heirs at two terms, at the feast of Saint Martin in winter twenty-one pence, and the same at Whitsuntide. All these with their appurtenances the monks shall hold and possess, &c., so that no service or exaction shall be hereafter demanded. Acquittance. The monks have given me in my great necessity thirty shillings of silver. Waranty. Seal. Witnesses.]

Sciant presentes et futuri quod ego Willelmus de Barevilla, pro salute anime mee et omnium antecessorum et heredum meorum, dedi, concessi, et hac presenti carta mea confirmavi deo et ecclesie sancti Johannis apostoli et ewangeliste de Pontefracto et monachis ibidem deo servientibus, in liberam, puram, et perpetuam elemosinam, sexdecim acras terre arabilis et dimidiam in territorio de Bilam cum releviis et wardis, et omnibus aliis pertinentiis suis. Quarum quinque acre terre jacent in Estfelda et quinque acre in Middelfelda et quinque acre in Westfelda et tres perticate terre que vocantur Riding et una perticata que buttat super crucem de Hikiltona et una dimidia acra in Estfeld que buttat super rivulum de Hotona. Et insuper dedi dictis monachis illum toftum cum crofto adjacente qui jacet ante portam Roberti de Aynesforda ex alia parte itineris sicut fossato circumcluditur. Quas quidem terras dictus Robertus de Aynesforda antea de me tenuit cum dictis et tofto et crofto pro annuo redditu quadraginta duorum denariorum. Quem redditum dicti monachi percipient annuatim pro omnibus supranominatis terris per manus dicti Roberti de Aynesforda et heredum suorum ad duos terminos, scilicet ad festum sancti Martini in hyeme viginti unum denarios, et totidem ad Pentecosten. Has omnes supradictas terras cum omnibus pertinentiis suis sicut predictum est tenebunt et habebunt dicti monachi in bene et pace sine alicujus contradictione vel molestia. Ita quod numquam per me vel per heredes meos vel per aliquem alium nisi per predictos monachos aliquid servicii vel exactionis exigetur a dictis terris in posterum. Set ego et heredes mei dictum toftum cum crofto et omnes alias prenominatas terras adquietabimus ab omnibus consuetudinibus, servitiis, sectis et demandis sicut nostram liberam, puram et perpetuam elemosinam. Pro hac autem donatione, concessione et confirmatione dederunt mihi dicti monachi in mea magna necessitate triginta solidos argenti p' manibus. Et ego dictus Willelmus de Barevilla et heredes mei omnia que prescripta sunt in carta ista cum omnibus pertinentiis suis dictis monachis contra omnes homines warentizabimus imperpetuum ac defendemus. Et ut hec mea donatio, concessio, et confirmatio perpetue firmitatis robur optineat, presenti scripto tam pro me quam pro heredibus meis sigillum meum apposui in testimonium. Hiis testibus, *domino Henrico Walensi, domino Roberto de Stapiltona, Gregorio de Camera, Roberto de Knaresburg, Nicolao ad eadem, Thoma filio Thome de Bilam,* et aliis.

CCCCXXX sexta.[1]   **Carta Everardi de Wich.**[2]

[To all the sons, &c., Everard de Wick greeting . . . . . . I have quit-claimed . . . . all the right which I claimed in the church of Catwick, or its appurtenances. Seal. Witnesses.]

Omnibus sancte matris ecclesie filiis presentibus et futuris Everardus de Wichie salutem. Noverit universitas vestra quod ego pro salute anime mee et antecessorum et heredum meorum remisi priori et monachis de Pontefracto[3] imperpetuum quietum clamavi de me et heredibus meis totum jus et clamium quod dicebam me habere in ecclesia de Cathwic aut ejus pertinentiis. Et in hujus rei testimonium presenti scripto sigillum meum pro me et heredibus meis apposui. Hiis testibus, *domino Petro de Falcumberga, Andrea fratre ejus, Willelmo Foliot, Petro persona de Risa, Alano capellano, Hugone clerico de Burtona, Ricardo de Martona,* et aliis.

----

(1) *Sic.*   (2) Catwick.   (3) "et" is omitted.

----

437.   **Carta Radulfi de Wich.**

[To all the sons, &c., Ralph de Wick greeting. I have confirmed . . . . . . all the alms which my predecessors have lawfully given. Namely, half the church of Catwick, with its appurtenances, that is, three bovates of land, and a rent of twelve pence in a certain piece of land which Gerald of Lutton holds from the monks. In pure and perpetual alms, free and quit, &c. Witnesses.]

Omnibus sancte matris ecclesie filiis tam presentibus quam futuris Radulfus de Withic salutem. Noverit universitas vestra me donasse et concessisse et hac presenti carta mea confirmasse deo et sancto Johanni et monachis de Pontefracto totam elemosinam quam antecessores mei eis rationabiliter dederunt. Scilicet medietatem ecclesie de Cathewic cum omnibus pertinentiis suis, id est cum tribus bovatis terre, et redditum xij denariorum in quadam portione terre quam Geraldus de Luttona[1] tenet de monachis. Harum predictarum rerum concessionem et confirmationem feci predictis monachis in puram et perpetuam elemosinam, liberam et quietam ab omni exactione seculari de me et de heredibus meis, pro salute anime mee et omnium antecessorum et heredum meorum. Hiis testibus, *Waltero de Faukeberga, Stephano et Roberto fratribus suis, Magistro Warino, Willelmo filio Eustachii, Magistro Raimundo, Willelmo de Horbir',* et aliis.

----

(1) See No. 148.

2 P

438.   Carta Thome Bilam.

[. . . . . I, Thomas, son of Thomas of Bilam, have demised . . . . the
bovate of land with its appurtenances which I have held of William de Bareville
in the territory of Bilham, for the term of six years, commencing in the year of
grace 1237, at Whitsuntide. For this the prior and monks have given me two
silver marks. Seal. Witnesses.]

Sciant presentes et futuri quod ego, Thomas filius Thome de
Bilama, dimisi domino priori de Pontefracto et ejusdem loci conventui illam bovatam terre cum pertinentiis suis quam tenui de
Willelmo de Barevilla in territorio de Bilam usque ad terminum sex
annorum, termino incipiente anno gratie m⁰.cc⁰.xxx⁰.vij⁰. ad Pentecosten, et pro hac dimissione et quieta clamatione dederunt mihi
predicti prior et monachi pre manibus duas marcas argenti. Et ne
ego dictus Thomas vel heredes mei in predicta bovata terre vel
ipsius pertinentiis aliquid juris vel clamii in posterum vendicare
possimus, huic scripto sigillum meum apposui. Hiis testibus, *magistro
Jo' de Hospitali*,[1] *Willelmo de Barevilla, Henrico de Camera, Waltero
Bercario, Johanne filio Michaelis de Pontefracto, Ricardo Janitore*[2] *de
eadem*, et aliis.

————

(1) St. Nicholas.

(2) Richard "Janitor," the porter, the last of these witnesses, was possibly Richard de Marton,
son of Alice de Marton, who in No. 417 gave himself so fully to the monks in life and death.

————————

439.   Carta Thome filii Thome de Bilam.

[. . . . . . I, Thomas, son of Thomas of Bilham, have demised . . . . . . that
bovate of land with its appurtenances which I have held of William de Bareville
in the territory of Bilham, for the term of twelve years, commencing in the year
of grace 1229, at the feast of St. Michael next following. To be held and possessed
to the end of the term named, &c. The prior and monks have given me two silver
marks. Seal. Witnesses.]

Sciant presentes et futuri quod ego, Thomas filius Thome de
Bilam, dimisi et omnino quietum clamavi domino priori et monachis
de Pontefracto illam bovatam terre cum pertinentiis suis quam tenui
de Willelmo de Barevilla in territorio de Bilam usque ad terminum
xij annorum, termino incipiente anno gratie m⁰.cc⁰.xx⁰.ix⁰. ad festum
sancti Michaelis proxime sequentis. Tenendam et habendam prefatis
monachis usque in finem termini prenominati sine aliqua contradictione
vel reclamatione mei vel heredum meorum. Pro hac vero dimissione
et quieta clamatione dederunt mihi dicti prior et monachi duas
marcas argenti pre manibus. Et ne ego dictus Thomas vel heredes
mei contra dimissionem et quietam clamationem in posterum venire

possimus, huic scripto sigillum meum apposui in testimonium. Hiis testibus, *domino Henrico capellano de Hotona, Willelmo de Barevilla, Henrico Camb',*[1] *Roberto de Heinesforda, Waltero Bercario, Ricardo Janitore de Pontefracto,* et multis aliis.

(1) If this is Henry de Camera, he tests also No. 441 and the two following charters.

---

440. Carta Willelmi de Bilam.

[. . . . . I, William of Bilham, have given . . . . to John, son of Matthew, half of a bovate of land in the territory of Bilham, which I have held from the Abbot of Roche. It lies near the land of Richard of Bilham, my grandson, and the toft which Philip of Bilham formerly held. To be held and possessed, &c. Paying yearly three silver shillings and six pence, half at Whitsuntide and half at the feast of St. Martin in winter. Warranty. Witnesses.]

Sciant omnes tam presentes quam futuri quod ego Willelmus de Bilam dedi, concessi et hac presenti carta mea confirmavi Johanni filio Mathei medietatem unius bovate terre in territorio de Bilam quam tenui de abbate de Rupe. Scilicet illam medietatem que jacet propinquior terre Ricardi de Bilam nepotis mei et toftum quod Philippus de Bilam quondam tenuit. Tenendam et habendam dicto Johanni et heredibus suis de me et heredibus meis in feudo et hereditate, libere et quiete, cum omnibus pertinentiis et libertatibus et aisiamentis infra villam et extra. Reddendo inde annuatim mihi et heredibus meis tres solidos argenti et sex denarios, scilicet medietatem ad Pentecosten et medietatem ad festum sancti Martini in hyeme, pro omni servitio et demanda. Et ego Willelmus et heredes mei warentizabimus predicto Johanni et heredibus suis predictam medietatem predicte bovate terre cum predicto tofto contra omnes homines inperpetuum. Hiis testibus, *Willelmo de Adwick, Jordano de Insula de Broddessword, Hugone de Scauceby, Willelmo de Balleby, Willelmo de Barevilla,* et aliis.

---

441. Carta Mathei[1] de Bilam.

[To all, &c., John, son of Matthew of Bilham, greeting. Thomas of Bilham, my nephew, has paid me five silver marks, in which he was bound, for the land which I sold him . . . . . . I have set my seal to this, and delivered it to the said Thomas. Witnesses.]

(1) *Sic.*

Omnibus hoc scriptum visuris vel audituris Johannes filius Mathei de Bilam salutem. Universitati vestre notum facio quod Thomas de Bilam, nepos[2] meus, fideliter mihi pacavit quinque marcas argenti in quibus mihi tenebatur pro terra quam ei vendidi et inperpetuum de me et heredibus meis quietam clamavi sibi et heredibus suis. Et ne ego Johannes vel aliquis ex parte mea aliquam calumpniam predicto Thome vel alicui suorum super solutione predictarum quinque marcarum in posterum inferre possimus, huic scripto sigillum meum apposui et eidem Thome tradidi. Hiis testibus, *Willelmo de Barevilla, Henrico de Camera, Ricardo de Bilam, Ricardo de Martona,* et aliis.

(2) There is an ambiguity here in the use of this word, which in this place seems to denote rather the son of a cousin than the son of a brother.

442.   Carta Mathei[1] de Bilam.

[. . . . . I, John, son of Matthew of Bilham, have granted . . . . . to Richard, son of John of Bilham, ... all my right in five acres of land in the territory of Bilham, with appurtenances, which I, John, formerly held of the same Richard. To be held and possessed, &c., so that I can have no claim therein. For this Richard has given me two and a half silver marks. Warranty. Seal. Witnesses.]

Sciant presentes et futuri quod ego Johannes filius Mathei de Bilam concessi et quietum clamavi de me et heredibus meis Ricardo filio Johannis de Bilam et heredibus suis vel assignatis suis totum jus et clamium quod habui vel habere potui in quinque acris terre in territorio de Bilam cum omnibus pertinentiis suis quas ego Johannes quondam tenui de eodem Ricardo. Tenendas et habendas libere et quiete, ita quod nec ego Johannes nec aliquis meorum aliquod jus vel aliquam calumpniam in predictis quinque acris terre cum pertinentiis de cetero numquam habere possimus. Pro hac autem concessione et quieta clamatione dedit mihi predictus Ricardus duas marcas et dimidiam argenti. Ego autem Johannes et heredes mei istam quietam clamationem et concessionem dicto Ricardo et heredibus suis contra omnes homines warentizabimus. In cujus rei testimonium huic scripto sigillum meum apposui. Hiis testibus, *Jordano de Insula, Willelmo de Barevilla, Henrico de Camera, Thoma filio Thome de Bilam, Radulfo de Cateby,* et aliis.

(1) *Sic.*

443.   Carta Mathei filii Johannis[1] de Bilam.

[. . . . . I, John, son of Matthew of Bilham, have sold and . . . . . confirmed
to Thomas, son of Thomas my uncle, a bovate of land with its appurtenances in
the territory of Bilham, for five silver marks, two acres which I have given to
Helen my sister being excepted. Half of it I formerly held from William of
Bilham, and the other half I held from Richard of Bilham. To be held and
possessed, &c., in wood and plain, &c. Paying yearly 32 pence, at Whitsuntide
16 pence and at the feast of St. Martin 16 pence. Warranty. Seal. Witnesses.]

Sciant presentes et futuri quod ego Johannes filius Mathei de
Bilam vendidi, concessi et hac presenti carta mea confirmavi Thome
filio Thome avunculi mei unam bovatam terre cum omnibus pertinentiis suis in territorio de Bilam pro quinque marcis argenti quas
ipse dedit mihi pre manibus, exceptis duabus acris quas dedi Helene
sorori mee. Illam scilicet bovatam cujus dimidiam tenui quondam
de Willelmo de Bilam et alteram dimidiam tenui de Ricardo de
Bilam. Tenendam et habendam de me et heredibus meis vel meis
assignatis sibi et heredibus suis vel suis assignatis cum omnibus
libertatibus et aisiamentis ad eandam bovatam spectantibus, in bosco
et plano, in pratis, in pasturis, in aquis, et molendinis, libere, quiete,
pacifice, et honorifice. Reddendo inde annuatim mihi et heredibus
meis vel meis assignatis xxxij denarios pro omni servitio seculari vel
demanda, videlicet ad Pentecosten xvj denarios et ad festum sancti
martini xvj denarios. Ego vero predictus Johannes et heredes mei vel
mei assignati predictam bovatam cum omnibus pertinentiis suis prefato
Thome et heredibus suis vel suis assignatis warantizabimus contra
omnes homines inperpetuum ac defendemus. In cujus rei testimonium
huic scripto sigillum meum apposui. Hiis testibus, *Jordano de Insula
de Hotona,*[2] *Henrico de Tancresley, Willelmo de Bilam, Willelmo de
Bareville, Henrico de Camera,* et aliis.

---

(1) *Sic.*   (2) See No. 244 and No. 440.

CCCCXL quarta.[1]   **Carta Petri de Falkebergia.**

[To all the sons, &c., Peter de Falkeberg greeting. . . . . . . By the advice of
Roger, Archbishop of York, I have given . . . . my half of the church of St.
Michael of Catwick, with its appurtenances, ... to be held in hand and
warranted against all men, ... my wife Beatrice and my sons consenting.
And may they who bring any injury on the monks concerning this alms have God's
curse and mine. The monks have granted me, at my death, funeral as for a monk

---

(1) No. 444 is in *Dodsworth*, vol. 135, and it is No. XVI in the *Monasticon*.

of that house. And they shall make my anniversary every year from the rent of the church aforesaid, and on the anniversary of my death the monks shall be provided from the aforesaid rent. And the monks have granted the same to my wife Beatrice on the day of her death. Also they have received us and our heirs into full fellowship. The witnesses of this deed are, &c.]

Omnibus sancte matris ecclesie filiis tam presentibus quam futuris Petrus de Falkebergia salutem. Universitati vestre notum fieri volo me consilio venerabilis Rogeri dei gratia Eboracensis Archiepiscopi dedisse et concessisse et presentis carte mee testimonio confirmasse deo et sancte marie et sancto Johanni evangeliste et priori et monachis de Pontefracto medietatem meam ecclesie sancte Michaelis de Catthevic cum omnibus pertinentiis suis in puram et perpetuam elemosinam, liberam et quietam ab omni seculari exactione, manu tenendam et warentizandam contra omnes homines, pro salute anime mee et uxoris mee Beatricis et filiorum meorum, Willelmi, Walteri, Stephani et omnium antecessorum et heredum meorum, predictis uxore mea Beatricia et filiis meis concedentibus et consentientibus. Qui autem super hanc elemosinam meam predictis monachis aliquam injuriam vel aliquod gravamen intulerint maledictionem dei et meam habeant. Pro hujus vero donationis beneficio concesserunt mihi predicti monachi in obitu meo tantum obsequii quantum pro uno de monachis ipsius domus. Insuper autem anniversarium meum singulis annis facient de redditu predicte ecclesie, scilicet elemosine mee de Catewic, et in die anniversaria obitus mei de predicto redditu predicti monachi procurabuntur, et hoc idem concesserunt prefati monachi uxori mee Beatricie in die obitus sui. Nos etiam in plenariam societatem domus sue et totius ordinis Cluniacensis et heredes nostros receperunt. Hujus rei testes sunt, *Rogerus dei gratia Eboracensis archiepiscopus, Johannes[2] filius Letoldi, Willelmus capellanus, Jordanus Folioth, Hugo de Perdevill, Toma dapifer monachorum, Jordanus de Aula.*

(2) He was not yet archdeacon.

---

445.   Carta Petri de Falkebergia.[1]

[To all the sons, &c., Peter de Falkeberg greeting. Having seen the documents which the prior and monks have from my ancestors concerning the church of Catwick, I have renounced and remitted to them for ever all the right which I claimed in the aforesaid church, to which they last presented Sir Eustace de Falkeberg, my uncle. Witnesses.]

(1) This is Peter de Falkenberg II.

Omnibus sancte matris ecclesie filiis presentibus et futuris Petrus de Falkebergia salutem. Noverit universitas vestra quod, inspectis et auditis instrumentis que prior et monachi de Pontefracto habent ab antecessoribus meis de ecclesia de Cattewic, renunciavi appellationem meam pro eadem ecclesia interpositam. Et remisi eis inperpetuum et quietum clamavi de me et de heredibus meis totum jus et clamium quod dicebam me habere in predicta ecclesia, ad quam ultimo presentaverunt dominum Eustachium de Falkebergia avunculum meum. Hiis testibus, *Magistro Rogero Marmiun canonico Beu'lac, Henrico hospitalo, Thoma elemosinario de Bederna, Moritio clerico, Willelmo Folioth, Ricardo de Martona*, et aliis.

---

446.   Carta Walteri de Falkebergia.

[To all the sons, &c., Walter de Falkeberg greeting.   I have granted . . . . . . half the church of Catwick, which my father gave them . . . . . Witnesses.]

Omnibus sancte matris ecclesie filiis tam presentibus quam futuris Walterus de Falkebergia salutem. Noverit universitas vestra me concessisse et hac presenti carta mea confirmasse deo et sancto Johanni et priori et monachis de Pontefracto medietatem ecclesie de Catthwic cum omnibus pertinentiis, quam pater meus eis dedit, in puram et perpetuam elemosinam, liberam et quietam ab omni seculari exactione, pro salute anime sue et uxoris sue Beatricis matris mee, et mee, et fratrum meorum, et omnium suorum. Hiis testibus, *Magistro Warino, Stephano de Falkeberga et Roberto fratre suo, Amando filio Willelmi, Radulfo de Wichis, Magistro Raimundo, Ricardo filio Ricardi de Stagno*, et aliis.

---

447.   Carta Osberti de Brettona.[1]

[. . . . . . I, Osbert de Bretton, ... have granted . . . . Alan son of Arnald, with his whole following and all his goods.   Seal.   Witnesses.]

Sciant presentes et futuri quod ego Osbertus de Brettona pro salute anime mee et omnium antecessorum et heredum meorum concessi et quietum clamavi inperpetuum deo et sancto Johanni de Pontefracto et monachis ibidem deo servientibus Alanum filium Arnaldi cum tota sequela sua et omnibus catallis suis. Et ne ego prefatus Osbertus vel heredes mei inposterum contra hanc meam quietam clamationem venire possimus huic carte sigillum meum pro

---

(1) The Bretton in which these interests lay was Burton Salmon.

me et heredibus meis apposui. Hiis testibus, *Willelmo filio Petri*,[2] *Waltero de Byrum, Ricardo de Suttona, Gaufrido de Ledeshama, Ricardo de Martona, Ricardo de Stagno*, et aliis.

(2) William, son of Peter, a grandson of Peter the eldest son of Asolf, appears to have been known as William de Bretton (afterwards Sir William), to have died early, and, according to No. 259, to have left a widow Alice and a daughter Matilda. The pedigree will be given in connection with No. 505.

448.   Carta Osberti[1] de Brettona.

[. . . . . . I, Osbert de Bretton, have granted . . . . the bovate of land in Bretton which Geoffrey de Ledsham has held of me and has given to the monks. Also I have given a rent of two shillings which Geoffrey has paid to me yearly for the aforesaid bovate of land, and all other services to which Geoffrey and his heirs were bound. To be held and possessed, &c. Warranty. Seal. Witnesses.]

Sciant presentes et futuri quod ego Osbertus de Brettona concessi et hac presenti carta mea confirmavi deo et sancto Johanni de Pontefracto et monachis ibidem deo servientibus in puram et perpetuam elemosinam illam bovatam terre in Brettona quam Galfridus de Ledeshama de me tenuit et eisdem monachis dedit. Insuper ego Osbertus dedi et concessi predictis monachis redditum duorum solidorum quos mihi et heredibus meis predictus Galfridus annuatim pro predicta bovata terre reddidit et omnia alia servitia que mihi et heredibus meis predictus Galfridus et heredes sui facere tenebantur. Tenendam et habendam prefatis monachis cum omnibus libertatibus et aisiamentis ad predictam bovatam terre infra villam de Brettona et extra pertinentibus, liberam et quietam et solutam ab omni servitio et seculari consuetudine. Et ego Osbertus et heredes mei deo et sancto Johanni de Pontefracto et monachis ibidem deo servientibus hec omnia predicta contra omnes homines warentizabimus. Et ut ista concessio et confirmatio inperpetuum predictis monachis firma et stabilis perseveret, huic carte pro me et heredibus meis sigillum meum apposui. Hiis testibus, *Willelmo filio Everardi, Willelmo de Camesala, Willelmo de Hameltona, Waltero de Birum, Jordano de la Landa, Rogero capellano de Pontefracto*, et aliis.

(1) Osbert, the grantor of No. 447 and No. 448, was the head of his family, and as Sir Osbert he witnessed No. 312. He was frequently followed by his brother Serlo (No. 204, No. 265, No. 300, No. 312), who married Agnes daughter of Geoffrey Pigot, the holder of the fee, which, as we learn from No. 204, had descended to him from his father Pigot, son of Hugh,—perhaps Hugh fitz Asolf.

449. **Carta abbatis Sancte Marie de Eboraco.**

[To all Christ's faithful . . . . Robert, abbot of St. Mary of York, and the convent there, greeting in the Lord. By the inspiration of divine love and from regard for holy religion we have unanimously granted . . . . . 13 perches in breadth and four feet to make a ditch, from the moor of Roger de Hook next the moor of William de Percy. towards the west, and in length as far as the moor of Roger extends towards the south-west, and two perches of land from the aforesaid moor down to the river Ouse to make their road, with the common pasture of Inklesmore, which the aforesaid Roger has given them. To be held for ever as the charter of the aforesaid Roger, which they have, witnesses. Paying yearly to our church a pound of pepper at the Nativity of the Blessed Mary at York. Witnesses.]

Omnibus Christi fidelibus has litteras visuris vel audituris Robertus[1] dei gratia Abbas Sancte Marie Eboracensis et ejusdem loci conventus salutem in domino. Noverit universitas vestra nos divini amoris intuitu et sacre religionis aspectu unanimiter concessisse et presenti carta nostra confirmasse deo et ecclesie sancti Johannis evangeliste de Pontefracto et monachis ibidem deo servientibus xiij perticatas in latitudine et quatuor pedes ad fossatum suum faciendum de mora Rogeri de Huuc juxta moram Willelmi de Percy versus occidentem, et in longitudine quantum predicta mora ejusdem Rogeri extenditur versus sud west, et duas[2] perticatas terre a supradicta mora usque ad flumen Vse ad faciendam viam suam, cum communi pastura de Inclesmora ad totam predictam terram pertinente, quas predictus Rogerus eis dedit. Tenendas inperpetuum sicut carta ejusdem Rogeri quam[3] ipsi inde habent testatur. Reddendo inde annuatim ecclesie nostre unam libram piperis ad Nativitatem beate Marie apud Eboracum. Hiis testibus, *domino Ricardo abbate de Seleby,*[4] *Johanne de Birkina,*[5] *Roberto Walensi,*[6] *Magistro Waltero de Seleby, Thoma de Wiltona,* et aliis. ———

(1) No doubt this is Abbot Robert de Longchamp.
(2) In No. 169 it is three perches.   (3) It is No. 451.   (4) He died in 1237.
(5) John de Birkin died in 1227. This is probably the uncle surviving him.
(6) Robert Wallis II. See No. 450.

CCCCL. Carta Johannis filii Rogeri filii Asketilli de Huck.

[. . . . . . I, John, son of Roger son of Asketil de Hook, have granted . . . . . 13 perches in breadth and four feet to make their ditch, from my moor of Hook, next the moor of William de Percy towards the west, and in length as far as the aforesaid moor extends towards the south-west, and two perches of land from the aforesaid moor down to the river Ouse, to make their road, with the common pasture of Inklesmoor. To be held and possessed, &c. Paying yearly four shillings, two at the feast of St. Martin and two at Whitsuntide. Warranty. So that it shall be allowed them to construct whatever they please without hindrance, as well from the moor as from the land within the above-written boundaries. Witnesses.]

Sciant presentes et futuri quod ego Johannes filius Rogeri filii Asketilli de Huke concessi et hac presenti carta mea confirmavi[1] pro salute anime patris mei et mee et animarum omnium predecessorum et successorum meorum deo et ecclesie sancti Johannis ewangeliste de Pontefracto et monachis ibidem deo servientibus xiij perticatas in latitudine et quatuor pedes ad fossatum suum faciendum de mora mea de Huck juxta moram Willelmi de Percy versus occidentem, et in longitudine quantum predicta mora extenditur versus sud west, et duas perticatas[2] terre a supradicta mora usque ad flumen Vse ad faciendam viam suam, cum communi pastura de Inclesmora. Habendas et tenendas de me et heredibus meis inperpetuum, libere, quiete et honorifice.   Reddendo mihi et heredibus meis annuatim quatuor solidos pro omni servitio, duos ad festum sancti Martini et duos ad Pentecosten.   Et ego Johannes filius Rogeri de Huck et heredes mei warentizabimus predictis monachis prenominatam moram contra omnes homines.   Ita quod licebit eis tam de mora quam de terra que est infra suprascriptas metas ad commodum suum facere quicquid eis placuerit sine impedimento.   Hiis testibus, *Ricardo abbate de Seleby, Thoma de Polingtona, Henrico Walensi,*[3] *Ada de Bella Aqua, Ada de Berlaya, Willelmo tunc vicario, Roberto Walensi,*[4] et aliis.

(1) It should be noted that here the grantor does not say that he "gives." His father had "given, granted, and confirmed ;" he himself merely grants and confirms.

(2) This word is repeated, and forms the junction of the two Fasciculi. See Introduction, page 496.   (3) Henry Wallis III.

(4) Robert Wallis II, afterwards parson of Methley and vicar of Fryston.

CCCCLI.[1]   Carta Rogeri filii Asketilli.

[. . . . . I, Roger, son of Asketil de Hook, have given . . . . 13 perches in breadth and four feet to make their ditch, from my moor of Hook, next the moor of William de Percy towards the west, and in length as far as the aforesaid moor extends towards the south-west, and two perches of land from the aforesaid moor down to the river Ouse to make their road, with the common pasture of Inklesmoor.   To be held and possessed, &c.   Paying to me and my heirs yearly four shillings for all service, two at the feast of St. Martin, and two at Whitsuntide.   Warranty.   So that it shall be allowed them to construct whatever they please without hindrance, as well from the moor as from the land within the above boundaries.   Witnesses.]

(1) These two charters are nearly identical in terms with No. 168, but this last (No. 168) seems to be later in date than either of them, for it contains an additional clause with regard to having the seal of the grantor affixed, which does not occur in those now before us.   Similar grants are on record to Drax and St. Leonard's of York, and each (with a short pedigree of this family) is printed in the *Yorkshire Archæological Journal*, xi, 66–8.

Sciant presentes et futuri quod ego Rogerus filius Asketilli de Huck dedi et concessi et hac presenti carta mea confirmavi, pro salute anime patris mei et mee et animarum omnium predecessorum et successorum meorum, deo et ecclesie sancti Johannis ewangeliste de Pontefracto et monachis ibidem deo servientibus xiij perticatas in latitudine et quatuor pedes ad fossatum suum faciendum de mora mea de Huck juxta moram Willelmi de Percy versus occidentem, et in longitudine quantum predicta mora extenditur versus sud west, et duas perticatas terre a supradicta mora usque ad flumen Vse ad faciendam viam suam, cum communi pastura de Inclesmora. Habendas et tenendas de me et heredibus meis inperpetuum, libere, quiete, et honorifice. Reddendo mihi et heredibus meis annuatim iiij*or* solidos pro omni servitio, duos ad festum sancti Martini et duos ad Pentecosten. Et ego Rogerus de Huck et heredes mei warantizabimus predictis monachis prenominatam moram contra omnes homines. Ita quod licebit eis tam de mora quam de terra que est infra superscriptas metas ad commodum suum facere quicquid eis placuerit sine impedimento. Hiis testibus, *Ricardo abbate de Seleby, Johanne de Birkina, Roberto Walensi, Hugone de Toulestona, Ada de Bella Aqua, magistro Waltero de Seleby*, et aliis.

CCCCLII.   **Carta Alani[1] filii Nicholai de Sypena.**   Circa 1212.

[To all, &c., Alan, son of Nicholas, of Shippen, greeting. Know that I have given . . . . pasture for two hundred sheep in my pasture of Shippen and its appurtenances, with my grange next my gate towards the east, with free outgoing and incoming. This grange, with the plot in which it is situate, I have given to the monks to shelter their sheep. The dung shall remain to me and my heirs. I and my heirs shall find litter, and they shall repair and maintain the grange at their own charge. Warranty. Witnesses.]

Omnibus hoc scriptum visuris vel audituris Alanus filius Nicholai de Sypena salutem. Noverit universitas vestra me dedisse et hac presenti carta mea confirmasse deo et ecclesie sancti Johannis de Pontefracto et monachis ibidem deo servientibus, pro salute anime mee et patris mee et omnium antecessorum et heredum meorum, in liberam, puram et perpetuam elemosinam, pasturam ad ducentos multones in pastura mea de Sypena et suis pertinentiis, cum grangia mea que sita est juxta portam meam versus partem orientalem, cum

---

(1) This Alan has already appeared in No. 162, No. 164, and No. 210. He was the grandson of the grandson of the great Ailric, the daughter of whose son Reginald was Alan's maternal grandmother.

libero exitu et introitu.   Hanc vero grangiam cum tota placia in qua
sita est dedi prefatis monachis ad multones suos hospitandos.   Ita ut
stercora mihi et heredibus meis remaneant.   Et ego et heredes mei
inveniemus stramuram et ipsi predictam grangiam cum necesse fuerit
ad custum suum emendabunt et sustinebunt.   Et ego A. et herèdes
mei predictam pasturam et grangiam cum tota placia contra omnes
homines inperpetuum warantizabimus ac defendemus.   Hiis testibus,
domino Hugone[2] tunc senescallo, Johanne de Rouecestria tunc constabulario,
Ricardo Lond', Waltero receptore, Johanne filio Michaelis, Ricardo de
Martona, et aliis.

(2) Sir Hugh Butler.

CCCCLIII.[1]   Carta Hugonis filii Willelmi filii Pagani.

[To all, &c., Hugh, son of William, son of Paganus, greeting.   Know that I
have confirmed . . . . . . whatever Alan, son of Nicholas, of Shippen, has charitably
conveyed to the monks from my fee in the territory of Shippen, in lands, pastures,
commonages and possessions.   Seal.   Witnesses.]

Omnibus hoc scriptum visuris vel audituris Hugo filius Willelmi
filii Pagani salutem.   Noverit universitas vestra me pro salute anime
mee concessisse et hac presenti carta mea in liberam, puram, et
perpetuam elemosinam confirmasse deo et ecclesie sancti Johannis de
Pontefracto et monachis ibidem deo servientibus quicquid Alanus
filius Nicholai de Sypena prefatis monachis de feodo meo in territorio
de Sypena, in terris, pasturis, cummunis, et possessionibus karitative
contulit.   In cujus rei testimonium huic scripto sigillum meum apposui.
Hiis testibus, *domino Hugone tunc senescallo, Waltero receptore, Hugone[2]*
fratre suo, Gaufrido tunc ballivo,[3] Symone de Rupe, Ricardo de Martona,
et aliis.

(1) No. 453 is the confirmation of the preceding charter by the lord of the fee.   Shippen is in
Hillam, as we learn from No. 210.   (2) Possibly Hugh de Batley. See No. 458.
(3) This is Geoffrey the clerk. See No. 162 and No. 261.

454.[1]   Carta Thome filii Roberti de Toulestuna.   Circa 1180.

[To all the faithful, &c., Thomas, son of Robert de Toulston, greeting.   Know
that I have granted . . . . . . a toft in Toulston, namely the toft of Stephen, with
all his following, ... with my brother Robert, when in the house of St. John
he has been made a monk.   And if any of my heirs shall diminish this alms or
cause disturbance therein, let him know that he is bound under my curse.   Of this
the witnesses are, &c.]

(1) The enumeration has in this case been omitted.

Omnibus fidelibus sancte matris ecclesie Thomas filius Roberti de Toulestona salutem.   Sciatis omnes quod ego concessi et donavi et hac mea carta confirmavi deo et sancto Johanni in Pontefracto et monachis ibidem deo servientibus unum toftum in Toulestuna, scilicet toftum Stephani, cum tota secta sua, libere et quiete de me et de heredibus meis, in puram et perpetuam elemosinam, cum fratre meo Roberto, quando in domo sancti Johannis factus est monachus in Pontefracto. Siquis autem heredum meorum hanc elemosinam predictis monachis abstulerit vel minuerit vel perturbationem inde eis fecerit, sciat se maledictione mea esse obstrictum.   Hujus rei testes sunt, *Herbertus de Archis, Willelmus filius Hervei, Robertus de Swinlingtona, Robertus de Stapiltona, Adam de Prestuna,*[2] *Thomas de Prestona.*[2]

(2) *Sic.*

454.[1]   Carta Petri de Toulestona.   Circa 1180.

[. . . . . I, Peter de Toulston, give and by this my charter and my seal confirm, ... with my brother Robert whom they have received as a monk, three shillings from the rent of the bovate which Roger, son of Syxtan, holds in Toulston . . . . Of which rent shall be paid to the monks half, that is to say, eighteen pence, on the feast of St. Martin and an equal half at Whitsuntide.   Whosoever shall hold that land shall observe each term aforesaid, paying to the cellarer the rent as appointed.   Witnesses.]

Sciant presentes et futuri quod ego Petrus de Toulistona do et concedo et hac mea carta et sigillo meo confirmo deo et sancto Johanni et monachis de Pontefracto, cum.fratre meo Roberto quem susceperunt in monachum, tres solidos de redditu de bovata illa quam Rogerus filius Syxtan tenet in Toulestona, in puram et perpetuam elemosinam de me et de heredibus meis, quicumque illam bovatam tenebit.   De quo redditu reddentur[2] eisdem monachis medietas, scilicet xviij denarii, in festo sancti Martini et alia medietas que tantundem est in Pentecosten.   Quicumque vero terram illam tenebit predictum terminum utrumque observabit, reddendo celerario eundem redditum sicut perfunctum est in domo sancti Johannis de Pontefracto eisdem terminis.   Testibus, *Herberto de Archis, Jordano de Ledestuna, et fratribus suis Hugone et Roberto,*[3] *Hugone herede Petri,*[4] et aliis.

(1) Thus enumerated, in error for 455.   (2) *Sic.*
(3) Probably the sons of Walter, who was King's bailiff in 1189.   (4) The donor.

CCCCLVI ta.[1]   **Carta Ade filii Rogeri de Croslanda.**[2]   **Circa 1212.**

[. . . . . . I, Adam, son of Roger de Crosland, have given . . . . . . a rent of
two shillings from Robert, my son, or his assigns, to be received for ever within
the octave of the Blessed John the apostle and evangelist at the Nativity of our
Lord yearly, from the land of the Hermitage next Caldwendenbrook towards the
south within the boundaries of Crosland. Witnesses.]

Sciant presentes et futuri quod ego Adam filius Rogeri de
Croslanda dedi, concessi, et hac presenti carta mea confirmavi in
puram et perpetuam elemosinam deo et ecclesie sancti Johannis de
Pontefracto et monachis ibidem deo servientibus, pro salute anime
mee et dominorum meorum Henrici, Roberti et Rogeri de Lascy et
omnium antecessorum et herêdum meorum et omnium fidelium,
redditum duorum solidorum de Roberto filio meo vel ipsius assignatis
infra octavam beati Johannis apostoli et ewangeliste in Nathali domini
annuatim, de terra heremitagie que jacet juxta Caldewenedenebroc[3]
versus australem partem infra divisas de Croslanda inperpetuum
percipiendum.   Hiis testibus, *Hugone Pincerna tunc senescallo domini
Johannis constabularii Cestrie, Johanne de Hotona, Roberto de Stapiltona,*[4]
*Waltero receptore, Henrico de Sewilla, Ivone de Medel', Hugone clerico,
Ricardo de Martona,* et aliis. _____

(1) I nowhere find copies of the charters from No. 445 to No. 455, but there is a short abstract.
of No. 456 in *Dodsworth* 155, and another in vol. 133.

(2) This Crosland is now merged in Lockwood, and the name of the Hermitage is still preserved
in Armitage Bridge, which crosses the Colne, a tributary of the Calder.   (3) *Sic.*

(4) If this is Robert I, he must have been a long liver.

_____

456*.[1]

[. . . . . . I, Hugh, son of Rayner, clerk of Darfield, have given . . . . . . to
Ralph de Wath, my uncle, and his heirs or assigns, half a carucate of land in
Menton, with its appurtenances . . . . for his homage and service and for a
mark of silver which Ralph gave me in acknowledgment. My father has held it
from the monks. To be held and possessed, &c. Paying yearly to me and my
heirs three shillings at the feast of St. Martin, for every service and for every
claim, and for every exaction, and for every cause, &c.]

Sciant presentes et futuri quod ego Hugo, filius Reyneri clerici de
Derfeudo, dedi, concessi et hac presenti carta mea confirmavi Radulfo
de Wath avunculo meo et heredibus suis vel assignatis dimidiam
carucatam terre in Mentona cum omnibus pertinentiis et cum omnibus

(1) This charter is a somewhat later insertion. It was never numbered, and there is no heading.
When the conclusion of No. 456 was reached, on the first column of the dorse of fo. 71, a space
remained sufficient for 34 lines, and on the last line of the column was placed the rubricated heading
for the charters of William the Receiver (No. 457), which commenced the second column. The first
half of these blank 34 lines was subsequently occupied by this charter of Hugh son of Rayner,
which I have numbered No. 456*.

liberis communitatibus et aisiamentis in bosco et plano ad predictam terram pertinentibus, pro homagio suo et servitio et pro una marca argenti quam predictus Radulfus dedit mihi pre manibus in recognitione. Illam scilicet quam pater meus R. tenuit de monachis de Pontefracto. Tenendam et habendam de me et heredibus meis libere, quiete, pacifice, et honorifice, in feodo et hereditate. Reddendo inde annuatim mihi et heredibus meis iij solidos ad festum sancti Martini pro omni servitio et pro omni querela et pro omni exactione et pro omni causa, et cetera.

---

457.   Carte quondam Walterii[1] receptoris de Pontefracto.   Circa 1220.[2]

[. . . . . . . I, John, son of Hugh the tanner, have given to Walter the clerk, or to whom he will assign it, an acre and a half in the Fields of Pontefract next the Waterfall, which Hugh, my father, has held from William, son of Geoffrey. To be held and possessed, &c. Paying yearly to William, son of Geoffrey, and his heirs, eighteen pence for all services and exactions, half at Whitsuntide and half at the feast of St. Martin. Walter the clerk has given me two silver marks in acknowledgment. Warranty. Witnesses.]

Sciant presentes et futuri quod ego Johannes filius Hugonis Tanatoris[3] dedi et concessi et hac presenti carta mea confirmavi Waltero clerico, vel cui assignare voluerit, unam acram terre et dimidiam in campis Pontisfracti juxta Watrefal, illam scilicet acram terre et dimidiam quam Hugo pater meus tenuit de Willelmo filio Galfridi.[4] Tenendam et habendam sibi et heredibus vel assignatis suis, in feodo et hereditate, libere, quiete, pacifice. Reddendo inde annuatim Willelmo filio Galfridi et heredibus suis xviij denarios pro omnibus servitiis et exactionibus, scilicet medietatem ad Pentecosten et medietatem ad festum sancti Martini. Pro ista vero donacione et confirmatione dedit mihi dictus Walterus clericus duas marcas argenti de recognitione. Et ego Johannes filius Hugonis Tanatoris et heredes mei predicto Waltero clerico, vel cui assignare voluerit, predictam acram terre et dimidiam contra omnes homines warentizabimus. Hiis testibus, *Roberto de Cantia tunc senescallo, Johanne de Birkina,[5] Thoma filio suo,[6] Jordano de sancta Maria, Henrico Walensi,[7] Waltero Scotico, Thoma de Knaresburg, Roberto Camerario*, et aliis.

---

(1) Walterius, like Rogerius, is a common form.

(2) It is of later date than the three following, and the heading is some twenty years later (see note to preceding charter).

(3) In No. 460 Hugh the tanner is called Hugh the son of Gilbert, and in No. 459, still more fully, Hugh the son of Gilbert of Cottingham.   (4) See No. 460.

(5) He died in 1227.   (6) In 1230 he was his successor.   (7) Jordan's son-in-law.

458.   Carta Alicie filie Willelmi de Horre.   Circa 1196.

[. . . . . . I, Alice, daughter of William Horre, have given . . . . . to William, son of Hervey, son of Kaskin, and his heirs, an assart in the Fields of Pontefract lying towards the north, next the land of Simon Butler on the north side, abutting on the way from Hardwick. To be held, &c. Paying thence to the chief lord of Pontefract 12 pence yearly, and to me and my heirs 2 pence at Easter for every service. For this William has given me 3 shillings in acknowledgment. Warranty. Witnesses.]

Sciant presentes et futuri quod ego Aliz filia Willelmi Horre dedi et concessi et hac mea carta confirmavi Willelmo filio Hervici filii Kaskin[1] et heredibus suis unum essartum in campis Pontisfracti[2] versus boream, jacens juxta terram Symonis Butellarii in boreali parte, abuttans etiam ad viam de Herdewic.[3] Tenendam[4] de me et de heredibus meis in feudo et hereditate, libere et quiete. Reddendo inde capitali domino Pontisfracti annuatim xij denarios, et mihi et heredibus meis ij denarios ad pascha pro omni servitio. Et pro hac donatione et concessione dedit mihi predictus Willelmus iiij solidos de recognitione. Ego vero et heredes mei warentizabimus prefatum essartum prenominato Willelmo et heredibus suis contra omnes homines. Hiis testibus, *Roberto Walensi tunc senescallo,*[5] *Ricardo de Stapiltona,*[6] *Magistro Raimundo, Hugone de Batelay, Willelmo de Daneport, Jordano Campione,* et aliis.

---

(1) The grandfather is named in order to distinguish him from William, son of Hervey, son of Jordan fitz Ailric.

(2) Under the "little Charter" for land on the moor, this Hervey held seven acres in the Fields, where also this assart, or clearing, was situate.   (3) Spital Hardwick.   (4) *Sic.*

(5) To Roger de Lascy. He became sheriff in 1205.   (6) Brother of Robert, the lord.

---

459.   Carta Raimundi clerici.   Circa 1190.

[. . . . . I, Raimond the clerk, have given . . . . . to Hugh, son of Gilbert, of Cottingham, and his heirs, for his homage and service, a toft with adjoining croft in Pontefract, in Monkhill, without any withholding. It lies between the house of Robert Paul and the house of Nigel, brother of this Hugh. To be held, &c., for 40 pence, to be paid yearly, ... at Whitsuntide 20 pence and at the feast of St. Martin 20 pence. Hugh has given me two besants in acknowledgment. Warranty. Witnesses.]

Sciant presentes et futuri quod ego Raimundus clericus[1] dedi, concessi et presenti carta mea confirmavi Hugoni filio Gilleberti de Cotinghama et heredibus suis pro homagio suo et servitio unum

---

(1) At the time of the "Little Charter" he was Master (of St. Nicholas' Hospital), but that was not yet.

toftum cum crofto adjacente in Pontefracto in monte monachorum, sine aliquo retenemento mei et heredum meorum.   Illud scilicet qui^2 jacet inter domum Roberti Palle et domum Nigelli fratris ejusdem Hugonis.   Tenendum de me et de heredibus meis in feudo et hereditate, libere, quiete, et honorifice, pro xl denariis michi et heredibus meis tantummodo pro omni servitio et consuetudine annuatim reddendis hiis terminis : In Pentecosten xx*d.* et in festo sancti Martini xx*d.*   Et pro hac donatione et concessione dedit mihi predictus Hugo duos bisantios de recognitione.   Et ego Raimundus et heredes mei warentizabimus predicto H. et heredibus suis prefatum toftum cum crofto contra omnes homines.   Hiis testibus, *Jacobo*^{3} *tunc temporis magistro hospitalis, Willelmo de Vescy persona de Berwic,*^{4} *Roberto Walensi,*^{5} *Benedicto presbitero,*^{6} *Ricardo de Stapiltona, Symone de Rupe, Roberto Camberlano,* et aliis.

(2) *Sic.*   (3) Raimond had a son James, but this was his own predecessor.
(4) Maternal uncle to the lord Robert de Lascy.
(5) Not yet seneschal, which he was when he tested the preceding charter.
(6) The grantor of No. 140.

---

460.   Carta Willelmi filii Galfridi.   Circa 1190.

[. . . . . . . I, William, son of Geoffrey, have given . . . . to Hugh, son of Gilbert, and his heirs, for their homage and service, an acre and a half of land towards the north side of the high road leading from Monkhill to the thieves' gallows ; it lies also between the land of Master Raimond above the Waterfall and the land which belonged to Baldwin, son of Serich.   To be held, &c.   Paying thence yearly to me and my heirs 18 pence, half at Whitsuntide and half at the feast of St. Martin.   Hugh has given me three and a half silver marks in acknowledgment.   Warranty.   Witnesses.]

Sciant presentes et futuri quod ego Willelmus filius Gefridi^1 dedi et concessi et hac presenti carta mea confirmavi Hugoni filio Gilliberti et heredibus suis pro homagio suo et servicio unam acram terre et dimidiam, scilicet versus borealem partem de magna via tendente de monte monachorum ad furcas latronum, scilicet et que jacent inter terram magistri Raimundi super Watrefal et terram que fuit Baldewini filii Serich.   Tenendam de me et heredibus meis in feodo et hereditate, libere et quiete, pacifice et integre.   Reddendo inde annuatim mihi et heredibus meis xviij denarios pro omni servitio et seculari

(1) *Sic.* This Geoffrey was a son of Walter, the youngest brother of Jordan of Ledstone, and his brother Edwin was an original tenant of land on the moor under the "little charter."

2 Q

exactione, scilicet medietatem ad Pentecosten et medietatem ad festum sancti Martini. Pro hac autem donatione et concessione dedit mihi predictus Hugo filius Gilleberti tres marcas argenti et dimidiam de recognitione. Et ego Willelmus filius Gaufridi et heredes mei warantizabimus hanc predictam terram predicto Hugoni filio Gilleberti et heredibus suis contra omnes homines. Hiis testibus, *Roberto Walensi*,[2] *Johanne de Birkina*,[3] *Jordano de sancta Maria, Roberto Camberlano, Symone Butiler, Radulfo filio Hugonis de Batelay, Roberto Tinctore*, et aliis.

(2) Not yet seneschal. See note (5) to preceding charter.　　　(3) This is the uncle.

461.　　　　　　　　Carta Raimundi clerici.　　　　　　**Circa 1220.**

[. . . . . . I, Raimond the clerk, have given . . . . . to Peter the chaplain, his heirs and assigns, the land to the west of the Castle of the fee of Cridling, which I held from the brethren of the Hospital of St. Michael. It lies next to the land which was William Campion's. To be held, &c. Paying thence yearly to me, my heirs or assigns, twelve pence, six pence at the feast of St. Martin and six pence at Whitsuntide. Warranty. Witnesses.]

Sciant presentes et futuri quod ego Raimundus clericus dedi, concessi, et hac presenti carta mea confirmavi Petro capellano et heredibus suis vel cui assignare voluerit illam terram in occidentali parte castelli que est de feodo de Crideling, quam ego tenui de fratribus hospitalis sancti Michaelis. Scilicet illam terram que jacet propinquior terre que fuit Willelmi Campiun. Tenendam sibi et heredibus suis vel cui assignare voluerit in feudo et hereditate, libere, quiete, pacifice, et honorifice. Reddendo inde annuatim mihi et heredibus meis vel cui assignare voluero duodecim denarios pro omnibus serviciis et exactionibus, scilicet sex denarios ad festum sancti Martini et sex denarios ad Pentecosten. Et ego Raimundus clericus et heredes mei predicto Petro Capellano et heredibus suis, vel cui assignare voluerit, predictam terram contra omnes homines warantizabimus. Hiis testibus, *Johanne de Birkin*,[1] *Gilleberto de Nottona, Willelmo de Stapiltona, Jordano de sancta Maria, Roberto Walensi, magistro Adam de Kelingtona, Symone de Rupe, Henrico de Goldale*,[2] et aliis.

(1) The nephew; he died in 1227.　　　　　(2) He tested No. 141 and No. 168.

CCCCLXII.   Carta Emme filie Beatricie.   Circa 1212.

[. . . . . . . I, Emma, daughter of Beatrice, daughter of Hugh of Pontefract, abiding in widowhood, and William, my son, have granted to Agnes, daughter of the same Beatrice, her heirs and assigns, all our right and claim . . . . in the tenements of the said Agnes in Pontefract, within the town and without. The said Agnes has granted . . . . to the said Emma and William, her son, their heirs and assigns, 18 acres of land in the Fields of Ferry, ten in Putthale, six near Wellsike, and two abutting on the Limepit. Seals. Witnesses.]

Sciant presentes et futuri quod ego Emma, filia Beatricie filie Hugonis de Pontefracto, in viduitate existens, et Willelmus filius meus, concessimus et quietum clamavimus Agneti filie ejusdem Beatricie et heredibus suis vel cui assignare voluerit totum jus et clamium si quid habuimus vel habere potuimus in tenementis dicte Agnetis in Pontefracto, tam in villa quam extra villam, de nobis et heredibus nostris, sibi et heredibus suis, inperpetuum. Pro hac autem concessione et quieta clamatione concessit et quietum clamavit pro se et heredibus suis dicta Agnes dicte Emme et Willelmo filio suo xviij acras terre in campis de Fereia, x in Putthale, et sex juxta Willeschis, et ij abbuttantes super Limpit, sibi et heredibus eorum vel cui assignare voluerint, in perpetuum. In cujus rei testimonium huic scripto signa sua apposuerunt. Hiis testibus, *Hugone Pincerna tunc senescallo, Waltero clerico, Roberto Camerario, Johanne de Lovain, Henrico filio Ranulfi, Johanne de Batelay*, et aliis.

---

463.   Carta Lisiardi.

[. . . . I, Lisiard, have granted . . . . to Peter, priest of St. Clement's, his heirs and assigns, that part of my toft which lies between my house and the house of Richard Lorimer, stretching from the main road to the lord's vivary in length, and 54 feet in breadth. To be held and possessed, &c. Paying yearly to me and my heirs twelve pence for all service, six pence at the feast of St. Martin and six pence at Whitsuntide. Peter has given me twenty-five shillings in hand. Warranty. Witnesses.]

Sciant presentes et futuri quod ego Lisiardus concessi et dedi et hac presenti carta mea confirmavi Petro sacerdoti de sancto Clemente et heredibus suis vel cui assignare voluerit illam partem tofti mei que jacet inter domum meam et domum Ricardi Lorimarii, que extendit se a via capitali usque in vivarium domini in longitudine, et in latitudine quinquaginta quatuor pedum. Tenendam et habendam de me et heredibus meis sibi et heredibus suis vel cui assignare voluerit libere et quiete, in feudo et hereditate. Reddendo annuatim mihi et heredibus meis duodecim denarios pro omni servitio, scilicet sex denarios ad festum sancti Martini et sex denarios ad Pentecosten. Pro hac autem concessione et donatione dedit mihi prefatus Petrus viginti quinque solidos pre manibus. Et ego et heredes mei warentizabimus predictam terram illi et heredibus suis vel cui assignare voluerit contra omnes homines. Hiis testibus, *Johanne de Birkina, Gilliberto de Nottona, Ada de Kellingtona, Eudone capellano, Rogero capellano, Willelmo capellano, Magistro Raimundo,* et aliis,[1] *Ricardo Lorimario,* et aliis.

(1) *Sic.*

464.   Carta Emme de Kanne.[1]

[. . . . . I, Emma de Calne, in the lawful power of my widowhood, have granted . . . . to Walter the clerk, his heirs and assigns, for his homage and service, an acre of land in the Fields of Pontefract, lying between the two high roads leading from Pontefract to the Hospital of St. Michael, between the land of Robert, son of Harold, and the land of Hervey, son of Kaskin. To be held and possessed, &c. Paying thence yearly to me and my heirs two pence at the feast of St. Michael. . . . . Walter has given me ten shillings in acknowledgment. Warranty. Witnesses.]

Sciant presentes et futuri quod ego Emma de Kanne in ligia potestate viduitatis mee dedi et concessi et hac presenti carta mea confirmavi Waltero clerico et heredibus suis vel cui assignare voluerit pro humagio et servitio suo, unam acram terre in campis de Pontefracto. Illam scilicet que jacet inter duas magnas vias tendentes de Pontefracto usque ad Hospitale sancti Michaelis, et inter terram Roberti filii Haraldi et terram Hervei filii Kaskini. Tenendam et habendam prefato Waltero et heredibus suis vel cui assignare voluerit de me et heredibus, in feodo et hereditate, libere et quiete et integre. Reddendo inde annuatim michi et heredibus meis duos denarios ad festum sancti Michaelis pro omni servitio et seculari exactione. Pro hac autem donatione et concessione dedit mihi prefatus Walterus decem solidos de recognitione. Et ego predicta Emma et heredes mei prefatam terram prenominato Waltero et heredibus suis vel cui assignaverit contra omnes homines warantizabimus. Hiis testibus, *Rogero tunc decano de Pontefracto, magistro Raimundo, Waltero de Castello, Petro capellano,*[2] *Willelmo de Kamesala, Alano Noel,* et aliis.

(1) Comparing No. 464 with a later charter (No. 475) of Agnes the daughter of Emma, in which the subject of this grant is one of three, and collating both charters with No. 468, from William the husband of Emma, it is evident that this version, "Emma de Kanne," is but a misreading for "Emma de Calne."   (2) Of St. Clement's.

467.[1]   Carta Lisiardi.   Circa 1220,

[. . . . . . . I, Lisiard, have granted . . . . to Walter the clerk, his heirs
or assigns, a messuage in Pontefract behind the Castle.   It lies between the
messuage of the aforesaid Walter which he holds of me and the messuage of
William, my brother, and extends from the main road to the lord's vivary.   I have
besides granted to him my workshop which stands before his house.   To be held
and possessed, &c.   Paying yearly to me and my heirs six pence, three pence at
the feast of St. Martin and three pence at Whitsuntide. . . . . . Walter has given
me two silver marks in acknowledgment.   Warranty.   Witnesses.]

Sciant presentes et futuri quod ego Lisyardus[2] dedi et concessi et
hac presenti carta mea confirmavi Waltero clerico et heredibus suis
vel ejus assignatis unum mesuagium in Pontefracto retro Castellum.
Illud scilicet quod jacet inter mesuagium predicti Walteri quod tenet
de me et mesuagium Willelmi fratris mei et extendit se a via capitali
usque in vivarium[3] domini.   Preterea dedi ei et concessi fabricam
meam que stat ante domum ipsius Walteri.   Tenendum et habendum
sibi et heredibus suis vel ejus assignatis de me et heredibus meis, in
feudo et hereditate, libere, quiete, pacifice, et integre.   Reddendo inde
annuatim mihi et heredibus meis sex denarios, scilicet tres denarios
ad festum sancti Martini et iij denarios ad Pentecosten, pro omni
servitio et seculari exactione.   Pro hac autem donatione et concessione
dedit mihi predictus Walterus duas marcas argenti de recognitione.
Ego vero Lysiardus[2] et heredes mei predictam terram predicto Waltero
et heredibus suis vel ejus assignatis contra omnes homines warantizabimus in perpetuum.   Hiis testibus, *Roberto de Kent tunc senescallo,*
Johanne de Byrkin, Henrico Walensi,[4] *Alano de Smythetona, Henrico*
Byset, Alano Noel, Waltero Scot, Willelmo Danepore, et aliis.

---

(1) The numbering of these charters was at this part of the Chartulary performed very
irregularly and hastily.   At this point there is neither No. 465 nor No. 466, and about sixteen
charters later on, between No. 480 and No. 490, there are still further irregularities, which, however,
balance each other.   (2) *Sic* in each case.

(3) No. 96 shows a gift to the monks by Robert de Stapleton I (*circa* 1170) of the fee of a toft
"above the Pool," wherewith to make his anniversary.   This charter probably related to this very
property, but no direct evidence that such was the case has yet emerged.

(4) Not yet seneschal.

---

468.   Carta Willelmi filii Willelmi de Calne.[1]   Circa 1212.

[. . . . . I, William de Calne, have granted . . . . . . to Walter, clerk of
Pontefract, his heirs and assigns, for his homage and service, two acres and a

---

(1) In this instance, as in No. 169, the rubricator, when inserting the headings to the charter,
drew upon his better knowledge.   The grantor was described in the document as William de Calne,
a description which was perfectly accurate, though ambiguous, since there were two Williams de
Calne, father and son.   The description in the charter therefore expresses the truth, though not all
the truth ; for the grantor was William de Calne, junior, and therefore, to avoid ambiguity, the
rubricator interposed with a more particular description than that which he found.   For the subject
of the grant see No. 475.

half in the Fields of Pontefract, next the Hospital of St. Michael on the south.
To be held and possessed, &c. Paying yearly to me or my heirs five pence at
the feast of St. Michael. Walter has given me two silver marks in acknowledgment.
Warranty. Witnesses.]

Sciant presentes et futuri quod ego Willelmus de Calne dedi et
concessi et hac presenti carta mea confirmavi Waltero clerico de
Pontefracto, pro homagio et servitio suo, duas acras terre et dimidiam
in campis de Pontefracto, propinquiores hospitali sancti Michaelis ex
parte australi. Tenendas et habendas sibi et heredibus suis vel cui
assignare voluerit libere et quiete, pacifice et integre. Reddendo inde
annuatim mihi vel heredibus meis quinque denarios pro omni servitio
seculari et exactione ad festum sancti Michaelis. Pro hac autem
donatione et concessione dedit michi dictus Walterus duas marcas
argenti de recognitione. Ego vero Willelmus et heredes mei dicto
Waltero et heredibus suis vel cui assignare voluerit dictam terram
contra omnes homines inperpetuum warantizabimus. Hiis testibus,
*Hugone Pincerna tunc senescallo, Willelmo capellano, Thoma de
Knaresburg, Roberto de eadem, Johanne de Bateleya, Johanne de
Lowayn, Willelmo de Aula*, et aliis.

469.[1]   **Carta Johannis filii Ricardi Pinfuel.**

[. . . . . I, John, son of Richard Pinfuel, of Pontefract, have granted . . . . . to
Walter the clerk, his heirs and assigns, two acres and a half in the Fields of
Pontefract, between the land of Richard Haliday and William Brown, abutting
upon Greavewellsike. To be held and possessed, &c. Paying yearly to the exchequer
of the lord of Pontefract five pence at the feast of St. Michael Walter has given
me 14 shillings in acknowledgment. Warranty. Witnesses.]

Sciant omnes tam presentes quam futuri quod ego Johannes filius
Ricardi Pinfuel de Pontefracto dedi et concessi et hac presenti carta
mea confirmavi Waltero clerico et heredibus suis vel cui assignare
voluerit duas acras terre et dimidiam in campis de Pontefracto,
adjacentes inter terram Ricardi Haliday et terram Willelmi Brun,[2]
abuttantes super Grevewellesic. Tenendas et habendas prefato Waltero
et heredibus suis vel cui assignare voluerit, in feudo et hereditate,
libere, quiete, pacifice, integre et honorifice. Reddendo inde annuatim
scaccario domini de Pontefracto quinque denarios ad festum sancti

---

(1) The plots of land dealt with in the earlier charters of Walter the receiver were in the North
Field, that is to say, to use the phrase of No. 103, those "which lie between Ralph's Cross (that is,
Stump Cross) and the thieves' gallows." No. 469 refers to land on the Greave Field, that is,
towards Knottingley. It ought, therefore, to be grouped with No. 474 and No. 477.

(2) This William Brun may possibly be the William Bern of No. 130, No. 131, and No. 474.

Michaelis pro omni servitio seculari et exactione.   Pro hac autem donatione et concessione dedit mihi prefatus Walterus xiiij solidos de recognitione.   Et ego prenominatus Johannes et heredes mei warentizabimus prefato Waltero et heredibus suis vel cui assignare voluerit predictas duas acras et dimidiam contra omnes homines.   Hiis testibus, *Willelmo de Nottona, tunc constabulario de Pontefracto, magistro Raimundo,*[3] *Ada de Kelingtona, Rogero decano de Ledeshaṁa, Roberto Camerario, Radulfo de Bateleia,* et aliis.

(3) He was not yet of Methley.

---

470.   **Carta Arnaldi filii Hormi de Feria.**

[. . . . . I, Arnald, son of Orm of Ferry, have granted . . . . . to Walter, clerk of Pontefract, his heirs and assigns, a rent of six pence in Ferry, which Richard of Methley has paid me yearly, a messuage near the house of John de Wakefield, and a rood and a half of land abutting upon the meadow.   To be held and possessed, &c. Paying yearly to me and my heirs a half-penny at the feast of St. Martin.   Walter has given me six shillings in acknowledgment.   Warranty.   Witnesses.]

Sciant presentes et futuri quod ego Arnaldus, filius Hormi de Feria, dedi et concessi et hac presenti carta mea confirmavi Waltero clerico de Pontefracto redditum sex denariorum in Feria quos Ricardus de Medelaya reddidit mihi annuatim et unum mesuagium juxta domum Johannis de Wakefeld et unam percatam terre et dimidiam abuttantem super pratum.   Tenendum et habendum sibi et heredibus suis vel cui assignare voluerit in feudo et hereditate, libere, quiete, pacifice, integre.   Reddendo inde annuatim mihi et heredibus meis unum obolum ad festum sancti Martini pro omnibus servitiis.   Pro ista vero donatione et confirmatione dedit mihi dictus Walterus de recognitione sex solidos.   Et ego Arnaldus et heredes mei dicto Waltero clerico et heredibus vel assignatis suis dictam firmam et dictum tenementum contra omnes homines warentizabimus. Hiis testibus, *Alano de Smythetona, Roberto Camerario, Henrico Biset, Willelmo de Daneport, Willelmo de Aula, Henrico filio Matildis, Waltero Scot, Hugone de Castelforda,* et aliis.

---

471.   **Carta Agnetis filie Rogeri de Ledestuna.**   **Circa 1216.**

[. . . . . . I, Agnes de Parlington, daughter of Roger of Ledstone, formerly wife of William de Parlington, in the power of my widowhood, have granted . . . . . to Walter, clerk of Pontefract, his heirs and assigns, nine acres with appurtenances in the Field of Hardwick, lying near the way by which we go from Pontefract to the mill of Hardwick towards the east. To be held and possessed, &c. Paying yearly to me and my heirs two shillings, twelve pence at the feast of St. Martin and twelve pence at Whitsuntide. Walter the clerk has given me five silver marks in acknowledgment. Warranty. Witnesses.]

Sciant presentes et futuri quod ego Agnes de Parlingtona, filia Rogeri de Ledestuna, uxor quondam Willelmi de Parlingtona, in propria potestate viduitatis mee concessi et dedi et hac mea presenti carta confirmavi Waltero clerico de Pontefracto novem acras terre cum pertinentiis in campo de Herdwic, adjacentes prope viam per quam itur a Pontefracto ad molendinum de Herdwic versus orientem. Tenendas et habendas et sibi et heredibus suis vel cui assignare voluerit in feudo et hereditate, libere et quiete, pacifice et integre. Reddendo inde annuatim mihi et heredibus meis duos solidos pro omni seculari servitio et consuetudine. Scilicet duodecim denarios ad festum sancti Martini et xij denarios ad Pentecosten. Pro ista vero donatione et concessione dedit mihi predictus Walterus clericus v marcas argenti de recognitione. Et ego Agnes et heredes mei predictam terram cum pertinentiis predicto Waltero clerico et heredibus suis vel cui assignare voluerit contra omnes homines inperpetuum warantizabimus. Hiis testibus, *Hugone Pincerna tunc senescallo, Roberto de Stapiltona, Henrico Biset, Roberto filio Hernisii, Waltero Scotico, Willelmo de Daneport*, et aliis.

---

472.   Carta Ricardi[1] Lorimarii.

[. . . . . . I, Hugh son of Richard Lorimer, have given . . . . . to Walter, clerk of Pontefract, and his assigns, the land behind the Castle which was Lisiard's and William his brother's. To be held and possessed, &c. . . . . . . Paying yearly to me and my heirs twenty-five pence for all services, half at Whitsuntide and half at the feast of St. Martin. Walter the clerk has given me twenty shillings in acknowledgment. Warranty. Witnesses.]

Sciant presentes et futuri quod ego, Hugo filius Ricardi Lorimarii, dedi et concessi et hac presenti carta mea confirmavi Waltero clerico de Pontefracto totam terram que fuit Lisiardi retro castrum et Willelmi fratris sui. Tenendam et habendam sibi vel cui assignare voluerit de me et heredibus meis in feodo et hereditate, libere, quiete, pacifice et integre. Reddendo inde annuatim mihi et heredibus meis viginti quinque denarios pro omnibus servitiis, scilicet medietatem ad Pentecosten et medietatem ad festum sancti Martini.

---

(1) *Sic*, in obvious error for *Hugonis filii Ricardi*.

Pro ista vero donatione et confirmatione dedit mihi Walterus clericus viginti solidos de recognitione. Et ego Hugo filius Ricardi Lorimarii et heredes mei predicto Waltero clerico vel assignatis suis predictam terram cum pertinentiis contra omnes homines warantizabimus. Hiis testibus, *Roberto de Cantia, tunc senescallo, Johanne de Byrkina, Alano de Smythetona, Henrico Biset, Waltero Scot, Willelmo de Daneport, Alano Noel, Willelmo de Aula*, et aliis.

---

473.   Carta Walteri Scotici.

[. . . . . . . I, Walter Scott, have given . . . . . . to Walter the clerk and his assigns a culture in the Fields of Pontefract, called The Waterfall, lying at the outskirts of the town above Monkhill towards the Gallows. To be held and possessed, &c. . . . . Paying yearly to me and my heirs two shillings, twelve pence at Whitsuntide and twelve pence at the feast of St. Martin. Walter the clerk has given me two silver marks in acknowledgment. Warranty. Witnesses.]

Sciant presentes et futuri quod ego Walterus Scottus[1] dedi et concessi et hac presenti carta mea confirmavi Waltero clerico unam culturam in campis Pontisfracti, que vocatur Watrefal, jacentem in exitum ville Pontisfracti super montem monachorum versus furcas. Tenendam et habendam sibi vel cui assignare voluerit de me et heredibus meis in feodo et hereditate, libere, quiete, pacifice et integre. Reddendo inde annuatim mihi et heredibus meis ii*os* solidos pro omnibus servitiis, scilicet xii denarios ad Pentecosten et xii denarios ad festum sancti Martini. Pro ista vero donatione et confirmatione dedit mihi Walterus clericus duas marcas argenti de recognitione. Ego vero Walterus Scott et heredes mei predicto Waltero clerico vel assignatis suis predictam culturam contra omnes homines warantizabimus. Hiis testibus, *Roberto Camerario, Johanne de Lovayn, Henrico Byset, Willelmo de Aula, Willelmo de Daneport, Hugone de Castelforda, Symone de Rupe*, et aliis.

(1) *Sic.*

---

474.   Carta Matildis filie Willelmi Bern.[1]

[. . . . . . . I, Matilda, daughter of William Bern, in power of my widowhood have granted . . . . to Walter, clerk of Pontefract, his heirs and assigns, two acres in the territory of Pontefract near the Greave, one near the land of William

---

(1) In No. 469 he is called Brun.

son of Hervey and another which abuts upon Wellsike. To be held and possessed,
&c. . . . . Paying yearly to me and my heirs four pence at the feast of
St. Michael. . . . . . . Walter the clerk has given me a silver mark in acknowledgment. Warranty. Witnesses.]

Sciant presentes et futuri quod ego Matildis filia Willelmi Bern, in
propria viduitatis mee,[2] concessi et dedi et hac mea presenti carta
confirmavi Waltero clerico de Pontefracto duas acras terre in
territorio de Pontefracto juxta Greve, unam acram scilicet que jacet
juxta terram Willelmi filii Hervei et aliam acram que abuttat super
Wellesik.[3] Tenendas et habendas sibi et heredibus vel cui assignare
voluerit in feodo et hereditate, libere, quiete, et pacifice. Reddendo
inde annuatim mihi et heredibus meis quatuor denarios ad festum Sancti
Michaelis pro omni servitio et exactione. Pro hac autem concessione
et donatione dedit mihi predictus Walterus clericus unam marcam
argenti de recognitione. Ego vero predicta Matildis et heredes mei
predicto Waltero clerico et heredibus suis vel ubi assignare voluerit
predictas duas acras terre contra omnes homines warantizabimus
inperpetuum. Hiis testibus, *Hugone Pincerna, tunc senescallo, Roberto
de Stapiltona, Jordano de Insula, Roberto Camerario, Johanne de
Lovayn, Gregorio de Camera, Roberto filio Silver*, et aliis.

(2) The word " potestate" is omitted.
(3) In No. 469 it is named Grevewellesic, while in No. 477 it is Grewellesic.

475 [1]   **Carta Agnetis filie Emme.**   **1240.**

[. . . . . . I, Agnes daughter of Emma, in my power as a maiden, have quit-
claimed to Walter, the clerk of Pontefract, his heirs and assigns, a messuage which
belonged to Robert White, the weaver, before the entrance of St. Nicholas' chapel in
Pontefract, and an acre of land between the two roads leading to the Hospital of
St. Michael, and two acres and a half behind the Hospital of St. Michael towards
Darrington. To be held and possessed, &c. . . . . . . Paying yearly to me and my
heirs six pence at the feast of St. Martin. . . . . I, Agnes and my heirs, will
warrant and defend, &c. . . . . . . This charter was made on St. Dunstan's Day, in
the 24th year of the reign of King Henry, in the court of Pontefract. Witnesses.]

Sciant presentes et futuri quod ego Agnes filia Emme, in ligia
puellari potestate mea, quietum clamavi Waltero clerico de Pontefracto
unum mesuagium quod fuit Roberti Albi textoris, quod jacet ante
hostium capelle sancti Nicholai in Pontefracto, et unam acram terre
que jacet inter duas vias que tendunt versus hospitale sancti Michaelis,

(1) This is the only charter between No. 455 and No. 480 which I have found copied or
abstracted.

et duas acras et dimidiam que jacent retro hospitale sancti Michaelis versus Dardingtonam.   Habendum et tenendum sibi et heredibus suis vel suis assignatis libere et quiete de me et heredibus meis. Reddendo inde annuatim mihi et heredibus meis sex denarios ad festum sancti Martini pro omni servitio seculari, exactione et demanda. Ego vero Agnes et heredes mei predictum mesuagium et totam predictam terram cum omnibus pertinentiis predicto Waltero vel suis assignatis contra omnes homines pro predicto servitio warantizabimus inperpetuum et defendemus.   Hec carta facta fuit die sancti Dunstani, anno regni Regis Henrici xx° iiij,[2] in curia de Pontefracto.   Hiis testibus, *domino Adam de Neirforda, tunc senescallo, domino Thoma de Pirhou, domino Rogero de Nottona, Symone de Rupe, Roberto persona de Medeley, Gregorio de Camera*, et aliis.

(2) May 19, 1240.

476.[1]   **Carta Symonis Pincerne.**

[. . . . . . I, Simon Butler, have granted . . . . . to Walter the clerk, his heirs and assigns, ... seven acres and three roods in the Fields of Pontefract, four acres and a half upon Dalebank, near the land of William de Campsall, and three acres and a rood under Hamelinroyd-end, near the land of Thomas son of Edwin. To be held and possessed, &c. . . . . . Paying yearly to me and my heirs 8 pence at the feast of St. Martin. . . . . Walter the clerk has given me five silver marks in acknowledgment.   Warranty.   Witnesses.]

Sciant presentes et futuri quod ego Symon Pincerna dedi et concessi et hac presenti carta mea confirmavi Waltero clerico et heredibus suis vel cui assignare voluerit pro homagio et servitio suo septem acras terre et tres percatas in campis de Pontefracto.   Scilicet quatuor acras et dimidiam super Dalebank propinquiores terre Willelmi de Kamesale et tres acras et unam percatam subtus Hamelinrodehend propinquiores terre Thome filii Edwini.   Tenendas et habendas sibi et heredibus suis vel cui assignare voluerit de me et de heredibus meis in feodo et hereditate, libere et quiete et honorifice.   Reddendo inde annuatim mihi et heredibus meis viij denarios ad festum sancti Martini pro omni servitio et seculari exactione.   Pro hac vero donatione et concessione dedit mihi prefatus Walterus clericus quinque marcas argenti de recognitione.   Et ego predictus Symon et heredes mei predictas vii acras terre et tres percatas prenominato Waltero

(1) This is an earlier charter ; and as John de Birkin, who died in 1227, witnesses it, we learn that Simon "Butler" had become "Pincerna" at least before that year.

clerico et heredibus suis vel cui assignare voluerit contra omnes homines inperpetuum warantizabimus.   Hiis testibus, *Gilleberto de Nottona, tunc senescallo, Johanne de Birkina, Radulfo de Bateleia, Willelmo de Camosala, Alano Noel, Willelmo de Aula, Radulfo de Northgate, Symone Beverege, Gilleberto filio Hugonis, Waltero Scot,* et aliis.

---

477.   **Carta Huctredi filii Andree.**

[. . . . . . . I, Uctred son of Andrew, and Beatrice daughter of Robert son of Astin, my wife, have sold . . . . to John son of Richard Pinful and his heirs two acres and a half in the Fields of Pontefract, lying between the land of Richard Haliday and the land of William Bern, abutting upon the Greavewellsike.   To be held by him, &c. . . . . . . Paying yearly to the lord's exchequer five pence at the feast of St. Michael . . . .   The aforesaid John has given us twelve shillings sterling.   Witnesses.]

Sciant presentes et futuri quod ego Huctredus filius Andree et Beatrix filia Roberti filii Astini, uxor mea, vendidimus et inperpetuum quietas clamavimus de nobis et heredibus nostris Johanni filio Ricardi Pinful et heredibus suis duas acras terre et dimidiam in campis Pontisfracti adjacentes inter terram Ricardi Haliday et terram Willelmi Bern, abuttantes super Grewellesic.   Tenendas sibi et heredibus suis, in feodo et hereditate, libere, quiete, pacifice, integre.   Reddendo inde annuatim scaccario domini quinque denarios ad festum sancti Michaelis pro omnibus servitiis.   Pro ista vero venditione et quieta clamatione dedit nobis predictus Johannes duodecim solidos sterlingorum.   Hiis testibus, *Rogero decano de Ledeshama, magistro Adam de Kellingtona, Johanne fratre suo, Roberto Camerario, Radulfo de Batelay, Thoma fratre suo, Radulfo de Northgate,* et aliis.

---

478.   **Carta Willelmi filii Hervei.**

[. . . . . . I, William, son of Hervey son of Kaskin, have granted . . . . . . to Walter, clerk of Pontefract, his heirs and assigns, ... an assart in the Fields of Pontefract, lying next the land of Simon Butler on the north, abutting on the road from Hardwick.   To be held and possessed, &c. . . . . . .   Paying yearly to me and my heirs thirteen pence at the feast of St. Michael. . . . . . .   The aforesaid Walter has given me five silver marks in acknowledgment.   Warranty.   Witnesses.]

Sciant presentes et futuri quod ego Willelmus filius Hervei filius Kaskini dedi et concessi et hac presenti carta mea confirmavi Waltero clerico de Pontefracto et heredibus suis vel cui assignare voluerit pro homagio et servitio suo unum assartum in campis Pontis fracti, jacens juxta terram Symonis Pincerne in parte boreali, abuttans super viam de Herdewic.[1] Tenendum et habendum de me et heredibus meis sibi et heredibus suis vel cui assignare voluerit in feodo et hereditate, libere, quiete.   Reddendo inde annuatim michi et heredibus meis ille et heredes sui tresdecim denarios ad festum sancti Michaelis pro omni servitio et seculari exactione.   Et pro hac donatione et concessione predictus Walterus dedit mihi quinque marcas argenti de recognitione.   Ego vero Willelmus et heredes mei predictum assartum prenominato Waltero et heredibus suis vel cui assignare voluerit contra omnes homines warantizabimus.   Hiis testibus, *Roberto de Cantia, tunc senescallo, Henrico Byseth, Waltero Scotico, Alano Noel, Willelmo de Daneport, Willelmo de Aula, Gilleberto filio Hugonis,* et aliis. _____

(1) Spital Hardwick.

---

479.   **Carta Hugonis filii Walteri quondam receptoris.**

[To all Christ's faithful. . . . . Hugh son of Walter, formerly receiver of Pontefract, greeting in the Lord. For the good of my soul and of the said Walter my father, ... I have granted . . . . all my land in the territory of Pontefract, with appurtenances, which the aforesaid W. my father formerly gave me, and with all the rents and buildings given me by the same my father, as well in the town of Pontefract as without, and with all the escheats which can fall to me, without any withholding. To be held and possessed, &c., as witness the charters of the said Walter my father which I had and which I have delivered to the monks together with my present charter. So that neither I nor my heirs . . . . shall hereafter be able to assert any right in the said land, &c. The monks have granted me a monk's corrody for my whole life, to be received in their house of Pontefract, and ten silver shillings yearly at Whitsuntide. Warranty. Seal. Witnesses.]

Omnibus Christi fidelibus presens scriptum visuris vel audituris Hugo filius Walteri quondam receptoris de Pontefracto salutem in domino. Noveritis me pro salute anime mee et dicti Walteri patris mei et omnium antecessorum et successorum meorum dedisse, concessisse, et hac presenti carta mea confirmasse deo et ecclesie sancti Johannis Apostoli et Evangeliste de Pontefracto et monachis ibidem deo servientibus totam terram meam in territorio de Pontefracto cum pertinentiis suis quam predictus W. pater meus mihi antea dedit, et cum omnibus redditibus et edificiis mihi ab eodem patre meo datis, tam in villa Pontisfracti quam extra, et cum omnibus eschaetis que mihi aliquo modo accidere possunt, sine aliquo retenemento. Tenendam et habendam dictis monachis in perpetuam elemosinam cum omnibus pertinentiis et libertatibus suis et cum omnibus redditibus, edificiis et eschaetis supranominatis, libere, quiete, pacifice, et honorifice, prout carte dicti Walteri patris mei, quas habui et quas dictis monachis una cum presenti carta mea tradidi, testantur. Ita quod nec ego nec heredes mei nec aliquis alius per me vel pro me in dicta terra, redditibus, edificiis et omnibus aliis supranominatis aliquod jus vel clamium in posterum vendicare poterimus vel exigere. Pro hac autem mea donatione, concessione et confirmatione, concesserunt me[1] dicti monachi unum corredium monachale in tota vita mea in domo sua de Pontefracto percipiendum et decem solidos argenti annuatim ad Pentecosten. Et ego dictus Hugo et heredes mei vel mei assignati totam predictam terram cum omnibus pertinentiis et cum omnibus redditibus, edificiis et eschaetis supranominatis, dictis monachis inperpetuum warantizabimus contra omnes homines ac defendemus. Et ut hec mea donatio, concessio et confirmatio perpetue firmitatis robur optineat, huic scripto sigillum apposui in testimonium. Hiis testibus, *domino Ricardo Walensi, domino Henrico fratre suo, Symone de Rupe, Symone filio suo, Willelmo de Fetherstana, Willelmo de Cell'o, Roberto filio Amabilie, Rogero filio Mabile,*[1] *Roberto fratre suo,* et aliis.

―――― ――――

(1) *Sic* in each case.

―――――――――

480.　　　**Carta Dalmatii Prioris de Pontefracto.**　　　**1248.**

[To all the sons, &c., brother Dalmatius, the humble minister of Pontefract, and the convent of that place, greeting in the Lord. We have granted . . . . . to our beloved Hugh son of Walter, formerly receiver of Pontefract, a monk's corrody, to be received all the days of his life in our house of Pontefract, whether he shall be present or absent, that is to say, a loaf and a gallon of monastery beer daily, and a mess from the kitchen such as a monk receives in our house. Also ten silver shillings yearly at Whitsuntide, without fraud and without failure. The said Hugh has given us all his land in the territory of Pontefract, which the said Walter his father formerly gave him, with all its appurtenances, &c. . . . . In witness this charter has been made in the manner of a cyrograph, one part of which sealed with our authentic seal shall remain in possession of the said Hugh, and the other part sealed with the seal of the said Hugh shall remain in our possession. Done in the year of grace one thousand two hundred and forty-eight, at the feast of St. Martin in winter. Witnesses.]

Omnibus sancte matris ecclesie filiis ad quos presens scriptum pervenerit frater Dalmatius humilis minister de Pontefracto et ejusdem loci conventus salutem in domino. Noveritis nos concessisse et hac presenti carta nostra confirmasse dilecto nostro Hugoni filio Walterii[1] quondam receptoris de Pontefracto unum corredium monachale omnibus diebus vite sue in domo nostra de Pontefracto percipiendum, sive presens fuerit sive absens, videlicet unam micam et unam galonem cervisie conventualis qualibet die et unum ferculum de coquina sicut unus monachus in domo nostra percipit, et insuper decem solidos argenti annuatim percipiendos ad Pentecosten sine fraude et sine defectu aliquo. Pro hac vero nostra concessione et confirmatione dedit nobis dictus Hugo totam terram suam in territorio Pontisfracti, quam dictus Walterus pater suus ei antea dederat, cum omnibus pertinentiis suis et cum omnibus redditibus, edificiis, et eschaetis, eidem a dicto patre suo infra dictam villam et extra datis et concessis. In cujus rei testimonium facta est hec carta in modum cyrographi, cujus una pars sigillata sigillo nostro auctentico remanebit penes dictum Hugonem. Et altera pars sigillata sigillo dicti Hugonis remanebit penes nos. Actum anno gratie millesimo ducentesimo quadragesimo octavo, ad festum sancti Martini in Hyeme. Hiis testibus, *domino Johanne de Hoderode, Hugone tunc decano de Pontefracto, Thoma de Reclusagio et Augustino capellanis, Symone de Rupe, Symone filio suo, Willelmo de Fetherstana*, et aliis.

(1) *Sic.*

480.[1]   1250.

[To all Christ's faithful . . . . . . John son of Walter the receiver, of Preston, greeting in the Lord. I have granted . . . . all right . . . . and suit which we had or might have in all that land in the town and in the territory of Pontefract, in messuage, rents, the services of free men, reliefs, homages, and all other things anywhere belonging, as well within the town of Pontefract as without, which Walter my father gave to Hugh the clerk my brother, and the said Hugh gave . . . . in free and perpetual alms. Also I confirm the gift of that Hugh, according to the charter of the said Hugh. Neither I, John, nor any of my heirs can have hereafter any right, claim, or suit in the aforesaid . . . . The monks shall hold these things well and in peace, quit from me and my heirs for ever. I grant also . . . . that if it shall happen to those monks (which God forbid) to be in any way impleaded in the court of the lord the king or elsewhere, ... concerning the aforesaid land, &c., and they shall wish to summon us, we will not refuse to go. To the monks and their men, whomsoever they shall have attornied, we will give faithful counsel and help. All the aforesaid shall be held and maintained without any gainsaying. If the monks shall wish to cyrograph the said land, &c., before the justice, we will assent without

(1) This charter, No. 480 *bis*, is really No. 479 (see note (1) to No. 467), and has been entered without any heading, as have the remainder of the charters in this Fasciculus. It is copied with a few literal errors, mainly arising from the difficult handwriting, into *Dodsworth*, vol. 151, and there is an abstract in vol. 138.

gainsaying. And that this my grant and obligation, in the form which shall have been above noted, shall be held for ever, I, John, have promised and sworn for myself and my heirs. Seal. Witnesses. Given at Pontefract on the morrow of St. Martin, in the 35th year of King Henry, son of King John.]

Omnibus Christi fidelibus ad quos presens scriptum pervenerit Johannes filius Walteri le recevour de Preston salutem in domino. Noverit universitas vestra me concessisse pro me et heredibus meis inperpetuum deo et ecclesie sancti Johannis evangeliste de Ponte-fracto et monachis ibidem deo servientibus totum jus si quod habuimus vel in aliquo tempore habere possemus, et similiter eisdem monachis remisisse et quietum clamasse totum clamium et omni-modam peticionem que habuimus vel umquam habere possemus in tota terra illa, in villa et in territorio de Pontefracto, messuagio, redditibus, servitiis liberorum, releviis, homagiis, et omnibus aliis rebus ad eandem terram et cetera prenominata tam infra villam de Pontefracto quam extra ubique pertinentibus, que Willielmus[2] pater meus dedit Hugoni le clerc fratri meo et idem Hugo dedit et carta sua confirmavit deo et prefate ecclesie sancti Johannis evangeliste de Pontefracto et prefatis monachis in liberam et perpetuam elemosinam. Cujus etiam Hugonis donum ego Johannes pro me et heredibus meis prefatis monachis per hoc meum scriptum plenius confirmo, secundum quod carta ejusdem Hugonis quam dicti monachi inde habent melius testatur. Et sciendum est quod nec ego Johannes nec aliquis heredum meorum aliquid juris, clamii, aut peticionis de cetero habere poterimus in predicta terra, messuagio, redditibus, servitiis, homagiis, aut aliis pertinentiis suis. Ea omnia tenebunt et habebunt prefati monachi, bene et in pace, quieta de me et heredibus meis inperpetuum. Concedo etiam pro me et heredibus meis, me et ipsos[3] prefatis monachis et eorum successoribus per hoc scriptum obligandos inperpetuum, quod si ab hac die contingat, quod absit, ipsis monachis de predicta terra, messuagio, redditibus, servitiis, homagiis aut aliquibus rebus ad ea pertinentibus, ab aliquibus in curia domini regis vel alibi quacumque videlicet curia vel loco,[4] unique inplacitari quicumque et ubicumque, iidem monachi nos dicti tamen eorum supraposita ducere vel vocare voluerint, ire non recusabimus nec contradicemus, scilicet eisdem monachis et eorum si quos fecerint attornatos fidele consilium et auxilium juxta omne post termini. Ad omnia predicta tenenda et defendenda sine aliqua

---

(2) This should be Walterus. The writer may have had " W." before him, and guessed thus.

(3) *Sic.* Both here and throughout the Latin is curious; occasionally it is unintelligible.

(4) These five words are omitted by Dodsworth.

contradictione conferemus. Si vero dicti monachi dictam terram, messuagium, redditus, servitium, homagium aut alia pertinentia coram justiciario inter nos cirographare voluerint, ubicunque et quocunque illis hoc facere placuerit, sine contradictione assenciemus. Hanc vero meam concessionem et obligationem in forma illa que superius notata fuerit, in prefatis monachis in perpetuum tenendam, pro me et heredibus meis ego Johannes affidavi et juravi. Et ad majorem omnium securitatem rerum predictarum presenti scripto sigillum meum apposui. Hiis testibus, *domino Johanne de Hoderode tunc senescallo, Henrico Biset clerico, Michaele de Dunestorp, Jordano de Insula, Willelmo de Assartil, Willelmo de Fetherstana, Willelmo filio Sabini de eadem, Stephano clerico de Waittham,* et aliis. Datum apud Pontefractum in crastino sancti Martini anno regni regis Henrici filii regis Johannis xxxv.[5]

(5) 12 November, 1250.

483.

[To all, &c., the prior and convent, &c., eternal greeting in the Lord. We have granted . . . . . . to Sir Richard Foliot the West Mill of Norton, with all the land belonging thereto, and the other appurtenances. We have held it of the gift of the predecessors of the same Sir Jordan Foliot. In exchange for twenty-seven shillings and six pence of annual rent, to be received yearly, half at the feast of St. Martin in winter, and the other half at Whitsuntide. That is to say, from the tenement which Nicholas de Norton has held from the said Sir Richard in Greater Norton twenty-five shillings and six pence sterling, by equal portions at the prescribed terms. Nicholas, for himself and his heirs, has performed fealty to us in the full court of Pontefract. The holding contains these parts: In Wayings three acres of land for six pence yearly. Also ten acres and a half rood, and a third acre of meadow which the said Nicholas has held for ten shillings. Also six acres which Nicholas has held for six shillings. Also three tofts in Norton, for each toft three shillings; one lies in the east of the town where Nicholas then resided, another lies from the west side of the King's highway leading from the hall of the lord towards Campsall, and the third lies from the west of the toft which Adam Smith held. Also from two acres which William son of Robert of Stubbs, the clerk, then held, two shillings; one acre lies between the land of Alan son of John of Little Smeaton on the south side, near the king's highway, and the land of Simon son of Alan the miller on the north side, and abuts upon the Field of Stubbs, and the other lies between the land of John de Quarmby on the south side and the land of William formerly serjeant to Eva de More, on the north side, and abuts similarly on the Field of Stubbs; for these a rent of two shillings is to be paid at the aforesaid terms. The aforesaid William has performed to us fealty. It is understood that the said Nicholas shall hold the aforesaid tenement of Greater Norton as above expressed for the rent mentioned for ever, and shall answer to us faithfully concerning the said rent at the terms above written, and shall do fealty to us and our successors. If Nicholas or his heirs shall fail in the

payment of the rent, we and our successors may distrain the said holding and
seize it into our hands, and hold it until there shall be full satisfaction to us.
William and his heirs shall hold from us the said two acres in manner prescribed.
Sir Richard and his heirs shall from henceforth peaceably possess the said mill
with all its appurtenances without reclaim from us or our successors. Saving to
Sir Richard and his heirs the homages of the said Nicholas and William and their
heirs, and to us the fealties of themselves and their heirs, so that the said Sir
Richard and his heirs will warrant . . . . . . the aforesaid rent to be received yearly
by us. Seal. Witnesses.]

Universis presens scriptum visuris vel audituris prior et conventus
monachorum sancti Johannis de Pontefracto eternam in domino
salutem. Noveritis nos remisisse, concessisse, sursum reddidisse, et
quietum clamasse, de nobis et successoribus nostris in perpetuum
domino Ricardo Folyot et heredibus suis vel assignatis westmolen-
dinum de Norton, cum tota terra pertinente ad ipsum molendinum
et ceteris pertinentiis. Quod quidem molendinum quondam habuimus
in puram et perpetuam elemosinam ex dono domini Jordani[1] Folyot
predecessorum ejusdem. In escambium scilicet xx*ti* septem solidos
et sex denarios annui redditus et perpetui annuatim percipiendos ad
duos anni terminos. Medietatem scilicet ad festum sancti Martini
in Yeme et alteram medietatem ad Pentecosten. Videlicet de
tenemento quod Nicholas de Nortona tenuit de dicto domino
Ricardo in Maiori Nortona et ejus territorio, videlicet xx*ti* quinque
solidos et sex denarios sterlingorum percipiendorum de predicto
Nicholao et heredibus suis vel assignatis, per equales portiones ad
terminos scriptos, unde predictus Nicholas pro se et heredibus suis
vel assignatis nobis prestitit fidelitatem in plena curia Pontisfracti.
Et quidem tenementum continet has partes. Scilicet in Wehynges
tres acras terre pro sex denariis annuatim solvendis. Item decem
acras et dimidiam perticatam et tertiam acram prati quas idem
Nicholas tenuit pro omnia bovata[2] pro decem solidis per annum.
Item sex acras quas dictus Nicholas tenuit de dominico dicti domini
Ricardi pro sex solidis per annum. Item tria tofta in predicta villa
de Nortona, quolibet tofto tres solidos, quorum unum jacet in orientali
parte dicte ville, ubi dictus Nicholas tunc habitavit, et alterum toftum
jacet ab occidentali parte vie regie que ducit ab aula domini versus
Campesaliam, et tertium toftum jacet ab occidente tofti quod Adam
Faber quondam tenuit. Item de duabus acris terre quas Willelmus
filius Roberti de Stubbes clericus tunc tenuit de dicto domino
Ricardo duos solidos per annum, quarum una acra jacet inter terram

---

(1) In apparent error for "Ricardi."   (2) *Sic.*

Alani filii Johannis de Smythetona minori ex parte australi, prope viam regiam et terram Simonis filii Alani molendinarii de eadem ex parte boreali, et buttat super campum de Stubbes. Et alia jacet inter terram Johannis de Querneby ex parte australi et terram Willelmi quondam servientis Eve de Mora ex parte boreali, et buttat similiter super campum de Stubbes, pro qua quidem firma duorum solidorum nobis et successoribus nostris solvenda predictis terminis annuis predictus Willelmus pro se et heredibus suis vel assignatis nobis prestitit fidelitatem. Hoc insuper intellecto quod dictus Nicholas et heredes seu assignati sui totum predictum tenementum de Maiori Nortona prout superius est expressum de nobis et successoribus nostris pro annua firma superius numerata in perpetuum tenebit, et nobis de dicta firma annua terminis suprascriptis fideliter respondebit, et inde nobis et successoribus nostris fidelitatem faciant successive. Et si contingat predictum Nicholaum vel heredes suos seu assignatos in solutione annue firme predicte suis terminis nobis solvende deficere, licebit nobis et successoribus nostris dictum tenementum distringere tam infra predictam villam de Nortona quam extra, et dictum tenementum in manus nostras saisire, et tam diu saisitum recevere[3] donec de dicta firma annua nobis fuerit plenarie satisfactio. Et dictus Willelmus et heredes sui vel assignati dictas duas acras terre in modo prescripto de nobis tenebunt. Dictus vero dominus Ricardus et heredes sui vel assignati ex nunc et in posterum dictum molendinum cum omnibus suis pertinentiis sine reclamatione nostri vel successorum nostrorum in perpetuum pacifice possidebunt. Salvis dicto domino Ricardo et heredibus suis vel assignatis homagiis predictorum Nicholai et Willelmi et heredum eorundem seu assignatorum, et nobis fidelitatibus eorundem et heredum suorum seu assignatorum. Ita videlicet quod predictus dominus Ricardus et heredes sui et assignati predictam firmam de predicto tenemento annuatim percipiendam nobis et successoribus nostris in puram et perpetuam elemosinam contra omnes homines warantizabit, acquietabit, et defendebit in perpetuum. In cujus rei testimonium ego predictus Ricardus Folioth pro me et heredibus meis vel assignatis presenti scripto priori et conventui tradito sigillum meum apposui. Hiis testibus, *domino W. le Vavasur tunc constabulario castelli Pontisfracti, domino Ada de Novo Mercato, Petro de Santona tunc senescallo Pontisfracti, domino Hugone Swinlingtona, Johanne de Hetona milite,* et multis aliis presentibus in plena curia Pontisfracti.

---

(3) *Sic.*

484.[1]

[. . . . . . I, Adam de Newmarch, son of John de Newmarch, for the good of
my soul and of Joanna my wife, and of my father and all my ancestors and heirs,
have granted . . . . . to God and St. Mary and the Monastery and Cluniac monks
of the York diocese, &c., the place of the blessed Nicholas of Cobcroft, with all
its appurtenances . . . . To be held and possessed, &c., ... by their finding a monk
to celebrate mass in Cobcroft, for the souls of the abovesaid and of all the faithful
departed.   If the said prior and convent fail in so finding a monk (which God
forbid), it shall be allowed me and my heirs to distrain upon them in Cobcroft to
full satisfaction.   And if in course of time it happen, through anyone's diligence,
that the said place of Cobcroft should be so increased that thereby three or more
monks can be sustained, their prior or guardian shall be presented to me or my
heirs, one or other in turn for one deposed, dead or removed.   And in their
vacancy, it shall be allowed to me and my heirs to have the custody of the place
without waste.   He who on that account shall receive it for me shall have his will
of it for the time.   And the place shall be vacant only for this purpose.   And if
the prior and convent can acquire anything in my fee, in the town and territory of
Womersley, they shall be permitted.   Warranty.   Seal.   Witnesses.]

Sciant presentes et futuri quod ego Adam de Novo Mercato, filius
Johannis de Novo Mercato, pro salute anime mee et Johanne uxoris
mee et patris mei predicti et omnium antecessorum et heredum
meorum in futurum, dedi, concessi, et hac presenti carta mea confirmavi deo et beate Marie virgini et monasterio sancti Johannis
evangeliste   de   Pontefracto   ac   monachis   ejusdem   loci   ordinis
Cluniacensis Eboracensis diocesis in eodem loco servientibus locum
beati Nicholai de Cobbecroft, cum omnibus pertinentiis suis, terris,
redditibus, possessionibus, juribus, libertatibus, communis, aisiamentis,
et estovariis, in boscis, planis, pascuis et pasturis, mariscis et moris,
stagnis et aquis, vivariis, molendinis et omnibus aliis commoditatibus
quibuscunque ad dictum locum de Cobecroft pertinentibus, in
puram, liberam et perpetuam elemosinam, sine ullo retenemento
mei vel heredum meorum in perpetuum.   Tenendum et habendum
et possidendum jure perpetuo dicto monasterio et monachis ibidem
deo servientibus ordinis supradicti, inveniendo unum monachum in
dicto loco de Cobbecroft divina celebrantem pro animabus supradictorum et omnium fidelium defunctorum.   Et sciendum est quod
si dicti prior et conventus de Pontefracto in inveniendo unum
monachum divina celebrantem in eodem loco de Cobbecroft, quod
absit, defecerint, licebit mihi et heredibus meis dictos priorem et
conventum in predicto loco de Cobbecroft distringere usque ad
satisfactionem plenariam.   Et si processu temporis contigerit per
cujuscunque industam[2] dictum locum de Cobbecroft in bonis

---

(1) There is an incomplete abstract of No. 484 in *Lansdowne* 207a.   (2) *Sic.*

temporalibus adeo augmentari quod inde tres vel plures monachi dicti monasterii et ordinis possint commodo sustentari, prior vel custos eorum mihi vel heredibus‑meis presentabitur, et alius successive alio deponito, mortuo, vel amoto.   Et quorum vacationis licebit mihi et heredibus meis custodiam dicti loci habere per aliquem de meis sine wasto aliquo aut destructione.   Qui mihi inde capiet, habebit suo termino nutum suum.   Et hoc solum gradui dictus locus vacaverit.   Et si dicti prior et conventus in posterum aliquid possint adquirere vel perquirere in feodo meo, in villa et territorio de Wylmersley, licebit eis cum voluntate tum mea et assensu meo et heredum meorum.   Ego vero dictus Adam et heredes mei predictam elemosinam meam ita puram, liberam et perpetuam sicut predictum est, quantum est de feodo meo, predictis monasterio et monachis contra omnes homines warantizabimus, adquietabimus et defendemus in perpetuum.   In cujus rei testimonium pro me et heredibus meis ac successoribus presenti scripto sigillum meum apposui.   Hiis testibus, *domino Ricardo Foliot, domino Jordano Foliot, domino Roberto de Wilmersly,[3] domino Umfrido de Veili militibus, Petro de Santona, Nicholao de Burtona, Petro de Giptona,* et multis aliis.

(3) I have come across nothing concerning this Robert of Womersley. His name as spelt here illustrates the continual tendency to introduce an "l" into the first syllable of Womersley, as if deriving the name from "William." Similarly Hemelesworth for Hemsworth is a frequent use.

483.[1]   Circa 1250.

[. . . . . . I, Dalmatius, the humble prior of Pontefract, and the convent, have granted . . . . . to Thomas de Manningham a bovate of land in the town of Denby, which Thomas de Thornton gave us and Robert de Denby has held from us.   To be held and possessed, &c.   Paying to us yearly, at the feast of St. Giles, twelve pence.   We have placed our common seal to the present writing.   The said Thomas . . . . . has placed his seal to the transcript which we retain in our charge. Witnesses.]

Sciant presentes et futuri quod ego Dalmatius, prior humilis de Pontefracto, et ejusdem loci conventus, dimisimus, concessimus et hac presenti carta nostra confirmavimus Thome de Mayingham unam bovatam[2] terre in villa de Deneby, illam scilicet quam Thomas de Thornethona[3] nobis dedit et Robertus de Deneby de nobis tenuit.

(1) In this charter—thus numbered—a hyphen at the commencement of the second line is used as an indication of a word divided between two lines.

(2) Doubtless the bovate which the monks acquired by No. 431.

(3) The name of Thomas de Thornton frequently appears as an attesting witness to deeds in the Chartulary ; partly, no doubt, because he was the king's bailiff (No. 181), perhaps in succession to Ranulph son of Alan, who held both Staincross and Osgoldcross (see No. 110 and No. 269) ; but mainly because he was a local man of importance as husband of the heir of William de Preston (see pedigree, *ante,* p. 226).

Tenendam et habendam prefato Thome et heredibus suis de nobis, libere, quiete, et pacifice, in feodo et hereditate, cum tofto et crofto et aliis asyamentis ad predictam bovatam terre pertinentibus. Reddendo inde nobis annuatim ad festum sancti Egidii duodecim denarios pro omnibus servitiis ad nos pertinentibus. In cujus rei testimonium presenti scripto sigillum nostrum commune apposuimus. Et ne idem Thomas vel heredes ejus in posterum contra tenorem hujus carte venire possint, transcripto quod penes nos retinemus pro se et heredibus suis sigillum suum apposuit. Hiis testibus, *domino J. de Hoderod tunc senescallo,*[4] *Hugone de Brodecrofts,*[5] *Johanne de Hawrd, Elya de Oxneap, Ricardo le Blomer de Bradeford,* et aliis.

(4) John de Hoderoyd was seneschal at least from 1250 to 1258.
(5) Hugh de Brodecroft was the first husband of Incella, one of the co-heirs of Thomas de Thornton.

Ante 1156.[1]

[Be it known . . . . . . that Sir Adam, prior of Pontefract, with the consent of the chapter, has granted to this Matthew his land of Shitlington, in wood and plain, as his father Saxe held it well, for 6 shillings to be paid yearly, free and quit from other services except what a free man is accustomed to do to his lord without exaction. Yet so that the monks may have as much wood as may suffice for their works. If Matthew should die before Edith his wife, then, by the same service which Matthew now renders, she may hold that land as if he had given it to her in dower. The witnesses are, &c.]

Notum sit omnibus tam presentibus quam futuris quod dominus Adam prior Pontisfracti, consensu totius capituli, concessit huic Matheo terram suam de Schitlingtona in bosco et plano, sicut pater ejus Saxe eam melius tenuit, pro vj solidis per annum solvendis, liberam et quietam ab aliis servitiis, preter ea que liberalis homo facere solet domino suo sine exactione. Ita tamen ut monachi tantum habeant de bosco quantum sufficiat propriis operibus eorum. Et si contigerit Matheum mori ante Edith uxorem suam, eodem servitio quod modo reddit Matheus teneat ipsa eandem terram, sicut ei in dote donaverit eam. Hujus rei testes sunt, *Adam filius Sywardi, Adam de Horbiri, Paulinus filius Walteri, Robertus filius Stanard, Paganus Parmentarius,* et aliis.[2]

(1) As Prior Adam was transferred to Monk Bretton in 1156, this charter, if genuine, must ante-date that year. But it was not placed in this record till about 1250, and then was unnumbered; so that, as in the case of No. 378, there is not even the usual guarantee for its accuracy, while it might easily have been manufactured or manipulated to serve a purpose.
(2) *Sic.*

CCCCLXXX sexta. 1192.

[. . . . . I, Hugh, prior of Pontefract, by the counsel and consent of the whole convent, have granted . . . . . . to Edwin son of Walter, and his heirs, two bovates of land in Flockton, with their appurtenances, which William de Hotton gave us, that Edwin may hold the bovates from us, freely, quietly, &c., paying to us yearly four shillings, ... half at the feast of St. Martin and half at Whitsuntide. Edwin and his heirs shall besides give to us, for Henry son of Edward and for all his following, in acknowledgment of his homage, six pence yearly, three pence at the feast of St. Martin and three pence at Whitsuntide. This Henry with all his following we have granted to the aforesaid Edwin and his heirs for the aforesaid six pence. Witnesses.]

Sciant presentes et futuri quod ego Hugo, prior de Pontefracto, consilio et consensu totius conventus, dedi, concessi, et hac presenti carta nostra confirmavi Edwino filio Walteri et heredibus suis duas bovatas terre in Floctona cum omnibus pertinentibus suis. Illas scilicet quas Willelmus de Hoctona dedit nobis, ut ipse Edwinus predictas bovatas habeat et teneat de nobis libere, quiete, et honorifice, in feodo et hereditate. Reddendo inde nobis ipse et heredes sui annuatim quatuor solidos pro omnibus que ad terram pertinent, medietatem solidorum ad festum sancti Martini et medietatem ad Pentecosten. Preterea idem Eduuinus et heredes sui dabunt nobis pro Henrico filio Eduuardi et pro omni secta sua in recognitione homagii sui sex denarios annuatim, tres scilicet denarios ad festum sancti Martini et tres denarios ad Pentecosten. Quem Henricum cum tota secta sua prefato Eduuino et heredibus suis concessimus, de nobis tenendos pro predictis sex denariis. Hiis testibus, *Eudone de Lungevilers tunc senescallo, Alano filio ejus, Willelmo de Lungevilers, Ada de Raynevilla, Thoma filio ejus, Ada filio Petri, Johanne filio ejus, Willelmo de Preston, Arnald Pigat,* etc.[1]

---

(1) Here all the Lungvilers precede the de Reinevilles and the Fitz Peters. In No. 211 and No. 233 they come before the de Arches, but in No. 231 and No. 248 they come after de Reinevilles. Of the last five witnesses to the present charter, the first (Thomas) died in 1218, the next in 1207, and the third in 1227.

Fasciculus XI.

THE ELEVENTH and last Fasciculus commences on the 76th folio with a charter of Prior Stephen, in the original hand as usual.

This Fasciculus shows more signs of wear than any other portion of the volume; the parchment is comparatively brittle and the edges are more torn. It evidences in many ways that the practical men of the monastery were more concerned with these living documents, by which they obtained their rents, than with the dead documents by which they had acquired their property.

In dealing with the contents, as to the nature of which we have already said something on page 519, we soon (No. 489) come upon the name "De Novoforo." It precedes the names of Henry Wallis (the son of the great seneschal of Roger de Lascy) and of Alan son of Ralph (the bailiff of Osgoldcross and Staincross), and it is noteworthy that it occurs in the charters of Roche Abbey and of Monk Bretton, at an interval of two generations, and in each case competent authorities consider that the person intended was a Newmarch. In the case of Roche Abbey, Adam de Novoforo, besides the gift of his own share of the manor of Newsom, was the first witness of each of the foundation charters of the two joint lords. It is true that this would not be gathered from the account of Roche Abbey printed by Mr. Hunter in *South Yorkshire*, i, 268, though I think he was quite justified in giving "de Newmarch" as a translation or equivalent of "de Novoforo"; and, while Dr. Aveling follows his example whenever in his history of Roche Abbey he has occasion to use the name, it is unfortunate that neither takes occasion to mention that the original document has "Novoforo." Its date was before 1186, for the gift was confirmed by Pope Urban III in that year, when he, apparently by way of inducing order and obtaining their registration, took occasion to confirm so many of such documents. Similarly, among the Monk Bretton charters there is one (*Monasticon Anglicanum*, v, 137, No. 4) from Sir John de Novoforo, dated at York on the morrow of the Translation of the Blessed Thomas the Martyr (7th July), 1239. It contains a concession to Sir John de Novoforo that he shall hold the manor of Alverthwaite from the monks, as his uncle Henry de Novoforo had held it, at a rent of $2\frac{1}{2}$ marks at the

Feast of St. Martin and $2\frac{1}{2}$ marks at Whitsuntide; but in the title
the charter is said to be from John de "Novo Mercato." This
cartographer also was doubtless justified in his indication; for
probably he knew the Novoforo only as Novo Mercato: but it must
be borne in mind that one of the divisions of Pontefract had been
the Novum forum or Newmarket, which name it retained till well
within the last hundred years. The locality is now called the Market
Place, and it is very probable that the Newmarches of Osgoldcross,
Strafford, and Tickhill took their names from their holding in it.
For it has never been clearly ascertained how these Newmarches
came into Yorkshire, but the fact that the local use of the name
was an alternative for New Market now affords a clue. They were
probably a family who used the distinction of "de Novo foro," as
derived from their property in the Pontefract New Market, while, a
concurrent appellation being "de Novo Mercato," they thus became
confused with the Newmarches proper, from whom they were widely
distinct.

We have seen one of the name testing No. 224; but the first
I trace of Adam de Novo Mercato at Campsall is that (1) on the
15th kal. February, 1227–8, Robert Gray was instituted to the
Reineville mediety of the Church of Campsall on his presentation,
showing that he had by some means succeeded the Reinevilles in
the possession of the advowson; (2) that on the 6th kal. November,
1230, the archbishop issued a charter of protection to the Chapel of
Cobcroft, "according to the charter of Adam de Novo Mercato"
(*ante*, No. 482); and (3) that he made a second presentation to his
moiety of Campsall on 6 nones July, 1231. These three transactions
from 1227 to 1231 are recorded in the Register of Archbishop
Gray, the patron being in each case styled "Nobilis vir" and acting
with the full powers of the lord of the manor and owner of the
advowson.

As I have said, it is not clear how he obtained the position; but
in 3 Henry III [1218] the manor had passed to the heirs of Thomas,
son of Adam de Reineville, Eva de Boby, the widow of Thomas,
claiming her dower in it. There is thus an interval of only nine
years between its ascertained possession by Reineville and its ownership by Newmarch, while the mode by which the transfer was

effected has hitherto baffled all enquiry. The Reinevilles had held the moiety of the manor of Campsall from the time of the foundation of St. Clement's Chapel, about 1080; and as four knights' fees of the new feoffment (that is, enfeoffed after the death of King Henry I), a William de Reineville held it and other properties in 1166, being also charged on the Pipe Roll of the same year with five marks in the wapentake of Morley. Thenceforward till the death of Thomas de Reineville (*inq. p. m.* 3 Henry III [1218]) Campsall descended in the possession of the Reinevilles with other manors of the Lascy fee, the whole holding continuing to be returned as of four knights' fees. There was also in the 1166 return a Harvey de Reineville who held half a knight's fee in the Fee of Skipton, likewise of the new feoffment; and during the later years of Thomas de Reineville there was a tenant of the same name, perhaps indeed the same man, who held half a knight's fee under the archbishop in 12 and 13 John [1214].

The heir of Thomas de Reineville was his son Adam. But Thomas's next brother, William, is generally considered the head of the new generation, and he might have been the successor at Campsall under some scheme for dividing the properties; for another brother, Geoffrey, who had tested No. 212 in 1206, appears in 1229 in possession of Upton, one of the family manors, and passing it to Archbishop Walter. There was also a William de Campsall, who at this time (as in No. 95, No. 98, No. 99, and many others) is found testing charters. But this latter uniformly signs in so inferior a position that he cannot be accepted as the owner of so large a property; he must be absolutely put aside; he cannot be William de Reineville inheriting Campsall and taking the name of the place as his surname.

Adam de Newmarch, however, was in full possession and presenting to his moiety of Campsall Church in 1227, and the still unanswered questions are, what Adam was he? and how did he get that and other Reineville manors?

The Newmarch family, like that of the Lascies, had a western and Welsh branch. The two branches of the Lascies have been connected, and prove to be descendants of two brothers, Roger of Gloucestershire, Herefordshire, Worcestershire, and Shropshire, and Ilbert of Yorkshire, Lincolnshire, and Oxfordshire. But no such connection has hitherto been found possible for the Newmarches. The Welsh and Gloucestershire line commences with Bernard, who is not named in the Survey but who appears as a later "Companion of the Conqueror," being a witness of the Foundation Charter of Battle Abbey. The monkish traditional history given in the *Monasticon* (319)—though it must be borne in mind that these traditional histories (generally written in the fourteenth or fifteenth century) are very inaccurate—makes it appear that the name died with him; but whether or not a descendant in a female line from Bernard, there was certainly a Henry de Newmarch, who held an important fee in Gloucestershire in 1166, and he had the same Christian name as the "de Novo foro" who afterwards gave Alverthwaite to Monk Bretton and to whom I shall presently return. But there was no Bernard among the Yorkshire Newmarches, so that even if there had been any connection between them and those of Gloucestershire they had not sought to keep it in remembrance. The great name in this district, at least in Osgoldcross and Tickhill, was Adam, which appears with bewildering frequency, and it was only with the last Adam in the second half of the thirteenth century that they adopted the obvious distinction of styling Adam "the son of John." The first was that Adam who before 1122 granted $3\frac{1}{2}$ bovates in "Histoft" (*Monasticon Anglicanum*, ii, 37; but "Halton," *Baronage*, i, 435) to the canons of Nostell. I find no subsequent mention of him during the remainder of the reign of Henry I and all that of Stephen, though the non-appearance of his name is not to be wondered at, considering the great destruction of state records before the reign of Henry II. In that reign, however, a William de Newmarch renders through the Yorkshire sheriff an account of £93 6s. 8d. for the custody of the land of his nephew, Adam de Newmarch, the gradual payment of which amount during seven years implied that the young heir was fourteen years old at the time of his father's death, some time before or during 1160–1, and that therefore he was born in or about 1146.

The following are the entries on the Pipe Rolls year by year with regard to this transaction:—

7 Henry II (year ending Michaelmas, 1161) William de Newmarch renders account for £93 6s. 8d. for the custody of the land of Adam de Newmarch; he paid into the Treasury £23 6s. 8d. in two tallies; and he owes   £70.

8 Henry II (year ending Michaelmas, 1162) William de Newmarch renders account for £70 for the custody of the land of Adam de Newmarch; he paid into the Treasury (during the year) £10 13s. 4d.; and he owes   £59 6s. 8d.

9 Henry II (year ending Michaelmas, 1163) William de Newmarch renders account for £59 6s. 8d. for the custody of the land of his nephew; he paid into the Treasury £24 6s. 8d.; and he owes   £35.

10 Henry II (year ending Michaelmas, 1164) William de Newmarch renders account for £35 for the custody of the land of his nephew; he paid nothing, and he owes   £35.

11 Henry II (year ending Michaelmas, 1165) William de Newmarch renders account for £35 for the custody of the land of his nephew; he paid £11 13s. 4d. in three tallies, and he owes   £23 6s. 8d.

12 Henry II (year ending Michaelmas, 1166) William de Newmarch accounts for £23 6s. 8d. for the custody of the land of his nephew; he paid into the Treasury £8 13s. 4d., and by the king's writ to Aaron the Jew [a well-known capitalist of Lincoln] £6 13s. 4d.; and he owes   £8.

13 Henry II (year ending Michaelmas, 1167) William de Newmarch owed £8 for the custody of his nephew; he paid £8, and is acquit.

These Newmarch entries afford an interesting illustration of the method in which such accounts were kept year by year, and, the young heir being called sometimes Adam de Newmarch, at other times William's nephew, enables us to frame the following scheme:—

NEWMARCH, OF YORKSHIRE.

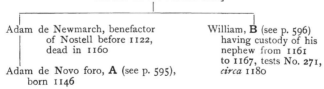

[? Ralph, a witness to the Blythe foundation charter, named by Hunter (i, 223), but not in the *Monasticon*.]

Adam de Newmarch, benefactor of Nostell before 1122, dead in 1160

William, **B** (see p. 596) having custody of his nephew from 1161 to 1167, tests No. 271, *circa* 1180

Adam de Novo foro, **A** (see p. 595), born 1146

As "Adam de Novo foro," the second Adam was a considerable benefactor to Roche Abbey, was a witness to their foundation charters, and before 1186, perhaps some time before, gave them the manor of Newsom. But nothing has emerged to show whether William his uncle and guardian had property in Yorkshire, under that or any other name He tested No. 271, *circa* 1180.

Since the first Adam, the benefactor to Nostell, was of age and in possession before 1122, Dugdale must be wrong when he implies, as he does, that his brother William was the William who in 10 Richard I [1198] paid £100 for livery of his father's lands in Dorsetshire and Somersetshire, and who in 6 John [1204], having fallen into leprosy, had the custody of his lands in Hampshire transferred to Godfrey St. Martin. But much of the account of the Newmarches in the *Baronage*, i, 435, is equally confused. This William the leper was clearly the son of the Henry de Newmarch who owned nearly eighteen knights' fees in Gloucestershire in 1166, in 1168 paid £11 14s. 2d. on their assessment, and in 6 Richard I [1194] paid £17 11s. 4d. as his scutage for the king's redemption and a fine of ten marks in order to be exempt from attendance upon the king in Normandy. It was clearly his son William who appears in 10 Richard I [1198] paying a hundred pounds for livery of his father's lands and a hundred marks for his relief.

Dugdale says that Henry ratified the grants of Winebald, "his grandfather," to the monks of Bermondsey. It may have been so, but the learned author of the *Baronage* gives no reference, and the statement is not confirmed by the evidence of the charters in the *Monasticon*, while Winebald would have been his great-grandfather.

William, son of Henry, was succeeded by James his brother, who in 6 John gave 200 marks for livery of his lands, and in 13 John paid £197 10s. for his relief and £24 4s. for his scutage. But James was dead in 17 John, without male heirs, for in that year the custody of his lands in Berkshire and of his daughters was granted to John Russell, Matilda, James's wife, surviving. And thus the name died out in this branch, with no apparent connection between them and those of Yorkshire.

In a later generation, the connection of the branches of such a family can sometimes be inferred or negatived by a comparison of the arms borne. But in the case of the Newmarches this resource is denied us, for the earlier branches died out before arms were on record, and accordingly only one coat, that of Adam de Newmarch— he of Womersley in 1250, now in Womersley Church,—is on record in Glover's Roll, *Goules, ung fece engrele d'or;* which, with a difference of tincture, implying connection of some sort, are the Percy arms : *Azure, a fess engrailed or.* In Camden's Roll (*circa* 1280) the arms of Adam de Newmarch are given as *Gules, five fusils, conjoined in fess or;* an identical blazon, though differently expressed.

The pedigree of this branch seems to be as follows, and the father of Henry might be a descendant of Mael, though the connection is not clear :—

NEWMARCH, OF GLOUCESTERSHIRE.

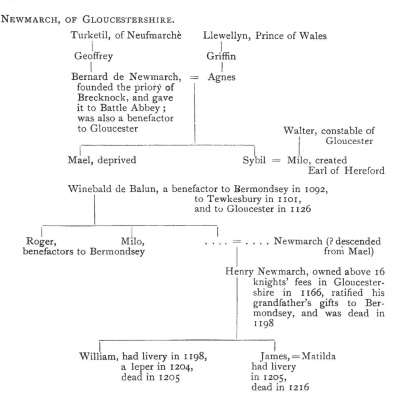

Thus the male line of the Gloucester Newmarches died out,— Otho Fitz William, on 18 August 3 Henry III [1219], making a fine of six palfreys for having to wife Matilda the widow.

James de Newmarch had followed the king in his Irish expedition in 1210, and after the party had landed he received as Imprest Money, or loan from the king to defray his expenses, two sums of 10 marks each, one at the encampment at Kells in Meath, and the other at Dublin (DE PRÆSTITO, 189, 225). Part of this money had remained unpaid for as long as twenty years, and on 5 March 14 Henry III [1230], long after the borrower's death, a requisition was made upon John de Baterell, who had married one of the daughters of James de Novo Mercato, for 18 marks on account of the balance. The reply being that the late King John had pardoned John de Baterell 6 marks, an order was made that he should pay the remainder into the Treasury at the rate of four marks yearly (EXCERPTA, 195). A Roger de Newmarch is named on the DE PRÆSTITO Roll of 1210 as receiving an Imprest of two marks, but I find no more of him.

And now to revert to the Yorkshire Newmarches. Adam de Newmarch appears in the first instance with Henry his brother as witnessing the confirmation of the grant of Boadley to Fountains by Roger de Lascy (*Fountains*, fo. 110*b*). He next appears on King John's DE PRÆSTITO Roll as a forgiven debtor on account of 20 silver marks, of 50 marks which he owed for trespass. The pardon is dated 16 November 3 John [1201], and he is entered on the Fine Roll of 6 John as one of the bail of Henry fitz Count in 1205. He accompanied King John to Ireland in 1210, and received four separate payments on account of his expenses: 100*s*. on the Friday after St. Swithin's Day (16 July) at the camp, which would have been at or near Downpatrick; 6 marks on 20 July at Carrickfergus; 100*s*. on the Sabbath after the Assumption (July 17); and 100*s*. (paid to Henry de Vernoil) at the camp near Dublin on Wednesday, the feast of St. Bartholomew (August 24). But in 1213 he came under the king's displeasure, the loss of some of the royal rolls for 1211, 1212, and 1213 perhaps hiding from us the reason why.

In October of the last-named year, his sons John and Adam, who had been detained in Corfe Castle as hostages for his good conduct, were released, Saher de Quency, Earl of Winchester (grandfather of Margaret, wife of John de Lascy, Earl of Lincoln), and Gerard de Furnival being bail for their production at the king's order. There is no indication as to Adam's offence or as to the part of the country to which he belonged; but, although Foss seems to think that this Adam was he of Tickhill, there can be no doubt, when the pedigree on page 595 is examined, that Adam the father was the Adam de Newmarch who afterwards appeared so suddenly at Campsall in possession of the advowson and presenting to the living in 1227 and 1231. There was at the time no Adam de Newmarch holding of the Tickhill fee.

It must also be he whose unrecorded charter concerning Cobcroft (Surtees, lvi, 15, 46) was confirmed by another Adam, his grandson, son of his elder son John, as we have seen in No. 482; and, as we learn from Foss, he was in the following year (16 John, 1214) employed with three others and the sheriff of Yorkshire to take an assise of mort d'ancestor between two parties in that county. Under Henry III he was engaged as a principal landed proprietor in collecting the king's fifteenths in Yorkshire, and he acted as a justice itinerant in various counties in 3, 9, 16, and 18 Henry III, as we have seen in vol. i. Altogether he was a somewhat important man in his time and locality.

Adam de Newmarch was followed by his son John, who, as he entered upon his inheritance somewhat late in life, appears to have had a comparatively short tenure. He died in 31 Henry III, on 25th September of which year the king took the homage of Adam son of John de Novo Mercato for the lands and tenements of Adam de Novo Mercato (the grandfather, as if John had never had full possession), and of all the lands of which Adam was seised when he died. And then (EXCERPTA, p. 19) follows the remark, "He holds of the king of the honour of Tickhill," which evidently misled Foss, who seems to have applied it to the grandfather, not to the grandson. There is, however, in the *Monasticon* (*ante*, p. 585) the record of the trial of a writ of novel disseisin concerning the manor of Alderthwait (near Skiers, a hamlet of Hoyland in Wath, which Mr. Stapleton in his paper on Holy Trinity, York, p. 125, incorrectly identifies as Alverley Grange in Wadworth). The trial of the action took place at York, on the morrow of the translation of St. Thomas the Martyr (8 July), 1239, before Pigot de Lasceles, Robert de Cokefield, Gerald Salvein, and William Constable, justiciars, all but the second being merely justiciars "ad hoc." Robert de Cokefield was, moreover, a local man; he was sheriff in 1226-9, and had married Nichola, daughter of Jordan de St. Maria by Alice, daughter of Geoffrey Haget, all of Frystone (ARCHÆOLOGIA, xxx, 485). The grandson of this Gerald Salvein is the earliest of that name mentioned by Foss as a justiciar, and he names his grandson also; after whom he puts it upon record that the united names have continued to designate every head of the family for above four centuries.

The decree, which was stated to be between the prior and convent of Monk Bretton, petitioners, and John de Newmarch (as I have said, called in the body of the deed "de Novo foro"), tenant, was that the said John shall hold the manor of Alwardethwait from the monks at a rent of five marks yearly, as his uncle Henry "de Novo foro" had held it. This fixes, approximately, the death of the uncle.

It may be as well to note that Alderthuait is called in the body of the charter (*Monasticon Anglicanum*, 661) Alwardethuait, Alverdethuait, and Alwardethueit, while in the rubricated heading it is Alverthuait; but Dodsworth indexed it correctly (*Monasticon Anglicanum*, 1116, third column), Alderthwait.

This Henry, the younger brother of Adam, had become an important personage in the fee of Tickhill in which Alderthwait was situate, holding four knights' fees there, a position he had mainly acquired by his marriage with Dionysia, daughter of Otto de Tilli and widow of Henry de Puteaco who died in 1211; though his second marriage with Frethesenta Paynell, widow of Geoffrey Luterel, for the marriage with whom, "if she will" (gallant man!), he gave to the king 40 marks at Westminster on 15 May, 2 Henry III [1218], may have contributed to this result. In his earlier years, Henry de Novo Mercato had followed King John to Ireland in 1210, where he received an imprest loan of 3 marks on the same day (16 July) on which his elder brother Adam had received one of 100s., the differing amount indicating the difference in rank and importance of the two brothers and the differing size of their following.

Mr. Hunter, however, quotes from the Monk Bretton Chartulary a charter of Rayner Malet of lands at Bolton, which is witnessed by Henry de Newmarch, Ralph de Newmarch, and Henry de Alderthwaite. This seems to militate against Henry de Newmarch being Henry de Alderthwaite. Henry and Adam usually come together, and several of the Finchale charters (*e.g.* No. 16 and No. 21) are witnessed by "Adam de Novo Marcheto, and Henry his brother" (SURTEES, vi, 15, 23, &c.), while in the White Book of Southwell (SURTEES, lvi, 195) there is a record of (1) the gift by Henry de Novo Mercato to Robert of Lexington of a bovate and other properties in Barnborough, together with the advowson of the church; (2) the confirmation by Adam his elder brother, which was witnessed by Adam's two sons, John and Adam; (3) the grant by Robert of Lexington of the advowson to the chapter of Southwell; and (4) its confirmation by Archbishop Gray. This last was in February, 1242. The chapter do not, however, seem to have presented, but by 1244 some great change had been made, probably owing to the death of Henry de Novo Mercato and his son Adam, involving a transference of the interest from the Tickhill fee to that of Pontefract. In the same year a presentation to Barnborough was made by Adam son of John, Henry's great nephew, of the elder branch, the great Adam of the

Lascy fee, who was then in the height of his power. He incurred a forfeiture in 1264, and his manors of Womersley, Campsall, Thorp, Bentley and Arksey were committed to the charge of Richard Foliot; but he was restored three years afterwards.

The following is the pedigree of this branch:—

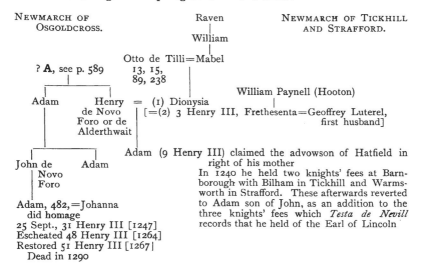

NEWMARCH OF OSGOLDCROSS. Raven NEWMARCH OF TICKHILL AND STRAFFORD.

William

Otto de Tilli=Mabel
13, 15, 89, 238

? **A**, see p. 589

Adam   Henry = (1) Dionysia   William Paynell (Hooton)
        de Novo   [=(2) 3 Henry III, Frethesenta=Geoffrey Luterel,
        Foro or de   first husband]
        Alderthwait

John de   Adam   Adam (9 Henry III) claimed the advowson of Hatfield in
Novo   right of his mother
Foro   In 1240 he held two knights' fees at Barn-
                    borough with Bilham in Tickhill and Warms-
Adam, 482,=Johanna worth in Strafford. These afterwards reverted
did homage   to Adam son of John, as an addition to the
25 Sept., 31 Henry III [1247]   three knights' fees which *Testa de Nevill*
Escheated 48 Henry III [1264]   records that he held of the Earl of Lincoln
Restored 51 Henry III [1267]
Dead in 1290

The following notes from *Kirkby's Inquest* relate to this younger or Tickhill branch of the Newmarches:—

MARR.—William de Hamilton holds a moiety from Adam de Novo Mercato, and he from Tickhill.

WENTWORTH.—Adam holds half, of the Honour (of Tickhill); and William de Fleming half, of Skipton.

BOLTON.—Half held from Adam de Novo Mercato, and half from Normanvile.

TURNSCOE.—Half held from Adam de Novo Mercato, and half from Robert Luterel.

[9 Hen. III (1224), Adam (son of Henry), apparently in his infancy, recovered seisin of the Church of Hatfield, in right of his mother, heir of Otto de Tilli.]

After the coming of age of his ward William de Newmarch seems to have disappeared, and there is no indication of his subsequent career. There is, however, one of his name who stands charged in the Pipe Roll of 17 Henry II [1170-1] with 100 marks "pro concord' duelli," of which amount he was the same year credited with £20 10s., leaving a balance of £46 3s. 4d., towards which he made no payment for some years, an indication of the low state of his exchequer. Although I have failed to find proof, it is very probable that he is the William de Newmarch who married Isabel, one of the co-heirs' in the following scheme, mainly compiled from *South Yorkshire*, ii, 133, as that was taken from *Dodsworth*, vol. 4.

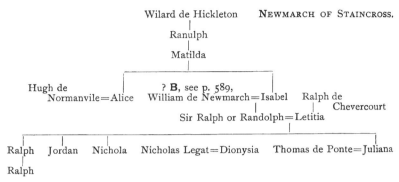

Wilard de Hickleton   NEWMARCH OF STAINCROSS.

This branch was of Staincross; and as Adam of Osgoldcross, his two sons, John and Adam, and his brother, Henry, appear as witnesses to several of their charters, the probability is that the two branches had some cousinly relation which· gave those of Osgoldcross a contingent interest in the property.

The charters are as follows :—

1.   Ralph (the second) gave six bovates at Hickleton to Monk Bretton. Witnessed by Sir Adam de Newmarch and Sir Henry his brother.

2.   Ralph (the third), son of Ralph (the second), confirmed.

3.   Adam (the first), prior of Monk Bretton, granted the six bovates to Nichola, daughter of Sir Randolph (the first).

4.   The lady Nichola de Hickleton quit-claimed the land at Hickleton which she held of the convent according to the charters of Randolph (the first), her father, and Ralph (the second), her brother.   Witnessed by Sir Adam de Newmarch (probably the father) and Sir John (probably his eldest son).

5.   Ralph (the second), son of Ralph (the first), grants to Nichola, his sister, two bovates at Hickleton which Jordan his brother held of the monks.

6.   Nichola, daughter of Randolph (the first), granted three acres in Hickleton, especially for the health of the soul of Jordan her brother, whose obit is to be kept on January 3rd.

The first Sir Ralph, or Randolph (two forms of the same name, here used indiscriminately), married one of the co-heiresses of Ralph de Chevercourt, founder of Wallingwells, whose rights in respect of that marriage were, as early as 4 John, a matter for settlement in the courts. He had also in 17 John a share through his wife in the right of presentation to the church of Carleton in Lindrick, which that year fell to the king, the lands of Richard de Furneaux, Ralph de Newmarch and Ralph de Eccleshill, the three husbands, being all in the king's hands. It would have been this Sir Ralph who was in Ireland with the king in 1210 and who received there three DE PRÆSTITO grants of 20*s.*, 2 marks, and 1 mark respectively, these small amounts showing the meagreness of his following.

Finally, the *Testa de Nevill* (page 364, printed edition) records among the fees of the honour of the Earl of Lincoln that three were held by Adam de Novo Mercato, who would be the first Adam, of Osgoldcross, the founder of Cobcroft, whose charter was confirmed by his grandson, as an original (No. 482); and among those of the Earl of Warenne that two were held by Adam de Novo Mercato in Barnborough, Bilham and Wermswrth (incorrectly transcribed on page 367 as Westmswrth), which would be Adam the son of Henry, of Strafford.

The circumstance that the name "de Newmarch" is represented by "de Novo foro" in independent charters belonging to three branches of the family is another reason for the presumption that all three had a common origin; and that the "de Novo foro" of the Alderthwait charter, made by the Staincross branch, the "de Novo foro" of the Roche charter, made by the Tickhill branch, and the attestation of No. 489 made by Adam of the Osgoldcross branch, point to a common tradition as to the early habitat of the family, which I suggest to have been the Market Place of Pontefract. This theory, if substantiated, would entirely disconnect those three branches from the western Newmarch, the benefactor of Brecknock and Gloucester, who witnessed the Conqueror's charters to Battle Abbey.

We pass on now to No. 492, which represents the settlement made by Roger Fullo of Malfaygate on Mabel, his mother, at her second marriage with William the dyer, son of Ace. The relationship between the parties would be thus represented :—

```
                        Ace, 120
                           |
    Simon Fullo, 120  =  Mabel  =  William, 120, 129
                  |              |
        120 [1253], 169, Roger   Robert, 169
```

The second marriage seems to have been fruitful and its issue to have lived to man's estate, the two half brothers being in 1253 co-witnesses in the important dated charter, No. 169.

The seat of John of Baghill, mentioned in charter No. 492, still remains as Baghill House. The Baghill family afterwards migrated to Featherstone, where the name is yet on record as that of the fifteenth-century donor of the church font. Malfaygate, which in the fifteenth century was apparently the name given to Southgate, is here very evidently what is now Walkergate. William son of Everard of Methley owned a toft in this street, which was worth tenpence a year, and which was the first named in No. 94 on the lengthy list of his bounties to the monks.

The property leased by No. 493 to William son of Gilbert of Ascham was that which had been given to the monks some two or three generations previously by Simon de Mohaut (see No. 331) and subsequently confirmed by William his grandson (see No. 228*, and the pedigree at page 398). It was afterwards exchanged with the nuns of Arthington for property in Pontefract, to the mutual convenience of the two houses; for the monks of Pontefract obtained a larger rent from a property near to their monastery, while the nuns of Arthington exchanged a distant toft for one in their immediate vicinity.

In the first of the three unnumbered charters which follow, the mention of the watercourse under the garden at Ledsham (see also No. 22) illustrates the manner in which the course of a stream was occasionally hidden, being protected by a sort of roof composed of plates of stone. These again were covered with soil, in which herbage grew, completely concealing the underground brook and affording firm footing for grazing cattle.

The second of these three charters was the originator of No. 43 and No. 53, and a collation and comparison of them with No. 42 (a century earlier than any of them) will throw much light upon the relations between such outlying dependencies as Fairburn and such a central body as the chapter of York.

The transaction belongs to the close of 1235 and the opening of 1236, as appears by the names of the officials; but I find no "W. Chancellor" at that time in Le Neve, the only chancellor which he gives between 1225 and 1237 being Richard of Cornwall. The treasurer at the time was William de Rotherfield, and it is probable that the name of his office was here incorrectly transcribed.

In No. 43, No. 53, and the corresponding document in Archbishop Gray's Register (pp. 181–2), the names of the Committee are given as

> Walter, the Archbishop.
> Robert de Winton, the precentor.
> Walter, archdeacon of the East Riding.
> John, the sub-dean, and
> William de Suwell.

But it does not appear how the last three were substituted for those originally named for the Commission in the charter now before us.

The part of Dodworth granted by No. 497 is very graphically described. It is the south-west portion of Dodworth, projecting between Silkstone and Stainborough and extending to Thurgoland. It was probably part of a Field common to all four manors but partitioned long before the date of this charter. Traces of the former character of the district are to be gathered from the mention of the "wood of Dodworth," of the name Haves-"hirst" in that manor, of " Moor " End in Silkstone, and of Berry " moor " in Thurgoland.

The mention of John son of John, chaplain of Silkstone, shows that this No. 497 was a generation later than No. 359. The first on its list of witnesses, Master Robert de Winton, was in 1218 presented by the archbishop to the living of Silkstone, on the failure of the monks to present. He was then a canon of York and afterwards precentor, being in No. 495 one of the Commissioners in the proceedings concerning the Church of Ledsham.

The history of the plots dealt with in No. 498 is interesting. They belonged (see No. 236) to Henry, son of William, the soldier, of Stubbs, who gave them to his brother Otto in trust, to bestow them in religion where he would. Otto accepted the trust and (see No. 328) granted them to St. John's monastery, that the monks might make an anniversary for him. They received the grant and, as this charter indicates, let the property to farm, first to Richard Ruffus, afterwards to Alexander de Norwich. According to the usual practice of the monks, they preserved no copy of the expired lease to Richard Ruffus, which had been superseded by that to Alexander de Norwich.

Sir Theobald, whose land was to the south of one of the properties, was the fourth heir in lineal descent from the Walding whose name was given to the manor.

No. 499 (in error numbered 490) groups with No. 402, No. 403, No. 419, No. 432, and No. 507, and belongs to the East Riding. But in this part of the Chartulary there is hardly an attempt to keep any order in the arrangement of the documents.

I have in the previous volume explained the interesting character of the original gift of Robert de Stapleton. By No. 503 we find it being leased in about 1228, but Walter Scot, who is at the head of its witnesses and therefore even then an important man, lived till at least 1253, in which year he made with the monks the useful exchange recorded in No. 169.

Prior Hugh, who makes the grant, is a second of that name, and an active, energetic, and vigorous administrator. His rule was but short, for his predecessor Robert appears in a fine in 1225, while he himself was similarly in the king's court at York in 1226 (see No. 243). The commencement of his priorate was thus clearly in the latter half of 1225 or the early part of 1226, while, as his successor Prior Walter (according to Mr. Baildon's useful list of priors) is named in 1230, he could not have had a complete five years of rule. But during that short space of time his influence was felt in all parts of the monastic domains, and he seems to have done much to put the management of the monastic lands and properties on a safe and lasting footing. For instance, by No. 492 and No. 503 he leased out properties in Pontefract; by No. 493 and No. 501, those at Wick; by No. 497, that at Hawkhirst; by No. 499, that at Scarborough; by No. 514; that at Broughton; by No. 489, that at Smeaton; by No. 524 and No. 525, some at the Mere; by No. 528, that at Bretton; by No. 529*, that at Kimberworth; by No. 540, a bovate at Slepehill; and by No. 541, part of the property at Ferriby. He thus put the monks beyond the risk of loss from distant agricultural operations and ensured a clear, if small, profit from each of their estates. The earlier monks had been themselves, in a large proportion, labourers, but as the generations rolled on the proportion of intellectual clerkly men increased among them, and hence it became increasingly less profitable for them to undertake on their own account the cultivation of their distant properties.

The following seems to be the relationship and connection between the Burton Salmon families who appear in No. 505 :—

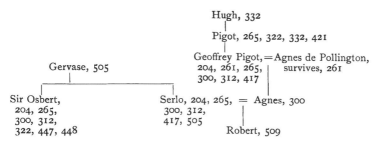

Hugh, 332

Pigot, 265, 322, 332, 421

Gervase, 505 Geoffrey Pigot,=Agnes de Pollington,
204, 261, 265, survives, 261
300, 312, 417

Sir Osbert, Serlo, 204, 265, = Agnes, 300
204, 265, 300, 312,
300, 312, 417, 505
322, 447, 448 Robert, 509

This illustrates the very general course of such properties. The manor remained in the owner of the fee and his descendants for some three generations, when the virility of the race failed and the male line expired, the heiress carrying the inheritance by marriage to the younger branch of a neighbouring family.

There was at this time another good family at Burton Salmon, a branch of that of the great Asolf. They also called themselves de Bretton, and failed similarly.

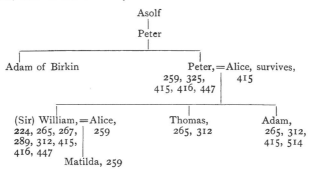

Asolf

Peter

Adam of Birkin Peter,=Alice, survives,
259, 325, 415
415, 416, 447

(Sir) William,=Alice, Thomas, Adam,
224, 265, 267, 259 265, 312 265, 312,
289, 312, 415, 415, 514
416, 447
Matilda, 259

The Beatricehill of No. 505 is now Betteros hill. It is in Hillam, and the extreme north of Burton Salmon township adjoins it on two - sides. It has probably changed very little since the days of Serlo son of Gervase, seven centuries ago.

The conditional promise in No. 506 affords just a glimpse of the method with which the original open space in the New Market of Pontefract was being steadily encroached upon and covered with buildings. In No. 136, a charter not much earlier in date than No. 506, the "placia" of Alexander was called a "stallum," and no claim was made as to the site ; now the site is the more important,

while the "buildings upon it" become a mere accompaniment, and
even an effort to turn the site into pure alms is hinted at. This
was effected some half a century, afterwards by the charter of
Henry de Lascy. Even to-day part of this district is called "The
Shambles."

The advowson of Slaidburn, transferred by No. 510, had been
acquired by the monastery from Hugh de Laval and seems to
have been his own gift from his own hereditary possessions, independent altogether of his rights as the temporary owner of the Lascy
honour. The charter exemplifies very clearly the rights which the
monks had in their advowsons. They had a practical ownership,
which they conferred upon their nominee, in exchange for a pension
out of the proceeds, very much as if they had granted a lease for
life of a freehold property at a rent, though in the case of an
advowson the presentee had to be qualified by holy orders. On his
death or resignation the ownership reverted to the patron, and the
natural abuse quickly sprang up that he delayed to present and
appropriated the revenue. This was met by the order of the third
Lateran Council, that on the failure of the patron to present within
a time limited the patronage should revert to the bishop or other
higher authority (see No. 50). On this basis the parsonage of
Slaidburn was held at least till 1291, the date of the Nonæ Rolls.
It was never appropriated and remains to this day a rectory. A list
of the rectors from 1294 is given in Whitaker's *Craven*, but as
Slaidburn seems to have been considered at the time as the eastern
portion of the diocese of Chester, this presentation of Stephen, clerk
of Hamerton, was not registered on the rolls of the diocese of York.

The term during which Prior Fulk ruled the house was but short.
He came between the third Prior Walter, who was prior in 1227, and
Prior Stephen, who had the grant of the chapelry of Cobcroft in
1235, so that 1231-4 may be taken as the extreme limits of his
priorate. At this time John de Birkin was dead (he died 1227), his
son Thomas had inherited and was dead (he died 1230, being the
last male of the elder branch of the Birkin family), and the estates
had come to Isabel, daughter of Thomas, whose husband, Robert de
Everingham, had received seisin in November, 1230. The John
de Birkin who signs last amongst those named in this charter was
John Fitz Peter, brother of Adam Fitz Peter of Birkin.

Falthwait, with which we meet in No. 512, is a hamlet in the west
part of Stainborough, of which Adam fitz Peter fitz Asolf was the
lord by marriage, and by the name of which he was sometimes

called. His third son, John de Birkin, inherited the manor of that name on the death of his father, in 1207, the elder sons Robert and Peter having their inheritance at Midgley and other places in the west, while his younger brothers, Roger and William, had lands to the east, in a certain degree dependent upon Birkin. But the John de Birkin who witnesses No. 510 and No. 512 was of an older generation, being, as already pointed out, the brother of Adam Fitz Peter and the uncle of the lord John, third son of the great Adam (see No. 325).

Adam's charter of gift of the subject of No. 512 and tested by the same witnesses is No. 344. Adam inherited in 1165 and was a very early benefactor to the monks from another part of Stainborough, having quite a generation earlier than No. 512 given them half the mill there (see No. 319).

The clause "saving to us our woods" serves to indicate the local value of the growing fuel of whose use we have already seen indications. But the far greater value of the coal in the ground seems not to have been yet discovered.

The provision by No. 514 against a possible, perhaps unfounded, claim from the Earls of Albemarle, the lords of Skipton, indicates how even in the time of Prior Hugh II (1226) there was still felt something of the former condition of disturbance and uncertainty through which the Skipton Fee had passed. But in fact the relations of that fee had become somewhat settled; for, after the heirless death of Baldwin de Bethune (see page 392 for the genealogy to that point), the third husband of Cecily de Rumelli, the fee had passed to the descendants of her second husband William de Fortibus, in the person of a son and grandson, a second and a third William de Fortibus, in which last the earldom expired.

Alexander, son of Thomas, who obtained the lease granted by the charter which follows, seems to have succeeded his father in the parsonage of Kellington; but in 1240 (Archbishop Gray's Register, No. 377,) he was superseded by Robert de Meleburn, on the presentation of the Knights Templars, to whom that church belonged. The respective rights of the two vicars, Alexander, the hereditary vicar, and Robert, who claimed the vicarage as having been instituted on the presentation of the Knights Templars, seem not to have been clearly defined for at least five years; for in 1245 (Archbishop Gray's Register, No. 427) there was a fresh institution of the same Robert, with a reservation to Alexander, the clerk, of his portion therein, which at his death was to go to the rector; and thus the claims of the hereditary vicars, which had lasted for four or five incumbencies, were finally disposed of. Incidentally it appears that the living of Kellington had not yet been appropriated.

The expression "versus partes de Medelay" in No. 518 satisfactorily shows that the locality indicated is Whitwood Mere, next Castleford, and not Marr, near Doncaster, as might be surmised. The course of the river Calder—the "Magna Aqua" of the charter—has been in this direction considerably diverted, and there is now no trace of the name "Sandbed," though much of the district is a modern alluvium consisting of a considerable proportion of river sand.

At Frystone (No. 176, No. 307, and No. 393) and at Allerton Bywater (No. 213) the Aire is similarly called "Magna Aqua." Here the phrase is applied to the Calder, which divides Methley from the Mere.

No..519 is the correlative of No. 174, No. 175, and No. 176; but the documents may be of three different dates. When Robert Wallis tested No. 175, he was described as sheriff of Yorkshire and seneschal of Pontefract, which must have been before 1209; for in that year he ceased to be sheriff. In No. 174 and No. 176 he was described as seneschal to Roger de Lascy, which might have been any time before 1211, in which year Roger died. And as he subscribes No. 519 with no affix, that charter was probably granted after 1211, the date of the death of Roger de Lascy, but must have been before 1218, the date of the death of Thomas de Reineville.

We have already seen how the descendants of the wealthy Lesing were gradually divesting themselves of their great inheritance. Of Lesing we know nothing and can gather nothing but that he was a tenant at Ledstone, of perhaps equal status to Ailric, the father of Jordan and his three brothers, and that the fate attended his family which generally follows an excess of expenditure over income unaccompanied by an increase of capital. Richard, his elder son, alienated to the monks the family messuage at Ledstone (No. 192), which appears to have been in that part of the manor which was in the parish of Kippax, and perhaps he received it subject to a mortgage to two neighbouring capitalists who were less improvident than his own family. This indebtedness he removed by the sale of some of his land to the monks (No. 174) by names which are now lost but which clearly point out the property as having been between Green Lane to the north, Moor Lane to the south, the upper part of Mill Lane to the east, and the Roman Road to the west. And there is one peculiarity about this tract; although it is within the township of Ledstone, it pays tithe to the parish of Kippax, its subjection to the parish of Kippax seeming to indicate that it had formerly been in the same ownership as either that manor or Allerton, on both of which it abuts; but there is no direct evidence of the fact. Nor is there now any trace aboveground of the house which was occupied by Lesing and his successors.

The two tofts of No. 523 are first named in the Chartulary in No. 236, where Henry son of William of Stubbs confirmed them to Otto his next elder brother, so that Otto might give them in religion as he would. They are then called "an assart named Rollescroft" and "a small messuage on the other side of the road within sight (coram) of the messuage of William Burnell." This was before 1218, as the document was tested by Thomas de Reineville, who died that year; and, moreover, William of Campsall is one of the witnesses.

Otto's choice was the monastery of St. John at Pontefract; and as No. 328, Otto's gift, is tested by nine witnesses, including the original grantor, Henry and his son, with as many as six who had tested No. 236, the two charters may be considered almost contemporaneous. The properties are very similarly described in the two documents, though in the second the messuage on the other side of the road is not called "small." But by the time of No. 523 the assart has become a toft, as have the messuages; and the tofts, in which are the messuages, are described as lying east and west of each other, while only Geoffrey Scorchbeef and William of Campsall remain as witnesses. Of those witnesses, Robert Wallis is probably not Robert Wallis the former seneschal, but his grandson Robert, the vicar of Methley, presented in 1248 to Frystone; William de Stapleton is the head of the Stapleton house and eldest brother of Hugh de Horton and Hameric of Mara; and William de Campsall is accompanied by an Elias, probably his son.

No. 524 evidently refers to two separate plots of three bovates, each in the Mere. The monks for twenty shillings confirm to Robert, son of Robert, the three bovates which he held from them at a rent of 6s. Robert, on the other hand, gives his contingent interest in those other three bovates which Robert his father (No. 250 and No. 252) had received from the mesne lord, William, son of Hameric, otherwise William of Whitwood (No. 256), and William of the Mere (No. 253); which the elder Robert had given to his elder son Peter (No. 256); for which Peter had received the confirmation of William (No. 255), and which Peter had in 1223 demised to the monks (No. 250) for sixty years, and afterwards granted to them absolutely (No. 257 and No. 258).

The second part of No. 524 was thus a confirmation of No. 252.

The grantee of the following charter, James son of Raimond of Methley, appears in No. 150 as selling to the monks for thirty shillings a rent of four shillings from a messuage in New Market, Pontefract, formerly belonging (see No. 151) to Walter Scot, that wealthy owner who made by No. 169 so considerable an exchange with the monks. This James of Methley, by No. 127 and No. 128, made to the monks other large donations of property in the same New Market.

The "territory" of the Mere, now dealt with, is the extreme east of Whitwood, and was bounded to the north by the river Calder and to the east by the "territory," that is, the Field, or the outskirts, of Castleford. At present, however, this latter description hardly holds good; for the northern boundary has been rectified by the construction of a new course for the river, while the buildings of Castleford are so advanced towards the west as to obliterate entirely part of the boundary between Castleford and the Mere,—Whitwood Mere, as it is called.

Whitwood Proper and the Mere were always considered to be but one manor and township. They have recently been formed into two distinct ecclesiastical districts, each with its church.

In the foundation charter No. 1, "Whitwood and the Mere" are granted as one, and in several of the subsequent confirming charters Whitwood alone is named, even when the context shows that the intention was to denote both Whitwood and the Mere. In No. 248, moreover, which is a grant from Roger Pictavus intended to settle the long-standing disputes of his family with the monks concerning the manor, although the Mere is not mentioned, the two bovates granted are said to be "from my demesne in Whitwood, next towards the east," i.e. the most easterly portion of Whitwood, which would be the Mere.

No. 526 refers to the bovate of Bramley which Adam de Reineville gave to the monks by No. 212, and the present eight witnesses were all among the sixteen who tested it.

We learn from a collation of the several charters concerned that Herbert, who is styled "de Mara" in No. 527 and was the former owner of two of the bovates there referred to, is Herbert son of William (No. 148) the baker (No. 101, No. 149, No. 159, and No. 167). William had also a son John (No. 386), a son Alexander (No. 101 and No. 331), and a son William (No. 147, No. 149, and No. 207); while, again, William the baker was the next brother (No. 241) of Thomas dapifer, and therefore son of the great Asolf.

This third owner in the Mere, styling himself "de Mara," is also called Herbert of Whitwood, and witnesses No. 147 and No. 167. The genealogy of this branch was as follows :—

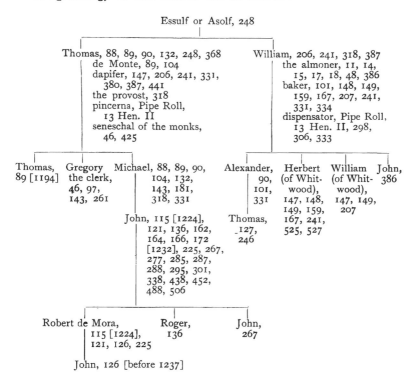

Essulf or Asolf, 248

Thomas, 88, 89, 90, 132, 248, 368
de Monte, 89, 104
dapifer, 147, 206, 241, 331,
380, 387, 441
the provost, 318
pincerna, Pipe Roll,
13 Hen. II
seneschal of the monks,
46, 425

William, 206, 241, 318, 387
the almoner, 11, 14,
15, 17, 18, 48, 386
baker, 101, 148, 149,
159, 167, 207, 241,
331, 334
dispensator, Pipe Roll,
13 Hen. II, 298,
306, 333

Thomas,   Gregory   Michael, 88, 89, 90,
89 [1194]   the clerk,   104, 132,
              46, 97,   143, 181,
              143, 261   318, 331

                            John, 115 [1224],
                            121, 136, 162,
                            164, 166, 172
                            [1232], 225, 267,
                            277, 285, 287,
                            288, 295, 301,
                            338, 438, 452,
                            488, 506

Alexander,   Herbert   William   John,
90,   (of Whit-   (of Whit-   386
101,   wood),   wood),
331   147, 148,   147, 149,
                  149, 159,   207
Thomas,   167, 241,
127,   525, 527
246

Robert de Mora,   Roger,   John,
115 [1224],   136   267
121, 126, 225

John, 126 [before 1237]

This, and the pedigree of the Burton Salmon branch on p. 601, will partially illustrate the manner in which this family spread through this neighbourhood, and indicate how the descendants of these twelfth century officials became the progenitors of the middle-age proprietors. For there is every reason to suppose that the Robert de Mora of 1224 and 1237, father of John, was the ancestor of a family of Mores, who continued in good position at Pontefract, even till the end of the Commonwealth period (see *Pontefract Book of Entries*).

No. 529, which is the foundation charter of the chapel of the Blessed Thomas, referred to in No. 171, seems to locate it within the court of the monastery. Probably, in consequence of the shrinkage of the rents so carefully provided for, the chapel did not last longer than the generation in which it was established, notwithstanding the promise of faithful observance enshrined in this document.

The John de Builli of No. 529 *bis* was the heir of the younger brother of the Domesday grantee of Kimberworth. That manor, with Brodsworth, Scawsby, Maltby, and Hillaby, had belonged to Alsi under the old regime, but under the new dispensation it had been granted to Roger de Busli, Buthlei, Bulli, Builli, or Bullay; for the name is to be found in each of these forms. Roger, whose fee was extensive, and who, very shortly after he had obtained them, must have enfeoffed his brother Ernald in Alsi's former possessions, was dead in 1099. He was succeeded in possession of the remainder of the large fee by his son, a second Roger, whose tenure lasted but a few months, his sister Beatrice being his heir. She married William, Count d'Eu, and the right to the fee remained in the family of the Count for four generations, though for various reasons it was during much of the time in the possession of the Crown. For whoever was the monarch, he seemed to think so rich a fee as that of De Busli too valuable for a subject.

John de Boulli, the grantor by No. 411 of this half acre, was constable of Scarborough Castle in 1202 and for some years afterwards. He was the great grandson of Ernald, brother of the first Roger, and his daughter and heiress was Idonea. She married Robert de Vipont, whereby the Kimberworth property, which, with much more, had been owned in pre-Norman times by Alsi, and which had been possessed for four generations by the descendants of Ernald de Busli, was continued in the female branch even till the time of the last Tudor.

But the principal part of the original Busli fee had extended into Nottinghamshire, and the enumeration of its manors in that county covered three folios, *i.e.* above twelve columns, of the Domesday volume. The whole of this was escheated in the time of Henry I, owing to the action of Robert de Belesme, the guardian and trustee of the younger Roger; for, notwithstanding Roger's death in 1099, Robert de Belesme had continued to hold the Honour, probably as the next male heir. But some portion of it, as we have seen, was possessed by the descendants of Ernald, whose great-grandson, a second Richard, rendered account in 1166 of £30, for relief of the Kimberworth six knights' fees, which were still technically described as being in the honour of Tickhill.

The great bulk of the Busli fee, however, had continued to vest in the descendants of Beatrice, daughter of the first Roger and sister of the second. And with respect to her a singular misapprehension arose, which is even now continued in many genealogical statements. It was alleged that Beatrice was the sister of the first Roger (in which case this John de Boulli would have been the rightful heir), and in 1219 an action was brought against Alice, the heiress of Beatrice, by Robert de Vipont, the husband of John's daughter (who had followed his father-in-law as Constable). His claim was for the whole of the Honour, as of right; and there were many pleadings and counter-pleadings, of which Roger Dodsworth obtained a complete copy, still among his MSS. in the Bodleian. It was only after three years' litigation that a result was attained in 1222 in favour of the defendant, on the ground that Beatrice, through whom the plaintiff claimed, was the daughter of the first Roger and not his sister, as the plaintiff mistakenly alleged.

The relation of the two branches is shown in the following genealogy, which will be found to differ from that generally given, even by Mr. Hunter (*Hallamshire*, chap. iii; *South Yorkshire*, i, 228, 285); for, as stated above, the bearing of the opposing pleadings has been overlooked :—

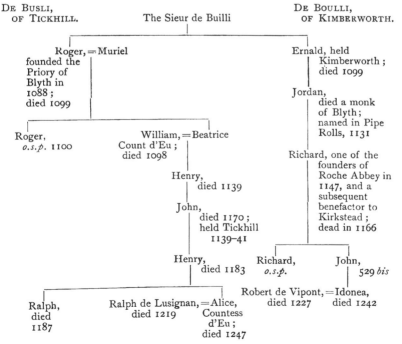

DE BUSLI, OF TICKHILL. The Sieur de Builli DE BOULLI, OF KIMBERWORTH.

Roger, = Muriel, founded the Priory of Blyth in 1088; died 1099

Ernald, held Kimberworth; died 1099

Jordan, died a monk of Blyth; named in Pipe Rolls, 1131

Roger, *o.s.p.* 1100

William, = Beatrice Count d'Eu; died 1098

Richard, one of the founders of Roche Abbey in 1147, and a subsequent benefactor to Kirkstead; dead in 1166

Henry, died 1139

John, died 1170; held Tickhill 1139–41

Henry, died 1183

Richard, *o.s.p.*

John, 529 *bis*

Ralph, died 1187

Ralph de Lusignan, = Alice, died 1219 Countess d'Eu; died 1247

Robert de Vipont, = Idonea, died 1227 died 1242

No connection can be traced between this line of Kimberworth lords and either the Otto, son of Robert de Bulli (see the Foliot charters, No. 87, No. 88, and No. 90), or the William de Bulli of the next generation, who tested No. 5, No. 12, No. 13, No. 89, No. 91, and No. 149, and who appears as de Copley in No. 148.

The Northcroft of No. 533 does not occur in Domesday, and I have failed to trace it elsewhere. It ought to have been a notable hamlet, having ten acres attached to a demesne-house, but I cannot localize it. It was probably only a portion of some larger manor, in which it had been absorbed. The names of most of the witnesses direct our search to somewhere in the neighbourhood of Barnsley or Cudworth. It would, however, be doubly interesting to ascertain its exact position; for there need be little doubt that the grantee, Adam, son of Geoffrey, was the husband of Goodwoman and the descendant by the spindle of Roger of Ledstone, the third son of the great Ailric. Geoffrey witnessed the dated charter No. 184 [1231].

The line of Roger of Ledstone, showing the descent from his two daughters, is given at page 506.

It is difficult to disentangle the various interests in the carucate of No. 534, all of which ultimately centred in the monks, and it is somewhat surprising to notice how scattered are the charters connected with it. By No. 421, Roger de Newby, who seems to have been the mesne tenant, demised to Henry Neeloth a carucate in Bretton which Pigot son of Hugh had held, with all Pigot's service. By No. 405, Henry Neeloth gave it to the monks. But as, notwithstanding his father's apparently unlimited gift, Ralph son of Roger had some hereditary rights in the property, of which his father's deed could not deprive him, and Pigot, son of Hugh, similarly had some latent possessory rights, the original deeds had to be confirmed by Ralph son of Roger (No. 434) and by Pigot son of Hugh (No. 332); while in the next generation Geoffrey son of Pigot (see page 601) made a gift to the monks of all his land from his patrimony (No. 204), and Agnes his wife, born Agnes de Pollington, granted (No. 261) all the claim she ever had in the name of dower in a bovate of her husband's land in Bretton, in exchange for a corrody. Finally, by No. 534 the prior of Pontefract grants to Ralph, son of Roger de Newby, a rent of twelvepence yearly, to be secured on the carucate on condition that he pays the forinsec service (which No. 421, the original charter, states to have been the twentieth part of a knight's fee, a remarkable contrast to the value of land in Bramley, according to No. 212) and all other exaction and demand; while, throughout, there is not the smallest reference or allusion to the interests of the lord of the fee, whether they are those of Henry de Lascy, or of his son Robert, or of his successor, Roger, Constable of Chester.

But there was other property in Bretton (Burton Salmon) in which the monks had interests. For by No. 265 Geoffrey, son of Pigot, gave to Robert, son of David, an acre dispersed in the Fields of Bretton, which by No. 429 Robert gave to the monks. Each charter specifies the portions of land which composed this acre; and, further, there was in Burton Salmon a carucate which Pigot, son of Hugh, had held (No. 421), and which Roger de Newby gave to Henry Neeloth. Of this carucate Ralph, son of Roger, afterwards quit-claimed (No. 404) to Henry Neeloth the service of four pence or half a pound of pepper therefrom arising, by which means the freehold became Neeloth's, who (No. 405) gave it to the monks,—a gift confirmed by Ralph (No. 434). Whereupon, being sole owners, the monks (No. 529) re-leased its rents and outgoings to Henry Neeloth, who then held for life only that which had been his own freehold. There was, moreover, another piece of 2 acres $3\frac{1}{2}$ roods, really in Hillam, though it projected into Burton Salmon, which Henry Neeloth acquired by No. 505 from Serlo, younger son of Gervase. They had also obtained by purchase from Solomon de Bretton, "in his great necessity," a bovate there which Solomon had purchased from Geoffrey, the second Pigot; while, concurrently, they had received from Sir Osbert, elder brother of Serlo (No. 447), the gift of a native, with all his goods, and had purchased from Sir Osbert a rent of 2s. arising from a bovate which had been held from Geoffrey of Ledsham. Thus the interests in Burton Salmon were very much subdivided, and those of the Pontefract monks were large. Hillam, on the other hand, for the most part looked towards Selby, although the Pontefract monks had some interest there, owing to the gifts of Paganus, son of Bucardus (see No. 210 and No. 270).

Burton Salmon seems not to have been surveyed in Domesday, unless it came under the head of Hunchilhuse (Brotherton). But the taxable land in Hunchilhuse comprised one carucate only. Hillam, on the other hand, was probably surveyed as one of the berewicks of Sherburn.

No. 536 and No. 537 were granted at different times, refer to land which had been acquired from different persons, and are signed by different witnesses, but they may fitly be considered together as winding up and completing two series of transactions by which two small estates, which had come to belong to the monks, were placed for profitable cultivation in the hands, as lessee, of Thomas, son of Thomas. (The genealogy of this family is given on page 494.) The rent was in each case to be payable, half at Christmas and half at Easter, the former being named first, implying that Christmas was the first coming rent day, as indeed is to be seen by referring to the datal clause of the second deed, 1 August, 1240. This was, moreover, a rather early instance of the mention of the year of our Lord in deeds of this description.

The five acres seem to have passed through the family. Richard, son of John, the second son of Hugh de Bilham and grantor to the monks, had originally (No. 273) leased them to his cousin John, son of Matthew, the third son. John, son of Matthew, having subsequently, in consideration of 2½ marks, by No. 442 quit-claimed to Richard all his right and claim therein, Richard granted them to Thomas his uncle, the fourth son, at a rent of fourteen pence, payable at Christmas and Easter. Thomas afterwards returned them in the presence of the parishioners assembled in Hooton Church; and then, finally, by No. 276, Richard granted them to the monks in pure alms, Thomas, son of Thomas, by No. 274 confirming the gift. Now, by No. 536, they are leased to Thomas, son of Thomas, the former holder, at the old rent of fourteen pence.

It may be noted that the final deeds, No. 442, No. 274, and No. 276, were sealed with the respective seals of their grantors. The others were simply signed in the ordinary way.

Of the other possessions of William de Bareville in this manor there were two separate bovates, of each of which Thomas, son of Thomas, had been the tenant. For to him the monks, by No. 438, gave two marks for the transfer of the lease of one which he had held for a term of six years from Whitsuntide, 1237, and by No. 439 they gave a similar sum for a similar transfer of one which he had held for a term of twelve years from St. Martin's, 1229

There was, moreover, a third bovate in the fee of this lord, called the Paganel bovate, which with an additional acre he granted to the monks by No. 277. But by No. 275 (a dated charter of 1238, with no month or day of the month named) this acre was enlarged to an acre and a half, with two foredales or head-lands, the boundaries of which are particularly described; though, owing probably to some of the plots among them having since been thrown together, they cannot now be easily identified.

Again, by No. 435, in "his great necessity," William de Bareville sells to the monks, for 30 shillings, 16½ acres and a toft with croft, "as it is closed in by a ditch," of which the rent had been 42 pence at Martinmas and Whitsuntide. This toft and croft was probably the plot on which was built in the last century a "summer house," now in ruins, and which communicates, by an underground tunnel beneath the road, with the property on which the Grange stands. This tunnel is an admirable example of early work, and is at the present time in as good condition as it was six or seven centuries ago.

There is, moreover, one feature named as a boundary in both No. 275 and No. 435, "the Cross between Hickleton and Bilham," of which what appear to be the foundations are still evident, not many yards from the enclosing ditch named in No. 435.

The witnesses of No. 277 and No. 275 were practically the same, though in the latter they were headed by Sir Andrew Luterel, the lord of Hooton.

In No. 435 all the three bovates appear to be combined with the contents of No. 277, No. 438, and No. 439, to make 16½ acres, and there is also the additional toft and croft which was leased by No. 513 to Robert de Aynesford.

But there was another ecclesiastical organisation which held property in Bilham; for by No. 440 William de Bilham gave to John, son of Matthew, half a bovate which he had held from the abbot of Roche. This may be part of the bovate which John parted with by No. 443 to Thomas his uncle, and for which the receipt was put on record in No. 441. Nothing more, however, occurs with regard to it, and it is difficult to see why a charter which concerned land belonging to Roche was enrolled among those which related to the properties of the monks of Pontefract.

No. 538 seems to relate to a subdivision of the bovate which, by No. 212, Adam de Reineville (dead 1218), son of Thomas, had given to the monks. There is a grant in No. 526 of the undivided bovate to Nurasius the clerk, who is the last of the witnesses whose names are affixed to No. 538.

The "Busceler" appears to be another name for Robert, son of Humphrey, the native who was by No. 211 transferred to the monks with all his chattels. He is called Robert Busceler in No. 214, Robert de Busceler in No. 215, and Robert le Busceler in No. 538; while in the third generation Robert's son Adam with all his household is by No. 214 and No. 215 confirmed to the monks by Thomas, son of Adam de Reineville, in the same manner as Robert, son of

Humphrey, had been by Adam de Reineville himself. But there is no clue to the assumption in the second generation of the name of Busceler by Robert, son of Humphrey.

The Buscelers were a family of Pickering Lithe, one of whom, Alan Buscel, the second husband of Aaliza de Percy, granted the church of Hooton there (Hutton Bushel) to the monks of Whitby (W 1). It is hard to see how this "native" came by their name; but it is well to note that for generation after generation the "native" slaves, that is, those born on the land, thus in the first half of the thirteenth century continued in hereditary slavery.

No. 539 is one of the oldest leases in the collection, and it is not easy to believe that, granted as it was to the priest of Catwick, it was still in force when the Chartulary was transcribed. For the signatures as witnesses of the three brothers, Jordan, Reginald, and Walter, stamp it at once as of quite as early a date as 1180,—at least half a century before its insertion as a still valid document among the muniments of the house of St. John. The small touch of circumstance embodied in its last clause is most interesting.

The bovate which is the subject of this charter is mentioned several times. In No. 71 it is called simply a bovate of land; in No. 73 it is a bovate of land with its appurtenances; while in No. 57 it is said to be a bovate of land of the gift of Simon, son of Ralph de Catwick; and here we have the added feature that in the course of years Simon, son of Ralph, who gave the gift, say two generations previously, perhaps in 1130 or 1140, when he married Albreda de Mara at Pontefract, had now become "old Simon." This seems to indicate the probability that Ralph, the father of Simon, Ralph de Wichis (No. 446) or Cattewick (No. 413), whose gift of the first moiety of Catwick Church to the monks of Pontefract was in No. 413 confirmed by Stephen, Earl of Albemarle, was the son of one of the two knights of Drogo de Bevere, if not the knight himself, who held Catwick at the time of the Domesday Survey, the Falconberg ancestor being the second (see pp. 486–7).

As with the name Falconberg, of Catwick, so with that of Wichis,— the orthography of the Chartulary is singular. In other documents this family is called Wytyk, and Sir Simon Wytyk of Catwick, knight, is said (Poulson's *Holderness*, i, 290) to have confirmed, about 1220, a grant of lands to the priory of Nunkeeling. This is the orthography which obtains also in *Kirkby's Inquest*.

The forge or ironworks of No. 542 had already become of importance, as we have seen by the care which the monks took to retain their oaks in their own hands. We shall see it again in No. 547. Indeed, it is probable that, even before Ralph de Capriolecuria gave the monks this manor, both (Monk) Bretton and Barnsley had been seats of an iron mining industry, which required a bountiful supply of wood fuel.

Except a casual indication in No. 108, pointing to lands near the Ris, there is (apart from No. 544) no reference in the Chartulary to anything owned or occupied by Eudo the chaplain. He was of Aberford (No. 97) before he came to Pontefract, and from the first he appears in conjunction with, and preceding, one William, a fellow chaplain ; in No. 463 Roger the chaplain is interposed between them. From the mention of his son Thomas in No. 116 and No. 152, William appears to be identical with that William who, as stated in No. 535, had given the grange to Thomas his son, whence probably the limitations here placed upon it were a recognition of the claims of the last named. The charter by William de Vesci the younger, granting the toft and croft in Bondgate, is No. 125, though from No. 228 we learn that the gift was really an exchange. The land at the hoppedic (No. 97 and No. 544), or more frequently hopedic (No. 98, No. 99, and No. 100), adjoins Steany Lane.

The formality with which the transaction was completed is very striking, the newly-elected prior placing his seal to the deed, not of his own authority, but at the request of the brotherhood, while the sub-prior, who had now, by the induction of the prior, become only the second officer of the convent, attaches his seal also. From this charter indeed, read in the light of No. 201, it appears as if the sub-prior of the Cluniac monks of Pontefract had an official seal of his own, though it may really be that the sub-prior of No. 201 was this same Alan, ruling during the interregnum between two priors.. Gregory de Camera is, however, the only common witness to the two charters.

It is somewhat singular that not one charter of this Prior Peter is on record in this portion of the Chartulary, specially devoted to such documents. Of his immediate predecessor Stephen, there are many; of his immediate successor Dalmatius, not a few ; but Peter is represented nowhere but in Fasciculus V, and then only by No. 180, dated St. John Baptist's day, 1238. There is, however, a declaration on the part of John de Lascy, Earl of Lincoln, that he had received on St. Botolph's day, 1238, from Prior Peter and the convent, the sum of thirty marks of silver which they had been bound to pay that day, and that he could not return them their charter, for it had been lost by the carelessness of Osbert his clerk. And these two documents fix the date at which Peter held the priorship, and show that his rule extended over at least ten months. Only the latter document gives his name in full; the rest preserved his initial only.

No. 544 *bis* is a later charter and gives a later development of the name of the second witness. He appears about 1210, in No. 220 and No. 221, as Richard Pistor; in the Final Concord, No. 154, under date 1235, he is Richard Panetarius; but here he is Ricardus de Behale, panetarius. That is to say, he has assumed a local designation in addition to that of his occupation; and, discarding the previous descriptive name, he has allowed it to become the mere indication of his occupation, which might be readily and finally cast off altogether. He is now Richard de Beal, a baker or pantryman by occupation, and his adoption of the name of a manor at some distance from the place of his former habitation, indicates that his greater interests had come to lie in the new direction. I do not connect him with the family of William the almoner, dispensator, and baker, whose genealogy and part of whose connections are given on page 607.

Adam de Hemsworth, who tests No. 546, was the parson of Hemsworth, the son of one squire, the brother of another, and the uncle of a third, each a William. He had, moreover, an uncle Ralph and a brother Ralph. They were all Warnevilles, though sometimes called simply de Hemsworth (see the pedigree on page 619).

The monks had no property in Hemsworth, but the Hemsworth rectors make several appearances in the Chartulary as witnesses to various deeds, and the existence of as many as three early parsons of Hemsworth can be proved from the Chartulary. These may thus be ranged in order of time: William, priest of Hemsworth, tests No. 334, about 1200; Adam, parson of Hemsworth, tests No. 95, about 1220, following John de Birkin, but taking precedence of Adam de Kellington and Master Raimond; and Ralph, parson of Hemsworth, tests No. 157, about 1230. Though no one of these belongs to the twelfth century, they are all earlier than the vicars recorded by Torre from Archbishop Gray's Register, who are Thomas de Brettegate (instituted 2 non. August, 1242, on presentation of Sir William de Werneville), and five years afterwards, in October, 1247, John de Bederna, at the presentation of William de Ebor, lord provost of Beverley, custos of the land and heir of Sir William. This would show, if we did not know it from other sources, that Sir William had died in the interval; but, as a matter of fact, his *inq. p. m.* was held in 1244, when his heir Adam was reported to be of the age of 14 years.

It is not a little remarkable that the only names of Wannerville lords of Hemsworth that have descended to us—or at least that I have met with—during the twelfth century have been William, Adam, and Ralph; certainly several Williams, and probably more than one Adam, and more than one Ralph; while these are the only names that occur among these thirteenth century parsons of Hemsworth. The inference is that they were all of the same family, and that Hemsworth also had developed into a family living, held hereditarily as Kellington and Darrington had been. But if so, Ralph was the last of the series, the tradition having been broken and the practice overcome by the stern determination of Archbishop Gray.

In the time of Edward the Confessor, Hameleswrde had been held as two manors by Ulf and Siward, who cultivated four carucates with three ploughs. It then contributed 60s. to the royal treasury. But during the Conquest settlement it fell to the share of Ilbert, who by the date of the Domesday Survey had subinfeudated to Gamel not only the two manors (probably Hemsworth and Bisett or Visett) into which Hemsworth was divided, but also that of Kinsley. From being himself a very large proprietor Gamel was thus reduced somewhat to the position of a yeoman in a district of which he had not long since been owner, farming some of his own lands and letting off another portion. He kept in his own hand two carucates, while he sublet a third to three villanes and a bordar. Here were four acres of meadow and a large area of uncleared woody pasture, half a mile long and half a mile broad. There was no Domesday church, but Gamel or his immediate successor erected one about equi-distant—a mile—from Hemsworth, Visett, and Kinsley. This church was dedicated to the early saint, St. Helen, and provided with an ample endowment which is still in possession of the rector. But the subinfeudatory, whether Saxon or Norman, not only created and endowed a church, but combined into one the three manors which had been hitherto separate ; and this united manor, having a church at the time of the constitution of the parochial system, with immediate neighbours similarly provided at Wragby, Ackworth, Badsworth, and South Kirkby, and being sufficiently large to constitute a parish by itself, was allowed to retain its own parson or rector, who held the whole living as the squire held the whole of the manor. Hemsworth was thus thoroughly independent; and was never held in mediety, either in Church or State.

The Wannerville family, the owners after Gamel of this combined manor, seem also to have been remarkably self-contained, restraining their sympathies in an unusual degree to their own church and their own manor. The consequence was that they left little impression upon what were practically the family records of the period, the monkish chartularies. And, what was very unusual at a time when appropriation to a religious house was almost a mania, they retained their one living of Hemsworth in their own hands, as an estate for the elder son and a means of occupation for a younger son or brother. And so the Hemsworth manor became the Hemsworth parish and was as one large family, the heads of which sought but little beyond its borders; with possibly one exception—a Ralph de Wannerville, whom the general historiographers have failed to trace up to his place of origin, but who, in the quiet, unostentatious spirit of his family, filled a somewhat conspicuous position in the world, with an absence of self-seeking that is really charming in so great a man. So little was known of him apart from his office that his name is spelt by various writers Varnnevilla, Varnevilla, Warneville, Vinevilla, and even Wadnevilla, though most of the varieties are probably only the usual mistakes of copyists when dealing with an unfamiliar name and alternating the French V with the English W.

Ralph de Wannerville was possibly brother of that Adam de Wannerville who held one knight's fee in 1166, which had been enfeoffed before 1135, and, as Adam de Winerville, he had been fined 13s. 4d. in 1166 for "concealing a king's plea," i.e. hiding the fact that he had inherited property on which a death‑duty had to be paid. He had probably some previous position in the diocese; for, when John Talvace was made bishop of Poitiers in 1163, he succeeded him as Treasurer of York, an important and lucrative office which had been held by such men as Bishop Hugh and Archbishop William, before they received their higher dignity. He seems to have been even then of mature age; for the mistake of appointing too young a man to the post, which had been committed when Hugh de Puiset was brought to York from Winchester, would not have been committed in the time of Henry II, who had at least approved the appointment; for, after the post of lord chancellor had been vacant for three years, that king selected him to fill it. He would appear also to have held the dignity of Treasurer of York till Buchard de Puiset, son of his more celebrated predecessor, Hugh de Puiset, then Bishop of Durham, was appointed to the office in 1189. But in 1173, the lord chancellorship having been held somewhat in abeyance after the murder of Archbishop Becket, Godfrey Ridel, archdeacon of Canterbury (who, though never called "chancellor," appears to have been the keeper of the king's seal), having been nominated to the bishopric of Ely, Ralph de Wannerville, as we learn from Roger de Wendover and Matthew Paris, was appointed chancellor, still, however, retaining his treasurership at York. His two earliest -charters seem to have been signed with a Yorkshire following at Lillebonne in the summer of that year (*Monasticon Anglicanum*, vii, 1067; viii, 1107), Sayer de Quency coming after him on each document, with Robert de Stuteville in one instance and Walter de Coutance, a canon of Rouen, in the other. He was sacrist of Rouen also, and appears to have loved the Norman city and its officials better than those of York; for he appointed this Walter de Constantiis, afterwards Archbishop of Rouen, to be his deputy chancellor, to which appointment we may attribute the rarity as chancellor of his own attestation. He terminated his English connection altogether when made Bishop of Liseux in 1180. Foss says that he was succeeded as Treasurer of York by Geoffrey, afterwards archbishop, but this is a mistake. His successor was Buchard de Puiset.

The following is an attempt at a pedigree of the Hemsworth squires, which is, however, very defective between William, the head of the family in 1090, and the three Williams who successively occupied that position for about a century, terminating in 1244 :—

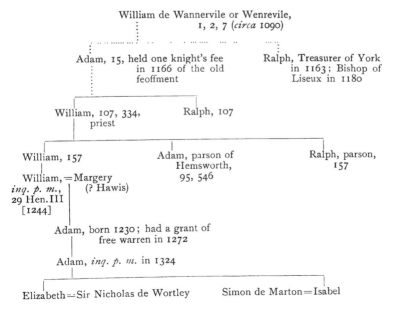

There was also a Henry de Hemsworth, said in No. 94 (*circa* 1200) to have owned a toft in Malfaygate, Pontefract; but in the absence of more evidence it is not possible to place him, though he was probably of this family.

It is noteworthy that a Nicholas de Wortley precedes Adam de Wannervile in No. 546. He was probably a collateral, if not direct, ancestor of the Nicholas de Wortley who married the elder of the two co-heiresses above a century afterwards.

No. 549 evidently relates to one of the Pontefract encroachments on the lord's highway, such as the buildings on the north side of the Market Place, which those concerned were not without hope would, in the end, be legalised. The legalisation was ultimately effected in 1278 by the second town charter, that of Henry de Lascy.

In the Hundred Rolls, some of these Pontefract encroachments are thus described (page 119):—

[The jurors say that Robert the goldsmith has taken from the king's highway seven feet in depth and fourteen in length for buildings. Robert Barefoot, ten feet in length and ten in depth. Robert, son of Mabel, six feet in depth and a hundred in length, from twenty years past.]

Dicunt quod Robertus Aurifaber appropriavit sibi de via regia in dicta villa septem pedes in latitudinem et quatuordecim in longitudinem, facienda ibidem edificia. Item Robertus Berfot in eadem decem pedes in longitudinem, et decem in latitudinem. Robertus filius Mabilie sex pedes in latitudinem, et centum in longitudinem, a xx annis elapsis.

The transaction recorded in No. 560 [550] would appear to have been commenced under the rule of Prior Stephen, been carried on during the short time of Prior Peter, and been completed in the very commencement of the rule of the successor of Prior Peter (Dalmatius); all being in accordance and agreement with the attesting signature of Alexander, "parson" of Kellington. For this Alexander seems to have obtained possession as by hereditary succession, and to have held till the patrons, the Knights Templars of Hirst, attempted to supersede him by the nomination of Robert de Melburn on 8 kal. May, 1239. He held possession, however, until— whether consequent on a legal action or by what other means I have not ascertained—a second nomination was made of the same Robert de "Malburn" on the nones of July, 1244, and division of the endowment effected. This was to continue until the death of Alexander, impliedly the older man, when the whole was to revert to Robert de Melburn as rector. This No. 550 is the only place in which I have found Alexander described as "parson" of Kellington.

The grantor of charter No. 554 was the then squire of Parlington and on his mother's side a grandson of Roger de Ledstone, third son of the great Ailric (see page 506 for the pedigree). His mother had taken Geoffrey of Ledsham for her second husband, but during her widowhood had by No. 469 parted with this property, which by No. 554 John, her son by her first husband, confirms to the monks in 1251, on his coming of age.

R. Rohet among the signatories is peculiar. If the name were intended for Ruet, the Roet coat armour being three Katherine wheels, this might possibly account for some of the Katherine wheels which are not infrequent on the parish churches in this particular district. But the name, either in the form of Rohet or Ruet, does not occur elsewhere in the Chartulary, and it is generally supposed that it made its first appearance in this neighbourhood when Sir Payne Roet came to England in 1328 as one of the suite of Philippa, queen of Edward III. Sir Payne's daughter Katherine was married to Hugh Swynford, lord of Kettlethorp in Lincolnshire, after whose death in 1372 she became mistress of John of Gaunt, whom she married at Lincoln, in January, 1396, having borne him four children, who were legitimised soon after the marriage.

Even at the time of the Domesday Survey Parlington had not been sub-infeudated, but was still jointly with Kiddal in the hands of Ilbert de Lascy as three carucates. It was, however, reported that three carucates of Kiddal and as many as six of Parlington were in the soke of the great fee of Kippax and Ledstone, so much of which, as we learn from this Chartulary, had been granted out by the king independently of the intervention of a mesne lord. This had been done perhaps at the time of the forfeiture of that powerful Earl of Mercia, Edwin, one of whose Yorkshire homes was at Ledstone, as a consequence of the Staffordshire insurrection in 1069, which so singularly finds no chronicler but Ordericus Vitalis. The suppression of this insurrection, it should be noted, immediately preceded the Conqueror's journey to York, in the course of which he was stopped at Pontefract by the swollen condition of the river Aire. The three stages of his march northward were Stafford to Nottingham, Nottingham to Pontefract, Pontefract to York. And, by the way, it may be remarked that Earl Edwin was escheated in 1069, that Earl Alan obtained a grant "of all his manors in Yorkshire" in 1071, that this latter did not obtain Ledstone or Kippax or their soke, and that therefore the assumption is warranted that, these being in the possession of Ilbert de Lascy in 1086, they had been granted to him in the interval which preceded the grant to Earl Alan, that is, between 1069 and 1071. This would have been in pursuance of the consistent policy of the Conqueror, to break up and distribute the large estates of these Saxon earls, who might otherwise have been powerful rivals in the affections of the people.

William of Parlington himself (see No. 147 and No. 148) seems to have been a son of Paganus, son of Bucardus, by whose name the fee of Hillam was known even in the time of Testa de Nevill, and who, as we learn from No. 57, gave 30 acres in Pontefract to the monks. Moreover, it was a Paganus, "his own liege man," of whom no more is recorded, who is said, after the death of King Henry, to have mortally wounded—in fact killed—the intruding lord, William Maltravers; so that, all the circumstances considered, it is not unlikely that the deed was done by this Paganus, son of Bucardus, than whom there is no one who can be made to fit in better with all the circumstances.

Another William of Parlington, son of Thomas of Parlington, appears as a witness to No. 194.

No. 556 is the last of a group of four charters concerning the Swillington Mill—between Swillington and Garforth, as it is described in No. 209. They were given by four successive lords of that manor during four generations, and not one of the many witnesses attests any two of the documents. In other words, so steady and peaceful was the life of these squires of Swillington in the twelfth and thirteenth centuries that each lord seems to have inherited his estate in due course, and so to have lived out his allotted term that, when he left it to his son, all the witnesses who testified to his own grant to the monks had departed on their long journey, and the new-coming lord had in each case to call forward an entirely new set of witnesses.

Here we reach the conclusion of the Chartulary proper, including three documents which were inserted on the dorse of folio 82 in the second and nearly contemporary hand. But to these others were afterwards added on four additional folios: No. 557 on folio 83, a charter from Prior Dalmatius, late, rather coarse, and written across the page at the upper part of a folio never otherwise occupied; No. 558, on its dorse, an agreement between the monks of Pontefract and those of Monk Bretton with regard to the tithes of Notton, an enumeration of the belongings of the church of Silkstone, and a copy of the Taxatio of the churches belonging to the priors of Pontefract. This last occupies the whole of folio 84 also, and part of the *recto* of folio 85. Folio 86 contains an inquisition taken at Christmas, 1259, after the death of Edmund de Lascy, as to the rights of the constables of Chester during the vacancy of the priory, and also a genealogy of the descendants of Swain fitz Ailric, which is transcribed into the *Monasticon* and is perhaps unique. All these are in a handwriting of the early part of the fourteenth century.

These conclude the original volume. But four folios of thicker vellum were afterwards added (the fourth of which has been cut away), and these contain fourteenth century documents, the third (and last) being initialled R: D: as indicative of the ownership at the time of Roger Dodsworth.

488.   Carta Stephani prioris.   Circa 1235.

[. . . . . I, Brother S., of Pontefract, and the convent have granted
. . . . to Hugh, son of Roger Long, of Darrington, and his heirs, a toft in
Darrington, next the toft of Walter the deacon, towards the east.   To be held, &c.,
for two shillings yearly, half at Whitsuntide and half at the feast of St. Martin.
Witnesses.]

Sciant presentes et futuri quod ego frater S. de Pontefracto et
ejusdem loci conventus dimisimus, concessimus, et hac presenti carta
nostra confirmavimus Hugoni filio Rogeri Longi[1] de Dardingtona et
heredibus suis unum toftum in Dardingtona juxta toftum Walteri
diaconi versus est.   Tenendum de nobis in feodo et hereditate, libere
et quiete ab omni servitio et consuetudine, pro duobus solidis
annuatim reddendis, medietatem ad Pentecosten et medietatem ad
festum sancti Martini.   Hiis testibus, *Gaufrido clerico tunc ballivo,*[2]
Ricardo Londinensi, Waltero receptore, Henrico filio Randulphi, Johanne
filio Michaelis, Ada filio Serlonis, Ricardo de Martona, et aliis.

(1) Roger Long, the father of this grantee, was incidentally mentioned in No. 216 as holding
a toft next that of Walter the priest.   Now we learn that the two were east and west of each other,
as we learned from No. 220 and No. 221 that such a toft was forty-five feet long by thirty-five broad.

(2) See No. 162, No. 217, No. 249, No. 253, and No. 261.

Carta Walteri prioris.[1]

[. . . . . . I, Walter the prior, and the convent have granted . . . . . to Merlin
Fleming and his heirs a toft in Pontefract which William of Stubbs has given us.
Baldwin Dyer has held it from us and has surrendered it to us in our court . . . .
To be held, &c., for ten pence yearly, half at Whitsuntide and half at the feast of
St. Martin.   Merlin has placed his seal to the counterpart which we retain.
Witnesses.]

[S]ciant presentes et futuri quod ego Walterus prior et conventus
de Pontefracto dedimus, concessimus et presenti carta nostra confirmavimus Merlino Flandrensi[2] et heredibus suis unum toftum in
Pontefracto quem Willelmus de Stubb dedit nobis.[3]   Illum scilicet
quem Baldewinus Tinctor de nobis tenuit et quem in curia nostra
nobis sursum reddidit et quietum de se et heredibus suis clamavit.
Tenendum de nobis sibi et heredibus suis, libere et quiete, pro x

(1) This charter (No. 488*) had a rubricated heading ; but, as it did not have the blue initial
letter which should have occupied the margin to the extent of six or eight lines, it was overlooked
in the numbering.   (2) Merlin Fleming was a landowner in Darfield and Wath.

(3) There is no trace of the charter by which William of Stubbs, the soldier, the son of
Walding, whose name was afterwards given to the manor, granted this toft to the monks.

denariis nobis annuatim reddendis pro omni servitio, medietatem ad Pentecosten et medietatem ad festum sancti Martini. Et ne ipse Merlinus vel heredes sui imposterum contra tenorem hujus carte venire possint, contrascripto ipsius quod penes nos retinemus sigillum suum apposuit. Hiis testibus, *Willelmo de Kamesal, Willelmo diacono, Roberto Camberlano, Radulfo de Batelay, Serlone de Munchil, Thoma de Stagno,* et aliis.

CCCCLXXX nona.   **Carta Hugonis prioris.**

[. . . . . . . I, brother Hugh, the humble prior of Pontefract, and the convent have granted . . . . to Thomas the miller of Smeaton the bovate of land with the tofts and all other easements and appurtenances in Smeaton which Herbert de Arches has given us and which Simon son of Alpais has holden of him. To be held and possessed, &c., in wood, in plain, in meadows and pastures, with all liberties, &c. Paying us two shillings yearly, twelve pence at the feast of St. Martin and twelve pence at Whitsuntide. Seal. Thomas has placed his seal to the counterpart which we retain. Witnesses.]

Sciant presentes et futuri quod ego frater Hugo, humilis prior de Pontefracto, et ejusdem loci conventus dimisimus, concessimus, et presenti carta nostra confirmavimus Thome molendinario de Smidetona illam bovatam terre cum toftis et omnibus aliis aisiamentis et pertinentiis suis in Smidetona quam Herebertus de Archis[1] nobis dedit in puram et perpetuam elemosinam et quam Symon filius Alpais[2] tenuit de predicto Herberto in eadem villa. Tenendam et habendam de nobis sibi et heredibus suis in feodo et hereditate, libere, quiete, et honorifice, in bosco, in plano, in pratis et pasturis, cum omnibus libertatibus et aisiamentis predicte terre pertinentibus. Reddendo inde nobis annuatim ij solidos, scilicet duodecim denarios ad festum sancti Martini et xij denarios ad Pentecosten. In cujus rei testimonium hoc scriptum sigillo nostro roboravimus. Et idem Thomas contrascripto quod penes nos retinemus sigillum suum apposuit in testimonium. Hiis testibus,[3] *Jordano Folioth, Willelmo de Crescy, Ada de Novo foro, Henrico Walensi, Alano filio Ranulphi, Alano filio Josien,[4] Roberto filio Gilleberti, Ricardo Noel,* et aliis.

---

(1) Herbert de Arches is described in No. 96 as "of Coniston" (probably the place of that name in Craven, near to which Osbern de Arches had possessions at the time of the Survey), and he was a frequent witness of charters connected with Swillington.   (2) ? Alphaeus.

(3) No. 205, the deed of gift of Herbert de Arches of this bovate in Smeaton, was witnessed by all these witnesses, with the further names of Maurice de Askern and Theobald de Stubbs, placed between Henry Wallis and Alan son of Ralph, and the addition, after all, of Robert de Stubbs and William son of Geoffrey.

(4) The Josian whose son Alan signed after Alan son of Ralph was a female owner of property at Smeaton. The name is spelt variously, and it is sometimes misread as Josiah. In this instance it is extended as "Josien."

490.   Carta Walteri prioris.

[. . . . . I, Walter, prior of Pontefract, and the convent have granted
. . . . to William de Campsall a toft in Pontefract under Baghill. Thomas
Dyer held it from us and in our court surrendered it. To be held and possessed,
&c., for twelve pence yearly, half at the feast of St. Martin and half at Whitsun‑
tide. Lest William or any other assigned to this tenement should hereafter, &c.,
he has placed his seal to the counterpart which we retain. Witnesses.]

Sciant presentes et futuri quod ego Walterus prior de Pontefracto
et ejusdem loci conventus dedimus, concessimus, et presenti carta
nostra confirmavimus Willelmo de Kamesala[1] unum toftum in Ponte‑
fracto subtus Baghil. Illum scilicet quem Thomas Tinctor de nobis
tenuit et in curia nostra nobis sursum reddidit et quietum de se et
heredibus suis clamavit. Tenendum et habendum prefato Willelmo
vel cui assignare voluerit, libere et quiete, pro duodecim denariis
nobis annuatim pro omni servitio reddendis, medietatem ad festum
sancti Martini et medietatem ad Pentecosten. Et ne ipse Willelmus
vel alius ad hoc tenementum assignatus in posterum contra tenorem
hujus carte venire possit, contrascripto quod penes nos retinemus
sigillum suum apposuit. Hiis testibus, *Osberto de Brettona, Willelmo
filio Everardi, Radulpho de Bateley, Symone Pincerna, Ricardo de
Stagno*, et aliis.

(1) This William de Campsall is very much in evidence as a witness to Pontefract charters
between 1220 and 1230. By No. 110 he also confirmed to the monastery ten acres which he had
acquired from Simon Butler, one of the witnesses of No. 490. Simon Butler's charter, No. 111,
names John as William's son and appointed heir. As in No. 269 he is preceded by Ralph de
Campsall, it may be that he was the William, son of Ralph, who, as we learn from No. 122, had a
house in Pontefract and who witnessed No. 167 ; while, again, he may be William the goldsmith
of No. 88.

Carta Walteri prioris.[1]

[. . . . . I, Walter, prior of Pontefract, and the convent have granted . . . . . .
to William de Horkestowe a toft in Ferriby and three acres and three perches of
land in the territory of that town which Alan the chaplain has held from us. To
be held and possessed, &c. Paying sixteen pence yearly, four pence at the feast
of St. Botolph, four pence at the feast of St. Michael, four at the feast of
St. Thomas the apostle before the Nativity of the Lord, and four on Palm Sunday.
He has placed his seal to the counterpart which we retain. Witnesses.]

Sciant presentes et futuri quod ego Walterus prior de Pontefracto
et ejusdem loci conventus dedimus, concessimus, et presenti carta
confirmavimus Willelmo de Horkestoue unum toftum in Feriby et

(1) This, like the document following, has been left unnumbered. There are many more such
cases, but in future they will pass unnoted.

tres acras et tres percatas terre in territorio ejusdem ville.[2] Illas
scilicet quas Alanus capellanus tenuit de nobis. Tenendas et
habendas prefato Willelmo et heredibus suis de nobis, libere et
quiete, in feodo et hereditate. Reddendo inde nobis annuatim
sexdecim denarios pro omni servitio hiis terminis, scilicet iiij*or* denarios
ad festum sancti Botulfi, et quatuor denarios ad festum sancti
Michaelis, et iiij*or* ad festum sancti Thome Apostoli ante Nativitatem
domini, et iiij*or* ad pascha floridum. Et ne idem Willelmus vel
heredes sui inposterum contra tenorem hujus carte venire possint,
contrascripto quod penes nos retinemus sigillum suum apposuit.
Hiis testibus, *Willelmo capellano de Feriby, Gervasio Coco, Benedicto
filio Geraldi, Roberto filio Rogeri, Waltero de Horkestowe*, et aliis.

---

(2) The property thus granted would have been part of the grant of Gilbert, Earl of Lincoln
(see No. 399), by which he redeemed himself from the payment of six librates of rent, an indemnity
given to the monks in compensation for the damage inflicted upon the monastery during the "war"
of succession between himself and Henry de Lascy, after the death of Ilbert the second.

Carta Hugonis prioris.

[To all to whom the present writing shall come, brother H., prior of Pontefract, and the convent, greeting. We have granted . . . . and held to be satisfactory the grant which Roger son of Simon Fullo of Malfaygate made to William
son of Ace the dyer and Mabel his mother, and their heirs who shall come from
himself and Mabel mother of the aforesaid R., namely a house in Malfaygate
with all its appurtenances of our fee. It lies between the house of the said
Roger and the fee of John of Baghill, and was given to Mabel his mother as
dower. To be held and possessed, &c., as the charter of the aforesaid R. witnesses.
Paying us 6*d.* yearly, half at Whitsuntide and half at the feast of St. Martin. . . . .
He has placed his seal to this writing which we retain. Witnesses.]

Omnibus ad quos presens scriptum pervenerit, frater H. prior de
Pontefracto et ejusdem loci conventus, salutem. Universitati vestre
notum facimus nos concessisse et confirmasse et gratam habuisse
donationem et concessionem quam Rogerus filius Symonis Fullonis
de Malfaigate fecit Willelmo filio Ace tinctoris et Mabilie matri sue
et heredibus eorum qui de ipso et Mabilia matre prefati R. exibunt ;
videlicet unam domum in Malfaigate cum omnibus pertinentiis suis
de feodo nostro. Illam scilicet que jacet inter domum dicti Rogeri
et inter feodum Johannis de Baghil et que data erat Mabilie matri
sue nomine dotis. Tenendam et habendam de nobis sibi et heredibus
suis de predicta Mabilia matre dicti R. genitis, in feodo et hereditate,
libere et quiete, pacifice et integre, pro ut carta predicti R. testatur.
Reddendo inde nobis annuatim vj*d.*, medietatem ad Pentecosten et

medietatem ad festum sancti Martini. Et ne ipsi contra tenorem hujus confirmationis et concessionis venire possint, huic scripto quod penes nos retinemus sigillum suum apposuit. Hiis testibus, *Willelmo capellano, Johanne de Lovain, Roberto de Knaresburg, Gregorio de Thalamo, Johanne filio Michaelis,*[1] et aliis.

----

(1) This may be John of Baghill.

----

493.   **Carta Hugonis prioris.**

[. . . . . I, brother H., prior of Pontefract, and the convent have granted . . . . . . to William son of Gilbert of Ascham two bovates of land in the town of Wick which Adam de Alwoodley has held from us. To be held and possessed, &c., both in fee and by heirship, ... within the town of Wick and without. Paying us yearly two shillings and 6*d.*, half at Whitsuntide and half at the feast of St. Martin. The said William . . . . . . has placed his seal to the transcript which we retain. Witnesses.]

Sciant presentes et futuri quod ego frater H. prior de Pontefracto et ejusdem loci conventus dimisimus, concessimus, et hac presenti carta nostra confirmavimus Willelmo filio Gilleberti de Ascham duas bovatas terre in villa de Wic. Illas scilicet quas Ada de Alwoldleia tenuit de nobis. Tenendas et habendas de nobis sibi et heredibus suis, in feodo et hereditate, libere, quiete, et honorifice, cum omnibus pertinentiis suis et aisiamentis infra villam de Wic et extra pertinentibus. Reddendo inde annuatim nobis duos solidos et vj*d.* pro omni servitio, scilicet medietatem ad Pentecosten et medietatem ad festum sancti Martini. Et ne idem Willelmus vel heredes sui in posterum contra tenorem hujus carte venire possit, transcripto quod penes[1] retinemus pro se et heredibus suis sigillum suum apposuit. Hiis testibus, *Ada de Wittona, Henrico de Westschov, Henrico de Alwoldleya, Willelmo de Lofthus, Rogero de Neuhal,* et aliis.

----

(1) The word "nos" is omitted.

Carta Dalmatii prioris.

[. . . . I, brother Dalmatius, the humble prior of Pontefract, and the convent have granted . . . . . . to Robert Cook, of Ledsham, a toft with adjoining croft in that town. It lies between the watercourse which flows under our garden and the toft of Adam Freeman. To be held and possessed, &c., paying us yearly four silver shillings, at Whitsuntide two shillings and at the feast of St. Martin in winter two shillings. We have placed our seal to this writing, and the said Robert has similarly placed his seal to the transcript which we retain. Witnesses.]

Sciant presentes et futuri quod ego frater Dalmatius prior humilis de Pontefracto et ejusdem loci conventus dimisimus, concessimus, et hac presenti carta nostra confirmavimus Roberto Coco de Ledesham unum toftum cum crofto adjacente in eadem villa. Quod toftum jacet inter cursum aque que currit sub, gardino nostro in dicta villa et toftum Ade Liberi. Tenendum et habendum de nobis dicto Roberto et heredibus suis libere, quiete, pacifice. Reddendo inde nobis annuatim quatuor solidos argenti ad hos terminos, videlicet ad Pentecosten duos solidos et ad festum sancti Martini in hieme duos solidos, pro omnibus servitiis. In cujus rei testimonium huic scripto sigillum nostrum apposuimus, et dictus Robertus transcripto quod penes nos retinemus sigillum suum similiter apposuit in testimonium. Hiis testibus, *Hugone tunc vicario de Ledeshama, Rogero Pateman, Rogero de Monte, Johanne Norreis, Adam Libero,* et aliis.

Carta Stephani prioris.

[To all the sons, &c., Stephen, prior of Pontefract, and the convent, eternal greeting in the Lord. Whereas a dispute between the chapter of York and ourselves concerning the church of Ledsham might by length of time lead to greater discord, we, wishing to provide for the good of souls and peace of minds, have entrusted it absolutely to the arrangement of our venerable father Walter, by the grace of God Archbishop of York, primate of England, and of G., dean, and of R., precentor, and of W., chancellor, and of W. de Laneham, Archdeacon of Durham, canons of York. We will receive gratefully whatever shall be ordered. Seals.]

Universis sancte matris ecclesie filiis has litteras visuris vel audituris, Stephanus prior de Pontefracto et ejusdem loci conventus salutem eternam in domino. Noveritis quod cum contentio inter capitulum Eborascense ex una parte et nos ex altera mota super ecclesiam de Ledeshama pro temporis diuternitate majoris discordie etiam esse possit, nos[2] saluti animarum et tranquillitati animorum providere volentes ordinationi venerabilis patris nostri W.[1] dei gratia Eborascensis archiepiscopi, primatis Anglie, et G. decani, et R. precentoris, et W. cancellatoris, et W de Lanum archidiaconi Dunolmensis, canonicorum Ebor', quantum ad predictam ecclesiam pure et absolute nos[2] commisimus. Ratumque habemus et gratanter accipiemus que per eos in dicto negotio fuerit ordinata. In cujus rei testimonium presenti scripto apposuimus sigilla nostra.

---

(1) The full names would be Walteri, Galfridi, Roberti. The archdeacon was William, but the chancellor I have not traced.   (2) Repeated thus.

Carta Walteri prioris.

[. . . . . I, Walter, prior of Pontefract, and the convent . . . . . . have granted
. . . . . to Hamon the merchant and his heirs the toft in Pontefract above the lord's
vivary which Henry son of Ranulph[1] formerly held from us. Paying us yearly
twelve pence, half at Whitsuntide and half at the feast of St. Martin. Hamon
. . . . . has placed his seal to the counterpart which we retain. Witnesses.]

Sciant presentes et futuri quod ego Walterus prior de Pontefracto
et ejusdem loci conventus dedimus, concessimus, et presenti carta
confirmavimus Hamoni mercatori et heredibus suis toftum illum in
Pontefracto super vivarium domini quem Henricus filius Ranulphi
de nobis ante tenuit. Reddendo inde nobis annuatim pro omni
servitio duodecim denarios, medietatem ad Pentecosten et medietatem
ad festum sancti Martini. Et ne ipse Hamo vel heredes sui in
posterum contra tenorem hujus carte venire possint, contrascripto
quod penes nos retinemus sigillum suum apposuit. Hiis testibus,
*Johanne de Birkina, Willelmo de Stapiltona, Jordano de Sancta Maria,
Magistro Raimundo, Radulpho de Nortgate, Merlino Wad*,[2] et aliis.

----

(1) The charter to Henry son of Ranulph, being superseded, was not preserved.

(2) Merlin Wath, otherwise Merlin Fleming, as we learn from No. 102, owned one of the tofts
at Baghill.

CCCCLXXXX septima.[1]   Carta Hugonis prioris.

[. . . . . . I, Hugh, prior of Pontefract, and the convent . . . . . . have granted
to John son of John, chaplain of Silkstone, all the land of Hawkhirst, in length
by the stream of Middlecliff to the boundaries of Thurgoland and in breadth from
the boundary of Silkstone to the boundary of Stainborough, and eighteen acres of
land in the territory of Dodworth, in the far end of Middlecliff towards the
west, between the land of Gilbert de Notton towards the north, and the land of
Matthew Pincher towards the east, and Hawkhirst towards the south. To be held
and possessed, &c., with all who are on the aforesaid lands. Paying us yearly
fourteen shillings and ten pence, half at the feast of St. John Baptist and half at
the feast of St. Andrew. John and his heirs shall have common of pasture
and easement of water from Dodworth, after our men have reaped their wheat
and carried their hay, saving to us our wood. And the men of the aforesaid
town shall common in the land of Hawkhirst when John and his heirs have
reaped and carried hay. . . . . . . He has placed his seal to the transcript which we
retain. Witnesses.]

Sciant presentes et futuri quod ego Hugo prior de Pontefracto
et ejusdem loci conventus dedimus, concessimus, et presenti carta
confirmavimus Johanni filio Johannis capellani de Silkestuna totam

----

(1) A copy of No. 497 occurs in *Dodsworth*, vol. 151, and there is an abstract both in vol. 135
and in vol. 138.

terram de Haueshirst per divisas istas in longitudine, scilicet per
rivulum aque de Midelclif usque ad divisas de Turgerland, et in
latitudine a divisa de Silkestona usque ad divisam de Stainburg, et
xviij acras terre in territorio de Doddewrd, in ultimo fine de
Midelclyf versus west, inter terram Gilleberti de Notton versus north
et terram Matheie Pinchewer versus est et Haueshirst versus suth.
Tenendam et habendam prefato Johanni et heredibus suis de nobis
libere et quiete, in feodo et hereditate, cum omnibus qui sunt in
prefatis terris. Reddendo inde nobis annuatim xiiij solidos et decem
denarios, medietatem ad festum sancti Johannis Baptiste et medietatem
ad festum sancti Andree. Idem vero Johannes et heredes sui
habebunt communam pasture et aisiamentum aque de de[2] Doddeworda
postquam homines nostri ejusdem ville messuerint bladum suum et
fenum suum kariaverint, salvo nobis per omnia bosco nostro de
Doddeuuorda. Et homines predicte ville communicabunt in predicta
terra de Haueshirst quando idem Johannes et heredes sui messuerint
et fenum kariaverint. Et ne ipse aut heredes sui inposterum contra
tenorem hujus carte venire possint, transcripto quod penes nos
retinemus sigillum suum apposuit. Hiis testibus, *Magistro Roberto
de Wincestria, Rogero clerico de Silkestona, Willelmo de Bretton,
Ricardo de Martona*, et aliis. ————

(2) The word is repeated thus.

---

498.   **Carta Stephani prioris.**

[. . . . . I, Stephen, prior of Pontefract, and the convent . . . . have
confirmed to Alexander de Norwich a toft in the territory of Stubbs which is called
Rollecroft, and a toft in the same town, lying next the toft of William Burnell
towards the west and the land of Sir Theobald, knight, towards the south. To be
held and possessed by the said A. and his heirs, in fee, as fully and well as
Richard Ruffus last held them from us, with the common easements of that town.
Paying yearly four shillings and two pence, half at the feast of St. Martin and half
at Whitsuntide. And . . . . A. has placed his seal to the transcript which we
retain. Witnesses.]

Sciant presentes et futuri quod ego Stephanus prior de Pontefracto
et ejusdem loci conventus dimisimus, concessimus, et hac presenti
carta nostra confirmavimus Alexandro de Norwich unum toftum in
territorio de Stubb qui nominatur Rollecroft,[1] et unum toftum
in eadem villa jacentem juxta toftum Willelmi Burnel versus

---

(1) In the early charters Rollecroft is called an assart; in this lease it has risen to the dignity
of a toft.

west et terram domini Teobaldi militis versus suth.   Tenendum et habendum dicto A. et heredibus suis in feodo et hereditate de nobis libere, quiete, et honorifice, cum pertinentiis suis, ita plenius et melius sicut Ricardus Ruffus de nobis illa ultimo tenuit, cum communibus aisiamentis ejusdem ville tanto tenemento pertinentibus.   Reddendo inde annuatim quatuor solidos et duos denarios pro omni servitio seculari, medietatem ad festum sancti Martini et medietatem ad Pentecosten.   Et ne ipse A. vel heredes sui in posterum contra tenorem hujus carte venire possint, transcripto quod penes nos retinemus sigillum suum apposuit.   Hiis testibus, *Gaufrido clerico, tunc ballivo, Alano de Smithetona, Willelmo de Archis, Henrico Burnel, Radulpho de Nortona, Ricardo de Martona,* et aliis.

490.[1]   **Carta Hugonis prioris.**

[To all Christ's faithful, &c., brother Hugh, prior, and the convent of Ponte-fract, greeting in the Lord. . . . . . We have confirmed to Robert son of Basilia and his heirs our toft in the new town of Scarborough, namely, that in which was formerly situated the granary of Siward Ruffus.   To be held and possessed by fee-farm rent.   Paying yearly to us and our house eighteen pence, at the feast of St. Martin nine pence and at Whitsuntide nine pence, saving the service of the lord king and everything else belonging to that land.   In witness we have delivered to him this our charter.   Witnesses.]

Omnibus Christi fidelibus ad quos presens scriptum pervenerit, frater Hugo prior et conventus de Pontefracto salutem in domino. Noscat universitas vestra nos dimisisse et hac presenti carta nostra confirmasse Roberto filio Basilie et heredibus suis toftum[2] nostrum in novo burgo de Scardeburga, scilicet in quo quondam situm fuit horreum Sywardi Ruffi.   Tenendum et habendum de nobis per feodi firmam inperpetuum.[3]   Reddendo inde annuatim nobis et domui nostre decem et octo denarios ad duos terminos, scilicet ad festum sancti Martini novem denarios, ad Pentecosten novem denarios, pro omni servitio.   Salvo servitio domini regis et aliis omnibus si qua sunt vel esse possunt ad istam terram pertinentibus.   Et in hujus rei testimonium ei hanc cartam nostram tradididimus.[4]   Hiis testibus, *Henrico de Hareford,*[5] *Huctredo de Winnertorph,*[6] *Roberto fratre suo, Willelmo de Boston, Thoma de Lingeberge, Toma Piscatore,* et aliis.

---

(1) It is thus numbered in error.

(2) This toft was afterwards, by No. 543, leased to Thomas Turs, also a burgess of Scarborough, at the advanced rent of 1s. 8d.   See also No. 507.

(3) Here the words "scilicet ad festum sancti Martini" were inserted in error, and afterwards erased in red.   (4) *Sic.*

(5) See No. 419 and No. 432.   (6) See No. 432.

D.   Carta Agnetis de Bradelay.[1]

[. . . . . . . I, Agnes de Bradley, who was wife of William son of Hameric de
Whitwood, have, in the power of my widowhood, ... foresworn and in
the court of Pontefract surrendered . . . . all the land which I had in
the territory of the Mere, in the name of dower, from the gift of William my
husband. To be held and possessed . . . . without reclaim from me or mine.
The monks have given me in hand a silver mark. Seal. Witnesses.]

Sciant presentes et futuri quod ego Agnes de Bradelay que fui
uxor Willelmi[2] filii Haymerici de Withewode in ligia potestate
viduitatis mee dedi, concessi, foris juravi, et in curia Pontisfracti
sursum reddidi et in perpetuum quietam clamavi de me et omnibus
meis deo et sancto Johanni de Pontefracto et monachis ibidem deo
servientibus totam terram quam habui in territorio de Mara nomine
dotis ex dono Willelmi sponsi mei. Tenendam et habendam prefatis
monachis in perpetuum sine reclamatione mei vel aliquorum meorum.
Pro hac autem quieta clamatione et concessione dederunt mihi
predicti monachi unam marcam argenti pre manibus. Et ne ego vel
aliquis meorum contra hanc meam quietam clamationem et concessionem in posterum venire possimus, vel aliquod jus in predicta
terra aut suis pertinentiis vendicare, huic carte sigillum meum pro
me et omnibus meis apposui in testimonium. Hiis testibus, *Henrico
Walensi, Umfrido de Millers, Henrico de Tancrelleia, Roberto de
Deneby, Radulpho de Rupe, Ricardo de Martona, Gerardo de Berneslay,*
et aliis.

(1) This is still the popular pronunciation of the word.

(2) No. 253 to No. 258, a series of charters from this William, show how he, an offshoot of the
Stapleton family, became first "of the Mere," and afterwards, as here, "of Whitwood." Whitwood
and Whitwood Mere are adjacent.

DI.[1]   Carta Hugonis prioris.

[. . . . . I, Hugh, prior of Pontefract, and the convent have . . . . . confirmed
to Adam de Alwoodley, son of William, two bovates of land in Wick, which
William son of Simon de Mohaut gave us. To be held and possessed by him and
his heirs, &c. Paying yearly two shillings for all service, half at Whitsuntide and
half at the feast of St. Martin . . . . He has placed his seal to the counterpart
which we retain. Witnesses.]

Sciant presentes et futuri quod ego Hugo prior de Pontefracto et
ejusdem loci conventus dedimus, concessimus, et presenti carta nostra
confirmavimus Ade de Alwaldeley filio Willelmi duas bovatas terre

---

(1) No. 501 would be intermediate in time between No. 331 and No. 228 *bis.*

in Wick. Illas scilicet quas Willelmus filius Symonis de Mohaut[2] nobis dedit. Tenendas et habendas de nobis libere et quiete sibi et heredibus suis in feodo et hereditate, cum omnibus pertinentiis suis et aisiamentiis ad prefatas bovatas terre infra villam de Wick et extra pertinentibus. Reddendo nobis annuatim duos solidos pro omni servitio, medietatem ad Pentecosten et medietatem ad festum sancti Martini. Et ne idem Adam vel heredes · sui in posterum contra tenorem hujus carte venire possint, contrascripto quod penes nos retinemus sigillum suum apposuit. Hiis testibus, *Symone de Mohaut, Willelmo de Mohaut, Roberto de Mohaut, Hugone de Witona, Gaufrido de Ardington, Roberto ad Bec,* et et[3] aliis.

(2) There is a small pedigree of the family of Mohaut on page 398.   (3) *Sic.*

502.[1]   Carta Walteri prioris.

[. . . . . I, Walter, prior of Pontefract, and the convent have . . . . confirmed to Ralph, brother of Richard of Stubbs, two acres in the Fields of Smeaton, which Alan, son of Robert, son of Oliver of Smeaton, gave us ; one acre and a half lie above Drakehough and reach on one side to the Went and on the other to the high road to Norton, and half an acre lies between the land of Siward of Norton and the land of Josiana mother of Alan, son of Robert, son of Oliver, and on one side borders upon the land of Alan son of Ranulf and on the other upon the high road to Norton. To be held and possessed by Ralph and his heirs, in fee and heirship, &c., paying us yearly six · pence for all service, half at Whitsuntide and half at the feast of St. Martin. . . . . Ralph has placed his seal to the counterpart which we retain. Witnesses.]

Sciant presentes et futuri quod ego Walterus prior de Pontefracto et ejusdem loci conventus dedimus, concessimus, et presenti carta nostra confirmavimus Radulpho fratri Ricardi de Stubbis duas acras terre in campis de Smithetona. Illas scilicet quas Alanus filius Roberti filii Oliverii de Smithetona nobis dedit in puram et perpetuam elemosinam. Ex quibus acris una acra et dimidia jacent super Drakehov et ex una parte extendunt se versus Went et ex alia parte versus magnam viam que tendit versus Nortonam, et dimidia acra jacet inter terram Sywardi de Nortona et terram Josiane[2] matris Alani filii Roberti filii Oliverii, et ex una parte percutit super terram Alani filii Ranulfi et ex alia parte super magnam viam que tendit versus Nortonam. Tenendas et habendas prefato Radulfo et heredibus suis

(1) No. 502 is almost identical in terms with No. 269 ; and, many of the witnesses being common, it appears to be an immediate lease of that which No. 269 granted to the monks in fee.
(2) See No. 489.

de nobis in feodo et hereditate, libere et quiete, cum communiis et libertatibus et aisiamentis ad tantum tenementum pertinentibus. Reddendo inde nobis annuatim sex denarios pro omni servitio, medietatem ad Pentecosten et medietatem ad festum sancti Martini. Et ne idem Radulphus vel heredes sui in posterum contra tenorem hujus carte venire possint, contrascripto quod penes nos retinemus sigillum suum apposuit. Hiis testibus, *Alano filio Ranulfi, tunc ballivo de Staincros et Osgotcros, Thebaudo de Stubbis, Petro de Archis,*[3] *Ricardo Noel, Radulpho de Kamesal, Ricardo de Martona,* et aliis.

---

(3) In No. 269 he is Peter de Stubbs.

---

503. **Carta Hugonis prioris.** **Circa 1228.**

[. . . . . I, Hugh, prior of Pontefract, with the consent of all the convent, have granted to William, son of Robert, son of Alice of Pontefract, and his heirs half the land of Southgate which Robert de Stapleton gave. William and his heirs shall hold it of us for two shillings yearly, at the feast of St. Martin twelve pence and at Whitsuntide twelve pence . . . . . . He has placed his seal to the counterpart which we retain. Witnesses.]

Sciant presentes et futuri quod ego Hugo prior de Pontefracto consensu totius conventus concessi Willelmo filio Roberti filio Aalicie de Pontefracto et heredibus suis medietatem terre de Suthgate quam Robertus de Stapiltona dedit deo et sancto Johanni. Hanc terram tenebunt prefatus Willelmus et heredes sui de nobis libere et quiete pro duobus solidis nobis annuatim reddendis pro omni servitio et consuetudine, ad festum sancti Martini xij*d.* et ad Pentecosten xij*d.* Et ne ipse Willelmus vel heredes sui in posterum contra tenorem hujus carte venire possint, contrascripto quod penes nos retinemus sigillum suum apposuit. Hiis testibus, *Waltero Scot, Willelmo de Daneport, Willelmo de Novo castello, Thoma de Dengge,*[1] *Roberto de Queldale, Symone Beverege, Martino de Seleby, Ricardo de Stagno,* et aliis.

---

(1) In No. 109 it is Dinga.

D quinta.[1] **Carta Serlonis filii Gervasii de Brettona.** **Circa 1194.**

[Agreement made between Serlo son of Gervase of Bretton, plaintiff, and Henry Neeloth, tenant, concerning two acres and three and a half roods in Beatricehill, in the eighth year of the reign of King Richard, as to which there was

---

(1) The numbering omitted 504. No. 505 was copied into *Dodsworth*, vol. 151, and *Lansdowne* 207. There is also an abstract in *Dodsworth*, vol. 136.

a plea between them. Serlo has quit-claimed the land from him and his heirs to Henry and his heirs for sixteen shillings sterling. That this may be held valid and unshaken and without deceit, each has confirmed it by the bond of the faith and the setting to of his seal. Witnesses.]

Hec est conventio facta inter Serlonem filium Gervasii de Brettona, petentem, et Henricum Neeloth,[2] tenentem, de duabus acris et de tribus rodis et dimidia rǫda terre in Beatrishil, anno regni regis Ricardi octavo.[3] Unde placitum fuit inter eos. Scilicet quod predictus Serlo prefatam terram quietam clamavit et abjuravit de se et heredibus suis predicto Henrico et heredibus suis pro sexdecim solidis sterlingorum quos idem Henricus ei dedit. Et ut ista quieta clamatio et abjuratio rata et inconcussa et sine fraude teneatur, uterque fidei religione et sigilli sui appositione confirmavit. Hiis testibus, *Radulfo filio Radulfi*,[4] *Johanne de Luttringtona*,[5] *Roberto Vavasore, Willelmo fratre, Ottone de Barkestona, Ricardo de Hudlestona.*

---

(2) See No. 332.   (3) 1197.

(4) This Ralph, son of Ralph, was one of the witnesses of the almost contemporary town charter of 1194, as was also Robert Vavasour.   (5) Lotherton.

---

506.   Carta Stephani prioris de Pontefracto.   Circa 1236.

[. . . . . . I, brother St., prior of Pontefract, and the convent have . . . . confirmed to Richard son of Jordan of Roall and his heirs a plot of land with its buildings in the New Market of Pontefract which Alexander the chaplain formerly held from us. It lies between the land of John de Selsey and the land of Marsand. To be held and possessed by him and his heirs, &c. Paying us yearly six silver shillings, half at Whitsuntide and half at the feast of St. Martin, and doing forinsec service to the chief lord. But if we can change the site into pure alms, Richard and his heirs shall pay us yearly half a mark at the aforesaid terms. Warranty. . . . . . . Richard has placed his seal to the transcript which we retain. Witnesses.]

Sciant presentes et futuri quod ego frater St. prior de Pontefracto et ejusdem loci conventus dimisimus, concessimus, et hac presenti carta nostra confirmavimus Ricardo filio Jordani de Rowella et heredibus suis unam placiam terre cum edificiis in ea positis in novo foro Pontisfracti. Illam scilicet quam Alexander capellanus quondam tenuit de nobis, que jacet inter terram Johannis de Sellesheya et terram Marsand. Tenendam et habendam sibi et heredibus suis in feodo et hereditate, libere, quiete, et honorifice. Redde[1] inde nobis annuatim sex solidos argenti, medietatem ad Pentecosten et medieta-

---

(1) *Sic.*

tem ad festum sancti Martini, faciendo forinseca servitia domino capitali pertinentia. Set si nos dictam placiam in puram potuerimus vertere elemosinam, prenominatus Ricardus et heredes sui reddent nobis annuatim dimidiam marcam ad prefatos terminos pro omni servitio. Nos vero predictam placiam cum edificiis in ea positis predicto Ricardo et heredibus suis contra omnes homines warentizabimus quam diu nobis fuerit warentizata. Et ne idem Ricardus vel heredes sui contra hanc cartam inposterum venire possint, transcripto quod penes nos retinemus sigillum suum apposuit. Hiis testibus, *Henrico Walensi, Waltero receptore, Johanne de Lovain, Johanne Vinitore, Johanne filio Michaelis, Ricardo de Martona,* et aliis.

SCARBURG.
507. **Carta Dalmatii prioris.**

[. . . . . I, brother Dalmatius, the humble prior of Pontefract, and the convent . . . . have confirmed to Robert Fareman, burgess of Scarborough, and his heirs or assigns my land in the New Town of Scarborough. It lies between the land which Godric Busceler has held from the house of Watton and the land which Stephen son of Roger Smith has held. To be held and possessed, &c., in all places and things. Paying us yearly three shillings sterling, eighteen pence at the feast of St. Martin in winter and eighteen pence at Whitsuntide. Saving the service of the lord king, which Robert Fareman or his heirs or assigns are bound to do. If the said Robert Fareman or his heirs or assigns fail in payment of the rent at the aforesaid terms, our messenger, sent at their cost, shall remain until he shall have fully received it. . . . . . . The oftnamed Robert has . . . . . . placed his seal to the transcript which we retain. Witnesses.]

Sciant presentes et futuri quod ego fr. Dalmatius humilis prior de Pontefracto et ejusdem loci conventus dimisimus, concessimus, et hac presenti carta nostra confirmavimus Roberto Fareman[1] burgensi de Scardeburg et heredibus suis vel assignatis terram meam in novo burgo de Scardeburga. Illam scilicet que jacet inter terram quam Godricus Busceler tenuit de domo de Wattona et terram quam Stephanus filius Rogeri Fabri tenuit. Tenendam et habendam dicto Roberto et heredibus suis vel assignatis in perpetuum libere, pacifice, honorifice, in omnibus locis et rebus. Reddendo inde annuatim nobis tres solidos sterlingorum ad eandem terram pro omni servitio et exactione pro omnibus rebus, scilicet octodecim denarios ad festum sancti Martini in yeme et xviij denarios ad Pentecosten.

, (1) There is nothing to show whether this Robert Fareman is or is not the Robert son of Basil of No. 499.

Salvo servitio domini regis ad dictam terram pertinente, quod servitium dictus Robertus Fareman vel heredes sui aut assignati facere tenentur. Si vero dictus Robertus Fareman vel heredes sui aut assignati in solutione dicte firme ad prefatos terminos defecerint, nuntius noster ad dictam firmam recipiendam missus sumptibus dicti Roberti vel heredis sui aut assignati qui pro ipso fuerit remanebit donec dictam firmam plenarie perceperit. Et ne dictus Robertus vel heredes sui aut assignati contra tenorem hujus carte possint in posterum venire, sepedictus Robertus transcripto quod penes nos retinemus pro se et suis et[2] heredibus et assignatis sigillum suum apposuit. Hiis testibus, *Rogero Huctred, Johanne de Waud', Adam de Tostona, Waltero Au'ni, Rogero Wbram, Galfrido Cottinghama, Rogero Cottinghama*, et aliis.

(2) *Sic.*

509.[1]   Carta Dalmatii prioris.

[To all Christ's faithful, &c., brother Dalmatius, the humble prior of Pontefract, and the convent of that place, greeting in the Lord. We have . . . . . . confirmed to Alice, formerly wife of Gilbert le Surrey of Sutton, and her heirs or assigns, two assarts in the territory of Byram, which Gilbert held of us. To be held and possessed, &c. Paying us yearly six silver shillings, three shillings at Whitsuntide and three at the feast of St. Martin in winter. We have placed our seal to the present charter, and the said Alice . . . . has placed her seal to the transcript which we retain. Witnesses.]

Universis Christi fidelibus ad quos presens scriptum pervenerit, frater Dalmatius humilis prior de Pontefracto et ejusdem loci conventus, salutem in domino. Noverit universitas vestra nos dimisisse, concessisse, et presenti carta nostra confirmasse Alicie, quondam uxori Gilleberti le Surreis de Suttona, et heredibus suis vel assignatis, duo assarta in territorio de Birum. Illa scilicet que dictus Gillebertus de nobis tenuit. Tenenda et habenda dicte Alicie et heredibus suis vel assignatis libere et quiete, pacifice et honorifice. Reddendo inde nobis annuatim sex solidos argenti pro omni servitio et exactione, scilicet tres solidos ad Pentecosten et tres solidos ad festum sancti Martini in hyeme. In hujus autem rei testimonium presenti scripto sigillum nostrum apposuimus, et dicta Alicia quod penes nos retinemus transcripto pro se et heredibus suis et assignatis sigillum suum apposuit. Hiis testibus, *domino Nichola de Queldale, Willelmo de Birum, Serlone de Brettona, Roberto filio ejus, Salomone de Brettona*,[2] et aliis.

(1) This charter was numbered both 508 and 509.
(2) It is probable that from him is derived the second name of Burton Salmon.

510.[1]   Carta Fulconis prioris.

[To all the sons, &c., brother Fulk, prior of Pontefract, and the humble convent, greeting in the Lord. With the common and unanimous consent of our chapter, we have in court of charity . . . . confirmed to Stephen, the clerk of Hamerton, our church of Slaidburn, with the lands and tithes and all things belonging to it, for his life. To be held and possessed at an annual pension of six marks, half within the octave of Pentecost and half within the octave of St. Martin. The said Stephen shall pay all episcopal dues and bear all church burdens. And he has sworn, touching the Holy Gospels, that he will conduct himself faithfully towards us as regards the pension and as regards the benefice. Witnesses.]

Omnibus sancte matris ecclesie filiis presentibus et futuris frater Fulco prior de Pontefracto et humilis conventus ejusdem loci, salutem in domino. Universitati vestre notum facimus nos communi et unanimi assensu capituli nostri caritatis in curia concessisse, dedisse, et hac presenti carta nostra confirmasse Stephano clerico de Hamerton ecclesiam nostram de Sleyteburna cum terris et decimis et omnibus ad eam pertinentibus in tota vita sua. Tenendam et habendam de nobis sub annua pensione sex marcarum, medietatem infra octavas Pentecosti et medietatem infra octavas sancti Martini. Idem vero Stephanus omnia episcopalia persolvet et omnia onera ecclesie sustinebit. Juravit etiam tactis sacrosanctis ewangeliis quod fideliter se habebit erga nos de pensione reddenda statutis terminis et de predicto beneficio. Hiis testibus, *Rogero de Ledesham, Benedicto de Millum, Adam de Arneclif, Bernard de Ripeleya, Ricardo capellano, Johanne de Berkin,* et aliis.

(1) In a brief abstract in *Dodsworth*, vol. 155, this charter is quoted as No. 509. It is placed also as No. 509 in the Index, so that the present numbering must be of a later date than either; for there is no appearance in the Chartulary itself that this document was ever numbered other than 510.

---

511.   Carta Dalmatii prioris.

[. . . . . I, brother Dalmatius, the humble prior of Pontefract, and the convent have . . . . . . confirmed to Roger, son of Matilda of Frystone, a bovate of land in the territory of Frystone, which William Marshall gave us with his body. To be held and possessed, &c. Paying us yearly during the life of Sigereda, formerly wife of the said William Marshall, whom the said Roger afterwards married, six pence, at Whitsuntide three pence and at the feast of St. Martin three pence. After the death of the said Sigereda, Roger and his heirs shall pay us yearly five shillings in equal parts at the aforesaid terms. But if he die without heir of his body, the bovate shall return to us. In testimony we have placed our seal to this writing, and the said Roger has placed his seal to the transcript which we retain. Witnesses.]

Sciant presentes et futuri quod ego frater Dalmatius humilis prior
de Pontefracto et ejusdem loci conventus dimisimus, concessimus, et
hac presenti carta nostra confirmavimus Rogero[1] filio Matildis de
Fristona unam bovatam terre in territorio de Fristona.   Illam scilicet
quam Willelmus Mariscallus nobis dedit cum corpore suo.   Tenendam
et habendam de nobis dicto Rogero et heredibus suis libere, quiete,
pacifice.   Reddendo inde nobis annuatim in vita Siggrede,[2] quondam
uxoris dicti Willelmi Marescalli, quam dictus Rogerus postea despon-
savit, sex denarios, videlicet ad Pentecosten iij*d.* et ad festum sancti
Martini iij*d.*, pro omnibus servitiis secularibus.   Post obitum vero
dicte Siggerede dictus Rogerus et heredes sui reddent nobis annuatim pro dicta bovata terre quinque solidos per equales partes ad
predictos terminos.   Si vero dictus Rogerus obierit sine herede de
corpore suo dicta bovata terre sine alicujus impedimento ad nos
revertetur.   In cujus rei testimonium huic scripto sigillum nostrum
apposuimus.   Et dictus Rogerus transcripto quod penes nos retinemus
sigillum suum apposuit.   Hiis testibus, *Nichola de Queldale, Symone
capellano de Pontefracto, Radulpho capellano de Feria, Roberto,*[3] *Waltero
de Pontefracto, Johanne de Lovain,* et aliis.

---

(1) From this charter is gathered the following pedigree, but nothing occurs to add to it:—

Matilda, of Frystone

William Marshall,=Sigereda=Roger
the donor

(2) Sigereda or Sigireda was a not uncommon name.   In No. 229 there is a Richard, son of
Sigereda, of about 1180, and in No. 239 a John, son of Sigereda, of a generation or so later.   But
there is nothing to identify this latter with the almost contemporary Sigereda of No. 511.

(3) Possibly the Robert de Monte Monachorum of No. 115, No. 121, and No. 125.

---

512.   Carta Walteri Prioris.

[. . . . . I, Walter, prior of Pontefract, and the convent . . . . have
confirmed to Adam de Falthwait and his heirs, or to whom he may assign
it, a toft in Barnsley of half an acre of land, between the land of Gerard son of
Bernard and the land of Pagan on the east side of the toft of Hugh de
Baghill, and half an acre in Collegrimewelleroyds, and half an acre upon
Kirktofts, and half an acre upon Langlands, and a rood upon Claylands.   To be
held and possessed, &c., with commonage of the town, as much as belongs to such
a holding.   Saving to us our woods.   Paying us yearly a pound of cummin at the
feast of St. Giles . . . . Adam has placed his seal to the transcript which
we retain.   Witnesses.]

Sciant presentes et futuri quod ego Walterus prior de Pontefracto
et ejusdem loci conventus dedimus, concessimus, et presenti carta
confirmavimus Ade de Falewait et heredibus suis vel cui assignare

voluerit unum toftum in Berneslay de dimidia acra terre inter terram Gerardi filii Bernardi et terram Pagani in orientali parte tofti Hugonis de Baggehill, et dimidiam acram in Collegrimewellerodes, et dimidiam acram super Kirke toftes, et dimidiam acram super Langelandes et unam percatam[1] super Claylandes. Tenendas et habendas prefato Ade et heredibus suis vel cui assignare voluerit, libere et quiete, cum communa prefate ville de Berneslay quantum ad tantum tenementum pertinet. Salvis nobis boscis nostris. Reddendo inde nobis annuatim unam libram cymini ad festum sancti Egidii pro omni servitio. Et ne prefatus Adam vel heredes sui sive assignati sui in posterum contra tenorem hujus carte venire possint, transcripto quod penes nos retinemus sigillum suum apposuit. Hiis testibus, *Johanne de Birkin, Rogero clerico de Silkestona, Roberto de Turs, Rainero de Wambewelle, Adam de Aldefeld, Ricardo de Martona,* et aliis.

_____

(1) " Perticata " is a rood and " Percata " a perch; but the two words are frequently used interchangeably. Strictly, perhaps, perticata belonged to area ; percata to length.

_____

Carta Dalmatii prioris.

[. . . . . I, brother Dalmatius, the humble prior of Pontefract, and the convent . . . . have confirmed to Robert of Aynesford a toft in the town of Bilham with the adjoining croft, surrounded by a fosse, before the gate of the said Robert on the other side of the way ; and sixteen acres and a half of arable land in the Fields of that town, with their appurtenances. The said Robert formerly held them from William de Bareville, who afterwards gave them to us. Five acres lie in Eastfield, five in Middlefield, five in Westfield ; three roods are called Riding, one rood abuts upon the Cross of Hickleton, and a half acre in Eastfield which abuts upon the boundary of Hooton. To be held and possessed, &c., in fee and in heirship, &c. Paying us yearly forty-two pence, half at the feast of St. Martin in winter and half at Whitsuntide. . . . . We have placed our seal to this, and the said Robert, for himself and his heirs, has placed his seal to the counterpart which we retain. Witnesses.]

Sciant presentes et futuri quod ego frater Dalmatius humilis prior de Pontefracto et ejusdem loci conventus dedimus, concessimus, et hac presenti carta nostra confirmavimus Roberto de Aynesford unum toftum in villa de Bilam cum crofto adjacente sicut fossato circumcluditur. Illum scilicet qui jacet ante portam dicti Roberti ex altera parte itineris, et sexdecim acras terre arabilis et dimidiam in campis ejusdem ville, cum omnibus pertinentiis suis. Illas scilicet quas dictus Robertus tenuit prius de Willelmo de Barevill et quas idem Willelmus postea nobis dedit. Quarum quinque acre jacent in

Estfeld, et quinque acre in Middelfeld, et quinque acre in Westfeld, et tres perticate que vocantur Riding, et una perticata que buttat super crucem de Hikilton,[1] et dimidia acra in Estfeld que buttat super bundum de Hoton.   Tenendas et habendas de nobis dicto Roberto et heredibus suis in feodo et hereditate, libere, quiete, pacifice, et honorifice.   Reddendo inde nobis annuatim quadraginta duos denarios, medietatem ad festum sancti Martini in hyeme et medietatem ad Pentecosten, pro omnibus servitiis, exactionibus, et secularibus demandis.   In cujus rei testimonium huic scripto sigillum nostrum apposuimus, et dictus Robertus tam pro se quam pro heredibus suis contrascripto quod penes nos retinemus sigillum suum apposuit.   Hiis testibus, *domino Ada de Neirford, Henrico Walensi, Roberto filio Ernis, Willelmo de Barevilla, Henrico de Camera,* et aliis.

---

(1) The Cross of Hickleton is referred to also in No. 275 and No. 537.

514.[1]   **Carta Hugonis prioris.**

[. . . . . I, Hugh, prior of Pontefract, by the advice and consent of the whole convent . . . . have confirmed to Adam son of Peter de Broughton and his heirs two bovates of land in Broughton with their belongings.   They were William, son of Ralph's, and he surrendered them to us in our court.   To be held and possessed, &c., for five shillings yearly, half at Whitsuntide and half at the Feast of St. Martin.   And if the lord of Skipton shall ask anything from us, Adam or his heirs shall acquit us, as much as belongs to such a holding.   Adam and his heirs shall build and dwell on it.   When they die the third part of their belongings shall remain to the church of St. John.   This Adam, for himself and his heirs, has sworn to keep faithfully for ever. . . . . He has placed his seal to this charter.   Witnesses.]

Sciant presentes et futuri quod ego Hugo prior de Pontefracto consilio et consensu totius conventus ejusdem loci dedi, concessi, et hac presenti carta confirmavi Ade filio Petri de Broctuna et heredibus suis duas bovatas terre in Broctuna cum pertinentiis suis, que fuerunt Willelmi filii Radulfi et quas idem Willelmus nobis sursum reddidit in curia nostra.   Tenendas et habendas de nobis libere et quiete ab omni servitio et consuetudine pro quinque solidis annuatim reddendis, medietatem ad Pentecosten et medietatem ad festum sancti Martini.   Et si dominus de Scyptona quisierit aliquid de nobis occasione tenementi nostri de Broctuna, ipse Adam vel heredes sui adquietabunt nos quantum pertinet ad tantum

---

(1) There is a brief abstract of No. 514 in *Dodsworth*, vol. 155.

tenementum. Predictus Adam et heredes sui prefatam terram edificabunt et manebunt in ea. Et cum ad obitum suum pervenerint tota tertia pars catallorum suorum remanebit ecclesie sancti Johannis de Pontefracto. Et hoc fideliter observaturum predictus Adam juravit et affidavit pro se et heredibus suis in perpetuum. Et ne ipse Adam vel heredes sui in posterum contra tenorem hujus carte venire possint huic carte sigillum suum apposuit. Hiis testibus, *Petro Gillot, Willelmo Hebbedene, Symone de Martona, Willelmo Graindeorge, Johanne de Estun, Ricardo de Martona, Roberto Camerario,* et aliis.

---

515. Carta Walteri prioris.

[. . . . . . . I, brother Walter, prior of Pontefract, and the convent . . . .
have confirmed to Alexander son of Thomas, parson of Kellington, and his heirs, two acres of meadow in the oatlands of Kellington, to be held and possessed, &c. Paying us yearly six pence on St. John's day at Christmas. Witnesses.]

Sciant presentes et futuri quod ego frater Walterus prior de Pontefracto et ejusdem loci conventus dedimus et concessimus et hac presenti carta nostra confirmavimus Alexandro filio Thome persone de Kellingtona et heredibus suis duas acras prati in avenamas[1] de Kellingtona. Tenendas et habendas de nobis sibi et heredibus suis, in feodo et hereditate, libere, quiete, pacifice. Reddendo inde annuatim nobis sex denarios pro omni servitio et exactione die sancti Johannis infra Nathale. Hiis testibus,[2] *Johanne de Birkina, Thoma filio suo, Willelmo filio Everardi, Rogero capellano, Johanne filio Willelmi, Willelmo Cusyn, Alexandro de Rugala,* et aliis.

(1) In No. 231 it is "avenanis," in No. 232 "avenames."

(2) The witnesses to No. 515 and No. 232 are practically the same, showing that the two documents are of nearly, if not quite, the same date. The appearance here of John de Birkin, who died in 1227, and Thomas his son (the mention of whom identifies this particular John as the lord, as clearly as if he had been called "the son of Adam fitz Peter"), fixes the priorate of Walter III as having commenced at least as early as the year of the death of John de Birkin.

---

516. Carta Fulconis prioris.

[To all the sons, &c., brother Fulk, prior of Pontefract, and the convent, greeting. . . . . With common and unanimous consent we have . . . . confirmed to Robert, son of Peter, chaplain of Bardsey, and Hodierna, his sister, and their heirs, two bovates of land in Keswick with their belongings, which Simon de Mohaut gave us. To be held, &c. Paying us yearly seven shillings, half at Whitsuntide and the other half at the feast of St. Martin. Witnesses.]

Omnibus sancte matris ecclesie filiis presentibus et futuris frater Fulco prior de Pontefracto et ejusdem loci conventus salutem. Universitati vestre notum facimus nos communi et unanimi assensu concessisse et presenti carta nostra confirmasse Roberto[1] filio Petri capellani de Berdesey[2] et Hodierne· sorori ejusdem Roberti et heredibus eorum duas bovatas terre in Keswic cum omnibus pertinentiis suis. Illas scilicet quas Symon de Mohaut dedit nobis. Tenendas de nobis libere et quiete et pacifice, in feudo et hereditate. Reddendo nobis annuatim pro omni servitio septem solidos, medietatem ad Pentecosten et alteram medietatem in festo sancti Martini. Hiis testibus, *Willelmo filio Everardi, Willelmo de Rivilla,*[3] *Ricardo de Toulestona, Ada de Lumby, Roberto de Milford, Jordano Campione*, et aliis. ————

(1) In the next generation, when the monks were parting with this land, Robert, son of Peter, was called Robert of Sicklinghall in No. 228* and Robert the Sergeant in No. 266. The present and earlier charter gives a glimpse of his family connections, but nothing emerges to show what became of Hodierna, his sister, or to give any hint as to the origin of her romantic name.

(2) Part of Wike was in the parish of Bardsey, to which place Robert's father belonged.

(3) *Sic.*

———————

517.   Carta Fulconis prioris.

[. . . . . I, Fulk, prior of Pontefract, and the convent . . . . have confirmed to Robert the carpenter and his heirs the bovate of land in Thornton, the acre of land in the culture of Howfleet towards the south, the acre of meadow, and those which Robert de Laland gave us in pure and perpetual alms, for the soul of Thomas his son. To be held from us, &c., for ten shillings to be paid yearly, half at the feast of St. Martin and half at Whitsuntide. Robert has given ten shillings to the house of St. John in acknowledgment. And the aforesaid Robert, touching the Holy Gospels, has sworn that he and his heirs will pay us faithfully at Pontefract the aforesaid rent at the appointed terms. Witnesses.]

Sciant presentes et futuri quod ego Fulco prior de Pontefracto et ejusdem loci conventus dedimus, concessimus, et presenti carta nostra confirmavimus Roberto Carpentario et heredibus suis illam bovatam terre in Thornetona,[1] et illam acram terre in cultura de Houflet versus solem, et illam acram prati, et quas Robertus de la Landa nobis dedit in puram et perpetuam elemosinam pro anima Thome filii sui. Tenendas de nobis in feudo et hereditate, libere et quiete ab omni servitio et consuetudine, cum omnibus ad eas pertinentibus, pro decem solidis annuatim reddendis, medietatem ad festum sancti Martini et medietatem ad Pentecosten. Pro hac autem

(1) Unless this bovate is the bovate in Denby, named in No. 431, there is no record as to how any of this land came to the monks. Denby is in Thornton. All, or nearly all, the witnesses are North Riding men.

donatione, concessione, et confirmatione dedit idem Robertus decem solidos domui sancti Johannis de Pontefracto de recognitione. Prefatus vero Robertus carpentarius tactis sacrosanctis evangeliis[2] juravit quod ipse et heredes sui predictam firmam terminis statutis nobis apud Pontemfractum fideliter persolvent. Hiis testibus, *Gilleberto de Torni, Gaufrido Fossard, Arnaldo de Upesale, Andrea de Magneby, Johanne de Romundeby, Hugone filio Arti,* et aliis.

(2) The addition of the kiss, when taking oath, is modern. The medieval custom was, as above, merely to touch, or to lay the hand on, the book.

518. DXVIII.[1] Carta ejusdem.

[. . . . . . . I, prior Fulk, and the convent . . . . . . have confirmed to Peter the clerk, of Methley, and his heirs, for his homage and service, the land in the Fields of the Mere towards Methley, next the bank of the great water called Sandbed. To be held, &c. Paying us yearly one penny on St. Martin's day. Witnesses.]

Sciant presentes et futuri quod ego Fulco prior et conventus de Pontefracto dedimus et concessimus et hac presenti carta nostra confirmavimus Petro clerico de Medelay et heredibus suis pro homagio et servitio suo illam terram in campis de Lamare versus partes de Medelay, juxta curbam magne aque que vocatur Sandbed. Tenendam de nobis in feudo et hereditate, libere et quiete ab omnibus serviis et consuetudinibus que ad nos pertinent. Reddendo inde nobis annuatim unum denarium in die sancti Martini. Hiis testibus, *Johanne de Birkina, Rogero fratre suo, Willelmo filio Everardi, Hugone de Toulestuna, Hugone de Stapiltona, Waltero de Stapiltona,* et aliis.

(1) I find no transcript in either of Dodsworth's volumes of any of the charters between No. 497 and No. 519. No. 518 is headed, as above, with both figures and Roman numerals.

519.[1] Carta ejusdem. Circa 1210.

[. . . . . . . I, Fulk, prior of Pontefract, and all the convent . . . . . . have confirmed to Hervey, son of Richard, son of Lesing, of Ledstone, and his heirs, in fee and heirship, four acres, a half rood, and two parts of a half rood in the nearer part of our culture called Greave, towards the town, in exchange for all his land which lies between our grange and our culture called Lidflat towards the north. Warranty. Witnesses.]

(1) There is an abstract of No. 519 in *Dodsworth*, vol. 136, and a transcript in vol. 151.

Sciant presentes et futuri quod ego Fulco prior de Pontefracto et totus conventus ejusdem loci dedimus et concessimus et hac presenti carta nostra confirmavimus Herveo filio Ricardi filii Laising de Ledestuna, et heredibus suis, in feodo et hereditate, libere et quiete, quatuor acras terre et dimidiam rodam et duas partes dimidie rode in propinquiori parte culture nostre que appellatur Greve versus villam, in excambium pro tota terra sua que jacet inter grangiam nostram et culturam nostram que vocatur Lidflat[2] versus north. Et nos warantizabimus predictum excambium predicto Herveo et heredibus suis contra omnes homines. H. testibus, *Roberto Walensi, Ada de Reinevill, Thoma filio ejus, Symone de Mohaut, Willelmo Gramatico, Gilleberto de Millum,[3] Jordano Campione,* et aliis.

(2) See No. 174 and No. 176.   (3) Possibly Middleham, or in mistake for Hillum (Hillam).

---

520.   **Carta Walteri prioris.**

[. . . . . I, Walter, prior of Pontefract, and the convent . . . . have confirmed to Elias, son of William son of Osbert, and his wife Cecily, daughter of Theobald de Barnby, a bovate of land in Barnby, which the aforesaid Thorald held from us and surrendered to us in our court and quit-claimed. To be possessed and held by the aforesaid Elias and Cecily and the heirs who shall come from them, &c. Paying us yearly five shillings, half at the Assumption of St. Mary and half at the feast of St. Martin, and doing the forinsec service as much as belongs to one bovate of land in the aforesaid town of Barnby. A carucate of land makes the tenth part of a knight's fee. Elias has placed his seal to the counterpart which we retain. Witnesses.]

Sciant presentes et futuri quod ego Walterus prior de Pontefracto et ejusdem loci conventus dedimus, concessimus, et presenti carta nostra confirmavimus Helye filio Willelmi filii Osberti, et uxori sue, Cecilie filie Theobaldi[2] de Barneby, unam bovatam terre in Barneby.[1] Illam scilicet quam prefatus Thoraldus[2] de nobis tenuit et nobis sursum in curia nostra reddidit et sine retenemento in perpetuum quietam clamavit. Habendam et tenendam prefatis Helie et Cecilie et heredibus qui de eis exibunt, in feodo et hereditate, libere et quiete, cum omnibus pertinentiis et aisiamentis ad eandem bovatam pertinentibus. Reddendo inde nobis annuatim quinque solidos pro omni servitio, medietatem ad assumptionem sancte Marie et

---

(1) This bovate of land in Barnby is clearly that which was granted to the monks by Gilbert de Lascy of Lancashire (No. 5), and the forinsec service here mentioned, being that of a bovate where a carucate is the tenth part of a knight's fee, is in the earlier charter valued in another way as the eightieth part of a knight's fee, eight bovates making a carucate.   (2) *Sic.*

medietatem ad festum sancti Martini, et faciendo forense servitium quantum pertinet ad unam bovatam terre in prefata villa de Barnebi. Una carucata terre facit decimam partem feodi unius militis. Et ne prefatus Helyas vel heredes qui[3] de eo et predicta Cecilia exibunt contra tenorem hujus carte in posterum venire possint, contrascripto quod penes nos retinemus sigillum suum apposuit. Hiis testibus, *Thoma de Sandala, Hugone filio Walteri, Rogero filio Ricardi de Holm, Willelmo filio suo, Symone de Barneby, Willelmo de Kamesal*, et aliis.

---

(3) The word "qui" is interlined.

---

521. Carta ejusdem.

[. . . . . . . I, Walter, prior of Pontefract, and all the convent . . . . have confirmed to William, chaplain of Ferriby, or to whom he shall have assigned it, a toft in Ferriby with all its appurtenances which Hugelina has held before him, next the toft of John Bustard towards the south. To be held, &c. Paying us yearly 32 pence at these terms: at the Annunciation of St. Mary, eight pence; at the feast of St. Botolph, eight pence; at the feast of St. Michael, eight pence; at the feast of the holy Apostle, eight pence. But the said William or another assigned to this tenement shall not be able to transfer that toft to any other house of religion than our house of Pontefract. Witnesses.]

Sciant presentes et futuri quod ego Walterus prior de Pontefracto et totus conventus ejusdem loci ˙ dedimus, concessimus, et hac presenti carta nostra confirmavimus Willelmo capellano de Feribi vel cui ipse assignaverit unum toftum in Feriby[1] cum omnibus pertinentiis suis quod Hugelina tenuit ante eum. Illud scilicet quod est juxta toftum Johannis Bustard proximum versus austrum. Tenendum de nobis libere et quiete, in feodo et hereditate. Reddendo inde nobis annuatim xxxij denarios ad hos terminos: ad annunciationem sancte Marie viij denarios, ad festum sancti Botulfi viij denarios, ad festum sancti Michaelis viij denarios, ad festum sancti apostoli[2] viij denarios. Idem vero Willelmus vel alius ad hoc tenementum assignatus alteri domui religionis quam domui

---

(1) This toft was probably one of those granted by Gilbert de Gaunt (No. 400), the second earl of Lincoln, in compensation to the monks for the damage accruing to them from his abortive attempt to seize the honour cf Pontefract, after the death of his father-in-law, the first earl (see p. 482).

(2) The blank in the date of the fourth payment should probably be filled with the name either of St. Thomas or of St. John the Evangelist. It was evidently intended that the rent should be a quarterly payment in March, June, September, and December, St. Botolph's Day being June 17, the same as St. Alban's in the English Prayer Book. In medieval kalendars June 17 marks the entrance of the sun into Cancer, the precession of the equinoxes and the alteration of the English Kalendar in 1751 accounting for the difference. The date of St. Botolph's Day has been the subject of a singular error, indeed of a pair of errors. In the history of William of Worcester, published by the eminent antiquary Hearne, with *Liber Niger* (p. 457), St. Botolph's

nostre de Pontefracto illud toftum conferre non potuerit. Hiis testibus, *Alano,*[3] *capellano de Feriby, Gaufrido diacono, Ivone filio Roberti, Johanne filio Ysac, Willelmo Cusyn,* et aliis.

Day is incidentally said to be 22 April, a statement which the learned editor corrects in a footnote, stating that according to the English Martyrology this feast was celebrated on 16 May. This second singular error (the substitution of 16 May for 17 June) probably arose from a misreading by the great antiquary himself; the 16th May is the 17th of the Kalends of June, and Hearne appears to have misread "Kalend" for "day",—"17 kal." for "17 day." It is remarkable that one of the Pontefract town charters bears to this day on its endorsement the record of a similar mistake. The document is dated "vi idibus" of June, but it is endorsed, in a modern hand, "6th June."

(3) There were thus two chaplains of Ferriby, the grantee, William, and this Alan.

522.[1]   Carta ejusdem.

[. . . . . I, brother Hugh, prior of Pontefract, and the convent . . . . . . have confirmed to Mauger, son of William of Dodworth, two bovates of land with their tofts and crofts in the territory of Dodworth, which William son of Ulf formerly held. To be held and possessed, &c., saving to us our woods. Paying us eight shillings, half at the feast of St. Andrew, half at the feast of St. John Baptist. . . . . . . Mauger has placed his seal to the counterpart which we retain. Witnesses.]

Sciant presentes et futuri quod ego frater Hugo prior de Pontefracto et ejusdem loci conventus dedimus, concessimus, et presenti carta confirmavimus Maugero filio Willelmi de Doddewrd duas bovatas terre cum toftis et croftis earum in territorio de Doddewrd. Illas scilicet quas Willelmus filius Ulfi antea tenuit. Tenendas et habendas prefato Maugero et heredibus suis libere et quiete, in feodo et hereditate, cum omnibus ad predictas bovatas pertinentibus, salvis nobis per omnia boscis nostris. Reddendo inde nobis octo solidos, medietatem ad festum sancti Andree, medietatem ad festum sancti Johannis Baptiste. Et ne idem Maugerus vel heredes sui inposterum contra tenorem hujus carte venire possint, contrascripto quod penes nos retinemus sigillum suum apposuit. Hiis testibus, *Henrico de Saivile,*[2] *Johanne de Haueshirst, Roberto de Altona, Ricardo de Cravene, Gerardo filio Thome, Roberto filio Gerardi,* et aliis.

---

(1) No. 522 is copied into *Dodsworth,* vol. 151, and there is an abstract in vol. 133. Vol. 151 has a corrected heading, "Carta Hugonis prioris de Pontefracto Maugero filio Willielmi (*sic*) de Doddeworth." The Prior was (as in *Dodsworth*) Hugh, not "the same," *i.e.* Walter; moreover the names of the witnesses show that the Prior was Hugh I, and that the date of the document was at the close of the twelfth century or the beginning of the thirteenth.

(2) I have already pointed out (p. 411) that this Henry de Savile was one of the small group of Saviles (cousins or brothers of Lady Avicia, who married Hugh Pincerna of Sandal), from whom sprang the widely-spread family of that name. In No. 340, a dated deed of 1222, he is preceded by a Ralph de Savile, probably a younger brother.

523. Carta Walteri prioris.

[. . . . . I, prior Walter, and the convent . . . . have confirmed to Richard son of Ralph a toft in Stubbs next the toft of William Burnell towards the west, and a toft in the territory of Stubbs called Rollescroft. To be held and possessed, &c., with all easements of that town, as much as belongs to our holding. Paying us yearly 4 shillings for all service, half at the feast of St. Martin and half at Whitsuntide. Richard . . . . has placed his seal to the counterpart which we retain. Witnesses.]

Sciant presentes et futuri quod ego Walter prior et conventus de Pontefracto dedimus, concessimus, et presenti carta nostra confirmavimus Ricardo[1] filio Radulfi toftum unum in Stubbis juxta toftum Willelmi Burnelli versus West et unum toftum in territorio ejusdem ville de Stubbis quod nominatur Rollescroft. Tenenda et habenda sibi et heredibus suis libere et quiete cum omnibus aisiamentis ejusdem ville quantum ad nostrum tenementum pertinet. Reddendo inde nobis annuatim iiij *or* solidos pro omni servitio, medietatem ad festum sancti Martini et medietatem ad Pentecosten. Et ne ipse Ricardus vel heredes sui inposterum contra tenorem hujus carte venire possint, contrascripto quod penes nos retinemus sigillum suum apposuit. Hiis testibus, *Roberto Walensi, Willelmo de Stapiltona, Umfrido de Veilli, Gaufrido Scorchebof, Gaufrido de Nortona, Willelmo de Kamesal, Helia de Kamesal,* et aliis.

---

(1) In No. 122 we had a grant by a William, son of Ralph, who also tests No. 167.

---

524. Carta Hugonis prioris.

[. . . . . . I, brother Hugh, prior of Pontefract, and the convent . . . . . . have confirmed to Robert de Mara and his heirs the three bovates of land with appurtenances in the territory of the Mere which he holds from us . . . . . Paying us yearly six shillings, half at Whitsuntide and half at the feast of St. Martin. For this Robert has given us twenty shillings. He has also quit-claimed to us for ever the three bovates in the territory of the Mere which Peter de Mara his brother gave and confirmed to us. Seals. Witnesses.]

Sciant presentes et futuri quod ego frater Hugh prior de Pontefracto et ejusdem loci conventus concessimus et presenti carta confirmavimus Roberto de Mara et heredibus suis illas tres bovatas terre cum pertinentiis in territorio de Mara quas tenet de nobis, libere et quiete, integre et honorifice. Reddendo inde nobis annuatim de se et heredibus suis sex solidos, medietatem ad Pentecosten et medietatem ad festum sancti Martini. Pro hac autem concessione et

confirmatione dedit nobis predictus Robertus viginti solidos.   Preterea
quietas clamavit nobis de se et heredibus suis in perpetuum illas
tres bovatas terre cum omnibus pertinentiis suis in territorio de Mara
quas Petrus de Mara frater ejusdem Roberti dedit nobis et carta[1] sua
confirmavit.   Et ne nos vel ipse aut heredes sui contra tenorem
istius carte venire possimus, hinc inde huic scripto sigilla nostra
apposuimus.   Hiis testibus, *Willelmo filio Everardi,*[2] *Ricardo
Londinensi, Jacobo de Medeley, Ranulfo de Castelford, Gilleberto de
Mara*, et aliis.

(1) It is No. 250, and was dated St. Michael's Day, 1223.   (2) It is written "Ev'r'."

---

525.   Carta Hugonis prioris.

[. . . . . . I, brother Hugh, prior of Pontefract, and the convent . . . . . . have
confirmed to James son of Raimond of Methley a piece of meadow in the territory
of the Mere ; it lies towards the west, between Herbert's meadow and the ditch,
as the road descends from the Mere to the bank of the Calder.   To be held and
possessed by the aforesaid James and his heirs, &c.   Paying us yearly six pence at
Whitsuntide for all service. . . . . The said James has placed his seal to the
counterpart which we retain.   Witnesses.]

Sciant presentes et futuri quod ego quod ego[1] frater Hugo prior
de Pontefracto et ejusdem loci conventus dedimus, concessimus, et
presenti carta nostra confirmavimus Jacobo filio Raimundi de
Medelay quandam particulam prati in territorio de Mara.   Illam
scilicet que jacet versus West inter pratum Hereberti et fossatum,
sicut via descendit de Mara usque ad ripam de Keldre.   Tenendam
et habendam prefato Jacobo et heredibus suis, in feodo et hereditate,
libere et quiete.   Reddendo inde nobis annuatim sex denarios ad
Pentecosten pro omni servitio.   Et ne idem Jacobus vel heredes sui
inposterum contra tenorem hujus carte venire possint contrascripto
quod penes nos retinemus sigillum suum apposuit.   Hiis testibus,
*Thoma de Kellington, Magistro Ada fratre suo, Ricardo Londinensi,
Henrico de Medeley, Henrico de Byset, Thoma Camberlano, Symone de
Rupe*, et aliis.

(1) The two words are repeated thus.

---

526.   Carta Walteri prioris.

[. . . . . I, Walter, prior of Pontefract, and the convent . . . . have
confirmed to Nurasius, clerk, and his heirs, for their homage and service, all the
land which Adam de Reineville gave us in Bramley and in the appurtenances, in

perpetual alms. Namely, a bovate of land which was Roger's, the son of Maurice, and the assart which Robert Water, the shoemaker, held, and the land of Thomas son of Ulfkel, and Thomas himself, with all his following, and his chattels without any withholding. To be held and possessed, &c., in ways and paths, in wood and plain, in waters and mills, in meadows and pastures, &c., reserving to Adam and his heirs the sale and assartment of his wood of Bramley. Paying yearly to our doorkeeper 40 pence, half at the feast of St. Martin and half at Whitsuntide, for all service and exaction, doing forinsec service as much as belongs to a bovate of land where six and a half carucates of land make a knight's fee. Witnesses.]

Sciant presentes et futuri quod ego Walterus prior de Pontefracto et ejusdem loci conventus dedimus, concessimus, et hac presenti carta nostra confirmavimus Nurasio clerico et heredibus suis pro homagio et servitio suo totam terram quam Adam de Reinevilla nobis dedit in Bramlay et in pertinentiis in perpetuam elemosinam. Scilicet unam bovatam terre cum pertinentiis que fuit Rogeri filii Mauricii, et totum sartum cum pertinentiis quod Robertus Water[1] sutor tenuit, et totam terram Thome filii Ulfkelli cum pertinentiis in eadem villa, et ipsum Thomam cum omni secta sua et catallis suis sine omni retinemento. Tenendas et habendas de nobis in feodo et hereditate, libere et quiete, infra villam et extra villam, in viis et semitis, in bosco et plano, in aquis et molendinis, in pratis et pascuis, et in omnibus asiamentis et libertatibus predicte ville de Bramlay, exceptis prefato Ade et heredibus suis venditione et assartatione bosci sui de Bramlay. Reddendo inde annuatim hostilario nostro xl denarios, medietatem ad festum sancti Martini et medietatem ad Pentecosten, pro omni servitio et exactione, faciendo forense servitium quantum pertinet ad unam bovatam terre ubi sex carrucate terre et dimidia faciunt feodum unius militis. Hiis testibus, *Roberto Walensi, Johanne de Birkin, Jordano de Sancta Maria, Willelmo de Stapiltona, Ada de Kellington, Ricardo de Stagno, Thoma fratre suo, Ada filio Serich*, et aliis.

----

(1) See No. 538.

----

527. Carta Stephani prioris.

[. . . . . I, Stephen, prior of Pontefract, and the convent . . . . have confirmed to Geoffrey, son of Alan de Mara, four bovates of land in the territory of the Mere, two bovates of the fee of William, son of Hameric, and two bovates of those which Alan formerly held from Herbert de Mara. To be held and possessed by Geoffrey and his heirs or his assigns, &c. Paying us yearly fourteen silver shillings and eight pence, half at Whitsuntide and half at the feast of St. Martin. For this demise and grant Geoffrey has given us three silver marks in hand, as for relief. And . . . . Geoffrey has placed his seal to the transcript which we retain. Witnesses.]

Sciant presentes et futuri quod ego St. prior de Pontefracto et ejusdem loci conventus dimisimus, concessimus, et presenti carta nostra confirmavimus Gaufrido filio Alani de Mara quatuor bovatas terre in territorio de Mara, scilicet duas bovatas de feodo Willelmi filii Hamerici, et ab eis duas bovatas quas . Alanus pater predicti G. prius tenuit de Hereberto de Mara. Tenendas et habendas prefato G. et heredibus suis vel suis assignatis cum omnibus pertinentiis suis, in feodo et hereditate, libere, quiete, pacifice et honorifice. Reddendo inde nobis· annuatim xiiij solidos argenti et viij denarios pro omni servitio vel demanda, medietatem ad Pentecosten et medietatem ad festum sancti Martini. Pro hac vero dimissione et concessione dedit nobis dictus G. tres marcas argenti pre manibus, tamquam pro relevio. Et ne idem G. vel heredes sui in posterum contra tenorem hujus carte venire possint, transcripto quod penes nos retinemus sigillum suum apposuit. Hiis testibus, *Ricardo de Londinio, Johanne clerico, magistro hospital', Henrico de Goldale, Jacobo de Medelay, Henrico de eadem villa*, et aliis.

528.[1]   **Carta Hugonis prioris.**

[. . . . . I, Hugh, prior of Pontefract, and the convent . . . . have confirmed to Lambert, the miller, a plot of land in the Field of Burton called Lund Furlong, 40 feet in length and as many in breadth, with free and reasonable exit and entrance to the path between Burton and Fairburn. To be held and possessed by him and his heirs, &c. Paying us yearly three shillings, half at the feast of St. Martin and half at Whitsuntide. Lambert has placed his seal to the present counterpart which we retain. Witnesses.]

Sciant presentes et futuri quod ego Hugo prior de Pontefracto et ejusdem loci conventus dedimus, concessimus, et presenti carta nostra confirmavimus Lamberto molendinario quandam placiam terre in campo de Brettona[2] que vocatur Lund Furlang, habentem in longitudine xl pedes et totidem in latitudine, cum libero et rationabili exitio et introitu de predicta placia usque ad semitam que jacet inter Brettona et Fareburne.[3] Tenendam et habendam sibi et heredibus suis de nobis libere et quiete et pacifice. Reddendo inde nobis

---

(1) No. 528 is abstracted in *Dodsworth*, vol. 135 and vol. 138.   (2) Burton Salmon.

(3) The Common Field must have been partitioned between Burton and Fairburn and this path well defined as a boundary between the portion allotted to Fairburn and that awarded to Burton long before the date of this document. The Fairburn portion is still called the Lund Fields.

annuatim tres solidos, medietatem ad festum sancti Martini et medietatem ad Pentecosten. Et ne idem Lambertus vel heredes sui in posterum contra tenorem hujus carte venire possint, presenti contrascripto quod penes nos retinemus sigillum suum apposuit. Hiis testibus, *Serlone de Brettona, Waltero de Birum, Salomone de Brettona, Ada de eadem villa, Roberto Fabro, Roberto filio Serlonis,* et aliis.

---

529. Carta Walteri prioris.

[To all the sons, &c., Walter the prior and the convent, greeting in the Lord. With unanimous counsel we have . . . . . confirmed to Henry Neeloth all the rent and outgoing of the carucate of land which he gave us in Burton, to be received from our house by the hand of our cellarer as long as he lives in secular habit. After his decease it shall remain to us freely, &c. And we, as well from the aforesaid carucate as from other rent which Henry is bound to assign to us out of the increase, ... on receiving 40 shillings yearly will provide and maintain a chaplain who shall celebrate service in psalms and in masses in the chapel of St. Thomas the martyr within our court, for the soul of Henry, &c. If for the security of the aforesaid rents, it shall behove us to be at any expense, all burdens shall be borne from those rents, so that our house may find itself burdened in nothing. We have committed to faithful observance all these things in good faith, as long as the rents remain quietly to us and suffice to the maintenance of the said chaplain. Seal. Witnesses.]

Universis sancte matris ecclesie filiis Walterus prior et conventus de Pontefracto, salutem in domino. Noveritis nos unanimi consilio concessisse et hac carta nostra confirmasse Henrico Neeloth totum redditum et exitum illius carrucate terre quam dedit nobis[1] in Brettona recipiendum de domo nostra per manum cellerarii nostri quamdiu in seculari habitu vixerit. Post ejus vero decessum totius ejusdem terre redditus et exitus nobis libere, quiete, et solute remanebit, sine omni impedimento et contradictione heredum suorum. Et nos tam de predicta carrucata terre in Brettona quam de alio redditu quem nobis ex incremento idem Henricus assignare tenetur, ut ex integro perficiantur nobis, xl solidos annuatim percipiendo providebimus et sustinebimus unum capellanum qui in capella sancti Thome Martiris infra curiam nostram, pro anima ipsius Henrici et pro animabus antecessorum suorum et pro animabus nostris et pro animabus omnium fidelium defunctorum, tam in psalmis quam in missis divina perpetuo celebrabit. Si vero pro defensione predictorum

---

(1) The charter of Henry Neeloth here referred to is No. 405, and the original charter of Roger de Newby, rehearsing the history of the carucate, is No. 421. But Henry Neeloth had other property in this neighbourhood at Beatrice (still called Betteros) Hill. (See No. 505.)

reddituum optûlerit nos aliquem sumptum facere, sic omnia honera contingentia de ipsis redditibus sustineantur, ut domus nostra in nullo se sentiat honeratam.   Hec autem omnia in bona fide permisimus nos fideli observationi quam diu sepedicti redditus nobis potuerint quiete remanere et ad dicti capellani sustentationem sufficere.   Et ne nos vel successores nostri contra formam hujus concessionis venire possimus eam presenti scripto et sigilli nostri appositione confirmavimus.   Hiis testibus, *Johanne de Birkin, Roberto Walensi, Willelmo filio Everardi, Hugone filii Walteri*, et aliis.

---

529 bis.   **Carta Hugonis prioris.**

[. . . . . I, Hugh, prior of Pontefract, and the convent . . . . have confirmed to John de Greasbrook half an acre of land with a toft in Kimberworth, which John de Busli has given us.   To be held and possessed by the aforesaid John and his heirs, &c.   Paying us yearly 12*d.* at Whitsuntide.   And John . . . . . has placed his seal to the counterpart which we retain.   Witnesses.]

Sciant presentes et futuri quod ego Hugo prior de Pontefracto et ejusdem loci conventus dedimus, concessimus, et presenti carta nostra confirmavimus Johanni de Gresebroc dimidiam acram terre cum tofto eidem terre pertinente in Kymberwrdia, quam terram Johannes de Builli nobis dedit.   Tenendam et habendam prefato Johanni et heredibus suis libere et quiete, in feodo et hereditate.   Reddendo inde nobis annuatim xii*d.* ad Pentecosten.   Et ne idem Johannes vel heredes sui in posterum contra tenorem hujus carte venire possint, contrascripto quod penes nos retinemus sigillum suum apposuit. Hiis testibus, *Johanne de Hoili, Willelmo fratre ejus, Osberto de Padehale, Willelmo Campiun, Ricardo de Martona*, et aliis.

---

530.   **Carta Walteri prioris.**

[. . . . . . I, Walter the prior and the convent of Pontefract . . . . have confirmed to Adam de Went a toft in Pontefract, on Baghill, which lies between the toft of Merlin Fleming towards the north and the toft of Jocelyn towards the south, and which Albert Fullo has held from us and in our court has surrendered . . . . To be held and possessed by the aforesaid Adam and his heirs, &c., for ten pence to be paid us yearly, half at the feast of St. Martin and half at Whitsuntide. . . . . Adam has placed his seal to the counterpart which we retain.   Witnesses.]

Sciant presentes et futuri quod ego Walterus prior et conventus de Pontefracto dedimus, concessimus, et presenti carta nostra confirmavimus Ade de Went unum toftum in Pontefracto super Baggehil. Illum scilicet qui jacet inter toftum Merlini Flandrensis versus north et toftum Gocelini versus suth, et quem Albertus Fullo de nobis tenuit et in curia nostra nobis sursum reddidit[1] et quietum de se et heredibus suis clamavit. Tenendum et habendum prefato Ade et heredibus suis libere et quiete, pro x denariis nobis annuatim reddendis pro omni servitio, medietatem ad festum sancti Martini et medietatem ad Pentecosten. Et ne ipse Adam vel heredes sui inposterum contra tenorem hujus carte venire possint, contrascripto quod penes nos retinemus sigillum suum apposuit. Hiis testibus, *Willelmo filio Everardi*, *Osberto de Brettona*, *Willelmo de Kamesala*, *Merlino Flandrensi*, *Roberto Camberlano*, *Symone Pincerna*, et aliis.

---

(1) No. 102 is the deed of surrender by Albert Fullo of the property to which Adam de Went thus succeeded. The two charters would be practically contemporaneous; for four of the six witnesses to No. 530 witnessed No. 102 also. There are some small differences between the two documents; particularly, in the earlier the toft is said to be "subtus Baggahil" and in the latter it is "super Baggehil."

---

[1][. . . . . I, Walter, prior of Pontefract, and the convent . . . . have confirmed to Henry, son of Roger of Barnsley, and his heirs a toft in Barnsley of two acres of land under Barnscliff, and fifteen acres of land in the Fields; in Udalecroft ten acres, and five acres in the assart which belonged to William son of Ralph. To be held and possessed, &c., with common pasture, except the oaks in Barnsley Wood. Paying us yearly half a silver mark, half at Whitsuntide and half at the feast of St. Martin. . . . . Henry has given us twenty shillings. Witnesses.]

Sciant presentes et futuri quod ego Walterus prior de Pontefracto et ejusdem loci conventus dedimus et concessimus et hac carta nostra confirmavimus Henrico filio Rogeri de Bernell et heredibus suis unum toftum in Berneslay de duabus acris terre subtus Bernesclif et quindecim acras terre in campis, scilicet in Wdalecroft decem acras, et quinque acras in sarto quod fuit Willelmi filii Radulfi. Tenendas et habendas de nobis libere et quiete cum communi pastura ejusdem ville exceptis quercubus in bosco de Berneslay. Reddendo inde nobis annuatim dimidiam marcam argenti pro omni servitio, medietatem ad Pentecosten et medietatem

---

(1) This charter has neither heading nor number. An owner of the same name as the owner of this assart at Barnsley is mentioned in No. 122 as the owner of a house in Gillygate, adjacent to one owned by his brother Richard. He also tested the grant of Hamelin's Mill, made to the monks by William of Fryston (No. 167).

ad festum sancti Martini.   Pro hac autem donatione et concessione
dedit nobis predictus Henricus xx *ti* solidos.   Hiis testibus, *Thoma de
Thornetona, Reinero de Wambewell, Johanne de Rokeleya, Ricardo de
Stagno, Thoma fratre suo,* et aliis.

---

531.   **Carta Henrici filii Rogerı.**

[. . . . . . I, Henry, son of Roger of Barnsley, and my heirs will never exact
any common in the oaks of Barnsley Wood on account of our holding in that
town from the prior and convent.   Witnesses.]

Sciant presentes et futuri quod ego Henricus filius Rogeri de
Bernesleya et heredes mei nunquam exigemus aliquam communam
in quercubus bosci de Bernesleya occasione tenementi quod de
priore et conventu de Pontefracto tenemus in eadem villa.   Hiis
testibus, *Thoma de Tornetona, Reinero de Wambewell, Ada filio
Rogeri, Thoma de Stagno, Ricardo de Baghil,* et aliis.

532.[1]   **Carta Walteri prioris.**

[. . . . . I, Walter, prior of Pontefract, and the convent . . . . . have confirmed
to Richard Palmer, son of Geoffrey of Barnsley, ten acres of land of the assarts in
the territory of Barnsley, in the place called Pogmoor.   To be held and possessed
by him and his heirs, &c.   Paying us yearly three shillings, half at Whitsuntide and
half at the feast of St. Martin.   But by reason of this holding, Richard or his heirs
shall not claim any common in our woods or lands of Barnsley, which we may give,
sell, and assart freely to our advantage . . . . . . Richard has placed his seal to the
counterpart which we retain.   Witnesses.]

Sciant presentes et futuri quod ego Walterus prior de Pontefracto
et ejusdem loci conventus dedimus, concessimus, et presenti carta
nostra confirmavimus Ricardo Palmario filio Galfridi de Bernesleya
decem acras terre de essartis in territorio de Bernesleya in loco qui
vocatur Poggemor.   Tenendas et habendas sibi et heredibus suis de
nobis, libere et quiete, in feodo et hereditate.   Reddendo inde nobis
annuatim tres solidos pro omni servitio, medietatem ad Pentecosten
et medietatem ad festum sancti Martini.   Occasione autem hujus
tenementi idem Ricardus vel heredes sui ullam[2] exigent communam
in boscis nostris aut terris de Bernesleya, quos possimus dare,

---

(1) No. 532 is abstracted in *Dodsworth,* vol. 117.

(2) *Sic :* a negative has clearly been omitted.   The determination of the monks (seen in these
three charters) to keep their Barnsley woods in their own hands was probably a consequence of
their knowledge of the mineral wealth of the district.   (See also No. 512.)

vendere, et essartare libere ad commodum nostrum ubicumque voluerimus sine impedimento vel contradictione prefati Ricardi et heredum suorum. Et ne ipse Ricardus vel heredes sui inposterum contra tenorem hujus carte venire possint, contrascripto quod penes nos retinemus sigillum suum pro se et heredibus suis apposuit. Hiis testibus, *Gilberto de Nottona, Roberto de Berch, Jeremia de Thornhil, Rogero de Derton, Radulfo de Rupe, Ricardo de Martona,* et aliis.

533.   Carta Stephani prioris.

[. . . . . I, brother Stephen, prior of Pontefract, and the convent . . . . . have confirmed to Adam son of Geoffrey of Northcroft ten acres of land in the territory of Northcroft with their messuage, which Mauger has held from us, &c. To be held and possessed by him and his heirs, paying us yearly four shillings, two shillings at the feast of St. Martin and two shillings at Whitsuntide. . . . . . Adam has placed his seal in witness to the transcript which we retain. Witnesses.]

Sciant presentes et futuri quod ego frater Stephanus prior de Pontefracto et ejusdem loci conventus dimisimus, concessimus, et hac presenti carta nostra confirmavimus Ade filio Gaufridi[1] de Northcroft decem acras terre in territorio de Nortcroft cum mesagio eisdem acris pertinente. Illas scilicet quas Mauger tenuit de nobis. Tenendas et habendas sibi et heredibus suis in feodo et hereditate, libere, quiete et integre, reddendo inde nobis annuatim iiij solidos, duos solidos ad festum sancti Martini et ij solidos ad Pentecosten. Et ne idem Ada vel heredes sui contra tenorem hujus carte in posterum possint venire, transcripto quod penes nos retinemus sigillum suum apposuit in testimonium. Hiis testibus, *Waltero de Brettona, Ada de Holand, Ricardo de Travers, Roberto filio Gerardi, Ada Norreis, Paulino de Estfeld,* et aliis.

(1) This may possibly be Geoffrey of Ledsham, and the ten acres may be those in Oldfield. (See No. 346 and No. 374.)

534.   Carta Dalmatii prioris.

[. . . . . I, brother Dalmatius, the humble minister of Pontefract, and the convent . . . . have confirmed to Ralph, son of Roger of Newby, and his heirs a rent of twelve pence, to be received yearly at Whitsuntide at our manor of Ledstone, without anyone's gainsaying. If we shall fail in the payment . . . . Ralph and his heirs shall be permitted to distrain our land of Burton, so that no grievance or prejudice concerning the said land shall accrue to us on account of the distraint. For this Ralph and his heirs are bound to defend that carucate of land with its appurtenances, which we have in the territory of Burton from the

2 W

grant of Henry Neeloth, and acquit it from forinsec service and from all other exaction and demand.   In witness of which we have placed our authentic seal to this charter.   Ralph has placed his seal to the transcript which we retain. Witnesses.]

Sciant presentes et futuri quod ego frater Dalmatius humilis minister de Pontefracto et ejusdem loci conventus concessimus et hac presenti carta nostra confirmavimus Radulfo filio Rogeri de Neuby et heredibus suis redditum duodecim denariorum annuatim ad Pentecosten, apud manerium nostrum de Lediston percipiendorum sine alicujus contradictione.   Et si defecerimus in solutione dictorum duodecim denariorum ad dictum terminum, licebit dicto Radulfo et heredibus suis distringere terram nostram de Brettona, donec eisdem plenarie dictos duodecim denarios solverimus.   Ita tamen quod pro districtione per eos facta nullum nobis gravamen vel prejudicium de dicta terra gravetur.   Pro hac vero concessione dictus Radulfus et heredes sui tenentur defendere totam illam carrucatam terre cum omnibus pertinentiis suis quam habemus in territorio de Brettona[1] ex dono Henrici Neeloth et eam de forinseco servitio et de omni alia exactione et demanda adquietare.   In cujus rei testimonium huic scripto sigillum nostrum autenticum apposuimus.   Et dictus Radulphus tam pro se quam pro heredibus suis transcripto quod penes nos retinemus sigillum suum apposuit.   Hiis testibus, *domino Waltero de Ludhama, seneschalo de Pontefracto, Roberto persona de Medelay, Hugone tunc vicario ejusdem ville, Gregorio de Camera, Serlone de Brettona*, et aliis.

(1) Burton Salmon.   (See page 611.)

535.   **Carta Stephani prioris.**

[. . . . . I, Stephen, prior of Pontefract, and the convent . . . . have confirmed to William the clerk, son of Gilbert of Pontefract, for his homage and service, a toft in the town of Pontefract with the buildings on it, which William the chaplain, uncle of the said W. the clerk, formerly held from us and afterwards during his life gave to him, lying between the toft of Hugh de Batley and the toft of Adam the cordwainer.   To be held and possessed from us, by him and his heirs, &c.   Saving the grange and its site, which William the chaplain gave to Thomas his son, with free exit and entrance.   William shall pay us yearly 12*d.*, half at the feast of St. Martin and half at Whitsuntide, and has given us in acknowledgment half a mark.   He has placed his seal to the transcript which we retain.   Witnesses.]

Sciant presentes et futuri quod ego Stephanus prior de Pontefracto et ejusdem loci conventus dimisimus et concessimus et hac presenti carta nostra confirmavimus Willelmo clerico, filio Gilberti de Pontefracto, pro homagio et servitio suo, unum toftum[1] in villa Pontisfracti cum edificiis in eo positis. Illud scilicet quod Willelmus capellanus avunculus ipsius W. clerici de nobis prius tenuit et sibi postea in vita sua dedit, jacens inter toftum Hugonis de Bateley et toftum Ade Cordwaner. Tenendum et habendum de nobis sibi et heredibus suis in feodo et hereditate, libere, quiete, et honorifice, salva grangia cum placia in qua est posita, quam prefatus Willelmus capellanus dedit Thome filio suo cum libero exitu et introitu. Idem vero Willelmus clericus reddet nobis annuatim pro dicto tofto xij*d*., medietatem ad festum sancti Martini et medietatem ad Pentecosten. Pro hac vero donatione et concessione dedit nobis predictus W. dimidiam marcam argenti de recognitione. Et[2] idem W. vel heredes sui contra tenorem hujus carte inposterum possint venire, transcripto quod penes nos retinemus sigillum suum apposuit in testimonium. Hiis testibus, *Roberto Camberlano, Johanne de Lovain, Johanne de Batelay, Henrico filio Ranulfi, Rogero filio Amabile, Willelmo filio Ace*,[3] et aliis.

(1) The names of the principal parties mentioned in this charter have frequently occurred in the Chartulary, but as witnesses only, so that there are not sufficient data to identify this property.

(2) The word "ne" has been omitted.

(3) The last two witnesses are the son-in-law and father-in-law mentioned in the small genealogy on page 597, the son-in-law taking precedence of his mother's second husband.

536. Carta Dalmatii prioris.

[. . . . I, brother Dalmatius, the humble prior of Pontefract, and the convent . . . . have confirmed to Thomas son of Thomas of Bilham those five acres of land with their appurtenances in the territory of Bilham, which Richard son of John conveyed to us. To be held and possessed by him and his heirs, &c. Paying us yearly fourteen pence, at Christmas seven pence and at Easter seven pence. Seal. Thomas has placed his seal to the transcript which we retain. Witnesses.]

Sciant presentes et futuri quod ego frater Dalmatius, humilis prior de Pontefracto, et ejusdem loci conventus dimisimus et hac presenti carta nostra confirmavimus Thome filio Thome de Bilam illas quinque acras terre cum pertinentiis suis in territorio de Bilam, quas Ricardus filius Johannis nobis in puram et perpetuam elemosinam contulit. Tenendas et habendas de nobis sibi et heredibus suis libere, quiete, pacifice, et honorifice. Reddendo inde nobis annuatim quatuordecim denarios pro omni servitio seculari vel demanda, videlicet ad Nathale domini vij*d*., et ad pascha septem denarios. In cujus rei testimonium huic scripto sigillum nostrum apposuimus, et ipse predictus Thomas pro se et heredibus suis transcripto quod penes nos retinemus sigillum suum apposuit. Hiis testibus, *domino Ada de Neirford,' Roberto de Stapiltona, Gregorio de Camera, Johanne de Lovain, Johanne Vinitore, Willelmo de Barevilla de Bilam*, et aliis.

537.[1]   **Carta Dalmatii prioris.**   **1240.**

[. . . . . . I, brother Dalmatius, the humble prior of Pontefract, and the convent . . . . . . have confirmed to Thomas son of Thomas of Bilham all the land which we have from the gift of William de Bareville, in the territory of Bilham, that is to say a bovate called the Painel bovate, and an acre and a half between the land of Walter the shepherd towards the west and the land of the parson of Hooton towards the east, and abutting upon the road to Brodsworth ; and two slips called headlands, lying towards the Cross between Hickleton and Bilham. To be held and possessed from us by him and his heirs, &c. Paying us yearly thirty pence, fifteen pence at Christmas and fifteen pence at Easter. For this Thomas has given us in hand nine silver marks. . . . Seal. . . . He has placed his seal to the transcript which we retain. Given at Pontefract, on the day of St. Peter ad Vincula, 1240. Witnesses.]

Sciant presentes et futuri quod ego frater Dalmatius, prior humilis de Pontefracto, et ejusdem loci conventus dimisimus, concessimus, et hac presenti carta confirmavimus Thome filio Thome de Bilam totam terram quam habemus ex dono Willelmi de Barevilla in territorio de Bilam, videlicet unam bovatam terre que vocatur bovata Painel, et unam acram terre et dimidiam que jacent inter terram Walteri Bercarii versus west et terram persone de Hoton versus est, et buttat super viam que tendit versus Broddeswrd, et duas seliones que vocantur fordeles et jacent versus crucem qui est inter Hikilton et Bilam. Tenendas et habendas de nobis sibi et heredibus suis libere, quiete, pacifice et honorifice, cum omnibus pertinentiis, libertatibus, et aisiamentis ad predictam terram infra villam et extra pertinentibus. Reddendo inde nobis annuatim triginta denarios, videlicet quindecim denarios ad Nathale domini et quindecim denarios ad Pascha pro omni servitio seculari et exactione. Pro hac autem dimissione, concessione et confirmatione dedit nobis dictus Thomas novem marcas argenti pre manibus. In cujus rei testimonium huic scripto sigillum nostrum apposuimus. Et ipse tam pro se quam pro heredibus suis transcripto quod penes nos retinemus sigillum suum apposuit. Datum apud Pontefractum in die sancti Petri ad Vincula, anno gratie m°.cc°.quadraginta. Hiis testibus, *Thoma filio Willelmi, Rogero fratre ejusdem, Willelmo de Bilam, Willelmo de Barevilla*, et aliis.

---

(1) No. 536 and No. 537 are copied into *Dodsworth*, vol. 151.

538. Carta Walteri prioris de Pontefracto.

[. . . . . I, Walter, prior of Pontefract, and the convent . . . . . have confirmed to Adam son of Robert le Busceler a toft with croft in Bramley and two assarts in the territory of that town, namely the toft and croft which lie between the toft of Thomas Forester and Adam Fisher, and the two assarts which the aforesaid Robert, father of Adam, held before Adam de Reineville gave them to us. To be held and possessed by Adam and his heirs, &c. Paying yearly to our doorkeeper eighteen pence, half at the feast of St. Martin and half at Whitsuntide. . . . . Adam has placed his seal to the counterpart which we retain. Witnesses.]

Sciant presentes et futuri quod ego Walterus prior de Pontefracto et ejusdem loci conventus dedimus, concessimus, et presenti carta nostra confirmavimus Ade filio Roberti le Busceler unum toftum cum crofto in Bramelay et duo essarta in territorio ejusdem ville. Illud scilicet toftum cum crofto quod jacet inter toftum Thome Forestarii et Ade Piscatoris, et illa duo essarta que prefatus Robertus pater predicti Ade antea tenuit, antequam Adam de Rainevilla illa nobis dedit. Tenenda et habenda predicto Ade et heredibus suis de nobis libere et quiete, in feodo et hereditate, cum omnibus communis libertatibus et aisiamentis predictis terris pertinentibus. Reddendo inde annuatim hostillario nostro octo decem denarios pro omni servitio, medietatem ad festum sancti Martini et medietatem ad Pentecosten. Et ne prefatus Adam vel heredes sui in posterum contra tenorem hujus carte venire possint, contrascripto quod penes nos retinemus sigillum suum apposuit. Hiis testibus, *Rogero Scot, Ricardo de Tanga, Petro de Alta Ripa, Roberto de Rainevilla, Hugone clerico de Kaverlay, Norasio clerico*, et aliis.

---

539. Carta Bertramini[1] prioris.

[. . . . . Sir Bertram, the prior of Pontefract, with the consent of all the convent, has granted to William, priest of Catwick, a bovate of land in Catwick with croft, and a toft. William will give every year two shillings, and for another toft twelve pence, eighteen pence at Whitsuntide and eighteen pence at the feast of St. Martin. If William wishes to demise the land to anyone without its appurtenances, he shall take him to the prior and he shall receive the land from the prior and convent and hold it from them. That it may be certain which that bovate may be, it is specified as that which old Simon, of Wick, gave to God and St. John on the day on which he married Albreda de Mara at Pontefract. Witnesses.]

Sciant presentes et futuri quod dominus Bertramus prior de Pontefracto consensu totius conventus concessit Willelmo, presbitero

---

(1) *Sic*.

de Cathewic, unam bovatam terre in Cathwic cum crofto et unum toftum, pro qua bovata cum tofto idem Willelmus dabit unoquoque anno ij solidos et pro alio tofto xij denarios, dimidiam scilicet viij decem denarios ad Pentecosten et xviij denarios ad festum sancti Martini. Si vero idem Willelmus hanc terram alicui ex pertinentibus suis dimittere voluerit, adducet eum ad priorem et a priore et conventu hanc terram accipiet et de eis tenebit. Et ut certum sit que bovata illa sit, illa est nominata quam Symon senex de Witic[2] dedit deo et sancto Johanni die qua disponsavit Albredam de Mara apud Pontefractum. Hiis testibus, *Waltero de Cathwic, Jordano, Rainaldo, Waltero de Ledestona, et toto conventu sancti Johannis.*

---

(2) Catwick.

539*.   Carta Stephani prioris.

[To all Christ's faithful . . . . . . Brother Stephen, prior of Pontefract, and the convent, greeting. . . . . . We have confirmed to Peter son of Lemar of Polis and his heirs all the lands which he holds of our fee within the town of Bretton and without, as the charter which he has of Henry Neeloth witnesses. . . . . Seal. Peter has placed his seal to the transcript which we retain. Witnesses.]

Omnibus Christi fidelibus ad quos litere presentes pervenerint, frater S. prior de Pontefracto et ejusdem loci conventus, salutem. Noverit universitas vestra nos concessisse et presenti carta nostra confirmasse Petro filio Lemer de Polis et heredibus suis omnes terras quas tenet de feodo nostro, infra villam de Brettona et extra, sicut carta quam habet de Henrico Neeloth testatur.[1] In cujus rei testimonium huic scripto sigillum nostrum apposuimus. Et ne idem P. vel heredes sui contra tenorem hujus carte in posterum venire possit, transcripto quod penes nos retinemus sigillum suum apposuit. Hiis testibus, *Serlone de Brettona, Waltero de Birum, Ada de Brettona, Thoma de Suttona, Ricardo Pateman,* et aliis.

---

(1) This charter of Henry Neeloth was not put on record in the Chartulary.

---

540.   Carta Hugonis prioris de Pontefracto.

[Be it known to all who shall see or hear this writing, that I, brother Hugh, the humble prior of Pontefract, and the convent have granted to the nuns of Hampole a bovate of land in Slepehill, which Ralph son of Hugh has held from us, holding to be valid and pleasing the gift which Hugh formerly made to them in the aforesaid bovate. The nuns shall pay us twelve pence yearly, six pence at the feast of St. Martin and six pence at Whitsuntide. Ralph and his heirs will warrant, &c. We have strengthened this with our seal. And at the foot the nuns have placed their seal. Witnesses.]

Notum sit omnibus hoc scriptum visuris vel audituris quod ego, frater Hugh, humilis prior de Pontefracto et ejusdem loci conventus dimisimus et concessimus monialibus de Hanepol unam bovatam terre in Sleiphil,[1] illam scilicet quam Radulphus filius Hugonis de nobis tenuit, ratam et gratam habentes donationem quam predictus H. in predicta bovata terre eis prius fecerat. Pro qua bovata terre predicte moniales reddent nobis annuatim xij*d.* pro omni servitio seculari vel demanda, scilicet vj*d.* ad festum sancti Martini et sex*d.* ad Pentecosten. Et prefatus Radulphus et heredes sui predictam bovatam terre sicut elemosinam suam perpetuam prefatis monialibus contra omnes homines inperpetuum warantizabunt. In hujus rei testimonium hoc scriptum sigillo nostro roboravimus. Et prefate moniales pedi hujus scripti ad majorem securitatem sigillum suum apposuerunt in testimonium. Hiis testibus, *Rogero decano de Ledeshama, Hugone de Treton, Hereberto de Archis, Thoma de Bilam, Henrico Biseth, Ricardo de Martona,* et aliis.

(1) Slepehill is in Hampole. The bovate seems to be that which nearly a century before had been given to the monks by William de Slepehill (see No. 206). In that manor the bovate was sixteen acres, so that a knight's fee of 640 acres comprised only five carucates.

---

541.   **Carta Hugonis prioris.**

[. . . . . . I, brother Hugh, prior of Pontefract, and the convent have confirmed to Robert Duvler and his heirs a toft in the town of Ferriby which Godfrey has held from us, and an acre of land in the Fields of that town, and half an acre in the Fields of Barton.[1] To be held and possessed from us, &c. Paying us three silver shillings yearly, at four terms, at Christmas 9*d.*, at Easter 9*d.*, at the feast of St. Botolph 9*d.*, at the feast of St. Michael 9*d.* . . . . . . R. has placed his seal to the transcript which we retain. Witnesses.]

Sciant presentes et futuri quod ego frater H. prior de Pontefracto et ejusdem loci conventus dimisimus, concessimus, et hac presenti carta nostra confirmavimus Roberto Duvler et heredibus suis unum toftum in villa de Feriby, illud scilicet quod Godefridus tenuit de nobis, et unam acram terre in campis ejusdem ville, et dimidiam acram in campis de Barton. Tenenda et habenda de nobis sibi et heredibus suis in feodo et hereditate, libere, quiete et honorifice.

(1) This Lincolnshire property was part of the grant of Gilbert, Earl of Lincoln (died 1156).

Reddendo inde annuatim nobis tres solidos argenti pro omni servitio ad quatuor anni terminos, scilicet ad Nathale domini ix*d*., ad Pascha ix*d*., ad festum sancti Butulfi ix*d*., ad festum sancti Michaelis ix*d*. Et ne idem R. vel heredes sui contra tenorem hujus carte in posterum venire possint, transcripto quod penes nos retinemus pro se et heredibus suis sigillum suum apposuit. Hiis testibus, *Willelmo capellano, Gervasio coco, Ivone filio Ysaac, Gocelino filio Benedicti, Nicholao Barin, Alano Husebonde,* et aliis.

542.[1]   **Carta Walteri prioris de Pontefracto.**

[. . . . . . . I, Walter, prior of Pontefract, with the consent and counsel of all the convent, have . . . . confirmed to Adam, son of Roger of Barnsley, and his heirs eight acres of land in the territory of Barnsley, namely, in Millcarr and in Millholm, and five acres near the forge of Ralph the clerk, towards the west. To be held, &c. Paying us for them every year 14*d*. for all service and custom belonging to us. He shall have the common easements of the town. Half of this rent he shall pay at Whitsuntide and half at the feast of St. Martin, saving to us our oaks. These before-written things we have granted to Adam and his heirs. Witnesses.]

Sciant presentes et futuri quod ego Walterus prior de Pontefracto, consensu et consilio totius conventus, concessi, dedi, et presenti carta nostra confirmavi Ade filio Rogeri de Berneslaya et heredibus suis viij acras terre in territorio de Bernesleya, scilicet in Milneker et in Milneholm, et quinque acras juxta forgiam Radulfi clerici versus west. Tenendas de nobis in feodo et hereditate, libere, quiete et honorifice. Reddendo pro eis nobis singulis annis xiiij*d*. pro omni servitio et consuetudine ad nos pertinente. Habebit autem communia aisiamenta ejusdem ville. Medietatem hujus firme reddet ad Pentecosten et medietatem ad festum sancti Martini, salvis nobis quercubus nostris. Hec prescripta prefato Ade et heredibus suis concessimus. Hiis testibus,[2] *Rogero decano de Ledeshama, Willelmo filio Everardi, Rogero de Silkistona, Roberto de Stainburc, Willelmo de Kamesal, Waltero de Birum, Petro fratre suo, Gerardo de Berneslaya,* et aliis.

---

(1) This and the two preceding are leases of property owned by the monks, which had been granted out previously on a lease now superseded and therefore unregistered.

(2) The witnesses are, with two additions, the same as those whose names are appended to No. 383, which concerns the eight acres only. In No. 382, the later of the two charters, which, like No. 542, includes the five acres near the forge, Roger is called " steward of Barnsley."

543. Carta Dalmatii prioris.

[To all Christ's faithful, &c., brother Dalmatius, the humble prior of Pontefract, and the convent, greeting in the Lord . . . . We have confirmed to Thomas Turs, burgess of Scarborough, our toft in the New Town of the town of Scarborough, in which the grange of Siward Ruffus was once situated. To be held and possessed by him and his heirs from us in fee-farm rent for ever. Paying us yearly twenty pence, at the feast of St. Martin in winter ten pence and at Whitsuntide ten pence. But Thomas and his heirs ought to acquit the service of the lord king. If Thomas or his heirs shall not have paid the rent at the aforesaid terms, they shall, as a fine, pay to the bailiff of Scarborough six pence and to the proctor of Pontefract appointed to receive the rent six pence, every term in which he shall fail. In witness, we have given him this our charter. Witnesses.]

Omnibus Christi fidelibus ad quos presens scriptum pervenerit frater Dalmatius humilis prior de Pontefracto et ejusdem loci conventus, salutem in domino. Noverit universitas vestra nos dimisisse et hac presenti carta nostra confirmasse Thome Ters, burgensi de Scardeburga, toftum nostrum[1] in novo burgo predictem[2] ville de Scardeburga in quo situm fuit quondam horreum Sywardi Ruffi. Tenendum et habendum sibi et heredibus suis de nobis in feodi firmam inperpetuum. Reddendo inde nobis annuatim viginti denarios ad duos terminos, scilicet ad festum sancti Martini in hyeme decem denarios et ad Pentecosten decem denarios. Predictus vero Thomas et heredes sui debent adquietare servitium domini regis quod ad predictum toftum pertinet. Si autem contingat quod predictus Thomas vel heredes sui firmam prefatam terminis predictis non persolverint, dabit ipse Thomas vel heredes[2] suus qui pro tempore fuit nomine pene ballivo ville de Scardeburg sex denarios et procuratori Pontisfracti ad firmam prefatam recipiendam constituto sex denarios, in omni termino in quo solvere prefatam firmam desierit. Et in hujus rei testimonium ei hanc cartam nostram tradidimus. Hiis testibus, *Roberto Fareman, Rogero Huctred, Thoma de Lindbergh, Rogero Haldan, Henrico de Haverford,* et aliis.

---

(1) This toft had been formerly leased by No. 499 to Robert son of Basil, at a rent of eighteen pence, and without the additional penal clause, which was probably inspired by some failure to pay on the part of Prior Hugh's grantee. In No. 507 there was a curious variant in this clause. In that case, if rent were not paid to the messenger sent to receive it, he was to remain at Scarborough at the tenant's expense till the claim was satisfied. (2) *Sic* in each case.

---

544. Carta Stephani prioris.

[To all, &c., brother Alan, sub-prior, and the convent, greeting. . . . . Sir Stephen, formerly our prior, and we, at the impulse of divine piety, have . . . . confirmed to God and the church of St. Clement of York and the nuns there serving God all the rents and possessions which Eudo the chaplain formerly held from us within the town of Pontefract.   Saving to us that toft with croft which William de Vesci has given us, which lies between Adam Divil and William of Wheldale in Bondgate, and saving two shillings for the land of Micklegate next the Upperdyke, and twelve pence for the grange above the vivary of the lord earl towards the south, to be paid yearly to us by the said nuns at these terms, namely at the feast of St. Martin 18 pence and at Whitsuntide 18 pènce.   To this the venerable P., successor of our aforesaid prior, has at our request placed his seal. In testimony of which a writing has been made in the manner of a cyrograph, of which one part, sealed with the seal of Sir P., our prior, together with our seal, shall remain in the charge of the aforesaid nuns, and the other part, sealed with the seal of the nuns, shall remain in our charge.   Witnesses.]

Universis hoc scriptum visuris vel audituris frater Alanus supprior et conventus de Pontefracto, salutem.   Noverit universitas vestra dominum Stephanum quondam priorem nostrum et nos divine pietatis intuitu concessisse et hac presenti carta nostra confirmasse deo et ecclesie sancti Clementis Ebor' et monialibus ibidem deo servientibus omnes redditus et possessiones quas Eudo capellanus quondam tenuit de nobis infra villam Pontisfracti.   Salvo nobis illo tofto cum crofto quem Willelmus de Vesci dedit nobis qui jacet inter Adam Dibbil et Willelmum de Queldale in Bondegate, et salvis duobus solidis pro terra de Miclegate que jacet juxta hoppedic, et duodecim denariis pro grangia que sita est super vivarium domini comitis versus suth, a dictis monialibus annuatim nobis ad hos terminos solvendis, videlicet ad festum sancti Martini xviij denarios et ad Pentecosten xviij denarios. Huic vero concessioni et confirmationi venerabilis P. predicti prioris nostri successor ad petitionem nostram sigillum suum apposuit.   In cujus rei testimonium confecta est scriptura in modum cyrographi. Cujus una pars signata sigillo domini P. prioris nostri una cum sigillo nostro penes prefatas sanctimoniales remanebit, et altera pars signata sigillo sanctimonialium penes nos residebit.   Hiis testibus, *Gregorio de Camera, Roberto filio Ernis, Thoma de Knaresburga, Jordano de Hamtona, Lamberto de Saxtona,* et aliis.

---

544 bis.   Carta Dalmatii prioris.

[. . . . . I, brother Dalmatius, the humble prior of Pontefract, and the convent . . . . . . have confirmed to William son of Hugh of Knottingley a plot of land in that town, with the buildings upon it.   It lies between the land of Jordan Clutera and the land of Richard Dikeman, and extends from our grange in Knottingley to the Aire.   To be held and possessed by the said William and his heirs, &c.

Paying us yearly twenty-seven pence at two terms, at Whitsuntide thirteen pence and a halfpenny, and the same at the feast of St. Martin. William and his heirs shall hold the land with its appurtenances by the aforesaid rent for ever. They shall preserve the freedom from damage of that part of our grange near their land. Seal. William . . . . has placed his seal to the transcript which we retain. Witnesses.]

Sciant presentes et futuri quod ego frater Dalmatius humilis prior de ·Pontefracto et ejusdem loci conventus dimisimus, concessimus, et hac presenti carta nostra confirmavimus Willelmo filio Hugonis de Knottinglay unam placiam terre in eadem villa cum omnibus edificiis in ea superedificatis. Illam scilicet placiam terre que jacet inter terram Jordani Clutere et terram Ricardi Dikeman et extenditur in longitudine a grangia nostra que sita est in villa de Knottinglay usque ad aquam de Air. Tenendam et habendam de nobis dicto Willelmo et heredibus suis libere, quiete, pacifice et integre. Reddendo inde nobis annuatim viginti et septem denarios ad duos terminos, videlicet ad Pentecosten tresdecim denarios et obolum et ad festum sancti Martini totidem, pro omnibus servitiis secularibus vel demandis. Dictus vero Willelmus et heredes sui tenebunt et habebunt dictam placiam terre cum omnibus pertinentiis suis per predictam firmam in perpetuum. Ita quod omnino conservabunt indempnitatem dicte grangie nostre ex illa parte que proximior est terre sue. In cujus rei testimonium huic scripto sigillum nostrum apposuimus. Et dictus Willelmus, tam pro se quam pro heredibus suis, transcripto quod penes nos retinemus sigillum suum apposuit. Hiis testibus, *Willelmo de Birum, Ricardo de Behale, panetario, Rogero de Rugala, Willelmo de Thirne, Serlone de Brettona, Rogero filio Walteri*, et aliis.

---

545.   Carta Stephani prioris.

[. . . . . . I, brother S., prior of Pontefract, and the convent . . . . have confirmed to William son of Hugh of Knottingley a plot of land in that town, which abuts upon the Aire and the land of Adam of Kellingley, between the toft of Jordan Clutera and the land of Richman towards the west. To be held and possessed by him and his heirs, in fee and heirship, &c. Paying us yearly thirteen pence at Whitsuntide . . . . William has in witness placed his seal to the transcript which we retain. Witnesses.]

Sciant presentes et futuri quod ego frater S. prior de Pontefracto et ejusdem loci conventus dimisimus, concessimus, et hac presenti carta nostra confirmavimus Willelmo filio Hugonis de Knottinglay pro homagio et servitio suo quandam placiam terre in eadem villa. Illam scilicet que[1] buttat super aquam de Ayr et terram Ade de Kellinglay, jacentem inter toftum Jordani Clutere et terram Richeman[2] versus west. Tenendam et habendam de nobis sibi et heredibus suis in feodo et hereditate, libere, quiete, et integre. Reddendo inde annuatim nobis xiij denarios in die Pentecostes pro omni servitio seculari vel demanda. Et ne idem Willelmus vel heredes sui contra tenorem hujus carte in posterum possint venire, transcripto quod penes nos retinemus sigillum suum apposuit in testimonium. Hiis testibus, *Thoma de Poulingtona, Johanne de Hek, Radulfo de Rugala, Ottone de Ruhale, Rogero filio Alexandri,*[3] *Ada de Lunda,* et aliis.

(1) The terms of this charter give four boundaries to the plot : (1) the water of Aire, which must be to the north, and therefore (2) the land of Adam de Kellingley was to the south ; (3) the land of Richman or Richard Dikeman to the west, and therefore (4) the toft of Jordan Clutera was to the east.

(2) Possibly a clerical error for " Ricardi Dikeman," as given in the preceding charter.

(3) They would seem to be the Roger and Alexander who witnessed No. 231.

---

546.   **Carta Walteri prioris de Pontefracto.**

[. . . . . I, Walter the prior, and the convent . . . . . . have confirmed to Henry, son of Waldef of Hawkehirst, and his heirs twelve acres of land from the assart under the Fallverchif, saving to us the oaks. To be possessed and held, &c. Paying us yearly two shillings, half at the feast of St. John the Baptist and half at the feast of St. Andrew. . . . . He has placed his seal to the counterpart of this charter. Witnesses.]

Sciant presentes et futuri quod ego Walterus prior et conventus de Pontefracto dedimus, concessimus, et hac presenti carta nostra confirmavimus Henrico filio Waldef de Haskehirst et heredibus suis xij acras terre de essarto sub Fallverckif, salvis nobis quercubus. Habendas et tenendas de nobis libere et quiete, in feodo hereditarie. Reddendo inde nobis annuatim duos solidos, medietatem ad festum sancti Johannis Baptiste et medietatem ad festum sancti Andree. Predictus vero huic sigillum suum contrascripto hujus carte apposuit ne contra tenorem ejus ipse vel heredes sui aliqua venire possint. Hiis testibus, *Thoma de Thorneton, Nichola de Wrthelay, Ada de Hymliswrd, Symone de Herdeslay, Hugone filio Alani,* et aliis.

---

547.   **Carta Walteri prioris.**

[. . . . . I, Walter prior of Pontefract, and the convent . . . . have confirmed to Gilbert de Hetiler nineteen acres of land in the territory of Dodworth. Ten acres are between the Wintelersike way and Breregrevehirst, five acres are between Spinkswell and Horclouf under Orreputes, three acres are between the way from Dodworth to the church of Silkstone and the wood of Gilbert de Notton, and one acre lies between the gate of Robert de Hethiler and the middle furlong of Dodworth. To be held and possessed by Gilbert and his heirs, &c., with commonage of the town as much as belongs to such a holding, always saving to us our woods. Paying us yearly three shillings and two pence, half at the feast of St. John Baptist and half at the feast of St. Andrew. . . . . . Gilbert has placed his seal to the transcript which we retain. Witnesses.]

Sciant presentes et futuri quod ego Walterus prior de Pontefracto et ejusdem loci conventus dedimus, concessimus, et presenti carta nostra confirmavimus Gilleberto de Hetiler novemdecim acras terre in territorio de Doddeworda. Ex quibus acris decem acre sunt inter viam Wintelersik[1] et Breregrevehirst, et quinque acre sunt inter Spinkeswelle et Horclouf subtus Orreputes, et tres acre sunt inter viam que tendit a Doddeworda usque ad ecclesiam de Silkeston et boscum Gilberti de Notton, et una acra jacet inter januam Roberti de Hethiler et middelfurlang de Doddeworda. Tenendas et habendas prefato Gilleberto et heredibus suis de nobis libere et quiete, cum communa prefate ville, quantum ad tantum tenementum pertinet, salvis nobis per omnia boscis nostris. Reddendo inde annuatim nobis a prefato Gilleberto et heredibus suis tres solidos et duos denarios pro omni servitio, medietatem ad festum sancti Johannis Baptiste et medietatem ad festum sancti Andree. Et ne prefatus Gilbertus vel heredes sui in posterum contra tenorem hujus carte venire possint, transcripto quod penes nos retinemus sigillum suum apposuit. Hiis testibus, *magistro Roberto de Wincestre, Rogero clerico de Silkestona, Rogero capellano, Ricardo de Martona, Johanne clerico, Gerardo de Bernesleya,* et aliis.

---

(1) Not one of the names of these properties has left a trace behind it; but the clause transferring the three acres is still a good description, pointing to a wood to the south of "the way which goes from Dodworth to the church of Silkstone" as being that of Gilbert de Notton.

---

548.   **Carta Stephani prioris.**   **Circa 1235.**

[. . . . . . I, brother Stephen, prior of Pontefract, and the convent . . . . . have confirmed to Hugh, son of Osbern of Castleford, thirteen acres of arable land and an acre of meadow called Hirst, namely five acres in the territory of Whitwood, in the culture called Blackflat, three acres and three roods between Stonewall row and Fulford, half an acre at Osolfpit, three roods in Cutsyke, two acres in Langlands, and one acre in the territory of the Mere at Trowbridge. Paying us yearly five silver shillings, half at Whitsuntide and half at the feast of St. Martin. Hugh or his heirs ought not by reason hereof to claim or have commonage in the Mere of Whitwood or in the territory of that town, except only in the aforesaid lands. And we have received Hugh into full brotherhood, granting to him a share of all the goods hereafter in our church, and after his decease burial honourably in our cemetery. For this gift, &c., and for the good of his soul, &c., Hugh has quit-claimed to us for ever . . . . . . all right and claim in eighteen acres of land in the Fields of Ferry, of the fee of Lady Alice Haget, of which we have the charter of John Vintner. . . . . . . Hugh has placed his seal to the transcript which we retain. Witnesses.]

Sciant presentes et futuri quod ego frater Stephanus prior de Pontefracto et ejusdem loci conventus dedimus, concessimus, et hac presenti carta nostra confirmavimus Hugoni filio Hosberni de Castelford tresdecim acras terre arabilis et unam acram prati que vocatur Hirst, videlicet quinque acras in territorio de Witewde, que jacent in cultura que vocatur Blakeflat, et tres acras et tres perticatas inter Stanwalrawe et Fulfort, et dimidiam acram ad Osolvepit, et tres perticatas in Cutthesik, et duas acras in Langelandes, et unam acram in territorio de Mara ad Trowebrigge.[1] Reddendo inde nobis annuatim pro omni servitio seculari vel demanda quinque solidos argenti, medietatem ad Pentecosten et medietatem ad festum sancti Martini. Dictus vero Hugo vel heredes sui occasione istarum terrarum ullarum omnino communiam in Mara de Witewode vel in territorio ejusdem ville vendicare nec habere debet, nisi tum modo in terris prenominatis. Nos vero ipsum Hugonem recepimus in plenariam fraternitatem, concedentos[2] ei participationem omnium bonorum que deinceps fient in ecclesia nostra, et post decessum ejus sepulturam honorifice in cimiterio nostro. Pro hac autem donatione, concessione et confirmatione, et pro salute anime sue et antecessorum et heredum suorum, prefatus Hugh nobis in perpetuum sine aliqua reclamatione de se et heredibus suis quietum clamavit totum jus et clamium quod habuit vel unquam habere potuit in decem et octo acris terre in campis de Feria que sunt de feodo domine Alicie Haget, de quibus habemus cartam Johannis Vinitoris.[3] Et ne idem Hugh vel heredes sui in posterum contra tenorem hujus carte venire possint, transcripto quod penes nos retinemus sigillum suum apposuit. Hiis testibus, *domino Johanne de Lascy, comite Lincolnie, Nicholao de Quatremars, Henrico Wallensi, Ricardo de Londinio, Gregorio de Camera, Johanne Vinitore,*[4] et aliis.

_____

(1) All these names have disappeared except Cutsyke, and perhaps a fragment of Stonewall Row remains in "Rawgate"; but there is no present trace in this neighbourhood—the district embracing the east of Whitwood Mere on the western border of Castleford—of Hirst, Black flat, Fulford, Osolve (? Asolf) pit, Langlands, or Trowbridge.

(2) *Sic.*   (3) See No. 284 and No. 285.

(4) The signatory, John Vintner, referred to also in the body of the charter, is called John of Batley in No. 287 and No. 288. As in other charters he is called John son of Hugh, the Hugh here named would appear to be his father, so that his pedigree is now carried up a generation.

549. Carta Stephani prioris.

[. . . . . I, Stephen prior of Pontefract, and the convent . . . . have confirmed to Henry Toye a plot of land in the town of Pontefract, which lies between the land of Isaac the Jew and the land of that Henry in Micklegate. To be held and possessed by Henry and his heirs, &c., by doing all forinsec service belonging to the chief lord. Paying us yearly twelve pence, half at Whitsuntide and the other half at the feast of St. Martin. If we shall be able to turn the said plot into pure alms, Henry and his heirs shall pay us yearly two silver shillings, at the before-named terms. Warranty, as it was formerly warranted to us . . . . . Henry has placed his seal in witness to the transcript which we retain. Witnesses.]

Sciant presentes et futuri quod ego Stephanus prior de Pontefracto et ejusdem loci conventus dimisimus, concessimus, et hac presenti carta nostra confirmavimus Henrico Toye unam placiam terre in villa Pontisfracti. Illam scilicet que jacet inter terram Ysaac Judei et terram ejusdem Henrici in Magno Vico. Tenendam et habendam prefato Henrico et heredibus suis in feodo et hereditate, libere, quiete, pacifice et honorifice, faciendo omnia servitia forinseca domino capitali pertinentia. Reddendo inde nobis annuatim duodecim denarios pro omni servitio seculari vel demanda, medietatem ad Pentecosten et alteram medietatem ad festum sancti Martini. Set si nos dictam placiam in puram potuerimus convertere elemosinam, prefatus Henricus et heredes sui reddent nobis annuatim duos solidos argenti ad terminos prenominatos. Nos vero dictam placiam dicto Henrico et heredibus suis contra omnes homines warantizabimus[1] quondam fuerit nobis warantizata. Et ne idem Henricus vel heredes sui in posterum contra tenorem hujus carte venire possint, transcripto quod penes nos retinemus sigillum suum apposuit in testimonium. Hiis testibus, *Henrico Walensi, Johanne de Rouecestria, Gregorio de Camera, Johanne de Lovain, Johanne Vinitore,* et aliis.

(1) Apparently "sicut" has been omitted, or "quondam" should be "quamdiu."

560.[1] Carta Stephani prioris.

[To all, &c., brother Alan, sub-prior, and the convent, greeting. Sir Stephen, formerly our prior, and we, with unanimous consent, have granted . . . . to Adam son of Henry of Kellingley and his heirs all the lands and possessions which Henry his father has held from us within the town of Kellingley and without, with all their appurtenances and easements, except the common and ancient turbary formerly belonging to them and now ours. To be held and possessed, &c. Paying

(1) In error for 550. A further confusion in the enumeration follows.

us yearly ten shillings and four pence, half at the feast of St. Martin and half at Whitsuntide, and three boon days in August, also one with two men. Peter, the successor of our aforesaid prior, has accepted this gladly and strengthened it with his seal. . . . . This charter is made in the manner of a cyrograph, of which one part, signed with the seal of P., our aforesaid prior, together with our authentic seal, shall remain in charge of the aforesaid A. and his heirs, and the other part, sealed with his seal, shall remain in our charge. Witnesses.]

Universis hoc scriptum visuris vel audituris frater Alanus supprior et conventus de Pontefracto, salutem. Noverit universitas vestra dominum Stephanum quondam priorem nostrum et nos unanimi assensu concessisse et hac presenti carta nostra confirmasse Ade filio Henrici de Kellinglay et heredibus suis omnes terras et possessiones quas Henricus pater suus tenuit de nobis infra villam de Kellinglay et extra, cum omnibus pertinentiis et aisiamentis suis, excepta communi et antiqua turbaria quondam ad eos sed nunc nos tamen spectante. Tenendas et habendas de nobis sibi et heredibus suis in feodo et hereditate, libere, quiete, pacifice et honorifice. Reddendo inde nobis annuatim x solidos et quatuor denarios pro omni servitio seculari vel demanda, medietatem ad festum sancti Martini et medietatem ad Pentecosten, et tres precarias[2] in Augusto, unam quoque cum duobus hominibus. Hanc vero concessionem et confirmationem venerabilis Petri[3] predicti prioris nostri successor gratanter acceptavit et sigillo suo roboravit. Et ut hec nostra concessio et confirmatio perpetue firmitatis robur obtineat, conficitur hec carta in modum cyrographi, cujus una pars signata sigillo P. predicti prioris nostri, una cum sigillo nostro autentico, penes predictum A. et heredes suos remanebit, et altera pars signata sigillo suo penes nos remanebit. Hiis testibus, *Magistro Ada de Kellingtona, Thoma de Polingtona, Roberto de Orthewrd, Ottone de Rugala, Ricardo de London', Alexandro persona de Kelingtona*, et aliis. ————

(2) The "precariae" were the boon days on which a tenant had to do gratuitous service to his lord. Such service had a well-defined value, and at the *inq. p. m.* of a deceased owner was duly assessed (see No. 286 and p. 319).   (3) This would seem to be in error for "Petrus."

————————

548 bis.[1]   **Carta Willelmi filii Petri de Broctona.**

[. . . . . I, William son of Peter de Broughton, have quit-claimed to my lords the prior and convent of the house of St. John of Pontefract all my right and claim . . . . . . in those two bovates of land which Ouskil formerly held of my said lords in the town of Broughton, with the toft and croft and all other things thereto belonging. Seal. Witnesses.]

Sciant presentes et futuri quod ego Willelmus filius Petri de Broctona[2] sursum reddidi et quietum clamavi dominis meis priori et conventui domus sancti Johannis de Pontefracto totum jus et clamium quod unquam habui vel habere potui in illis duabus bovatis terre quas Ouskil[3] quondam de dictis dominis meis priore et conventu in villa de Broctona tenuit, cum tofto et crofto et omnibus aliis infra predictam villam de Broctona et extra ad prefatas bovatas pertinentibus. Et ne ego Willelmus vel heredes mei contra tenorem hujus scripti in posterum venire possimus, presentem paginam pro me et heredibus meis sigilli mei appositione roboravi. Hiis testibus, *Symone de Martona, Godefrido de Karletona, Johanne de Estuna, Ricardo Tempest, Roberto filio Ricardi, Roberto filio Willelmi*, et aliis.

(2) William son of Peter of "Bretton," that is Burton Salmon, is thus passing into William son of Peter of Brocton, that is "Broughton." He was really both. This Broughton is near Skipton. See No. 514. It is the place where, on the invitation of Alice de Rumelli, the monks found refuge while their buildings were being rebuilt after their destruction during the "war" between Gilbert de Gaunt and Henry de Lascy (see No. 399).

(3) The tenant, here called Ouskil and in the next charter Onskil, is in No. 415 called Ulkel.

---

549 bis.   **Carta Dalmatii prioris.**

[To all, &c., brother Dalmatius, the humble prior of Pontefract, and the convent, greeting in the Lord. We . . . . have confirmed to Amabel, formerly wife of Meldred of Broughton and Richard her son, whom she had by Meldred, and to their heirs, two bovates of land in the territory of Broughton, with toft and croft, and all easements and liberties within the town of Broughton and without, except those two acres and that portion of the aforesaid toft which Elias de Broughton holds from us. They are those bovates and that toft and croft which Onskil formerly held from us. To be held and possessed, &c. Paying us yearly four shillings and eight pence, half at Whitsuntide and half at the feast of St. Martin. And when the holder shall die, the third part of his goods shall revert to us fully and entirely. Seal. . . . . Amabel and Richard have placed their seals to the transcript which we retain. Witnesses.]

Universis hoc scriptum visuris vel audituris frater Dalmatius humilis prior de Pontefracto et ejusdem loci conventus, salutem in domino. Noverit universitas vestra nos dimisisse, concessisse et presenti carta nostra confirmasse Amabilie quondam uxori Meldredi de Broctona et Ricardo filio ejus quem habuit dicto Meldredo et heredibus suis duas bovatas terre in territorio de Broctona, cum tofto et crofto et omnibus aisiamentis et libertatibus infra villam de Broctona et extra ad dictas bovatas pertinentibus, exceptis illis duabus acris et illa portione prefati tofti que Helias de Broctona de nobis in eadem villa tenet. Illas scilicet bovatas et illud toftum et croftum que Onskil quondam de nobis tenuit.   Tenenda et habenda dictis Amabilie et Ricardo et heredibus suis libere, quiete, pacifice et honorifice.   Reddendo nobis inde annuatim quatuor solidos et viij denarios pro omni servitio et exactione et demanda.   Scilicet medietatem ad Pentecosten et medietatem ad festum sancti Martini.   Cum autem predictas bovatas tenens obierit, tercia pars bonorum tenentis qui pro tempore fuerit plenarie et integre absque ulla diminutione ad nos revertetur.   In hujus autem rei testimonium presenti scripto sigillum nostrum apposuimus.   Et ne dicti Amabilia et Ricardus vel heredes sui contra tenorem hujus pagine possint venire, sepedicti Amabilia et Ricardus pro se et heredibus suis transcripto quod penes nos retinemus sigilla sua apposuerunt.   Hiis testibus, *Symone de Martona, Godefrido de Karletona, Johanne de Estuna, Roberto filio Ricardi, Roberto filio Willelmi, Johanne filio Walteri,* et aliis.

550 bis. [1]   **Carta Dalmatii prioris.**

[Let all . . . . . know that I, brother Dalmatius, the humble prior of Pontefract, and the convent . . . . . have confirmed to Elias de Broughton and his wife Amabel and the heirs of their body two acres of land in the territory of Broughton.   Half an acre lies upon Morbeck, half an acre upon Northflat, half an acre upon Middlebirch, and half an acre in Westbotham of Micklethrene.   And a portion of the toft which Ouskil formerly held from us in that town, namely from the ditch in the said toft up to the public way, with all easements and liberties, &c.   To be held and possessed, &c.   Paying us yearly eight pence, half at Whitsuntide and half at the feast of St. Martin.   When the holder of the toft and acres shall die, the third part of all his goods shall revert to us, fully and entirely and without any diminishing.   But if it happens that Elias and Amabel pass away without heir of their body, the acres and toft shall revert to Richard son of Meldred and his heirs for the aforenamed rent.   Seal.   And Elias and Amabel have placed their seals to the transcript which we retain.   Witnesses.]

Noverint universi hoc scriptum visuri vel audituri quod ego frater Dalmatius humilis prior de Pontefracto et ejusdem loci conventus dimisimus, concessimus, et presenti carta nostra confirmavimus Helie de Broctona et uxori sue Amabilie et heredibus quos de corpore suo habebunt duas acras terre in territorio de Broctona, quarum jacet

---

(1) There is a brief abstract of No. 549* and No. 550* in *Dodsworth*, vol. 155.   It is not only curious that these two documents, one a pre-nuptial deed by the widow and son of Meldred, the other post-nuptial by her second husband, should have exactly the same witnesses, but that Elias, the second husband, should occur in the first deed as a tenant of an adjoining plot.   The two neighbours had probably already planned their marriage when the first deed was executed.   For Elias seems to have been the second husband of Amabel; and the relationship of the parties named would stand thus :—

```
Meldred,=Amabel=Elias,
 first    |      second
husband   |      husband
          |
       Richard
```

dimidia acra super Morebech et dimidia acra super Northflat et dimidia acra super Middelberch et dimidia acra in Westbotheme de Mikilthrene, et quandam portionem tofti quod Ouskil quondam de nobis in predicta villa tenuit, scilicet a fossato quod est in dicto tofto usque ad publicam arateam² cum omnibus aisiamentis et libertatibus infra villam de Broctona et extra ad dictum toftum et dictas acras pertinentibus. Tenendas et habendas dictis Helye et Amabilie et heredibus suis, libere, quiete, pacifice et honorifice. Reddendo nobis inde annuatim viij denarios pro omni servitio et exactione et demanda, scilicet medietatem ad Pentecosten et medietatem ad festum sancti Martini. Cum autem predictum toftum et predictas acras tenens obierit, tercia pars omnium bonorum tenentis qui pro tempore fuerit plenarie et integre absque aliqua diminutione ad nos revertetur. Si autem contingat quod sepedicti Helias et Amabilia sine herede corporis sui in fata discesserint, tam dicte due acre quam prefatum toftum ad Ricardum filium Meldredi et heredes suos pro firma prenominata revertentur. Et ut hujus scripti tenor perpetuum robur optineat, presentem paginam sigilli nostri appositione duximus roborandam. Et dicti Helyas et Amabilia transcripto quod penes nos retinemus pro se et et³ heredibus suis sigilla apposuerunt. Hiis testibus, *Symone de Martona, Godefrido de Carletuna, Johanne de Estun, Roberto filio Ricardi, Roberto filio Willelmi, Johanne filio Walteri, Roberto Cemetario,*³ et aliis.

---

(2) This is what we make the word out to be.   (3) *Sic* in both cases.

---

551.   Carta Dalmatii prioris.[1]

[. . . . . I, Dalmatius prior of Pontefract, and the convent . . . . . . have confirmed to William de Featherstone and his heirs or assigns all the land which Hugh the park-keeper, son of Ralph of Methley, and Alice his wife formerly gave us in the town and in the Field of Featherstone, lying between the toft which was John Durward's and the toft of Nicholas of Featherstone, containing in breadth three perches and in length eleven perches; two acres and one rood upon Brekeflat, between the land of Nicholas of Featherstone and the land of the aforesaid William, abutting towards the east and west; two acres between the land of William son of Odo and the land of Alan of Thornhill, extending from the Featherstone road towards Pontefract Park; half an acre in Featherstone Moor, between the land of William son of Roger of Featherstone and the land of Alexander Brown of Pontefract; one acre between the land of Nicholas of Featherstone and the land

---

(1) This is practically a putting to farm of the properties acquired under No. 245. But the only common witness is Walter de Ludham, the seneschal, who receives the knightly title of "Sir" in this later charter.

of Hervey of the same town, abutting on the house which belonged to Alice and Tibba, daughters of John Durward, stretching towards the east and west; a rood and a half on the hill between the land of Ralph of Featherstone and the land of William of the said town, between the Park and Featherstone; a half of the Woodroyd next the town of Featherstone, with all its appurtenances within the town and without. To be held and possessed, &c. Paying us yearly two shillings at two terms, at Whitsuntide twelve pence and at the feast of St. Martin twelve pence; and to Alan of Thornhill and his heirs six pence, at Whitsuntide three pence and at the feast of St. Martin three pence; to Alice and Tibba, daughters of John Durward, three pence at Christmas; and to the heirs of Henry Fresel one penny at Whitsuntide. . . . . Seal. And William has placed his seal to the transcript which we retain. Witnesses.]

Sciant presentes et futuri quod ego Dalmatius, prior de Pontefracto, et ejusdem loci conventus dedimus, concessimus, et hac presenti carta nostra confirmavimus Willelmo de Fethrestona et heredibus suis vel assignatis suis totam terram quam Hugo filius Radulfi de Medelay, parcarius, et Alicia uxor ejus quondam nobis dederunt in villa et in campo de Fethirstona, videlicet jacentem inter toftum quod fuit Johannis Durward et toftum Nicholai de Fethirstana continentem in latitudine tres perticatas terre et in longitudine undecim perticatas terre, et duas acras et unam perticatam super Brekeflat que jacent inter terram Nicholai de· Fethirstana ex una parte et terram predicti Willelmi ex altera, abuttantes versus orientem et occidentem. Et duas acras jacentes inter terram Willelmi filii Odonis et terram Alani de Thornhil, extendentes a via de Fethirstana versus parcum de Pontefracto. Et dimidiam acram terre in mora de Fetherstana, jacentem inter terram Willelmi filii Rogeri de Fetherstana et terram Alexandri Brun de Pontefracto. Et unam acram terre jacentem inter terram Nicholay de Fethirstana et terram Hervei de eadem villa abuttantem super domum que fuit Alicie et Tibbe filiarum Johannis Durward, tendentem versus orientem et occidentem. Et unam perticatam terre et dimidiam jacentem super Hil, inter terram Radulfi de Fetherstana et terram Willelmi de eadem villa, scilicet inter parcum et Featherstanam. Et medietatem de Woderode propinquiorem ville de Fethirstana, cum omnibus pertinentiis suis infra villam et extra. Tenendas et habendas dicto Willelmo et heredibus suis vel assignatis suis de nobis libere et quiete et pacifice. Reddendo inde nobis annuatim duos solidos ad duos terminos, scilicet ad Pentecosten xij*d.* et ad festum sancti Martini xij*d.*, et Alano de Thornhil et heredibus suis vj*d.*, scilicet ad Pentecosten iij*d.* et ad festum sancti Martini iij*d.*, et Alicie et Tibbe filiabus Johannis Durward iij*d.* ad Nathale domini, et heredibus Henrici Fresel j*d.* ad Pentecosten, pro omni servitio ad nos et ad alios supranominatos pertinenti. In cujus rei testimonium huic scripto sigillum nostrum apposuimus, et supradictus Willelmus transcripto quod penes nos retinemus sigillum suum apposuit. Hiis testibus, *domino Waltero de Ludham tunc senescallo, Roberto receptore, Magistro Warnero, Gregorio de Camera, Rainero le Ferur,* et aliis.

552.[1]   Carta Dalmatii prioris.

[. . . . . I, brother Dalmatius, the humble prior of Pontefract, and the convent
. . . . . have confirmed to John, son of Robert the Chamberlain of Pontefract and his heirs a house with croft in Bondgate, within the town of Pontefract, which Ralph the carpenter has held from us. To be held and possessed, &c. Paying us yearly two shillings and six pence, fifteen pence at Whitsuntide and fifteen pence at the feast of Saint Martin in winter. John has placed his seal to the transcript which we retain. Witnesses.]

Sciant presentes et futuri quod ego frater Dalmatius humilis prior de Pontefracto et ejusdem loci conventus dimisimus, concessimus, et presenti carta nostra confirmavimus Johanni filio Roberti Camerarii de Pontefracto et heredibus suis unam domum cum crofto in Bondegate[2] infra villam Pontisfracti, illam scilicet quam Radulphus carpentarius tenuit de nobis. Tenendam et habendam dicto Johanni et heredibus suis libere, quiete, pacifice et honorifice. Reddendo inde nobis annuatim duos solidos et vj*d.* pro omni servitio et exactione, scilicet xv*d.* ad Pentecosten et xv denarios ad festum sancti Martini in hyeme. Et ne dictus Johannes vel heredes sui contra tenorem hujus scripti possint in posterum venire, dictus Johannes transcripto quod penes nos retinemus pro se et heredibus suis sigillum suum apposuit. Hiis testibus, *Roberto filio Ernis, Roberto de Knaresburg, Gerardo Duvle, Willelmo filio Gerardi, Willelmo filio Helye, Roberto Camerario, Thoma filio Willelmi capellani,* et aliis.

(1) I have met with no transcript of either No. 551 or No. 552.

(2) No. 552 clearly refers to the toft and croft in Bondgate confirmed to the monks by the second William de Vesci in the time of Robert de Kent, seneschal, but which had been originally given to them by John de Vesci, in exchange for an outlying two bovates at Wick (see No. 228* and No. 266).

DE LEDESHAM.
553.[1]   1251.

[. . . . . . I, Robert Francis, son of William Goki of Ledsham, have . . . . . . surrendered . . . . . . to my lords the prior and monks of Pontefract a bovate of land in the territory of Ledsham, with toft and croft and meadow and all other its

(1) No. 553 is transcribed into *Dodsworth*, vol. 151. Robert Francis, the grantor, had been a witness to No. 180, which also dealt with properties in Ledsham but twenty years before. This present charter, like the three remaining ones, had neither heading nor rubrication.

appurtenances, which my father bought of William de Batley. To be held and possessed, &c., without gainsaying, &c. So that neither I nor my heirs, nor any other, shall hereafter assert or demand any right, &c. . . . . The monks have given me in hand six silver marks and a quarter of corn. Warranty. Done at Ledsham in the year of grace 1251, within the octave of Saint John the Baptist. Seal. Witnesses.]

[S]ciant presentes et futuri quod ego Robertus Franciscus, filius Willelmi Goki de Ledesham, sursum reddidi et hac presenti carta mea confirmavi atque omnino de me et heredibus meis inperpetuum quietam clamavi dominis meis priori et monachis de Pontefracto unam bovatam terre in territorio de Ledeshama cum tofto et crofto et prato ad dictam terram pertinentibus et cum omnibus aliis pertinentiis suis. Illam scilicet bovatam terre quam pater meus emit de Willelmo de Batelay. Tenendam et habendam dictis monachis libere, quiete, pacifice et honorifice in perpetuum sine alicujus contradictione, gravamine vel impedimento. Ita quod nec ego prenominatus Robertus nec heredes mei nec aliquis alius per me vel pro me in dicta bovata terre nec in dictis tofto et crofto et prato vel pertinentiis suis aliquid juris vel clamii in posterum vendicabimus aut exigemus. Pro hac autem sursum redditione, confirmatione, et mea presenti quieta clamatione dederunt mihi predicti monachi sex marcas argenti et unum quarterium frumenti in manibus. Et ego dictus Robertus et heredes mei dictam bovatam terre cum dictis tofto et crofto et prato et cum omnibus aliis ad dictam terram infra villam de Ledesham et extra pertinentibus dictis monachis in perpetuum contra omnes homines warantizabimus ac defendemus. Actum apud Ledesham anno gratie millesimo ducentesimo l° primo infra octavas sancti Johannis Baptiste. In cujus rei testimonium huic scripto sigillum meum apposui. Hiis testibus, *domino Johanne de Hoderode, tunc senescallo de Pontefracto, domino Roberto de Stapeltona, domino Ricardo Walensi, Willelmo de Fetherstan, Hugone Biset, Rogero Pateman de Ledesham,* et aliis.

DE TERRA NOSTRA DE HERDEWICKE.[1]
554.   **1251.**

[. . . . . . . I, John, son of William of Parlington, for the health of my soul, ... have confirmed to God and the church of St. John the apostle and evangelist of Pontefract and the monks there serving God those nine acres of land with their appurtenances which Agnes my mother formerly sold to Walter the clerk of Pontefract, lying near the road which leads from Pontefract to the mill of

---

(1) The word "Hospitala" has been added.

Hardwick on the east, between the land which belonged to Simon Beveridge towards the west and the land of the monks towards the east. To be held and possessed, &c., without gainsaying, &c. Paying me and my heirs two silver shillings yearly, twelve pence at the feast of St. Martin and twelve pence at Whitsuntide. All my right . . . . in the nine acres . . . . . which the monks have of my fee of the gift of Hugh, son of the aforesaid Walter the clerk, I have remitted, &c. If at any time the monks shall be impleaded or be troubled or burdened concerning the aforesaid nine acres, I and my heirs will go and stand with them at their expense wherever they will, without any contradiction, dealing out counsel to them and assistance as far as we can. Done at Pontefract in the year of grace 1251, at the feast of St. Michael the Archangel. Seal. Witnesses.]

Sciant presentes et futuri quod ego Johannes filius Willelmi de Parlingtona, pro salute anime mee et omnium antecessorum et heredum meorum, concessi et hac presenti carta mea confirmavi deo et ecclesie sancti Johannis apostoli et evangeliste de Pontefracto et monachis ibidem deo servientibus illas novem acras terre cum pertinentiis suis quas Agnes mater mea quondam vendidit Waltero clerico de Pontefracto, jacentes prope viam que ducit a Pontefracto ad molendinum de Herdewic in parte orientali, scilicet inter terram que fuit Symonis Bevereche versus occidentem et terram supradictorum monachorum versus orientem. Tenendas et habendas dictis monachis in perpetuam elemosinam, libere, quiete, pacifice, et integre, sine alicujus contradictione, gravamine vel impedimento. Reddendo inde mihi et heredibus meis annuatim duos solidos argenti, videlicet duodecim denarios ad festum sancti Martini, et duodecim denarios ad Pentecosten, pro omni servitio seculari et demanda et pro omni re. Et insuper omne jus et clamium quod habui vel unquam habere potui in prenominatis novem acris terre vel earum pertinentiis, quas dicti monachi habent ex dono Hugonis filii supradicti Walteri clerici de feodo meo, dictis monachis remisi et omnino imperpetuum de me et heredibus meis quietum clamavi. Ita quod nunquam ego Johannes nec heredes mei nec aliquis alius per nos vel pro nobis in predictis terris vel earum pertinentiis aliquid juris vel clamii vendicabimus vel exigemus in posterum. Set si contingat in aliquo tempore quod dicti monachi ab aliquo vel ab aliquibus de predictis novem acris terre inplacitati fuerint aut aliquo alio modo vexati vel gravati, ego et heredes mei cum eis ad expensas eorundem ibimus et stabimus ubicumque voluerint, sine aliqua contradictione, consilium eisdem et auxilium in quantum poterimus inpendentes. Actum apud Pontefractum anno gracie m°cc°l°primo ad festum sancti Michaelis archangeli. Et ut omnia predicta perpetue firmitatis robur obtineant, huic scripto tam pro me quam pro heredibus meis sigillum meum apposui. Hiis testibus, *domino Johanne de Hoderode, tunc senescallo Pontefracti, domino Roberto de Stapiltona, domino Ricardo Walensi, Gilberto de Parlingtona, R. Rohet, Willelmo de Fethirstona, Willelmo filio Helye,* et aliis.

DE SWINLINGTONA.

556.[1]   1251.

[. . . . . . . I, Hugh, son of William of Swillington, for the health of my soul, &c., have confirmed to God and the church of Saint John the apostle and evangelist of Pontefract and to the monks there serving God the annual rent of five shillings which Robert son of Hugh de Swillington formerly gave the said monks and which William my father granted to those monks. To be held and possessed, &c. I and my heirs will faithfully pay it to the said monks yearly, by equal parts at Whitsuntide and at the feast of St. Martin. Warranty. Seal. Given at York on the morrow of Saints Fabian and Sebastian, in the year of grace 1251, in the month of January. Witnesses.]

[S]ciant presentes et futuri quod ego Hugo filius Willelmi de Swinlintona, pro salute anime mee et patris mei et matris mee et omnium antecessorum et heredum meorum, concessi et hac presenti carta mea confirmavi deo et ecclesie sancti Johannis apostoli et evangeliste de Pontefracto et monachis ibidem deo servientibus illum annuum redditum quinque solidorum quem Robertus filius Hugonis de Swinlinton dictis monachis prius dedit et quem Willelmus pater meus eisdem monachis concessit et carta sua confirmavit. Tenendum et habendum predictis monachis in liberam, puram et perpetuam elemosinam. Quem redditum ego prenominatus Hugo et heredes mei fideliter persolvemus dictis monachis annuatim ad Pentecosten et ad festum sancti Martini per equales partes inperpetuum. Et contra omnes homines dictum redditum dictis monachis inperpetuum warantizabimus et defendemus. In cujus rei testimonium huic scripto sigillum meum apposui. Datum apud Eboracum in crastino sanctorum Fabiani et Sebastiani, anno gratie milesimo ducentesimo quinquagesimo primo, mense Januario.[2] Hiis testibus, *domino Waltero de Ludam, domino Nicholayo Devias, Magistro Warnero de Pontefracto, Roberto de Knaresburga, Willelmo filio Helye, Ricardo Seman, Jacobo de Methelay, Ada clerico de Swinlinton, Johanne de Cailli,* et aliis.

---

(1) No. 555 was omitted in the enumeration. Of No. 556 there is a copy both in *Dodsworth,* vol. 151, and in *Lansdowne,* vol. 207.   (2) January 21, 1251-2.

PRIORS OF PONTEFRACT.[1]

1. Martin; *temp.* Hen. I.
2. Walter; 1135; Abbat of Selby.
3. Reginald or Roger; 1139.
4. Adam; 1156; first prior of Monk Bretton.
5. Bertram; 116-.
6. Hugh; 1184.
7. Walter; Fine, 1219.
8. Robert; Fine, 1225.
9. Hugh; Fine, 1226.
10. Walter; 1230.
11. Fulk.
12. Stephen; Fine, 1235.
13. Peter; 1238.
14. Dalmatius; Fines, 1241–52.
15. Geoffrey; Fine, 1268.
16. Rayner.
17. William; 1300.
18. Guichard de Cherlen; elected 1311.
19. Simon de Castleford; 1316.
20. Stephen; 1342.
21. John Tunstal; 1387.
22. William Helagh; succeeded 1404.
23. Richard Haigh; 1413.
24. William; 1442.
25. John; 1439.
26. Nicholas [Hall]; pardon, 1452.
27. John Flint; 1499.
28. Richard [Brown]; 1507.
29. James Thwayts; last prior.

---

(1) This list is taken, by Mr. W. Paley Baildon's kind permission, from his *Monastic Notes*, which is Vol. XVII of this series. See pages 166-172 of that volume.

INDEX.

3 A

SUBSCRIBERS TO THE RECORD SERIES.

AMHERST (of Hackney), LORD, Didlington Hall, Brandon, Norfolk.
ANDERTON, HERBERT F., Bolton Royd, Manningham, Bradford.
APPLETON, HENRY, M.D., 19, Regent's Terrace, Hull.
ARMITAGE, the Revd. E., Westholm, Rawdon, near Leeds.
ARMYTAGE, Sir G. J., F.S.A., Kirklees Park, Brighouse.
ATHILL, CHAS. H., Richmond Herald, Herald's College, E.C.
AYRTON, WM., 9, Cook Street, Liverpool.

BAILDON, W. PALEY, F.S.A., 5, Stone Buildings, Lincoln's Inn, W.C.
BARBER, JOHN, Oakerbank, Ripon Road, Harrogate.
BARKWORTH, Dr. A. B. WILSON, Kirk Ella House, Kirk Ella, near Hull.
BARRACLOUGH, THOS., 69, Ashley Gardens, Victoria Street, London, S.W.
BELL, HUGH, Red Barns, Coatham, Redcar.
BILSON, JOHN, F.S.A., Hessle, E.R. Yorkshire.
BOLTON, LORD, Bolton Hall, Wensley, S.O., Yorkshire.
BRIGG, WM., Harpenden, Herts.
BRIGG, W. A., Kildwick Hall, near Keighley, Yorkshire.
BRIGGS, ARTHUR N., c/o Messrs. Milligan, Forbes & Co., Bradford.
BROOKE, JOHN ARTHUR, Fenay Hall, Huddersfield.
BROOKE, Sir THOS., Bart., F.S.A., Armitage Bridge, Huddersfield.
BROOKE, The Ven. Archdeacon, Halifax.
BROOKE, WM., Northgate Mount, Huddersfield.
BROWN, WM., F.S.A., Whitehouse, Northallerton.
BUCHANNAN, GEORGE, Solicitor, Whitby.
BUCKLEY, G. F., Linfitts House, Delph, Oldham.
BURKE, H. FARNHAM, Somerset Herald, Herald's College, E.C.
BURR, GEORGE, Solicitor, Keighley.

CAREY-ELWES, V. D., F.S.A., Brigg, Lincolnshire.
CARR, WM., F.S.A., Ditchingham Hall, Norfolk.
CARTWRIGHT, JAS. J., F.S.A., Public Record Office, Chancery Lane, London, E.C.
CASTLE, SEPTIMUS, 12, Devonshire Place, Claughton, Birkenhead.
CHADWICK, S. J., F.S.A., Lyndhurst, Dewsbury.
CHAMBERS, J. E. F., The Hurst, Alfreton, Derbyshire.
CHEESEMAN, W. N., The Crescent, Selby.
CHOLMLEY, A. J., Place Newton, Rillington, York.
CLARK, E. K., F.S.A., 9, Hyde Terrace, Leeds.
CLARK, E. T., The Goddards, Snaith, R.S.O., Yorkshire.

CLAY, A. T., Holly Bank, Rastrick, Brighouse, Yorkshire.
CLAY, J. W., F.S.A., Rastrick House, Brighouse.
COKAYNE, G. E., F.S.A., Norroy King of Arms, Herald's College, E.C.
COLLINS, F., M.D., Pateley Bridge, Yorkshire.
COLLYER, Rev. Dr., 1672, Broadway, New York, U.S.A.
COMBER, JOHN, Abermaed, near Aberystwith.
COMBER, THOS., Leighton, Park Gate, Chester.
CREYKE, RALPH, Rawcliffe Hall, Selby.
CROSSLEY, E. W., Dean House, Triangle, near Halifax.

DARWIN, FRANCIS, Creskeld, Arthington, Leeds.
DENISON, SAMUEL, 4, St. George's Terrace, Far Headingley, Leeds.
DENT, Major J. W., Ribston Hall, Wetherby.
DENT, R. J., 28, Mount Street, Oatlands, Harrogate.
DICKONS, J. NORTON, 12, Oak Villas, Manningham, Bradford.
DYSON, GEORGE, Springfield Terrace, Marsden, near Huddersfield.

ECKERSLEY, J. C., Carlton Manor, Yeadon, near Leeds.
ELAND, JOHN, 12, New Court, Lincoln's Inn, W.C.
EMPSON, C. W., 11, Palace Court, Bayswater Hill, London, W.
ESHELBY, H. D., F.S.A., 80, Shrewsbury Road, Oxton, Birkenhead.

FARRAH, JOHN, Jefferies Coate, York Road, Harrogate.
FARRER, WM., Marton House, Skipton.
FERRAND, W., St. Ives, Bingley, Yorkshire.
FLETCHER, JOHN CARR, 330, Glossop Road, Sheffield.
FORD, J. R., Quarrydene, Weetwood, Leeds.
FOWLER, Rev. J. T., D.C.L., F.S.A., Bishop Hatfield's Hall, Durham.
FRANK, F. B., Campsall Hall, Doncaster.

GATTY, A. S., York Herald, Herald's College, E.C.
GILL, FREDK., 38, John Street, Bedford Row, London, W.C.
GLEADOW, FREDK., 38, Ladbroke Grove, London, W.
GREENWOOD, JOHN ANDERTON, Funtington House, near Chichester.

HAIGH, CHAS., 1, Elm Court, Temple, London, E.C.
HANSOM, JOSH. S., 27, Alfred Place West, South Kensington, S.W.
HARDING, WM. AMBROSE, Histon Manor, Cambridge.
HARPLEY, R. W., 19, Sidney Road, St. Margaret's, Twickenham, Middlesex.
HARVEY, WM. MARSH, 58, Queen's Gate Terrace, Kensington, S.W.
HAWKESBURY, LORD, Kirkham Abbey, York.
HAWKYARD, ARTHUR, 138, Jack Lane, Hunslet, Leeds.
HEBBLETHWAITE, RHODES, Maryland House, Grosvenor Road, Headingley, Leeds.
HEMSWORTH, The Rev. BENJN., Monk Fryston Hall, South Milford.
HIRST, S. EDGAR, Crow Trees, Rastrick, Brighouse.
HOLMES, Rev. H. C., Birkby Rectory, Northallerton.
HOLMES, LAMPLEY, Hook, Goole.

HOVENDEN, R., F.S.A., "Heathcote," Park Hill Road, Croydon.

JACKSON, W. F. M., Smethwick, Staffordshire.

KAYE, W. J., c/o G. S. Brooke, Esq., Edgerton Cottage, Huddersfield.
KENDELL, D. B., M.B., Thornhill House, Walton, near Wakefield.
KITSON, Sir JAS., Bart., M.P., Gledhow Hall, Leeds.

LANCASTER, W. T., Yorkshire Banking Coy., Leeds.
LEA, J. H., 18, Somerset Street, Boston, Mass., U.S.A.
LEADMAN, A. D. H., F.S.A., Pocklington, Yorkshire.
LEES, WM., Solicitor, 10, Norfolk Street, Manchester.
LEGARD, ALBERT G., Glan-y-Mor, Penarth.
LISTER, JOHN, Shibden Hall, Halifax.
LUMB, G. D., 65, Albion Street, Leeds.

LIBRARIES :

BOSTON PUBLIC LIBRARY, Boston, Mass., U.S.A.
BRADFORD FREE LIBRARY, Yorkshire.
BRADFORD HISTORICAL SOCIETY, 5, Bond Street, Bradford, Yorkshire.

CHETHAM LIBRARY, Manchester.

DEWSBURY FREE LIBRARY, Yorkshire.

HARVARD COLLEGE LIBRARY, Cambridge, Mass., U.S.A.
HULL PUBLIC LIBRARIES.
HULL SUBSCRIPTION LIBRARY.

LEEDS FREE LIBRARY.
LEEDS INSTITUTE OF SCIENCE, ART, AND LITERATURE.
LEEDS SUBSCRIPTION LIBRARY.
LONDON LIBRARY, St. James's Square, London.

MANCHESTER FREE LIBRARY.
MIDDLESBROUGH FREE LIBRARY.

NEW ENGLAND HISTORIC GENEALOGICAL SOCIETY, 18, Somerset Street,
    Boston, U.S.A.
NEW YORK PUBLIC LIBRARY.
NEW YORK STATE LIBRARY.

PUBLIC RECORD OFFICE, London, E.C.

ROCHDALE FREE PUBLIC LIBRARY.

SHEFFIELD DISTRICT INCORPORATED LAW SOCIETY.
SHEFFIELD FREE PUBLIC LIBRARY.
SOCIETY OF ANTIQUARIES, Burlington House, London, W.

The HISTORICAL SOCIETY OF PENNSYLVANIA, U.S.A.

LIBRARIES (*continued*) :—

The LIBRARY COMPANY OF PHILADELPHIA, U.S.A.

The LIBRARY OF CONGRESS, Washington, U.S.A.

The LIBRARY OF THE CORPORATION OF THE CITY OF LONDON, Guildhall, E.C.

The LIBRARY OF THE DEAN AND CHAPTER OF YORK.

WAKEFIELD MECHANICS' INSTITUTE, Yorkshire.

YORKSHIRE ARCHÆOLOGICAL SOCIETY, 10, Park Street, Leeds.

YORK SUBSCRIPTION LIBRARY.

MARSHALL, G. W., LL.D., Sarnesfield Court, Weobley, R.S.O.

MASHAM, LORD, Swinton, Masham.

MENNELL, PHILIP, 11 and 13, Wool Exchange, E.C.

MITCHELL, T. CARTER, F.S.A., Topcliffe, Thirsk, Yorkshire.

MOORE, Miss AMELIA, Dyneley Hall, Bramhope, near Leeds.

MORKILL, J. W., M.A., Newfield Hall, Bell Busk, Leeds.

MORRISON, WALTER, Malham Tarn, Bell Busk, near Leeds.

NORFOLK, HIS GRACE THE DUKE OF, Norfolk House, St. James's Square, S.W.

NEVIN, JOHN, Littlemoor House, Mirfield, Yorkshire.

OXLEY, Rev. W. H., Petersham Vicarage, Surrey.

PARKER, Lieut.-Col. JOHN, Browsholme Hall, Clitheroe.

PATCHETT, ALFRED, 37, York Road, Birkdale, Southport.

PEACOCK, JAS., 47, West Sunnyside, Sunderland.

PEASE, A. E., Pinchinthorpe House, Guisborough, Yorkshire.

POWELL, Sir F. S., Bart., Horton Old Hall, Bradford.

RAMSDEN, Sir J. W., Bart., Byram Hall, Ferrybridge, Yorkshire.

RICHARDSON, GEO., Wedderburn, Harrogate, Yorkshire.

RICHARDSON, WM. RIDLEY, Ravensfell, Bromley, Kent.

RIPON, THE MARQUIS OF, Studley Royal, Ripon.

ROBINSON, W. P., c/o C. L. Woodward, Esq., 78, Nassau Street, New York.

RONKSLEY, J. G., Sale Hill, Sheffield.

SALTMARSHE, Lieut.-Col. P., R.A., R.A. House, Sheerness.

SANDWITH, Capt. L., Rowlers, Croughton, Brackley.

SCOTT, JOHN, Jnr., Gargrave Road, Skipton.

SCOTT, JOSEPH, 98, Albion Street; Leeds.

SHEARD, MICHAEL, Sutton House, Sutton, Isle of Ely.

SLINGSBY, F. W., Thorpe Underwood Hall, Ouseburn, York.

SLINGSBY, J. A., Carla Bank, Skipton-in-Craven.

SPOFFORTH, MARKHAM, 15, St. George's Place, Hyde Park Corner, London, S.W.

STANSFELD, JOHN, Dunninald, Montrose, N.B.

STECHERT, G. E., 2, Star Yard, Carey Street, W.C.

STEPHENSON, MILL, F.S.A., 14, Ritherdon Road, Upper Tooting, London, S.W.

TAYLOR, The Rev. R. V., Melbecks Vicarage, Richmond, Yorkshire.

TEMPEST, Mrs. ARTHUR, Broughton Hall, Skipton.

TENISON, CHAS. M., Barrister-at-Law, Hobart, Tasmania.

TINKER, C. S., Meal Hill, Hepworth, Huddersfield.

TINKLER, The Rev. JNO., Caunton Vicarage, near Newark, Notts.

TOLSON, LEGH, Elm Lea, Dalton, Huddersfield.

TUKE, WM. MURRAY, Saffron Walden.

TURTON, R. B., F.S.A., Kildale Hall, Grosmont, York.

TWEEDALE, JOHN, The Moorlands, Dewsbury.

VINCENT, The Rev. M., Great Ouseburn, York.

WADDINGTON, JOHN, Ely Grange, Frant, Sussex.

WAGNER, H., F.S.A., Half Moon Street, Piccadilly, London, W.

WAKEFIELD, THE BISHOP OF, Bishopgarth, Wakefield.

WALKER, J. W., F.S.A., The Elms, Wakefield.

WARD, J. WHITELEY, South Royde, Halifax.

WEDDALL, G. E., Thornton House, Brough, E. Yorkshire.

WHARNCLIFFE, THE EARL OF, Wortley Hall, Sheffield.

WHITAKER, B. J., Hesley Hall, Tickhill, Rotherham.

WHITEHEAD, TOM, Alfred Street, Boar Lane, Leeds.

WHITHAM, JNO., Solicitor, Ripon.

WHITLEY, ALFRED, Greenroyd, Halifax.

WILKINSON, JOSH., The Hollies, Victoria Road, Barnsley.

WILSON, DARCY B., Seacroft Hall, Leeds.

WILSON, EDMUND, F.S.A., Red Hall, Leeds.

WILSON, E. B., Bank House, Mirfield, Yorkshire.

WILSON, E. S., Melton, Brough, East Yorkshire.

WITHINGTON, Mrs., Woolley Park, Wakefield.

WOODD, BASIL A. H., 35, Tite Street, Chelsea.

WOODS, Sir ALBERT W. (Garter), Herald's College, E.C.

WURTZBURG, J. H., Clavering House, 2, De Grey Road, Leeds.

PRINTED BY

J. WHITEHEAD AND SON, ALFRED STREET, BOAR LANE,

LEEDS.

Printed in Great Britain
by Amazon